A Treatise
on the
Measure of Damages

A Treatise
on the
Measure of Damages

OR

AN INQUIRY INTO THE PRINCIPLES WHICH GOVERN
THE AMOUNT OF PECUNIARY COMPENSATION
AWARDED BY COURTS OF JUSTICE

BY

THEODORE SEDGWICK

AUTHOR OF " A TREATISE ON STATUTORY AND CONSTITUTIONAL LAW "

CUM PRO EO QUOD *INTEREST* DUBITATIONES ANTIQUAE IN INFINITUM PRODUCTAE SINT,
MELIUS NOBIS VISUM EST, HUJUSMODI PROLIXITATEM, PROUT POSSIBLE EST, IN ANGUSTUM COARCTARE.
Cod. De sent. quce pro eo quod int. prof. lib. vii, tit. xlvii

NINTH EDITION

REVISED, REARRANGED, AND ENLARGED
BY
ARTHUR G. SEDGWICK
AND
JOSEPH H. BEALE

Volume I

BeardBooks
Washington, D.C.

DANIEL LORD, ESQ.

DEAR SIR:

IF you find no fault, I am very sure that I shall not be elsewhere censured for placing your name (although without any previous permission) upon the dedication page of this work.

Your opinion of the importance of the subject, is one of the circumstances that have most strongly urged me to proceed with it. But I have other reasons for requesting you to accept this volume.

You show us all, by a teaching far better than barren precept, how much true dignity and usefulness, as well, if we may be allowed to judge, as real happiness, attend a life assiduously, intelligently, and above all, honorably devoted to that profession of which we are the votaries.

I am, dear Sir,

With sincere regard and respect,

Your obedient servant,

THEODORE SEDGWICK

New York, January, 1847.

PREFACE TO NINTH EDITION

The last edition of Sedgwick on Damages appeared in 1891, and the work on the present edition was begun five or six years ago. Although several assistants have been employed, the enormous accumulation of cases, decided meantime, has made the labor involved unusually great.

It proved impossible to go to press until the spring of 1911, and in seeing it through the press and completing it, so as to bring in the latest cases, nearly a year has been consumed. So far as possible the cases have been brought down to January 1st, 1912. Besides this, a large volume of cases, which had for different reasons been omitted from the eighth edition, have been incorporated in this one, and another quantity of cases, omitted from all previous editions, have been collected and inserted. The number of cases in the present edition is about 30,000, of citations nearly 60,000.

With each succeeding edition of the book, it is now found necessary to leave out new passages of the original text, either because they consist of statements of cases, which in the light of modern decisions have lost their early importance, or else because the discussion of the authorities needed to be revised and put into a new form. This treatise, which made its appearance in 1847, is one of the few survivors of the numerous systematic law books of the 19th century, a period productive of so many valuable expositions of the common law. Apart from the fact that it was the first systematic treatise on the subject, and besides its excellent juridical style, its success was due to three features which gave it among law books a definite distinction,—a careful and interesting historical presentation and comparison with civil-law principles, a discussion of the reasons suggested by history or analogy, or laid down by the courts, for existing rules; and, for the purpose of this discussion, the collection, and where it was necessary, the examination in detail, of the cases. The historical and comparative presentation we have left untouched; the discussion and examination of cases also is retained in substance so far as practicable. In this way, the main features of the original treatise and in great part the author's text are preserved, as the small but substantial basis of the present edition.

To live on, and to be useful to a practising lawyer, such a book must now (owing to the constantly increasing stream of cases) be not only a treatise, but so far as may be, a cyclopædia as well. If it does not give substantially all the cases on the subject treated, it will do badly what the general cyclopædias do well; if it does not as far as possible continue to expound the law by giving a rationale of the principles underlying the decisions, it shirks the function originally undertaken by the author—the most useful function in our opinion of a writer on law. The proportions of a work expanded in this way can never be so symmetrical as the original. Without entirely rearranging the book (a task for which, were it worth while, there was not time), the perspective cannot be preserved. Every new edition, it is always found, must have as its basis the edition next preceding, and such will be found to be the case with the present one. We have therefore retained the general arrangement of the eighth edition, and as far as possible, the section numbers.

Although the size of the page and volume is much enlarged, and although wherever it seemed possible we have reduced the number and length of the passages from the original treatise, (designated by asterisks), the actual number of pages of text and notes is increased by nearly one-half. Had the form of the last edition been retained, the number of volumes would have been five and perhaps six. The notes are continuous, i. e., no attempt has been made to separate the earlier notes from our own.

In the present edition there are 520 more sections and 15 more chapters than in the last edition. All the English and American cases to January 1st, 1912, have been included. This means in the greater part of the book all cases on damages that could be found down to 1912. In the chapters on torts to person and property, to include all the cases would have been to make the chapters unnecessarily long, as there are so many merely cumulative cases. We have therefore confined ourselves to adding the latest decisions with a selection of the earlier cases. In the Practice chapters, i. e., XLV and LV–LVIII, since practice so rapidly changes, no attempt has been made to add cases before the date of the last edition.

A great deal of the discussion is new. In Chapter II there is a new and full treatment of compensation for mental suffering, with several entirely new sections. There is also much new matter in the chapter on Nominal Damages. Chapter VII on Consequential Damages has been entirely rearranged and rewritten. In this chapter there are several instances of new and full treatment of difficult points. An attempt has been made to explain the nature of the distinctions between causation in nature and causation as a ground of legal liability. In Chapter VIII on Natural Consequences the introductory general matter is new. The whole of Chapter X on Avoidable Consequences has been rearranged. Chapter XI on Replacement is new, as well as much of the chapters on Higher Intermediate Value and Conversion. Chapter XVII on Liquidated Damages contains several new sections, and the subject of Alternative Contracts has been re-examined. Chapters XVIII to XX on Tort have been rearranged and rewritten. Chapter XXVII on Contract has been entirely rewritten and greatly enlarged. New sections on Repudiation of Contract (embodying the substance of an article upon this subject by Professor Beale, published in the Yale Law Journal for April, 1908), have been added, and a part of the old chapter, very greatly enlarged, has been taken out to form new chapters, viz.: Chapters XXVIII, XXIX and XXX. In connection with this the increasingly important subject of Forward Contracts is treated. Chapter XXXII on Bonds has been rewritten and greatly enlarged. Chapters XLIV on Landlord and Tenant, LIV on Damages in Equity, LVIII on Excessive Damages, and LIX on the Conflict of Laws, are entirely new. Every chapter has been carefully studied and such enlargement has been made as was necessary.

We are glad to take this opportunity to express our thanks for work done in examining the authorities, and in the arrangement of them in chapters, and also for contributions of value, to Mr. William Parkin, of the New York Bar, who began the work by copious annotations on chapters in the third volume of the old edition, and whose assistance was of much value in the chapter on Admiralty; for information and criticism of great value, to Mr. Austen G. Fox, of the New York Bar; to Mr. R. E. McMath, of the New York Bar—Chapters XXXV (Sales—especially for a valuable dissipation of the confusion surrounding the leading case of Smith v. Bolles)—; and XXXVIII (Carriers), and parts of Chapters XVIII, XIX (Torts); to Mr. A. M. Beale, of the Massachusetts Bar— Chapter XXVI (Admiralty); to Mr. R. T. Swaine, of the New York Bar—Chapters XXXIV (Insurance) and XLII (Real Covenants); to Mr. W. H. Pollak, of the New York Bar—Chapter XXXVII (Agency), and part of Chapter XIX (Slander); to Mr. J. W. Plaisted, of the Massachusetts Bar— Chapters XXXIX (Telegraph Companies) and XLVI, XLVII and XLVIII (Eminent Domain).

In this edition, in citation of cases, the references are to the current National West Reporter System, i. e., the Supreme Court, Atlantic, Pacific, Northeastern, Northwestern, Southeastern, Southwestern, Southern, Federal, and New York Supplement, to the Lawyers' Reports Annotated, including the New Series, to the American Decisions, American Reports, and American State Reports, as well as to the regular authorized series.

It is proper to say that there is no other connection between this book and the "Elements of the law of Damages" often cited here, than that the author of the latter is one of the editors of the other. The design and scope of the two books are radically different. In two or three cases the statements of conclusions in the two differ; it should be understood that those in these pages, as being the result of later and more mature consideration, represent the view now arrived at by both editors. In reflecting on the extent of the field covered, it is a satisfaction to find that the most recent study of the subject by one editor is confirmed at every point but one by the conclusions of the other, while this point is one on which the courts have for fifty years been in conflict.

In the twenty years elapsed since the publication of the last edition, the development of what may be called the substantive law of damages, *i. e.*, the body of rules which regulate the measure of compensation, the course of decision has been steadily in the direction of subordinating technicality to reason and logic. As we get further and further away from the old common-law actions, it is more clearly seen that they were the principal obstacles in the way of making the redress depend, in the language of the author, "solely on the right." This field furnishes an interesting proof of the fact that the natural action of judges, when they are independent and untrammeled, is to simplify and improve the law, and not to befog it. Judges have neither the disposition nor the power to manufacture new rules, and where an apparently new growth of law is seen, it is usually found to be based on the application of old rules to novel states of facts produced by novel social changes, inventions and discoveries, but above all, by new acts of legislation with which they have nothing to do and over which they have no control.

In the last twenty years, to give a few illustrations, the courts have been much occupied with the subject of Liquidated Damages; but the result has been in the direction of simplification. They found a number of "canons of interpretation" designed to aid in the wilderness of cases in distinguishing contractual liquidation from "penalties," the distinction having grown out of an antiquated technicality relating to a fictitious intention imputed to the parties, invoked for the purpose of counteracting their real intention, when to have given effect to the latter would have been against public policy. The recent decisions of the English courts and the Supreme Court of the United States in Clyde Bank E. & S. Co. *v.* Castenada, and Sun Printing & Publishing Assn. *v.* Moore, have thrown into such strong relief the real nature of contractual valuation and pre-ascertainment of damages that there should be hereafter less and less necessity to resort to the still technically authoritative "canons" to distinguish between the allowed and the prohibited in contracts providing for liquidation.

So, the confusion which for a long time caused the courts to divide on the question of recovery for physical injury, produced by the effects of negligence, through the nervous system of the person injured, producing every year a quantity of irrecon-

cilable cases, has been finally dispelled by the cases of Dulieu *v.*
White and Simone *v.* Rhode Island, in which it has been established (wherever the question is not unfortunately held to
be foreclosed by authority), that wherever physical injury is
proved to have resulted from fright or nervous shock *proximately
caused* by negligence, there is no escape from the conclusion
that an action will lie. These decisions, illuminating as argument and essential to the ends of justice, should be compared
with the curious logical devices in obstruction of the action
which they undermine. This is not at all an instance of new
law, but of new light expelling darkness in the old law, a darkness fostered by the old way of not looking at the real connection of the wrong to be redressed with its cause in fact, but at
the prescribed forms for ascertaining an artificial connection.

To take another instance—for which we may refer to the
chapter on Replacement, the sections on the Repudiation of
Contract, and also those on Reinstatement in Eminent Domain, modern decisions, examining the subject of avoidable
consequences in all its different aspects, and freed from the
necessity of asking whether their conclusions would apply
equally in trover, assumpsit and replevin, and having all the
issues before them, uncomplicated by pleadings, have been
able to dispose of two questions which had produced a mass of
litigation, and threatened to produce more—and which are
found essentially to be very simple—is there in law a "duty" of
replacement in the market, and does the doctrine of ordinary
care and prudence underlying that of avoidable consequences
establish a general rule of law requiring one whose contract
has been broken by the defendant to set immediately about
making another?

So distinct is the modern tendency to simplification that it
is a comparatively easy matter now to state succinctly the
hundred or more rules which in common-law actions determine
the limits of compensation. It is easy to codify the law of
Damages, and this has been done in one or more States, but
the statutory enactment of a code is of comparatively little
importance; indeed, since a code is statutory and not judicial,
it generally leads with us to an increase rather than a diminution of the *volumina legis.*

But this tendency is obscured by causes so powerful that, except to those who look closely into the judicial course of decision on purely substantive points of law, it is not recognized. The volume of decisions is constantly increasing, and thousands of cases in the law of damages, as elsewhere, multiply points of what goes by the name of law, until the courts are clogged, and some rule of thumb remedy, like the increase of judges or the creation of new courts, gives temporary relief, and serves the illusory purpose of masking the fact that the process continues to go on exactly as before.

In the last twenty years, therefore, in the United States, the bulk of the law has become more swollen than ever; the annual volume of decided and reported cases being greater every year; and this is peculiarly noticeable in the field of Damages to anyone who watches it closely, as it is in the field of Evidence. The principles of compensation, like those of proof, have never before been studied by judges and writers with so close a view to simplification and harmony, but it is the swollen volume which clogs and obstructs and confuses the law, and furnishes a measure of "the law's delay."

The congestion is due to causes which are immensely difficult for the general public to understand, but by judges and lawyers they are generally comprehended and they are not irremediable; nor is there now any lack of public attention to the evil, nor of an outcry for reform.

It may possibly be of use to point out a few facts which an examination of the recent development of the law of damages forces upon the mind.

First: The relief to be expected from not reporting cases (or from memorandum decisions) or from limiting the citation of cases in court to a few jurisdictions, is so trifling that it is hardly worth considering. It has no appreciable effect upon the professional demand for reports, treatises and cyclopædias, and is only a palliative; it does not touch the causes of the evil.

Second: Codification of the substantive law is no cure. Wherever the code alters the law, it promotes new litigation and a new crop of decisions; wherever it merely restates the law, as judicially laid down, it tends to prevent that natural growth through advancing knowledge and adaptation to changed conditions, which is the life and soul of the best "judge-made" law. In the field of eminent domain, for instance, the principle of natural justice, that private property must not be taken for public use without just compensation (one of our fundamental constitutional guarantees) was codified in our constitutions and then complicated by additional legislation, on the subject of benefits, so that every word used in the constitutional provision and in the statutes has been for two generations a painful source of conflicting opinions and rules, and it is only within the last twenty years that it has been possible to say that an approach to harmony in the *ratio decidendi* has been reached. Compare the course of decision in this statutory field with the course of decision on consequential damages in contract, under the rule in Hadley *v.* Baxendale, both in England and America, and a good measure is given of the difference in simplicity and conciseness between the growth of law under independent judges, and the extraordinary complications, obscurities and litigation produced by the apparently most simple and elementary legislative enactments.

Third: One great cause of the evil, so far as the measure of damages is concerned, is clearly due to the complication of our procedure, the fact that *we have actually made it part of our substantive law*, and the fact that this fosters new trials. It requires no argument to show that whatever promotes new trials promotes the multiplication of decisions and reports, and whatever diminishes the former reduces the volume of the latter.

Fourth: One reason why new trials are a prolific cause of the multiplication of cases and reports is connected with the doctrine of judicial error, and that again with the jury system, and with the law of evidence. As regards damages, whether it be gain prevented or loss suffered, proof is offered to the jury, which the trial judge decides is admissible, or not admissible; as to any rule of law, he gives or refuses such instructions as may be asked for. If an exception is taken to any such admission or rejection, or request, the party taking the exception, on appeal, if he can show that, had the ruling been the other way, the jury might possibly have rendered a verdict in his favor, is entitled to a new trial. This, or substantially this, was the doctrine of judicial error in England from 1830 to 1875; when it was recognized as an abuse which had perverted the earlier doctrine that a new trial could not be had unless it was perceived by the tribunal of review that a substantial injustice had been done. If the verdict were supported by the necessary weight of evidence required by the nature of the case, and if the probable conclusion would still be the same, even with the error corrected, then, there should be no new trial. The whole matter will be found fully explained by Professor Wigmore in his lucid chapter on Admissibility of Evidence. The erroneous English rule became incorporated in the jurisprudence of this country, and the abuse, notwithstanding some attempts at reform, became a fixed principle of procedure. It has led to the practice so well known with us, of trying a case "for exceptions," and made "requests to charge" a trap by which a trial on the merits is converted into a contest to upset an opponent on matters of procedure, and so obtain a new trial. It is one of the matters which is gradually making it clear that when we swept away the old forms of actions and the old system of pleading, we reserved to ourselves at the same time in procedure a plague which was predestined to become a curse. The abuse of new trials is an instance of what may be produced (through the exaltation of procedure) by what was originally a harmless principle as to the admissibility of evidence.

But besides all this, for reasons which it is needless to consider here, we resorted to the extraordinary expedient of taking all procedure out of the hands of the judges and putting it into the hands of the legislature. This was going directly counter to the teachings of experience and has greatly aggravated our difficulties, wasting the time of our superior courts and filling their reports with matters which (but for the fact that our practice act is a maze of constantly changing legislation) would never come before them at all.

Fifth: In England, not only was the abuse of compulsory new trials for "error" which the appellate court could itself see ought not to be a ground of reversal and merely because the jury might by possibility have decided the other way (so contrary to the general principle that perversions of justice by

the jury are always under judicial control) done away with by
the Judicature Act of 1875, and the Rules of Court of 1883;
but the whole subject of procedure is now so regulated that
it does not come up before the superior courts whose opinions
are reported.

"In England to-day," as Professor Wigmore says (and what
he says applies to damages no less than to evidence), "the whole
odious practice of misusing the rules of evidence as petty
stratagems in litigious tactics has passed away. In the reports
of decisions, there now occur annually not more than five
rulings upon points of evidence, as against more than five
hundred in the reports of the United States,—and that in a
community almost half as populous as ours but more than
twice as litigious. The reformatory legislation in England,
commencing with the Common Law Procedure Act of 1852
and culminating in the Judicature Act of 1875, and the Rules
of Court of 1883, seems to have been based upon a profound
professional revolution, and to have signified not merely a
change of rules but a change of spirit. The same thing is possible among us."

Sixth: Professor Wigmore goes into some of the causes which
have produced this curious feature in the development of our
law as compared with that of England, some of which are political, and some professional. But the practical question is
whether we will recognize that what has been done with regard
to procedure in general in the original home of the common
law can be done here. The proof is conclusive that it can be
done only in one way. Procedure must no longer be confounded
with substantive law, nor the result of grave questions of life,
liberty and property made to hinge on the formal regularity of
the method of trial. Such law is not that of civilized communities, but precisely the fetish worshipped by our simple and
barbarous ancestors who did not know the nature of proof and
could not distinguish between substance and form in law.
The technical absolute doctrine of judicial error as developed
in the United States, and such monstrous structures of legislative procedure as the New York Code, must be swept away.
A people who, knowing the way, cannot reform its law so as to
make it simple, concise, easily ascertained and certain, has

PREFACE TO FIRST EDITION

THE subject of damages, in other words, the pecuniary compensation awarded by the tribunals of justice, in the widest acceptation of the term, embraces the whole field of redress by legal means; and in this sense includes the entire philosophy of the Law, at least so far as it is distinguished from Equity. In taking this view of the matter, we should be led to consider questions which lie at the very basis of our system of jurisprudence—to what extent compensation ought on principle to be carried—whether full and complete remuneration should be provided for every case of civil injury; or whether, as now, the reparation should be confined within much narrower limits. Again, for what particular wrongs reparation should be provided; should the crime of seduction be punished by a civil action on a fiction of service? Should the injured husband have compensation in an action for criminal conversation? In what cases should redress be furnished for slanderous or libellous publications? Ought the malicious refusal to fulfil contracts for the mere payment of money be more severely punished than honest incapacity?

These and similar inquiries would, as I say, embrace the whole philosophy of legal relief. But I have by no means in this volume intended to occupy ground so extensive; my aim has been much humbler; and if not more useful, at least more practical.

My purpose has been to examine those cases only, where, a wrong having been done, or, in more technical language, a right of action existing, the question remains, What is the amount of compensation to be awarded? In other words, what is the rule or measure of damages in courts of law?

In doing this, my principal purpose has been to present the law as it is; while, at the same time, I have thought it my duty to exhibit the contradictions and discrepancies which exist in this, as indeed in almost every part of our jurisprudence; and which must exist so long as those changes take place in the administration of justice, which sometimes furnish a theme for well-grounded censure, but more frequently exhibit its capacity of self-adaptation to the perpetual fluctuations of our social and commercial conditions.

In the execution of the work, I may be thought to have given the decisions of the courts too much at large. It is not unadvisedly that I have adopted the course pursued in this volume. Our law is so truly to be found in our reports, that it seems to me always better to give the very words of judicial opinions than to attempt to put them in different language. In regard to the subject of damages, too, this course has seemed to me particularly expedient. It is in the course of a trial that questions of this class generally present themselves, and my object has been to make a work which should be practically useful at nisi prius; while, at the same time, I have endeavored to clear the way to a correct appreciation of the whole subject.

I have found another reason for this course in the unsettled state of this branch of the law. The contradictions are so numerous, the discrepancies so great, and the subject in a connected shape so new, that I have hesitated to affirm any position without citing my authority at large. And in collating the decisions, I have found so much variance of opinion in the numerous tribunals which follow the course of the common law that it is with great difficulty in many cases that I have been able to do more than state the doubts as they exist.

I do not by any means flatter myself with the hope of complete success. But if this volume tend in any degree to reduce to greater certainty this department of our jurisprudence—to stimulate the inquiries, or to abridge the toil of those who painfully devote themselves to the great science of justice— my labor will be abundantly repaid.

TABLE OF CONTENTS

CHAPTER I

CHAPTER II

CHAPTER III

CHAPTER IV

CHAPTER V

CHAPTER VI

CHAPTER VII

CHAPTER VIII

CHAPTER IX

CHAPTER X

CHAPTER XVI

CHAPTER XVII

VOLUME IV

CHAPTER I

GENERAL VIEW OF THE SUBJECT

GENERAL INTRODUCTION

HISTORY OF DAMAGES IN OUR LAW

DAMAGES UNDER OTHER SYSTEMS OF LAW

GENERAL PRINCIPLES ADOPTED IN THE COMMON-LAW SYSTEM

(1)

GENERAL INTRODUCTION

§ 1. The subject a branch of the law of redress.

*The subjects of legal investigation, when practically considered, generally resolve themselves into three great heads of inquiry: the right of the parties or the cause of action, the forms of proceeding, and the mode of relief. It is of the last only of these three divisions that these pages are intended to treat; nor are they intended to discuss the whole topic of redress; on the contrary, they will be confined to a single head of this extensive branch.

§ 2. Legal relief consists of damages.

The relief afforded by a tribunal may be either preventive or remedial. If remedial, it may again be either specific, or it may consist in the mere award of pecuniary remuneration. The common law, as it exists in England, and as it was introduced into the United States, is generally remedial in character, and its remedies are of a pecuniary description. It has few preventive powers; it can rarely compel the performance of contracts specifically; its relief, for the most part, consists in the award of pecuniary damages. Whether it punishes wrongs, or remunerates for breach of contract, in either case its judgment simply makes compensation, by awarding a certain amount of money by way of damages to the sufferer.[1] The rules which in this matter govern its action, *i. e.*, the amount of compensation awarded by common-law tribunals, or in other words the Measure of Damages, will be the subject of this treatise.

A mere enumeration of the forms of action and proceedings at common law, when we consider them in contradistinction to equitable relief, is sufficient to show that the powers of the former tribunals are almost solely remedial, and confined, with few exceptions, to the infliction of pecuniary damages.

---

[1] And all the questions growing out of these subjects are investigated in one and the same proceeding. "It is incident to every common-law complaint of injury and damage, that the existence of the injury and right to compensation and the amount of damage alleged to have been sustained are tried and decided in one proceeding and upon one trial." East and West India D. & B. J. Ry. *v.* Gattke, 3 McN. & G. 155, 170; 15 Jur. 261.

§ 3. Equitable relief.

Equity operates by injunction; it restrains the aggressor from the contemplated violation of right; it gives specific relief by decreeing the very thing to be done which was agreed to be done; it compels the unwilling party to give testimony; it executes trusts, expounds testaments, and adapts its plastic hand with ease to the varied wants and complaints of man in a state of society. But, as a general rule, it refrains from awarding pecuniary reparation for damage sustained.[2] **

§ 4. Difference between them.

*With the common law the case is very different. The end at which it arrives is, in almost all instances, one and the same; in the actions founded upon contract, account, assumpsit, covenant, debt, the only object of the plaintiff is to obtain, and the only power of the court is to make, a judgment awarding a certain amount of money, by way of redress for the breach of the agreement. In the case of an action brought for the breach of a contract for the payment of money only, a suit for damages does, indeed, as Lord Mansfield has observed,[3] from the nature of the case, become a *suit for specific performance*.[4] But this is almost the only instance where a suit at law compels the very thing to be done which the defendant agreed to do. In the actions of tort, case and trespass, trover, replevin and det-

[2] It is true that a court of equity will sometimes give damages in lieu of the specific performance of a contract, but that is only, as a general rule, where it has obtained jurisdiction of the cause on other grounds. Wiswall v. M'Gown, 2 Barb. (N. Y.) 270. For a consideration of the exceptional cases where equity gives damages by way of relief see *post*, ch. 58.

[3] Robinson v. Bland, 2 Burr. 1077, 1086. See Lord Loughborough, in Rudder v. Price, 1 H. Bl. 547, 554.

[4] Yet, even in this case, the true theory of the recovery on a money demand is "not that the party recovers the particular note or chose in action, as is commonly imagined, but that he recovers damages for the non-perform-

ance of the contract." Guy v. Franklin, 5 Cal. 416. If any other provision is contained in the contract, there is no specific performance, in a court having only common-law powers, as to that. For instance, where in a suit on a note promising to pay $300, "without the benefit of the stay of execution," judgment was rendered that the plaintiff recover, etc., and that the defendant have no stay of execution. It was held, on appeal that the court could not enforce the specific performance of the agreement, but could only award damages for the breach of it, and that the part of the judgment prohibiting stay of execution must therefore be reversed. McLane v. Elmer, 4 Ind. 239.

inue, the rule is the same, with the exception that in the two latter the law makes a feeble and partial attempt to enforce the return of the specific chattels, for the taking or detention of which the suit is brought.

To this general rule, however, there are some further exceptions, which must be borne in mind. In the action of eject- ment, and in the proceedings to recover dower, as well as in cases of nuisance by abating the grievance complained of, the common law gives a specific remedy. By the proceedings of quo warranto, mandamus, and prohibition, and the ancient and now obsolete writ of *estrepement*, and the great writ of habeas corpus also, these tribunals exercise powers very analo- gous to those of a court of equity. But of these, so far as they belong to our subject, more particularly hereafter.

§ 5. Damages a species of property.

Blackstone, in his Commentaries, ranks damages among that "species of property that is acquired and lost by suit and judg- ment at law." "The primary right to a satisfaction for injuries is given by the law of nature, and the suit is only the means of ascertaining and recovering that satisfaction." "The injured party has unquestionably a vague and indeterminate right to some damages or other, the instant he receives the injury; and the verdict of the jurors, and the judgment of the court there- upon, do not, in this case, so properly vest a new title in him, as fix and ascertain the old one. They do not give, but define the right." [5] In Robert Pilfold's case, it is said, [6] "It is to be known that this word *Damna* is taken in the law in two several signifi- cations, the one properly and generally, the other *relative* and *stricte*. *Damna pro injuria illata*, and *expensæ litis*"—in other words, damages and costs—"for *damnum*, in its proper and general signification, *dicitur a demendo, cum deminutione res deterior fit*." [7] It is of the *Damna pro injuria illata*, or of dam-

---

[5] Book ii, ch. 29, p. 438.

[6] 10 Rep. 115.

[7] The origin of the word *Damnum* is thus given by Grotius: *Damnum forte a demendo dictum. Ita Varro, Libro V: Damnum a demptione, cum minus er factum quam quanti constat. Alii magis probant derivare a Græco δαπανη, ut sit dapnum, deinde damnum; ut ὑπνος, sop- nus, somnus. Nec absurde deducas a Græco δαμνω, quod est βιάζω, aut ex ζημια, damia, damnum; ut regia, reg-*

ages as now known by that phrase in opposition to costs, that we are here speaking, and the rules which govern this species of property form the subject of these volumes, under the name of the Measure of Damages.**

§ 6. General arrangement of the subject.

The subject will be arranged in the following general order of topics:

1. The origin of damages under the English system, and the tribunals by which they are now imposed.

2. The general principles by which they are regulated.

3. The measure of damages in particular cases.

4. Set-off and recoupment.

5. The rule of damages under special statutes.

6. Pleading, practice, and evidence, as applicable to the subject.

7. The control exercised by the court over the jury in regard to damages.

HISTORY OF DAMAGES IN OUR LAW

§ 7. Our law of damages originated with the Anglo-Saxons.

*In investigating the origin of our present system of pecuniary compensation, it is not difficult to trace it back to those Anglo-Saxons, whose marked and peculiar character has so deeply impressed itself on every quarter of the globe. Under the civil law, we shall see hereafter that the rights and remedies of the subjects of the imperial government of Rome were carefully protected in regard to the matters of which we now speak. But when that beautiful and elaborate structure shared the fate of its creators, the rules of right sank with it; and the law but slowly emerged from the wreck and chaos of empire. For nearly ten centuries the intellectual progress of Europe was arrested, or retarded; and during that period the earlier processes of civilization had necessarily to be worked out anew.

8. Damages under Anglo-Saxon jurisprudence.

English jurisprudence finds its earliest monument in the sixth

num.—De Juro Bell. et Pac. lib. ii, cap. 17. The Digest says, *Damnum et damnatio ab ademtione et quasi deminutione* *patrimonii dicta sunt.*—De Damno Inecto, l. xxxix, tit. 2, § 3.

century, in the laws of Ethelbert, king of Kent; and this code, known as *Leges Æthelbirhti*, illustrates our present subject too curiously to be unnoticed here. In this code we find the attention of the lawgiver confined almost exclusively to wrongs, or, as we should now say, to actions of tort; and the *were, weregildum*, or *weregild*,—literally a man's money, or the price of a man—is the earliest award of damages to be found in our jurisprudence. The antiquity of compositions for murder is illustrated by Homer (Iliad Σ., 498), where, in the description of the shield of Achilles, two disputants are represented wrangling before the judge for the weregild or price of blood, εἵνεα ποινῆς ἀνδρὸς ἀποφθιμένου.[8]

"The passion of revenge," says Mr. Hallam, "always among the most ungovernable in human nature, acts with such violence upon barbarians that it is utterly beyond the control of their imperfect arrangements of polity. It seems to them no part of the social compact, to sacrifice the privileges which nature has placed in the arm of valor. Gradually, however, these fiercer feelings are blunted, and another passion, hardly less powerful than resentment, is brought to play in a contrary direction. The earlier object of jurisprudence is to establish a fixed atonement for injuries, as much for the preservation of tranquillity as the prevention of crime. Such were the weregilds of the barbaric codes."[9]

§ 9. Damages in Anglo-Saxon law compensatory.

"Damages," says Sir Francis Palgrave, "recovered in a civil action for an assault, or any personal injury not being a felonious act, correspond to the Anglo-Saxon *were*. When Alfred enacts that the seduction of the wife of a Twelf hændman, or an Eorl, is to be compensated by payment of one hundred and twenty shillings; of the wife of a Six hændman, by payment

---

[8] Hallam's Middle Ages, vol. i, p. 154, ch. ii, part ii.

[9] Hallam, *ut supra*. "La Composition," says Guizot, "est le premier pas de la législation criminelle, hors du régime de la vengeance personnelle. . . . La composition est une tentative pour substituer un régime légal a la guerre; c'est la faculté donnée a l'offenseur, de se mettre, en payant une certaine somme à l'abri de la vengeance de l'offensé; elle impose à l'offensé l'obligation de renoncer à l'emploi de la force." —*Hist. de la Civilization en France*, tom. i, pp. 275 and 276 (Deuxième ed.).

of an hundred shillings; and of the wife of a Ceorl, by payment of forty shillings, he does nothing more whatever than fix and declare the amount of the verdict, instead of leaving the assessment of damages, as we do, to the direction of the judge and the discretion of the jury." [10]

The *were* is not to be confounded with the *wite*, the one answering to our civil damages for personal trespasses,[11] the other to our criminal mulct or fine. It is to both the *were* and the *wite* that Tacitus refers when, speaking of the Germans, he says, "*Sed et leviorbus delictis pro modo, pœna; equorum pecorumque numero convicti mulctantur, pars mulctæ regi vel civitati, pars ipsi qui vindicatur, vel propinquis ejus, exsolvitur.*" [12]

It is a curious fact that the laws of remote and barbarous periods show the most minute care in fixing the amount of compensation to be recovered by way of damages. We have the laws of twelve Anglo-Saxon monarchs, from the middle of the sixth century to the Norman Conquest. Of these, the earliest, as has been said, are those of Ethelbert, in the latter part of the sixth century; and his application of the *were*, or in other words, his rule of damages, is singularly minute.

"If the hair be plucked, or pulled, let fifty sceattas [13] be paid

[10] Palgrave's Rise and Progress of the English Commonwealth, vol. i, pp. 205 and 32.

[11] "The *wite* was a penalty paid to the crown by a murderer. The *were* was the fine a murderer had to pay to the family or relatives of the deceased; and the *wite* was the fine paid to the magistrate who presided over the district where the murder was perpetrated. Thus the *wite* was the satisfaction to be rendered to the community for the public wrong which had been committed, as the *were* was to the family for their private injury."—Bosworth's *Anglo-Saxon Dictionary in voc.* Were and Wite.

Dr. Lappenberg, in his History of England under the Anglo-Saxon Kings (see B. Thorpe's translation, London, 1845, vol. i, p. 336, *Particular and Penal Laws*), mentions several other fines imposed, besides the *were* and the *wite*, in cases of homicide. He says, "The relations of the slain received the whole *weregild* annexed to his rank in the community." "Previously to paying the *weregild*, the king's *mund*, a fine to the king for the breach of his protection, was to be levied; after which, within twenty-one days, the *heals fang* (apprehensio colli, collistrigium), a mulct in commutation of the pillory, or some similar punishment, was to be discharged, and after that, within twenty-one days, the *manbot*, or indemnity to the lord of the slain, for the loss of his man. In addition to all these, there was still the *fyht wite*, due to the crown for the breach of the peace, which, as well as the *manbot*, could never be remitted."

[12] De Moribus Germaniæ, ch. 12. Palgrave, vol. i, p. 99.

[13] A silver coin, weight 19 gr. *Vide* Hawkins' English Silver Coins, p. 18.

in compensation. If the scalp be cut to the bone [of the skull] so that the latter appear, let compensation be made by payment of three shillings.

"If an ear be cut off, let compensation be made by payment of twelve shillings.

"If a piece of the ear be cut off, let compensation be made by payment of six shillings.

"Whoever fractures the chin bone, let him forfeit twenty shillings for the offence.

"For each of the front teeth, six shillings.

"For the tooth that stands by the front teeth (on either side), four shillings.

"For every [finger] nail, one shilling.

"If the great toe be cut off, let a fine of ten shillings be incurred.

"If the great toe nail be cut off, let thirty sceattas be paid for compensation. For every other toe nail, ten sceattas." [14]

§ 10. Anglo-Saxon compensation pecuniary.

It will be noticed that the *were*, or damages, in the laws of Ethelbert, is assessed in money. But, says Sir Francis Palgrave, "until a metallic currency was introduced, the legal fines and penalties were paid in kind; in the laws of Hoel Dda all such fines are reckoned in cattle, and the same mode of computation prevails in the *Brehon* laws of Ireland, and the '*Assythments for Slauchter*' of the Scots. An intermediate stage is denoted by the laws of the Continental Saxons. Their *weres* are fixed in *solidi*, or shillings. But the *solidus* was an imaginary denomination; and instead of counting down the coin, the offending party might drive his legal tender into the farm of the

[14] The above extract is taken from Sir Francis Palgrave, vol. ii, page cvii. The last Latin translation of the Anglo-Saxon laws was by Wilkins, in 1721. The Record Commission, among its most valuable and important labors in the field of early English jurisprudence, have published, under the direction of Mr. Thorpe, the first English translation of these curious codes. The history of no part of the law should be written without giving them a careful examination.

Besides the folio edition of the Anglo-Saxon laws, published by the Record Commission, there is an edition in two volumes, 8vo; the translation of the passage above is substantially the same as that of Palgrave, with the exception that, in the former, "*Bote*" is used for its equivalent "*compensation*."

plaintiff. An ox passing sixteen months old, represented the greater solidus; the lesser solidus was a yearling ox, or a ewe and her lamb. Amongst some Saxon tribes, the solidus was reckoned in corn; thirty bushels of oats, forty of rye, and sixty of wheat, being each its equivalent; and it is most probable that the necessity of adjusting the ancient fines to the standard of Roman Britain, was the cause which produced the enactment of the Kentish laws." [15] "The coined money in England," says Mr. Sergeant Heywood, speaking of the Saxon period, "was so trifling in quantity, that most of the transactions of commerce, and all buying and selling, were carried on by barter, and cattle obtained the name of *Viva pecunia*, from being received as money upon most occasions, at certain regulated prices." [16]

§ 11. Amount of compensation carefully defined.

The laws of the Anglo-Saxon monarchs, which we have from the period of Ethelbert of Kent to the Norman Conquest, contain all, more or less, the application of the *were;* but in none, with the exception of those of Alfred, between A. D. 871 and 901, do we find the same minute classification of wrongs and remedies which we have just had occasion to notice.

In the laws of Alfred, the rates are higher, whether owing to a better appreciation of personal rights, or to the increase and consequent depreciation of the currency. In the laws of the Conqueror, the *weres* become very few. Perhaps this is evidence of a civilization gradually increasing, and a jurisprudence slowly improving; for feeble certainly, and unreliable, must be the tribunal charged with the task of imposing damages in civil suits, if the legislator considers it unsafe to be trusted with the assessment of the amount. This elaborate and minute specification, therefore, though on its face it appears to indicate the care and watchfulness of the lawgiver, on a closer examination furnishes stronger proof of his distrust of the judiciary. Arbitrary rules, which do not bend to the justice of the par-

---

[15] Palgrave's History, vol. i, p. 44.

[16] The Ranks of the People under the Anglo-Saxon Government, by Samuel Heywood, Sergeant, Introd., p. lii. *In Wera reddere poterit quis*, says the law of the Conqueror, § 10, *equum non castratum pro XX solidis, et taurum pro X solidis, et jumentum pro V solidis.* And see Lex Saxonum, tit. xviii, De Solidis.

ticular matter, especially when used to fix values, are always a misfortune and a defect in jurisprudence: they should never be tolerated, unless on account of some peculiar and extraordinary difficulty in arriving at the truth of the individual case.

§ 12. Anglo-Saxon judiciary.

What the judiciary was under the Anglo-Saxon government, it is now apparently impossible to learn. Palgrave says,[17] "Some kind of adjudication probably took place amongst the Anglo-Saxons before the *were* could be required." But any inquiry into this matter, even if practicable, would lead us far beyond our proper limits. It may not, however, be foreign to our subject to notice that if the *were* or the *wite* could not be paid, slavery (it seems) was the consequence. "The criminal whose own means were insufficient, and whose relatives or lord would not assist him to make up the legal fine he had incurred, was either compelled to surrender himself to the plaintiff or to some third party, who paid the sum for him by agreement with the injured party. Such a serf was called criminal slave. These are the *servi redemptione* of Henry the First." [18]

§ 13. Later modes of trial.

We now come to the examination of the tribunals which, under our present system, are charged with the duty of assessing the amount of damages. Various modes of trial have obtained at different periods of English jurisprudence; trials by ordeal, by battle, by wager of law, and by jury.

§ 14. Trial by ordeal.

The trial by ordeal, finally prohibited in the early part of the thirteenth century [19] was the creature of a superstitious age. It was the offspring of the clergy, and perhaps one among their many efforts to counteract the violence of the military portion of the community. In this aspect, it may not have been without its uses.

[17] Vol. i, p. 205.
[18] The Saxons in England, by J. M. Kemble, 1849, vol. i, p. 197.
[19] Ordeals were prohibited by the

18th Canon of the Fourth Lateran Council, A. D. 1215. Palgrave, vol. i, p. 66.

§ 15. By battle.

The trial by battle was the natural growth of the period at which we find it existing. "Man," says the learned and sagacious writer whom we have already several times quoted, "never begins by introducing any law which is entirely unreasonable; but he very frequently allows a law to degenerate into folly, by obstinately retaining it after it has outlived its use and application." [20] We should naturally expect, in a barbarous and disturbed state of society, where every man's house was a castle, and the whole structure of society upon a martial basis, that questions of right would originally be decided by an appeal to force, and that the first efforts of the legislator and the jurist would only be to systematize and solemnize this mode of determining a controversy by subjecting it to fixed rules, and decreeing the result to determine the right forever. [21] This mode of trial naturally gave way [22] before the advancing spirit of order, and little trace of it appears after the fourteenth century. [23]

[20] Palgrave's Rise and Progress, vol. i, p. 229.

[21] Ainsi, says M. Guizot, s'est introduit dans la legislation le combat judiciare, comme une regularization du droit du guerre, une arène limitée ouverte à la vengeance.—Guizot, *Hist. de la Civilization en France*, tom. i, p. 294 (deuxième ed.).

[22] Although singular as it appears, the appeal of death was not abolished in England till 1819. See Ashford *v.* Thornton, 1 B. & Ald. 405, which resulted in an act of Parliament, 59 Geo. III, ch. 46. The reign of Richard II, 1398, saw one famous trial by battle (being an appeal of treason) between two great lords, Hereford and Norfolk; and Shakespeare's genius has fixed it in our literature:

" What my tongue speaks, my right drawn sword may prove."

In France, trials by battle, *le gage de bataille*, were abolished as far as regarded the Royal Domains, by St. Louis (Louis IX), by his ordinance of the year 1260. He prohibited *les batailles en justice, mettant en leur place preuves par temoins, sans ôter les autres bonnes et loyales preuves usitées en cour laique jusqu' à ce temps.* So as to appeals or *faussements de jugements*, as they were called, and which were effected by a challenge to the judge to mortal combat: they were done away by the 8th Article of the same ordinance: *Si aucun veut fausser jugement, en pays là ou faussement de jugement affiert, il n'y aura point de bataille; mais les clameurs, les repons, et autres erremens du plaid seront rapportés en notre cour.* These provisions were intended to apply only to the Royal Domains, but the influence of the lawyers (*les Légistes*) gradually established the prohibition throughout the kingdom. See Sismondi's *Hist. des Francs*, tom. viii, ch. xi; Guizot's *Hist. de la Civiliz. en France*, vol. iv, p. 162 (*deuxième* ed.); Stephens' Lectures on the Hist. of France, lecture viii, for an interesting and picturesque description of the manner in which the lawyers ousted the barons out of their own courts.

[23] See Sismondi's Precis de l'Histoire de France, vol. i, p. 366, and Guizot's

§ 16. By wager of law.

The wager of law, or trial by compurgators, of which we see constant traces in the Anglo-Saxon laws, and which existed till a very recent period,[24] may claim a more reasonable origin. A party accused of an offence exonerated himself from the charge by the oaths of a certain number of witnesses; and as Palgrave well observes: "In criminal cases the whole theory of this trial resolves itself into the ordinary practice of our modern courts of justice. Evidence has been given by which a presumption is raised against the accused; but not being conclusive, it is rebutted by the proofs of general good character." [25]

§ 17. By jury.

Of the four modes of trial of which we have spoken, then, the one that has survived them all, after undergoing, however, very material modifications in its construction, is the *trial by jury*. But it is not within the scope of our present subject to trace the gradual formation of this institution. Suffice it to say, that trial by jury, originally a trial by witnesses, the jury being themselves the witnesses,[26] gradually supplanted the various modes of trial by battle, ordeal, and wager of law, and from the time of the reign of Henry II, seems to have begun to acquire stability, if not its present form.[27] At all events, at the period of the earliest systematic records of judicial proceedings in England, the jury had become the tribunal which disposed of

---

Hist. de la Civilization, vol. iv, p. 162. M. Guizot calls private wars and judicial duels (p. 159), "*les deux bases essentiels de la féodalité.*"

[24] 3 Black. Com., ch. 22, p. 345. In New York, by 2 Revised Statutes, p. 410, part iii, ch. vii, tit. iv, art. i, § 4, "Trials by battle, and by the grand assize, and all other modes of trial except by a jury or by referees, are forever abolished." Wager of law existed in England till recent times. It was abolished in all cases by 3 and 4 W. 4, ch. 42, sec. 13; Chitty on Pleadings, vol. i, *128.

[25] Vol. i, p. 233.

[26] "The ancient jurymen were not impanelled to examine into the credibility of the evidence; the question was not discussed and argued before them; they, the jurymen, were the witnesses themselves, and the verdict was substantially the examination of these witnesses, who of their own knowledge, and without the aid of other testimony, afforded their evidence respecting the facts in question to the best of their belief. In its primitive form, a trial by jury was therefore only a trial by witnesses."—Palgrave, vol, i, p. 244.

[27] Palgrave, vol. i, pp. 66 and 243. The whole subject is elucidated in J. B. Thayer's Preliminary Treatise on Evidence.

the question of fact, and the amount of damages became a principal part of their jurisdiction. All hope of discovering the precise date is now, perhaps, lost, as is the case in regard to the epoch of still greater interest, that of the origin of parliamentary representation.[28] It is certain that damages, by their present name, were known at a very early period of the English law. The statute of Gloucester, passed 6 Edward I, A. D. 1278,[29] after giving damages in certain real actions in which they were not previously recoverable, goes on to give costs in the same cases, and closes by enacting that the act shall apply to all cases where the party is to recover damages. " *Et tout ceo soit tenu en tout cas ou homme* recover damages." [30]

§ 18. Modern tribunals.

The jury in its present form dates, as has been already said, from about the period of the reign of Henry II (1150).[31] Previous to that time, the great mass of business was transacted in the county courts, where the freeholders were judges of both law and fact. The *Aula* or *Curia Regis*, of which the King's Bench is a remnant,[32] disposed of the causes of the great Lords only. The exchequer already existed, but was a part of the *Aula Regis.*[33] It would seem that this freeholders' court became very obnoxious, as ignorant of law, rendering it multiform, unequal, and unjust; and these abuses were remedied by the appointment of justices in eyre, who settled the questions of law, leaving to the jury the questions of fact.[34] The precise origin of this curious division of power, it is, as has been said, now impossible to trace with accuracy. A similar or analogous distinction existed in the republican age of the Roman Law un-

[28] Turner's Anglo-Saxons, book viii, ch. iv, vol. iii, p. 185, and Appendix III, ch. ix, vol. ii, p. 236.

[29] 6 Edw. I, c. i.

[30] See Barrington's Observations on the Statutes, p. 109. "After verdict given of the principal cause, the jury are asked touching *costs and damages.—* Jacob's *Law Dict. "Damage."*

[31] "Although Henry II was not in strictness the inventor of that legal constitution which succeeded to the Anglo-Saxon policy, yet 'Trial by the country' owes its stability, if not its origin, to his jurisprudence."—Palgrave, ch. viii, vol. i, p. 243.

[32] Bl. Com., bk. 3, ch. iv, § 6, p. 41.

[33] Hale's History C. Law, ch. vii; Sullivan's Lect. 32, p. 300; Bl. Com., bk. 3, ch. iv, § 6.

[34] Sullivan's Lectures, Lect. 32, p. 296; Hale's Hist of. Com. Law, ch. vii, vol. i, p. 246.

der the procedure by *formula;* but that feature of their jurisprudence disappeared when the formula, together with the
office of the *Judex,* or Referee, was abolished, and the magis-
trates, under the despotic innovations of the Empire, disposed
of the entire litigation *extra ordinem.* To this we shall have occasion hereafter to advert; suffice it for the present to say that
since the period to which we have referred, the maxim has generally held good in the English law, *ad questiones legis respondent
judices; ad questiones facti juratores.*

§ 19. Quantum of damages a question for the jury.

The quantum of damages being in most cases intimately
blended with the questions of fact, must have been from the
outset generally left with the jury. It is very certain that the
limits of their power over the amount of remuneration were not
at first as clearly defined as they have since become.   In one
case, as late as the reign of James I,[35] it is said that "the jury
are chancellors," and that they can give such damages as "the
case requires in equity," as if they had the absolute control of
the subject.   So an early text-writer puts the case of sheep passing the Severn, and, one of them being forced into the water, all
the rest follow and are injured, and asks whether he shall have
damages for all or for one; but the only solution he can find for
the difficulty is, that the "jury must well consider of it." [36] Yet,
on the other hand, the old books are full of cases, where, on
judgment by default and even on demurrer, the courts themselves fix the amount of damages; [37] and the remains of this we
see in the power still exercised by the English courts in cases of
mayhem.[38]   Indeed, for a long time after the distinction between law and fact was clearly established, and the separate
province of judge and jury defined with considerable accuracy,
there appears to have been an almost total want of any clear

[35] Sir Baptist Hixt's case, 2 Rol. Abr.
703, pl. 15.

[36] Shepherd's Epitome, p. 70.

[37] Rolles' Abr. tit. Damages.   The
court has still power to assess damages
on demurrer, or default, without the
intervention of a jury.   Whitaker *v.*
Harrold, 12 Jur. 395.

[38] In cases of a wound which is apparent, even though not a maim, the
court could anciently assess, decrease,
or increase damages.   Cook *v.* Beal, 1
Ld. Raym. 176.

and definite understanding of those rules of damages which we are about to consider.[39]

Before commencing the more practical part of this treatise, however, it will be well to bear distinctly in mind the general principle which the English law has in view in this matter, and how in this respect it differs from other systems of jurisprudence.**

Damages Under Other Systems of Law

§ 20. Jewish law.

*We have seen in the early laws of the Anglo-Saxons, that with the most minute care, specific damages were arbitrarily assessed in each class of cases, without reference to the actual injury sustained in the particular case. We find in codes yet more ancient, rules equally arbitrary in this respect. In the Jewish law (Exodus, ch. xxi, ver. 32) various provisions of a similar nature are incorporated; thus, "If a man's ox push (gore) a man servant or maid servant, he shall give unto their master *thirty shekels of silver*, and the ox shall be stoned." So, again, ch. xxii, ver. 9: "For all manner of trespass, whether it be for ox, or ass, for sheep, for raiment, or for any manner of lost thing which another challengeth to be his, the cause of both parties shall come before the judges, and whom the judges shall condemn, he shall *pay double* unto his neighbor." So, again, by a rough equity, ch. xxi, ver. 35: "If one man's ox hurt another's that he die, then they shall sell the live ox, and divide the money of it, and the dead ox also shall they divide."

§ 21. Hindoo law.

The same principle is to be found in the laws of the Hindoos: "Where a claim is proved, the person who gains the suit is put in possession, and the judge exacts a fine of equal value from the defendant. And if the plaintiff loses his cause, he in the like manner pays double the sum sued for." And in regard to torts the same principle was applied.[40]

---

[39] For a very full and able description of the powers and duties of court and jury under our system, see Commonwealth *v.* Porter, 10 Met. (Mass.) 263, and many cases there cited.

[40] Ayeen Akberry, by Gladwin, vol. ii, pp. 498, 504.

§ 22. Roman law.

When we come to the Roman law, we find the subject elaborately, but not very clearly nor very harmoniously treated. To understand its provisions, it is necessary to bear in mind the fact to which we have already adverted, that until the despotic centralization of the Empire had completely subverted the early institutions of the Republic, the same line was drawn in their administration of justice, as with us, between questions of law and questions of fact. The magistrate who heard the statements of the parties did not decide the cause. He turned the litigants over to a *judex*, or single juror, or referee, as he may be regarded, giving him at the same time a *formula* or charge by which his decision was to be controlled. This control was, however, not an absolute one, and in some aspects of the cause, and particularly as to the extent of the defendant's liability, and the *litis æstimatio*, or measure of damages, the *judex* seems to have been clothed with a large discretion. This discretion was, however, restrained and limited to a certain extent by several special statutes.[41]

The general definition of damages, *id quod interest* or *utilitas* of the civil law, in the Code of Justinian, is the actual loss sustained and the profit which might have been made—*in quantum mea interfuit, id est quantum mihi abest, quantumque lucrari potui.*[42] A more distinct subdivision of the subject is into *damnum emergens* or loss arising, and *lucrum cessans*, or profit prevented.[43] But how far in each case the party is liable, when for *damnum emergens* only, when for *lucrum cessans*, and to what extent, the texts of the Roman law leave us greatly in doubt. They inquire in each case whether the party is to be considered guilty of *dolus*, fraud or evil design, or of *culpa* only; if of *culpa*, whether *culpa lata*, or *culpa levis* merely; and the nice shades of distinction which they attempt to define, have at once excited and baffled the ingenuity of modern commentators. In all

---

[41] See as to the three stages of the Roman procedure,—the *Legis actiones;* the *Formula* introduced about 650 A. U. C.; and the forms of the Empire,—Das Romische Privat Recht von Wilhelm Reim, book 5.

[42] Rat. Rem. Hab. Dig. 46, tit. viii, § 13.

[43] Dig. de Damno Inf. lib. 26 (39, 2).

these questions the *judex* appears to have exercised a very considerable discretion.[44]

§ 23. How awarded under Roman law.

In the award of compensation, or damages, as we term it, the *litis æstimatio*, the *judex* seems also to have been little bound by any settled rules. In cases of fraud or gross negligence, which is as near as we can render *dolus* and *culpa lata*, the plaintiff or *actor* was permitted himself to swear to the amount of injury sustained; and there seems originally to have been no check on this prerogative, *in infinitum jurari potuit;* but this license was restrained by positive provisions, which gave the power of assessment to the *judex*.[45] To check still more effectually the abuses which would necessarily flow from such a state of things, various statutory provisions were introduced, and an effort was made to obviate the difficulty by fixed valuations not to be departed from.[46]

§ 24. Arbitrary rules of reparation under Roman law.

An arbitrary rule of a very singular character was established by the *Lex Aquilia*,[47] which provided by its first chapter, that in case of the killing of any slave or cattle, unless by mere chance, the trespasser should pay the master as much as the property had been worth at any time within the year. *Damni injuriæ actio constituitur per legem Aquiliam; cujus primo capite*

[44] Ueber die Frage wie weit in einem jeden Falle das Interesse praestirt werde, ist in dem Römischen Rechte wenig vorhanden, woraus sich bestimmte Grundsätze ableiten liessen. Doch geht die gewöhnliche Meinung dahin, dass in Fallen, wo *Dolus* oder *Culpa lata* oder *Contumacia insignis* die Ursache des Schadens sei, so wohl *damnum* als *lucrum*, hingegen wo nur eine gewöhnliche culpa zum Grunde liege, bloss das *damnum emergens* vergütet werde.—Haenel, *vom Schandenersatze*, Leipzig, 1823, § 81. The books of the German scholars are numerous; see "Die Culpa des Römischen Rechts," von J. C. Hasse, edited by Bethmann Holweg, Bonn: 1838. But the writers of this class, though profound scholars

and acute reasoners, appear to lose themselves in a maze of contradictory and obscure citations from the vast storehouse of the Pandects, and in a perhaps still more hopeless metaphysical labyrinth of abstract discussions on the different shades of fraud and fault. Nothing do they less resemble than the clear and practical manner of our writers.

[45] D. de in Lit. Jur. 1, 4, § 2 (12, 3); l. 5, § 1 cod. Haenel, § 95, p. 110.

[46] Rat. Rem. Hab. Dig. lib. 46, tit. viii, § 13.

[47] Inst. lib. iv, tit. iii, De Lege Aquiliâ, Dig. lib. ix, tit. ii, Ad Legem Aquiliam. This law is said to have been passed as early as 467 A. U. C.

2

cautum est, ut si quis alienum hominem, alienamve quadrupedem, quæ pecudum numero sit, injuriâ occiderit, quanti ea res in eo anno plurimi fuerit, tantum domino dare damnetur.[48] So that if a slave was killed who at the time of his death was a cripple, but within the year had been sound and valuable, his full value as sound was to be paid. By the third chapter of this law, other kinds of intentional or negligent injury to property were punished; but in these cases the estimate of damages was limited to the highest value of the thing injured within thirty days previous. *Non quanti in eo anno, sed quanti in diebus triginta proximis res fuerit, obligatur is, qui damnum dederit.*[49] The remedy given by the *Lex Aquilia* may be considered as very analogous to our actions of trespass and case,[50] but it was limited to wrongs actively perpetrated, and mere acts of nonfeasance did not come within its scope.[51] In consequence, other enactments were made, and the same principle of arbitrary and fixed valuation was applied to matters of contract for sums certain,[52] in which cases it was provided that damages should not be given beyond the double of the amount in question: *hoc quod interest dupli quantitatem minime excedere.*[53]

§ 25. Civil law.

The civil law, as introduced into modern Europe, seems to have retained the early features of its original, in the respect of which we are now speaking, and, instead of laying down any fixed or arbitrary rule, to have left the matter very much to the discretionary consideration of the tribunal which has cogni-

[48] See, on this subject, in the works of Molinæus (Dumoulin, ed. 1861, vol. iii, p. 422), his "Tractatus de eo quod interest." It is frequently referred to by Pothier as one of the most valuable expositions of the civil law on the measure of damages.

[49] Inst. lib. iv, tit. iii, § 14.

[50] Inst. lib. iv, tit. iii, § 9; Brown's Civil and Admiralty Law, bk. iii, ch. i, vol. ii, p. 401; Cooper's Justinian, in notes: Hugo, § 238. The provisions of the law are very curious, and worthy of a more careful examination than the scope of this work permits.

[51] Zuvöderst waren alle Beschädigungen ausgeschlossen die in einem blossen Nichtthun bestehen.—Hasse, *Culpa des Römischen Rechts*, § 6, p. 21.

[52] Code, lib. vii, tit. 46. De sent. quæ pro eo quod int. prof.

[53] The original of this rule is probably to be found in the Twelve Tables. *Si quid endo deposito dolo malo factum escit, duplione luito. Si depositarius in re deposita dolo quid fecerit in duplum condemnetur.* See Pothier's Pandects, by Bréard Neuville, vol. i, pp. 332, 364, 366.

zance of the cause. So, under this system as established in France, and previous to the adoption of the Code Napoleon, damages were divided into interest and damages (*intérêts* and *dommages-intérêts*). *Intérêt* answers precisely to our interest, and is the measure of damages inflicted for the breach of a mere pecuniary obligation, as in the common cases of bills and notes. *Dommages-intérêts* correspond with our term damages in its application to all other forms of action; and in this respect it is that the system appears loose and uncertain.[54]

§ 26. Dommages-intérêts indefinite.

After laying down the rule in regard to interest, which, as with us, is limited to a fixed rate, Domat says,[55] "The other kinds of damages are undefined, and are increased or diminished, at the discretion of the judge, according to the facts and circumstances of the particular case; thus, in the case of a tenant who omits to make the repairs to which he is bound by his lease, or of a contractor who does not perform his contract, or performs it ill,—in either case they owe an indefinite amount of damages resulting from the default, and these damages are differently regulated according to the diversity of the losses which happen, the nature of the facts, and the attendant circumstances." And he illustrates these rules by one or two cases as to profits claimed as loss, where he says, "It must be left to the discretion of the judge to arrive at some measure of compensation according to the circumstances and the particular usages, if there are any." [56]   And again,[57] "It results from all

[54] In addition to the two heads of Interest and Damage, Domat makes a third, of "Restitution des Fruits," which we shall consider under the head of Mesne Profits, it being fairly a branch of the great subject of damages.

[55] Loix Civiles, part i, liv. 3, tit. v, vol. i, p. 259. Les autres sortes de dommages sont *indefinis*, et ils s'étendent ou se bornent différemment par la prudence du juge, à plus ou à moins selon la qualité du fait et des circonstances. Ainsi, un locataire qui manque aux réparations qu'il doit par son bail, un entrepreneur qui manque de fair l'ou-

vrage qu'il a entrepris, ou qui le fait mal, doivent *indefiniment* les dommages et les intérêts qui peuvent suivre du défaut d'avoir executé leur engagement; et on les régle différemment, selon la diversité des pertes qui arrivent, la qualité des faits qui les causent, et les autres circonstances.

[56] P. 262: Il doit dépendre de la prudence du juge d'arbitrer et de modérer quelque dédommagement, selon les circonstances et les usages particuliers, s'il y en avoit.

[57] Book iii, tit. v, sec. 2, § 13, vol. i, p. 270. Il résulte de toutes les régles

the preceding rules, that as questions of damages depend on the attendant facts and circumstances, they must be decided by a sound discretion, exercised as well with regard to the circumstances of the case as to general principles."

§ 27. Limited only by the discretion of the judge.

And so says Pothier: [58] "It is necessary to exercise a certain degree of moderation in estimating the amount of damages, according to the particular case." And again,[59] "Damages are to be moderated where they would otherwise be excessive, by leaving the computation to the arbitrament of the judge." So, again,[60] "Where the damages are considerable in amount, they should not be rigorously assessed, but with a certain degree of moderation." And again, even in cases of fraud: [61] "It must be left to the discretion of the judge, even in cases of fraud, to exercise a certain degree of indulgence in fixing the amount of damages." Merlin uses substantially the same language; he says,[62] "It is to be observed that the law of Justinian, so far as

précédentes, que comme les questions des dommages et intérêts naissent toujours des faits que les circonstances diversifient, c'est par la prudence du juge qu'elles se décident, en joignant aux lumières que les principes doivent donner, le discernement des circonstances et des égards qu'on doit y avoir. In an old French work, 1637, "Recueil des Arrests Notables," is found a curious illustration of the looseness of the old French law in this respect. It says, En estimation des dommages et intérêts quand les experts sont discordans, le juge d'office doit prendre un tiers, et s'ils ne s'accordent, le "juge ne doit suivre ni la haute ni la moindre estimation." So, again, in the Journal des Audiences, t. 6, p. 252, on the question whether a promise given by a female to marry under a *dédit*, or forfeit of a fixed sum, was to be regarded as liquidated damages: "La proposition *stipulatio pœnae in contractu sponsalium apposita improbatur*, est écrite dans tous nos livres qui ont traité de la matière— Dans la jurisprudence on ne s'arrête

point à ces stipulations de peine—Les Dommages-intérêts ne sont adjugez que *ad arbitrium boni viri*—suivant que le meritent les cas de mauvaise foi, de la condition des personnes, de la depénse, perte, ou deshonneur.

[58] Traité des Obl. part i, ch. ii, art. 3, § 160. Il faut même, selon les differens cas, apporter une certaine modération à la taxation et estimation des dommages dont le débiteur est tenu.

[59] § 164. Nous devons modérer les dommages et intérêts, lorsqu'ils se trouvent excessifs, en laissant cette modération à l'arbitrage du juge.

[60] Quand les dommages et intérêts sont considérables, ils ne doivent pas être taxés et liquidés en rigueur, mais avec une certaine modération.

[61] § 168. Il doit être laissé à la prudence du juge, même en cas de dol, d'user de quelque indulgence sur la taxation des dommages et intérêts.

[62] Repertoire; Dommages et Intérêts, vol. viii. Il faut observer que la loi de Justinien, en ce qu'elle réduit précisément au double de la valeur de la chose

it limits exorbitant or excessive damages to precisely double the value of the thing in controversy, has not the force of law with us [and the Code has not incorporated it among its provisions]; but the principle on which it is founded, being one of natural equity, should be adhered to, by moderating the damages wherever they are too great, by leaving them to the arbitrament of the judge."

§ 28. Methods of avoiding injustice in the systems considered.

In the various systems of jurisprudence which we have thus cursorily examined, we see that the difficulty inherent in the subject is sought to be avoided, either by fixing on an arbitrary valuation of the loss sustained applicable to all cases, or by leaving the whole matter largely to the discretion of the tribunal which has cognizance of the subject.**

§ 28a. Damages under modern Codes.

Under the modern European codes, beginning with the Code Napoleon, the general rules for recovering damages for breach of contract are clearly and concisely laid down. The provisions of the Civil Code of France are typical:

"Damages and interest are due, as a rule, to the creditor for the loss which he has suffered and the gain of which he has been deprived (in consequence of the breach of contract), subject to the exceptions and modifications of this rule to be given hereafter. The debtor is only liable for such damage and to pay for such loss of interest as was foreseen or might have been foreseen, provided that the obligation has not been broken owing to his own fraud. Even where the non-performance of the contract is due to the fraud of the debtor, in arriving at the amount of damages and interest to be paid regard must, in estimating the loss which the creditor has suffered or the gain of which he has been deprived, only be had to the immediate and direct results of the breach of contract." [63]

les dommages et intérêts exorbitans, n'a pas force de loi parmi nous [et le Code Civil ne l'a pas remise en vigueur]; mais le principe sur lequel elle est fondée, étant un principe qui émane de l'équité naturelle, on doit s'y conformer, et en conséquence, modérer les vommages et intérêts lorsqu'ils se troudent excessifs, en laissant cette modération à l'arbitrage du juge.

[63] Code Civil, §§ 1149, 1150, 1151. Substantially similar provisions of the Spanish civil code, which is the basis of the law of Porto Rico, Cuba and the

On the other hand, the provisions governing the damages recoverable for a tortious wrong are very brief and general. "Any act by which a person causes damage to another binds the person by whose fault the damage occurred to repair such damage." [64]

The provisions of the new German Civil Code are more detailed, and are well worth the consideration of a common lawyer.

"A person who is bound to make compensation shall bring about the condition which would exist if the circumstances making him liable to compensate had not occurred. If compensation is required to be made for injury to a person or damage to a thing, the creditor may demand, instead of restitution in kind, the sum of money necessary to effect such restitution. The creditor may fix a reasonable period for the restitution in kind by the person liable to compensate with a declaration that he will refuse to accept restitution after the expiration of the period. After the expiration of the period the creditor may demand the compensation in money; if the restitution is not effected in due time the claim for restitution is barred. In so far as restitution in kind is impossible or is insufficient to compensate the creditor, the person liable shall compensate him in money. The person liable may compensate the creditor in money if restitution in kind is possible only through disproportionate outlay. The compensation required to be made includes also lost profits. Profit is deemed to have been lost which could have been expected with probability according to the ordinary course of things or according to the particular circumstances, e. g., according to the preparations and provisions made. For an injury which is not an injury to property compensation in money may be demanded only in the cases specified by law. If any fault of the injured party has contributed in causing the injury, the obligation to compensate the injured party and the extent of the compensation to be made depends upon the circumstances, especially upon how far the injury has been caused chiefly by the one or the other party. This applies also even if

Philippines, may be found in Walton, Civil Law of Spain, pp. 326, 327.

[64] Code Civil, § 1382; for the provision of the Spanish law, Walton, p. 458.

the fault of the injured party consisted only in an omission to call the attention of the debtor to the danger of an unusually serious injury which the debtor neither knew nor ought to have known, or in an omission to avert or mitigate the injury. A person who is required to make compensation for the loss of a thing or of a right is bound to make compensation only upon assignment to him of the claims which belong to the person entitled to compensation by virtue of his ownership of the thing or by virtue of his right as against third parties." [65]

The Code of Mexico also lays down certain general principles, and contains interesting provisions:

"By damages is understood the loss or detriment which the contracting party has suffered in his patrimony through the default in the fulfillment of the obligation. By loss is meant the deprivation of a lawful profit which would have been gained had the obligation been fulfilled.

"The 'damage' and 'loss' must be an immediate and direct result of the default in the fulfillment of the obligation, either because it has already caused, or must necessarily cause the same. If the thing has been lost, or has suffered a deterioration so great that in the opinion of experts it cannot be employed to the use to which it was naturally destined, the owner shall be indemnified to the extent of the full legitimate value of the thing. If the deterioriaton be less serious, then on restoring the thing, the amount of the 'damage' only shall be credited the owner. The value of the thing shall be that which it had at the time it was returned to the owner, except in the cases in which the law or the contract indicates another epoch.

"On assessing the deterioration of a thing, attention shall be given not only to the diminution in the absolute value thereby caused, but also to the expenses which the repairs necessarily give rise to. On fixing the value and the deterioration of a thing, no attention shall be given to the fancy or sentimental value, except it be proved that the person responsible destroyed or injured the thing with the object of hurting the feelings of the owner; the increase which for this reason may be awarded cannot exceed a third part of the ordinary value of the thing." [66]

[65] B. G. B., §§ 249–255.   [66] Art. 1464–1471.

GENERAL PRINCIPLES ADOPTED IN THE COMMON-LAW SYSTEM

§ 29. Damages consist in compensation for loss sustained.

* Our law differs very materially from all these systems. By the general system of our law, for every invasion of right there is a remedy, and that remedy is *compensation*. This compensation is furnished in the damages which are awarded.

"Wherever," says Blackstone, "the common law gives a right or prohibits an injury, it also gives a remedy by action." [67] "If a statute gives a right," said Lord Holt, "the common law will give a remedy to maintain that right; *a fortiori*, where the common law gives a right, it gives a remedy to assert it. This is an injury, and every injury imports a damage." [68] "It is the pride of the common law," says the Supreme Court of New York, "that wherever it recognizes or creates a private right, it also gives a remedy for the wilful violation of it." [69] "Another species of property," says Blackstone,[70] "acquired and lost by suit and judgment at law, is that of damages, given to a man by a jury as a compensation and satisfaction for some injury sustained." "Every one," said Lord Holt,[71] "shall recover damages in proportion to the prejudice which he hath sustained." "Damages—*damna* in the common law," says Lord Coke,[72] "hath a special signification for the recompense that is given by the jury to the plaintiff, for the wrong the defendant hath done unto him." "It is a general and very sound rule of law," said Sedgwick, J., delivering the opinion of the Supreme Court of Massachusetts,[73] "that where an injury has been sustained, for which the law gives a remedy, that remedy shall be commensurate to the injury sustained." "It is a rational and a legal principle," said Shippen, Chief Justice of the Supreme Court of Pennsylvania,[74] "that the compensation should be equivalent to the injury." "The general rule of law," said

[67] 3 Bl. Com., ch. viii, p. 123.
[68] Ashby *v.* White, 1 Salk. 19.
[69] Yates *v.* Joyce, 11 Johns. (N. Y.) 136. See also *Massachusetts:* Lamb *v.* Stone, 11 Pick. 527; *Ohio:* Allison *v.* McCune, 15 Ohio, 726, 45 Am. Dec. 605; *United States:* Webb *v.* Portland Manuf. Co., 3 Sum. 189.

[70] 2 Bl. Com., ch. xxix, p. 438.
[71] Ferrer *v.* Beale, 1 Lord Raym. 692.
[72] Co. Litt. 257*a*.
[73] Rockwood *v.* Allen, 7 Mass. 254.
[74] Bussy *v.* Donaldson, 4 Dallas, 206, 1 L. ed. 802.

Story, J., to the jury on the Rhode Island circuit,[75] "is, that whoever does an injury to another is liable in damages to the extent of that injury. It matters not whether the injury is to the property or the person, or the rights or the reputation of another." **

§ 30. Both in contract and in tort.

In all cases, then, of civil injury and of breach of contract [76] the declared object of awarding damages is to give compensation for pecuniary loss; that is, to put the plaintiff in the same position, so far as money can do it, as he would have been if the contract had been performed or the tort not committed.[77] Thus, in the case of a breach of contract, the plaintiff should recover "what the pecuniary amount is of the difference between the present state of things and what it would have been if the contract had been performed." [78] For example, where the United States Government suspended work on a contract which the plaintiff had with it to supply materials and labor, it was held that the proper method was to estimate what sum would place the claimant in the same condition that he would have been in if he had been allowed to proceed without interference.[79] So, in actions of tort, the damages awarded should be an amount sufficient to indemnify the plaintiff for the loss which he has suffered at the hands of the defendant.[80] In short, the purpose of awarding damages is the same whatever

[75] Dexter v. Spear, 4 Mason, 115.

[76] With the exception of breach of promise of marriage, where the amount to be recovered is left largely to the discretion of the jury and of those cases of torts in which the jury are permitted to inflict exemplary or vindictive damages. In Milwaukee & St. Paul Ry. v. Arms, 91 U. S. 489, 23 L. ed. 374, Davis, J., treating of exemplary damages, said: "It is undoubtedly true that the allowance of anything more than an adequate pecuniary indemnity for a wrong suffered is a great departure from the principle on which damages in civil suits are awarded."

[77] New York: Griffin v. Colver, 16

N. Y. 489; Texas: Smith v. Sherwood, 2 Tex. 460; England: Robinson v. Harman, 1 Ex. 850.

[78] Blackburn, J., in Wall v. City of London R. P. Co., L. R. 9 Q. B. 249. Again, in Hobbs v. London & S. W. Ry., L. R. 10 Q. B. 111, he expresses the same idea, saying, "What the passenger is entitled to recover is the difference between what he ought to have had and what he did have."

[79] U. S. v. Smith, 94 U. S. 214, 24 L. ed. 115. This rule, however, is not always applied to a breach of contract concerning real property. Post, ch. 43.

[80] Baker v. Drake, 53 N. Y. 211, 13 Am. Rep. 507.

the form of action. "In civil actions the law awards to the party injured a just indemnity for the wrong which has been done him, and no more, whether the action be in contract or tort; except in those special cases where punitory damages are allowed, the inquiry must always be, what is an adequate indemnity to the party injured, and the answer to that inquiry cannot be affected by the form of the action in which he seeks his remedy." [81]   Hence it follows that the consideration for the contract does not furnish the measure of damages. Accordingly, in an action against an attorney for failure to perform certain services at an agreed price, it was held error to charge that the plaintiff could recover the sum paid less the value of services actually rendered, and Rapallo, J., said that the damages should be measured by the injury done and not by the fee paid.[82] On the same principle, in an action for covenant not to manufacture, it was held that the measure of damages was what the plaintiff had lost, and that though what the defendant had gained might be evidence of what the plaintiff had lost, it would be evidence only.[83]   In an action on a penal bond given to the State by the defendant in consideration for a loan, one of the conditions of the bond being that the debtor should make annual reports to the governor, it was held that the measure of damages was the loss actually sustained, and not the amount of the loan.[84]

§ 31. The amount determined by rules of law.

* The amount of the compensation is not governed by any arbitrary method of assessment, nor, on the other hand, left to fluctuating discretion of either judge or jury. It is awarded

---

[81] Rapallo, J., in Baker v. Drake, 53 N. Y. 211, 220, 13 Am. Rep. 507. In admiralty, also, the rule is *restitutio in integrum*. The Clyde, Swabey, 23, 24; The Gazelle, 2 W. Rob. 279; The Baltimore, 8 Wall. 377, 385, 19 L. ed. 463; Clifford, J., in The Atlas, 93 U. S. 302, 308, 23 L. ed. 863.

[82] Quinn v. Van Pelt, 56 N. Y. 417; *acc.*, Bennett v. Buchan, 61 N. Y. 222.

[83] Peltz v. Eichele, 62 Mo. 171.

[84] Jemison v. Gov. of Alabama, 47 Ala. 390; acc., Murray v. Jennings, 42 Conn. 9, 19 Am. Rep. 527. In Indiana, it has been said that the measure of damages for the violation of a simple contract, where vindictive damages are not authorized, is the amount necessary to put the party injured in as good a condition as if he had not made the contract. Jones v. Van Patten, 3 Ind. 107. This, however, is clearly wrong. Wilson v. Whitaker, 49 Pa. 114, is also inconsistent with the above principles.

(except in those cases to which we have referred) according to certain rules of law which the jury are not at liberty to disregard, and which equally control the conduct of the court. "In cases," said Washington, J., on the Pennsylvania circuit,[85] "where a rule can be discovered, the jury are bound to adopt it. That rule is, that the plaintiff should recover so much as will repair the injury sustained by the misconduct of the defendant." In regard to the rate of damages on a foreign bill of exchange, the New York Court of Errors said, "In this, as in other cases of contract, the rule by which the amount or extent of redress should be ascertained, is a question of law," [86] The amount of compensation, or, in other words, the measure of damages, is, therefore, as a general rule, matter of law, to be disposed of by the court.

§ 32. Damnum absque injuria and injuriâ sine damno.

It is not, however, to be understood that legal relief is to be had for every species of loss that individuals sustain by the acts of others. It is undoubtedly true that damage resulting from fraud, deceit, or malice, always furnishes a good cause of action.[87] "This principle," says the Supreme Court of Ohio, "is one of natural justice, long recognized in the law." [88] But where the injury is not to be traced to any evil motive, the rule is by no means universal that injury is always entitled to redress. In addition to the great class of moral rights and duties which the law does not attempt to protect or enforce,[89] there are many sufferings inflicted by human agency, where the immediate instruments of the injury are free from fault, or the act beyond their control. In these cases the law does not seek to interfere.[90] It is only legal injury that sets its machinery in

[85] Walker v. Smith, 1 Wash. C. C. 152.

[86] Graves v. Dash, 12 Johns. (N. Y.) 17.

[87] Pasley v. Freeman, 3 T. R. 51; Upton v. Vail, 6 Johns. (N. Y.) 181, 5 Am. Dec. 210; Barney v. Dewey, 13 Johns. 224, 7 Am. Dec. 372.

[88] Bartholomew v. Bentley, 15 Ohio, 659, 666, 45 Am. Dec. 596.

[89] Pasley v. Freeman, 3 T. R. 51; Freund v. Murray, 39 Mont. 539, 104 Pac. 683.

[90] Such are the cases governed by the maxim, *Salus populi suprema lex.* "There are many cases," says Mr. Broom, in his work on Legal Maxims, p. 1, "in which individuals sustain an injury for which the law gives no action, as where private houses are pulled down, or bulwarks raised on private property for the preservation and de-

operation; and this is meant by the maxim that *damnum absque injuriâ* gives no cause of action.[91]   So, if in the prudent and reasonable exercise, by an owner of property, of his right of dominion, another sustains damage, it is *damnum absque injuriâ*.[92]   So it has been said in regard to a corporation charged with committing a nuisance, "If the defendants have only pursued the path presented for them by the laws from which they derive their existence, they have committed no wrongful act.   Though the plaintiffs may have sustained damage, it is indeed *damnum absque injuriâ;* for the act of the law, like the act of God, works no wrong to any one." [93]   There must not only be loss, but it must be injuriously brought about by a violation of the legal rights of others.   "No one, legally speaking," says the Supreme Court of New York, "is injured or damnified

fence of the kingdom against the king's enemies."   Such, again, are those which fall within the maxim *Necessitas inducit privilegium quoad jura privata.* "As a general rule," says Mr. Broom, in his work above cited p. 6, "the law charges no man with default where the act done is compulsory and not voluntary, and where there is not a careful selection on his part; and, therefore, if either there be an impossibility for a man to do otherwise, or so great a perturbation of the judgment and reason, as in presumption of law man's nature cannot overcome, such necessity carries a privilege in itself."

[91] Ashby *v.* White, 1 Salk. 19; s. c. 2 Ld. Raym. 938; Lamb *v.* Stone, 11 Pick. (Mass.) 527; Broom's Legal Maxims, 93. "In point of law," said Rolfe, B., in Davies *v.* Jenkins, 11 M. & W. 745, 756, where process had been by mistake served on the wrong person, "if the proceedings have been adopted purely through mistake, though injury may have resulted to the plaintiff, it is *damnum absque injuriâ*, and no action will lie." "This is one of those unfortunate cases," says the same learned judge, in Winterbottom *v.* Wright, 10 M. & W. 109, 116,—a suit by a mail coachman against a contractor for sup-

ply of mail coaches for injury resulting from a coach breaking down,— "in which there certainly has been *damnum*, but it is *damnum absque injuriâ*."   So in Massachusetts, where the owner of land made an excavation therein near the street, and a person in the nighttime fell in; held, that the owner was not liable.   "Where neither party is in fault," said the Supreme Court "and an accident takes place, it is *damnum absque injuriâ*."—Howland *v.* Vincent, 10 Met. (Mass.) 371, 374, 43 Am. Dec. 442; Gardner *v.* Heartt, 2 Barb. (N. Y.) 165. See *New York:* Talbot *v.* N. Y. & H. R. R., 151 N. Y. 155, 45 N. E. 382; *Pennsylvania:* Robb *v.* Carnegie, 145 Pa. 324, 22 Atl. 649, 27 A. S. R. 694, 14 L. R. A. 329.

[92] Donovan *v.* The City of New Orleans, 11 La. Ann. 711; First Baptist Church *v.* Sch'y & Troy R. R., 5 Barb. (N. Y.) 79, 84.

[93] Mahan *v.* Brown, 13 Wend. (N. Y.) 261, 265, 28 Am. Dec. 461, where it was held that an action will not lie for obstructing a neighbor's lights, if they be not ancient lights, and no right has been acquired by grant or occupation and acquiescence. See Steuart *v.* State of Maryland, 20 Md. 97.

unless some *right* is infringed. The refusal or discontinuance of a favor gives no cause of action." [94]   The prosecution of this inquiry, however, would lead us directly into the great field of causes of action. Suffice it for our present purposes to say that whenever loss is coupled with legal injury, the law gives compensation.

It is further to be borne in mind, that if loss without legal injury goes unredressed, the correlative proposition is equally true, that the infringement of a legal right, when unattended by any positive injury, furnishes no ground for other than nominal relief. It is not sufficient that an act unauthorized by law has been committed. For *Injuria sine damno* there is no compensation. Substantial loss to the party plaintiff must have ensued to entitle him to substantial relief. *De minimis non curat lex.*[95]   But of this we shall have occasion to take notice again, when we come to consider the subject of nominal damages.**

§ 33. Fletcher v. Rylands.

In Fletcher *v.* Rylands [96] the plaintiffs were owners of a mine which they had worked under the defendants' land. The defendants erected on their own land a reservoir for the purpose of working their mill. There were some old shafts in the defendants' land which had become partly filled, but connected below with the plaintiffs' mine. Of these the defendants knew nothing. The reservoir was not made sufficiently strong with regard to the shafts, and, in consequence, the water burst into the shafts and flooded the plaintiffs' mine. In the Court of Exchequer, it was held, Bramwell, B., dissenting, that the plaintiffs could not recover without showing want of due care on the part of the defendants.[97]   On appeal to the Exchequer Chamber, this decision was reversed, Blackburn, J., delivering the opinion. He said: "We think that the true rule of law is that the person, who for his own purposes brings on his lands and collects and keeps there, anything likely to do mischief if it escapes, must keep it in at his peril, and, if he does not do so,

---

[94] Paul *v.* Slason, 22 Vt. 231, 54 Am. Dec. 75.

[95] *De minimis non curat lex* does not prohibit the allowance of nominal damages. Fullam *v.* Stearns, 30 Vt. 443.

[96] L. R. 1 Ex. 265.

[97] 3 H. & C. 774.

is *prima facie* answerable for all the damage which is the natural consequence of its escape." In support of this doctrine, he cited the rule in the case of cattle escaping from control, without negligence on the part of the owners, and the case of Tenant *v.* Goldwin,[98] where a defendant was held liable for filth flowing from his cellar through defects in the wall. On appeal to the House of Lords, this judgment was affirmed.[99] Lord Cairns drew a distinction between a natural and a non-natural user of land, defining the latter as "introducing into the close that which in its natural condition was not in or upon it;" and held that, in the latter case, the defendant acted at his peril. In Losee *v.* Buchanan [100] the plaintiff's house was injured through the bursting of a boiler on the defendant's land. It was held that the defendant was only liable for negligence. Earl, C., said that the rule in the case of the escape of animals did not furnish analogies absolutely controlling in reference to inanimate objects. He considered Fletcher *v.* Rylands in conflict with the law of this country, especially those cases holding that if one light a fire on his land and it spread to his neighbor's, the former is liable only in case of negligence. He then said: "This examination has gone far enough to show that the rule is, at least in this country, a universal one, which, so far as I can discern, has no exceptions or limitations, that no one can be made liable for injuries to the person or property of another, without some fault or negligence on his part." In a case in New Jersey, precisely like the last case in its facts, the same conclusion was reached.[101] Beasley, C. J., after saying that in principle the case could not be distinguished from Fletcher *v.* Rylands, said that the fallacy in that case consisted in extending into a general principle the rule relating to cattle, a class of cases to be regarded as in a great degree exceptional. He then referred to the case of Tenant *v.* Goldwin, and remarked, that allowing the cellar to get out of repair was in itself negligence, and that nothing was said as to the defendant's liability, had he taken all proper precautions to prevent the escape of the filth. He said that this case partook largely of the character of nuisances.

---

[98] 6 Mod. 311.
[99] L. R. 3 H. L. 330.
[100] 51 N. Y. 476, 10 Am. Rep. 623.

[101] Marshall *v.* Welwood, 38 N. J. L. 339, 48 Am. Rep. 394.

He then said: "The common rule, quite institutional in its character, is, that in order to sustain an action for a tort, the damage complained of must have come from a wrongful act." In New Hampshire, the doctrine of Fletcher v. Rylands has also been disapproved.[102] The defendant's horses became frightened by a locomotive, and escaping from the defendant's control, ran upon the plaintiff's land and injured a post. Doe, J., in a very elaborate opinion, endeavored to show the consequences to which the doctrine of Fletcher v. Rylands must lead. After quoting the language of Blackburn, J., cited *supra*, he said: "This seems to be substantially an adoption of the early authorities, and an extension of the ancient practice of holding the defendant liable in some cases, on the partial view that regarded the misfortune of the plaintiff upon whom a damage had fallen, and required no legal reason for transferring the damage to the defendant. The ancient rule was, that a person in whose house or on whose land a fire accidentally originated, which spread to his neighbor's property and destroyed it, must make good the loss. . . . One result of such a doctrine is, that every one building a fire on his own hearth, for necessary purposes, with the utmost care, does so at the peril, not only of losing his own house, but of being irretrievably ruined if a spark from his chimney starts a conflagration which lays waste the neighborhood." [103] But in Massachusetts the doctrine seems to have been regarded with more favor. In Shipley v. Fifty Associates [104] the defendant built a house in Boston, with a high pitched roof, so situated that anything falling off the roof would naturally fall into the street. During the winter some ice slid off the roof and injured a passer. It was held that the defendant was liable. Ames, J., cited the opinions of Lord Cairns and of Blackburn, J., but he also put the decision on the ground that, from the position and style of the building it was highly probable the accident would occur. It was therefore a clear case of negligence, and in that distinguishable from Fletcher v. Rylands. In Wilson v. New Bedford [105] the de-

[102] Brown v. Collins, 53 N. H. 442, 16 Am. Rep. 372.

[103] See further Sweet v. Cutts, 50 N. H. 439, 9 Am. Rep. 276; Bassett v. Salisbury Mfg. Co., 43 N. H. 569, 82 Am. Dec. 179.

[104] 106 Mass. 194, 8 Am. Rep. 318.

[105] 108 Mass. 261, 11 Am. Rep. 352.

fendants had built a dam and made a reservoir under a power conferred by statute, but owing to the increased pressure, the water percolated through the soil and flooded the plaintiff's cellar. The statute made the defendant liable for all damage caused by the construction of the reservoir. The plaintiff had repeatedly, during two years, demanded payment for the damage sustained by him. The court, on the authority of several Massachusetts cases, in which damages sustained through artificial percolation had been recovered, and on the authority of a New York case, and of Fletcher v. Rylands, held the defendants liable. This case is clearly distinguishable from Fletcher v. Rylands, as the defendant continued the use of the land after it had notice of the injury it was causing. Although nothing is said in the opinion on this point, it is to be noticed that one of the cases cited in support of the judgment, and in which Fletcher v. Rylands was cited, Ball v. Nye,[106] was decided expressly on this ground. The other two Massachusetts cases on which Wilson v. New Bedford was decided, were actions for damages for percolation, arising from flowing lands for mills, and it was held that damages by percolation were the natural consequences of flooding the lands, no question of *damnum absque injuriâ* being raised. The case cited from New York, Pixley v. Clark,[107] was one where the defendants dammed a stream, and caused percolation on the plaintiff's land. Peckham, J., in an elaborate review of the cases, held the defendants liable. But he placed his decision on the ground that there was no difference between flooding land from the direct overflow of the stream and from percolation, and in Losee v. Buchanan, *supra*, this decision was said to be an application of the principle, *aqua currit et debet currere*, to the facts of the case. Peckham, J., also pointed out the fact that the defendants continued their works without change, after they knew the injury it was causing, saying: "These defendants tried an experiment for their own benefit and found it seriously injured the plaintiff. When they see the injury they insist upon continuing it." A second distinction to be drawn between Wilson v. New Bedford and Fletcher v. Rylands seems to be, that in the former the injury was a direct and natural consequence, flowing from the

[106] 99 Mass. 582, 97 Am. Dec. 56.   [107] 35 N. Y. 520, 91 Am. Dec. 72.

use of the defendant's land in the very manner in which it was intended to be used, whereas, in Fletcher v. Rylands, the use to which the defendant intended to put his land was by a wholly unforeseen circumstance entirely destroyed, and the injury resulted not from the use for which he intended it, but from the destruction of this use. This same distinction was drawn in Losee v. Buchanan between the facts of that case and of Hay v. Cohoes Co.[108] In the latter case, the defendants were authorized to dig a canal. In blasting, a piece of rock was thrown against the plaintiff's house; it was held that the defendant was liable without any proof of negligence on his part. Earl, C., said of this decision, in Losee v. Buchanan, that it was based upon the soundest principles. "The damage was the necessary consequence of just what the defendant was doing." In McKeon v. See [109] the defendant was held liable for injury caused by his machinery jarring the walls of the plaintiff's houses. And in Gray v. Harris,[110] Chapman, C. J., says: "The degree of care which a person is bound to use in constructing a dam across a stream . . . must be in proportion to the extent of the injury which will be likely to result to third persons, provided it should prove insufficient." In Smith v. Fletcher [111] the defendants by working their mines had caused hollows to form in the surface of the land. A watercourse ran across their land which they had diverted from its original channel. In an extraordinary freshet the water overflowed the banks of the stream, into the hollows, thence through openings made into the defendant's mines, and thence into the plaintiff's mine. The Court of Exchequer held the case not to be distinguishable from Fletcher v. Rylands, but on appeal to the Exchequer Chamber this decision was reversed and sent back for a new trial. Lord Coleridge said that the case was not in every respect within the authority of Fletcher v. Rylands, and thought it desirable that the opinion of the jury should be taken whether the defendant's acts were done in the ordinary reasonable and proper mode of working the mine. On a new trial the jury found that the flooding was caused by the diversion of the

[108] 2 N. Y. 159, 51 Am. Dec. 279; acc., Colton v. Onderdonk, 69 Cal. 155.

[109] 51 N. Y. 300, 10 Am. Rep. 659.
[110] 107 Mass. 492, 6 Am. Rep. 61.
[111] L. R. 7 Ex. 305.

stream, and that the diverted channel was insufficient, and more likely to overflow than in its original condition. The case was carried to the House of Lords,[112] and Lord Penzance held the findings of the jury to be conclusive against the defendant. He said that apart from these findings there would have been a question what obligations the defendants took upon themselves in diverting the channel. He expressed the opinion that the new course must be in itself capable of conveying such rainfalls as might reasonably be anticipated, and that the defendants were not bound to make provision for any quantities of rain however heavy that might be discharged into it. In Wilson v. Waddell [113] the defendant's mining operations caused the surface land to split so that in rain-storms the water passed through and flooded the plaintiff's land. This was held not to create any cause of action, but to be a case of *damnum absque injuriâ*, on the ground that the use of the land was a natural one, and necessarily caused the cracking of the surface. In Nichols v. Marsland [114] the defendant's reservoir through an extraordinary fall of rain gave way and carried off some bridges. It was held on appeal that the law imposed a duty upon the defendant to keep the water within bounds, but that it was a general rule that if an act of God prevented the performance of a duty imposed by rule of law, the defendant was excused from liabilities, and it was held that the unusual rainfall must be considered an act of God. In Jones v. Festiniog Ry. Co.[115] the court, following Fletcher v. Rylands, held that the defendant was liable for the escape of sparks from an engine without any negligence on his part, the use of engines not being especially provided for in the company's charter. The case was distinguished from Vaughan v. Taff Vale Ry. Co.,[116] where the Exchequer Chamber held that there was no liability for the escape of sparks where the use of engines was authorized by statute, and there was no negligence on the defendant's part. If these cases hold that there was no liability for damages resulting necessarily from the use of the engines, they were properly decided on the ground that a grant by the Legislature carries

---

[112] 2 App. Cas. 781.
[113] 2 App. Cas. 95.
[114] 2 Ex. Div. 1.

[115] L. R. 3 Q. B. 733.
[116] 5 H. & N. 679.

with it the incidents of the grant, one of which here would be immunity from liability for damage necessarily caused. But if it was intended to decide that the legislative sanction relieved the defendant from the duty to restrain under all circumstances the dangerous element it was employing, it seems difficult to understand why the sanction of the common law should not have the same effect. In Cattle *v.* Stockton Water Works [117] the plaintiff was working under a contract with one Knight; the defendant's water-pipes, which their charter had authorized them to construct, burst, flooded Knight's land, and delayed the plaintiff in his work. The court refused to pass upon the question whether the defendants were relieved from liability on the ground of the sanction of their charter, but held that there was no liability to the plaintiff, although there might have been to Knight.

§ 34. No compensation for loss by nuisance common to all.

* To this general principle, that where loss and legal injury unite, relief will be given by suit, the law recognizes one exception: that where the wrong is on so great a scale that the whole community, or a large portion of them, suffer from it. "Here," says Blackstone, "I must premise that the law gives no *private* remedy for anything but a *private* wrong." [118] And so the law is laid down by Lord Coke in regard to nuisances on the highway: "A man shall not have an action on the case for a nuisance done in the highway, for it is a common nuisance, and then it is not reasonable that a particular person should have the action, for by the same reason that one person might have an action for it, by the same reason every one might have an action, and then he would be punished a hundred times for one and the same cause." In such case the remedy is by indictment.

§ 35. Unless particular damage results.

But Coke goes on immediately to make this distinction: "But if any particular person afterwards, by the nuisance done, has more particular damage than any other, then for that particular injury he shall have a particular action on the case." [119]

[117] L. R. 10 Q. B. 453.   [119] Williams's case, 5 Rep. 72.
[118] 3 Bl. Com. 219; 4 ib. 167; Broom's Legal Maxims, 206.

The rule and the exception have both been repeatedly recognized in England and in the courts of this country, though there has been much controversy as to the nature and amount of the "particular damage" that will support the action.[120] It has been held in England that an obstruction of a navigable creek, by which the plaintiff's vessel was arrested in her course, was sufficient to maintain a suit;[121] and where a corporation

[120] Where the nuisance consists of an obstruction of the highway, an interference with plaintiff's passage along the highway, and the necessity of making a détour, is not special damage, since all passers suffer alike.

Massachusetts: Nichols v. Richmond, 162 Mass. 170, 38 N. E. 501.

Minnesota: Shaubut v. St. Paul Ry., 21 Minn. 502.

New York: Masterson v. Short, 3 Abb. Pr. (N. S.) 154.

Pennsylvania: Saylor v. Pennsylvania Canal Co., 183 Pa. 167, 38 Atl. 598.

England: Greasly v. Codling, 2 Bing. 263.

But if the nuisance interferes with plaintiff's access from the highway to his own land he suffers special damage for which he may sue.

California: Schulte v. North Pacific Transportation Co., 50 Cal. 592.

Illinois: Pekin v. Brereton, 67 Ill. 477.

Ohio: Farrely v. Cincinnati, 2 Disn. 516 (though plaintiff was in the omnibus business and lost custom).

Rhode Island: Clark v. Peckham, 10 R. I. 35.

Washington: Brazell v. Seattle, 55 Wash. 180, 104 Pac. 155.

So of the obstruction of a navigable stream. Drews v. E. P. Burton & Co., 57 S. E. 176, 76 S. C. 362.

The fact that plaintiff paid an assessment for building a highway does not give him the right to special damages upon a discontinuance of it.

Illinois: Chicago v. Union Bldg. Assoc., 102 Ill. 379, 393.

Indiana: Stout v. Noblesville & E. Gravel R. R., 83 Ind. 466.

The fact that stagnant water is caused to stand in the highway in front of plaintiff's land is not in itself special damage for which he may sue. Hatch v. Vermont Cent. R. R., 28 Vt. 142.

But sickness caused by such stagnant water is special damage. Hamilton v. Mayor, 52 Ga. 435. And so is any permanent injury caused by the pollution of a stream. Drake v. Lady Ensley Coal, Iron & R. Co., 102 Ala. 501, 48 Am. St. 77, 14 So. 749, 24 L. R. A. 64.

It seems that loss of a tenant by reason of the nuisance would be special damage; but refusal of a tenant to pay rent, while he continues in occupation, is not special damage, since he is legally bound to pay. Baker v. Boston, 12 Pick. (Mass.) 184.

Where plaintiff had let a balcony and windows to view a procession and her view was cut off by an obstruction of the highway, so that she could not get the agreed compensation for her balcony and windows, this was held special damage for which she could recover. Campbell v. Paddington, [1911] 1 K. B. 869.

[121] Rose v. Miles, 4 Maule & Sel. 101, which virtually overruled Hubert v. Groves, 1 Esp. 148, and Paine v. Partrich, Carth. 191; and the doctrine of Rose v. Miles was affirmed in Greasly v. Codling, 2 Bing. 263, as to a highway. The authority of Hubert v. Groves has also been denied in this country. Lansing v. Wiswall, 5 Denio (N. Y.), 213.

bound to repair certain banks, mounds, sea-shores, and piers neglected to do so, in consequence of which the plaintiff's house was injured, it was also held that the action lay.[122] So, again, where a bookseller, having a shop by the side of a public thoroughfare, suffered loss in his business in consequence of passengers having been diverted from the thoroughfare by the defendant's continuing an unauthorized obstruction across it for an unreasonable time, this was held a sufficient particular damage to be the foundation of an action.[123] The doctrine of these cases has been substantially adopted in this country, as we shall have occasion to see when we come to treat of trespasses to real estate.[124]

---

[122] The Mayor and Burgesses of Lyme Regis v. Henly, 1 Bing. N. C. 222.

[123] Wilkes v. Hungerford Market Company, 2 Bing. N. C. 281, where the authority of Hubert v. Groves was again denied.

[124] *Massachusetts:* Stetson v. Faxon, 19 Pick. 147, 31 Am. Dec. 123.

New York: Pierce v. Dart, 7 Cowen, 609; Lansing v. Smith, 8 Cowen, 146; s. c. 4 Wend. 9; Mills v. Hall, 9 Wend. 315, 24 Am. Dec. 160; The Mayor, etc., v. Furze, 3 Hill, 612; Myers v. Malcolm, 6 Hill, 292, 41 Am. Dec. 744; Lansing v. Wiswall, 5 Denio, 213; First Baptist Church v. Sch'y & Troy R. R., 5 Barb. 79.

Vermont: Baxter v. Winooski Turnpike Co., 22 Vermont, 114, 52 Am. Dec. 84.

In the Proprietors of the Quincy Canal v. Newcomb (7 Met. 276), it was said, that if a party "had suffered damage from the filling up of a canal and want of cleansing, by means of which he was unable to enter it, it would have been a damage suffered in common with all other members of the community, and therefore redress must be sought by a public prosecution. Where one suffers in common with all the public, although from his proximity to the obstructed way, or otherwise, from his more frequent occasion to use it he may suffer in a greater degree than others, still he cannot have an action, because it would cause such a multiplicity of suits as to be itself an intolerable evil. But when he sustains a special damage differing in kind from that which is common to others, as where he falls into a ditch unlawfully made in a highway, and hurts his horse, or sustains a personal damage, then he may bring his action."

In Pennsylvania, the rule has been applied to an obstruction in the Big Schuylkill, which prevented the plaintiff's rafts from descending. Hughes v. Heiser, 1 Binney, 463, 2 Am. Dec. 459. In that State, when a private person suffers some extraordinary damage beyond other citizens, by a public nuisance, he shall have a private satisfaction by action, even if his special damage be merely consequential. Pittsburgh v. Scott, 1 Barr, 309. In Kentucky, it has been said that it is not enough that one be turned out of the way. Barr v. Stevens, 1 Bibb, 292. In Connecticut, see Bigelow v. Hartford Bridge Co., 14 Conn. 565, 36 Am. Dec. 502, and O'Brien v. Norwich & W. R. R., 17 Conn. 372. The doctrine is the same in regard to abatement: "The ordinary remedy for a public nuisance is itself public—that of indict-

We shall be obliged to make a more minute examination of this subject when we come to speak particularly of the subject of Nuisances; but we should not omit to notice here that in cases like these, in which the right to relief depends upon the amount of injury, we may be said to approach a vanishing point, where all distinctions between the cause of action and the rule of compensation are confounded and lost.

§ 36. Nor by way of settlement for crime.

It is proper here to call attention to the distinction maintained between those cases of a criminal character which can be compromised by the parties themselves, and those in which no such private interference is permitted. It was early held, that a contract to withdraw a prosecution for perjury is founded on an unlawful consideration and void. If the party charged were innocent, the law was abused for the purpose of extortion; if guilty, it was eluded by a corrupt compromise, screening the criminal for a bribe.[125] The subject has been much considered in subsequent cases; and it seems now to be well settled that the right to compromise depends on the right to recover damages in a civil action. "The law permits a compromise of all offences, though made the subject of a criminal prosecution, for which offences the injured party might sue and recover damages in an action. It is often the only manner in which he can obtain redress. But if the offence is of a public nature only, no agreement can be valid that is founded on the consideration of stifling a prosecution for it;" therefore, although the party injured may lawfully compromise an indictment for a common assault, yet an agreement to pay the costs of a prosecution of an assault on the plaintiff and riot, and of an action for a wrongful levy under a *fi. fa.*, which agreement was founded partly on compromise of the prosecution, and partly on an undertaking to withdraw the execution, is altogether invalid as founded on an illegal consideration.[126] **

---

ment—and each individual who is only injured as one of the public can no more proceed to abate than he can bring an action." Mayor of Colchester *v.* Brooke, 7 Q. B. 339, 377.

[125] Collins *v.* Blantern, 2 Wils. 341, 347.

[126] Keir *v.* Leeman, 6 Q. B. 308, 321.

§ 36a. Apportionment of damage between wrongdoers.

There can be no apportionment of the damage between joint wrongdoers, and consequently where two or more persons are concerned together in the commission of a tort, acting in concert, each is responsible for the entire amount of the damage.[127] The plaintiff may join all as defendants, or select such as he wishes to hold. This is true even where the wrong was a conversion, and each party took a part only of the property converted; each is liable for the entire value of the property taken by their joint act, not merely for the value of what he took himself.[128] But where two or more parties are concerned in the damage, and they acted entirely independently of one another, they are not jointly liable, but each is liable for the damage he himself caused.[129] Upon this principle where two

---

[127] *Georgia:* Hunter *v.* Wakefield, 97 Ga. 543, 25 S. E. 347 (joint libel).

Indiana: Everroad *v.* Gabbert, 83 Ind. 489; Block *v.* Haseltine, 3 Ind. App. 491, 29 N. E. 937 (principal and agent).

Iowa: Turner *v.* Hitchcock, 20 Iowa, 310.

Kansas: Kansas City *v.* Slangstrom, 53 Kan. 431, 36 Pac. 706.

Maine: Allison *v.* Hobbs, 96 Me. 26, 51 Atl. 245.

Massachusetts: Kennebeck Co. *v.* Boulton, 4 Mass. 419.

New Jersey: Jenne *v.* Sutton, 43 N. J. L. 257, 39 Atl. 578 (subscribers to illegal display of fireworks). See *post*, § 431.

[128] *Colorado:* Mason *v.* Sieglitz, 22 Colo. 320, 44 Pac. 588.

Kansas: Westbrook *v.* Mize, 35 Kan. 299, 10 Pac. 881.

New York: Williams *v.* Sheldon, 10 Wend. 654.

Cf. the equitable rule that there is always contribution between co-trustees, if equity requires it, although the *cestui que trust* has the right to make the whole loss out of any one or more of them as for a joint and several tort.

California: Bermingham *v.* Wilcox, 120 Cal. 467.

Illinois: Fellrath *v.* Peoria German School Assn., 66 Ill. App. 77.

New York: Sherman *v.* Parish, 53 N. Y. 483.

England: Edwards *v.* Hood-Barrs [1905], 1 Ch. 20; 2 Perry on Trusts, § 848.

[129] *California:* Durgin *v.* Neal, 82 Cal. 595 (injury by flowage; part of damage caused by defendant's obstruction, part by that of others).

Massachusetts: Wheeler *v.* Worcester, 10 All. 591.

New York: Wallace *v.* Drew, 59 Barb. 413 (injury by flowage; part of water thrown on land by defendant's structure, part of it by another structure). Whalen v. Union B. & P. Co., 129 N. Y. Supp. 391,— App. Div.— (pollution of stream: several persons independently polluted it).

Pennsylvania: Bard *v.* Yohn, 26 Pa. 482 (each defendant wrongfully placed a horse and carriage on opposite sides of road; plaintiff kicked by one horse against the other carriage; no joint liability). Little Schuylkill R. R. *v.* Richards, 57 Pa. 142, 98 Am. Dec. 209 (obstruction of stream by throwing in

dogs or other animals trespass and do damage together, the owners of the animals not being jointly concerned in the trespass, are not jointly liable; each is responsible only for the damage caused by his own animal.[130]

Where it is clear that part of the damage only was caused by the defendant, and it is impossible to show with a satisfactory degree of certainty just what part this was, the jury must estimate as well as they can what part of the damage was caused by the defendant, and find a verdict for that amount.[131]

The apportionment of damage between the wrongdoers is possible only when each in fact caused part of the damage and did not cause the rest. It commonly happens that the act of one of the wrongdoers is in fact a contributing cause to the whole damage; and in that case he is liable for the whole amount of the loss, and cannot escape any part of the liability by showing that an independent wrongdoer contributed to the result. A wrongdoer is responsible for the whole of any damage which he has himself caused, in whole or in part.[132] Upon this princi-

dirt; several threw it in; each responsible only for the damage caused by the dirt he himself threw in).

Wisconsin: Karns *v.* Allen, 135 Wis. 48, 115 N. W. 357 (nuisance caused by a dam erected by A and continued by B; B not liable for damage caused during A's ownership).

[130] *Massachusetts:* Buddington *v.* Shearer, 20 Pick. 477.

New Jersey: Nierenberg *v.* Wood, 59 N. J. L. 112, 35 Atl. 654.

New York: Van Steenburgh *v.* Tobias, 17 Wend. 562.

Tennessee: Dyer *v.* Hutchins, 87 Tenn. 198, 10 S. W. 194.

If there is no evidence as to the amount of damage done by each animal, it has been held that the amount will be presumed to be equal. Ogden *v.* Lucas, 48 Ill. 492; Partenheimer *v.* Van Order, 20 Barb. (N. Y.) 479.

And where the animals were different in size, it has been held that the jury might apportion the damage according to size. Wilbur *v.* Hubbard, 35 Barb. (N. Y.) 303.

In some States the owners are made jointly liable by statute.

Pennsylvania: Kerr *v.* O'Connor, 63 Pa. 341.

Vermont: Fairchild *v.* Rich, 68 Vt. 202, 34 Atl. 692.

[131] *California:* Learned *v.* Castle, 78 Cal. 454, 18 Pac. 872, 21 Pac. 11.

Illinois: Chicago & N. W. Ry. *v.* Hoag, 90 Ill. 339.

Maine: Washburn *v.* Gilman, 64 Me. 163.

New Jersey: Jenkins *v.* Pennsylvania R. R., 67 N. J. L. 331, 51 Atl. 704.

New York: Schriver *v.* Johnstown, 71 Hun, 232, 24 N. Y. Supp. 1083.

Contra, Ohio: Beiser *v.* Grever & Twaite Co., 11 Ohio Dec. 444, where in such a case the court refused to allow any damages.

[132] *New York:* Slater *v.* Mersereau, 64 N. Y. 138.

ple, when an action is brought by a wife, under the civil damage act, for an injury caused by selling liquor to her husband whereby he became intoxicated, each person who sold part of the liquor which caused the intoxication is liable, though the intoxication was in part caused by liquor sold independently by another, since the liquor sold by each was an active cause of the intoxication complained of.[133] Where plaintiff suffered a personal injury from defendant, and a short time afterwards an independent injury from another, and in an action against the latter had concealed the fact of the preceding injury and recovered compensation for the loss caused by both injuries, in an action now brought against the defendant it was held that each wrongdoer was liable for the damage which he had independently caused and that the wrong of the plaintiff in obtaining too great damages from the other did not bar him from now recovering from defendant the damages due from him.[134]

Wisconsin: Folsom v. Apple River L. D. Co., 41 Wis. 602.

Two buildings, one on each side of plaintiff's building, simultaneously fell, by the negligence of their owners, and crushed plaintiff's building. He may hold either wrongdoer liable for the whole damage. Johnson v. Chapman, 43 W. Va. 639, 28 S. E. 744.

[133] *Illinois:* Tetzner v. Naughton, 12 Ill. App. 148.

Iowa: Kearney v. Fitzgerald, 43 Iowa, 580.

Kansas: Werner v. Edmiston, 24 Kan. 147.

Massachusetts: Bryant v. Tidgewell, 133 Mass. 86.

Michigan: Steele v. Thompson, 42 Mich. 594, 4 N. W. 536.

Ohio: Boyd v. Watt, 27 Ohio St. 259.

Persons whose liquor merely put the victim into a besotted condition are too remote from the consequences of the final intoxication.

Illinois: Tetzner v. Naughton, 12 Ill. App. 148.

Iowa: Hitchner v. Ehlers, 44 Iowa, 40.

Kansas: Werner v. Edmiston, 24 Kan. 147.

Massachusetts: Bryant v. Tidgewell, 133 Mass. 86.

Unless the complaint is of the besotted condition of the husband; for in that case all whose sales contributed to cause the condition are liable. Rantz v. Barnes, 40 Ohio St. 43.

On this section see further, Sedgwick, Elements, p. 150.

[134] Post v. Hartford St. Ry., 72 Conn. 362, 44 Atl. 547.

CHAPTER II

COMPENSATION

§ 37. The elements of injury.

* It has been said that the effect of our law is to give in damages what it calls compensation. When, however, we come to analyze this phrase, we shall find its juridical interpretation a very restricted one. Injury resulting from the acts or omissions of others, free from any taint of fraud, malice, or wilful wrong, consists:—

First. Of the *actual pecuniary loss directly sustained;* as the amount for the note unpaid; the value of the property paid for, but not delivered.

Second. Of the *indirect pecuniary loss* sustained in conse-

42

quence of the primary loss; the derangement and disturbance produced by the failure of others to comply with their engagements, and the consequent inability of those who depend on them to adhere to their own; loss of credit; loss of business; insolvency.

Third. Of the *physical and mental suffering* produced by the act or omission in question; pain; vexation; anxiety.

Fourth. The *value of the time* consumed in establishing the contested right by process of law, if suit become necessary.

Fifth. The *actual expenses* incurred to obtain the same end—costs and counsel fees.

To these one further element is to be added in those cases where the aggressor is animated by a fraudulent, a malicious, or an oppressive intention, and that is—

Sixth. The *sense of wrong or insult,* in the sufferer's breast, resulting from an act dictated by a spirit of wilful injustice, or by a deliberate intention to vex, degrade, or insult. This constitutes the difference, and the only difference between the injury produced by inability and that produced by design. All the other constituents are the same. The pecuniary loss, direct and indirect, the anxiety, the time and expense, are the same whether a wrong be done through the honest inability, the wilful fraud, or the deliberate malice of the offending party. But in the two latter cases, the last element is superadded; a sense of wrong or insult which does not exist in the former.[1]

§ 38. Perfect compensation impossible.

All the items must, therefore, be taken into the account in any effort to make complete *compensation,* in the ordinary acceptation of the word. But we shall find that the legal

---

[1] The Scotch law has endeavored practically to analyze the elements of injury. By the jurisprudence of Scotland, in actions for personal torts, the damages are divided into *special damages,* the actual pecuniary loss, and *solatium,* solace, or recompense for the wounded feelings. So in Forgie *v.* Henderson, 1 Murray, 410, in assault and battery, the Lord Chief Commissioner Adam said, "There are, first, *special damages,* consisting of the surgeon's account, and the person being kept from his work. Second, the *solatium,* which is peculiarly within the province of the jury." So in Cameron *v.* Cameron, 2 Murr. 232, "If no damages are proved, you cannot find them; but there is a claim for *solatium,* and you must consider what evidence there is of the injury to the mind and feelings."

meaning of the term is very different. In fact, unless the word is used in a technical sense, it is altogether inaccurate to speak of damages as always resulting in *compensation;* and whatever restricted meaning this term may be supposed to have technically acquired, it is at all events entirely incorrect to say in the language which we have above seen used by various eminent judges, that "the remedy is commensurate to the injury." This language attributes to legal relief a degree of perfection which it is very far from possessing. "It would be going a great way," said Chief-Justice Marshall,[2] "to subject a debtor, who promises to pay a debt, to *all the loss* consequent on his failure to fulfil his promise. The general policy of the law does not admit of such strictness; and although in morals a man may justly charge himself as the cause of any loss occasioned by the breach of his engagement, yet, in the course of human affairs, such breaches are so often occasioned by events which were unforeseen, and could not easily be prevented, that interest is generally considered as compensation which must content the injured." "It has been contended," said another eminent judge, "that the true measure of damages, in all actions of covenant, is the loss actually sustained. But this rule is laid down too generally. In an action of covenant for non-payment of money on a bond or mortgage, no more than the principal and legal interest of the debt can be recovered, although the plaintiff may have suffered to a much greater amount by the default of payment."[3] And it is to be borne in mind, that the same deficiency of compensation exists in the case of defendants as well as plaintiffs. If the party who receives the injury is obliged to bear his proportion of the loss—so, •on the other hand, the party wrongfully charged recovers his costs only, and no allowance is made for his time, indirect loss, annoyance, or counsel fees. "Every defendant," says Mr. Broom, "against whom an action is brought, experiences some injury or inconvenience beyond what the costs will compensate him for."[4] **

To say nothing of the anxiety and pain of mind which often result from a breach of contract, and which the law is power-

---

[2] Short *v.* Skipwith, 1 Brock. 103, 114.
[3] Tilghman, C. J., in Bender *v.* Fromberger, 4 Dall. 436, 444.

[4] Broom's Legal Maxims, 199; Davies *v.* Jenkins, 11 M. & W. 745, 756.

less to assuage, all lawyers know that in most cases of the non-payment of money when due, where the creditor has no means of replacing it, and indeed, in a large proportion of all lawsuits, the mere delay in obtaining such redress as can be had, entails on the sufferer consequential damages often serious, sometimes ruinous, for which there is no legal compensation. To quote the language of an article [5] entitled "The Rule of Damages in Actions ex delicto," published in the Law Reporter in June, 1847, "In the most ordinary case of a suit on a note of hand, the damages do not amount to compensation. Who pays the counsel fees? Who pays for the time of the plaintiff? Who pays for his annoyance and vexation? The most successful lawsuit is too often a Barmecide feast."

But although the law does not attempt the impossibility of replacing the plaintiff in exactly the position he was in before the injury, yet within the bounds of possibility its aim is compensation.

§ 39. The injuries for which compensation is given.

The injuries for which the common law affords a remedy, and for which, therefore, in a proper case it gives reparation by way of damages, are all comprised in the following classes:

> Injuries to property.
> Physical injuries.
> Mental injuries.
> Injuries to family relations.
> Injuries to personal liberty.
> Injuries to reputation.

It may be laid down as a general rule that *an injury to any right protected by the common law will,* if the proximate or direct consequence of an actionable wrong, *be a subject for compensation.*

§ 40. Compensation for injuries to property.

For an injury to property resulting in its total loss compensation is recoverable, measured by the value of the property at the time of loss: the principles governing the admeasurement of the value of property will be stated in a later chapter.

[5] By the author.

For an injury to property resulting in a permanent diminution of value, compensation may be recovered for such diminution. Other forms of pecuniary loss may be compensated in a proper case, such as the loss of use of property, the loss of time, etc. All these questions will be discussed at large in later chapters.

Where the basis of recovery is a pecuniary loss, an actual pecuniary damage must be shown to justify recovery of substantial damages. So in an action for wrongful occupation by defendant of a public office belonging to plaintiff, where it appeared that no salary or other emolument was attached to the office and no actual pecuniary damage was shown, no damages could be recovered for exclusion from the office.[6] The same principle was applied in an action for wrongful exclusion of plaintiff from a public school. There was nothing to show that the plaintiff, the boy himself, paid anything for tuition elsewhere; but the amount was probably paid by his parents. It was held, in the absence of evidence that he was personally obliged to pay for tuition elsewhere, that he could not recover damages.[7]

§ 41. For physical pain.

Physical pain is always regarded as a subject for compensation, this compensation being its pecuniary equivalent as measured by the jury.[8] Of necessity the measurement of such

[6] Palmer v. Darby, 64 Ohio St. 520, 60 N. E. 626.

[7] Morrison v. Lawrence, 181 Mass. 127, 63 N. E. 400; acc., Douglass v. Campbell, 89 Ark. 254, 116 S. W. 211, 20 L. R. A. (N. S.) 205.

[8] *United States:* Wade v. Leroy, 20 How. 34, 15 L. ed. 813; Beardsley v. Swann, 4 McLean, 333; Hanson v. Fowle, 1 Sawy. 539; Boyle v. Case, 9 Sawy. 386; Paddock v. Atchison, T. & S. F. R. R., 37 Fed. 841; Carpenter v. Mexican N. R. R., 39 Fed. 315; Campbell v. Pullman P. C. Co., 42 Fed. 484.

Alabama: South & N. A. R. R. v. McLendon, 63 Ala. 266.

Arkansas: Ward v. Blackwood, 48 Ark. 396; Cameron v. Vandegriff, 53 Ark. 381, 13 S. W. 1092.

California: Fairchild v. California S. Co., 13 Cal. 599; Masters v. Warren, 27 Conn. 293; Lawrence v. Housatonic R. R., 29 Conn. 390.

District of Columbia: Larmon v. District, 16 D. C. (5 Mackey) 330; Johnson v. Baltimore & P. R. R., 17 D. C. (6 Mackey) 232.

Georgia: Cooper v. Mullins, 30 Ga. 146, 76 Am. Dec. 638; Atlanta & W. P. Ry. v. Johnson, 66 Ga. 259.

Illinois: Pierce v. Millay, 44 Ill. 189; Indianapolis & S. L. R. R. v. Stables, 62 Ill. 313; Chicago v. Jones, 66 Ill. 349; Chicago v. Langlass, 66 Ill. 361; Chicago v. Elzeman, 71 Ill. 131; Sheridan v. Hibbard, 119 Ill. 307; Chicago & E. R. R. v. Holland, 122 Ill. 461.

Indiana: Indianapolis v. Gaston, 58

compensation must be left entirely to the jury. The pain for which the plaintiff recovers is only what is found by the jury, although by reason of a peculiarity of his constitution his pain would be greater than that of the ordinary man.[9]

§ 41a. Impairment of physical power.

This is a subject for compensation, entirely apart from the capacity to earn money by exercise of the power.

Therefore in a case of physical injury one is entitled to be compensated for loss of power to work,[10] and for loss of child-bearing power or power to beget offspring.[11]

Ind. 224; Ohio & M. Ry. v. Dickerson, 59 Ind. 317; Huntington v. Breen, 77 Ind. 29.

Iowa: Muldowney v. Illinois C. Ry., 36 Ia. 462; McKinley v. Chicago & N. W. Ry., 44 Ia. 314, 24 Am. Rep. 748; Reddin v. Gates, 52 Ia. 210; Stafford v. Oskaloosa, 64 Ia. 251; Fleming v. Shenandoah, 71 Ia. 456.

Kansas: Tefft v. Wilcox, 6 Kan. 46; Kansas P. Ry. v. Pointer, 9 Kan. 620; Missouri, K. & T. Ry. v. Weaver, 16 Kan. 456.

Kentucky: Kentucky C. R. R. v. Ackley, 87 Ky. 278, 12 Am. St. Rep. 480, 8 S. W. 691.

Louisiana: Rutherford v. Shreveport & H. R. R., 41 La. Ann. 793.

Maine: Mason v. Ellsworth, 32 Me. 271; Verrill v. Minot, 31 Me. 299.

Maryland: McMahon v. Northern C. Ry., 39 Md. 438.

Massachusetts: Hawes v. Knowles, 114 Mass. 518, 19 Am. Rep. 383.

Michigan: Ross v. Leggett, 61 Mich. 445, 28 N. W. 695, 1 Am. St. Rep. 608.

Mississippi: Memphis & C. R. R. v. Whitfield, 44 Miss. 466, 7 Am. Rep. 699, *n.*

Missouri: Stephens v. Hannibal & S. J. R. R., 96 Mo. 207, 9 S. W. 589, 9 Am. St. Rep. 336, *n;* Ridenhour v. Kansas C. C. Ry., 102 Mo. 270, 13 S. W. 889; Steiner v. Moran, 2 Mo. App. 47; McMillan v. Union P. B. W., 6 Mo. App. 434.

Nevada: Cohen v. Eureka & P. R. R., 14 Nev. 376.

New York: Morse v. Auburn & S. R. R., 10 Barb. 621; Brignoli v. Chicago & G. E. Ry., 4 Daly, 182.

North Carolina: Wallace v. Western N. C. R. R., 104 N. C. 442.

Oregon: Oliver v. Northern P. T. Co., 3 Ore. 84.

Pennsylvania: Pennsylvania R. R. v. Allen, 53 Pa. 276; Pennsylvania & O. C. Co. v. Graham, 63 Pa. 290, 3 Am. Rep. 549; McLaughlin v. Corry, 77 Pa. 109, 18 Am. Rep. 432; Scott v. Montgomery, 95 Pa. 444; Lake Shore & M. S. Ry. v. Frantz, 127 Pa. 297, 18 Atl. 22.

Texas: Houston & T. C. Ry. v. Boehm, 57 Tex. 152.

Utah: Giblin v. McIntyre, 2 Utah, 384.

Vermont: Fulsome v. Concord, 46 Vt. 135.

Wisconsin: Goodno v. Oshkosh, 28 Wis. 300.

England: Phillips v. Southwestern Ry., 4 Q. B. Div. 406.

[9] Fitzgerald v. Dobson, 78 Me. 559, 7 Atl. 704.

[10] *Georgia:* Atlanta St. R. R. v. Jacobs, 88 Ga. 647, 15 S. E. 825.

Missouri: Perrigo v. St. Louis, 185 Mo. 274, 84 S. W. 30.

New York: Austin v. Bartlett, 67 App. Div. 312, 73 N. Y. Supp. 156.

[11] *United States:* Denver & R. G. Ry.

§ 42. For inconvenience.

Damages will not be given for mere inconvenience and annoyance, such as are felt at every disappointment of one's expectations, if there is no actual physical or mental injury.[12] Thus where the plaintiff was delayed on the defendant's railway, and was obliged to remain overnight in a place distant from his destination, it was held that he could recover only the cost of his night's lodging, not his disappointment and annoyance on account of the delay.[13] In an action for breach of contract to give a lease of a house, the fact that the plaintiff is not so conveniently situated in the house subsequently procured as he would have been in the house the defendant agreed to lease him, has been held not to be a cause of damage where the plaintiff is not shown to have lost money by the inconvenience.[14]

But inconvenience amounting to physical discomfort is a subject of compensation.[15] "The injury must be physical, as distinguished from one purely *imaginative;* it must be something that produces real discomfort or annoyance through the medium of the senses, not from delicacy of taste or a refined

v. Harris, 122 U. S. 597, 7 Sup. Ct. 1286, 30 L. ed. 1146; Patridge *v.* Boston & M. R. R., 184 Fed. 211, C. C. A.

Alabama: Alabama G. S. R. R. *v.* Hill, 93 Ala. 514, 9 So. 722, 30 Am. St. Rep. 65.

West Virginia: Normile *v.* Wheeling T. Co., 57 W. Va. 132, 49 S. E. 1030, 68 L. R. A. 901.

[12] *Michigan:* Detroit Gas Co. *v.* Moreton Truck & Storage Co., 111 Mich. 401, 69 N. W. 659 (by wrongful deprivation of gas, plaintiff was obliged to use oil lamps which were cheaper; the merely mental inconvenience was not subject of compensation).

[13] Hamlin *v.* Great Northern Ry., 1 H. & N. 408.

[14] Hunt *v.* D'Orval, Dudley (S. C.), 180.

[15] *Illinois:* Chicago & A. R. R. *v.* Flagg, 43 Ill. 364, 92 Am. Dec. 133, *n.*

Kansas: Southern K. Ry. *v.* Rice, 38 Kan. 398, 16 Pac. 817, 5 Am. St. Rep. 766.

Massachusetts: Emery *v.* Lowell, 109 Mass. 197.

Michigan: Ross *v.* Leggett, 61 Mich. 445, 28 N. W. 695, 1 Am. St. Rep. 608.

Missouri: McRae *v.* Metropolitan St. Ry., 125 Mo. App. 562, 102 S. W. 1032.

New Jersey: Luse *v.* Jones, 39 N. J. L. 707.

New York: Ives *v.* Humphreys, 1 E. D. Smith, 196.

Pennsylvania: Scott *v.* Montgomery, 95 Pa. 444.

Texas: Gulf, C. & S. F. Ry. *v.* Overton, 101 Tex. 583, 110 S. W. 736.

But in Walsh *v.* Chicago, M. & S. P. Ry., 42 Wis. 23, 24 Am. Rep. 376, the court refused to allow damages for the annoyance of being kept out late at night, though physical discomfort existed.

fancy."[16]   It must be "such as is capable of being stated in a *tangible form*, and assessed *at a money value*,"[17] and is more than mere annoyance.[18]

In a case in the Supreme Court of the United States the defendant, a railroad company, had built a roundhouse near the church edifice of the plaintiff, and interrupted the church services by noise, smoke, and other discomforts.   Field, J., said: "The plaintiff was entitled to recover because of the inconvenience and discomfort caused to the congregation assembled, thus tending to destroy the use of the building for the purposes for which it was erected and dedicated.   The property might not be depreciated in its salable or market value, if the building had been entirely closed for those purposes by the noise, smoke, and odors of the defendant's shops.   It might then, perhaps, have brought in the market as great a price to be used for some other purpose.   But, as the court below very properly said to the jury, the congregation had the same right to the comfortable enjoyment of its house for church purposes that a private gentleman has to the comfortable enjoyment of his own house, and it is the discomfort and annoyance in its use for those purposes which is the primary consideration in allowing damages.   As with a blow on the face, there may be no arithmetical rule for the estimate of damages.   There is, however, an injury the extent of which the jury may measure."[19]

So where a railroad track was wrongfully laid along the rear of the plaintiff's land, it was held that he might recover compensation for the loss and inconvenience in the prosecution of his business.[20]   And in general compensation may be recovered for the discomfort caused by a nuisance.[21]

In Hobbs v. London & S. W. Ry. Co., [22] the plaintiff, a passenger on the defendant's railway, was set down at the wrong station, and a verdict of £8 for inconvenience suffered by hav-

[16] Bird, V. C., in Westcott v. Middleton, 43 N. J. Eq. 478, 486; affirmed, 44 N. J. Eq. 297.

[17] Baltimore & O. R. R. v. Carr, 71 Md. 135, 17 Atl. 1052.

[18] Georgia R. & E. Co. v. Baker, 1 Ga. App. 832, 58 S. E. 88.

[19] Baltimore & P. Ry. v. Fifth Baptist Church, 108 U. S. 317, 335, 27 L. ed. 739.

[20] Hatfield v. C. R. R., 33 N. J. L. 251.

[21] Labasse v. Piat, 121 La. 601, 46 So. 665.

[22] L. R. 10 Q. B. 111.

4

ing to walk home was sustained on appeal. Cockburn, C. J., said that Hamlin *v.* Great Northern Ry. Co.[23] did not, as was contended for by the defendants, decide that personal inconvenience could not be taken into account as a subject-matter of damage on a breach of contract. Blackburn, J., cited Burton *v.* Pinkerton [24] as an authority to the effect that a recovery can be had for inconvenience.   Mellor and Parry, JJ., distinguished the inconvenience appearing in this case, calling it physical inconvenience, which they said could be estimated in damages, from annoyance, loss of temper, vexation, disappointment, which they thought could not be.

Where the plaintiff, a woman, was carried beyond her station by the defendant's fault, it was held that she might recover compensation for the discomforts of a long walk over a dusty road in a hot day, in the course of which she had to wade across creeks and pass at nightfall through a piece of dark woods.[25]

In most cases of contract, there is no specific recovery for inconvenience, which may be regarded as merged in the pecuniary injury.   In some cases it has been suggested that personal inconvenience which is the direct consequence of tort would be an item of compensation in such action, but that if an action for the same injury were in form an action of contract, the inconvenience, not being contemplated at the time the contract was entered into, could not be considered in estimating damages.[26]   This is a question which will be discussed in connection with the subject of natural consequences.

§ 43. For mental suffering—Early misconception of rule.

The importance of the question whether mental suffering, as distinct from physical suffering, is ever a subject for com-

[23] 1 H. & N. 408.

[24] L. R. 2 Ex. 340.

[25] *Indiana:* Cincinnati, H. & I. R. R. *v.* Eaton, 94 Ind. 474, 48 Am. Rep. 179; *acc., Georgia:* Seals *v.* Augusta So. R. R., 102 Ga. 817, 27 S. E. 116.

Missouri: Triggs *v.* St. L., K. C. & N. Ry., 74 Mo. 147, 41 Am. Rep. 305. But in Texas Tr. Co. *v.* Hanson, Tex. Civ. App. , 124 S. W. 494, the court held that the recovery for physical and mental pain included the inconvenience of a walk home, and that an additional recovery for inconvenience could not be allowed.

[26] *Indiana:* Cincinnati, H. & I. R. R. *v.* Eaton, 94 Ind. 474, 48 Am. Rep. 179. *Massachusetts:* Murdock *v.* B. & A. R. R., 133 Mass. 15, 43 Am. Rep. 480*n.* *Wisconsin:* Brown *v.* C., M. & St. P. Ry., 54 Wis. 342, 41 Am. Rep. 41*n.*

pensation, and the more or less doubtful state of the law, call for a careful discussion.

It was early settled that substantial damages might be recovered in a class of torts where the only injury suffered is mental, namely, in cases of assault without physical contact.[27] Moreover, in actions for false imprisonment where the plaintiff was not touched by the defendant substantial damages have been recovered, though physically the plaintiff did not suffer any actual detriment.[28]   But when the question of allowing damages for mental pain came directly before the courts, these cases seem to have been entirely lost sight of, and it has been assumed that mental suffering generally is not a subject for compensation.

This opinion apparently arose from a misconception of Lord Wensleydale's *dictum* in the case of Lynch v. Knight, [29] where he said: "Mental pain or anxiety the law cannot value, and does not pretend to redress, when the unlawful act complained of causes that alone: though where a material damage occurs, and is connected with it, it is impossible a jury, in estimating it, should altogether overlook the feelings of the party interested."   Taking this language in connection with the facts of the case, the meaning is clear; but the case was an action of slander, brought for an imputation on the plaintiff's chastity, and the decision was that such an imputation was not actionable without special damages and that mental pain alone is not such special damage.   No question of the measure of damages was under consideration, and the opinion is no authority for

[27] *Maine:* Goddard v. G. T. Ry., 57 Me. 202.

Maryland: Handy v. Johnson, 5 Md. 450.

New Hampshire: Beach v. Hancock, 27 N. H. 223, 59 Am. Dec. 373.

Vermont: Alexander v. Blodgett, 44 Vt. 476.

England: I. de S. v. W. de S., Y. B. Lib. Ass., fol. 99, pl. 60; s. c. Ames, Cas. on Torts, 1; Mortin v. Shoppee, 3 C. & P. 373.

[28] *United States:* Fotheringham v. Adams Ex. Co., 36 Fed. 252.

Georgia: Courtoy v. Dozier, 20 Ga. 369.

Illinois: Hawk v. Ridgway, 33 Ill. 473.

New York: Gold v. Bissell, 1 Wend. 210, 19 Am. Dec. 480n.

North Carolina: Mead v. Young, 2 Dev. & Bat. 521.

Texas: Davidson v. Lee, 139 S. W. 904.

England: Wood v. Lane, 6 C. & P. 774; Peters v. Stanway, 6 C. & P. 737; Grainger v. Hill, 4 Bing. N. C. 212.

[29] 9 H. L. C. 577, 598.

the proposition that mental suffering which is the result of an actionable wrong is not in any case a proper subject for compensation. Lord Wensleydale's general proposition was wholly *obiter*.[30]

§ 43a. Ambiguity of the term " Mental Suffering."

The confusion which still surrounds the question as to liability for mental suffering is also partly due to the fact that the term is used to cover a variety of injuries of very different kinds. Thus, mental suffering may consist of annoyance, distress or anxiety; among its most serious forms is fright or terror. It may also spread from the brain to the whole nervous system, and so become nervous shock or nervous prostration. Nervous shock and prostration, again, may produce specific bodily illness and irreparable mental disorder, or even death. There may be also a long or short interval of time, or no appreciable interval between the first and the last stage. Under the head of mental suffering come also injuries to the feelings and affections—shame, humiliation, and grief. In the decisions, the various species of suffering produced through the brain or nervous system are not carefully distinguished from one another, yet it is obvious that they form a series, of which the two extremes are very different. All this is matter of fact of which the courts must take cognizance. The law is not a metaphysical or philosophical system bound to any *a priori* theory of the nature of the mind or its connection with the body. It takes both as they are found inseparably linked together, the brain and nervous system being part of the physical organism.

Injuries to the feelings and mental suffering are of such frequent occurrence in daily life that it is impossible that an action for damages should be allowed wherever they are caused to one person by the wrong or negligence of another. As has been pointed out with regard to recovery for fright, in a class of cases of constant occurrence, fright is an incident of every railroad accident. If negligence producing fright were enough to state a cause of action, every passenger, though not in any other way sustaining damage, would have a cause of action

[30] 9 H. L. C. 591. See for further consideration of this subject Sedg. El. Dam. (2d ed.) 100.

against the company for the fright to which he had been subjected.[31]   In much the same way in cases involving the family
affections, if an action in all cases is sustained, every relative
of the injured person would have an action, on the ground of
sympathetic suffering, although as a matter of fact in the case of
the nearest relatives there may be no actual suffering at all.
Consequently, it has been repeatedly laid down that the mere
allegation of a wrong or act of negligence on the part of A
through which B, to whom A owes a duty of care, suffers from
fright, does not state a cause of action.   So also, as we shall
see presently, in an action for breach of an ordinary contract,
although the breach obviously occasions distress and anxiety,
there can be no recovery for these as heads of damage.   All
such cases fall within that vast field of damage of which the
law can take no notice whatever.   But there is no *rule of law*
which declares that there can be no recovery for fright, nor that
damages for mental suffering cannot be recovered in an action
of contract.   At the other end of the scale, where terror produces nervous shock and ensuing bodily ailment, is there any
reason why there should not be a recovery?   Suppose that the
nervous shock results in serious physical injury, *e. g.*, a miscarriage or premature birth and consequent illness, on what
ground can the defendant be relieved from liability?

This brings before us one difficulty which for a long time
escaped the attention of the courts—that while in most cases
the mere allegation of fright will not sustain a cause of action,
the allegation of fright followed by serious physical consequences may entitle the plaintiff to recover for these as *proximate consequences of the tort or negligence*, the medium of causation being the mind or nervous system affected by the fright.
This makes the question one of proximate cause.   The recovery, if any, is not for the fright, but for the physical injury
caused by the negligence or tort,[32] in which case the cause of
action is clearly physical injury, while the fright, like physical
pain in an ordinary accident case, is inevitably allowed for as
an element or head of damage.

---

[31] Ewing *v.* Pittsburgh, C. & S. L.
Ry., 147 Pa. 40, 43, 23 Atl. 340, 14 L.
R. A. 666, 30 Am. St. Rep. 709.

[32] Dulieu *v.* White, [1901] 2 K. B.
669.

§ 43b. Physical impact theory.

A great source of confusion in the cases' is the idea that to recover at all, the plaintiff must have suffered external physical damage (or at least a technical battery) at the time of the accident; this theory being derived, at least in part, from Lord Wensleydale's *dictum* in Lynch *v.* Knight.[33]

This idea has been seized upon by courts as a means of ridding themselves of the burden of the mass of doubtful cases in which plaintiffs are likely to rely on questionable proof in support of their claims; and they have gone the length of holding that no matter how demonstrable the connection between the physical consequences and the wrong are, yet that there can be no recovery unless there is proof of at least what is called *physical impact* or physical contact.[34]

It may perhaps now be definitely said that there is no foundation for this theory at all on principle. "That fright—where physical injury is directly produced by it—cannot be a ground of action merely because of the absence of any accompanying impact, appears to me to be a contention both unreasonable and contrary to the weight of authority."[35]

§ 43c. Public policy theory.

To support the theory of physical contact or impact, another theory has been developed in several jurisdictions, to the effect that *public policy* demands its adoption as a sort of legal dogma, on the ground that otherwise the door would be opened to illimitable litigation. In the view here taken, any such recourse to public policy is wholly unnecessary. Fictitious and speculative claims for damages are effectively provided against by the rules of certainty and proximate cause. To quote Kennedy, J., again, "My experience gives me no reason to suppose that a jury would really have more difficulty in weighing

---

[33] 9 H. L. C. 577, 598; for a full consideration of this case, see Sedg. El. Dam. 100.

[34] Spade *v.* Lynn & B. R. R., 168 Mass. 285, 47 N. E. 88, 60 Am. St. Rep. 393, 38 L. R. A. 512; 172 Mass. 488, 52 N. E. 747; Cameron *v.* New England T. & T. Co., 182 Mass. 310, 65 N. E. 385.

[35] Kennedy, J., in Dulieu *v.* White, [1901] 2 K. B. 669, 673. This case and Simone *v.* Rhode Island Co., 28 R. I. 186, 66 Atl. 202, 9 L. R. A. (N. S.) 740, throw the clearest light on the whole subject.

the medical evidence as to the effects of nervous shock through fright than in weighing the like evidence as to the effects of nervous shock through a railway collision or a carriage accident, where, as often happens, no palpable injury, or very slight palpable injury, has been occasioned at the time."[36]

§ 43d. The course of decision.

A collation of the following cases, especially the last two, will give a fair *conspectus* of the course of decision:

In Ewing *v*. Pittsburgh, Chicago and St. Louis Railway [37] it was held that an averment that through the negligence of defendant's employees, cars were derailed and thrown against plaintiff's dwelling, subjecting her to fright and to nervous excitement, permanently disabling her, stated no cause of action. Mitchell *v*. Rochester Railway [38] follows this case and holds that for injuries sustained by fright occasioned by the negligence of another, where there is no immediate personal injury, no action lies. The injury was a miscarriage and consequent illness. Three reasons for the decision are given. 1st, that as no recovery can be had for fright, the defendant cannot be liable for its consequences; 2d, that if a cause of action be granted to exist, it would result in a flood of litigation in cases where the injury can be easily feigned without detection, and where the damages must rest on mere conjecture and speculation. To establish such a doctrine would be contrary to public policy; 3d, it cannot be said that the injury was proximate, because it was plainly the result of an accidental or unusual combination of circumstances which could not have been reasonably anticipated, and over which the defendant had no control. Here the action is supposed to be solely for fright, the injury is regarded only as its consequence. In Spade *v*. Lynn & Boston Railroad [39] the action was to recover damages for an injury sustained through the negligence of another, and it was held that there could be no recovery for the bodily injury caused by mere fright and mental disturbance,

[36] Dulieu *v*. White, [1901] 2 K. B. 681.

[37] 147 Pa. 40, 23 Atl. 340, 14 L. R. A. 666, 30 Am. St. Rep. 709.

[38] 151 N. Y. 107, 45 N. E. 354, 34 L. R. A. 781, 56 Am. St. Rep. 604.

[39] 168 Mass. 285, 47 N. E. 88, 60 Am. St. Rep. 393, 38 L. R. A. 512.

where there is no injury to the person *from without.* On a second trial [40] a distinction was taken, and it was held that if a passenger upon a street car suffers physical injury from fright caused by the removal of a drunken man, and by a slight unintentional battery of her person, she can recover only for the pain and fright caused by the battery, not for that which was due to the general disturbance. In Homans *v.* Boston Elevated Railway [41] the rule of physical impact was ameliorated by holding that where a slight injury to the person is accompanied by a nervous shock due to the same wrongful cause, the injured person may recover for the consequences of the nervous shock, whether the shock was due to the physical injury or merely accompanied it.[42]

In Dulieu *v.* White [43] a case of negligence, nervous shock and a miscarriage resulting from fright, on a careful examination of English and American cases, it was held that damages resulting from a nervous shock occasioned by fright *unaccompanied by any actual impact,* are recoverable in an action for negligence if physical injury has been caused to the plaintiff.[44]

In Simone *v.* The Rhode Island Company [45] the subject was thoroughly reviewed, and the law laid down that where the negligence of a defendant causes fright, and as a natural effect bodily ills follow, or if the fright as a cause produces nervous disturbance, and these in turn physical ailments, the defendant is liable for the physical results, although there was no actual external physical injury at the time of the accident.

§ 43e. Conclusion to which the course of decision points.

The theory which amply and most simply justifies these two last cases, and all similar decisions, is not that the cause of action is for negligence producing fright or nervous shock, damages for physical injuries being allowed as proximate consequences of the fright, but that the action is founded on neg-

---

[40] 172 Mass. 478, 52 N. E. 744, 70 Am. St. Rep. 298.

[41] 180 Mass. 456, 62 N. E. 737, 57 L. R. A. 291.

[42] See further Cameron *v.* New England T. & T. Co., 182 Mass. 310, 65 N. E. 385.

[43] [1901] 2 K. B. 669.

[44] The court refused to follow Victorian Railways Commissioners *v.* Coultas, 13 App. Cas. 222 (1888).

[45] 28 R. I. 186, 66 Atl. 202, 9 L. R. A. (N. S.) 740.

ligence and physical damage, the connection between the two being through the fright or nervous shock as *causa causans*. It leaves the question of proximate cause to the jury, where it belongs, disposes of the fantastic theory of the necessity of proof of physical impact, and the theory of public policy requiring the rejection of well founded claims lest ill founded claims should be feigned, and demands only proof of the certain, normal connection of effect with cause, which of itself excludes all speculative and hypothetical damages.

Cases where the action is based on a statute, and recovery for merely mental suffering is refused because it does not fall within the language of the statute, do not bear upon the general question, and must be distinguished.[46]

§ 43f. Mental suffering alone not usually a cause of action.

As has been already explained, for an infliction of mere mental suffering by an assault or an act of false imprisonment an action may be sustained, although the damage is purely mental. But for wrongs, which do not fall within the class of wilful trespasses a different rule prevails. Such wrongs are not usually actionable unless they result in some tangible physical or pecuniary damage; not for instance where they result in mere mental suffering unaccompanied by physical effect.[47] Nor are

[46] *Illinois:* Schertz v. Indianapolis R. R., 107 Ill. 577.

Indiana: Peru & I. R. R. v. Hasket, 10 Ind. 409, 71 Am. Dec. 335.

Missouri: Lafferty v. Hannibal & S. J. R. R., 44 Mo. 291.

[47] *Arkansas:* Hot Springs R. R. v. Deloney, 65 Ark. 177, 45 S. W. 351, 67 Am. St. Rep. 913; Texarkana & F. S. Ry. v. Anderson, 67 Ark. 123, 53 S. W. 673.

California: Sloane v. So. Cal. Ry., 111 Cal. 668, 44 Pac. 320, 32, L. R. A. 193 (*semble*).

Illinois: Illinois Cent. R. R. v. Siddons, 53 Ill. App. 607; North Chicago St. R. R. v. Deubner, 85 Ill. App. 602.

Indiana: Gaskin v. Runkle, 25 Ind. App. 584, 58 N. E. 740.

Kansas: Atchison, T. & S. F. R. R.

v. McGinnis, 46 Kan. 109, 26 Pac. 453.

Kentucky: Morse v. Chesapeake & O. Ry., 117 Ky. 11, 77 S. W. 361, 25 Ky. L. R. 1159.

Maine: Wyman v. Leavitt, 71 Me. 227.

Massachusetts: Spade v. Lynn & B. R. R., 168 Mass. 285, 47 N. E. 88, 60 Am. St. Rep. 393, 38 L. R. A. 512.

Missouri: Trugg v. St. Louis, K. C. & N. Ry., 74 Mo. 147; Spolin v. Mo. Pac. Ry., 116 Mo. 617, 22 S. W. 690.

New Jersey: Westcott v. Middleton, 43 N. J. Eq. 478, 11 Atl. 490 (following Cleveland v. Citizens' Gaslight Co., 20 N. J. Eq. 201).

Texas: Gulf, C. & S. F. Ry. v. Trott, 86 Tex. 412, 25 S. W. 419, 40 Am. St. Rep. 816.

they actionable unless the mental suffering is the natural and proximate result of the defendant's act.[48] In the ordinary course of life many annoying and disturbing things happen, which the sufferer must bear as the necessary incidents of existence; for such annoyances, however disturbing to the mind, there can be no recovery.[49]

Wisconsin: Summerfield v. Western U. T. Co., 87 Wis. 1, 57 N. W. 973.

England: Lynch v. Knight, 9 H. L. C. 577; see § 43 above.

[48] *United States:* Haile v. Texas & P. Ry., 60 Fed. 557, 23 L. R. A. 774, 9 C. C. A. 134.

Arkansas: St. Louis, I. M. & S. Ry. v. Bragg, 69 Ark. 402, 64 S. W. 226, 86 Am. St. Rep. 206 (train stopped at wrong place; plaintiff's fright at having to cross a cattle guard not natural consequence).

Indiana: Indianapolis St. Ry. v. Ray, Ind. , 78 N. E. 978 (personal injury; grief at being deprived of social intercourse remote).

Massachusetts: White v. Dresser, 135 Mass. 150, 46 Am. Rep. 454 (causing land to fall; land was intended by plaintiff for use as burial place, but defendant did not know it; plaintiff's grief not natural consequence).

Minnesota: Renner v. Canfield, 36 Minn. 90, 30 N. W. 435 (defendant shot dog in street; plaintiff, standing unseen near by, frightened; fright too remote).

Mississippi: Dorrah v. Ry., 65 Miss. 14, 3 So. 36, 7 A. S. R. 629 (separation from family by failure to stop train).

Texas: Southern Pac. Co. v. Ammons (Tex. Civ. App.), 26 S. W. 135 (wrongful expulsion from ferryboat; fright from apprehension that there would not be sufficient means of egress too unnatural); Jones v. Texas & N. O. R. R., 23 Tex. Civ. App. 65, 55 S. W. 371 (grief at separation from family as result of defendant's failure to stop at station).

Canada: Rock v. Denis, 4 Montreal

L. R. (Super. Ct.) 356 (plaintiff frightened by falling of bundle of laths).

So in an action for fraud in inducing plaintiff to subscribe for shares of stock in a company, the plaintiff cannot recover for disappointment or disgrace, injuring his feelings, in being induced to purchase stock of that kind. Cable v. Bowlus, 21 Ohio Cir. Ct. 53, 11 Ohio Cir. Dec. 526.

In Watson v. Augusta Brewing Co., 124 Ga. 121, 52 S. E. 152, 1 L. R. A. (N. S.) 1178, the plaintiff suffered personal injury by defendant getting broken glass into soda water bottle while he was preparing it for sale. Plaintiff had the glass removed from his stomach. It was held that the damage included the mental suffering from fear of death while the glass was in his stomach, but after the glass had been removed, and he was completely restored, he could recover no more for mental suffering for fear of what might happen in the future. "He may not continue for an indefinite period to vex his soul with dread on account of having been cut on the inside."

It will be noticed that the question in this case is one concerning the existence of a cause of action, and therefore though the action sounds in tort, the injury must be a natural as well as a proximate consequence of the defendant's act. *Post,* § 139.

[49] *Georgia:* Georgia Ry. & E. Co. v. Baker, 58 S. E. 88, 1 Ga. App. 832 (annoying language about herself overheard by a woman).

South Carolina: Taylor v. Atlantic Coast Line R. R., 59 S. E. 641, 78 S. C. 552 (woman left alone at night in sta-

§ 43g. **No recovery for sympathetic mental suffering.**
As a corollary from the rule that there can be no cause of action when the mental suffering does not result proximately from the defendant's act, it follows that there can be no recovery for sympathetic mental distress, whatever its result, which was caused by injury directed towards *a third party*, whether a near relative of the plaintiff [50] or a stranger.[51] So one cannot recover for mental anguish caused by thought of the extraneous suffering or inconvenience which might be entailed on members of his family.[52] In an action for malicious prosecution, it appeared that the plaintiff had suffered loss through the illness and insanity of his wife, caused by the arrest. This loss was held too remote.[53] Nor can the mother of a libelled person recover for mental anguish caused to her by the libel.[54] For the same reason, no damages can be recovered for mental suffering caused by seeing an injury to a pet animal.[55] And

tion with a boisterous crowd of persons who did not in fact harm her).

[50] *Alabama:* Bube v. Birmingham Ry. L. & P. Co., 140 Ala. 276, 37 So. 285, 130 A. S. R. 33 (injury to child); Reaves v. Anniston Knitting Mills, 154 Ala. 565, 45 So. 702 (injury to child).

Louisiana: Black v. Carrollton R. R., 10 La. Ann. 33, 63 Am. Dec. 586 (accident to minor son); Sperier v. Ott, 116 La. Ann. 1087, 41 So. 323, 7 L. R. A. (N. S.) 518 (malicious arrest of child).

Minnesota: Sanderson v. Northern Pac. Ry., 88 Minn. 162, 92 N. W. 542, 60 L. R. A. 403 (wrongful removal of child from train); Bucknam v. Great N. Ry., 76 Minn. 373, 79 N. W. 98 (abusive language to husband).

New York: Hutchinson v. Stern, 115 App. Div. 791, 101 N. Y. Supp. 145 (assault on husband).

Texas: Gulf, C. & S. F. Ry. v. Overton, 101 Tex. 583, 110 S. W. 736, 19 L. R. A. (N. S.) 500 (injury to invalid sister); Pacific Exp. Co. v. Black, 8 Tex. Civ. App. 363, 27 S. W. 830 (suffering of wife by delay of package of medicine).

[51] *Illinois:* Phillips v. Dickerson, 85

Ill. 11, 28 Am. Rep. 607 (defendant and another seen quarrelling in street); Braun v. Craven, 175 Ill. 401, 51 N. E. 657, 42 L. R. A. 199 (attempt to eject stranger from house).

Kentucky: Reed v. Ford, 112 S. W. 600, 33 Ky. Law Rep. 1029, 19 L. R. A. (N. S.) 225 (assault on lodger in plaintiff's house).

England: Smith v. Johnson (1907), 2 Q. B. 61 (cited) (illness from shock of seeing person killed by defendant).

[52] *Kansas:* Atchison, T. & S. F. R. R. v. Chance, 57 Kan. 40, 45 Pac. 60.

Minnesota: Bahr v. N. Pac. Ry. 101 Minn. 314, 112 N. W. 267.

Nebraska: Dennison v. Daily News Pub. Co., 82 Neb. 675, 118 N. W. 568, 23 L. R. A. (N. S.) 362.

Oregon: Maynard v. Oregon R. R. & N. Co., 46 Ore. 15, 78 Pac. 983, 68 L. R. A. 477.

Texas: Texas Mexican Ry. v. Douglass, 69 Tex. 694, 7 S. W. 77.

[53] Hampton v. Jones, 58 Ia. 317; acc., Ellis v. Cleveland, 55 Vt. 358.

[54] Bradt v. New Nonpareil Co., 108 Ia. 449, 79 N. W. 122, 45 L. R. A. 681.

[55] Buchanan v. Stout, 123 App. Div.

there can be no recovery by an injured mother for mental suffering caused by fear of deformity or imperfection of her unborn child.[56]

§ 43h. Mental suffering resulting in physical harm.

Where, however, any wrongful act of the defendant causes the plaintiff fright, and leads him to attempt to escape from danger, and he is injured physically in this attempt, he is allowed everywhere to recover compensation for his physical injury as a proximate result, though it originated in a purely mental cause. The physical injury is the damage, the fear a link in the chain of causation.[57] And by the prevailing view when a tortious act directly causing a purely mental injury results proximately in physical harm, such as nervous prostration, miscarriage, etc., the party may recover compensation for his entire loss, both physical and mental;[58] though in a

648, 108 N. Y. Supp. 38 (pet cat hurt by defendant's dog).

[56] Sullivan v. Old Colony St. Ry., 197 Mass. 512, 83 N. E. 1091.

[57] So where a frightened passenger jumped from the vehicle and was hurt.

United States: Stokes v. Saltonstall, 13 Pet. 181, 10 L. ed. 810.

Georgia: Southwestern R. R. v. Paulk, 24 Ga. 356.

Minnesota: Wilson v. Northern Pac. R. R., 26 Minn. 278, 3 N. W. 333, 37 Am. Rep. 410; Smith v. St. Paul, M. & M. Ry., 30 Minn. 169, 14 N. W. 797.

Missouri: McPeak v. Missouri Pac. Ry., 128 Mo. 617, 30 S. W. 170.

Nebraska: St. Joseph & G. I. R. R. v. Hedge, 44 Neb. 448, 62 N. W. 887.

New Jersey: Tuttle v. Atlantic City Ry., 66 N. J. L. 327, 49 Atl. 450, 54 L. R. A. 582, 88 Am. St. Rep. 491.

New York: Twomley v. Central, P. N. & E. R. R. R., 69 N. Y. 158.

Texas: Gallagher v. Bowie, 66 Tex. 265, 17 S. W. 407; Missouri, K. & T. Ry. v. Rogers, 91 Tex. 52, 40 S. W. 956.

England: Jones v. Boyce, 1 Stark. 402.

And so of other similar injuries:

Massachusetts: Cameron v. New England T. & T., 182 Mass. 310, 65 N. E. 385 (stumbled on rising to escape when frightened by explosion of dynamite).

Nebraska: Ellick v. Wilson, 58 Neb. 584, 79 N. W. 152 (plaintiff injured knee in effort to escape).

New Jersey: Buchanan v. West Jersey R. R., 52 N. J. L. 265, 19 Atl. 254 (plaintiff threw herself down to avoid being hit by timber projecting from train).

New York: Coulter v. Merchants' Union Ex., 56 N. Y. 585 (plaintiff attempting to escape wagon hurt her head against building).

Pennsylvania: Vallo v. U. S. Exp. Co., 147 Pa. 404, 14 L. R. A. 743, 23 Atl. 594, 30 Am. St. 741 (leaping to avoid missile, fell over defendant's obstruction); Baker v. North East Borough, 151 Pa. 234, 21 Atl. 1079 (defendant frightened plaintiff's horse; plaintiff grasped wrong rein and injured herself).

[58] *California:* Sloane v. Southern Cal. R. R., 111 Cal. 668, 32 L. R. A. 193, 44 Pac. 320.

few jurisdictions it is held that where the intervening cause of the suffering is purely mental, though actual physical harm supervenes, there can be no recovery.[59]

Georgia: Louisville & N. R. R. v. Wilson, 123 Ga. 62, 51 S. E. 24.

Iowa: Watson v. Dilts, 116 Ia. 249, 89 N. W. 1068, 57 L. R. A. 559, 93 Am. St. Rep. 239.

Louisiana: Stewart v. Arkansas So. R. R., 112 La. 764, 36 So. 676.

Maryland: Green v. Shoemaker & Co., 111 Md. 69, 73 Atl. 688.

Minnesota: Purcell v. St. Paul City Ry., 48 Minn. 134, 50 N. W. 1034, 16 L. R. A. 203; Lindh v. Great N. Ry., 99 Minn. 408, 109 N. W. 823, 7 L. R. A. (N. S.) 1018.

North Carolina: Watkins v. Kaolin Mfg. Co., 131 N. C. 536, 42 S. E. 983, 60 L. R. A. 617; Kimberly v. Howland, 143 N. C. 398, 55 S. E. 778, 7 L. R. A. (N. S.) 545.

Rhode Island: Simone v. Rhode Island Co., 28 R. I. 186, 66 Atl. 202, 9 L. R. A. (N. S.) 740.

South Carolina: Mack v. South Bound R. R., 52 S. C. 323, 29 S. E. 905, 40 L. R. A. 679, 68 Am. St. Rep. 913; Taber v. Seaboard Air Line Ry., 81 S. C. 317, 62 S. E. 311.

Texas: Hill v. Kimball, 76 Tex. 210, 13 S. W. 59, 7 L. R. A. 618; Gulf, Col. & Santa Fe Ry. v. Hayter, 93 Tex. 239, 54 S. W. 994, 47 L. R. A. 325, 77 Am. St. Rep. 856; El Paso El. Ry. v. Furber, 45 Tex. Civ. App. 348, 100 S. W. 1041; St. Louis Southwestern Ry. v. Murdock, 00 Tex. Civ. App. 000, 116 S. W. 139.

Wisconsin: Koerber v. Patek, 123 Wis. 453, 102 N. W. 453, 68 L. R. A. 956; Pankopf v. Hinkley, 141 Wis. 146, 123 N. W. 625.

England: Wilkinson v. Downton, [1897] 2 Q. B. 57; Dulieu v. White, [1901] 2 K. B. 669; Yates v. South Kirby, etc., Collieries, [1910] 2 K. B. 538.

Ireland: Bell v. Great N. Ry., 26 L. R. (Ir.) 428.

Canada: Fitzpatrick v. Great W. Ry., 12 U. C. Q. B. 645.

Scotland: Gilligan v. Robb, [1910] S. C. 856.

Whether the physical injury is proximately caused by the mental suffering is a question of fact for the jury. Dreyfus v. St. Louis & S. Ry., 124 Mo. App. 585, 102 S. W. 53.

[59] *United States:* Haile v. Texas & P. Ry., 60 Fed. 557, 23 L. R. A. 774, 9 C. C. A. 134.

Illinois: Braun v. Craven, 175 Ill. 401, 51 N. E. 657, 42 L. R. A. 199.

Iowa: Lee v. Burlington, 113 Iowa, 356, 85 N. W. 618, 86 Am. St. Rep. 379.

Massachusetts: Smith v. Postal T. C. Co., 174 Mass. 576, 55 N. E. 380, 47 L. R. A. 323.

Michigan: Nelson v. Crawford, 122 Mich. 466, 81 N. W. 335, 80 Am. St. Rep. 577.

Missouri: Strange v. Missouri Pac. Ry., 61 Mo. App. 586; Deming v. Chicago, R. I. & P. Ry., 80 Mo. App. 152 (but see Shellabarger v. Morris, 115 Mo. App. 566, 91 S. W. 1005).

New Jersey: Ward v. W. Jersey & S. R. R., 65 N. J. L. 383.

New York: Mitchell v. Rochester Ry., 151 N. Y. 107, 45 N. E. 354, 34 L. R. A. 781, 56 Am. St. R. 604; Hack v. Dady, 134 App. Div. 253, 118 N. Y. Supp. 906.

Ohio: Miller v. B. & O. S. W. R. R., 78 Ohio St. 309, 85 N. E. 499.

Pennsylvania: Ewing v. Pittsburgh, C. & S. L. Ry., 147 Pa. 40, 23 Atl. 340, 14 L. R. A. 666, 30 Am. St. R. 709; Linn v. Duquesne, 204 Pa. 551, 54 Atl. 341; Huston v. Freemansburg, 212 Pa. 548, 61 Atl. 1022, 3 L. R. A. (N. S.) 49;

§ 43i. Mental suffering consequent upon an independent actionable wrong.

If a cause of action exists independently of the mental suffering, so that an action will lie at any rate, there can be no doubt of the right to compensation for any mental suffering which proximately follows. Thus damages may be recovered for mental suffering resulting from a technical assault [60] or battery,[61] for the slightest bodily injury produced by negligence,[62] or resulting from the circumstances of an actual trespass on land [63]

Morris v. Lackawanna & W. V. R. R., 228 Pa. 198, 77 Atl. 445.

England: Victorian Rys. Comrs. v. Coultas, 13 App. Cas. 222 (Privy Council).

[60] *Indiana:* Kline v. Kline, 158 Ind. 602, 64 N. E. 9, 58 L. R. A. 397.

Missouri: Carmody v. St. Louis Transit Co., 122 Mo. App. 338, 99 S. W. 495; Hickey v. Welch, 91 Mo. App. 4.

New York: Williams v. Underhill, 63 App. Div. 223, 71 N. Y. Supp. 291.

Ohio: Kear v. Garrison, 13 Ohio C. C. 447.

Texas: Leach v. Leach, 11 Tex. Civ. App. 699, 33 S. W. 703.

[61] *Kansas:* Wm. Small & Co. v. Lonegan, 81 Kan. 48, 105 Pac. 27, 25 L. R. A. (N. S.) 967.

New Hampshire: Cooper v. Hopkins, 70 N. H. 271, 279, 48 Atl. 100.

Wisconsin: Craker v. Chicago & N. W. Ry., 36 Wis. 657.

[62] *United States:* Denver & R. G. R. R. v. Roller, 100 Fed. 738; Armour & Co. v. Kollmeyer, 161 Fed. 78.

Massachusetts: Homans v. Boston E. Ry., 180 Mass. 456, 62 N. E. 737, 57 L. R. A. 291; Spade v. Lynn & B. R. R., 172 Mass. 488, 52 N. E. 747, 70 Am. St. Rep. 298.

New Jersey: Consolidated Traction Co. v. Lambertson, 59 N. J. L. 297, 36 Atl. 100 (affirmed in 60 N. J. L. 457, 38 Atl. 684); Shay v. Camden & S. Ry., 66 N. J. L. 334, 49 Atl. 547; Porter v.

D., L. & W. Ry., 73 N. J. L. 405, 63 Atl. 860.

New York: Jones v. Brooklyn Heights R. R., 23 N. Y. App. Div. 141, 48 N. Y. Supp. 914, 5 N. Y. Annot. Cas. 124; O'Flaherty v. Nassau Electric R. R., 34 N. Y. App. Div. 74, 54 N. Y. Supp. 96; Lofink v. Interborough R. R., 102 App. Div. 275, 92 N. Y. Supp. 386.

Contra, Washington & G. R. R. v. Dashiell, 7 D. C. App. Cas. 507.

The bodily injury may be of the slightest nature.

Maryland: Philadelphia, B. & W. R. R. v. Mitchell, 107 Md. 600, 69 Atl. 422.

Massachusetts: Driscoll v. Gaffey, 207 Mass. 102, 92 N. E. 110. But the mental suffering must be consequent on the injury. Hack v. Dady, 127 N. Y. Supp. 22, App. Div.

[63] *Alabama:* Bessemer Land & I. Co. v. Jenkins, 111 Ala. 135, 18 So. 565, 56 Am. St. Rep. 26; Engle v. Simmons, 148 Ala. 92, 41 So. 1023, 7 L. R. A. (N. S.) 96.

Iowa: Watson v. Dilts, 116 Ia. 249, 89 N. W. 1068.

Minnesota: Lesch v. Great Northern Ry., 91 Minn. 503, 106 N. W. 955.

Missouri: Hickey v. Welch, 91 Mo. App. 4; Bouillon v. Laclede G. L. Co., 148 Mo. App. 462, 129 S. W. 401.

Texas: Hill v. Kimball, 74 Tex. 210; Ft. Worth & N. O. Ry. v. Smith (Tex. Civ. App.), 25 S. W. 1032; Alexander

or for the tortious treatment of a dead body,[64] for actionable defamation,[65] or for false imprisonment or malicious prosecution.[66]

§ 43j. Mental suffering for intentional wrong.

In several jurisdictions recovery for fright or other mental suffering resulting in physical harm is made by the courts (though wrongly, we think, on principle) to depend upon whether the infliction of the mental suffering was intentional or was caused by the defendant's negligence; and in almost every jurisdiction recovery would probably be allowed for such injury where the defendant intentionally caused the fear or mental suffering.[67]   So, even in a jurisdiction which generally denies an action for mental suffering, however proximately it results, where the defendant, as a practical joke, falsely told the plaintiff that her husband had met with an accident and she suffered a nervous shock, he was held responsible.[68]   So a mental shock, even without injurious physical consequences, which results from intentionally insulting language or conduct of the defendant, is a ground for recovery, assuming the existence of a cause of action.[69]   And mental suffering caused by the wanton and deliberate act of a conductor in putting off a passenger at the wrong place may be recovered.[70]   In a case

[64] *Georgia:* Medical College of Ga. *v.* Rushing, 1 Ga. App. 468, 57 S. E. 1083.

Illinois: Palenzke *v.* Bruning, 98 Ill. App. 644.

Minnesota: Larson *v.* Chase, 47 Minn. 307, 50 N. W. 238, 28 Am. St. Rep. 370, 14 L. R. A. 85.

Wisconsin: Koerber *v.* Patek, 123 Wis. 453, 102 N. W. 40, 68 L. R. A. 956.

[65] Davis *v.* Mohn (Ia.), 124 N. W. 206.

[66] Gibney *v.* Lewis, 68 Conn. 392, 396, 36 Atl. 799.

[67] Preiser *v.* Weilandt, 48 App. Div. 569, 62 N. Y. Supp. 890.

v. St. Louis Southwestern Ry. Co. of Texas, (Tex. Civ. App.), 122 S. W. 572; St. Louis S. W. Ry. *v.* Alexander, 141 S. W. 135.

Vermont: Newell *v.* Whitcher, 53 Vt. 589, 38 Am. Rep. 702.

[68] Wilkinson *v.* Downton, [1897] 2 Q. B. 57.

[69] *Connecticut:* Treat *v.* Barber, 7 Conn. 274.

Georgia: Dunn *v.* W. U. Tel. Co., 2 Ga. App. 845, 59 S. E. 189.

Nebraska: Kurpgeweit *v.* Kirby, 88 Neb. 72, 129 N. W. 127.

Texas: Gulf, C. & S. F. Ry. *v.* Luther, 40 Tex. Civ. App. 517, 90 S. W. 44.

Washington: Davis *v.* Tacoma & P. Ry., 35 Wash. 203, 77 Pac. 209, 66 L. R. A. 800.   *Contra,* however, in *Arkansas:* St. Louis, I. M. & S. R. R. *v.* Taylor, 84 Ark. 42, 104 S. W. 551, 13 L. R. A. (N. S.) 159; Chicago, R. I. & P. Ry. *v.* Moss, 89 Ark. 187, 116 S. W. 192; Pierce *v.* St. Louis, I. M. & S. Ry., 94 Ark. 489, 127 S. W. 707.

[70] *Georgia:* Williamson *v.* Central of Ga. Ry., 127 Ga. 125, 56 S. E. 119.

in Wisconsin, however, plaintiff hired a hearse for his child's funeral; the defendants, being members of a union, ordered the hearse away because of the rules of the union. It was held that plaintiff could *not* recover against the defendants, although their act was wrongful, since there was no actual damage except injuries to the feelings and no action could be maintained for such injuries alone.[71] This case obviously called for a different decision, while the cases supporting an action (if the views here exposed are sound) are made to rest on an erroneous principle. The true question is not whether the injury to feelings and mental suffering were *intentional,* but whether they were natural and proximate in view of the nature of the act, it being assumed that the defendant owes a duty in the premises. Hurt feelings are a normal and natural consequence of hoaxes and practical jokes of a certain sort; but it is not, therefore, to be assumed that every April fool can maintain an action.

§ 43k. What persons can suffer mentally.

It is not every person recognized by law who is capable of mental suffering. Thus, it is clear that a corporation, being incapable of feeling, is incapable of mental suffering,[72] but a child, however young, might suffer fright or some other variety of mental discomfort; and it has been held that a child only four years old might feel not only fright but other kinds of mental suffering.[73] And a person of unsound mind may suffer mentally.[74] It may be at least questionable in fact whether a Christian Scientist can so suffer.[75]

§ 44. Damages for mental suffering in actions for personal injury.

Mental suffering as a distinct element of damage in addition

Missouri: Harless v. Southwest Mo. Electric Ry., 123 Mo. App. 22, 99 S. W. 793.

[71] Gatzow v. Buening, 106 Wis. 1, 81 N. W. 1003, 80 Am. St. Rep. 1, 49 L. R. A. 475. And see Richmond Gas Co. v. Baker, 146 Ind. 600, 41 N. E. 1049, 36 L. R. A. 683 (apprehension of death from injury; not independent ground of recovery, as no damages can be recovered for death).

[72] Farbenfabriken of Elberfield Co. v. Beringer, 158 Fed. 802, 86 C. C. A. 62.

[73] Gulf, C. & S. F. Ry. v. Sauter, 46 Tex. Civ. App. 309, 103 S. W. 201.

[74] Gulf, W. T. & P. Ry. v. Holzheuser (Tex. Civ. App.), 45 S. W. 188.

[75] Fort Worth & D. C. Ry. v. Travis,

to bodily suffering has been held not to be a subject for compensation.[76] Other cases, however, have allowed recovery.[77] There would be great difficulty in upholding a rule refusing recovery. The result of it would seem to be that if A sees B lying in the street, and threatens him with a club, he is liable in an action of assault for the fright caused; but if A sees B standing, and first knocks him down and then threatens him, he is not liable for the fright, for it is "mental suffering as a distinct element of damage in addition to bodily suffering." It is, however, often true in this sort of case, that the suffering is not the direct result of the injury, and is not a subject of compensation for that reason. So where a physical injury results directly in a miscarriage, physical or mental suffering attending the miscarriage is a proper subject for compensation; but grief for loss of the child cannot be considered, because it is too remote a result of the injury,[78] though it has been held that the woman may recover for mental distress for fear the child would

45 Tex. Civ. App. 117, 99 S. W. 1141.

[76] *Kansas:* Salina *v.* Trosper, 27 Kan. 544.

Nevada: Johnson *v.* Wells, 6 Nev. 224, 3 Am. Rep. 245.

[77] *United States:* Denver & R. G. Ry. *v.* Roller, 100 Fed. 738, 49 L. R. A. 77.

Alabama: Lunsford *v.* Dietrich, 86 Ala. 250, 5 So. 461, 11 Am. St. Rep. 37.

Arkansas: Arkansas M. Ry. *v.* Robinson,   Ark.   , 130 S. W. 536.

California: Malone *v.* Sierra Ry. Co. of California,   Cal.   , 91 Pac. 522.

Colorado: Denver City Tramway Co. *v.* Martin, 44 Colo. 324, 98 Pac. 836.

Connecticut: Mastes *v.* Warren, 27 Conn. 293.

Illinois: Indianapolis & S. L. R. R. *v.* Stables, 62 Ill. 313; Chicago City Ry. *v.* Taylor, 170 Ill. 49, 57, 48 N. E. 831; Chicago Consol. Traction Co. *v.* Schritter, 222 Ill. 364, 78 N. E. 820 (affirming 124 Ill. App. 578); (the contrary intimation in Joch *v.* Dankwardt, 85 Ill. 331, must be regarded as overruled).

Indiana: Pittsburg, C. & St. L. Ry. *v.* Sponier, 85 Ind. 165; Moyer *v.* Gordon,

113 Ind. 282, 14 N. E. 476; Vandalia Coal Co. *v.* Yemm,   Ind.   , 92 N. E. 49.

Iowa: Parkhurst *v.* Masteller, 57 Ia. 474; Shepard *v.* Chicago, R. I. & P. Ry., 77 Ia. 54.

Minnesota: Jansen *v.* Minneapolis & S. L. Ry., 112 Minn. 496, 128 S. W. 826.

Missouri: Porter *v.* H. & St. J. Ry., 71 Mo. 66, 36 Am. Rep. 454.

Montana: Hosty *v.* Moulton Water Co., 39 Mont. 310, 102 Pac. 568.

[78] *California:* Thomas *v.* Gates, 126 Cal. 1, 58 Pac. 315.

Minnesota: Morris *v.* St. Paul C. Ry., 105 Minn. 276, 117 N. W. 500, 17 L. R. A. (N. S.) 598.

Montana: Hosty *v.* Moulton Water Co., 39 Mont. 310, 102 Pac. 568.

Texas: Western U. T. Co. *v.* Cooper, 71 Tex. 507, 9 S. W. 598, 10 Am. St. Rep. 772, *n.*

Vermont: Bovee *v.* Danville, 53 Vt. 183.

Washington: Hawkins *v.* Front S. C. R. R., 3 Wash. 592, 28 Pac. 1021, 28 Am. St. Rep. 72, 16 L. R. A. 808.

be deformed in consequence of the injury.[79] Recovery may be had for the reasonable apprehension of insanity resulting from the injury;[80] or for apprehension of future injury to health,[81] such as blood poisoning.[82] So fear of death resulting directly from the injury itself is a proper subject for compensation;[83] and it has been held that where the plaintiff fell into a hole between the rails of a street railway track he could recover compensation for the fear of death from passing cars.[84] But where the result of the wrongful ejection of a passenger was a cold, fear of death from tuberculosis was held too remote for recovery.[85] Business anxiety because of being disabled has been held not to be a proper subject for recovery.[86] So where a man brings an action for personal injuries by being thrown from a carriage, his anxiety for the safety of others who were driving with him is too remote a result of the injury for compensation.[87] So in Chicago v. McLean,[88] where it was held that the mental suffering which is inseparable from the bodily injury can be recovered for, without allegation of special damage, the court added: "Any mental anguish which may not have been connected with the bodily injury, *but caused by some conception arising from a different source*," could not be taken into consideration.

In other cases which are often cited in connection with this

[79] Prescott v. Robinson, 74 N. H. 460, 69 Atl. 522, 17 L. R. A. (N. S.) 594. But see *ante*, § 43g.

[80] Walker v. Boston & M. R. R., 71 N. H. 271, 51 Atl. 918.

[81] Watson v. Augusta Br. Co., 124 Ga. 121, 52 S. E. 152, 18 L. R. A. (N. S.) 1178, 110 Am. St. Rep. 157.
As apprehension of hydrophobia from bite of dog. Warner v. Chamberlain, 7 Houst. (Del.) 18, 30 Atl. 638; Godeau v. Blood, 52 Vt. 251, 36 Am. Rep. 751.

[82] *Missouri:* Butts v. Nat. Exch. Bank, 99 Mo. App. 168, 72 S. W. 1083.
Texas: Southern K. R. R. v. McSwain,   Tex. Civ. App.   , 118 S. W. 874.

[83] St. Louis, I. M. & S. Ry. v. Leamons, 82 Ark. 504. 102 S. W. 363.

[84] Lowe v. Metropolitan St. Ry., Mo. App.   , 130 S. W. 119.

[85] St. Louis, I. M. & S. Ry. v. Buckner, 89 Ark. 58, 115 S. W. 923, 20 L. R. A. (N. S.) 458.

[86] Statler v. George A. Ray Mfg. Co., 195 N. Y. 478, 88 N. E. 1063 .
But mental suffering from consciousness that one has become incapable of earning a living is ground for recovery.
Georgia: Brush E. L. & P. Co. v. Simonsohn, 107 Ga. 70, 32 S. E. 902.
Texas: Citizens' Ry. v. Branham, Tex. Civ. App.   , 137 S. W. 403.

[87] Keyes v. Minneapolis & S. L. Ry., 36 Minn. 290.

[88] 133 Ill. 148, 24 N. E. 527, 8 L. R. A. 765.

rule, the defendant's negligence, for which action was brought, infringed no right of the plaintiff's, and therefore gave no right of action to the plaintiff, though as a matter of fact it frightened him.[89] These cases are entirely analogous to Lynch v. Knight.[90]

§ 44a. For tortious injury to property.

Mental suffering resulting from an injury to property has been held not to be a subject for compensation.[91] But where mental pain was the natural and proximate result of the injury, compensation has been allowed for it. Thus where the defendant entered the plaintiff's land and removed the dead body of his child, it was held that the plaintiff might recover compensation for the mental anguish caused thereby.[92] Where the plaintiff and his family were wrongfully turned out of their house, it was held that he could recover compensation for his sense of shame and humiliation.[93] Where the defendant maliciously injured the plaintiff's horse, it was held that the plaintiff might recover compensation for his wounded feelings;[94] and the same decision was reached where the defendant maliciously beat the plaintiff's slave.[95] For wrongful and malicious attachment or levy of execution damages may be obtained for the mental suffering of the owner.[96] And where the plaintiff was injured by the defendants by an illegal boycott he was allowed damages for mental suffering.[97]

§ 45. In actions of contract.

Mental suffering resulting from breach of contract has been held not to be a subject for compensation.[98]

[89] *Maine:* Wyman v. Leavitt, 71 Me. 227, 36 Am. Rep. 303, *n.*
Massachusetts: Canning v. Williamstown, 1 Cush. 451.
[90] 9 H. L. C. 577, *supra.*
[91] Smith v. Grant, 56 Me. 255.
[92] Meagher v. Driscoll, 99 Mass. 281, 96 Am. Dec. 759.
[93] *Indiana:* Moyer v. Gordon, 113 Ind. 282, 14 N. E. 476.
Massachusetts: Fillebrown v. Hoar, 124 Mass. 580.
[94] Kimball v. Holmes, 60 N. H. 163.
[95] West v. Forrest, 22 Mo. 344.

[96] *Alabama:* Pollock v. Gantt, 69 Ala. 373, 44 Am. Rep. 519.
Louisiana: Byrne v. Gardner, 33 La. Ann. 6.
Contra, Ainsa v. Moses (Tex. Civ. App.), 100 S. W. 791.
[97] Carter v. Oster, 134 Mo. App. 146, 112 S. W. 995.
[98] *Dakota:* Russell v. Western U. T. Co., 3 Dak. 315.
Minnesota: Beaulieu v. Great Northern Ry., 103 Minn. 47, 114 N. W. 353, 19 L. R. A. (N. S.) 564.

Undoubtedly in most cases of contract, where the basis of the agreement involves the delivery of articles or the rendering of services having a recognized pecuniary value, or the payment of money, that is, in the great body of cases of contract, the question of mental suffering is excluded. This is very likely a consequence of those general rules governing the allowance of damages, to be discussed hereafter, that damages must be certain, and not remote, and must represent the natural and probable consequences of the act complained of. From the fact that this is the general rule, the consequence has been deduced that there is something in the nature of an action of contract which makes it impossible that the plaintiff should recover damages for injury to feelings. It has been necessary to recognize a supposed exception to the universality of the rule in cases of breach of promise of marriage, where damages for mental suffering are allowed,[99] though it is hard to see any distinction, except that mental suffering is usually the natural and proximate result of a breach of that contract, while it is usually not the natural and proximate result of a breach of an ordinary contract.

In many cases, if mental suffering cannot be compensated, only nominal damages can be recovered for a total breach of contract. For instance, if a defendant contracts not to disturb the plaintiff, ill with nervous prostration, by making a noise, either the court must allow compensation for mental suffering upon breach or else only nominal damages can ever be recovered on the contract. If the latter is the true rule, such a contract can never be enforced.

The true rule seems to be that laid down by the Supreme Court of Tennessee: "Where other than pecuniary benefits are contracted for, other than pecuniary standards will be applied to the ascertainment of damages flowing from the

[99] *Arkansas:* Collins *v.* Mack, 31 Ark. 684.

Maine: Tobin *v.* Shaw, 45 Me. 331, 71 Am. Dec. 547.

Massachusetts: Coolidge *v.* Neat, 129 Mass. 146.

Michigan: Vanderpool *v.* Richardson, 52 Mich. 336.

Missouri: Wilbur *v.* Johnson, 58 Mo. 600.

New York: Southard *v.* Rexford, 6 Cow. 254; Wells *v.* Padgett, 8 Barb. 323.

North Carolina: Allen *v.* Baker, 86 N. C. 91, 41 Am. Rep. 444; *post,* § 638*b*.

breach." [100]   And this rule seems now to be accepted by the courts. Thus the later cases tend to establish the rule that where the contract naturally involves mental suffering in case of breach, damages may be recovered for such suffering; [101] but that such damages cannot ordinarily be recovered for breach of contract because not usually the natural consequence of a breach. [102] So for failure to pay money, according to agreement, there can be in the ordinary case no recovery of damages for mental suffering; [103] but where there is special notice of circumstances that make mental suffering a natural consequence of the breach recovery may be had. [104] So in an action for a violation of a contract for the transportation, care, or burial of a corpse, damages may be recovered for mental suffering. [105] In an Indiana case of this sort the defendant, an under-

[100] Wadsworth v. Western U. T. Co., 86 Tenn. 695, 703, 8 S. W. 574.

[101] *Louisiana:* Lewis v. Holmes, 109 La. 1030, 34 So. 66 (failure to furnish trousseau for bride).

New York: Smith v. Leo, 92 Hun, 242, 36 N. Y. Supp. 949 (expulsion from dancing class).

Rhode Island: Vogel v. McAuliffe, 18 R. I. 791, 31 Atl. 1 (failure to furnish proper furnace; the action seems to have been in form an action of tort).

Texas: Galveston, H. & S. A. Ry. v. Rubio (Tex. Civ. App.), 65 S. W. 1126 (failure to furnish medical attendance); Dunn v. Smith (Tex. Civ. App.), 74 S. W. 576 (failure to furnish coffin).

[102] *United States:* Morse v. Duncan, 14 Fed. 396 (failure to stop train at station); Wilcox v. Richmond & D. R. R., 52 Fed. 264, 3 C. C. A. 73, 17 L. R. A. 804 (failure to furnish special train).

Kansas: Cole v. Gray, 70 Kan. 705, 79 Pac. 654 (failure to deliver postal card).

Kentucky: American Nat. Bk. v. Morey, 113 Ky. 857, 69 S. W. 759, 58 L. R. A. 956 (dishonor of check).

[103] *Iowa:* Smith v. Sanborn State Bank,   Ia.   , 126 N. W. 779.

Kentucky: Robinson v. Western U. T. Co., 24 Ky. L. Rep. 452, 68 S. W. 656, 57 L. R. A. 611.

[104] Western U. T. Co. v. Wells, 50 Fla. 474, 39 So. 838, 2 L. R. A. (N. S.) 1072 (wrongful refusal to pay money to a man known to be destitute).

[105] *Indiana:* Renihan v. Wright, 125 Ind. 536, 25 N. E. 822, 21 Am. St. Rep. 249, 9 L. R. A. 513 (wrongful disposition of dead body).

Kentucky: Louisville & N. R. R. v. Hull, 113 Ky. 561, 68 S. W. 433, 57 L. R. A. 771 (delay in transporting corpse).

Washington: Wright v. Beardsley, 46 Wash. 16, 89 Pac. 172 (failure to bury in usual manner).

In Beaulieu v. Gr. N. Ry., 103 Minn. 47, 114 N. W. 353, 19 L. R. A. (N. S.) 564, the opposite view was taken by the court, and a distinction was taken between active injury to the body, where the injury was tortious (as in Lindh v. Ry., 99 Minn. 408, 109 N. W. 823, 7 L. R. A. (N. S.) 1018, where the corpse was exposed to the weather), and cases of mere breach of contract. The dissenting opinion of Jaggard, J., may be referred to as stating a sounder view than that of the majority.

taker, agreed to keep the body of the plaintiff's daughter in a vault till the plaintiff should be ready to inter it. Instead of doing so, he allowed a third party to inter the body. It was held that the plaintiff could recover compensation for his mental anguish.[106] The court, after referring to the telegraph cases, said: "The cases rest upon the reasonable doctrine that where a person contracts, upon a sufficient consideration, to do a particular thing, the failure to do which may result in anguish and distress of mind on the part of the other contracting party, he is presumed to have contracted with reference to the payment of damages of that character in the event such damages accrue by reason of a breach of the contract on his part. . . . When the appellants contracted with the appellees to safely keep the body of their daughter until such time as they should desire to inter the same, they did so with a knowledge of the fact that a failure on their part to comply with the terms of such contract would result in injury to the feelings of the appellees, and they must, therefore, be held to have contracted with reference to damages of that character, in the event of a breach of the contract on their part."

§ 45a. In actions against public service corporations.

The same rule is, by the better view, applicable to actions against public service companies. Thus in actions for the wrongful ejection of passengers damages may be recovered for injured feelings and sense of humiliation arising out of the circumstances of the ejection;[107] but where the ejection is in good faith and without any circumstances which would lead to feel-

---

[106] Renihan v. Wright, 125 Ind. 536, 25 N. E. 822, 21 Am. St. Rep. 249, 9 L. R. A. 514. This case has, however, been overruled in Indiana: see § 45a.

[107] *Alabama:* Alabama & G. S. R. R. v. Tapia, 94 Ala. 226, 232, 10 So. 236.

England: Coppin v. Braithwaite, 8 Jur. 875; *post,* § 865.

So a passenger may recover for mental suffering caused by insulting language of the conductor addressed to him. Bleecker v. Colorado & S. Ry., 50 Colo. 140, 114 Pac. 481.

But in Kyle v. Chicago, R. I. & P. Ry., 182 Fed. 613, recovery for mental suffering from failure to carry a person to the bedside of her sick mother was refused, the court saying that it is a settled rule in the federal courts that there can be no recovery for mental suffering where that is the only damage; and the same decision was reached in *Iowa,* in an action for refusal of passage on a steamship. Zabron v. Cunard S. S. Co., 151 Ia. 345, 131 N. W. 18.

ings of humiliation, such damages cannot be recovered.[108] For breach of contract to provide a special train nothing can be recovered on account of disappointment and mental suffering;[109] but in an action against steamship company for breach of contract to give a certain stateroom, the stateroom given instead being in the stern of vessel where plaintiff was unable to sleep and consequently suffered nervous sickness, causing much pain and suffering, it was held that if plaintiff was given no choice before the vessel sailed she could recover for the consequential illness. Her mental suffering, the court said, arose from physical discomfort and loss of sleep. Had it arisen from mere vexation and disappointment or something that would not have disturbed the ordinary person the company would not have foreseen it, but loss of sleep was a probable consequence of the change and she could recover.[110] For damage to goods carried[111] and for delay in transportation [112] or refusal to deliver [113] mental suffering is not an element of recovery, since it is not within the contemplation of the parties, and not a proximate result of the injury. So in an action against a water company for failure to furnish water, recovery cannot be had for mental suffering.[114]

When a telegraph company contracts to deliver a message, and has notice that failure to deliver it will cause mental pain, it is in some jurisdictions held that in an action against it for failure to deliver the message, the plaintiff may recover compensation for his mental pain.[115] But by the prevailing view

[108] Glover v. Atchison, T. & S. F. Ry., 129 Mo. App. 563, 108 S. W. 105.

[109] Wilcox v. Richmond & D. R. R., 52 Fed. 264, 3 C. C. A. 73, 17 L. R. A. 804.

[110] North German Lloyd Steamship Co. v. Wood, 18 Pa. Super. Ct. 488.

[111] Chicago, R. I. & P. Ry. v. Whitten, 90 Ark. 462, 119 S. W. 835. In Long v. Chicago, R. I. & P. Ry., 15 Okla. 512, 86 Pac. 289, 6 L. R. A. (N. S.) 883, damages were refused for mutilation of a corpse while in transit.

[112] Eller v. Railway Co., 140 N. C. 140, 52 S. E. 305, 3 L. R. A. (N. S.) 225 (delay in transporting a corpse). But see Louisville & N. R. R. v. Hull, 113 Ky. 561, 68 S. W. 433, 57 L. R. A. 771.

[113] Gates v. Bekins, 46 Wash. 14, 87 Pac. 505.

[114] Birmingham Water Works Co. v. Vinter, 164 Ala. 490, 51 So. 356.

[115] *United States:* Beasley v. Western U. T. Co., 39 Fed. 181.

Alabama: Lay v. Postal T. C. Co. (Ala.), 54 So. 529 (refusing to follow the Indiana court in repudiating the doctrine).

Iowa: Cowan v. Western U. T. Co., 122 Iowa, 379, 98 N. W. 281, 64 L. R. A. 545, 101 Am. St. Rep. 268.

Kentucky: Chapman v. Western U. T. Co., 90 Ky. 265, 13 S. W. 880; Western U. T. Co. v. Van Cleave, 107 Ky. 464, 54 S. W. 827, 92 Am. St. Rep. 366; Postal T. C. Co. v. Terrell, 124 Ky. 822,

such damages cannot be recovered for negligence in transmitting a telegram.[116] The reasoning upon which this result is reached is not altogether satisfactory; and the doctrine appears to be an application of the general doctrine disallowing a cause of action for a negligent wrong where the only damage is mental,[117] the courts losing sight of the fact that there is here a cause of action for breach of the public duty entirely apart from the damage.[118] The subject will be more fully dealt with in the chapter on Telegraph and Telephone Companies.[119]

§ 46. Difficulty of estimating in money no objection.

The chief objection urged against the allowance of compen-

100 S. W. 292, 14 L. R. A. (N. S.) 927; Western U. T. Co. v. Witt, 33 Ky. L. Rep. 685, 110 S. W. 889.

Nevada: Barnes v. Western U. T. Co., 27 Nev. 438, 76 Pac. 931, 103 Am. St. Rep. 776, 65 L. R. A. 666.

North Carolina: Young v. Western U. T. Co., 107 N. C. 370, 11 S. E. 1044, 9 L. R. A. 669, 22 Am. St. Rep. 883.

Tennessee: Wadsworth v. Western U. T. Co., 86 Tenn. 695, 8 S. W. 574, 6 Am. St. Rep. 86.

Texas: So Relle v. Western U. T. Co., 55 Tex. 308, 40 Am. Rep. 805; Stuart v. Western U. T. Co., 66 Tex. 580, 18 S. W. 351, 59 Am. Rep. 623 (explaining Gulf, C. & S. F. Ry. v. Levy, 59 Tex. 563, 46 Am. Rep. 278); Western U. T. Co. v. Cooper, 71 Tex. 507, 9 S. W. 598, 10 Am. St. Rep. 772, *n.* In South Carolina a telegraph company is made liable by statute to damages for mental suffering which were within the contemplation of the parties; but this does not extend to an action against the operator in fault, and no damages for mental suffering can be recovered in an action against him. Fail v. W. U. Tel. Co., 80 S. Car. 207, 60 S. E. 697.

[116] *United States:* Chase v. Western U. T. Co., 44 Fed. 554, 10 L. R. A. 464; McBride v. Sunset Telephone Co., 96 Fed. 81; Rowan v. Western U. T. Co., 149 Fed. 550.

Alabama: Blount v. Western U. T. Co., 126 Ala. 105, 27 So. 779.

Arkansas: Peay v. Western U. T. Co., 64 Ark. 538, 43 S. W. 965, 39 L. R. A. 463.

Dakota: Russell v. Western U. T. Co., 3 Dak. 315.

Indiana: Western U. T. Co. v. Ferguson, 157 Ind. 64, 60 N. E. 674, 1080 (overruling Reese v. Western U. T. Co., 123 Ind. 294, 24 N. E. 163); Kazy v. Western U. T. Co., 37 Ind. App. 73, 76 N. E. 792.

Kansas: West v. Western U. T. Co., 39 Kan. 93, 17 Pac. 807, 7 Am. St. Rep. 530.

Missouri: Connell v. Western U. T. Co., 116 Mo. 34, 22 S. W. 345, 38 Am. St. Rep. 575, 20 L. R. A. 172.

North Carolina: Thompson v. Western U. T. Co., 107 N. C. 449, 12 S. E. 427.

Ohio: Kester v. Western U. T. Co., 8 Ohio Cir. Ct. 236; Connelly v. Western U. T. Co., 100 Va. 51, 40 S. E. 618, 56 L. R. A. 663.

Oklahoma: Western U. T. C. v. Choteau, 115 Pac. 879.

Wisconsin: Summerfield v. Western U. T. Co., 87 Wis. 1, 57 N. W. 973, 41 Am. St. Rep. 17.

[117] *Ante,* § 43f.

[118] *Ante,* § 43j.

[119] Chap. xxxix.

sation for mental suffering is that it is not capable of being estimated in money; but that argument might as well be urged against awarding damages for physical pain. "Wounding a man's feelings," said Beckley, C. J.,[120] "is as much actual damage as breaking his limbs. The difference is, that one is internal and the other external; one mental, the other physical; in either case the damage is not measurable with exactness. There can be a closer approximation in estimating the damage to a limb than to the feelings, but at the last the amount is indefinite." "That the amount of damages allowable in such a case as this is not capable of easy and accurate mathematical computation is freely conceded; but that should not be a sufficient reason for refusing or defeating the right of action altogether; for the same objection may be urged with the same force in all cases where mental and bodily suffering are treated as proper elements of damage."[121]

The Supreme Court of Massachusetts, in a carefully reasoned opinion, has effectually disposed of the objection. The plaintiff claimed compensation for diminution of mental capacity caused by the injury. The court said:[122]

"In all actions of this description, and particularly in those in which damages for mental suffering or loss of mental capacity are sought to be recovered, the difficulty of furnishing by evidence the means of measuring the extent of the injury, so that the jury may be able to award with any certainty a pecuniary equivalent therefor, is at once apparent; and in this difficulty the defendants find argument for the support of their objection. But the answer is, that the law does not refuse to take notice of such injury on account of the difficulty of ascertaining its degree. In a variety of actions founded on personal torts, and in many where no positive bodily harm has been inflicted, the plaintiff is permitted to recover for injury to the feelings and affections, for mental anxiety, personal insult, and that wounded

[120] Head v. G. P. Ry., 79 Ga. 358, 360, 7 S. E. 217, 11 Am. St. Rep. 434.
[121] Caldwell, J., in Wadsworth v. Western U. T. Co., 86 Tenn. 695, 711, 8 S. W. 574, 6 Am. St. Rep. 864. Acc. Indiana: Indiana Ry. v. Orr, 41 Ind. App. 426, 84 N. E. 32.

North Carolina: Young v. Western U. T. Co., 107 N. C. 370, 11 S. E. 1044. 9 L. R. A. 669, 22 Am. St. Rep, 883.
[122] Ballou v. Farnum, 11 All. (Mass.) 73, 77, per Colt, J.

sensibility which follows the invasion of a large class of personal rights. The impossibility, in all such cases, of precisely appreciating in money mental suffering of this description is certainly as great as is suggested where the question is what shall be allowed for a permanent injury to mental capacity. The compensation for personal injury occasioned by the negligence or misconduct of others, which the law promises, is indemnity, so far as it may be afforded in money, for the loss and damage which the man has suffered as a man. Some of its elements may be bodily pain, mutilation, loss of time, and outlay of money; but of more important consideration oftentimes is the mental suffering and loss of capacity which ensues. Of these several items of injury, if compensation is to be confined to those capable of accurate estimate it will include but a small part, and must exclude all those injuries commonly regarded as purely physical; for the difficulty in ascertaining a pecuniary equivalent for the last named is precisely the same and quite as great as any that have been suggested. In fact, it will be found impossible to fix a limit to injuries of a physical nature so as to exclude from consideration their effect on the mental organization of the sufferer. The intimate union of the mental and physical, the mutual dependence of each organization—if, indeed, for any practical purpose in this regard, they can be considered as distinct—the direct and mysterious sympathy that exists whenever the sound and healthy condition of either is disturbed, render useless any attempt to separate them for the purpose indicated."

§ 46a. Mental injury must be real.

Mental injury for which recovery can be had must be real suffering or damage. It must be more than mere vexation or loss of temper for being disappointed in a particular thing on which the mind was set.[123] "For mere inconveniences,

[123] *Arkansas:* Western U. T. Co. v. Archie, 92 Ark. 59, 121 S. W. 1045.

Kentucky: Robinson v. Western U. T. Co., 24 Ky. L. Rep. 452, 57 L. R. A. 611, 68 S. W. 656.

North Carolina: Hancock v. Western U. T. Co., 137 N. C. 497, 49 S. E. 952,

69 L. R. A. 403; Gerock v. Western U. T. Co., 147 N. C. 1, 60 S. E. 637.

South Carolina: Johnson v. Western U. T. Co., 81 S. C. 235, 62 S. E. 244.

Wisconsin: Walsh v. C., M. & St. P. Ry., 42 Wis. 23, 24 Am. Rep. 376.

such as annoyance and loss of temper or vexation, or for being disappointed in a particular thing which you have set your mind upon, without real physical inconvenience resulting, you cannot recover damages. That is purely sentimental."[124] Nothing so vague as "inability to enjoy life" should be allowed to furnish a basis of recovery.[125]

§ 47. Kinds of mental injury compensated.

It remains to consider the various kinds of mental suffering for which compensation has been awarded in the proper case.

1. *Loss of mental capacity* is a proper subject of compensation.[126]

2. *Mental suffering accompanying physical pain* is a subject of compensation.[127] It is difficult in most cases to distinguish

England: Hamlin v. Great N. Ry., 1 H. & N. 408, 411.

[124] Mellor, J., in Hobbs v. L. & S. W. Ry., L. R. 10 Q. B. 111.

[125] South Bend Brick Co. v. Goller, 46 Ind. App. 531, 93 N. E. 37 (see, however, Pittsburgh, C., C. & St. L. Ry. v. Cozatt, 39 Ind. App. 682, 79 N. E. 534).

[126] *Massachusetts:* Ballou v. Farnum, 11 All. 73.

New York: Williams v. Underhill, 63 App. Div. 223, 71 N. Y. Supp. 291.

North Carolina: Wallace v. Western N. C. R. R., 104 N. C. 442.

Texas: Houston & T. C. R. R. v. Shapard,   Tex. Civ. App.   , 118 S. W. 596 (mind less accurate than before).

Utah: Nichols v. Oregon S. L. R. R., 28 Utah, 319, 78 Pac. 866 (loss of memory).

[127] *United States:* Wade v. Leroy, 20 How. 34, 15 L. ed. 813; McIntyre v. Giblin, 131 U. S. clxxiv; Hanson v. Fowle, 1 Sawy. 539; Boyle v. Case, 9 Sawy. 386; Carpenter v. Mexican N. R. R., 39 Fed. 315.

Alabama: South & N. A. R. R. v. McLendon, 63 Ala. 266.

California: Fairchild v. California S. Co., 13 Cal. 599; Jones v. The Cortes,

17 Cal. 487, 79 Am. Dec. 142; Malone v. Hawley, 46 Cal. 409.

Colorado: Wall v. Cameron, 6 Colo. 275.

Connecticut: Seger v. Barkhamsted, 22 Conn. 290; Masters v. Warren, 27 Conn. 293; Lawrence v. Housatonic R. R., 29 Conn. 390.

District of Columbia: Larmon v. District, 16 D. C. (5 Mackey) 330.

Georgia: Cooper v. Mullins, 30 Ga. 146, 76 Am. Dec. 638; Smith v. Overby, 30 Ga. 241; City & S. Ry. v. Findley, 76 Ga. 311.

Illinois: Pierce v. Millay, 44 Ill. 189; Indianapolis & S. L. R. R. v. Stables, 62 Ill. 313; Chicago v. Jones, 66 Ill. 349; Chicago v. Langlass, 66 Ill. 361; Chicago v. Elzeman, 71 Ill. 131; Sorgenfrei v. Schroeder, 75 Ill. 397; Hannibal & S. J. R. R. v. Martin, 111 Ill. 219; Sheridan v. Hibbard, 119 Ill. 307.

Indiana: Taber v. Hutson, 5 Ind. 322, 61 Am. Dec. 96; Nossaman v. Rickert, 18 Ind. 350; Wright v. Compton, 53 Ind. 337; Indianapolis v. Gaston, 58 Ind. 224.

Iowa: Muldowney v. Illinois C. Ry., 36 Ia. 462; McKinley v. Chicago & N. W. Ry., 44 Ia. 314, 24 Am. Rep. 748; Ferguson v. Davis Co., 57 Ia. 601; Gronan v. Kukkuck, 59 Ia. 18; Staf-

the mental from the physical pain, but compensation may be recovered for both.

3. *Mental anxiety and distress*, which, though the direct and natural result of the injury, are independent of it, are subjects of compensation.[128] So one who has been mutilated or crippled by the defendant's fault may recover for the distress of mind because of the disfigurement.[129] So where one was bitten by a

ford *v.* Oskaloosa, 64 Ia. 251; Kendall *v.* Albia, 73 Ia. 241.

Kansas: Tefft *v.* Wilcox, 6 Kan. 46; Kansas P. Ry. *v.* Pointer, 9 Kan. 620; Missouri, K. & T. Ry. *v.* Weaver, 16 Kan. 456; Manser *v.* Collins, 69 Kan. 290, 76 Pac. 851.

Kentucky: Alexander *v.* Humber, 86 Ky. 565; Kentucky C. R. R. *v.* Ackley, 87 Ky. 78, 8 S. W. 691, 12 Am. St. Rep. 480.

Maryland: Stockton *v.* Frey, 4 Gill, 406, 45 Am. Dec. 138; McMahon *v.* Northern C. Ry., 39 Md. 438.

Massachusetts: Tyler *v.* Pomeroy, 8 All. 480; Smith *v.* Holcomb, 99 Mass. 552.

Mississippi: Memphis & C. R. R. *v.* Whitfield, 44 Miss. 466, 7 Am. Rep. 699.

Missouri: West *v.* Forrest, 22 Mo. 344; Porter *v.* Hannibal & S. J. R. R., 71 Mo. 66, 36 Am. Rep. 454; Ridenhour *v.* Kansas C. C. Ry., 102 Mo. 270, 13 S. W. 889; McMillan *v.* Union P. B. W., 6 Mo. App. 434; Fell *v.* Rich H. C. M. Co., 23 Mo. App. 216.

New Hampshire: Holyoke *v.* Grand T. Ry., 48 N. H. 541; Clark *v.* Manchester, 64 N. H. 471.

New York: Matteson *v.* New York C. R. R., 62 Barb. 364; Brignoli *v.* Chicago & G. E. Ry., 4 Daly, 182.

North Carolina: Wallace *v.* Western N. C. R. R., 104 N. C. 442; Britt *v.* Carolina N. R. R., 147 N. C. 1, 67 S. E. 601.

Pennsylvania: Pennsylvania & O. C. Co. *v.* Graham, 63 Pa. 290, 3 Am. Rep. 549; McLaughlin *v.* Corry, 77 Pa. 109,

18 Am. Rep. 432; Scott *v.* Montgomery, 95 Pa. 444.

South Carolina: Robinson v. St. Mathews,   S. C.   , 71 S. E. 234.

Texas: Houston & T. C. Ry. *v.* Boehm, 57 Tex. 152; Texas & P. Ry. *v.* Curry, 64 Tex. 85.

Vermont: Bovee *v.* Danville, 53 Vt. 183.

Virginia: Richmond & D. R. R. *v.* Norment, 84 Va. 167, 4 S. E. 211, 10 Am. St. Rep. 827.

West Virginia: Vinal *v.* Core, 18 W. Va. 1; Riley *v.* West V. C. & P. Ry., 27 W. Va. 145.

Wisconsin: Goodno *v.* Oshkosh, 28 Wis. 300; Stewart *v.* Ripon, 38 Wis. 584.

England: Phillips *v.* London & Southwestern Ry., 4 Q. B. Div. 406.

[128] *California:* Procter *v.* Southern Cal. R. R., 130 Cal. 20, 62 Pac. 306 (worry at being separated from baggage); Merrill *v.* Los Angeles G. & E. Co.,   Cal.   , 111 Pac. 534.

Idaho: Lindsay *v.* Oregon Short Line R. R., 13 Idaho, 477, 90 Pac. 984, 12 L. R. A. (N. S.) 184 (anxiety at being separated from wife).

New York: Webb *v.* Yonkers R. R., 51 N. Y. App. Div. 194, 64 N. Y. Supp. 491 (worry over an injury).

Texas: Pullman Co. *v.* Cox,   Tex. Civ. App.   , 120 S. W. 1058 (distress at not being carried to destination); Western U. T. Co. *v.* Rich,   Tex. Civ. App.   , 126 S. W. 686 (distress through fear of being quarantined and kept away from family).

[129] *United States:* McDermott *v.* Se-

dog suspected of being mad, he was allowed to recover for his fear of evil results,[130] and compensation has been recovered for anxiety caused by the non-arrival of a physician, a telegram summoning him not having been delivered, owing to the defendant's negligence.[131]

4. *Fright caused by apprehension of physical harm* is a subject of compensation.[132] Thus, where the plaintiff, put off the defendant's train wrongfully at night in a freight yard before reaching his station, fell into a culvert, and was frightened by trains backing over the culvert, he was allowed to recover for his fright.[133]   So recovery is allowed for a shock to the nervous system.[134]

5. *Loss of peace of mind and happiness* is a subject of compensation.[135]

6. *Sense of insult or indignity, mortification, or wounded pride* is a subject of compensation.[136]   A common instance is where

vere, 202 U. S. 600, 26 Sup. Ct. 709, 50 L. ed. 1162; Patridge *v.* Boston & M. R. R., 184 Fed. 211,   C. C. A.   .
Indiana: Harrod v. Bisson, 000 Ind. App.   , 93 N. E. 1093.
Missouri: Shortridge v. Scarritt Estate Co., 145 Mo. App. 295, 130 S. W. 126.
North Carolina: Britt v. Carolina N. R. R., 147 N. C. 1, 61 S. E. 601.
[130] Godeau *v.* Blood, 52 Vt. 251, 36 Am. Rep. 751, *n.*
[131] Western U. Tel. Co. *v.* Cooper, 71 Tex. 507, 9 S. W. 598, 10 Am. St. Rep. 772, *n.*
[132] *Alabama:* Louisville & N. R. R. *v.* Whitman, 79 Ala. 328.
Connecticut: Seger *v.* Barkhamsted, 22 Conn. 290.
Maine: Fitzgerald v. Dobson, 78 Me. 559, 7 Atl. 704.
Missouri: Butts v. Nat. Exch. Bank, 99 Mo. App. 168, 72 S. W. 1083 (fear of blood poisoning).
Texas: Southern K. Ry. *v.* McSwain, Tex. Civ. App.   , 118 S. W. 874; Pullman Co. *v.* Cox,   Tex. Civ. App.   , 120 S. W. 1058; Western U. T. Co. *v.* Rich,   Tex. Civ. App.   , 126

S. W. 686 (fear of contagion.)   But see Missouri, K. & T. Ry. *v.* Linton, Tex. Civ. App.   , 126 S. W. 678, where the apprehension was not of physical harm, but a fear (which proved groundless) that a body would not arrive in time for burial.
[133] Stutz v. C. & N. W. Ry., 73 Wis. 147, 40 N. W. 653, 9 Am. St. Rep. 769, *n.*
[134] Kendall *v.* Albia, 73 Ia. 241, 34 N. W. 833.
[135] Cox v. Vanderkleed, 21 Ind. 164, and the cases of breach of promise of marriage above.
[136] *United States:* Quigley v. C. P. R. R., 5 Sawy. 107; Boyle *v.* Case, 9 Sawy. 386.
Alabama: Birmingham Ry. & E. Co. *v.* Ward, 124 Ala. 409, 27 So. 471; Mattingly *v.* Houston, 167 Ala. 167, 52 So. 78.
Arkansas: Ward v. Blackwood, 48 Ark. 396.
California: Thomas v. Gates, 126 Cal. 1, 58 Pac. 315; Merrill *v.* Los Angeles G. & E. Co.,   Cal.   , 111 Pac. 534.
Louisiana: Bonneval v. Am. Coffee Co., 127 La.   , 53 So. 426.

a passenger is wrongfully ejected from a railroad train.[137] So, where the plaintiff was wrongfully ejected from his house, it was held that he could recover compensation for mortification.[138] So the plaintiff may recover compensation for wounded pride in actions for malicious prosecution [139] or false imprisonment [140] or in an action for assault and battery committed in arresting the plaintiff illegally.[141]

On the same ground the plaintiff recovers in actions of libel and slander; [142] but when in an action of slander the words are

Maine: Wadsworth *v.* Treat, 43 Me. 163.

Maryland: Philadelphia, B. & W. R. R. *v.* Crawford, 112 Md. 508, 77 Atl. 278.

Michigan: Robinson *v.* Stimer, 154 Mich. 244, 117 N. W. 634.

New York: Binns *v.* Vitagraph Co., 130 N. Y. Supp. 876.

Wisconsin: Craker *v.* Chicago & N. W. R. R., 36 Wis. 657, 17 Am. Rep. 504.

[137] *Alabama:* Louisville & N. R. R. *v.* Whitman, 79 Ala. 328.

California: Sloane *v.* Southern Cal. R. R., 111 Cal. 668, 44 Pac. 320, 32 L. R. A. 193.

Georgia: Head *v.* Georgia P. Ry., 79 Ga. 358, 7 S. E. 217, 11 Am. St. Rep. 434.

Illinois: Chicago & A. R. R. *v.* Flagg, 43 Ill. 364, 92 Am. Dec. 133, *n;* Chicago & N. W. Ry. *v.* Williams, 55 Ill. 185, 8 Am. Rep. 641; Chicago & N. W. Ry. *v.* Chisholm, 79 Ill. 584; Pennsylvania R. R. *v.* Connell, 112 Ill. 295, 54 Am. Rep. 238, *n.*

Indiana: Lake E. & W. Ry. *v.* Fix, 88 Ind. 381, 45 Am. Rep. 464.

Iowa: Shepard *v.* Chicago, R. I. & P. Ry., 77 Ia. 54; Southern K. Ry. *v.* Rice, 38 Kan. 307, 16 Pac. 695, 5 Am. St. Rep. 744.

Kentucky: Tennessee C. R. R. *v.* Brasher, 29 Ky. L. Rep. 1277, 97 S. W. 349.

New York: Gillespie *v.* Brooklyn Heights R. R., 178 N. Y. 347, 70 N. E. 857, 66 L. R. A. 618.

Ohio: Smith *v.* Pittsburgh, F. W. & C. Ry., 23 Oh. St. 10.

Washington: Davis *v.* Tacoma R. & P. Co., 35 Wash. 203, 77 Pac. 209, 66 L. R. A. 802.

Wisconsin: Stutz *v.* Chicago & N. W. Ry., 73 Wis. 147, 40 N. W. 653, 9 Am. St. Rep. 169, *n.*

England: Coppin *v.* Braithwaite, 8 Jur. 875.

It is, however, held in some jurisdictions that if the conductor acted considerately, the plaintiff should have felt no sense of insult, and therefore that he can recover nothing for sense of indignity. Paine *v.* C., R. I. & P. Ry., 45 Ia. 569; Fitzgerald *v.* C., R. I. & P. Ry., 50 Ia. 79; Batterson *v.* C. & G. T. Ry., 49 Mich. 184; but *contra*, Chicago & A. R. R. *v.* Flagg, 43 Ill. 364, 92 Am. Dec. 133, *n;* Carsten *v.* Northern P. Ry., 44 Minn. 454, 47 N. W. 49.

[138] Moyer *v.* Gordon, 113 Ind. 282.

[139] *Alabama:* Lunsford *v.* Dietrich, 86 Ala. 250, 5 So. 461, 11 Am. St. Rep. 37.

Iowa: Parkhurst *v.* Masteller, 57 Ia. 474.

West Virginia: Vinal *v.* Core, 18 W. Va. 1.

[140] *Connecticut:* Gibney *v.* Lewis, 68 Conn. 392, 36 Atl. 799.

Michigan: Ross *v.* Leggett, 61 Mich. 445, 28 N. W. 695, 1 Am. St. Rep. 608.

Texas: Hays *v.* Creary, 60 Tex. 445.

[141] Morgan *v.* Curley, 142 Mass. 107.

[142] *Connecticut:* Swift *v.* Dickerman, 31 Conn. 285.

Illinois: Adams *v.* Smith, 58 Ill. 418.

not actionable in themselves, and special damage must be shown, recovery cannot be had for mental suffering alone.[143]

So where a plaintiff suffered bodily mutilation through the defendant's tort, he may recover compensation for mortification which he has suffered and will suffer by reason of the mutilation, and of the fact that he may become an object of curiosity and ridicule among his fellows.[144] And recovery may be had for the mortification and sense of indignity suffered by reason of defendant's unlawful mutilation of the body of plaintiff's mother.[145]

7. *Sense of shame and humiliation* is a subject of compen-

Iowa: Prime v. Eastwood, 45 Ia. 640.

Louisiana: Miller v. Roy, 10 La. Ann. 231; Dufort v. Abadie, 23 La. Ann. 280.

Maryland: Blumhardt v. Rohr, 70 Md. 328, 17 Atl. 266.

Massachusetts: Hastings v. Stetson, 130 Mass. 76; Mahoney v. Belford, 132 Mass. 393; Chesley v. Tompson, 137 Mass. 136.

Michigan: Scripps v. Reilly, 38 Mich. 10; Newman v. Stein, 75 Mich. 402, 42 N. W. 956, 13 Am. St. Rep. 447.

New Hampshire: Barnes v. Campbell, 60 N. H. 27.

Wisconsin: Hacker v. Heiney, 111 Wis. 313, 87 N. W. 249.

[143] Lynch v. Knight, 9 H. L. C. 577.

[144] *United States:* McDermott v. Severe, 202 U. S. 600, 26 Sup. Ct. 709, 50 L. ed. 1162; United States Ex. Co. v. Wahl, 168 Fed. 848, 94 C. C. A. 260.

Iowa: Newbury v. Getchell & Martin Lumber & Manuf. Co., 100 Iowa, 441, 69 N. W. 743, 62 Am. St. Rep. 582; Rice v. Council Bluffs, 124 Iowa, 639, 100 N. W. 506.

Maine: Coombs v. King,   Me. , 78 Atl. 468.

Michigan: Sherwood v. Chicago & W. M. Ry., 82 Mich. 374, 46 N. W. 773; Beath v. Rapid Ry., 119 Mich. 512, 78 N. W. 537.

Pennsylvania: Rockwell v. Eldred, 7 Pa. Super. Ct. 95.

Texas: Galveston, H. & S. A. Ry. v.

Clark, 21 Tex. Civ. App. 167, 51 S. W. 276.

Washington: Gray v. Washington Water Power Co., 30 Wash. 665, 71 Pac. 206.

Wisconsin: Heddles v. Chicago & N. W. Ry., 77 Wis. 228, 46 N. W. 115.

In a few jurisdictions the courts, falsely following the analogy of the cases where recovery is refused for mere mental suffering, refuse to give what are called the merely "sentimental" damages, that is, the anguish caused by the contemplation of one's disfigurement.

United States: Chicago, etc., R. R. v. Caulfield, 63 Fed. 396, 11 C. C. A. 552; Southern Pac. Co. v. Hetzer, 135 Fed. 272, 68 C. C. A. 26, 1 L. R. A. (N. S.) 288.

Idaho: Giffen v. Lewiston, 6 Ida. 231, 55 Pac. 545.

Illinois: Chicago Ry. v. Anderson, 182 Ill. 298, 55 N. E. 366; Chicago, B. & Q. R. R. v. Hines, 45 Ill. App. 299; West Chicago St. R. R. v. James, 69 Ill. App. 60; Decatur v. Hamilton, 89 Ill. App. 561; Lake St. El. R. R. v. Gormley, 108 Ill. App. 59.

Indiana: Harrod v. Bisson,   Ind. App.   , 93 N. E. 1903.

Oregon: Maynard v. Oregon Ry., 46 Ore. 15, 78 Pac. 983, 68 L. R. A. 477.

[145] Koerber v. Patek, 123 Wis. 453, 102 N. W. 40, 60 L. R. A. 956.

sation.[146]   So where a father brings an action for the seduction of his daughter, he may recover compensation for the shame it caused him; [147] and in jurisdictions where, by statute, the woman may recover for her seduction, her shame is an element of compensation.[148]   In an action for indecent assault, the woman may recover compensation for her sense of shame and humiliation; [149] so may the plaintiff in an action for the unlawful execution of a search warrant.[150]

So where a physician brought with him a layman to help him deliver the plaintiff of a child, and they were admitted upon the supposition that both were physicians, it was held that the plaintiff, on learning the truth, might recover compensation from the physician for her sense of shame.[151]   And where a female passenger was kissed by a conductor, it was held that she could recover compensation for her sense of humiliation.[152]

8. *A blow to the affections* is a subject for compensation,[153]

[146] *Illinois:* Palmer v. Baum, 123 Ill. App. 584 (indecent assault on daughter).
Kentucky: Postal T. C. Co. v. Terrell, 124 Ky. 822, 100 S. W. 292, 14 L. R. A. (N. S.) 927; Adkins v. Kendrick, 131 Ky. 779, 115 S. W. 814 (alienation of affections of husband).
Missouri: Johnson v. Daily, 136 Mo. App. 534, 118 S. W. 530 (assault and battery).
Texas: Missouri, K. & T. Ry. v. Ball, 25 Tex. Civ. App. 500, 61 S. W. 327 (white woman placed in car for colored persons).
Virginia: Norfolk & W. Ry. v. Stone, Va.   , 69 S. E. 927 (white woman placed in car for colored persons).
[147] *United States:* Barbour v. Stephenson, 32 Fed. 66.
Massachusetts: Hatch v. Fuller, 131 Mass. 574.
Minnesota: Russell v. Chambers, 31 Minn. 54.
New Hampshire: Lunt v. Philbrick, 59 N. H. 59.

West Virginia: Riddle v. McGinnis, 22 W. Va. 253.
[148] *Indiana:* Simons v. Busby, 119 Ind. 13.
Oregon: Breon v. Henkle, 14 Ore. 494, 500.
Wisconsin: Giese v. Schultz, 53 Wis. 462, 65 Wis. 487.
[149] *United States:* Campbell v. Pullman P. C. Co., 42 Fed. 484.
Indiana: Wolf v. Trinkle, 103 Ind. 355.
Michigan: Fay v. Swan, 44 Mich. 544.
New York: Ford v. Jones, 62 Barb. 484.
[150] Melcher v. Scruggs, 72 Mo. 407.
[151] De May v. Roberts, 46 Mich. 160, 9 N. W. 146, 41 Am. Rep. 154.
[152] Craker v. C. & N. W. Ry., 36 Wis. 657, 17 Am. Rep. 504.
[153] *Colorado:* Stark v. Johnson, 43 Colo. 243, 95 Pac. 930, 16 L. R. A. (N. S.) 674 (crim. con.).
Kentucky: Adkins v. Kendrick, 131 Ky. 779, 115 S. W. 814 (alienation of affections).

as in the case of breach of promise of marriage.[154]   Compensation is awarded for this cause in those jurisdictions which permit recovery for the grief caused by non-delivery of a telegram announcing the illness or death and funeral of a relative.[155]

9. *Nervous prostration* or any diseased condition of the nerves, though shown only through the mind, is the subject for compensation when the result of an actionable wrong.[156]

§ 48. Compensation for injuries to family relations.

The relations existing between the members of a family are protected by the common law, and for injuries to such relations compensation may be had; thus, damages may be recovered for the loss by a husband or wife of the *consortium* of the other, and by a parent for the society and services of his child.   In such cases there is injury independent of pecuniary loss; indeed, recovery may be had though there is no pecuniary loss.

The right of a husband to the *consortium* of his wife includes not only a right to the services of the wife, but also to her affection, comfort, and fellowship, and to an undefiled marriage-bed.   A husband has therefore been allowed to recover damages for a rape on his wife, though their relations were uninterrupted and her household services continued to be performed,[157] and for alienating the affections of his wife, though she continued to live with him.[158]   And a father, suing for the seduction of his daughter, may recover compensation for "loss of society of a virtuous daughter," [159] and for the "destruction of his domestic peace."[160]

So in an action for malicious prosecution, it was held that the plaintiff could recover compensation for the loss of society of his family.[161]

<hr/>

[154] *Post,* § 638a.   [155] *Post,* § 894.

[156] *California:* Sloane v. Southern C. R. R., 111 Cal. 668, 44 Pac. 320, 32 L. R. A. 193.

New York: Williams v. Underhill, 63 App. Div. 223, 71 N. Y. Supp. 291.

Texas: Weatherford M. W. & N. N. W. Ry. v. Cutcher, 141 S. W. 137.

So for suffering due to imagination, resulting from neurotic condition. Chicago, R. I. & G. Ry. v. Barnes, 50 Tex. Civ. App. 46, 111 S. W. 447.

[157] Bigaouette v. Paulet, 134 Mass. 123, 45 Am. Rep. 307.

[158] Heermance v. James, 47 Barb. (N. Y.) 120.

[159] Russell v. Chambers, 31 Minn. 54.

[160] Kendrick v. McCrary, 11 Ga. 603.

[161] Hamilton v. Smith, 39 Mich. 222.

The loss of society of one's family is not necessarily caused by direct assaults upon the family relation. A husband who suffers a loss of his wife's society by reason of a personal injury to the wife is entitled to compensation for the loss. Although she still remained with him, if she was so injured that her strength, health and usefulness as a helpmate were impaired, he is entitled to recover for such loss of society. By the term society, is meant such capacities for usefulness, aid and comfort as a wife as she possessed at the time of the injury. Any diminution of those capacities constituted a just basis for an award of compensatory damages.[162]

So in an action for trespass on land, in the course of which the defendant attempted to seduce the wife, a husband may recover compensation for injury to the family relations; [163] and in an action by a wife for alienating her husband's affections she may recover for the loss of *consortium*.[164]

§ 49. To personal liberty.

For an illegal restraint of the plaintiff's personal liberty compensation may be recovered.[165] This is something different from either the loss of time or the physical injury or mental suffering caused by the imprisonment. It is of the same general character as the latter, and the measurement of the compensation must necessarily be left entirely to the jury.

§ 50. To reputation and standing in society.

For an injury to the plaintiff's reputation, honor, and standing in society, caused by the defendant's wrongful act, compensation may be recovered.[166] So, in a case of indecent assault, the court said the plaintiff could recover compensation for "loss of honor and good name." [167] The same decision was made

[162] Furnish *v.* Missouri Pac. Ry., 102 Mo. 669, 15 S. W. 315, 22 Am. St. Rep. 800.

[163] Brame *v.* Clark, 148 N. C. 364, 62 S. E. 418.

[164] Scott *v.* O'Brien, 129 Ky. 1, 110 S. W. 260.

[165] Fotheringham *v.* Adams Ex. Co., 36 Fed. 252; Hamilton *v.* Smith, 39 Mich. 222.

[166] *Michigan:* Andrews *v.* Booth, 111 N. W. 1059, 148 Mich. 333, 14 Detroit Leg. N. 241.

Wisconsin: Barnes *v.* Martin, 15 Wis. 240, 82 Am. Dec. 670; and in all actions for defamation.

[167] Wolf *v.* Trinkle, 103 Ind. 355.

So in an action for seduction.

Iowa: Hawn *v.* Banghart, 76 Ia. 683, 39 N. W. 251, 14 Am. St. Rep. 261.

Oregon: Breon *v.* Henkle, 14 Ore. 494, 500.

where the defendant wrongfully entered the plaintiff's premises with the avowed purpose of searching for stolen money.[168] And where the plaintiff and his family were wrongfully turned into the street, it was held that he could be compensated for "injury to his pride and social position." [169]

A plaintiff may also recover compensation if prevented from gaining an advantage in worldly position. Thus, in an action for breach of promise, of marriage the plaintiff may recover damages for "loss of station." [170] And so where the defendant's defamation has deprived the plaintiff of a marriage, the plaintiff may recover compensation for the "advantages" of it.[171]

§ 51. Aggravation and mitigation.[172]

In all actions where the damages are not capable of exact pecuniary measurement—that is, where the amount is to a certain extent within the control of the jury—all circumstances may be shown in evidence which will in any way assist the jury in forming its estimate of the amount of damages. In all cases where the amount of damages depends upon the effect of the injury on the feelings, the circumstances of the injury and the position in life of the parties have a bearing on the amount which should be awarded as compensation. So in the case of an injury to liberty, to family relations, to reputation and social standing. And where exemplary damages are to be given, such circumstances have great bearing on the defendant's malice, and may be shown in evidence for the purpose of increasing or decreasing the exemplary damages. Circumstances shown by the plaintiff for the purpose of increasing the amount either of compensatory or of exemplary damages are said to be shown in *aggravation* of the damages; circumstances shown by the defendant for the purpose of cutting down the amount

---

[168] Anon., Minor (Ala.), 52, 12 Am. Dec. 31.

[169] Moyer *v.* Gordon, 113 Ind. 282.

[170] Kelly *v.* Renfro, 9 Ala. 325, 44 Am. Dec. 441.

[171] Davis *v.* Gardiner, 4 Co. 16*b*.

[172] For cases deciding what evidence may be introduced in aggravation or mitigation of damages, see §§ 430 (torts in general), 445–453 (defamation), 460 (malicious prosecution), 465, 466 (false imprisonment), 475, 476 (seduction), 479, 480 (criminal conversation), 487–490 (personal injury) 548 (actions against officers), 639–641 (breach of promise of marriage), 929 (injury to land).

allowed as damages are said to be shown in *mitigation*. These terms, often misused, are properly applied only where evidence is presented to the jury for the purpose of affecting its estimate of damages in this class of cases.

§ 52. Matter of evidence, not of law.

It will be observed that matters of aggravation or mitigation are properly matters of evidence only; and it is not really a question of law whether or not a circumstance is one of aggravation or mitigation. In fact, it is easily conceivable that a circumstance that would aggravate the damages in one case would mitigate them in another. Even in the same form of action the same circumstances might be in one instance an aggravation, in another a mitigation of the injury. In an action of slander the high position of the plaintiff usually aggravates the damages, since it puts an unusually high value on the reputation injured; but it has been held to be a matter of mitigation if the plaintiff's character were so high as to be above the reach of the slander.[173]

The court is called upon to decide whether evidence offered by a party is admissible in his favor, either in aggravation or in mitigation. But counsel for the other party might desire to argue before the jury that the evidence offered in aggravation should really be considered by the jury as a matter of mitigation, or *vice versa*. It seems that in fairness this privilege should be allowed him, on the same principle that he is allowed to argue that the evidence is not of any weight at all. But if so, the court would not be justified in charging that the evidence *must* be taken in one way or the other; to do so would be to take from the jury the decision of a controverted question of fact. It would, therefore, seem that, in any case where the effect of evidence admitted is reasonably contested by the parties, the court should not charge in favor of either side, but should leave the matter to the jury. It is rarely, however, a matter of any doubt whether a circumstance tends to mitigate or aggravate damages, and in the ordinary case the court is justified in charging that certain facts are to be considered by the jury in aggravation or mitigation.

[173] Broughton *v.* McGrew, 39 Fed. 672.

The question, in short, is one as to the admissibility and effect of evidence, and not strictly one as to the legal measure of damages. Nevertheless, certain rules as to the effect of some common circumstances (such as provocation, good faith, the position of the parties, etc.) in aggravating or mitigating the damages have been laid down, and are followed in ordinary cases; though, as has been said, they should not be regarded as conclusive. These rules are applied in actions of breach of promise of marriage and of tort for personal injury, and in all actions where exemplary damages are allowed, and will be stated and discussed in connection with those actions.

CHAPTER III

§ 53. Offer of specific reparation.

A court of law cannot, as has been seen, decree specific reparation for a wrong; nor can it require the injured party to accept such reparation in lieu of damages. The right to damages is absolute upon the happening of the wrong, and nothing but the act of the injured party can release it. Consequently an offer of specific reparation, unaccepted, will not reduce the plaintiff's damage. For instance, the plaintiff is not obliged to receive converted property which the defendant desires to return.[1] And of course the plaintiff cannot be obliged to buy back his property, though offered to him at less than the market

---

[1] *Arkansas:* Norman v. Rogers, 29 Ark. 365.

Maine: Carpenter v. Dresser, 72 Me. 377, 39 Am. Rep. 337.

Massachusetts: Stickney v. Allen, 10 Gray, 352.

Michigan: Bringard v. Stellwagen, 41 Mich. 54.

Missouri: Gilbert v. Peck, 43 Mo. App. 577.

New Jersey: Wooley v. Carter, 7 N. J. L. (2 Halst.) 85, 11 Am. Dec. 520.

New York: Hanmer v. Wilsey, 17 Wend. 91; Livermore v. Northrup, 44 N. Y. 107; Carpenter v. Manhattan Life Ins. Co., 22 Hun 47; Smith v. Hartog, 51 N. Y. Supp. 257; Lyon v. Yates, 52 Barb. 237.

Vermont: Green v. Sperry, 16 Vt. 390; Morgan v. Kidder, 55 Vt. 367.

price,[2] nor to accept other property in lieu of that converted.[3] So in an action of trover [4] it was said: "No tender or offer to restore the property after conversion, will defeat the action or mitigate the damages.   If the injured party accept the property when tendered, this may be shown in mitigation of damages, but will not defeat the action entirely.   Nor will a mere agreement without consideration to receive the property, defeat the action or mitigate the damages where the injured party thinks proper to disregard the agreement and bring his suit for the conversion."

And if a contract to marry is broken, a subsequent offer to marry will not mitigate the damage.[5]   Nor in the case of a contract to deliver property, once the contract is broken, can a subsequent offer to deliver the property be shown in mitigation of damages.[6]

Where, however, the conversion was not wilful, but merely technical, there is a tendency in the later cases to allow a tender of the property to be shown in reduction of damages.[7]   And in an action for not conveying all the land covered by an agreement to convey, a tender of a deed of the land was allowed to be shown to reduce the damages.[8]

§ 54. Bringing converted property into court.

The practice of staying proceedings in certain cases upon bringing converted property into court was not unknown in England.   The question was early considered by Lord Mansfield,[9] where a motion was made to stay proceedings on bringing the chattel into court, with costs to that time.   The rule was refused on the circumstances of the particular case; but his lordship said:

[2] *New York:* Weld v. Reilly, 48 N. Y. Super. Ct. 531.

Utah: Hecht v. Metzler, 14 Utah, 408, 48 Pac. 37.

[3] *Connecticut:* Munson v. Munson, 24 Conn. 115.

Georgia: Woods v. McCall, 67 Ga. 506.

[4] *Arkansas:* Norman v. Rogers, 29 Ark. 365, 369.

[5] *Indiana:* Kurtz v. Frank, 76 Ind. 594, 40 Am. Rep. 275.

Michigan: Bennett v. Beam, 42 Mich. 346, 36 Am. Rep. 442, n.

Contra, Kelly v. Renfro, 9 Ala. 325.

[6] Colby v. Reed, 99 U. S. 560, 25 L. ed. 484.

[7] *United States:* Colby v. Reed, 99 U. S. 560, 25 L. ed. 484 (*semble*).

Missouri: Ward v. Moffett, 38 Mo. App. 395.

[8] Towle v. Lawrence, 59 N. H. 501.

[9] Fisher v. Prince, 3 Burr. 1363.

"Where trover is brought for a specific chattel, of an ascertained quantity and quality, and unattended with any circumstances that can enhance the damages above the real value, but that its real and ascertained value must be the sole measure of the damages, there the specific thing demanded may be brought into court; where there is an uncertainty either as to the quantity or quality of the thing demanded, or that there is any tort accompanying it that may enhance the damages above the real value of the thing, and there is no rule thereby to estimate the additional value, then it shall not be brought in." The case of Whitten v. Fuller [10] was a motion to defendant, in an action of trover for a bond, to have proceedings stayed on delivering up the bond and paying costs. But the plaintiff objecting, that he had sustained great loss by the detention of the bond till after the death of the obligor, and insisting on his right to go for special damages, the motion was denied.

This practice of staying proceedings, though known in England much later than the time of Lord Mansfield,[11] is little known in this country.[12]   In Stevens v. Low,[13] Cowen, J., said, however: "It is quite common for the courts to make a rule stopping the action on a redelivery and payment of costs." The reports of our decisions would not seem to warrant the remark; but the practice seems still to prevail in Vermont [14] and Wisconsin.[15]

In Maine, by statute, defendant may tender the goods and thus reduce damages when the trespass was involuntary and by mistake.[16]

§ 55. Reparation accepted.

Where, however, the injured party accepts reparation, it operates as a reduction of damages.   Thus where goods wrong-

[10] 2 W. Black. 902.

[11] Earle v. Holderness, 4 Bing. 462; Tucker v. Wright, 3 Bing. 601; Gibson v. Humphrey, 1 Cr. & M. 544.

[12] Shotwell v. Wendover, 1 Johns. (N. Y.) 65.

[13] 2 Hill (N. Y.), 132.

[14] Rutland & W. R. R. v. Bank of Middlebury, 32 Vt. 639; Bucklin v.

Beals, 38 Vt. 653 (semble). No order will be made where the goods had been greatly damaged by the defendant's negligence. Giffin v. Martel, 77 Vt. 19, 58 Atl. 788.

[15] Churchill v. Welsh, 47 Wis. 39, 1 N. W. 398.

[16] Brown v. Neal, 36 Me. 407.

fully taken from the owner are returned to him and accepted, damages are reduced by the value of the goods when accepted,[17] and the same is true where the goods are sold and the proceeds returned to the owner and accepted by him.[18]   It is enough if the property is returned to a co-owner of the plaintiff, who has a right to the goods.[19]   The return or reparation must, it has been held, be previous to bringing the action.[20]

The same rule applies in actions of contract.   Thus where

[17] Actions of trover:

United States: Bates *v.* Clark, 95 U. S. 204, 24 L. ed. 471.

Alabama: Renfro *v.* Hughes, 69 Ala. 581.

Colorado: Murphy *v.* Hobbs, 8 Colo. 17.

Connecticut: Cook *v.* Loomis, 26 Conn. 483; Lazarus *v.* Ely, 45 Conn. 504.

Illinois: Barrelett *v.* Bellgard, 71 Ill. 280.

Massachusetts: Long *v.* Lambkin, 9 Cush. 361; Lucas *v.* Trumbull, 15 Gray, 306; Delano *v.* Curtis, 7 All. 470; Perham *v.* Coney, 117 Mass. 102.

New Hampshire: Hackett *v.* B. C. & M. R. R., 35 N. H. 390; Gove *v.* Watson, 61 N. H. 136.

New Jersey: McFadden *v.* Whitney, 51 N. J. L. 391.

New York: Bowman *v.* Teall, 23 Wend. 306, 35 Am. Dec. 551; McCormick *v.* P. C. R. R., 80 N. Y. 353; Dyett *v.* Hyman, 129 N. Y. 351, 29 N. E. 261; Johnson *v.* Marks, 66 Misc. 153, 121 N. Y. Supp. 294; Dailey *v.* Crowley, 5 Lans. 301.

Vermont: Yale *v.* Saunders, 16 Vt. 243.

England: Willoughby *v.* Backhouse, 2 B. & C. 821; Bayliss *v.* Fisher, 7 Bing. 153; s. c. 4 M. & P. 790; Moon *v.* Raphael, 2 Bing. N. C. 310.

Actions of trespass:

Alabama: Grisham *v.* Bodway, 111 Ala. 194, 20 So. 514; Stephenson *v.* Wright, 111 Ala. 579, 20 So. 622.

Arkansas: Walker *v.* Fuller, 29 Ark. 448.

Massachusetts: Gibbs *v.* Chase, 10 Mass. 125; Kaley *v.* Shed, 10 Met. 317 (*semble*).

New York: Vosburgh *v.* Welch, 11 Johns. 175; Hanmer *v.* Wilsey, 17 Wend. 91; Hibbard *v.* Stewart, 1 Hilt. 207.

Oregon: Lowenberg *v.* Rosenthal, 18 Ore. 178, 22 Pac. 601.

Upper Canada: Loucks *v.* McSloy, 29 U. C. C. P. 54.

The goods must actually be accepted by the owner; merely turning cattle converted back on the owner's range is not enough. Keiffer *v.* Smith, 16 S. Dak. 433, 93 N. W. 645.

[18] Van Brunt *v.* Schenck, 13 Johns. (N. Y.) 414; Ferguson *v.* Buchell, 101 App. Div. 213, 91 N. Y. Supp. 724.

[19] Nightingale *v.* Scannell, 18 Cal. 315.

Where the vendor under a conditional contract for the sale of goods sold his interest, and the goods were taken by a third person and returned to the vendor, this did not reduce the amount of the vendee's recovery, since the vendor had ceased to have any interest in the goods. Wooley *v.* Edson, 35 Vt. 214.

[20] Rundle *v.* Little, 6 Q. B. 174, 13 L. J. Q. B. 311, 8 Jur. 668. This seems to have turned on a question of pleading. A mere offer to return, after suit brought, can of course not be made so as to reduce damages to a nominal amount and affect costs. Hanmer *v.* Wilsey, 17 Wend. (N. Y.) 91.

machinery sold by the defendant to the plaintiff was not delivered in good condition, evidence that the plaintiff allowed the defendant after delivery to remedy the defect is admissible to reduce damages.[21]

The measure of damages is the difference in the value of the goods at the time and place of taking and the time and place of return [22] plus the value of the use,[23] and in any case nominal damages at least may be recovered.[24]   But where part only is recovered, which is greatly enhanced in value, the enhancement cannot be used to reduce recovery of the value of the goods not returned.[25]

When the goods taken are inclosed in boxes, the mere opening of the boxes subsequently by the owner, to enable a witness to appraise the value of the goods, is not such a resumption of the property as will justify a mitigation of damages.[26]

§ 55a. Return to the general owner.

A return of the goods to the general owner and an acceptance by him may be shown in reduction of the damages recoverable by the owner of a special interest.[27]   So in an action by a lien-

[21] Marsh v. McPherson, 105 U. S. 709, 26 L. ed. 1139.

[22] *Dakota:* Clark v. Bates, 1 Dak. 42, 46 N. W. 510.

Missouri: Green v. Stephens, 37 Mo. App. 641.

[23] *Alabama:* Fields v. Williams, 91 Ala. 502, 8 So. 808.

Maryland: Warfield v. Walter, 11 G. & J. 80.

Michigan: Hart v. Blake, 31 Mich. 278.

South Carolina: Jones v. McNeil, 2 Bail. 466.

Texas: Hance v. Burke, 73 Tex. 62, 11 S. W. 135.

[24] The language of the oldest authority on this point is as follows: "*Si home prist mon cheval et ceo chevaucha et puis ceo rediliver al moy uncore jeo poio aver cest action vers luy; car ceo est un convercion, et le redelivery nest ascun barr del action mes solement serra un mitigacion de damages. Per Cur., in the Countess of Rutland's Case, 1 Roll. Abr. 15.*

Baldwin v. Cole, 6 Mod. 212; 5 Bac. Ab. Trover, D., § 39; Esp. N. P. 190, 191; Cook v. Hartle, 8 Car. & Payne, 568. So, in Murray v. Burling, 10 Johns. (N. Y.) 172, Thompson, J., said: "It is every day's practice to sustain this action for the injury suffered, although the owner has repossessed himself of his property." And the same point was held in Reynolds v. Shuler, 5 Cowen (N. Y.), 323.

The same has been held in Massachusetts. Wheelock v. Wheelright, 5 Mass. 104; Gibbs v. Chase, 10 Mass. 125; Greenfield Bank v. Leavitt, 17 Pick. (Mass.) 1. See also Austin v. Miller, 74 N. C. 274.

[25] Gaskins v. Davis, 115 N. C. 85, 20 S. E. 188.

[26] Connah v. Hale, 23 Wend. (N. Y.) 462.

[27] Champion v. Smith, 1 Brev. (S. C.) 243. *Contra*, King v. Orser, 4 Duer (N. Y.), 431.

holder the defendant may show that he returned the goods to the owner,[28] and if he has accepted payment of the amount of his lien, the lien-holder in such a case can recover only nominal damages.[29]   Upon a similar principle, a return to a receiver of the plaintiff's property may be shown.[30]

§ 56. Reparation preventing actual loss.

In some cases the reparation has absolutely prevented the happening of damage from the injury.   In such cases this is allowed to be shown, not, properly speaking, in reduction of damages, but in proof of the actual amount of damages.   Acceptance by the injured party need not be shown, for no right ever accrued to him to recover more than the original and actual loss.   In Dow v. Humbert [31] the defendants, supervisors of a town, being sued for refusing to put two judgments of the plaintiff on the tax list, were allowed to show in mitigation that they were subsequently placed on the list.   So where a lien is discharged and the discharge enures to the benefit of the plaintiff, the amount paid may be deducted.[32]   Where the grantor of land bought in an outstanding incumbrance, the grantee, not having been actually injured by the incumbrance, could recover only nominal damages.[33]   Such a case was Hartford and Salisbury Ore Co. v. Miller,[34] an action for breach of covenant of seisin contained in a deed purporting to convey certain mineral rights which the defendant in fact could not convey, not having the consent of his co-tenants.   They afterwards consented, so that the plaintiffs acquired the same rights which they would have had if there had been no breach; and it was held that the plaintiff could only recover nominal damages.

In an action for the diversion of a water course, the fact that part of the water diverted was returned to the stream above the plaintiff's land was to be considered in estimating the amount of damages.[35]

[28] Huning v. Chavez, 7 N. Mex. 128, 34 Pac. 44.

[29] Bisson v. Joyce, 66 N. H. 478, 30 Atl. 1120.

[30] Aylesbury Mercantile Co. v. Fitch, 22 Okla. 475, 99 Pac. 1089, 23 L. R. A. (N. S.) 573.

[31] 91 U. S. 294, 23 L. ed. 368.

[32] Stollenwerck v. Thacher, 115 Mass. 224.

[33] McInnis v. Lyman, 62 Wis. 191.

[34] Mannville Co. v. Worcester, 138 Mass. 89, 52 Am. Rep. 261.

[35] 41 Conn. 112.

§ 57. Reparation by a third party.

Reparation, not by the wrongdoer, but by a stranger, will reduce the damages if it was accepted by the injured party or was of a nature to prevent loss. So, where, by the defendant's procurement, the plaintiff's wife had left the plaintiff, taking a quantity of his personal property, but afterwards returned to the vicinity of his house, and delivered to him the baggage checks given by the railway for his goods, so that these came under his control, it was held that this delivery should go in reduction of his damages, and a verdict for the full value of the property was held wrong.[36]

Where goods were misdelivered by a carrier, the latter may show in reduction of damages that the owner has accepted compensation from the person to whom they were delivered.[37] Similarly, in a suit on an administrator's bond for failure to account for the proceeds of a sale of property, it may be shown in reduction of damages that payment has been made by the purchaser to the administrator *de bonis non*.[38] And so in an action by a sheriff on a bond indemnifying him from damage in levying execution, where he had been required to pay $1,600 in a suit by the owner for conversion, it was held that the sureties could show, in mitigation of damages, that he had received $1,000 on a sale of the goods, for his injury was the difference between those sums.[39]

Where an action is brought against one of two joint tortfeasors, it may be shown in reduction of damages that the other tortfeasor has made part compensation.[40]

§ 58. Recovery of property by the injured party.

If the owner has recovered property taken from him by the

[36] Dailey *v.* Crowley, 5 Lans. (N. Y.) 301.

[37] *United States:* Rosenfield *v.* Express Co., 1 Woods, 131.

Minnesota: Jellett *v.* St. P., M. & M. Ry., 30 Minn. 265.

[38] Probate Court *v.* Bates, 10 Vt. 285.

[39] O'Brien *v.* McCann, 58 N. Y. 373.

[40] *New York:* Knapp *v.* Roche, 94 N. Y. 329.

England: Burn *v.* Morris, 2 C. & M. 579.

But in a case where a sheriff wrongfully attached a mortgaged crop and paid over a balance to the mortgagor, who with it paid his rent, which had been a lien on the crop, it was held in an action by the mortgagee against the sheriff that damages could not be reduced by the amount so paid, be-

wrongdoer, that fact will reduce the damages; but the owner is allowed compensation for his expenditure in recovering the property.[41] Thus where the plaintiff's property was seized and sold by the defendant, a sheriff, and was repurchased by the plaintiff from the one who bought it at the sheriff's sale, it was held that the measure of damages was the amount paid to repurchase the property.[42] Where the defendant secured a loan from the plaintiff by fraud, and was sued for the fraud, it was held that the amount of a judgment previously obtained by the plaintiff in an action to recover the money loaned should be deducted from the compensation given for the fraud.[43] So in an action for breaking into the plaintiff's house and removing his furniture, the amount of a judgment for the value of the use of the furniture, recovered by the plaintiff in a replevin suit previously brought by him against the defendant, is to be recovered.[44] And so where a surplus received on a wrongful sale of the goods is turned over to the owner, the damages are

---

cause it was paid by the mortgagor and not by the defendant. Keith v. Ham, 89 Ala. 590, 7 So. 234.

[41] *Alabama:* Ewing v. Blount, 20 Ala. 694.

Connecticut: Baldwin v. Porter, 12 Conn. 473.

Maine: Merrill v. How, 24 Me. 126.

Missouri: Alexander v. Helber, 35 Mo. 334.

Nebraska: Watson v. Coburn, 35 Neb. 492, 63 N. W. 477.

New York: Ford v. Williams, 24 N. Y. 359; McDonald v. North, 47 Barb. (N. Y.) 530; Sprague v. McKinzie, 63 Barb. (N. Y.) 60; Vedder v. Van Buren, 14 Hun (N. Y.), 250; Hough v. Bowe, 51 N. Y. Super. Ct. 208.

Pennsylvania: Forsyth v. Palmer, 14 Pa. 96, 53 Am. Dec. 519; McInroy v. Dyer, 47 Pa. 118.

Texas: Hogan v. Kellum, 13 Tex. 396.

Vermont: Hurlburt v. Green, 41 Vt. 490; Chase v. Snow, 52 Vt. 525.

Wisconsin: Johannesson v. Borschen-

ius, 35 Wis. 131; Sprague v. Brown, 40 Wis. 612.

England: Tamvaco v. Simpson, 19 C. B. (N. S.) 453.

But it was held in Vermont, in an action of trover for a pair of oxen, which had been stolen from the plaintiff, and were found in the defendant's possession in New York, that the expenses incurred by the plaintiff in regaining possession of the cattle, by legal process in New York, could not be included in the damages recoverable for the conversion. Harris v. Eldred, 42 Vt. 39.

See also *post*, § 226c.

[42] *Kansas:* Dodson v. Cooper, 37 Kan. 346.

New Hampshire: Felton v. Fuller, 35 N. H. 226.

North Carolina: Winburne v. Bryan, 73 N. C. 47.

Pennsylvania: McInroy v. Dyer, 47 Pa. 118.

Texas: Brown v. Leath, 17 Tex. Civ. App. 262, 42 S. W. 655.

[43] Whittier v. Collins, 15 R. I. 90.

[44] Briggs v. Milburn, 40 Mich. 512.

reduced by the amount so returned.[45]   And the same thing
is true where the proceeds are turned over to his assignee in
insolvency.[46]

§ 59. Application of property to the benefit of the injured party.

The rules are the same where the defendant attempts to
show not that he has made specific reparation, but that he has
applied the proceeds of his wrong to the benefit of the injured
party.   The injured party has ordinarily the right to refuse
to accept such application, and in that case, if he does refuse,
there can be no reduction of damages.[47]   So the defendant cannot show, in reduction of damages, that he has applied the proceeds of the sale to the payment of a debt of the plaintiff.[48]   So
a defendant cannot show that he has paid the plaintiff's note
with the proceeds of the converted property.[49]   But where
the owner was liable to defendant for breach of contract to
build a dam, it was held that the use of the tools and supplies
taken in completing the contract could be shown to reduce the
damages for taking them.[50]

If the injured party consents to the application, it may be
shown in reduction of damages.[51]   Thus, in Torry v. Black,[52]
the defendant had unlawfully cut timber from the plaintiff's
land.   It was held that he might show, in mitigation of damages,
that he had, with the assent of the infant's guardian, applied
part of the proceeds to the payment of taxes upon and debts
against the infant's estate, but could not show payments made

[45] Ingram v. Hartz, 48 Pa. 380.
Not if it is turned over to the owner
and accepted by him as agent for another.   Locke v. Garrett, 16 Ala. 698.
[46] Chesapeake & O. Ry. v. Lavin,
136 Ky. 205, 124 S. W. 274.
[47] Torry v. Black, 58 N. Y. 185.
[48] *Alabama:* East v. Pace, 57 Ala. 521;
Bird v. Womack, 69 Ala. 390.
Arkansas: Parham v. McMurray, 32
Ark. 261.
New York: Price v. Keyes, 1 Hun,
177.
Pennsylvania: Dallam v. Fitler, 6

W. & S. 323; M'Michael v. Mason, 13
Pa. 214.
[49] Northrup v. McGill, 27 Mich. 234.
[50] Montgomery Co. v. William A. C.
Co., 126 Fed. 68.
[51] *Illinois:* Davenport v. Ledger, 80
Ill. 574.
Michigan: Bringard v. Stellwagen, 41
Mich. 54.
New Jersey: Hendrickson v. Dwyer,
70 N. J. Law, 223, 57 Atl. 420.
Ohio: Doolittle v. McCullough, 7 Oh.
St. 299.
[52] 58 N. Y. 185.

without such consent.   Grover, J., said: "A trespasser cannot
mitigate the damages by an offer to return the property to its
owner; but if the owner accept the property, or otherwise re-
gains possession of it, it may be proved for that purpose, as
in that case he is not deprived of his property.   The inquiry
is, what is the amount of damage sustained by the plaintiff
from the wrongful act of the defendant.   But to warrant this
evidence, the property must be received by the plaintiff or
applied to his use with his assent.   The law will not permit a
wrongdoer to take the property of another and apply the same
to his use without his assent, and if so applied, the damages
recoverable for the injury will not be thereby affected.   When
the owner voluntarily receives the proceeds of the property
wrongfully taken or directs or assents to their application to
his use, such facts may be shown in mitigation, the same as the
receipt or application of the identical property taken by the
trespasser."

§ 60. Application authorized by law—Seizure on execution, etc.

In certain cases the injured party cannot object to the application made of the property; in such cases the property is to
be considered as returned to him,[53] and damages will be reduced, not by the actual proceeds of the property, as would
be the case if the doctrine of recoupment were invoked, but by
the value of the property thus applied.   In other words, no
damages can be recovered, in the absence of special circumstances, for the original taking of property afterwards so applied.[54]

Thus where goods in the possession of a wrongdoer are
seized by a sheriff on a writ against the owner, sold, and the
proceeds applied to discharge the owner's debt, the damages
recoverable against the wrongdoer for conversion of the goods
will be reduced by the value of the goods.[55]   In some States

[53] Kaley v. Shed, 10 Met. (Mass.) 317.
[54] *New York:* Ward v. Benson, 31 How. Pr. 411.   Unless the property is sold for less than its value. Empire Mill Co. v. Lovell, 77 Ia. 100, 41 N. W. 583, 14 Am. St. Rep. 272.

[55] *Connecticut:* Lazarus v. Ely, 45 Conn. 504.
Illinois: Perkins v. Freeman, 26 Ill. 477; Bates v. Courtwright, 36 Ill. 518.
Massachusetts: Squire v. Hollenbeck, 9 Pick. (Mass.) 551, 20 Am. Dec. 506.

this may be done even when the process was in favor of the wrongdoer himself;[56] but the better view is that to enable the wrongdoer to obtain a reduction of damages the process must be in favor of a third person.[57] So in Edmondson v. Nuttall,[58] Willes, J., said: "Subsequently to the conversion the defendant acquired a right to the goods, but this is a right which he could not have exercised but for a wrongful act of his own in taking possession of the goods, and it would be against the plainest principles to allow a man to take advantage of his own wrong." And where the property seized is exempt from execution, an application of it to the payment of the debt cannot be shown in reduction of damages, since the effect of such a course would be to annul the exemption law.[59]

Minnesota: Howard v. Manderfield, 31 Minn. 337; Beyersdorf v. Sump, 39 Minn. 495, 41 N. W. 101, 12 Am. St. Rep. 678.

New Hampshire: Howard v. Cooper, 45 N. H. 339.

New York: Ball v. Liney, 48 N. Y. 6, 7 Am. Rep. 511; Wehle v. Spelman, 25 Hun, 99; Parker v. Connor, 44 N. Y. Super. Ct. 416.

Oregon: Morrison v. Crawford, 7 Ore. 472.

Texas: Mayer v. Duke, 72 Tex. 445.

Vermont: Stewart v. Martin, 16 Vt. 397; Montgomery v. Wilson, 48 Vt. 616.

Wisconsin: Cotton v. Reed, 2 Wis. 458.

Contra, upon assumed statutory grounds, Nash v. Noble, 46 Tex. Civ. App. 369, 102 S. W. 736.

[56] *United States:* McAfee v. Crawford, 13 How. 447, 14 L. ed. 217.

Connecticut: Curtis v. Ward, 20 Conn. 204; Lazarus v. Ely, 45 Conn. 504.

New Jersey: Hopple v. Higbee, 23 N. J. L. 342.

Oregon: Morrison v. Crawford, 7 Ore. 472.

Texas: Mayer v. Duke, 72 Tex. 445; Mississippi Mills v. Meyer, 83 Tex. 433, 18 S. W. 748.

[57] *Vermont:* Collins v. Perkins, 31 Vt. 624.

Massachusetts: Stickney v. Allen, 10 Gray, 352.

Minnesota: Beyersdorf v. Sump, 39 Minn. 495.

New York: Otis v. Jones, 21 Wend. 394; Higgins v. Whitney, 24 Wend. 379; Sherry v. Schuyler, 2 Hill, 204; Ball v. Liney, 48 N. Y. 6; Wehle v. Butler, 61 N. Y. 245; Tiffany v. Lord, 65 N. Y. 310; Wehle v. Spelman, 25 Hun, 99; Smith v. Healey, 64 Misc. 177, 121 N. Y. Supp. 230.

See Lobenstein v. Hymson, 90 Tenn. 606, 18 S. W. 250.

But where a sale of goods was made by a debtor in violation of the State insolvent laws, and the goods, while in the purchaser's hands, were attached by a creditor, who held them till the institution of proceedings in insolvency and choice of an assignee, and then delivered them to the assignee, these facts were allowed in mitigation, in an action of tort brought by the purchaser against the attaching creditor. Leggett v. Baker, 13 Allen (Mass.), 470.

[58] 34 L. J. (C. P.) 102, 104. In the regular reports this language is not found, but the substance of it is given. 17 C. B. (N. S.) 280.

[59] Hill v. Loomis, 6 N. H. 263.

§ 61. Informal sale after legal seizure.

Where there is an informal sale by one who has rightfully seized the plaintiff's property under authority of law, but by the informality becomes a trespasser *ab initio*, the case is different. There is no return of the goods in that case either to the owner or to his use; and the defendant is obliged to rely upon the principle that he is legally discharging the plaintiff's debt. The damages are reduced, therefore, not by the value of the goods seized, but by the amount of the debt paid. So in the case of an illegal distress without the statutory appraisement required, it was intimated that the measure of damages would be the difference between the fair value of the goods and the amount of rent discharged by the proceeds of the sale.[60] So where goods were seized by a tax-collector, for non-payment of taxes, but a subsequent irregularity rendered all the proceedings void, the collector was held liable for the value of the goods less the amount applied to the payment of the tax.[61]

Where a sheriff rightfully seized property on execution, but wrongfully sold it without due notice, it was held that though he became a trespasser *ab initio*, yet he might show his authority in reduction of damages; and that damages would be reduced to the increase of price that would have been obtained if due notice of the sale had been given.[62] And where a sheriff lawfully attaches goods, but becomes a trespasser *ab initio* by a subsequent misuse of the property; he may show in reduction of damages a levy on execution upon the property to satisfy a judgment obtained in the suit in which the attachment had been made.[63]

So in the case of an executor *de son tort*, who is liable for the value of goods appropriated by him, it was long ago held by Lord Holt, that although "he cannot plead payment of debts,

[60] *Pennsylvania:* Mickle *v.* Miles, 1 Grant, 320.

England: Wilson *v.* Nightingale, 8 Q. B. 1034 (*semble*); Biggins *v.* Goode, 2 Cr. & J. 364; Proudlove *v.* Twemlow, 1 Cr. & M. 326; Knight *v.* Egerton, 7 Ex. 407.

[61] *Maine:* Cressey *v.* Parks, 76 Me. 532.

Massachusetts: Pierce *v.* Benjamin, 14 Pick. 356, 25 Am. Dec. 396.

[62] *Alabama:* Wright *v.* Spencer, 1 Stew. 576.

Pennsylvania: Carrier *v.* Esbaugh, 70 Pa. 239.

[63] Lamb *v.* Day, 8 Vt. 407, 30 Am. Dec. 479.

etc., to the value, etc., or that he hath given the goods, etc., in satisfaction of the debts, . . . nevertheless, upon the general issue pleaded, such payments shall be recouped in damages." [64] But where an officer, by selling the attached property unlawfully, had become a trespasser *ab initio*, and it did not appear that judgment had been, or would be, rendered in the original suit, and the proceeds of the sale of the attached property applied on the execution, the defendant was held not entitled to a reduction of damages.[65]

§ 62. Reparation which would prevent further loss.

If the reparation offered would prevent further loss, the injured party is bound to accept it. This is, however, not a reduction of damages for a loss already inflicted, but rather a prevention of future loss, and it will be discussed later as part of the subject of Avoidable Consequences.

§ 63. Benefit conferred on the injured party by the wrongful act.

If the wrongful act of the defendant at once confers a benefit and inflicts an injury, the loss actually caused will be the net result of the act to the plaintiff; and this net result will be the measure of damages. Thus, where the defendant placed earth on the plaintiff's land, the damages will be measured by the actual damage caused to the land from having the earth there. In Mayo *v.* Springfield,[66] Field, J., said: "In determining the extent of the injury to the plaintiff's land, the court had a right to consider the benefits, if any, arising from placing the earth upon the land. An allowance for such benefits is not in the nature of recoupment or set-off, but a method of determining the actual damages sustained." So where the tres-

---

[64] *Alabama:* Carpenter *v.* Going, 20 Ala. 587.

Pennsylvania: Saam *v.* Saam, 4 Watts, 432.

South Carolina: Cook *v.* Sanders, 15 Rich. 63.

England: Whitehall *v.* Squire, Carthew, 103; Mountford *v.* Gibson, 4 East 441, 447.

[65] Ross *v.* Philbrick, 39 Me. 29.

[66] 138 Mass. 70; *acc., Minnesota:* Schroeder *v.* De Graff, 28 Minn. 299.

Wisconsin: Murphy *v.* Fond du Lac, 23 Wis. 365, 99 Am. Dec. 181.

Contra, Hurley *v.* Jones, 105 Pa. 34, 30 Atl. 499.

See *post,* § 107d.

passer dug drains, he was allowed to prove in reduction of damages that the drains benefited the land.[67]

In an action against a railroad for a nuisance caused by running its tracks near the plaintiff's land, and thereby incommoding his business, the defendant was allowed to reduce damages by showing that the plaintiff could carry on his business to greater advantage in certain respects on account of the railroad; [68] but not that his tenants thereby derived a benefit which plaintiff was not shown to share.[69]   Similarly, where a highway was obstructed by the building of a railroad station, the measure of damages is the net diminution in value of the land on the highway, considering the advantage of the station as well as the disadvantage of the obstruction.[70]

§ 64. In an action for flooding lands.

There is some conflict of authority on the question whether in an action for flooding lands the defendant can be allowed for benefit, if any, caused by the flowing.   All allowance for benefit was denied in Gerrish v. The New Market Mfg. Co.[71]   But in Massachusetts, in an action for damages occasioned by the filling up by the defendants of their land lying adjacent to that of the plaintiff, whereby the free flow of water off the plaintiff's land as formerly existing had been obstructed, it was held that instructions to the jury, that "they should take into consideration the evidence on both sides bearing on this point, and if they were satisfied that the filling up had actually benefited the plaintiff's estate in any particular, they would, in assessing the

---

[67] Burtraw v. Clark, 103 Mich. 383, 61 N. W. 552.

[68] Jeffersonville, M. & I. R. R. v. Esterle, 13 Bush (Ky.), 667.

[69] Leigh v. Garysburg Mfg. Co., 132 N. C. 167, 43 S. E. 632.

In Loomis v. Green, 7 Me. 386, an action for cutting and carrying off timber (not for injury to the land), it was held that damages could not be reduced by showing that the trespass opened up the forest and thus increased the value of the land.   In Baillio v. Burney, 3 Rob. (La.) 317, the defend-

ant was not allowed to reduce damages by showing that the trespass had resulted in clearing the land where there was no evidence to show that the land would not be equally valuable with the timber on it.

[70] Meighan v. Birmingham Terminal Co., 165 Ala. 591, 51 So. 775.

[71] 30 N. H. 478.

And see to the same effect:

Georgia: Farkas v. Towns, 103 Ga. 150, 29 S. E. 700.

New Hampshire: Tillotson v. Smith, 32 N. H. 90, 64 Am. Dec. 355.

damages, make an allowance for such benefit, and give the plaintiff such sum in damages as they found upon the evidence would fully indemnify and compensate him for all the damages he had actually sustained," were correct.[72] So where the defendant at first erected a dam which benefited the plaintiff's property, and the subsequent heightening of the dam caused the injury, it was said that the benefits should be deducted, and therefore, that the value of the plaintiff's property before any dam had been erected would be the standard, and not the value before the heightening.[73] The Massachusetts rule seems to be somewhat restricted by late decisions. The allowance must be confined to benefits resulting from the overflow itself, and does not include those incidentally received from the defendant's operations in other respects. So the benefit to the complainant's land by being drained by a ditch made by the respondent on his own land to draw water from a pond to the projected dam, cannot be offset against the damage caused by the overflow of the dam after its erection.[74] So where a riparian proprietor, by obstructing a river and thereby setting back the water, becomes liable to a mill owner for the injury sustained, he cannot, in an action by the injured party, offset the benefit to the plaintiff's lands by the removal of obstructions in the river at another time and place.[75] Benefit from the neighborhood of a mill cannot be considered in an action for flooding land.[76] Where in consequence of the wrongful construction of a railway embankment the plaintiff's lands were flooded, but would have been flooded in a lesser degree had the embankment not been constructed, the measure of damages was held to be the difference between the two amounts of damage.[77]

[72] *Massachusetts:* Luther *v.* Winnisimmet Co., 9 Cush. 171

See to the same effect:

Georgia: Imboden *v.* Etowah & B. B. Co., 70 Ga. 86, 116.

Washington: Koch *v.* Sackmann-Phillips Inv. Co., 9 Wash. 405, 37 Pac. 703.

Wisconsin: Brower *v.* Merrill, 3 Chand. 46.

[73] Howe *v.* Ray, 113 Mass. 88.

[74] Gile *v.* Stevens, 13 Gray (Mass.), 146.

[75] Talbot *v.* Whipple, 7 Gray (Mass.), 122.

[76] Marcy *v.* Fries, 18 Kan. 353.

[77] *Arkansas:* St. Louis, I. M. & S. Ry. *v.* Morris, 35 Ark. 622.

Nebraska: Stewart *v.* Schneider, 22 Neb. 286.

England: Workman *v.* Great N. Ry., 32 L. J. Q. B. 279.

§ 65. On the injured party in common with others.

But even where the value of a benefit would be deducted, it has been held that the value of one which accrues to many others with the plaintiff, cannot. Kellogg *v.* Malin [78] was an action on a covenant against incumbrances, the incumbrance being a right of way in a railroad corporation over part of the land. It was held that the defendant could not show that the railroad raised the value of all land thereabouts, including the plaintiff's, for that was a common benefit. [79]

So in an action for maintaining a nuisance, the nuisance being a factory, the defendant was not allowed to show, in reduction of damages, that the rental value of the plaintiff's premises was increased by the increase of population, that increase consisting of employees of the defendant. [80] This qualification applies generally to benefits which, by statute, are allowed to be set off. The allowance of benefits in condemnation proceedings is governed by special rules hereafter to be considered.

§ 66. Not caused directly by the wrongful act itself.

If the benefit is not caused by the wrongful act itself, the defendant cannot claim a reduction of damages on account of it. [81] So the benefit to the plaintiff's land by being drained by a ditch dug by the defendant to draw water from a certain pond to his dam will not reduce the damages recoverable by the plaintiff for injury caused by the overflow of the dam; [82] and

[78] 62 Mo. 429.

[79] *Acc., Georgia:* Gilbert *v.* S. G. & N. A. Ry., 69 Ga. 396.

Indiana: Martinsville *v.* Shirley, 84 Ind. 546.

Iowa: Koestenbader *v.* Peirce, 41 Ia. 204.

Kansas: Marcy *v.* Fries, 18 Kan. 353.

Kentucky: Jeffersonville, M. & I. R. R. *v.* Esterle, 13 Bush, 667.

Michigan: Fisher *v.* Naysmith, 106 Mich. 71, 64 N. W. 19.

[80] Francis *v.* Schoellkopf, 53 N. Y. 152. *Acc.,* Harvey *v.* Georgia, S. & F. R. R., 90 Ga. 66, 15 S. E. 783.

And where a railroad had been illegally built in front of plaintiff's premises, diminishing the rental value, it was not permitted to set off any increase in the market value. Davis *v.* East Tennessee, V. & G. Ry., 87 Ga. 605, 13 S. E. 567.

[81] Burcky *v.* Lake, 30 Ill. App. 23.

So in an action against a city for negligent grading and construction of a drain, the city cannot set off the increased value of the land by reason of the improvement. Mayor of Brunswick *v.* Tucker, 103 Ga. 233, 29 S. E. 701.

[82] Gile *v.* Stevens, 13 Gray (Mass.), 146.

where land was overflowed because of the construction of a street, damages for the overflow will not be reduced because the value of the land was increased by reason of the greater accessibility caused by the street.[83] Nor can the defendant in an action for obstructing a water course show that he removed obstructions at another time and place.[84] Nor can the defendant in an action for injuring the plaintiff's land take advantage of a benefit conferred on other land of the plaintiff.[85] A defendant in an action for the seduction of the plaintiff's daughter cannot prove in reduction of damages presents or money given by him to the daughter,[86] or the amount of a judgment recovered against him by the daughter for the same act.[87]

Nor can benefits only indirectly caused by the wrongful act be shown to reduce damages. In an English case, by the defendant's delay in discharging a vessel the plaintiffs lost profits in the loss of the passage-money of emigrants who were booked to sail in her. Some of the plaintiffs were part owners of another vessel which derived a benefit by receiving these emigrants; but it was held that the plaintiffs' damages could not be reduced at all by these profits.[88]

In an action for failure to accept a certain number of bricks manufactured by the plaintiff, the defendant cannot show that the plaintiff, at the time fixed for delivery, sold bricks at a higher price than the defendant was to pay; for as many bricks might have been sold at the higher price, even if the defendant had received the bricks he contracted for.[89] So where, through the master's wrongful act, the delivery of a cargo of sugar was

[83] Ewing v. Louisville,   Ky.   , 131 S. W. 1016.

[84] Talbot v. Whipple, 7 Gray (Mass.), 122.

[85] Gerrish v. New Market Manuf. Co., 30 N. H. 478. So where without a legal taking a town built a highway across plaintiff's land, the measure of damages was the value of the land taken, without deducting the increase in value to the remaining land by reason of the increased accessibility. Pinney v. Winchester, 83 Conn.   , 76 Atl. 994.

And see Mayo v. Springfield, 138 Mass. 70.

[86] Russell v. Chambers, 31 Minn. 54.

[87] Pruitt v. Cox, 21 Ind. 15; Sellars v. Kinder, 1 Head (Tenn.), 134.

[88] Jebsen v. E. & W. Ind. Dock Co., L. R. 10 C. P. 300; acc., Coffin v. The Osceola, 34 Fed. 921. Contra, Leathers v. Sweeney, 41 La. Ann. 287. The English case was decided on the analogy of the cases discussed in the next section.

[89] Canda v. Wick, 49 N. Y. Super. Ct. 497.

delayed and part of the sugar lost by leakage, it was held that the master could not reduce the damages recovered for the sugar that was lost by showing that during the delay the market price of sugar had increased.[90]

The defendant, in examining the title to land for the plaintiff, negligently failed to find an incumbrance. The plaintiff took a mortgage on the land, and in order to protect his mortgage was obliged to buy the land at a sale made to satisfy the prior incumbrance. The value of the land advanced so much that the plaintiff, before bringing this action, had sold it for more than he had paid out in all; but it was held that this fact could not be shown in reduction of damages.[91] So where the plaintiff, a lessee of the defendant, was obliged, in order to protect his possession, to take out a new lease from the holder of the paramount title, it was held in an action on the covenant for quiet enjoyment that the defendant could not show, in reduction of damages, that the plaintiff had sold his new lease at a profit.[92]

Defendant, who was excavating in land adjoining plaintiff's building, employed a contractor to shore up plaintiff's wall (as he was not legally bound to do), and thereby saved plaintiff from considerable damage to his building; but in shoring up the wall the contractor entered the plaintiff's premises without permission and put beams through the wall, whereby plaintiff's property was injured. It was held that plaintiff was entitled to recover the amount of the injury, without deducting the amount plaintiff had been saved by shoring up his wall.[93]

§ 67. Benefit received from third parties on account of the injury.

Damages cannot be reduced by an amount which the plaintiff may have received from third parties, acting independently of the defendant, though it is given to the plaintiff on account of the injury. For it is given either as a pure gift, not intended by the giver to be in lieu of damages, or else it is given in per-

---

[90] Elwell v. Skiddy, 77 N. Y. 282; acc., Morrison v. Florio S. S. Co., 36 Fed. 569.

[91] Harrison v. Brega, 20 Up. Can. Q. B. 324.

[92] Fitzgibbons v. Freisem, 12 Daly, (N. Y.) 419.

[93] Ketcham v. Cohn, 2 N. Y. Misc. 427, 22 N. Y. Supp. 181.

formance of a contract, the consideration of which was furnished by the plaintiff. In neither case has the defendant any equitable or legal claim to share in the benefit.

So no reduction of damages is made because of any charitable aid the plaintiff has received on account of the injury.[94] Nor is he precluded from recovering the value of the time he has lost by reason of the injury, though his employer has in fact continued his salary.[95] In a few jurisdictions it is held that in such a case there can be no recovery, on the ground that if he recovers it is for the loss of wages, which were not in fact lost.[96] But it seems clear that the recovery is for loss of time, and the injury did in fact occasion this loss; and the amount of wages or salary which had been paid is evidence only of the value of the time. If the salary or wages are continued, it is not in payment for services, but as a gratuity, by which the defendant has no right to profit.

A similar difference of opinion has developed with regard to charging the defendant with the value of physicians' or nurses' services which have in fact cost the plaintiff nothing. By the better view the defendant is liable for the reasonable value of the services.[97] In a few jurisdictions, however, the

[94] *Pennsylvania:* Norristown v. Moyer, 67 Pa. 355.

New Zealand: Greymouth, P. E. R. & C. Co. v. McIvor, 16 N. Z. L. R. 258.

[95] *Georgia:* Nashville, C. & S. L. Ry. v. Miller, 120 Ga. 453, 47 S. E. 959, 67 L. R. A. 87.

Indiana: Ohio & M. Ry. v. Dickerson, 59 Ind. 317.

Kentucky: Louisville & N. R. R. v. Carothers, 23 Ky. L. R. 1673, 65 S. W. 833.

Massachusetts: Elmer v. Fessenden, 154 Mass. 427, 28 N. E. 299.

[96] *Alabama:* Montgomery & E. Ry. v. Mallette, 92 Ala. 209, 9 So. 363.

Missouri: Elphland v. Missouri Pac. Ry., 57 Mo. App. 147.

New York: Drinkwater v. Dinsmore, 80 N. Y. 390, 36 Am. Rep. 624, reversing s. c., 16 Hun, 250.

In Pennsylvania it is held that where the plaintiff is employed on a regular salary which continues necessarily during the disability, there can be no recovery. Quigley v. Pennsylvania R. R., 210 Pa. 162, 59 Atl. 958.

But where the salary or wages are continued merely as a gift from the employer, the wrongdoer has no right to any advantage from this gift, and full recovery may be had. Stahler v. Philadelphia & R. Ry., 199 Pa. 383, 49 Atl. 273; Bundle v. State Belt Elec. Ry., 33 Pa. Super. Ct. 233.

[97] *United States:* Denver & R. G. R. R. v. Lorentzen, 79 Fed. 291, 24 C. C. A. 592, 49 U. S. App. 81.

Indiana: Pennsylvania R. R. v. Marion, 104 Ind. 239; Brosnan v. Sweetser, 127 Ind. 1, 26 N. E. 555; Indianapolis & E. Ry. v. Bennett, 39 Ind. App. 141, 79 N. E. 389.

Iowa: Varnham v. Council Bluffs, 52

plaintiff is not allowed to recover the value of the services, since he has not been obliged to pay out the money for them.[98] But evidently the services were either rendered by members of the plaintiff's household to whose services he had a right, in which case he lost the value of the services and was actually at the expense, though not in money actually paid out, or they were given to him as a pure gratuity, in which case again the defendant has no right to benefit by the charity extended to him.

Other cases depend upon the same general principle. So in an action for breach of a covenant of warranty under a mortgage, it was held that the plaintiff, having paid the mortgage before judgment, might recover the whole amount of it, although he had previously conveyed the estate to one who assumed, as a part of the consideration of that conveyance, to pay part of the mortgage.[99] So when a rebate of duties on damaged goods is allowed, this does not go to reduce the amount of any recovery in a suit against the vessel for the diminution in market value.[100] And so where the defendant, whose shop had been burned by the defendant's negligence, circulated a paper and obtained by subscription a large amount of money to help him rebuild, this was not allowed to reduce the damages.[101]

Iowa, 698, 3 N. W. 792; Scurlock v. Boone, 142 Ia. 580, 121 N. W. 369.

Kansas: Lewark v. Parkison, 73 Kan. 553, 85 Pac. 601, 5 L. R. A. (N. S.) 1069.

Massachusetts: Sibley v. Nason, 196 Mass. 125, 81 N. E. 887 (obligation discharged in bankruptcy).

Ohio: Klein v. Thompson, 19 Oh. St. 569; Ohligher v. Toledo, 20 Oh. Cir. Ct. 142.

Texas: Missouri, K. & T. Ry. v. Holman, 15 Tex. Civ. App. 16, 39 S. W. 131; Fort Worth & D. C. Ry. v. Walker, 48 Tex. Civ. App. 86, 106 S. W. 400; Houston & T. C. R. R. v. Girald, 128 S. W. 166,   Tex. Civ. App.   .

Wisconsin: Crouse v. Chicago & N. W. Ry., 102 Wis. 196, 78 N. W. 446, 778.

[98] *Alabama:* Southern Ry. v. Crowder, 135 Ala. 417, 33 So. 335.

Illinois: Chicago, B. & Q. R. R. v. Johnson, 24 Ill. App. 468 (*semble*).

Missouri: Morris v. Grand Ave. Ry., 144 Mo. 500, 46 S. W. 170; Gibney v. St. Louis Tr. Co., 103 S. W. 43, 204 Mo. 704.

Pennsylvania: Goodhart v. Pennsylvania R. R., 177 Pa. 1, 35 Atl. 191, 55 Am. St. Rep. 705.

[99] Estabrook v. Smith, 6 Gray, 572, 66 Am. Dec. 445.

[100] The Eroe, 17 Blatchf. 16; The Umbria, 11 U. S. App. 612, 59 Fed. 489, 8 C. C. A. 194.

[101] Citizens' G. & O. M. Co. v. Whipple, 32 Ind. App. 203, 69 N. E. 557.

§ 67a. Amount received on insurance policy.

The amount received by the plaintiff on an insurance policy cannot be shown to reduce the damages,[102] either in case of a burning of the plaintiff's property[103] or an injury to his vessel,[104] or a personal injury to the plaintiff himself.[105]   In Perrott v. Shearer,[106] Cooley, C. J., said of the defendant in

[102] *United States:* Propeller Monticello v. Mollison, 17 How. 152, 15. L. ed. 68; Cannon v. The Potomac, 3 Woods, 158.

Connecticut: Regan v. New York & N. E. R. R., 60 Conn. 124, 22 Atl. 503.

Indiana: Cunningham v. E. & T. H. R. R., 102 Ind. 478.

Massachusetts: Hayward v. Cain, 105 Mass. 213.

New Jersey: Weber v. M. & E. R. R., 35 N. J. L. 409.

New York: Kingsbury v. Westfall, 61 N. Y. 356; Carpenter v. Eastern Transp. Co., 71 N. Y. 574; Briggs v. N. Y. C. & H. R. R. R., 72 N. Y. 26.

North Carolina: Hammond v. Schiff, 100 N. C. 161.

Texas: Texas & P. Ry. v. Levi, 59 Tex. 674.

Vermont: Harding v. Townshend, 43 Vt. 536, 5 Am. Rep. 304.

England: Yates v. Whyte, 4 Bing. N. C. 272.

Canada: Brown v. McRae, 17 Ont. 712.

[103] *Alabama:* Long v. Kansas City, M. & B. R. R.,   Ala.   , 54 So. 62.

Georgia: City of Rome v. Rhodes, 134 Ga. 650, 68 S. E. 330.

Illinois: Wabash, C. & W. Ry. v. Oetting, 147 Ill. App. 179.

Indiana: Lake Erie & W. R. R. v. Griffin, 8 Ind. App. 47, 35 N. E. 396, 52 Am. St. Rep. 465.

Iowa: Allen v. Barrett, 100 Iowa, 16, 69 N. W. 272.

Missouri: Dillon v. Hunt, 105 Mo. 154, 16 S. W. 516, 24 Am. St. Rep. 374; Foster v. Missouri Pac. Ry., 128 S. W. 36,   Mo. App.   .

New York: Collins v. New York C. & H. R. R. R., 5 Hun 503.

Pennsylvania: Lindsay v. Bridgewater Gas Co., 14 Pa. Co. Ct. 181.

Vermont: Cushman & Rankin Co. v. B. & M. R. R., 82 Vt. 390, 73 Atl. 1073. The case is of course different when the plaintiff sues on a contract of indemnity against loss by fire. So where a water company contracted to protect plaintiff against loss by fire; the amount he had recovered on an insurance company was deducted from the total loss in an action against the water company. Georgetown Water, Gas, Electric & Power Co. v. Neale, 125 S. W. 293,   Ky.   .

[104] *United States:* The Yeager, 20 Fed. 653, 4 Woods, 18.

California: White v. The Mary Ann, 6 Cal. 462, 65 Am. Dec. 523.

[105] Accident insurance:

Illinois: Pittsburg, C. & S. L. Ry. v. Thompson, 56 Ill. 138.

Kentucky: Louisville & N. R. R. v. Carothers, 23 Ky. L. R. 1673, 65 S. W. 833.

New Jersey: Cornish v. New Jersey S. Ry., 73 N. J. Law, 273, 62 Atl. 1004.

New York: Chernick v. Independent American Ice Cream Co., 121 N. Y. Supp. 352, 66 Misc. 177.

Tennessee: Prewitt-Spurr Mfg. Co. v. Woodall, 115 Tenn. 605, 90 S. W. 623.

Texas: Missouri, K. & T. Ry. v. Rains (Tex. Civ. App.), 40 S. W. 635; Missouri, K. & T. Ry. v. Flood, 35 Tex. Civ. App. 197, 79 S. W. 1106.

Relief fund:

Maryland: Baltimore City Pass. Ry. v. Baer, 90 Md. 97, 44 Atl. 992.

Canada: Farmer v. Grand Trunk Ry., 21 Ont. 299.

[106] 17 Mich. 48, 56.

such a case: "His equitable claim to a reduction of damages, if he could have any, would spring from the fact that the plaintiff recovers pay for his property twice; but the answer to this is, that he recovers but once for the wrong done him, and he receives the insurance money upon a contract to which the defendant is in no way privy, and in respect to which his own wrongful act can give him no equities."

In Bradburn v. Great Western R. Co.[107] it was held, in an action for injuries suffered by the defendant's negligence, that a sum received by the plaintiff on an accident insurance policy could not be taken into account in reduction of damages, the court saying: "The plaintiff is entitled to recover the damages caused to him by the negligence of the defendants, and there is no reason or justice in setting off what the plaintiff has entitled himself to under a contract with a third party."

Where an action is brought (under a statute) for damages causing death, the rule in England is different. There it is held that since the ground of the plaintiff's recovery is loss of support, it may be shown that the wrongful act has given to the plaintiff a certain amount of money from an insurance company to apply to his support.[108] In the United States, however, the ordinary rule is followed, and the amount recovered is not reduced by the amount of insurance money.[109] In Canada the

---

[107] L. R. 10 Ex. 1.

[108] *England:* Blake v. M. Ry., 18 Q. B. 93; Hicks v. N. A. & H. R. R., 4 B. & S. 403, *n.* In New Zealand the court, accepting this doctrine, held that it did not apply to a fund raised by subscription by sympathetic friends for the benefit of the family of the deceased.

New Zealand: Greymouth P. E. R. & C. Co. v. McIvor, 16 N. Z. L. R. 258.

[109] *United States:* Clune v. Ristine, 94 Fed. 745, 36 C. C. A. 450.

Georgia: Western & A. R. R. v. Meigs, 74 Ga. 857.

Illinois: Illinois Cent. R. R. v. Prickett, 210 Ill. 140, 71 N. E. 435, 109 Ill. App. 468.

Indiana: Sherlock v. Alling, 44 Ind. 184, 199.

Missouri: Carroll v. Missouri Pac. Ry., 88 Mo. 239, 57 Am. Rep. 382.

New York: Kellogg v. Ry., 79 N. Y. 72; Althorf v. Wolfe, 22 N. Y. 355; Terry v. Jewett, 17 Hun 395.

Pennsylvania: North Pennsylvania R. R. v. Kirk, 90 Pa. 15; Coulter v. Pine Twp., 164 Pa. 543, 30 Atl. 490.

Texas: Tyler S. E. Ry. v. Rasberry, 13 Tex. Civ. App. 185, 34 S. W. 794 (accident policy); Houston & T. C. R. R. v. Weaver (Tex. Civ. App.), 41 S. W. 846; Houston & T. C. R. R. v. Lemair, 55 Tex. Civ. App. 237, 119 S. W. 1162.

Vermont: Harding v. Townshend, 43 Vt. 536, 5 Am. Rep. 305.

Virginia: Baltimore & O. R. R. v. Wightman, 29 Grat. 431, 26 Am. Rep. 384.

English rule was at first followed,[110] but the contrary rule has been laid down by the Privy Council in a Canadian appeal,[111] and followed in Canada.[112]

Nor will recovery be reduced by the amount of a pension received by his widow, Geary v. Metropolitan St. Ry., 73 App. Div. 441, 77 N. Y. Supp. 54; or by benefit received from relief department of defendant railroad, to which deceased had become entitled by premiums paid by him during his lifetime.

Boulden v. Pennsylvania R. R., 205 Pa. 264, 54 Atl. 906.

[110] Beckett v. Grand T. Ry., 13 Ont. App. 174.

[111] Grand T. Ry. v. Jennings, 13 App. Cas. 800.

[112] Grand T. Ry. v. Beckett, 16 Can. 713.

CHAPTER IV

§ 68. Damages as affected by limited ownership.

Property may be injured in which two or more persons have an interest, and the amount of compensation recoverable by one of the owners will not usually be the whole amount which the wrongdoer should pay. In no case should the fact that there are two owners put upon the wrongdoer the liability of paying increased damages; and if (as will sometimes be the case) one party in interest recovers compensation for the entire injury, this is a bar to an action, or at least to the recovery of more than nominal damages by anyone else. But where one owner recovers less than the amount of the injury, the exact measure of his recovery is often a matter difficult to settle.

§ 69. Damages recoverable by owner of limited interest in land.

Any one having an interest in land is liable to suffer injury with respect to this right; and accordingly, if his right, however

109

limited it be, is injured, he may recover compensation equal to his individual loss. The general rule may be said to be that the extent of the injury to the plaintiff's proprietary right, whatever it may be, furnishes the measure of damages. The owner of a freehold may recover for an injury which permanently depreciates his property, while a tenant, or one having only a possessory right, may recover for an injury to the use and enjoyment of that right.[1] If there is a reversionary interest, and the defendant is answerable over in part to the reversioner, the defendant must show that fact.[2] Where the plaintiff's only right is to take stone or ore from the land of another, it would seem that he could not recover from a trespasser the value of the ore or stone taken from the land.[3] But where the amount that could be taken from the land in one year was limited, the plaintiff may recover the full value of what was taken by the trespasser.[4]

It is a general principle that a wrongdoer cannot set up a title outstanding in a third party to protect himself. If therefore the occupant of land claims title, this claim cannot be disputed by a trespasser, who must therefore pay to the occupant the entire damages where no one has disputed his claim or interfered with his possession.[5]

---

[1] *Georgia:* Brown v. Woodliff, 89 Ga. 413, 15 S. E. 491.

Indiana: Sunnyside, C. & C. Co. v. Reitz, 14 Ind. App. 478, 43 N. E. 46.

Michigan: Gilbert v. Kennedy, 22 Mich. 5.

New York: Gourdier v. Cormack, 2 E. D. Smith, 200.

North Carolina: Gwaltney v. S. C. T. Co., 115 N. C. 579, 20 S. E. 465.

Ohio: Johnson v. Meyer, 2 Cleve. L. Rep. 81, 4 Oh. Dec. 383.

South Carolina: Jefcoat v. Knotts, 13 Rich. L. 50.

Texas: Texas & P. Ry. v. Torrey, 4 Tex. Civ. App. 445, 16 S. W. 547; Texas & P. Ry. v. Saunders, 4 Tex. Civ. App. 528, 18 S. W. 793.

West Virginia: Jordan v. Benwood, 42 W. Va. 312, 26 S. E. 266.

[2] Todd v. Jackson, 26 N. J. L. 525.

[3] O'Connor v. Shannon (Tex. Civ. App.), 30 S. W. 1096. But see *contra* Ganter v. Atkinson, 35 Wis. 48.

[4] Attersoll v. Stevens, 1 Taunt. 183, 9 R. R. 731.

[5] *Illinois:* Illinois & S. L. R. R. & C. Co. v. Cobb, 94 Ill. 55.

Kansas: Nelson v. Mather, 5 Kan. 151.

Kentucky: North v. Cates, 2 Bibb, 591; Owings v. Gibson, 2 A. K. Marsh. 515; Hall v. Deaton, 24 Ky. L. Rep. 314, 68 S. W. 672.

Missouri: Reed v. Price, 30 Mo. 442.

New Hampshire: Woods v. Banks, 14 N. H. 101 (see Poor v. Gibson, 32 N. H. 415).

New Jersey: Todd v. Jackson, 24 N. J. Law (2 Dutch.), 525.

New York: Dewey v. Osborn, 4 Cow. 329.

§ 70. By an occupant of land.

The mere occupant of premises is entitled to damages to an amount sufficient to indemnify him for the interest he had in the premises.[6] Thus a *cestui que trust* in possession may recover the damages actually caused to him—that is, such loss as he suffered through loss of the bare possession—which, in the absence of special damages, would be nominal merely.[7] But one in possession of land under a contract for the purchase of it is entitled to full damages,[8] since the risk of loss or deterioration is upon him.

On the general principle a husband in possession of his wife's land, or a wife of her husband's, cannot recover damages for injury to the freehold;[9] a vendor in possession is in the same position;[10] one who has a mere right to use the land temporarily can recover no more than the value of such use;[11] a tenant on sufferance can recover nominal damages only,[12] and in gen-

---

Texas: Beaumont Lumber Co. *v.* Ballard (Tex. Civ. App.), 23 S. W. 920; Paraffine Oil Co. *v.* Berry (Tex. Civ. App.), 93 S. W. 1089.

Canada: Caverhill *v.* Robillard, 2 Can. S. C. 575.

England: Glenwood *v.* Phillipps, [1904] A. C. 405, 73 L. J. P. C. 62, 90 L. T. 744, 20 T. L. R. 531.

And this although the possession was forbidden by statute, as where the land was public land not yet thrown open to entry. Oklahoma *v.* Hill, 4 Okla. 521, 50 Pac. 242.

[6] *New York:* Brown *v.* Bowen, 30 N. Y. 519, 86 Am. Dec. 406.

North Carolina: Frisbee *v.* Marshall, 122 N. C. 760, 30 S. E. 21.

Tennessee: Garland *v.* Aurin, 103 Tenn. 555, 53 S. W. 940, 48 L. R. A. 862.

[7] *North Carolina:* Salisbury *v.* Western N. C. R. R., 98 N. C. 465.

Ohio: Van Buskirk *v.* Dunlap, 2 Oh. Dec. 233, 2 W. L. Mag. 125. But in Watkins *v.* Kaolin Manuf. Co., 131 N. C. 536, 42 S. E. 983, one who had conveyed his premises in trust to secure a debt, remaining in possession,

was allowed to recover for damages to the freehold.

[8] *Nebraska:* Gartner *v.* Chicago, R. I. & P. R. R., 71 Neb. 444 , 98 N. W. 1052.

Vermont: Hunt *v.* Taylor, 22 Vt. 556.

Canada: Johnston *v.* Christie, 31 U. C. C. P. 358.

Contra, Southern Ry. *v.* Ethridge, 108 Ga. 121, 33 S. E. 850.

So one in possession of public lands under an application for entry may recover entire damages.

Indian Territory: Gulf, C. & S. F. Ry. *v.* Clark, 2 Ind. Terr. 319, 51 S. W. 962.

Louisiana: Mott *v.* Hopper, 116 La. 629, 40 So. 921.

[9] *Nebraska:* Nebraska City *v.* Northcutt, 45 Neb. 456, 63 N. W. 807.

Wisconsin: Ford *v.* Schliessway, 107 Wis. 479, 83 N. W. 761.

[10] Wallace *v.* Goodall, 18 N. H. 439.

[11] Delamater *v.* Folz, 50 Hun, 528, 3 N. Y. Supp. 711; Farnsworth *v.* Western U. T. Co., 53 Hun, 636, 6 N. Y. Supp. 735.

[12] *Illinois:* Reeder *v.* Purdy, 41 Ill. 279.

eral one who has possession merely cannot recover damages for an injury to the freehold, but is restricted to compensation for injury to his mere possessory right.[13] *A fortiori* a mere possessor can recover only nominal damages against the owner even if the latter enters upon his possession in violation of law.[14]

§ 71. By a lessee of land.

The injury to a lessee may consist in a definite and particular loss in the enjoyment of demised premises, or in an act permanently depreciating the value of the lease. In the former case the extent of the particular loss, not the diminished value of the entire lease or of the injured portion of the premises, is the measure of damages.[15] In estimating the injury to the tenant's right of possession, it may be necessary to allow full compensation for the injury on the ground that the whole loss falls on the tenant by the terms of the lease. Thus where the plaintiff was the lessee for years of certain premises at an annual rent, with liberty to dig half an acre of brick annually, and covenanted that he would not dig more, or that, if he did, he would pay an increased rent of £375 per half acre, being after

New Jersey: Thiel *v.* Bull's Ferry Co., 58 N. J. L. 212, 33 Atl. 281.

Texas: International & G. N. Ry. *v.* Ragsdale, 67 Tex. 24, 2 S. W. 515; Texas & P. Ry. *v.* Torrey, 4 Tex. Civ. App. 445, 16 S. W. 547.

[13] *Illinois:* Advance E. & W. Co. *v.* Eddy, 23 Ill. App. 352.

Minnesota: Rau *v.* Minn. V. R. R., 13 Minn. 442 (Gil. 407); Hueston *v.* Mississippi & R. R. B. Co., 76 Minn. 251, 79 N. W. 92.

New York: Kelly *v.* New York & M. B. R. R., 81 N. Y. 233.

North Carolina: Frisbee *v.* Marshall, 122 N. C. 760, 30 S. E. 21.

North Dakota: Russell *v.* Meyer, 7 N. D. 335, 75 N. W. 262.

Texas: Forst *v.* Rothe (Tex. Civ. App.), 66 S. W. 575.

Wisconsin: Wadleigh *v.* Marathon Bank, 58 Wis. 546, 17 N. W. 314.

England: Twyman *v.* Knowles, 13 C. B. 222, 22 L. J. C. P. 143, 17 Jur. 238.

So of one in possession under the homestead act. McLeod *v.* Spencer, 21 Okla. 165, 95 Pac. 754, 17 L. R. A. (N. S.) 958.

[14] *Georgia:* Bass *v.* West, 110 Ga. 698, 36 S. E. 244.

Iowa: Donald *v.* Lightfoot, Morris 450.

Kansas: Mitchell *v.* Woods, 17 Kan. 26.

Texas: Baker *v.* Cornelius, 6 Tex. Civ. App. 27, 24 S. W. 949.

[15] *Kansas:* Chicago, K. & W. R. R. *v.* Watkins, 43 Kan. 50, 22 Pac. 985 (destruction of crops).

New York: Terry *v.* New York, 8 Bosw. 504.

Wyoming: Painter *v.* Stahley, 15 Wyo. 510, 90 Pac. 375 (destruction of year's pasturage).

the rate that all the brick earth was sold for, and a stranger dug and took away brick earth; the lessee recovered against him the full value of the earth dug, on the ground that by the terms of the lease the tenant would be liable over for the waste to the landlord.[16]   So where the tenant sues for an injury to the building demised, and by the terms of the tenancy the plaintiff is bound to make repairs, and to restore the premises to the landlord at the end of the term in as good a condition as when they were leased, then the defendant is bound to enable the plaintiff to put the building in as good a condition as it was when the trespass was committed.[17]   So where a tenant erected a building with a right to remove it at the termination of the lease, he may recover compensation for a destruction of the building.[18]

In the ordinary case, however, the injury will be to the reversioner as well as to the lessee, and the latter can recover only the loss to his interest, which is the diminished value of the lease.[19]   Thus Heath, J., said, in Attersoll v. Stevens: [20] "If trees are demised and a stranger cuts them, the lessee shall have his action of trespass; but the measure of damages is not the value of the trees, but the loss of the shade and fruit during his term." So the measure of damages for an injury to a tenant for years caused by flooding his lands was held to be the loss of the use of the lands and their yearly products.[21]   And where in an

[16] Attersoll v. Stevens, 1 Taunt. 183.

[17] Cook v. Champlain Tr. Co., 1 Denio (N. Y.), 91; Gourdier v. Cormack, 2 E. D. Smith (N. Y.), 202; Walter v. Post, 4 Abb. Pr. 382, 6 Duer, 363.

In Weston v. Gravlin, 49 Vt. 507, it was held that a tenant could recover for all the damage done to a house where the acts directly interfered with the plaintiff's enjoyment of the premises, the court saying that, as the facts appeared in the case at bar, the tenant would ordinarily have to repair the injuries in order to make the house habitable.

[18] Eten v. Luyster, 60 N. Y. 253.

[19] *Alabama:* Snedecor v. Pope, 143 Ala. 275, 39 So. 318.

California: Hawthorn v. Siegel, 88 Cal. 159, 25 Pac. 1114, 22 Am. St. R. 291; Sacchi v. Bayside Lumber Co., Cal.   , 108 Pac. 885.

Delaware: Nivin v. Stevens, 5 Harr. 272.

New York: Holmes v. Davis, 19 N. Y. 488; Sheldon v. Van Slyke, 16 Barb. 26; Van Buren v. Fishkill & M. W. W. Co., 50 Hun, 448.

Texas: Steger v. Barrett,   Tex. Civ. App.   , 124 S. W. 174.

Canada: Drew v. Baby, 1 Up. Can. Q. B. 438; Fisher v. Grace, 27 Up. Can. Q. B. 158; Atkinson v. Beard, 11 Up. Can. C. P. 245.

[20] 1 Taunt. 182, 189.

[21] Grand Rapids Booming Co. v. Jarvis, 30 Mich. 308.

8

action of trespass by a tenant against his landlord, the premises had been in the possession of subtenants, who before the end of the term left them for a consideration paid by the defendant, and the defendant thereupon removed the houses with a view to rebuilding, the measure of the tenant's damages was held to be the rent or value of the use of the premises for the rest of the term only.[22] If, however, the defendant's wrongful act (such as a nuisance) began before the lease, and it appears that the lease was given at a reduced rent because of the nuisance, the landlord is entitled to the entire damages.[23]

§ 72. By a life-tenant of land.

A life-tenant, like a tenant for years, is entitled to recover for the damage to himself only. In the ordinary case, therefore, he recovers only for the injury to his enjoyment of the premises,[24] leaving to the reversioner the recovery for an injury to the freehold.[25] The injury to the life-tenant is measured by the present value of the rents and profits of the premises, multiplied by the probable number of years of the plaintiff's life, less the probable amount of taxes, repairs, and insurance, and a rebate of interest.[26]

If, however, the tenant is answerable to the reversioner for the damage,[27] or if he is entitled to the property which the defendant took or destroyed,[28] he may recover the whole damage.

§ 73. By a mortgagee or mortgagor of land.

The mortgagee of real estate out of possession may bring an

---

[22] Schlemmer v. North, 32 Mo. 206.

[23] Yoos v. Rochester, 36 N. Y. Supp. 1071.

[24] *Maryland:* Zimmerman v. Shreeve, 59 Md. 357.

West Virginia: Jordan v. Benwood, 42 W. Va. 312, 26 S. E. 266, 36 L. R. A. 519; Yeager v. Fairmont, 43 W. Va. 259, 27 S. E. 234.

But see St. L., I. M. & S. Ry. v. O'Baugh, 49 Ark. 418, 5 S. W. 711, where the life-tenant was allowed to recover the entire damage which appears to have included injury to the freehold.

[25] Willey v. Laraway, 64 Vt. 559, 25 Atl. 436.

[26] Greer v. New York, 1 Abb. N. S. (N. Y.) 206.

[27] *Massachusetts:* Fay v. Brewer, 3 Pick. 203.

Vermont: Willey v. Laraway, 64 Vt. 559, 25 Atl. 436.

[28] *Massachusetts:* Rockwood v. Robinson, 159 Mass. 406, 34 N. E. 521 (tenant for life with power to sell any part of the reversion for her own use).

South Carolina: Perry v. Jeffries, 61 S. C. 292, 39 S. E. 515.

action for the impairment of his security, and may recover the amount by which his security is impaired, not, however, exceeding the amount of the injury.   This is generally held to be all he can recover, whether his action is against the mortgagor or his assignee,[29] or against a stranger.[30]

In Massachusetts, however, it has been held that the mortgagee, as legal owner, is not limited in his recovery to the amount by which the security may be impaired, but is entitled to recover the whole loss.   While there are perhaps technical grounds for supporting this decision, where the action is by a first mortgagee against a stranger,[31] yet the doctrine is carried further and the junior mortgagee is allowed to recover the whole amount of the loss,[32] even against the mortgagor or his assignee.[33] There seems to be a conclusive objection to such recovery; the junior mortgagee, having no legal title and no possession, can bring no action of trespass or waste, but is restricted to an action on the case for the impairment of his security; and in such an action, as impairment is the gist of it, so recovery should be had for such injuries only as cause impairment.   But even in Massachusetts it was held that the trespasser should be allowed to show, in mitigation of damages, that the plaintiff had, since the taking, under his power of sale, sold the property for more than his debt and prior incumbrances.[34]   The court said: "The general rule is that the damages must be precisely commensurate with the injury which the plaintiff suffers by the act of wrong at the time it was committed; but under this rule the defendant is constantly permitted to give in evidence the plaintiff's subsequent change of relation to the property for the purpose

---

[29] *Colorado:* Belmont, M. & M. Co. *v.* Costigan, 21 Colo. 471, 42 Pac. 647.

Indiana: Cory *v.* Silcox, 6 Ind. 39.

New York: Lane *v.* Hitchcock, 14 Johns. 213; Van Pelt *v.* McGraw, 4 N. Y. 110.

South Carolina: Heath *v.* Haile, 45 S. C. 642, 24 S. E. 300.

Wisconsin: State *v.* Weston, 17 Wis. 107.

[30] *New Jersey:* Jackson *v.* Turrell, 39 N. J. L. 329; Schalk *v.* Kingsley, 42 N. J. L. 32; Delaware & A. T. & T. Co.

v. Elvins, 63 N. J. Law, 243, 43 Atl. 903.

New York: Yates *v.* Joyce, 11 Johns. 136; Gardner *v.* Heartt, 3 Den. 232; Morgan *v.* Waters, 122 App. Div. 340, 106 N. Y. Supp. 882.

Wisconsin: Atkinson *v.* Hewett, 63 Wis. 396.

[31] Jackson *v.* Turrell, 39 N. J. L. 329.

[32] Gooding *v.* Shea, 103 Mass. 360.

[33] Byrom *v.* Chapin, 113 Mass. 308.

[34] King *v.* Bangs, 120 Mass. 514.

of showing that the damages, to which he would otherwise have been entitled, have been thereby diminished."

A practical difficulty arises in case of recovery by a junior mortgagee. It may be impossible to decide, in the absence of the first mortgagee, whether the security of the junior mortgagee alone, or of the prior mortgagee also, has been impaired. If the injury was so great as to impair the security of the first mortgage, he has a right to compensation which cannot be barred by judgment in favor of the junior mortgagee. In New Jersey,[35] though the question was not passed upon by the court, it has been suggested that the money should be paid into court, and that if the prior mortgagee should not come in to present his claim, the junior mortgagee may be required, before taking it out, to give a bond of indemnity. In Massachusetts it has been held, as just stated, that the junior mortgagee's measure of damages is not affected by the existence of a prior mortgage;[36] but how the defendant can be protected against his liability to the prior mortgagee is a question not disposed of by the courts of that State.

The mortgagor of land in possession is entitled to recover the entire damages, irrespective of the mortgage.[37] A court of equity should, however, so deal with the proceeds as to preserve the security of the mortgagee;[38] as for instance, in case of the proceeds of land taken by eminent domain, by impressing upon the money the lien of the mortgage.[39]

One who has conveyed his land to a creditor as security for the debt may recover against the creditor, in an action for conveying the land to a *bona fide* purchaser so as to cut off all right of redemption, the value of the land less the amount of the debt for which the creditor held it.[40]

§ 74. By a reversioner.

In actions brought by reversioners for injuries to their inheritance (the remedy being by an action on the case), it was at

[35] Jackson *v.* Turrell, 39 N. J. L. 329.

[36] Gooding *v.* Shea, 103 Mass. 360.

[37] Kunkel *v.* Utah Lumber Co., 29 Utah, 13, 81 Pac. 897.

[38] Delaware & A. T. & T. Co. *v.*

Elvins, 63 N. J. Law, 243, 43 Atl. 903.

[39] Lumbermen's Ins. Co. *v.* St. Paul, 77 Minn. 410, 80 N. W. 357.

[40] Ullman *v.* Devereux, 102 S. W. 1163, 46 Tex. Civ. App. 459.

first doubted whether the reversioner's remedy was not limited to the case of an absolute and permanent diminution of the value of the property; and in an action for erecting a wall, whereby the plaintiff's lights were obstructed, the declaration counting for the plaintiff as reversioner, it was insisted that a temporary nuisance could not be an injury to the inheritance; but the court held otherwise, being of opinion that an action might be brought by the tenant in respect of his possession, and by the landlord or reversioner in respect of his inheritance, for the injury done to the value of it.[41] It is now well settled that, if the act complained of works any injury to the inheritance, or affects in any way the reversioner's title, the law will remunerate him in damages.[42] For example, building a roof with eaves which discharge rain water by a spout into the adjoining premises is an injury for which the landlord of such premises may recover as reversioner, while they are under demise, if the jury think there is a damage to the reversion.[43]

But the injury must always be to the reversion, and the reversioner cannot recover for damage to tenants merely;[44] so

[41] Jesser v. Gifford, 4 Burr. 2141. In Massachusetts it was held, previous to the revision of the statutes of that State, that the owner of real estate in the possession of a lessee, other than at will, could not maintain trespass for an injury to his reversionary interest, and that case was the only remedy. Lienow v. Ritchie, 8 Pick. 235. But if the lessee were at will only, it was held that trespass would lie. Now, however, since the provision first introduced in the revision of the statutes (in 1836) requiring three months' notice to be given in order to determine estates at will, this distinction is held to be done away, and case is considered the proper remedy for any injury to the landlord's reversionary interest in estates at will as well as others. French v. Fuller, 23 Pick. 104.

[42] *Illinois:* Cooper v. Randall, 59 Ill. 317; Indianapolis, B. & W. Ry. v. Mc-

Laughlin, 77 Ill. 275; Illinois & S. L. R. R. & C. Co. v. Cobb, 94 Ill. 55.

Maryland: Western M. R. R. v. Martin, 110 Md. 554, 73 Atl. 267.

New York: Van Deusen v. Young, 29 N. Y. 9.

North Carolina: Dorsey v. Moore, 100 N. C. 41.

Ohio: Dutro v. Wilson, 4 Oh. St. 101.

Pennsylvania: Schnable v. Koehler, 28 Pa. 181; Green v. Sun Co., 32 Pa. Super. Ct. 521.

West Virginia: Jordan v. Benwood, 42 W. Va. 312, 26 S. E. 266, 36 L. R. A. 519.

England: Shadwell v. Hutchinson, 3 C. & P. 615; s. c. 4 C. & P. 333.

Canada: Drew v. Baby, 1 Up. Can. Q. B. 438; Atkinson v. Beard, 11 Up. Can. C. P. 245.

[43] Tucker v. Newman, 11 A. & E. 40.

[44] *California:* Uttendorffer v. Saegers, 50 Cal. 496.

a reversioner cannot maintain an action on the case against a stranger for merely entering upon his land held by a tenant on lease, though the entry be made in exercise of an alleged right of way.[45]   But case lies by reversioner against one who erects a dam on the adjacent land and backs the water on the plaintiff's mill race.[46]

So, where the defendant, being a lessee for years, without leave opened a door in the house owned by the plaintiff as landlord, and the jury found that the house was not in any way weakened or injured by the act, the court refused to allow a verdict for nominal damages to be entered, and directed a new trial to be had on this point, saying: "We cannot say that the opening of the door in this case affects the evidence of the plaintiff's title.   That is a question of fact." [47]   But as it is evident that injuries of this character are often of a nature very difficult to be estimated, the courts have uniformly exhibited great caution in requiring the fact of damage to the reversionary interest to be clearly established.   Thus it is held that, in actions of this nature, it must be distinctly averred in the declaration that the act complained of has been done to the damage of the reversion, or must state an injury of such permanent nature as to be necessarily injurious to the reversion,[48] and where a verdict was obtained on a declaration alleging that the defendant had constructed a wall so as to overhang the yard of which the plaintiff was reversioner, and to produce a water drip in the yard, but without alleging any injury to the plaintiff's reversionary estate and interest in the premises, the judgment was arrested by the King's Bench.[49]   So, again, it has been held that the obstruction of a public navigable river is not a damage to a reversioner out of possession of premises abutting thereon.[50]

Illinois: Cooper *v.* Randall, 59 Ill. 317; Dixon *v.* Baker, 65 Ill. 518, 16 Am. Rep. 591; I. & St. L. R. R. & C. Co. *v.* Cobb, 94 Ill. 55.

Missouri: Thurmond *v.* Ash. G. W. L. Assoc., 125 Mo. App. 73, 102 S. W. 617.

[45] Baxter *v.* Taylor, 4 B. & A. 72.

[46] Ripka *v.* Sargeant, 7 W. & S. 9.

[47] Young *v.* Spencer, 10 B. & C. 145.

[48] *Illinois:* Chicago *v.* McDonough, 112 Ill. 85.

New Jersey: Tinsman *v.* B. D. R. R., 25 N. J. L. 255; Halsey *v.* L. V. R. R., 45 N. J. L. 26.

[49] Jackson *v.* Pesked, 1 M. & S. 234.

[50] Dobson *v.* Blackmore, 9 Q. B. 991.

As in previous instances, the market value of the reversion cannot be taken as the measure of damages where the injury to be compensated is not a permanent continuing one, but consists in specific past damage.   Thus in an action by a reversioner for damages done to the reversion, by cutting off the eaves of a building belonging to him, and by erecting a wall with a drip over his premises, it was held that, as there might be repeated actions for continuing the nuisance, evidence for the purpose of showing the diminution in the salable value of the premises should be rejected.[51]

Where there are several reversioners, as tenants for life, in tail, or in fee, each can recover compensation for the injury to his own estate.[52]

§ 75. By a tenant in common of land.

One tenant in common of land may maintain an action for injury to the land if the non-joinder of the other tenants in common is not pleaded in abatement, and may recover his share of the damages.[53]   So one of two reversioners may maintain an action, if the defendant does not plead in abatement, and recover his share of the damages.[54]

Where, under the old practice in ejectment, a recovery was effected on the demise of two only, out of several tenants, and suit was afterward brought for mesne profits, it was held that none but the shares of the mesne profits to which those two

[51] Battishill v. Reed, 18 C. B. 696.

[52] Zimmerman v. Shreeve, 59 Md. 357.

[53] *Alabama:* Lowery v. Rowland, 104 Ala. 420, 16 So. 88.

Illinois: Baltimore & O. S. W. Ry. v. Higgins, 69 Ill. App. 412.

New Hampshire: Daniels v. Brown, 34 N. H. 454, 69 Am. Dec. 505, n.

New Jersey: Jackson v. Todd, 25 N. J. Law (1 Dutch.), 121.

Pennsylvania: McGill v. Ash, 7 Pa. 397.

Tennessee: Winters v. McGhee, 3 Sneed, 128.

Texas: Rowland v. Murphy, 66 Tex. 534; Gulf, C. & S. F. Ry. v. Cusenberry, 86 Tex. 525, 26 S. W. 43.

Contra, Vermont: Hibbard v. Foster, 24 Vt. 542.

A fortiori damages are so restricted where the defendant acted by permission of the co-tenant.

Texas: Gulf, C. & S. F. Ry. v. Mc-Murrough, 41 Tex. Civ. App. 216, 91 S. W. 320.

West Virginia: McDodrill v. Pardee Co., 40 W. Va. 564, 21 S. E. 878.

[54] *Alabama:* Lowery v. Rowland, 104 Ala. 420, 16 So. 88.

Massachusetts: Putney *v.* Lapham, 10 Cush. 232.

tenants were entitled could be recovered.[55]   So, where a plaintiff in ejectment was tenant in common of the premises withheld, with one not a party to the suit, he was entitled to recover as damages for the detention a part of the mesne profits only, in proportion to his interest, and not the whole.[56]

Where one tenant in common sues the other for excluding him from the land, the measure of damages is the proportional part of the rental value, and not of the profits which may in fact have been received by the defendant.[57]

§ 76. By a possessor of chattels against a stranger.

By a peculiar doctrine of the law of personal property, the possessor of such property is endowed, for the purpose of protecting it against strangers, with all the rights of ownership. It follows from this general principle that one in possession of a chattel may recover from a stranger who injures it full damages, without the question of title being at all material,[58] and in that case he will be held responsible at law to the owner [59]

---

[55] Holdfast v. Shepard, 9 Ired. (N. C.) 222.

[56] Clark v. Huber, 20 Cal. 196. Compare the doctrine by which a tenant in common, bringing ejectment against a stranger, is let into possession of a half interest in common with the defendant. Williams v. Gold Creek M. & M. Co., 115 Tenn. 578, 93 S. W. 572, 6 L. R. A. (N. S.) 710.

[57] Cutter v. Waddingham, 33 Mo. 269.

[58] *United States:* Conard v. Pacific Ins. Co., 6 Pet. 262, 8 L. ed. 392; Northern Pac. Ry. v. Lewis, 51 Fed. 658.

In Guttner v. Pacific Steam Whaling Co., 96 Fed. 617, plaintiff was a seaman and remained behind in an icebound vessel after she had been abandoned by the master and rest of the crew. Held, that plaintiff was in possession and was entitled to recover compensation for the value of goods taken from the vessel by the defendant. Plaintiff's interest in goods was immaterial when the defendant was a mere stranger.

Maine: Barker v. Chase, 24 Me. 230.

Massachusetts: Gibbs v. Chase, 10 Mass. 125.

New York: King v. Orser, 4 Duer 431.

North Dakota: Mathews v. Great Northern Ry., 7 N. Dak. 81, 72 N. W. 1085.

Tennessee: Criner v. Pike, 2 Head, 398.

Utah: Rhemke v. Clinton, 2 Utah, 230.

Vermont: Fisher v. Cobb, 6 Vt. 622; Wooley v. Edson, 35 Vt. 214.

West Virginia: Wustland v. Potterfield, 9 W. Va. 438.

Upper Canada: Irving v. Hagerman, 22 U. C. Q. B. 545.

[59] *United States:* Pabst Co. v. Greenberg, 117 Fed. 135, 55 C. C. A. 151.

California: Treadwell v. Davis, 34 Cal. 601.

Connecticut: White v. Webb, 15 Conn. 302.

Georgia: Schley v. Lyon, 6 Ga. 530.

Illinois: Atkins v. Moore, 82 Ill. 240.

for all the damages above the amount of his own interest. And so it has been held in the various cases of consignors,[60] depositaries,[61] factors,[62] lessees,[63] lienors,[64] pledgees,[65] sheriffs,[66] finders of property,[67] and bailees in general,[68] and trustees.[69]

Thus, where the plaintiff was a collector and transmitter of small parcels and responsible for their safe delivery, he was

Michigan: Davidson *v.* Gunsolly, 1 Mich. 388; Burk *v.* Webb, 32 Mich. 173.

New Hampshire: Chesley *v.* St. Clair, 1 N. H. 189.

England: Heydon & Smith's Case, 13 Co. 67.

[60] *Massachusetts:* Finn *v.* W. R. R., 112 Mass. 524, 17 Am. Rep. 128.

New Jersey: Garretson *v.* Brown, 26 N. J. L. 425.

England: Crouch *v.* L. & N. W. Ry., 2 C. & K. 789; The Charlotte, [1908] P. 206, 77 L. J. P. 132, 99 L. T. 380, 24 T. L. R. 416.

[61] Rooth *v.* Wilson, 1 B. & Ald. 59; Burton *v.* Hughes, 2 Bing. 173; Mason *v.* Morgan, 24 U. C. Q. B. 328.

[62] Groover *v.* Warfield, 50 Ga. 644.

[63] *Arkansas:* St. L., I. M. & S. Ry. *v.* Biggs, 50 Ark. 169.

Maine: Freeman *v.* Underwood, 66 Me. 229.

Maryland: Harker *v.* Dement, 9 Gill, 7.

Massachusetts: Caswell *v.* Howard, 16 Pick. 562.

New York: Baker *v.* Hart, 52 Hun, 363.

[64] *Maryland:* Arnd *v.* Amling, 53 Md. 192.

Michigan: Davidson *v.* Gunsolly, 1 Mich. 388.

Nebraska: Fred Krug B. Co. *v.* Healey, 71 Neb. 662, 99 N. W. 489, 101 N. W. 329.

New York: Hays *v.* Riddle, 1 Sandf. 248.

Vermont: Hill *v.* Larro, 53 Vt. 629.

[65] *California:* Treadwell *v.* Davis, 34 Cal. 601, 94 Am. Dec. 770.

Illinois: U. S. Ex. Co. *v.* Meints, 72 Ill. 293.

Maine: Soule *v.* White, 14 Me. 436.

Massachusetts: Pomeroy *v.* Smith, 17 Pick. 85; Ullman *v.* Barnard, 7 Gray, 554; Adams *v.* O'Connor, 100 Mass. 515.

New York: Mechanics' & Traders' Bank *v.* Farmers' & Mechanics' Bank, 60 N. Y. 40; Alt *v.* Weidenberg, 6 Bosw. 176; Hanover Nat. Bk. *v.* Amer. D. & T. Co., 43 N. Y. Supp. 544, 14 App. Div. 255.

Pennsylvania: Lyle *v.* Barker, 5 Binn. 457.

England: Swire *v.* Leach, 18 C. B. (N. S.) 479.

[66] *Massachusetts:* Robinson *v.* Ensign, 6 Gray, 300.

Michigan: Burk *v.* Webb, 32 Mich. 173.

New Hampshire: Poole *v.* Symonds, 1 N. H. 289, 8 Am. Dec. 71.

New York: Buck *v.* Remsen, 34 N. Y. 383; Phillips *v.* Hall, 8 Wend. 476.

Vermont: Fisher *v.* Cobb, 6 Vt. 622.

[67] Armory *v.* Delamirie, 1 Stra. 504.

[68] *Connecticut:* Gillette *v.* Goodspeed, 69 Conn. 363, 37 Atl. 973.

Massachusetts: Brewster *v.* Warner, 136 Mass. 57.

England: The Winkfield, [1901] P. 42 (overruling Claridge *v.* South S. T. Co., [1892] 1 Q. B. 422).

[69] *North Carolina:* Murphy *v.* Moore, 4 Ire. Eq. 118.

Texas: Martin-Brown Co. *v.* Henderson, 9 Tex. Civ. App. 130, 28 S. W. 695.

allowed to recover the full value against a railway company, in an action of case for negligence, on the ground of his liability to pay their value to the true owner, whether he had actually paid it or not.[70]

Again, where unredeemed pledges deposited with the plaintiff in the way of his trade as a pawnbroker, and which were held under the English law to be protected from distress, had been seized by his landlord under a distress warrant, it was held in an action of trover for the goods, that as the defendant was an absolute wrongdoer, without color of right, the bailee was entitled to recover their full value.[71]

And where certain formalities are required by statute for the attachment of pledged property, and a sheriff pretends to attach pledged property without following out the method prescribed, he is liable to the pledgee for the whole value of the property.[72]

The plaintiff was lessee of a quarry, with the right to take out stone. The defendant wrongfully quarried and carried away stone, and the plaintiff sued him for conversion. It was held that the plaintiff had sufficient interest in the stone to bring trover, and could recover the whole value of it.[73] In a similar action by a lessee against a trespasser who carried away fruit, it was held that the lessee could recover the full value of the fruit.[74]

In a few isolated cases, intimating that he who has a bare possessory right is not entitled to full damages, the facts are not clearly reported.[75] They can hardly be regarded as authority on the point under discussion.

[70] Crouch v. L. & N. W. Ry., 2 C. & K. 789.

[71] Swire v. Leach, 18 C. B. (N. S.) 479.

[72] *Massachusetts:* Pomeroy v. Smith, 17 Pick. 85.

South Carolina: Compton v. Martin, 5 Rich. L. 14.

[73] Baker v. Hart, 52 Hun (N. Y.), 363.

[74] Freeman v. Underwood, 66 Me. 229.

[75] *Alabama:* Sterrett v. Kaster, 37 Ala. 366.

Indiana: Anthony v. Gilbert, 4 Blackf. 348.

North Carolina: Gwaltney v. Scottish C. T. & L. Co., 115 N. C. 579, 20 S. E. 465.

United States: In McDowell v. McCormick, 121 Fed. 61, 57 C. C. A. 401, the court held that where the plaintiff's possession was merely colorable and not *bona fide* he could not recover entire damages.

§ 77. In replevin by one who counts on possession merely.

The same rule should prevail in replevin; the person from whose possession goods have been taken wrongfully by a stranger should recover the full value of the goods, either in an action on the bond, or, in those States permitting such a proceeding, in the original action. And such is the doctrine generally held.[76]

But there seems a disposition on the part of some courts to hold that the mere possessor can recover in this case compensation for his own interest only.[77] And so it has been held in Iowa that where goods in the possession of a sheriff are wrongfully replevied by a stranger, the damages are limited to the amount of the execution.[78] Unless these cases are to be justified by local usage (on which the Maryland court seemed to rely) or on the form of the statute, they can hardly be supported.

In Ohio the statute authorizes the jury to give one who has a mere right of possession such damages as he has sustained. It is held that according to this statute the prevailing party is limited to the value of his interest,[79] or if that exceeds the value of the goods replevied, to the value of the goods.[80]

§ 78. By the possessor of chattels in an action against the owner.

The rule which puts the possessor of chattels in the position of the owner in actions against strangers does not apply where the wrongdoer is himself the owner. In such a case, according to the general principle, the possessor wrongfully deprived of the possession can recover only the amount by which he is

[76] *Illinois:* Broadwell *v.* Paradice, 81 Ill. 474; Atkins *v.* Moore, 82 Ill. 240.

Michigan: Burt *v.* Burt, 41 Mich. 82.

Missouri: Dilworth *v.* McKelvy, 30 Mo. 149; Fallon *v.* Manning, 35 Mo. 271; Frei *v.* Vogel, 40 Mo. 149; Miles *v.* Walther, 3 Mo. App. 96.

Nebraska: Frey *v.* Drahos, 7 Neb. 194.

New York: Buck *v.* Remsen, 34 N. Y. 383.

[77] *Indiana:* Noble *v.* Epperly, 6 Ind. 468.

Maryland: Cumberland Coal and Iron Co. *v.* Tilghman, 13 Md. 74.

[78] *Iowa:* Hayden *v.* Anderson, 17 Ia. 158, 165.

Contra, New York: Buck *v.* Remsen, 34 N. Y. 383.

[79] *Michigan:* Darling *v.* Tegler, 30 Mich. 54.

Ohio: Jennings *v.* Johnson, 17 Ohio, 154, 49 Am. Dec. 451.

[80] Latimer *v.* Motler, 26 Oh. St. 480.

actually damaged; that is, the amount of his interest in the property.[81]

"If the defendant, in the assertion and vindication of his supposed rights, and not for fraudulent purposes, or as a mere stranger, replevied the property, the measure of damages in this action is not necessarily the value of the property, but the extent of the plaintiff's injury by being deprived of such right as he in fact had in the property when return thereof should have been made. . . . The true question is, what has the plaintiff lost, or to what amount is he injured by the failure of the defendant to return the property? and to determine this, it is material to know the extent of his interest."[82]

Accordingly, when goods are replevied by the owner from one having the right of possession, the latter can recover as

[81] In general:
United States: Pabst Brewing Co. v. Greenberg, 117 Fed. 135, 55 C. C. A. 151.
Colorado: Sopris v. Lilley, 2 Col. 496.
Georgia: Schley v. Lyon, 6 Ga. 530.
Illinois: Benjamin v. Stremple, 13 Ill. 466.
Michigan: Davidson v. Gunsolly, 1 Mich. 388.
New York: Fitzhugh v. Wiman, 9 N. Y. 559; Seaman v. Luce, 23 Barb. 240; Rhoads v. Woods, 41 Barb. 471; Decker v. Decker, 17 Hun, 13.
Tennessee: Collomb v. Taylor, 9 Humph. 689; Bogard v. Jones, 9 Humph. 739.
Pennsylvania: Where a color mixer in a carpet manufactory, without the knowledge of his employers, entered the recipes in his own, instead of his employers', color books, and, on the employee's discharge, his employers, believing the books their own, refused to let the employee take them away, the employee could not recover the value of the recipes. Dempsey v. Dobson, 174 Pa. 122, 34 Atl. 459, 52 Am. St. R. 816, 32 L. R. A. 761.
Factor:
New York: Frost v. Willard, 9 Barb. 440.

Lessee:
South Carolina: Compton v. Martin, 5 Rich. L. 14.
Vermont: Hickok v. Buck, 22 Vt. 149.
Lienor:
Maryland: Albert v. Lindau, 46 Md. 334.
Massachusetts: Jarvis v. Rogers, 15 Mass. 389.
New York: Ingersoll v. Van Bokkelin, 7 Cow. 670.
Ohio: Case v. Hart, 11 Ohio, 364.
Pennsylvania: Lyle v. Barker, 5 Binn. 457, 460.
Pledgee:
United States: Hurst v. Coley, 15 Fed. 645.
Georgia: Clark v. Bell, 61 Ga. 147; Bradley v. Burkett, 82 Ga. 255.
New York: Hays v. Riddle, 1 Sandf. 248.
Texas: Payne v. Lindsley,   Tex. Civ. App.   , 126 S. W. 329.
Sheriff:
Massachusetts: Bartlett v. Kidder, 14 Gray, 449.
New York: Spoor v. Holland, 8 Wend. 445, 24 Am. Dec. 34; Scrugham v. Carter, 12 Wend. 131.
[82] Warner v. Matthews, 18 Ill. 83.

damages only the amount of his interest.[83]   Thus, in Illinois it appeared that one B. distrained for rent.   D., the owner, replevied the property, but did not prosecute the action, and a return of the property was decreed to B.   D. did not return, and B. sued on the replevin bond.   His damages were held to be, not the full value of the property, but only the value of his special interest, *i. e.*, the rent.[84]   Where goods were sold by the defendant to the plaintiff, and delivered, but the title was not to pass until complete payment was made, the plaintiff in an action for conversion by wrongfully resuming possession of the goods can recover only his interest; that is, the amount of his payments.[85]

§ 79. By a possessor of chattels where the owner cannot recover the full value.

The possessor, even if he is suing a stranger, cannot recover more than the value of his own interest where the owner would not have been entitled to recover more.   In Sheldon *v.* Southern Express Co.[86] it appeared that one T., being indebted to the plaintiff, transferred a note to the defendant express company (which the company agreed to collect), giving the receipt for it to the plaintiff as security for his debt.   The defendant, failing to collect it, allowed it to go into the hands of T., who collected it and paid the plaintiff a portion of his debt.   The measure of damages was held to be the unpaid portion of T.'s debt to the plaintiff.

So although as a general rule a bailee, *e. g.*, a warehouseman, may insure goods and recover the full value on the policy, yet if the owner has also insured them the loss must be apportioned between the companies insuring.[87]   Where goods were taken from the plaintiff, a naked bailee, and restored by the wrong-

---

[83] *Colorado:* Witkowski *v.* Hill, 17 Colo. 372, 30 Pac. 55.

Iowa: Harman *v.* Goodrich, 1 Greene, 13; Hawley *v.* Warner, 12 Ia. 42.

Maryland: Belt *v.* Worthington, 3 G. & J. 247.

Mississippi: Jones *v.* Hicks, 52 Miss. 682.

Nebraska: Cruts *v.* Wray, 19 Neb. 581.

New York: Dows *v.* Greene, 24 N. Y. 638; Weaver *v.* Darby, 42 Barb. 411.

Texas: Fowler *v.* Stonum, 6 Tex. 60.

[84] David *v.* Bradley, 79 Ill. 316.

[85] Levan *v.* Wilten, 135 Pa. 61, 19 Atl. 945.

[86] 48 Ga. 625.

[87] Home Ins. Co. *v.* Baltimore Warehouse Co., 93 U. S. 527, 23 L. ed. 868.

doer to the owner, nominal damages only can be recovered.[88] And a pledgee in a suit against a warehouseman for wrongful delivery to the pledgor recovers the amount of his loan, being less than the value of the property.[89]

And the rule is the same where the defendant claims under the owner,[90] as a vendee,[91] or an attaching sheriff.[92] Where an officer had paid freight due on goods attached by him, and afterwards, on demand of a person who had a lien on them for advances, refused either to pay the amount of the lien or to release the attachment, it was held, in an action against him for conversion of the property, that the amount he had paid for the freight must be deducted from its value.[93]

But of course the amount that can be recovered is limited by the injury done or the goods taken.[94]

§ 80. By an owner of chattels out of possession.

An owner of chattels, though out of possession, can generally recover full compensation for any injury done to them; and such recovery will bar action by the possessor.[95]

Where, however, the defendant has a beneficial interest in

---

[88] *United States:* Pabst B. Co. v. Greenberg, 117 Fed. 135, 55 C. C. A. 151.

Massachusetts: Squire v. Hollenbeck, 9 Pick. 551, 20 Am. Dec. 506; Lowell v. Parker, 10 Met. 309, 43 Am. Dec. 436.

Michigan: Mears v. Cornwall, 73 Mich. 78.

Tennessee: Criner v. Pikes, 2 Head, 398.

[89] Fifth National Bank v. Providence Warehouse Co., 17 R. I. 112, 20 Atl. 203.

[90] Temple v. Duran (Tex. Civ. App.), 121 S. W. 253.

[91] *Illinois:* Belden v. Perkins, 78 Ill. 449.

Kentucky: Linville v. Black, 5 Dana, 177.

New York: Chadwick v. Lamb, 29 Barb. 518.

[92] *Illinois:* Baldwin v. Bradley, 69 Ill. 32.

New Jersey: Outcalt v. Durling, 25 N. J. L. (1 Dutch.) 443.

North Carolina: Penland v. Leatherwood, 101 N. C. 509, 8 S. E. 234, 9 Am. St. Rep. 38.

Vermont: Chaffee v. Sherman, 26 Vt. 237.

Wisconsin: Clark v. Lamoreux, 70 Wis. 508.

[93] Clark v. Dearborn, 103 Mass. 335.

[94] *Michigan:* Burk v. Webb, 32 Mich. 173.

Nebraska: Hamilton v. Lau, 24 Neb. 59.

Texas: Boydston v. Morris, 71 Tex. 697.

[95] *Illinois:* Eisendrath v. Knauer, 64 Ill. 396.

New Hampshire: Chesley v. St. Clair, 1 N. H. 189.

New York: Green v. Clarke, 12 N. Y. 343.

the property, the measure of damages is reduced by the amount of the defendant's interest. Thus, a pledgor or other lienor can recover of the pledgee, in an action for a wrongful sale or other conversion of the pledged goods, only the excess of the value of the property over the amount of the debt.[96]

In an English case, a bankrupt had deposited certain dock warrants for brandy in dock as security for a loan, and it was agreed that the pledgee might sell the brandy if the loan were not repaid on the 29th of January following. The pledgee sold the brandy on the 28th, and on the 29th delivered the warrants to the purchaser, who took possession of the brandy on the 30th. This was held by all the court to be a conversion, although the bankrupt could not have redeemed the property. But the majority of the court held that the wrongful acts of the pawnee did not annihilate the contract between the parties, nor the interest of the pawnee in the goods under it. The pawnee had the right to have his debt deducted from the value of the property in estimating damages. Mr. Justice Williams, dissenting, held that the bailment having been terminated by the wrongful act of the pledgee, the property reverted to the pledgor as its absolute owner, and as such absolute owner he was entitled to full damages.[97] So where a corporation wrongfully sold stock of a stockholder for non-payment of calls, in an action for the conversion it was held that the plaintiff's recovery must be diminished by the amount of the calls.[98]

A note payable twelve months after date, given to an in-

[96] *Illinois:* Baldwin v. Bradley, 69 Ill. 32; Loomis v. Stave, 72 Ill. 623; Belden v. Perkins, 78 Ill. 449; Ludden v. Buffalo Belting Co., 22 Ill. App. 415.
Indiana: Shaw v. Ferguson, 78 Ind. 547; Rosenzweig v. Frazer, 82 Ind. 547.
Kentucky: First Nat. Bank of Louisville v. Boyce, 78 Ky. 42, 39 Am. Rep. 198.
Maryland: Baltimore Mar. Ins. Co. v. Dalrymple, 25 Md. 269.
Massachusetts: Chamberlain v. Shaw, 18 Pick. 278, 29 Am. Dec. 586; Fowler v. Gilman, 13 Met. 267; Briggs v. B. & L. R. R., 6 All. 246; Fisher v. Brown, 104 Mass. 259, 6 Am. Rep. 235.

New York: Stearns v. Marsh, 4 Den. 227; Levy v. Loeb, 47 N. Y. Super. Ct. 61; Van Schaick v. Ramsey, 35 N. Y. Supp. 1006.
Pennsylvania: Craig v. McHenry, 35 Pa. 120.
Oregon: Swank v. Elwert,   Or.   , 105 Pac. 901.
Wisconsin: Wheeler v. Pereles, 43 Wis. 332.
England: Bac. Abr. *Bailment,* B.; Halliday v. Holgate, L. R. 3 Ex. 299.
[97] Johnson v. Stear, 15 C. B. (N. S.) 330, 33 L. J. C. P. 130.
[98] Stollenwerck v. Thacher, 115 Mass. 224.

surance company for premiums, was pledged by the company
as collateral security for a loan less than its face. The maker
of the note paid the loan, taking up the note before its maturity.
The company, becoming insolvent, assigned their property
to assignees, who brought trover for the note. The action was
held maintainable, as the note was by its terms liable for the
company's losses up to its maturity, and the measure of recovery was the balance of the note over the amount of the loan.[99]
So it was held in Boutell v. Warne,[100] that where property was
adjudged to the defendant, the jury should deduct from the
value of the property the amount paid by the plaintiff for the
property on a contract to purchase.

So where an agent pawned his principal's watch, and waived
notice without authority, and the pledgee sold it without
notice, it was held that the principal could recover the excess
of the value of the watch over the money received by the
agent.[101] So a pledgee who has converted stock can recoup
the amount of assessments rightfully paid on the stock.[102]

The same principle is applied where the action is brought by
the owner of chattels against one who has succeeded to the rights
of the lienor or other possessor.[103] Thus it was held that a defendant who had received goods from the plaintiff's agent,
which were intended for sale, but were sold contrary to the
instructions of the principal, could have deducted from the
market value of the goods the amount paid by him to discharge
a lien of a common carrier.[104]

By the law of Massachusetts an assignment in trust for creditors is valid as to those creditors only who assent to it. Property so assigned having been attached by a creditor of the
assignor, it was held that the trustee to whom the assignment
was made could recover only the amount of his own debt.[105]
Indeed, wherever the defendant, although in the wrong in assuming or retaining a possession which rightfully belongs to
the plaintiff, has yet a legal or equitable interest in the chattel,

[99] Fell v. McHenry, 42 Pa. 41.
[100] 62 Mo. 350.
[101] Van Arsdale v. Joiner, 44 Ga. 173.
[102] McCalla v. Clark, 55 Ga. 53.
[103] Bradley Land & Lumber Co. v.

Eastern Mfg. Co., 104 Me. 203, 71 Atl. 710.
[104] Stollenwerck v. Thacher, 115 Mass. 224.
[105] Boyden v. Moore, 11 Pick. (Mass.) 362.

the action is now treated on equitable principles, and the recovery limited to the actual net amount of the plaintiff's claim.[106]

So where one having bought sheep on credit left them in custody of the vendor, and without default of the vendee the vendor resold them, it was held by the English Court of Exchequer that the measure was not their value, but merely the actual damage sustained.[107] And where the lessor of sheep sued the lessee for conversion of the wool, on which the lessee had a lien, it was held that the amount of the lien should be deducted from the damage.[108]

This doctrine applies only where the defendant has an interest in the goods; and in that case, the reduction allowed is only the amount of such interest. So where the conversion sued for is by an unlawful sale of goods by one having a lien on them, the expenses of the sale cannot be allowed the defendant.[109] So where a bailee wrongfully retained the property until he secured judgment against the owner, and then levied on the property, the owner was allowed to recover the whole value, for at the time of the injury the defendant had no interest in the property.[110]

§ 80a. By a party to a conditional sale.

The same principle applies to an action by a party to a conditional sale. If the vendee in possession sues a stranger, he may recover the entire value of the property destroyed; and this rule was applied in a case where the consignee of goods billed to him straight, being in fact a conditional vendee, was allowed to recover the full value of the goods from the carrier, who had lost them.[111] In an action between the parties the vendor can recover from the vendee no more than the unpaid

[106] Baltimore Mar. Ins. Co. v. Dalrymple, 25 Md. 269.

[107] Chinery v. Viall, 5 H. & N. 288, 2 L. T. R. (N. S.) 466.

[108] Chamberlain v. Shaw, 18 Pick. (Mass.) 278.

[109] Briggs v. B. & L. R. R. 6 All. (Mass.) 246.

[110] Edmundson v. Nuttall, 17 C. B. (N. S.) 280; and see St. John v. O'Connel, 7 Port. (Ala.) 466; Hatheway v. F. R. Nat. Bank, 131 Mass. 14.

[111] Texas & P. Ry. v. Wilson Hack Line, 46 Tex. Civ. App. 38, 101 S. W. 1042.

purchase money,[112] while the vendee's recovery from the vendor is reduced by that amount.[113]

Where, however, the vendee's rights will be forfeited if he departs from the terms of the agreement, it has sometimes been held that, the vendee having no right in the goods after the wrongful act, the vendor may recover the entire value. So where the property is sold or mortgaged to a third party or attached by the vendee's creditors, the vendor is held entitled to recover the full value and interest from the time of the conversion, without any deduction for payments made on account by the original vendee; for the vendee has no interest in the property which could be conveyed to a third party or attached, and the defendant in this case has therefore no interest in the property.[114]

§ 81. By the mortgagor or mortgagee of chattels.

The right of a party to a mortgage of chattels to recover for injury inflicted by a stranger depends usually on possession. It is often held that a chattel mortgage does not pass the legal title, but only an interest in the property, to the mortgagee. But if the mortgagee takes possession of the property, he stands in the same position as a pledgee with reference to damages, and therefore a mortgagee in possession can recover full compensation from a stranger.[115]   And so a mortgagor left in pos-

[112] *Alabama:* Hall v. Nix, 156 Ala. 423, 47 So. 335.

New York: Davis v. Bliss, 187 N. Y. 77, 79 N. E. 851, 10 L. R. A. (N. S.) 458.

[113] *Georgia:* Roper Wholesale Grocery Co. v. Favor,   Ga. App.   , 68 S. E. 883.

Rhode Island: Smith v. Goff, 29 R. I. 439, 72 Atl. 289.

Vermont: Clark v. Clement, 75 Vt. 417, 56 Atl. 94.

[114] *Maine:* Brown v. Haynes, 52 Me. 578.

Massachusetts: Angier v. Taunton Paper Manufacturing Co., 1 Gray, 621, 61 Am. Dec. 436; Colcord v. McDonald, 128 Mass. 470.

Wisconsin: Lillie v. Dunbar, 62 Wis. 198.

But *contra, Vermont:* Chaffee v. Sherman, 26 Vt. 237.

[115] *Colorado:* Stevenson v. Lord, 15 Colo. 131, 25 Pac. 313.

Connecticut: White v. Webb, 15 Conn. 302.

Dakota: Madison Nat. Bank v. Farmer, 5 Dak. 282.

Maine: Warren v. Kelley, 80 Me. 512.

Masschusetts: Barry v. Bennett, 7 Met. 354; Allen v. Butman, 138 Mass. 586.

Michigan: Densmore v. Mathews, 58 Mich. 616.

Minnesota: Adamson v. Petersen, 35 Minn. 529.

session of the goods, no matter whether he is regarded as the legal owner or merely as having an equitable interest in them, can recover full compensation for injuries inflicted by a stranger.[116]

If a mortgagee brings suit against a wrongdoer, and pending the suit the mortgage is redeemed, it has been held that the plaintiff can recover only nominal damages; for no longer having an interest in the property, he would not hold the proceeds in trust for the owner.[117]   If the decision is sound, it would apply to any case where suit is brought by a bailee, and possession is resumed by the bailor pending the suit.

The party out of possession should, if regarded as owner, be allowed to recover full compensation from a stranger; and if not the owner, compensation to the amount of his interest, if he recovers judgment before the other party.[118]

So where, under an execution against a mortgagor of chattels rightfully in possession, the chattels are, without notice to the mortgagee, sold to various purchasers so as to injure or sacrifice the interest of the mortgagee, although the latter cannot maintain an action in the nature of trespass or trover for the value of the goods, he may, it seems, in an action in the nature of

South Carolina: Wylie v. Ohio R. & C. R. R., 48 S. C. 405, 26 S. E. 676.

[116] *Connecticut:* Becker v. Bailies, 44 Conn. 167.

Massachusetts: Cram v. Bailey, 10 Gray, 87.

New Jersey: Luce v. Jones, 39 N. J. L. (10 Vroom) 707.

Rhode Island: Brown v. Carroll, 16 R. I. 604.

Tennessee: Turnpike Co. v. Fry, 88 Tenn. 296, 12 S. W. 720.

England: Turner v. Hardcastle, 11 C. B. (N. S.) 683.

Ireland: Haggan v. Posley, 2 L. R. Ir. 573.

In a case in England at *nisi prius* the court, in its anxiety to punish the plaintiff for fraud, seems to have lost sight of the rights secured by possession. The plaintiff, in order to baffle his creditors, made a colorable transfer of property to a third party, but remained in possession; and the property was injured by the defendant. It was left to the jury to find a verdict for the plaintiff's real and *bona fide* interest, and though the property taken was worth £21, the verdict was for one farthing. Cameron v. Wynch, 2 C. & K. 264.

Where the proceeds of the property were turned over in payment of the mortgage, the damages recoverable by the mortgagor are reduced by the amount so turned over. Bowman v. Davis, 13 Colo. 297, 22 Pac. 507.

[117] King v. Bangs, 120 Mass. 514. This was, to be sure, a mortgage of land; but the reasoning of the court would apply equally well to a mortgage of chattels.

[118] Watkins v. Citizens' Nat. Bk., 56 Tex. Civ. App. 138, 115 S. W. 304.

case, recover damages to the extent of the injury to his interest.[119] In such an action by a mortgagee against the receiver of the mortgaged property and others for an injury to his interest, the damages should be confined to the loss he has suffered by the dispersion of the property among the several purchasers.[120] A junior mortgagee, suing for the conversion of the mortgaged property, recovers the value of his interest, that is, he can be compensated only for the value of the property above the prior mortgage.[121]

§ 82. Between the parties to a mortgage of chattels.

When the suit is between the parties to the mortgage, the plaintiff, whether he has been in possession or not, can, on the equitable principle already explained, recover compensation only for the injury done to his interest. Thus, when a mortgagor sues a mortgagee for prematurely seizing or selling the mortgaged chattel, his recovery is diminished by the amount of the debt.[122] And where a mortgagee sues a mortgagor for conversion of the mortgaged property, the measure of damages is the amount of the debt and interest[123] up to the value of the

[119] *Colorado*: Citizens' C. & C. Co. v. Stanley, 6 Colo. App. 181, 40 Pac. 693.

New York: Goulet v. Asseler, 22 N. Y. 225.

Wyoming: Cone v. Ivinson, 4 Wyo. 203, 35 Pac. 933.

[120] *Maine:* Welch v. Whittemore, 25 Me. 86; Googins v. Gilmore, 47 Me. 9, 77 Am. Dec. 246.

Massachusetts: Ayers v. Bartlett, 9 Pick. 156; Forbes v. Parker, 16 Pick. 462.

New York: Manning v. Monaghan, 28 N. Y. 585.

[121] Straw v. Jenks, 6 Dak. 414, 43 N. W. 941.

[122] *Alabama:* Street v. Sinclair, 71 Ala. 110.

Arkansas: McClure v. Hill, 36 Ark. 268; Jones v. Horn, 51 Ark. 19, 9 S. W. 309, 4 Am. St. Rep. 17.

Kentucky: Swigert v. Thomas, 7 Dana, 220.

Maine: Treat v. Gilmore, 49 Me. 34.

Massachusetts: Dahill v. Booker, 140 Mass. 308, 5 N. E. 496, 54 Am. Rep. 465.

Michigan: Bearss v. Preston, 66 Mich. 11; Rall v. Cook, 77 Mich. 681, 43 N. W. 1069.

Minnesota: Torp v. Gulseth, 37 Minn. 135.

Nebraska: Lusch v. Huber Mfg. Co., 79 Neb. 45, 112 N. W. 284.

New Hampshire: Kimball v. Marshall, 8 N. H. 291.

New York: Russell v. Butterfield, 21 Wend. 300.

Oregon: Swank v. Elwert, Or. , 105 Pac. 901.

England: Brierly v. Kendall, 17 Q. B. 937; Toms v. Wilson, 32 L. J. (N. S.) Q. B. 382, 4 B. & S. 442.

Upper Canada: McAulay v. Allen, 20 Up. Can. C. P. 417.

[123] *Colorado:* Perrigo G. M. & T. Co. v. Grimes, 2 Colo. 651.

property; [124] and the measure of recovery is the same against one who stands in place of the mortgagor, as his vendee or attaching creditor.[125]

In an action of trover by a mortgagee of chattels against one who had bought them from the mortgagor, the defendant may show, in diminution of the mortgagee's special interest in the property, that other property was embraced in the mortgage, and that the plaintiff has reduced the same to possession.[126] So in an action by the mortgagee of goods, against an officer who has taken a part of them out of his possession under an attachment against the mortgagor, the defendant may show in mitigation that the mortgagee has collected his debt out of the residue.[127]   On the other hand, where the mortgagee took possession of mortgaged property prematurely, and the mortgagor brought replevin, but the mortgagee's right to the property soon after vested, it was held that the mortgagor could only recover damages for detention of the property until the mortgagee's right to it became vested.[128]

The rule in this case is the same, whether the plaintiff is the

Illinois: Bailey *v.* Godfrey, 54 Ill. 507, 5 Am. Rep. 157.

Indiana: McFadden *v.* Hopkins, 81 Ind. 459.

New York: Parish *v.* Wheeler, 22 N. Y. 494; Hinman *v.* Judson, 13 Barb. 629.

Rhode Island: Warner *v.* Vallily, 13 R. I. 483.

South Carolina: Williams *v.* Dobson, 26 S. C. 110.

Wisconsin: Ward *v.* Henry, 15 Wis. 239; Lowe *v.* Wing, 56 Wis. 31.

[124] *Dakota:* Keith *v.* Haggart, 4 Dak. 438, 33 N. W. 465.

Illinois: Mantonya *v.* Martin E. O. Co., 172 Ill. 92, 48 N. E. 721.

Michigan: Ganong *v.* Green, 71 Mich. 1.

Minnesota: Deal *v.* Osborne, 42 Minn. 102.

Wisconsin: Smith *v.* Phillips, 47 Wis. 202.

[125] *California:* Sherman *v.* Finch, 71 Cal. 68.

Maryland: Albert *v.* Lindan, 46 Md. 334.

Massachusetts: Boyden *v.* Moore, 11 Pick. 362; Howe *v.* Bartlett, 8 All. 20.

Michigan: Ganong *v.* Green, 71 Mich. 1.

Minnesota: Becker *v.* Dunham, 27 Minn. 32.

Nebraska: Hamilton *v.* Lau, 24 Neb. 59.

New Hampshire: Carpenter *v.* Cummings, 40 N. H. 158.

South Carolina: Williams *v.* Dobson, 26 S. C. 110.

Texas: Boydston *v.* Morris, 71 Tex. 697.

Vermont: Chaffee *v.* Sherman, 26 Vt. 237.

Wisconsin: Clark *v.* Lamoreux, 70 Wis. 508.

[126] Bailey *v.* Godfrey, 54 Ill. 507.
[127] Ward *v.* Henry, 15 Wis. 239.
[128] Deal *v.* Osborne, 42 Minn. 102.

legal owner or not; but the reduction rests on different grounds
in the two cases. If the plaintiff has a lien only, his legal property is the lien, and he recovers damages for injury done to
that: if he is the legal owner of the property he would on general
principles be entitled to full damages, but to avoid circuity
of action the amount he recovers is reduced by the amount of
the defendant's interest.[129] If the plaintiff has neither legal
ownership nor lien, but only an equitable interest in the property, he can recover nothing for injury to the property: his recovery must be upon the contract between the parties.

§ 83. By the part owner of chattels.

Where the interest of the plaintiff is a particular estate or a
reversion in a chattel he can recover from one who injures the
property only to the extent that he is personally injured,
though he may be in possession; for his possession is for himself
alone, and he has no fiduciary relation with the other owners.
Thus the life-tenant of a chattel can recover, in an action for
injury to it, only the amount of injury done to his interest;[130]
and the remainder-man can recover compensation for the injury done to the reversion. In an instructive case of this sort [131]
stock was converted during the continuance of the life, and the
remainder-man brought action; but before trial the life-tenant
died. It was held that the measure of damages was the value
of the stock at the expiration of the life, not at the time of conversion. Where a party is entitled to recover on a bond as the
cestui que trust, he can recover only the amount of his interest,
although the obligee might have recovered for him a greater
sum.[132]

Where one of two joint owners sues for injury to the property
jointly owned, the defendant, though he neglect to plead in
abatement, may show that the plaintiff is only a part owner,

[129] *Kentucky:* Peck *v.* Inlow, 8 Dana 192.

New York: Parish *v.* Wheeler, 22 N. Y. 494, 511.

[130] *Alabama:* McGowen *v.* Young, 2 Stew. 160; Strong *v.* Strong, 6 Ala. 345.

Georgia: Russell *v.* Kearney, 27 Ga. 96.

Kentucky: Glascock *v.* Hays, 4 Dana, 58.

Mississippi: Lloyd *v.* Goodwin, 12 Sm. & M. 223.

[131] Caulkins *v.* Gas-Light Co., 85 Tenn. 683. 4 S. W. 287.

[132] Sweeney *v.* Lomme, 22 Wall. 208, 22 Led. 727.

and the plaintiff can then recover damages only in proportion to his interest.[133]   Since at law partners hold property simply as joint owners, one partner can recover from one who injures the partnership property his proportionate share of the full compensation, no matter whether the partnership is or is not solvent, and without regard to the state of the partnership accounts.[134]   Thus in an Illinois case the plaintiff, and one of the partners of the defendant's firm, purchased from the defendant a distillery business.   The stock was represented to be much more valuable than it really was.   The plaintiff and his partner gave their partnership notes for the amount.   The partner absconded.   It was held, that the plaintiff could only recover his proportion of the excess of the notes over the value of the property, although he had been obliged to pay all the notes.[135]

In these cases the possession is joint.   In tenancy in common the possession, instead of being in both owners, may be in one only.   If that is the case the part owner out of whose possession a chattel is wrongfully taken by a stranger recovers full compensation.[136]

Where one tenant in common sues another for an injury to the property, the damages are confined to the amount of the plaintiff's interest.[137]

---

[133] *Connecticut:* Hillhouse v. Mix, 1 Root, 246.

Maine: Jones v. Lowell, 35 Me. 538.

Maryland: Bailey v. Grimes, 27 Md. 440, 451.

Massachusetts: Thompson v. Hoskins, 11 Mass. 419; Bartlett v. Kidder, 14 Gray, 449; Sherman v. F. R. Iron Works Co., 5 All. 213.

Michigan: Michand v. Grace H. L. Co., 122 Mich. 305, 81 N. W. 93.

Minnesota: Peck v. McLean, 36 Minn. 228, 30 N. W. 754, 1 Am. St. Rep. 665.

New York: Zabriskie v. Smith, 13 N. Y. 322, 64 Am. Dec. 55, *n;* Green v. Edick, 66 Barb. 564.

Tennessee: Turnpike Co. v. Fry, 88 Tenn. 296, 12 S. W. 720.

Vermont: Chandler v. Stear, 22 Vt. 388.

Wisconsin: Lefebre v. Utler, 22 Wis. 189.

[134] *Maine:* Crabtree v. Clapham, 67 Me. 326.

New York: Walsh v. Adams, 3 Den. 125; Berry v. Kelly, 4 Robt. 106.

Pennsylvania: Foster v. Weaver, 118 Pa. 42.

[135] Schwabacker v. Riddle, 84 Ill. 517.

[136] *Arkansas:* Phillips v. Pennywit, 1 Ark. 59.

New Jersey: Hasbrouck v. Winkler, 48 N. J. L. 431.

[137] *Kansas:* Sayers v. Missouri Pac. Ry., 82 Kan. 123, 107 Pac. 641.

New Hampshire: Daniels v. Brown, 34 N. H. 454.

§ 83a. Interest of creditor in property fraudulently transferred.

When a transfer of personal property is set aside as fraudulent, and it appears that the property was pledged to secure a valid debt, and the fraudulent transferee has only received the surplus, the creditors recover the value of the property, deducting the amount of the debt, and equity has no power to award more by way of punishment.[138]

New York: Felts *v.* Collins, 73 N. Y. Supp. 796, 67 App. Div. 430.

[138] Hamilton Nat. Bank *v.* Halsted, 134 N. Y. 520, 31 N. E. 900.

Prima facie plaintiff may recover the full value of the property the burden being on the defendant to reduce recovery by showing the exact amount of the superior lien, Hamilton *v.* Phillips, 120 Ala. 177, 24 So. 587, 74 Am. St. Rep. 29.

CHAPTER V

ENTIRE AND PROSPECTIVE DAMAGES

§ 83b. Cause of action cannot be split.

A creditor cannot split a single obligation, so as to subject the debtor to two claims where only a single obligation was undertaken. Therefore an assignment of a portion of a claim is entirely inoperative, so far as the debtor is concerned, and he is under no obligation toward the partial assignee.[1] So when a permanent injury is done to land, and before recovery of damages the owner dies, the entire right to damages passes to the ex-

[1] *Illinois:* Chicago & N. W. Ry. v. Nichols, 57 Ill. 464.

Maine: National Exchange Bank v. McLoon, 73 Me. 498, 40 Am. Rep. 388.

Missouri: Loomis v. Robinson, 76 Mo. 488 (judgment); Fourth Nat. Bank v. Noonan, 88 Mo. 372.

New York: Secor v. Sturgis, 16 N. Y. 548.

Oregon: Little v. Portland, 26 Ore. 235, 37 Pac. 911.

With the consent of the debtor, of course, a partial assignment may be made, and it will then be binding on the debtor.

New York: Mills v. Garrison, 3 Keyes, 40.

Oregon: Little v. Portland, 26 Ore. 235, 37 Pac. 911.

ecutor or administrator, and the heir or devisee has no right to recover even for the permanent injury.[2]   The most important consequence of this principle is that a cause of action cannot be split.

§ 84. All damages for an injury must be recovered in a single action.

As a consequence of this general principle, a plaintiff must in a single suit recover, once for all, all damages sustained as a result of the injury for which he sues.[3]   So several suits cannot be brought for a single personal injury, even though new damage appear.   All the damage must be estimated in one action.[4]   The question was early considered by Lord Holt in a case of tort.[5]   The plaintiff declared for a battery, alleging that he had previously brought an action for it against the defendant, and recovered £11, and no more; and that afterward part of his skull, by reason of the said battery, came out of his head, and for this subsequent damage the suit was brought. The defendant pleaded the recovery in bar and demurrer. And Shower, *pro querente*, argued, "that if a consequence will take away an action, for the same reason it will give an action." But judgment was given for the defendant, the whole court being of opinion "that the jury, in the former action, considered the nature of the wound, and gave damages for all the damage that it has done the plaintiff."   The case was moved again, when Holt, C. J., said: "If this matter had been given in evidence as that which *in probability might have been* the consequence of the battery, the plaintiff would have *recovered damages for it*.   The injury, which is the foundation of the action, is the battery, and the greatness or consequence of that is only in *aggravation of damages*."

And where, in an action for breaches of a covenant, the

[2] Barton Coal Co. *v.* Cox, 39 Md. 1, 17 Am. Rep. 525.

[3] *Georgia:* Atlanta Elevator Co. *v.* Fulton B. & C. Mills, 106 Ga. 427, 32 S. E. 541.

New York: John D. Park & Sons Co. *v.* Hubbard, 198 N. Y. 136, 91 N. E. 261.

North Carolina: Eller *v.* Carolina & N. W. Ry., 140 N. C. 140, 52 S. E. 305, 3 L. R. A. (N. S.) 225; Sloan *v.* Hart, 150 N. C. 269, 63 S. E. 1037.

[4] Howell *v.* Goodrich, 69 Ill. 556.

[5] Fetter *v.* Beale, 1 Ld. Raym. 339. 692, s. c. 1 Salk. 11.

plaintiff was entitled to damages accruing subsequently to the bringing of the suit, but under the erroneous instruction of the court, damages to the time of the trial only were given, it was held that this afforded no ground for bringing another action for the same breaches.[6]

It thus appears that fresh damages merely will not give a fresh action, and a judgment in a suit founded on a single act of tort, will be a conclusive bar to a second suit for the same injury, although harmful consequences have made themselves apparent subsequent to the first suit; as it will be held that in the first verdict the plaintiff recovered all he was entitled to claim. Hence the statute of limitations runs from the time of the breach. So where the plaintiff sued the defendant on a contract made in 1810, to deliver spring wheat, alleging that the plaintiff had resold the wheat to one Shephard as spring wheat, but that it was in fact winter wheat, and that in consequence thereof it failed; hereupon Shephard sued the plaintiff, and recovered a judgment, which the plaintiff paid in 1818, and then brought this suit. The statute of limitations was pleaded, and the Court of King's Bench held it a good bar, saying that the breach of contract was the gist of the action, and that the special damage was stated merely as a measure of the damages resulting from that cause of action; and Bailey, J., said: "If the plaintiff had failed in proving the special damage in the case, it would not have been a ground of nonsuit." [7]

It makes no difference that the former partial recovery was due to a mistake of counsel [8] or an error of law of an inferior court,[9] or to a belief of the plaintiff at the time of the prior suit that defendant was unable to pay the full amount of the claim.[10]

§ 84a. Joinder of similar causes in a single suit.

Not only must all damages from a single injury be recovered in one action; where a series of similar injuries is inflicted, the plaintiff must sue in a single action for all such injuries inflicted

[6] Winslow *v.* Stokes, 3 Jones L. (N. C.) 285.

[7] Battley *v.* Faulkner, 3 B. & Ald. 288.

[8] Folsom *v.* Clemence, 119 Mass. 473.

[9] Stodghill *v.* Chicago, B. & Q. R. R., 53 Ia. 341; Baird *v.* U. S., 96 U. S. 430, 24 L. ed. 703.

[10] Bagot *v.* Williams, 3 B, & C. 235.

before the date of his writ. Thus where successive performances are called for in the same contract, and there were several breaches before the date of the writ, recovery must be had for all the breaches in a single action; and there can be no second recovery for any breach prior to the date of the former writ.[11] And so where a continuous tort has been committed, recovery must be had in one action for all acts prior to the date of the writ. Thus, in an action against a railroad for failing to fence, as a result of which plaintiff's stock was killed in 1885, it appeared that plaintiff had already recovered for stock killed in 1886; this was held to bar the later action.[12] The recovery for different injuries must of course be had upon different counts.[13]

§ 85. Entire damages for breach of contract.

Where there is a breach of a single indivisible contract, even though the performance of it calls for several distinct acts or series of acts, only one action can be maintained for the breach; and the entire damages must therefore be recovered in the action, and if this is not done the remainder can never be recovered.[14] And if there be a partial breach of a divisible contract, all the damages growing out of that particular breach must be recovered, and no part of them can be recovered in a subsequent action.[15] Where there is a single contract of employment, compensation for all services under it, though of different sorts and rendered at different times, must be recovered in a single action.[16] And where there is a running account for goods

[11] *Illinois:* Casselberry v. Forquer, 27 Ill. 170.

Indiana: Indiana, B. & W. Ry. v. Koons, 105 Ind. 507, 5 N. E. 549.

[12] Steiglider v. Missouri Pac. R. R., 38 Mo. App. 511.

[13] Pucket v. St. Louis, etc., Ry., 25 Mo. App. 650.

[14] *Alabama:* Campbell v. Hatchett, 55 Ala. 548 (action to recover rent).

Arkansas: Reynolds v. Jones, 63 Ark. 259, 38 S. W. 151 (use and occupation).

Minnesota: Geiser T. M. Co. v.

Farmer, 27 Minn. 428, 8 N. W. 141 (sale with warranty).

New York: Stevens v. Lockwood, 13 Wend. 644 (goods sold); Smith v. Jones, 15 Johns. 229 (goods sold).

Ohio: Stein v. Steamboat Prairie Rose, 17 Ohio St. 471, 93 Am. Dec. 631 (hire of barge for voyage); North British & Mercantile Ins. Co. v. Cohn, 17 Ohio Ct. Ct. 185 (policy of insurance).

[15] Crabtree v. Hagenbaugh, 25 Ill. 233, 79 Am. Dec. 324.

[16] *United States:* Hughes v. Dundee Mortgage Trust Investment Co., 26 Fed. 831 (attorney).

sold, all items prior to the date of the writ must be included in the recovery.[17]

§ 85a. Separate contracts.

If, however, the claims in the two suits are distinct, separate actions may be brought and successive recoveries had. This will always be the case, of course, in an action on a running account for items which accrued after the date of the prior action.[18] And there may be distinct accounts between the same parties, upon which separate actions may be brought.[19] Thus where an agent at various times sold different pieces of property for the plaintiff, a former recovery of the money obtained by selling a portion of the property would not bar a suit for money obtained for other property separately sold.[20] On this ground it was held that where plaintiff had been wrongfully discharged from service, and had sued and recovered damages for the breach of the contract, he might maintain another action for the wages which had accrued before the discharge; the claims being distinct.[21] And where in a former action on a contract of employment the recovery had by consent covered the period

Alabama: Oliver v. Holt, 11 Ala. 574, 46 Am. Dec. 228 (physician).

Georgia: Atlanta Elevator Co. v. Fulton Bag & Cotton Mills, 106 Ga. 427, 32 S. E. 541.

Missouri: Wagner v. Jacoby, 26 Mo. 532.

Pennsylvania: Logan v. Caffrey, 30 Pa. 196.

[17] *Kansas:* Bolen Coal Co. v. Whittaker Brick Co., 52 Kan. 747, 35 Pac. 810.

Minnesota: Memmer v. Carey, 30 Minn. 458, 15 N. W. 877.

North Carolina: Magruder v. Randolph, 77 N. C. 79.

Wisconsin: Borngesser v. Harrison, 12 Wis. 544.

[18] Avery v. Fitch, 4 Conn. 362.

[19] *Missouri:* Alkire Grocer Co. v. Tagart, 60 Mo. App. 389 (separate charges, different length of credit).

New York: Gentles v. Finck, 23 N. Y. Misc. 153, 50 N. Y. Supp. 726 (contracts for doing labor of different kinds

and at different prices on the same house); Secor v. Sturgis, 16 N. Y. 548 (distinct sales of goods from separate shops).

In the following cases the circumstances were held not to be sufficient to make the accounts distinct:

New York: Colvin v. Corwin, 15 Wend. 557 (sale of goods; deliveries from different offices at different times).

Pennsylvania: Buck v. Wilson, 113 Pa. 423, 6 Atl. 97 (different notes given as conditional payment).

Courts seem sometimes ready to find separate contracts on rather slight evidence.

Massachusetts: Badger v. Titcomb, 15 Pick. 409.

Ohio: Wren v. Winter, 6 Ohio Dec. 176.

[20] Sweeny v. Daugherty, 23 Iowa, 291.

[21] Perry v. Dickerson, 85 N. Y. 345, 39 Am. Rep. 663.

to the date of the trial, in a later action the plaintiff was allowed to recover damages subsequently accruing.[22]

§ 85b. Entire damages for a tort.

So where a tort is committed, and part of the damage has been recovered, the remainder cannot be recovered in a subsequent action.[23] If goods were converted at one time, a recovery for part of the goods will bar a subsequent action for the remainder;[24] if two libellous statements were contained in a single publication, recovery must be had in a single suit for both;[25] and if several animals are killed at the same time by the defendant railroad, separate actions cannot be maintained.[26] So where replevin had been brought for part of the goods, trespass cannot be maintained for the rest.[27] And where two actions are pending for different portions of the property taken, one must be dismissed as soon as judgment has been rendered in the other.[28]

[22] Flanders v. Canada, A. & P. S. S. Co., 161 Fed. 378. The court said that the cause of action was not so clearly indivisible that the parties could not split it by agreement.

[23] United States: Child v. Boston & F. I. Works, 19 Fed. 258 (infringement of patent).

Missouri: Darby v. Missouri, K. & T. Ry., 156 Mo. 391, 57 S. W. 550 (failure to maintain fence, resulting in injury to crop).

England: Furness, Withy & Co. v. Hall, 25 T. L. Rep. 233 (former recovery for delay in completing repairs on vessel; second action cannot be brought for costs of action by third person on account of delay).

[24] California: Herriter v. Porter, 23 Cal. 385.

Kansas: Westbrook v. Mize, 35 Kan. 299, 10 Pac. 881; Thisler v. Miller, 53 Kan. 515, 36 Pac. 1060.

Massachusetts: Folsom v. Clemence, 119 Mass. 473.

New York: Farrington v. Payne, 15 Johns. 432.

[25] New York: Galligan v. Sun Printing & Pub. Assoc., 25 N. Y. Misc. 355, 54 N. Y. Supp. 471.

England: Macdougall v. Knight, 25 Q. B. Div. 1.

[26] Indiana: Brannenburg v. Indianapolis, P. & C. R. R., 13 Ind. 103, 74 Am. Dec. 250.

Missouri: Binicker v. Hannibal & S. J. R. R., 83 Mo. 660.

But in Missouri Pac. R. R. v. Scammon, 41 Kan. 521, 21 Pac. 590, an action for killing stock, where a mare and colt strayed on the track at the same time, the colt was killed by the train, and the mare, after running ahead about 30 rods from where the colt was struck, was also struck, and recovery had already been had for killing the colt, an action was allowed for the killing of the mare. The court said that there was a difference of time and locality, and these make separate and distinct causes of action. This seems questionable.

[27] Funk v. Funk, 35 Mo. App. 246.

[28] Marble v. Keyes, 9 Gray (Mass.), 221.

This principle applies to all cases where the plaintiff might have had complete recovery in the former action, though the damages might have been held partly for the use of another; [29] as where he owned part of the property in his own right and part as trustee; [30] and the same is true where he owned part of the land injured and was a tenant of the rest. [31] But where he owned part of the goods absolutely and part as tenant in common he could and must bring separate actions, since he was not entitled to full compensation for the goods owned in common. [32]

§ 85c. Distinct torts.

Where the defendant commits two distinct torts, recovery may be had in separate actions; the damages recovered in each action being confined to those resulting from the tort in question. [33] So where the same accident resulted in damage to the plaintiff's person and to his property it is usually held that he may recover separately for the separate injuries, [34] though in a few jurisdictions it is held that there is but one cause of action. [35]

---

[29] Trask v. Hartford & E. R. R., 2 Allen (Mass.), 331.

[30] O'Neal v. Brown, 21 Ala. 482.

[31] Stickford v. St. Louis, 7 Mo. App. 217.

[32] Huffman v. Knight, 36 Ore. 581, 60 Pac. 207.

[33] *New York:* Brooks v. Rochester Ry., 156 N. Y. 244, 50 N. E. 945 (two distinct accidents; damages for second confined to injuries attributable to that one, including aggravation of first injury); Lee v. Kendall, 56 Hun, 610, 11 N. Y. Supp. 131 (obtaining at different times several pieces of property as result of same false representation).

Texas: Millikin v. Smoot, 71 Tex. 759, 10 Am. St. 814, 12 S. W. 59 (separate seizure on the same day of herd of stock horses from the range and of work horses from the stable.)

[34] *New York:* McAndrew v. Lake Shore & M. S. R. R., 7 Hun, 46; Reilly v. Sicilian Asphalt Paving Co., 170 N. Y. 40, 62 N. E. 772, 88 Am. St. 636.

Texas: Watson v. Texas & P. R. R., 8 Tex. Civ. App. 144, 27 S. W. 924.

Vermont: Newbury v. Connecticut & P. R. R. R., 25 Vt. 377.

England: Brunsden v. Humphrey, 11 Q. B. Div. 712, 14 Q. B. Div. 141.

So in *New Jersey:* Ochs v. Public Service Ry., 80 Atl. 495.

In Jackson v. Emmons, 19 D. C. App. Cas. 250, where there was an injury to plaintiff's wife on one day and plaintiff's house on another day by negligence in blasting, the blasting going on during successive days under a single permit, it was held that the two suits were separate and the suit for injury to wife might be barred by the statute although the later injury was not yet barred.

[35] *Massachusetts:* Doran v. Cohen, 147 Mass. 342, 17 N. E. 647.

Minnesota: King v. Chicago, M. & S. P. Ry., 80 Minn. 83, 82 N. W. 1113, 50 L. R. A. 161.

Missouri: Von Fragstein v. Windler, 2 Mo. App. 598.

And so where the representative of a deceased person has an action for his death by the defendant's wrongful act, and also for a destruction of his personal property by the same act, separate actions may be brought.[36]   And a husband, having recovered for personal injury to himself, may recover for an injury to his wife by the same act,[37] though he has but one cause of action for injury by the same act to his wife and child.[38] The same is true of personal injury to a partner and injury by the same act to partnership property.[39]   And so of successive injuries to real and personal property.[40]

When an injury is done to different portions of a single tract of land there can be but one recovery.[41]   The defendant obstructed a water course and so overflowed the plaintiff's land,

New Jersey: Ochs v. Public Service Ry., 80 N. J. L. 148, 77 Atl. 533.

In any jurisdiction injury to clothing worn on the person would probably be held not to be separate from injury to the person. See Bliss v. New York C. & H. R. R. R., 160 Mass. 447, 36 N. E. 65. The doctrine of the cases cited in the preceding note seems preferable.   In Birmingham S. Ry. v. Lintner, 141 Ala. 420, 38 So. 363, where the court held that damages to person and personal property might be recovered in a single suit, they intimated that, while the cases were distinguishable, they did not accept the doctrine that separate actions might be brought. Among the reasons for thinking the causes of action different are the following: 1. Negligence is no cause of action at all, and only becomes so when united with damage. 2. Different periods of limitation apply. 3. The right of action for injury to the person is not assignable; that for injury to property is assignable, and may be seized by creditors. This difficulty does not seem to exist in actions of trespass to land, because in them, the entry being proved, all subsequent injuries are treated as matters of aggravation (*post*, § 929).

But in trespass on the case, where negligence combined with damage is necessary to constitute the cause of action, there seems to be no escape from the reasoning of the English and the New York courts.

[36] *United States:* Peake v. Baltimore & O. R. R., 26 Fed. 495.

Ireland: Barnett v. Lucas, Ir. R. 6 C. L. 247.

[37] *Minnesota:* Skogland v. Minneapolis S. R. R., 45 Minn. 330, 47 N. W. 1071, 25 Am. St. Rep. 733.

Texas: St. Louis, I. M. & S. Ry. v. Edwards, 3 Tex. App. C. C. § 346; Texas & P. Ry. v. Nelson, 9 Tex. Civ. App. 156, 29 S. W. 78.

Vermont: Newbury v. Connecticut & P. R. R. R., 25 Vt. 377.

[38] Cincinnati & H. & D. R. R. v. Chester, 57 Ind. 297.

[39] Taylor v. Manhattan Ry., 53 Hun (N. Y.), 305.

[40] *Virginia:* Southside R. R. v. Daniel 20 Grat. 344.

Wisconsin: Hazen v. Casey, 30 Wis. 553.

[41] Lamm v. Chicago, etc., Ry., 45 Minn. 71, 47 N. W. 455, 10 L. R. A. 268; Pierro v. St. Paul & N. P. Ry., 39 Minn. 451.

which comprised a tract of half a section.   The plaintiff brought suit for the injury done to part of this land and recovered: he then brought another suit for the injury done another portion of the same half section.   It was held that he could recover nothing more; for he must recover in the first suit all the damage he suffered from the defendant's act.[42]   But where the injury was to different tracts of land, different recoveries could be had.[43]

§ 86. Damages for prospective loss.

Since all damages for an injury must be recovered in one suit, and the whole damage may not accrue at once, it follows that a plaintiff in an action must recover compensation not only for such loss as has already accrued, but also for such loss as he can with reasonable certainty show will accrue in future.

The principle of allowing prospective loss to be compensated was not always recognized.   "The general rule in personal actions," says Chief Baron Comyn, "is that damages are allowed only to the time of the action commenced." [44]   And though this statement, and the decisions which follow it, are directed rather to denying the right to bring in evidence of matters occurring after action brought than to setting the principles of recovery, they had the effect of denying recovery for prospective damages.[45]

In time, however, the right to recover prospective damages became fully established.   So in an action of assumpsit against an attorney for negligence, the Supreme Court of the United States said: "When the attorney was chargeable with negligence, his contract was violated, and the action might have been sustained immediately.   Perhaps, in that event, no more than nominal damages may be proved, and no more recovered; but, on the other hand, it is perfectly clear that the proof of actual damages may extend to facts that occur and grow out

[42] Wichita & W. R. R. v. Beebe, 39 Kan. 465.

[43] Illinois Cent. R. R. v. Wilbourn, 74 Miss. 284, 21 So. 1.

[44] Comyn's Digest, Damages, D.; see Pilfold's Case, 10 Coke, 115b.

[45] *Massachusetts:* Powers v. Ware, 4 Pick. 106; Pierce v. Woodward, 6 Pick. 206.

South Carolina: Duncan v. Markley, 1 Harp. 276.

England: Catherwood v. Caslon, 1 Car. & M. 431; Goslin v. Corry, 7 M. & G. 343; Charles v. Altin, 15 C. B. 46.

of the injury, even up to the day of the verdict." [46]   And the rule was also early recognized in Kentucky that loss accruing subsequent to the suit may be recovered, where the subsequent damages are the very incident or accessory of the principal thing demanded, and no action can be maintained for them.[47]

§ 86a. Damages accruing between time of action brought and trial.

It is now universally recognized that a loss that happens after action brought, as a direct consequence of the wrong for which the action was brought, may be compensated, though it had not happened or could not be foreseen when the action was brought.[48]   So in suits on the covenant of warranty and against incumbrances, the plaintiff may recover the amount fairly and justly advanced to remove the incumbrance, though paid after the suit begins; [49] and so in an action for personal injury, expenses of cure incurred after the bringing of the suit are allowed.[50]   So where the defendant wrongfully allowed water to overflow plaintiff's land, where it froze several feet deep, it was held that the plaintiff might recover for damages resulting from the melting of the ice in the spring, after action brought.[51] By the better view, any aggravation of an entry on land (as

---

[46] Wilcox v. Plummer, 4 Pet. 172, 182, 7 L. ed. 821.

[47] Trigg v. Northcut, Lit. Sel. Cas. (Ky.) 414.

[48] United States: Jones v. Allen, 85 Fed. 523, 527; Fort v. Union Pacific R. R., 2 Dill. 259.

Indiana: Pendergast v. M'Caslin, 2 Ind. 87.

Kentucky: Louisville & N. R. R. v. Gormley, Ky.   , 109 S. W. 346.

Maine: Gennings v. Norton, 35 Me. 308; Whitney v. Slayton, 40 Me. 224.

Maryland: Corner v. Mackintosh, 48 Md. 374.

Massachusetts: Hagan v. Riley, 13 Gray, 515.

Minnesota: Hayden v. Albee, 20 Minn. 159 (overflow complained of caused loss of trees after action brought).

Missouri: Williams v. Missouri Furnace Co., 13 Mo. App. 70.

New York: Filer v. N. Y. Central R. R., 49 N. Y. 42, 45.

North Carolina: Frisbee v. Marshall, 122 N. C. 760, 30 S. E. 21.

Texas: Coles v. Thompson, 7 Tex. Civ. App. 666, 27 S. W. 46.

See Nevada, Patchen v. Keeley, 19 Nev. 404, 14 Pac. 347.

[49] Massachusetts: Leffingwell v. Elliott, 10 Pick. 204; Brooks v. Moody, 20 Pick. 474.

New Hampshire: Dickey v. Weston, 61 N. H. 23.

[50] Illinois: Sturm v. Consolidated Coal Co., 248 Ill. 20, 93 N. E. 345.

New Hampshire: Hopkins v. A. & St. L. R. R., 36 N. H. 9.

[51] Chicago & N. W. Ry. v. Hoag, 90 Ill. 339.

by carrying away timber) which happens after action brought may be considered in damages.[52]

§ 86b. Prospective damages for torts.

This principle is applicable generally in actions of tort.[53] In a statutory action for the death of a human being, the plaintiff may recover compensation for the loss of future support.[54] So where the defendant was employed as an attorney, to investigate securities on which a loan was to be made, and it was alleged that he had neglected to use proper care, and that the securities had proved defective, that a large amount of interest was lost, and that probably a portion of the principal would be also lost; the statute of limitations was pleaded, and it appeared that the examination of the title took place in 1814, but that the insufficiency was not discovered till 1820, up to which time the interest was paid. It was insisted that the statute ran, not from the time when the insufficient security was taken, but from the period when the special damage alleged in the declaration—namely, the loss of interest—accrued. But the statute was held a good bar, and Holroyd, J., said: "If the action had been brought immediately after the insufficient security had been taken, the jury would have been bound to give damages for the *probable loss* which the plaintiff was likely to sustain from the invalidity of the security."[55] And the authority of this case was recognized in the Court of Chancery, by Mr. Vice-Chancellor Wigram.[56]

In Goodrich v. Dorset Marble Co.,[57] the defendant, by obstructing a stream, caused the water to overflow the plaintiff's

[52] Wolf v. Wolf, 158 Pa. 621, 28 Atl. 164.
But see Archibald v. Davis, 49 N. C. 133.
[53] Cook v. Redman, 45 Mo. App. 397 (trespass in April, grass destroyed continuously till November).
[54] *Kansas:* U. P. Ry. v. Dunden, 37 Kan. 1.
New York: Houghkirk v. Del. & Hudson Canal Co., 92 N. Y. 219, 44 Am. Rep. 370.
Vermont: Eames v. Brattleboro, 54 Vt. 471.

Wisconsin: Hoppe v. C., M. & St. P. Ry., 61 Wis. 357, 21 N. W. 227; Lawson v. C., St. P. M. & O. Ry., 64 Wis. 447, 24 N. W. 618, 54 Am. Rep. 634; Johnson v. C. & N. W. Ry., 64 Wis. 425, 25 N. W. 223.
[55] Howell v. Young, 5 B. & C. 259, 268; *acc.,* Gillon v. Boddington, 1 R. & M. 161.
[56] Smith v. Fox, 6 Hare, 386, 12 Jur. 130. See 12 Wms. Saund. 169.
[57] 60 Vt. 280; *acc.,* Mayor of Baltimore v. Merryman, 86 Md. 584, 39 Atl. 98.

meadow. It was held that he might recover compensation for a loss caused by the overflow, which did not become apparent until after the bringing of the action. So where the defendant negligently set fire to the plaintiff's grass-land, and the roots of the grass were destroyed, damages for the entire injury were held to be recoverable at once.[58]

§ 86c. Prospective damages for personal injury.

Prospective damages are frequently recovered in actions for personal injuries.[59] Thus in such actions the plaintiff may recover for permanent loss of earning power, which includes both the pecuniary loss he has sustained and that he is likely to sustain during the remainder of his life,[60] or for future pain or permanent physical injury.[61] In an action for loss of service, the

[58] Fort Worth & N. O. Ry. v. Wallace, 74 Tex. 581.

[59] *United States:* Washington & G. R. R. v. Harmon, 147 U. S. 571, 13 S. Ct. 557, 37 L. ed. 284.
Alabama: Bay Shore R. R. v. Harris, 67 Ala. 6.
Iowa: Russ v. Steamboat War Eagle, 14 Iowa, 363.
Kansas: Chicago, R. I./& P. Ry. v. Kennedy, 2 Kan. App. 693, 43 Pac. 802.
New York: Filer v. New York Cent. R. R., 49 N. Y. 42.
So in the case of a child, he may recover for impairment of earning capacity, though he cannot be affected by such damage until he comes of age. *Missouri:* Rosenkranz v. Lindell Ry., 108 Mo. 9, 17, 18 S. W. 890, 32 Am. St. Rep. 588.
Texas: Gulf, C. & S. F. Ry. v. Grisom, 36 Tex. Civ. App. 630, 82 S. W. 671.

[60] *Alabama:* Barbour Co. v. Horn, 48 Ala. 566.
California: Malone v. Hawley, 46 Cal. 409.
Delaware: Wallace v. Wilmington R. R., 8 Houst. 529, 18 Atl. 818.
Illinois: Chicago v. Jones, 66 Ill. 349; Chicago v. Elzeman, 71 Ill. 131.

Indiana: Pittsburgh, C. & St. L. Ry. v. Sponier, 85 Ind. 165; Ind. Car Co. v. Parker, 100 Ind. 181.
New York: Ayres v. Delaware, L. & W. R. R., 158 N. Y. 254, 53 N. E. 22; Sheehan v. Edgar, 58 N. Y. 631.
Pennsylvania: McLaughlin v. Corry, 77 Pa. 109, 18 Am. Rep. 432.
Vermont: Fulsome v. Concord, 46 Vt. 135.

[61] *Georgia:* Atlanta & W. P. R. R. v. Johnson, 66 Ga. 259.
Iowa: Russ v. Steamboat War Eagle, 14 Ia. 363; Wilberding v. Dubuque, 111 Ia. 484, 82 N. W. 957.
Kansas: Townsend v. Paola, 41 Kan. 591.
Kentucky: Alexander v. Humber, 86 Ky. 565.
Minnesota: Johnson v. Northern Pac. R. R., 47 Minn. 430, 50 N. W. 473.
Missouri: Gorham v. Kansas City & S. Ry., 113 Mo. 408, 20 S. W. 1060.
New York: Caldwell v. Murphy, 11 N. Y. 416; Curtis v. Rochester & S. R. R., 18 N. Y. 534; Filer v. New York C. R. R., 49 N. Y. 42: Strohm v. New York, L. E. & W. R. R., 96 N. Y. 305; Kane v. New York, N. H. & H. R. R., 132 N. Y. 160, 30 N. E. 256; Ayres v. Delaware, L. & W. R. R., 158 N. Y. 254, 53 N. E.

plaintiff may recover compensation for probable future loss during the continuance of the term of service.[62] So where one had let a slave for a specified time to another, from whose possession it was immediately taken by a third party, it was held, in Missouri, that the lessee might recover the value of the slave's services from the wrongdoer for the whole term, although the suit was brought before it had ended.[63] And in an action against a surgeon for negligence in healing the plaintiff's broken leg, the plaintiff may recover compensation for inability to use the leg in the future.[64]

§ 87. Prospective damages for breach of contract.

Where an agreement covers a long period and is broken, prospective damages for the whole time covered by the contract may be obtained.[65]

Thus in an action of covenant by trustees of a wife against the husband, on his covenant to pay off certain incumbrances within twelve months, although no special damage was laid or proved, it was held that the plaintiffs were entitled to a verdict for the whole amount of the incumbrances.[66] And where a tenancy at will is wrongfully terminated by the landlord, the tenant's damages are not restricted to the beginning of the suit, but he may recover such damages as are the direct result of his

22; Ganiard v. R. C. & B. R. R., 50 Hun, 22; Crank v. Forty-second St., M. & S. N. A. Ry., 53 Hun, 425.

Wisconsin: Birchard v. Booth, 4 Wis. 67.

Canada: Fox v. St. John, 23 N. B. 244.

Recovery may be had for future pain though it is not likely to be permanent. Haxton v. Kansas City, 190 Mo. 53, 88 S. W. 714.

[62] *Massachusetts:* Hatch v. Fuller, 131 Mass. 574.

New York: Drew v. Sixth Ave. R. R., 26 N. Y. 49; Plate v. N. Y. C. R. R., 37 N. Y. 472; Cuming v. B. C. R. R., 109 N. Y. 95.

Vermont: Whitney v. Clarendon, 18 Vt. 252, 46 Am. Dec. 150.

England: Hodsoll v. Stallebrass, 11 A. & E. 301.

[63] Moore v. Winter, 27 Mo. 380.

[64] Chamberlain v. Porter, 9 Minn. 260.

[65] *Florida:* Griffing Bros. Co. v. Winfield, 53 Fla. 589, 43 So. 687.

Iowa: Russell v. Polk County Abstract Co., 87 Iowa, 233, 54 N. W. 212, 43 Am. St. Rep. 381.

New York: Amerman v. Deane, 132 N. Y. 355, 30 N. E. 741; Crain v. Beach, 2 Barb. 120.

North Carolina: Wilkinson v. Dunbar, 149 N. C. 20, 62 S. E. 748.

England: Roper v. Johnson, L. R. 8 C. P. 167.

[66] Lethbridge v. Mytton, 2 B. & A. 772.

expulsion, up to the time when the tenancy might be lawfully determined.[67]

§ 88. Renewed injury requires a new action.

Both in contract and tort, where the injury for which suit has been brought is repeated, a new action must be brought to recover compensation for the new injury. No action can be brought to redress an injury before it happens; consequently no injury will be redressed which was inflicted after the date of the writ.[68] So, in slander, no evidence can be given of words spoken after the commencement of the action.[69]

The renewed injuries may consist of a series of similar acts, as, for instance, trespassing upon the plaintiff's land every day. In such a case each act is plainly a new injury, and successive actions must be brought in order to obtain redress. But the renewed injuries may be caused by a single continuing act, as, for instance, obstructing a stream and flowing the plaintiff's land. In such a case, if the right of the plaintiff continues to exist, each moment's continuance of the wrong is a new injury. "In the case of a personal injury, the act complained of is complete and ended before the date of the writ. It is the damage only which continues and is recoverable, because it is traced back to the act; while in the case of a nuisance it is the act which continues, or, rather, is renewed day by day. The duty which rests upon the wrongdoer to remove a nuisance causes a new trespass for each day's neglect." [70]

§ 89. Continuing or successive breaches of contract.

A single act of the defendant may be of such a nature as to give rise to a continuous breach of his contract with the plaintiff, which, however, the defendant may bring to a close by resuming performance. In such a case each moment during which the injury is allowed to continue is really a new breach;

[67] *Indiana:* Palmer *v.* Crosby, 1 Blackf. 139.

Massachusetts: Ashley *v.* Warner, 11 Gray, 43.

[68] *Kansas:* Haskell County Bank *v.* Bank of Santa Fe, 51 Kan. 39, 32 Pac. 624.

Mississippi: Gulf & C. Ry. *v.* Hartley, 88 Miss. 674, 41 So. 382.

[69] Root *v.* Lowndes, 6 Hill (N. Y.), 518; Keenholts *v.* Becker, 3 Den. (N. Y.) 346.

[70] Danforth, J., in Rockland Water Co. *v.* Tillson, 69 Me. 255, 268.

and if action is brought during the continuance of the injury, compensation can be recovered for such loss only as is caused before the beginning of the action.[71] So, on breach of contract not to engage in business in a certain place, compensation can be recovered only for loss suffered before the date of the writ.[72] So, on breach of contract to keep a gate in repair, damages are recoverable only to the date of the writ, and for disrepair after that time a new action may be brought.[73] Additional damage from the continued withholding of the conveyance of real estate sustained after the commencement of a suit for breach of a contract to convey it cannot be recovered in that action, but may in a subsequent one.[74]

In the same way a contract may call for the doing of several successive acts, so that there may be successive breaches; and in such a case compensation can be recovered only for such breaches as happened before action brought, and for subsequent breaches a new action will lie. Such a case is that of a contract performable in installments.[75]

§ 90. Damages recoverable for act destroying a contract.

The wrongful act of the defendant may be of such a nature as to put an end to the plaintiff's right at once, though the conse-

[71] *Illinois:* Lake Shore & M. S. Ry. v. Richards, 152 Ill. 59, 38 N. E. 773, 30 L. R. A. 33 (to weigh grain); Camp v. Morgan, 21 Ill. 255 (to furnish water for a pasture).

Indiana: Basler v. Nichols, 8 Ind. 260 (to cultivate land for two years).

Kansas: Curry v. Kansas & C. P. Ry., 58 Kan. 6, 48 Pac. 579, followed in Kansas & C. P. Ry. v. Curry, 6 Kan. App. 561, 51 Pac. 576 (to furnish plaintiff with a railroad pass during his life).

Kentucky: Keith v. Hinkston, 9 Bush 283 (to keep switch in repair and furnish cars).

New York: Miles v. Barton, 107 N. Y. Supp. 885 (payment of proportionate rate during time leased property was retained).

[72] *Illinois:* Just v. Greve, 13 Ill. App. 302.

Maine: Hunt v. Tibbets, 70 Me. 221.

[73] Beach v. Crain, 2 N. Y. 86, 49 Am. Dec. 369, n.

[74] Warner v. Bacon, 8 Gray (Mass.), 397, 69 Am. Dec. 253.

[75] *Alabama:* Ryall v. Prince, 82 Ala. 264, 2 So. 319 (debt payable in installments).

Massachusetts: Nathan v. Leland, 79 N. E. 793, 193 Mass. 576 (debt payable in installments).

Nebraska: Beck v. Devereaux, 9 Neb. 109, 2 N. W. 365 (monthly payments for goods sold).

South Carolina: Coggeshall v. Coggeshall, 2 Strobh. 51 (annual payments during life).

Tennessee: Coleman v. Hudson, 2 Sneed, 463 (certain number of cattle deliverable monthly); Barnes v. Coal Co., 101 Tenn. 354, 47 S. W. 498 (payments on a lease).

quence is a continuing one. In such a case compensation may be recovered at once for the whole loss.

Thus where a breach of contract, though of a sort to be regarded as a continuing one, so goes to the essence of the contract and destroys its object as to justify the plaintiff in considering the contract at an end, compensation may be recovered in one action for the entire loss. Whether or not a breach puts an end to the contract is, in case of doubt, a question of fact for the jury.[76] Where a defendant was sued on a contract to keep certain cattle-passes in repair, the court refused to allow prospective damages, since, if in the future the defendant should fail to repair, there would be a new injury and a new cause of action would accrue;[77] but in another case, where the contract was to repair machinery in a mill, it was held that entire damages could be recovered, both past and prospective,[78] for the facts showed that the contract could not be kept alive.

[76] Shaffer v. Lee, 8 Barb. (N. Y.) 412; Remelee v. Hall, 31 Vt. 582, 76 Am. Dec. 145.

In the following cases the breach was held to be entire, and damages were recovered for the whole contract:

Alabama: Mason v. Alabama Iron Co., 73 Ala. 270 (to furnish supplies for workmen doing certain work: no supplies furnished for preliminary work).

Kentucky: Standard Oil Co. v. Denton, 24 Ky. L. Rep. 906, 70 S. W. 282 (to keep retail dealer supplied with oil for five years; refusal to furnish any oil).

Massachusetts: Walton v. Ruggles, 180 Mass. 24, 61 N. E. 267 (to pay off a mortgage payable in installments; first installment unpaid); Speirs v. Union Drop Forge Co., 180 Mass. 87, 91, 61 N. E. 825 (to keep shop supplied with work for a year; failure to furnish work for several months).

Minnesota: Ennis v. Buckeye Pub. Co., 44 Minn. 105, 46 N. W. 314 (to print defendant's magazine for two years: contract cancelled); Bowe v. Minn. Milk Co., 44 Minn. 460, 47 N. W. 151 (by corporation, to take entire

production of milk for a year. Corporation was dissolved); Kalkhoff v. Nelson, 60 Minn. 284, 62 N. W. 332 (corporation agreed to make release, and was then dissolved).

New York: Crane v. Powell, 19 N. Y. Supp. 220 (to furnish board and lodging for a time certain).

Oregon: Salzgeber v. Mickel, 37 Ore. 216, 60 Pac. 1009 (wrongful termination of lease by notice to quit).

In Van Keuren v. Miller, 78 Hun, 173, 28 N. Y. Supp. 971, the plaintiff was to erect a building for defendant and was to receive a commission on the cost, with certain monthly payments. The plaintiff had previously sued before the termination of the work, and recovered partial compensation. The court held the contract entire, and that but one recovery should have been had; but the former action did not bar recovery because it was prematurely brought.

See *post,* §§ 636g et seq.

[77] Phelps v. N. H. & N. Co., 43 Conn. 453.

[78] Cooke v. England, 27 Md. 14, 19 Am. Dec. 618, n.

A breach of contract to support the plaintiff for life is often of such a nature that the plaintiff could not reasonably be expected to return and live with the defendant afterwards even if he were allowed to do so. In such a case the breach would be a total one, and the plaintiff could recover compensation for prospective as well as past loss.[79] So in the common case of a contract of service, the plaintiff may usually bring suit before the term of service expires and recover compensation for his whole loss.[80] And if he may do so, a subsequent suit as for wages accruing later is barred although in fact his recovery was for services up to the date of the writ.[81] In a few jurisdictions,

[79] *Indiana:* Shover v. Myrick, 4 Ind. App. 7, 30 N. E. 207.

Massachusetts: Amos v. Oakley, 131 Mass. 413; Parker *v.* Russell, 133 Mass. 74.

Michigan: Wright *v.* Wright, 49 Mich. 624.

New York: Schell *v.* Plumb, 55 N. Y. 592; Shaffer *v.* Lee, 8 Barb. 412; Empie *v.* Empie, 35 App. Div. 51, 54 N. Y. Supp. 402.

Oregon: Tippin *v.* Ward, 5 Ore. 450; Morrison *v.* McAtee, 23 Ore. 530, 2 Pac. 400.

In Paro *v.* St. Martin, 180 Mass. 29, 61 N. E. 268, plaintiff conveyed to defendant a lot of land on condition (contained in the deed) that he should maintain the plaintiff during life. The conveyance was subject to a mortgage which defendant agreed to pay. Defendant did not pay mortgage, and it was foreclosed and the security of the condition on which the land was conveyed was thereby lost. On plaintiff's suit he was allowed to recover the present value of his support during the rest of his life, that being less than the value of the land conveyed. If that agreement had been performed, plaintiff would have had the unincumbered land as security for the performance of the promise to support. By neglect of this the security was lost and the damage was the value of the security up to the amount of the debt.

A breach of the contract to support is not necessarily an entire breach. In a proper case the plaintiff recovers only to the date of the writ, and may bring action later for a continued breach.

Massachusetts: Fay *v.* Guynon, 131 Mass. 31.

New York: Carpenter *v.* Carpenter, 66 Hun, 177, 20 N. Y. Supp. 928.

See *post,* § 636*i.*

[80] *Indiana:* Richardson *v.* Eagle Machine Works, 78 Ind. 422, 41 Am. Rep. 584.

Maine: Sutherland *v.* Wyer, 67 Me. 64.

Maryland: Dugan *v.* Anderson, 36 Md. 567, 11 Am. Rep. 509.

New Hampshire: Lamoreux *v.* Rolfe, 36 N. H. 33.

Tennessee: East T., V. & G. R. R. *v.* Staub, 7 Lea, 397.

[81] *United States:* Pierce *v.* Tenn. Coal, Iron & R. Co., 173 U. S. 1, 19 Sup. Ct. 335, 43 L. ed. 591.

Indiana: Richardson *v.* Eagle Machine Works, 78 Ind. 422, 41 Am. Rep. 584.

Maine: Alie *v.* Nadeau, 93 Me. 282, 44 Atl. 891, 74 Am. St. Rep. 346.

Maryland: Olmstead *v.* Bach, 78 Md. 132, 27 Atl. 501, 2 L. R. A. 74, 44 Am. St. Rep. 273.

Mississippi: Williams *v.* Luckett, 77 Miss. 394, 26 So. 967.

Nebraska: Kahn *v.* Kahn, 24 Neb. 709, 40 N. W. 135.

however, he is allowed to sue from time to time as for wages continually accruing.[82]

§ 91. Continuing tort.

Just as a single wrongful act may give rise to an indefinite number of breaches of contract, so it may give rise to a continuous series of torts which can be brought to an end by the defendant discontinuing the act.

As stated above, a wrongful act may create a nuisance which will continue, and each moment of its continuance will be a new tort. If in such case action is brought, compensation can be had only for loss caused before the bringing of the action.[83] Thus in an action for flowing lands,[84] or for diverting [85] or pol-

New York: Waldron v. Hendrickson, 40 App. Div. 7, 57 N. Y. Supp. 561.

Ohio: James v. Allen County, 44 Ohio St. 226, 6 N. E. 246.

[82] *United States:* Schroeder v. California Y. T. Co., 95 Fed. 296.

Minnesota: McEvoy v. Bock, 37 Minn. 402, 34 N. W. 740.

Wisconsin: Gordon v. Brewster, 7 Wis. 355.

[83] *Colorado:* Denver C., I. & W. Co. v. Middaugh, 12 Colo. 434, 21 Pac. 565, 13 Am. St. Rep. 234.

South Carolina: Duncan v. Markley, 1 Harper, 276.

Wisconsin: Cobb v. Smith, 38 Wis. 21; Stadler v. Grieben, 61 Wis. 500.

In North Carolina by interpretation of a provision of the code it has been held that in a case of continuing trespass damages may be recovered to the time of trial; but this is recognized to be a departure from the common law. Pearson v. Carr, 97 N. C. 194; Dailey v. Dismal Swamp Canal Co., 2 Ired. L. 222.

In Carmichael v. City of Texarkana, 94 Fed. 561, 575, the time of the *decree* is referred to as the limit, but no reason is given by the court.

In Marlborough v. Sisson, 31 Conn. 332, defendant wrongfully brought a pauper into plaintiff town and left him

there. Plaintiff sued defendant and recovered damages, including expenses up to time of judgment. They called upon defendant to remove the pauper, which defendant did not do. A new suit was now brought for damages accruing subsequently. It was held that plaintiff could recover, the causes of action being distinct.

[84] *Alabama:* Polly v. McCall, 1 Ala. Sel. Cas. 246, 37 Ala. 20.

Georgia: Savannah & O. C. Co. v. Bourquin, 51 Ga. 378.

Massachusetts: Aldworth v. Lynn, 153 Mass. 53, 26 N. E. 229.

Mississippi: Mississippi Cent. R. R. v. Magee, 93 Miss. 196, 46 So. 716.

Missouri: Benson v. Chicago & A. R. R., 78 Mo. 504.

Tennessee: Nashville v. Comar, 88 Tenn. 415; Chattanooga v. Dowling, 101 Tenn. 342, 47 S. W. 700.

[85] *Illinois:* Greenup v. Stoker, 7 Ill. 688.

Kentucky: Langford v. Owsley, 2 Bibb, 215.

Maine: Dority v. Dunning, 78 Me. 381.

North Carolina: Shaw v. Etheridge, 3 Jones L. 300.

Pennsylvania: Irving v. Media, 10 Pa. Super. Ct. 132.

luting [86] a water course, or for other nuisance,[87] compensation can be had only for loss accruing before the date of the writ; and the same is true in the case of an action for wrongfully placing a structure on the plaintiff's land,[88] or other trespass,[89] and for recovery of rents and profits against a disseizor.[90]

So in an early action on the case, where the plaintiff declared for procuring his apprentice to depart from his service, and for the loss of his service for the whole residue of the term of his apprenticeship, and the jury assessed damages generally, judgment was arrested, because it appeared that the term was not expired at the commencement of the suit.[91]

In New York, in an action to recover damages for enticing the plaintiff's son away, and inducing him to enlist in the army for three years, as a substitute for the defendant, it was held by the Supreme Court that the plaintiff could only recover to the time of the commencement of the action, or at most to the time of the trial.[92]

So in an action for enticing an apprentice where it appeared that the apprentice was still in the neighborhood, it was held in North Carolina that damages could be recovered only to the date of the writ.[93]

Where, however, an action is brought to abate a nuisance, and the nuisance is in fact abated before the trial, damages are given up to the time the nuisance was abated, and not merely to

[86] *Kentucky:* Kinnaird v. Standard Oil Co., 89 Ky. 468, 25 Am. St. Rep. 545, 7 L. R. A. 451, 12 S. W. 937.

New York: Whitmore v. Bischoff, 5 Hun, 176.

Pennsylvania: Sanderson v. Pa. Coal Co., 102 Pa. 370.

[87] *Missouri:* Beauchamp v. Taylor, 132 Mo. App. 92, 111 S. W. 609 (obstructing water course).

New Jersey: Delamarre v. Bott, 78 N. J. L. 234, 73 Atl. 74 (obstructing drain).

Texas: Sanders v. Miller, 113 S. W. 996, 52 Tex. Civ. App. 372 (maintaining stagnant pool).

[88] *Maine:* Esty v. Baker, 48 Me. 495; Russell v. Brown, 63 Me. 203.

New York: Stowers v. Gilbert, 156 N. Y. 600, 51 N. E. 282.

England: Holmes v. Wilson, 10 A. & E. 503.

[89] *Alabama:* Louisville & N. R. R. v. Higginbotham, 44 So. 872, 153 Ala. 334 (pumping water from plaintiff's spring).

District of Columbia: Cooper v. Sillers, 30 App. D. C. 567 (making improper use of party wall).

[90] Larrabee v. Lumbert, 36 Me. 440.

[91] Hambleton v. Veere, 2 Saund. 169; acc., Lewis v. Peachy, 1 H. & C. 518.

[92] Covert v. Gray, 34 How. Pr. (N. Y.) 450 (recovery should clearly not be allowed to time of trial).

[93] Moore v. Love, 3 Jones (N. C.) L. 215.

the date of the writ, although the tort was a continuing one.[94] This is probably because the action is essentially a real action, the abatement being the principal relief, and the award of damages being merely incidental.

§ 92. By trespass on plaintiff's land.

Where injury is caused by a continuous trespass on the plaintiff's land, since the defendant cannot remedy the wrong without another trespass, the injury is not continuing, but inflicted once for all, and full compensation is to be recovered in one action. So where the defendant made an excavation in the plaintiff's land, the entire damage was awarded in a single action.[95] Where the defendant broke through into the plaintiff's mine, which afterwards was flooded through the breach, it was held that the entire damage must be recovered in one action;[96] and the same decision was reached where the defendant wrongfully filled up the plaintiff's pond,[97] and where he threw up an embankment on the plaintiff's land, wrongfully claiming that it was a highway.[98]

But where the trespass is committed by constantly repeated acts of the defendant, recovery may be allowed from time to time; as for instance against a railroad running its trains over the land,[99] or against one who in blasting repeatedly injures plaintiff's house.[100]

§ 93. By unauthorized private structure or use of land.

If a private structure or other work on land is the cause of a nuisance or other tort to the plaintiff the law cannot regard it as permanent, no matter with what intention it was built; and

---

[94] *Texas:* Comminge v. Stevenson, 76 Tex. 642.

England: Fritz v. Hobson, 14 Ch. D. 542.

[95] *Kansas:* Kansas P. Ry. v. Mihlman, 17 Kan. 224.

England: Clegg v. Dearden, 12 Q. B. 576.

[96] *Michigan:* National Copper Co. v. Minn. Mining Co., 57 Mich. 83.

New Jersey: Lord v. Carbon Iron Mfg. Co., 42 N. J. Eq. 157.

Ohio: Williams v. Pomeroy Coal Co., 27 Oh. St. 583.

[97] Finley v. Hershey, 41 Ia. 389.

[98] Ziebarth v. Nye, 42 Minn. 541, 44 N. W. 1027.

[99] Savannah, etc., R. R. v. Davis, 25 Fla. 917, 7 So. 29.

[100] *District of Columbia:* Jackson v. Emmons, 25 App. D. C. 146.

New York: Morgan v. Bowers, 17 N. Y. Supp. 22.

damages can therefore be recovered only to the date of the action.[101] So where a stream is wrongfully obstructed by a private embankment, dam or canal, the plaintiff injured by it can recover compensation only to the date of the writ.[102] So in an action for obstructing the plaintiff's lights the plaintiff can recover only to the date of the writ;[103] and the same is true where the defendant wrongfully filled a canal,[104] flowed the plaintiff's land,[105] erected a building which was a nuisance,[106] laid out a highway wrongfully around the plaintiff's toll-gate, thus depriving the plaintiff of tolls.[107]

In one case, however, where the defendant on his own land maintained a "dirt dump," consisting of waste from his mine, which was a nuisance, it was held that the plaintiff might elect

[101] *Georgia:* Farley v. Gate City G. L. Co., 105 Ga. 323, 31 S. E. 193.

Illinois: Joseph Schlitz Brewing Co. v. Compton, 142 Ill. 511, 32 N. E. 693 (casting water on land from eaves of adjacent building).

West Virginia: Hargreaves v. Kimberly, 26 W. Va. 787 (pollution of atmosphere).

But where in an action for obstructing plaintiff's right of way by a building permanent damages had been recovered in a former action, it was held impossible to maintain a second action. Hodge v. Shaw, 85 Ia. 137, 52 N. W. 9, 29 Am. St. Rep. 290.

[102] *Illinois:* Chicago, B. & Q. R. R. v. Schaffer, 26 Ill. App. 280.

Kentucky: Langford v. Owsley, 2 Bibb, 215.

Maine: Williams v. Camden and Rockland Water Co., 79 Me. 543.

Missouri: Van Hoozier v. Hannibal & St. J. R. R., 70 Mo. 145; Dickson v. Chicago, etc., R. R., 71 Mo. 575.

New York: Phillips v. Terry, 3 Keyes, 313; Uline v. New York C. & H. R. R. R., 101 N. Y. 98, 4 N. E. 536; Duryea v. Mayor, 26 Hun, 120.

Ohio: Thayer v. Brooks, 17 Oh. 489.

Pennsylvania: Bare v. Hoffman, 79 Pa. 71, 21 Am. Rep. 42.

Texas: Galveston, H. & S. A. Ry. v. Norsky, 2 Tex. Civ. App. 545, 21 S. W. 1011.

West Virginia: Rogers v. Coal, R. B. & D. Co., 39 W. Va. 272, 19 S. E. 401.

[103] *Kansas:* Union Trust Co. v. Cuppy, 26 Kan. 754.

New York: Blunt v. McCormick, 3 Den. 283.

North Carolina: Spilman v. Roanoke Nav. Co., 74 N. C. 675.

Wisconsin: Winchester v. Stevens Point, 58 Wis. 350.

Canada: Pugsley v. Ring, Cass. Can. Dig. 138.

[104] *Maine:* Cumberland & Oxford Canal v. Hitchings, 65 Me. 140.

West Virginia: Watts v. Norfolk & W. R. R., 39 W. Va. 196, 19 S. E. 521.

[105] *Georgia:* Danielly v. Cheeves, 94 Ga. 263, 21 S. E. 524.

West Virginia: Hargreaves v. Kimberly, 26 W. Va. 787.

[106] Barrick v. Schifferdecker, 48 Hun (N. Y.), 355.

[107] Cheshire Turnpike Co. v. Stevens, 13 N. H. 28.

to treat the nuisance as permanent and to recover entire damages.[108]

§ 93a. By causing land to fall.

An excavation by the owner of land is not a tort, but causing another's land to fall by such an excavation is a tort. So where one excavation causes land to fall several times, each fall is a separate tort, and action may be brought for it.[109] But all the damages caused by one fall must be recovered in a single action.[110]

But where the plaintiff has an easement of support for its structure in the defendant's land, and the defendant by his excavation causes the structure to fall, the injury caused by the excavation is committed once for all, and entire damages may be recovered for it, since the structure has been destroyed.[111] If, however, the structure was not destroyed by the first fall, a new action may be brought for damages caused by a subsequent fall.[112]

The right of support at common law, irrespective of negligence, is a right to the support of the land in its natural state, without buildings; and action can be brought only if the land

---

[108] Risher v. Acken Coal Co., Ia. , 124 N. W. 764.

[109] *New Jersey:* McGuire v. Grant, 25 N. J. L. (1 Dutch.) 356, 67 Am. Dec. 49.

South Dakota: Ulrick v. Dakota Loan & Trust Co., 2 S. D. 285, 49 N. W. 1054.

England: Mitchell v. Darley Main Colliery Co., 14 Q. B. Div. 125, 11 App. Cas. 127, overruling Lamb v. Walker, 3 Q. B. D. 389.

Canada: Snarr v. Granite Curling and Skating Co., 1 Ont. 102.

In Pennsylvania the doctrine of the earlier English cases, that the injury takes place when the support is removed, and all damages must then be recovered, appears to be adopted. Noonan v. Pardee, 200 Pa. 474, 50 Atl.

255, 55 L. R. A. 410, 86 Am. St. Rep. 722.

Nevertheless if the removal of underground support causes different portions of the land to fall successively, it has been held that different actions could be brought, though not for successive falls of the same portion. Pantall v. Rochester & P. C. & I. Co., 204 Pa. 158, 53 Atl. 751, 18 Pa. Super. Ct. 341

[110] *Missouri:* Williams v. Missouri Furnace Co., 13 Mo. App. 70.

Pennsylvania: Pantall v. Rochester & P. C. & I. Co., 18 Pa. Super. Ct. 341, 53 Atl. 751, 204 Pa. 158.

[111] *Maine:* Rockland Water Co. v. Tillson, 69 Me. 255.

Michigan: Conlon v. McGraw, 66 Mich. 194.

[112] McConnel v. Kibbe, 33 Ill. 175, 85 Am. Dec. 265.

in its natural state would have fallen,[113] unless the defendant becomes liable through negligence.[114]

§ 94. For tort causing permanent injury.

The chief difficulty in this subject concerns acts which result in what effects a permanent change in the plaintiff's land, and is at the same time a nuisance or trespass. The subject is one which has become of much importance in the last few years, in connection with the construction of railroads and great public works.

Courts of the highest authority have differed on the question. It is urged on the one hand, with much propriety, that the law will not proceed upon the assumption that a nuisance or illegal conduct will continue forever, and therefore that entire damages will not be given, as for a permanent injury, no matter how lasting it seems destined to be. On the other hand, it is urged that the law will not allow the unnecessary multiplication of suits, and will if possible settle the entire controversy in a single suit; and that if the injury is proved with reasonable certainty to be permanent, damages should be allowed for the whole loss, past and future. If this view is adopted it is to be noted that as a result the defendant will by satisfaction of the judgment acquire a right to do the act previously wrongful; but this is no anomaly, for the same is true, for instance, on satisfaction of a judgment in an action of trover for refusal to deliver a chattel, which is of a very analogous nature.

§ 95. For injury caused by lawful permanent structure or use of land.

If the injury is caused by erecting a structure or making a use of land which the defendant has a right to continue, the injury is regarded as committed once for all, and action must be brought to recover the entire damage, past and future.

[113] *United States:* Transportation Co. v. Chicago, 99 U. S. 635, 640, 25 L. ed. 336.

Massachusetts: Thurston v. Hancock, 12 Mass. 220.

New York: White v. Nassau Trust Co., 168 N. Y. 149, 61 N. E. 1135; Lasala v. Holbrook, 4 Paige, 169, 25 Am. Dec. 524.

England: Wyatt v. Harrison, 1 B. & Ad. 871.

[114] Bohrer v. Dienhart Harness Co., 19 Ind. App. 489, 49 N. E. 296.

So in Stodghill *v.* Chicago, Burlington & Quincy Railroad [115] the Supreme Court of Iowa said: "When a nuisance is of such character that its continuance is necessarily an injury, and that when it is of a permanent character that will continue without change from any cause but human labor, the damage is original and may be at once fully estimated and compensated; . . . . successive actions will not lie. The damages being entire and susceptible of immediate recovery, plaintiff could not divide his claim and maintain successive actions. . . . It was the duty of plaintiff to have excepted and appealed."

A typical instance is an action against a railroad company for a nuisance caused by its embankment or other permanent structure. In such case, when the Constitution permits recovery, the great weight of authority is to the effect that the injured party may, and therefore must, recover compensation in one action for the entire loss. [116] And where the building and operation of the railroad produces a nuisance, as by polluting the air by smoke, or by obstructing a street by its tracks lawfully located, the rule is generally held to be the same. [117] In

[115] 53 Ia. 341; *acc.*, Van Orsdol *v.* B. C. R. & N. Ry., 56 Ia. 470; Fowler *v.* Des Moines & K. C. Ry., 91 Ia. 533, 60 N. W. 116.

[116] *Alabama:* Highland A. B. R. R. *v.* Matthews, 99 Ala. 24, 10 So. 267.

Colorado: Denver, T. & F. W. Ry. *v.* Pulaski I. D. Co., 19 Colo. 367, 35 Pac. 910.

Florida: Jacksonville, T. & K. W. Ry. *v.* Lockwood, 33 Fla. 573, 15 So. 327.

Illinois: Chicago & E. I. R. R. *v.* Loeb, 118 Ill. 203, 8 N. E. 460, and cases cited; Kankakee & S. R. R. *v.* Horan, 131 Ill. 288, 23 N. E. 621; Centralia *v.* Wright, 156 Ill. 561, 41 N. E. 217; Hart *v.* Wabash S. R. R., 238 Ill. 336, 87 N. E. 367, affirming 143 Ill. App. 503.

Indiana: Indianapolis, B. & W. Ry. *v.* Eberle, 110 Ind. 542; Elkhart & W. R. R. *v.* Waldorf, 17 Ind. App. 29, 46 N. E. 88.

Kentucky: Elizabethtown, L. & B.

S. R. R. *v.* Combs, 10 Bush, 382, 19 Am. Rep. 67; Fidelity Tr. Co. *v.* Shelbyville W. & L. Co., 33 Ky. L. Rep. 202, 110 S. W. 239; Board of Park Comrs. *v.* Donahue, Ky. , 131 S. W. 285.

Massachusetts: Fowle *v.* New Haven & N. R. R., 112 Mass. 334.

Nebraska: Gartner *v.* Chicago, R. I. & P. R. R., 71 Neb. 444, 98 N. W. 1052.

New Hampshire: Troy *v.* Cheshire R. R., 23 N. H. 83, 55 Am. Dec. 177.

Canada: Knapp *v.* Great W. Ry., 6 Up. Can. C. P. 187. So in case of the erection of a dock: Rust *v.* Victoria Graving Dock Co., 36 Ch. Div. 113.

In Texas if the structure is such as to cause damage only at times, separate actions may be brought for each injury, but if the damage produced is continuous and permanent, the plaintiff must obtain the redress in one action. Missouri, K. & T. R. R. *v.* Graham, 33 S. W. 576, 12 Tex. Civ. App. 54.

[117] *Illinois:* Chicago & E. I. R. R. *v.*

some cases it is held that the plaintiff *may* recover prospective damages, treating the injury as a permanent one;[118] and this election is not infrequently allowed in case of intermittent injury as by successive floods.[119] But if he may, it is clear that he must.[120] Where, however, the company can institute condemnation proceedings, and especially if such proceedings have actually been instituted since the bringing of the action,[121] it has been held that damages in the action of trespass can be recovered only to the date of the writ.[122] In a few States it is held that even a nuisance caused by a permanent railroad structure is continuous, and compensation can be recovered only for loss to the date of the action.[123] Of course, if the struc-

Loeb, 118 Ill. 203, 8 N. E. 460, 59 Am. Rep. 341, *n.*

Indiana: Porter v. Midland Ry., 125 Ind. 476, 25 N. E. 556.

Iowa: Cadle v. Muscatine W. R. R., 44 Ia. 11.

Kentucky: Jeffersonville, M. & I. R. R. v. Esterle, 13 Bush, 667; Covington & C. E. Ry. v. Kleymeier, 105 Ky. 609, 49 S. W. 484; Chesapeake & O. Ry. v. Gross, 19 Ky. L. Rep. 1926, 43 S. W. 203.

[118] *Kansas:* Central B. U. P. R. R. v. Andrews, 26 Kan. 702; Wichita & W. R. R. v. Fechheimer, 36 Kan. 45.

Virginia: Virginia Hot Springs Co. v. McCray, 106 Va. 461, 56 S. E. 216, 10 L. R. A. (N. S.) 465.

[119] *Arkansas:* St. Louis, I. M. & S. Ry. v. Biggs, 52 Ark. 240, 12 S. W. 331, 6 L. R. A. 804, 20 Am. St. Rep. 176.

Illinois: Strange v. Cleveland, C., C. & St. L. Ry., 245 Ill. 246, 91 N. E. 1036.

Iowa: Harvey v. R. R., 129 Iowa, 476, 105 N. W. 958, 3 L. R. A. (N. S.) 973, 113 Am. St. Rep. 483; Hughes v. Chicago, B. & O. Ry., 141 Ia. 273, 119 N. W. 924.

Virginia: American Locomotive Co. v. Hoffman, 108 Va. 363, 61 S. E. 759.

[120] *California:* Beronio v. Southern Pacific R. R., 86 Cal. 415, 21 Am. St. Rep. 57, 24 Pac. 1093.

Illinois: Galt v. Chicago & N. W. Ry., 157 Ill. 125, 140, 41 N. E. 643.

Nebraska: Gartner v. Chicago, R. I. & P. R. R., 71 Neb. 444, 98 N. W. 1052.

Texas: International & G. N. Ry. v. Gieselman, 12 Tex. Civ. App. 123, 34 S. W. 658.

So now by statute in North Carolina. Ridley v. Seaboard A. L. R. R., 124 N. C. 34, 32 S. E. 379.

[121] *Indiana:* Anderson, L. & St. L. R. R. v. Kernodle, 54 Ind. 314.

South Carolina: Woodstock, H. & S. M. Co. v. Charleston L. & W. Co., 84 S. C. 306, 63 S. E. 548.

Wisconsin: Sherman v. Milwaukee, L. S. & W. R. R., 40 Wis. 645.

[122] Callanan v. Port Huron & N. W. Ry., 61 Mich. 15.

[123] *Michigan:* Addison F. M. Co. v. Lake Shore & M. S. Ry., 160 Mich. 330, 125 N. W. 347, 16 Det. L. N. 1075 (explaining Harper v. Detroit, 110 Mich. 427, 68 N. W. 265, and Keyser v. Lake Shore & M. S. Ry., 142 Mich. 143, 105 N. W. 143).

Minnesota: Lamm v. Chicago, St. P., M. & O. Ry., 45 Minn. 71, 47 N. W. 455.

Nebraska: Omaha & R. V. R. R. v. Standen, 22 Neb. 343.

New York: Uline v. New York C. & H. R. R. R., 101 N. Y. 98, 4 N. E. 536, 54 Am. Rep. 657, following a long line

11

ture or the use of it is unauthorized by law, it is not to be supposed permanent, and compensation is recovered only for loss to date of writ.[124]

Where any other lawful work of a permanent nature causes injury to the plaintiff for which he may recover, the rule is the same, and he must recover all his damages in one action. So damages for the enlargement of a public canal [125] or for constructing a sewer [126] or a culvert through a railway embankment [127] must be recovered in a single action.[128]

If a permanent work rightfully done by public authority is

of New York cases. In Pond v. Met. El. Ry., 112 N. Y. 186, 19 N. E. 487, 8 Am. St. Rep. 734, the court seemed to regret that the law was so established by authority, and the rule is practically neutralized by allowing a petition for injunction to be inserted, making it an equitable action; damages are then given to the time of trial, and the defendant is required to give reasonable compensation for the future or to be enjoined, as in Henderson v. New York C. R. R., 78 N. Y. 423, or by allowing the parties to agree upon damages for the whole period, as in Lahr v. Met. El. R. R., 104 N. Y. 268. Uline v. N. Y. C. & H. R. R. R. is followed in the later cases: Ottenot v. New York, L. & W. Ry., 119 N. Y. 603, 23 N. E. 169. This whole subject is discussed at length in a later chapter in connection with the rules relating to condemnation proceedings.

[124] *Iowa:* Frith v. Chicago, D. & M. Ry., 45 Ia. 406; Cain v. C., R. I. & P. Ry., 54 Ia. 255.

Kansas: Interstate C. R. T. Ry. v. Early, 46 Kan. 197, 26 Pac. 422; Chicago, K. & W. R. R. v. Union I. Co., 51 Kan. 600, 33 Pac. 378; Ottawa, O. C. & C. G. R. R. v. Peterson, 51 Kan. 604, 33 Pac. 606.

Maine: Attwood v. Bangor, 83 Me. 582, 22 Atl. 466.

Minnesota: Adams v. H. & D. R. R., 18 Minn. 260.

Tennessee: Harmon v. L. N. O. & T. R. R., 87 Tenn. 614.

Wisconsin: Ford v. Chicago & N. W. R. R., 14 Wis. 609, 80 Am. Dec. 791; Carl v. Sheboygan & F. R. R., 46 Wis. 625.

[125] Queen v. Hubert, 14 Can. 737.

[126] *Kentucky:* Maysville v. Stanton, 14 S. W. 675.

Missouri: Kellogg v. Kirksville, 149 Mo. App. 1, 129 S. W. 57 (pollution of stream by sewer).

[127] *Kansas:* Kansas P. Ry. v. Mihlman, 17 Kan. 224.

Canada: Patterson v. G. W. Ry., 8 Up. Can. C. P. 89.

[128] *Illinois:* Centralia v. Wright, 156 Ill. 561, 41 N. E. 217 (waterworks).

Indiana: Lafayette v. Nagle, 113 Ind. 425, 15 N. E. 1 (change of grade of highway).

Iowa: Hempstead v. Des Moines, 63 Iowa, 36, 18 N. W. 676 (change of grade of highway); Bizer v. Ottumwa Hydraulic P. Co., 70 Iowa, 145, 30 N. W. 172 (dam).

Maryland: Baltimore v. Merryman, 86 Md. 584, 39 Atl. 98 (dam).

Where an electric light plant, the operation of which permanently injures adjoining land, is built by one and then sold to and operated by another, but one suit for damages, both past and prospective, may be maintained, and both may be sued jointly. Hyde Park T. H. E. L. Co. v. Porter, 167 Ill. 276, 47 N. E. 206.

yet so negligently done as to cause continuing injury to the plaintiff, it is to be supposed that the negligence will be remedied, and the plaintiff can therefore recover only for loss to the date of his writ.[129]   And so where the plan of the work is such that the defendant is committing the nuisance only temporarily, the same is true.   Thus where a city committed a nuisance by discharging its sewage near plaintiff's land, but the plan adopted by the city contemplated a discharge in another place, and the discharge near the plaintiff's land was temporary, he was held entitled to maintain successive actions.[130]

[129] *Alabama:* Eufaula *v.* Simmons, 86 Ala. 515.

Illinois: Fields *v.* Johnston, 143 Ill. App. 485.

Indiana: Por'er *v.* Midland Ry., 125 Ind. 476, 25 N. E. 556 (but see North Vernon *v.* Voegler, 103 Ind. 314).

Iowa: Powers *v.* Council Bluffs, 45 Ia. 652, 24 Am. Rep. 782.

New York: Duryea *v.* Mayor, 26 Hun, 120.

Texas: Gulf, C. & S. F. Ry. *v.* Hepner, 83 Tex. 136, 18 S. W. 441; Heilbron *v.* St. Louis S. W. Ry. (Tex. Civ. App.), 113 S. W. 979.

[130] Chattanooga *v.* Dowling, 101 Tenn. 342, 47 S. W. 700.

CHAPTER VI

§ 96ª. Nominal damages distinguished from substantial damages.

Before proceeding to consider the measure of legal compensation in cases where actual loss is sustained, it will be proper to examine the rule of *Nominal* Damages as contra-distinguished from *Substantial* Damages.

"Nominal damages," said the Connecticut court, "mean no damages at all. They exist only in name and not in amount. In the quaint saying of an old writer they are a mere peg to hang costs on." [1]

(a) For § 96 of the 8th edition see § 86a.

[1] Stanton *v.* N. Y. & E. Ry., 59 Conn. 272, 21 Am. St. 110, 22 Atl. 300.

"Some small amount sufficient to carry the costs." Ransone *v.* Christian, 56 Ga. 351.

When a case is made out for nominal damages it is error to instruct the jury that "some damages must be given."[2]

An allowance for nominal damages usually means an allowance of one cent, or six cents,[3] or some such very small sum; but an allowance of one dollar has been treated as nominal damages.[4] Any larger amount could hardly be held nominal.[5]

The term is contrasted with substantial damages, which means an amount assessed as the equivalent of an actually proved loss, however small. Small damages awarded as compensation for an actually proved but slight loss are not nominal damages.[6]

§ 96a. The common law relieves only from actual injury.

*We shall have frequent occasion hereafter to notice that the common law, as a general rule, only gives actual compensation in cases of actual injury. The object of the suit is to obtain remuneration for loss actually sustained. If it appear that though the defendant is in fault, still that the plaintiff is not injured, he can have no relief. It is *injuria sine damno*. As far back as the Year Books, it is said, "If a man forge a bond in my name, I can have no action on the case yet; but if I am sued, I may, for the wrong and damage, though I may avoid it

[2] Dady v. Condit, 188 Ill. 234, 58 N. E. 900.

[3] *New York:* Segelke v. Finan, 48 Hun, 310, 1 N. Y. Supp. 381.
Delaware: Bennum v. Coursey, 7 Pen. 74, 76 Atl. 53.

[4] Moe v. Chesrown, 54 Minn. 118, 55 N. W. 832.

[5] *Indiana:* Glass v. Garber, 55 Ind. 336 (three dollars and a half).
Michigan: Phenix v. Clark, 2 Mich. 327 (fifteen dollars).
Washington: Trumbull v. School Dist., 22 Wash. 631, 61 Pac. 714 (twenty-six dollars).
But in Western U. T. Co. v. Glenn, Ga. App.   , 68 S. E. 881, the court allowed a verdict for $250 to stand, after a charge that only nominal damages could be recovered. The court said that the amount that could be called nominal damages would vary according to the nature of the case and what would be trivial in one suit would not be in another. There is no maximum amount. See to the same effect Southern Ry. v. Johnson, Ga. App.   , 70 S. E. 69. And in Stanley v. Schumpert, 117 La. 255, 41 So. 565, 6 L. R. A. (N. S.) 306, a verdict of $25 as nominal damages was allowed. But in these cases the court appears to have confused small but real actual damages with nominal damages.

[6] *North Dakota:* Tri-State T. & T. Co. v. Cosgriff,   N. Dak.   , 124 N. W. 75, 26 L. R. A. (N. S.) 1171.
E n g l a n d: Steamship Mediana v. Lightship Comet, [1900] A. C. 113, 9 Aspin. Mar. 41, 69 L. J. P. 35, 82 L. T. Rep. 95, 48 W. R. 398.

by plea." [7]   And so Lord Hobart, C. J., says, "There must be not only a thing done amiss, but also a damage either already fallen upon the party, or else inevitable." [8]   Equity often proceeds, *quia timet*, in the exercise of her preventive powers to arrest the threatened injury, and there were some early and now obsolete proceedings of the same character at law; [9] but, as a general rule, it may at present be considered well settled that the relief of the common law is only to be obtained by those who have suffered actual injury.   This proposition is, however, subject to the modification which we shall now proceed to consider in relation to nominal damages.

§ 97. Damage inferred from the fact of wrong done.

Wherever the breach of an agreement or the invasion of a right is established, the English law infers some damage to the plaintiff; and if no evidence is given of any particular amount of loss, it declares the right by awarding what it terms nominal damages, being some very small sum, as a farthing, a penny, or sixpence—*Ubi jus, ibi remedium.*   "Every injury," said Lord Holt, "imports a damage." [10]   So again, in the same case as elsewhere reported, his Lordship said:

"My brother Powell, indeed, thinks that an action upon the case is not maintainable, because there is no hurt or damage to the plaintiff; but surely, every injury imports a damage, though it does not cost the party one farthing, and it is impossible to prove the contrary; for a damage is not merely pecuniary, but an injury imports a damage where a man is thereby hindered of his right.   As in an action for slanderous words, though a man does not lose a penny by reason of the speaking them, yet he shall have an action.   So if a man gives another a cuff on the ear, though it cost him nothing, no, not so much as a little *dia-*

---

[7] 19 H. 6, 44.

[8] Waterer *v.* Freeman, Hobart, 266.

[9] "And note," says Lord Coke, "that there be six writs in law that may be maintained, *quia timet*, before any molestation, distresse or impleading, as 1. A man may have his writ of *mesne* (whereof Littleton here speaks), before he be distreyned. 2. A *Warrantia Cartæ* before he be impleaded. 3. A

Monstraverunt before any distresse or vexation. 4. An *Audita Querela* before any execution sued. 5. A *Curia Claudenda* before any default of inclosure. 6. A *ne injuste vexes* before any distresse or molestation.   And these be called *brevia anticipantia*, writs of prevention."—Coke, Lit. 100*a.* Story's Equity Jurisprudence, §§ 730 and 825.

[10] Ashby *v.* White, 1 Salk. 19.

chylon, yet he shall have his action, for it is a personal injury. So a man shall have an action against another for riding over his ground, though it do him no damage, for it is an invasion of his property, and the other has no right to come there." [11]

"Wherever," says Mr. Sergeant Williams, "any act injures another's right, and would be evidence in future in favor of the wrongdoer, an action may be maintained for an invasion of the right, without proof of any specific injury." [12] **

§ 98. Nominal damages for the infringement of a right.

It is now well established that nominal damages may be recovered for the bare infringement of a right, or for a breach of contract, unaccompanied by any actual damage. [13]   To state

[11] 2 Ld. Raym. 938, 955.

[12] Mellor *v.* Spateman, 1 Saund. 346*b.*

[13] *United States:* Troy L. M. Co. *v.* Dolph, 138 U. S. 617, 623, 34 L. ed. 1083, 11 Sup. Ct. 412; Watts *v.* Phœnix Mut. L. Ins. Co., 16 Blatch. 228.

Alabama: Bagby *v.* Harris, 9 Ala. 173; Drum *v.* Harrison, 83 Ala. 384.

Arkansas: Barlow *v.* Lowder, 35 Ark. 492.

California: Browner *v.* Davis, 15 Cal. 9; Hancock *v.* Hubbell, 71 Cal. 537.

Delaware: Quillen *v.* Betts, 1 Pennew. 53, 39 Atl. 595.

Georgia: Kenny *v.* Collier, 79 Ga. 743.

Illinois: Burnap *v.* Wight, 14 Ill. 301; McConnel *v.* Kibbe, 33 Ill. 175, 85 Am. Dec. 265; Dent *v.* Davison, 52 Ill. 109.

Indiana: Rosenbaum *v.* McThomas, 34 Ind. 331; Wimberg *v.* Schevegeman, 97 Ind. 528.

Iowa: Madison County *v.* Tullis, 69 Ia. 720.

Kansas: Curtis *v.* Paggett, 97 Kan. 86, 27 Pac. 109.

Maine: Webb *v.* Gross, 79 Me. 224.

Massachusetts: Brown *v.* Perkins, 1 All. 89; Smith *v.* Whiting, 100 Mass. 122; McKim *v.* Bartlett, 129 Mass. 226; Shattuck *v.* Adams, 136 Mass. 34.

Minnesota: Cowley *v.* Davidson, 10 Minn. 392; Potter *v.* Mellen, 36 Minn. 122.

New Hampshire: Runlett *v.* Bell, 5 N. H. 433; French *v.* Bent, 43 N. H. 448; Golden *v.* Knapp, 41 N. J. L. 215.

New York: Taylor *v.* Read, 4 Paige 561; Quin *v.* Moore, 15 N. Y. 432; Pierce *v.* Hosmer, 66 Barb. 345; Colt *v.* Owens, 47 N. Y. Super. ·Ct. 430; Lawrence *v.* Kemp, 1 Duer 363; Shannon *v.* Burr, 1 Hilt. 39.

North Carolina: Bond *v.* Hilton, 2 Jones L. 149; Ledbetter *v.* Morris, 3 Jones L. 543; Kimel *v.* Kimel, 4 Jones L. 121; White *v.* Griffin, 4 Jones L. 139; Anders *v.* Ellis, 87 N. C. 207.

Ohio: Coe *v.* Peacock, 14 Oh. St. 187; Coopers *v.* Wolf, 15 Oh. St. 523.

Pennsylvania: Hutchinson *v.* Schimmelfeder, 40 Pa. 396, 80 Am. Dec. 582.

South Carolina: Hogg *v.* Pinckney, 16 S. C. 387.

Tennessee: Seat *v.* Moreland, 7 Humph. 575.

Texas: Hope *v.* Alley, 9 Tex. 394; Lawless *v.* Evans (Tex. App.) 14 S. W. 1019.

Vermont: Collins *v.* St. Peters, 65 Vt. 618, 27 Atl. 425.

Wisconsin: Eaton *v.* Lyman, 30 Wis. 41.

England: Marzetti *v.* Williams, 1 B. & A. 415; Feize *v.* Thompson, 1 Taunt.

when rights are infringed, and consequently when nominal damages are recoverable, would be to recapitulate the whole *corpus juris*. A few additional illustrations, however, may be given. In Tootle *v.* Clifton,[14] the wrong complained of was the erection by the defendant of an embankment on his own land, whereby the surface water accumulating on the land of the plaintiff was prevented from flowing off in its natural course and caused to flow off in a different direction over land of the plaintiff. The plaintiff was allowed to maintain the action, and recover nominal damages, although not actually injured. So the reversioner can recover nominal damages on the general covenant to repair, although he has not suffered any substantial damage.[15] If a passenger on a railroad train is carried beyond his destination he can recover nominal damages.[16] In libel the plaintiff can recover nominal damages.[17]

If the defendant pending suit pays the debt or returns the property converted, and the payment or return is accepted by the plaintiff, nominal damages may be recovered.[18]

§ 99. Nominal damages establish title.

* In regard to the right invaded, a verdict and judgment for the smallest amount is as effectual as any sum, however large; for it establishes the fact of the plaintiff's title. And in the common case of trespass to lands, the main object usually being to determine the right, this principle becomes very important. In many of these cases it might seem at first sight that the maxim *injuria sine damno* applied, and that the law would refuse redress.** But besides enforcing the principle that

121; Barker *v.* Green, 2 Bing. 317; Nosotti *v.* Page, 10 C. B. 643.

Canada: M'Leod *v.* Boulton, 3 Up. Can. Q. B. 84; Doan *v.* Warren, 11 Up. Can. C. P. 423; Doe *v.* Ausman, 1 R. & J. Ont. Dig. 989; Morrow *v.* Waterous, 24 N. B. 442.

[14] 22 Oh. St. 247, 10 Am. Rep. 732.

[15] Williams *v.* Williams, L. R. 9 C. P. 659.

[16] Thompson *v.* N. O., J. & G. N. R. R., 50 Miss. 315.

[17] *Delaware:* Bennum *v.* Coursey, 7 Pen. 74, 76 Atl. 53.

Louisiana: Levert *v.* Daily S. P. Co., 123 La. 594, 49 So. 206, 23 L. R. A. (N. S.) 726.

England: Kelly *v.* Sherlock, L. R. 1 Q. B. 686.

[18] *California:* Conroy *v.* Flint, 5 Cal. 327.

Massachusetts: Shattuck *v.* Adams, 136 Mass. 34.

England: But in England it is decided that judgment should be given for the defendant. Thame *v.* Boast, 12 Q. B. 808.

wherever there is a wrong there should be a remedy, this rule of giving nominal damages for the infliction of any legal wrong may settle the question of title or determine rights of the greatest importance.[19]   As has been clearly said by the Supreme Court of Connecticut, in an action for flowing lands, "An act which occasions no other damage than putting at hazard those rights, which, if the act were acquiesced in, would be lost by lapse of time, is a sufficient ground of action." [20]   So, again, it has been said in Maine, speaking of the flowage of lands, "Generally, when one encroaches on the inheritance of another the law gives a right of action, and even if no actual damages are proved, the action will be sustained and nominal damages recovered; because, unless that could be done, the encroachment acquiesced in might ripen into a legal right, and the trespasser, by a continuance of his encroachments, acquire a perfect title." [21]   So, in Pennsylvania, in trespass for flowing lands, it was held "that the law implies damage from flooding the ground of another, though it be in the least possible degree, and without actual prejudice.   But where the law implies the injury, it also implies the lowest damage." [22]   And the rule is generally recognized.[23]

[19] *Georgia:* Price v. High Shoals Mfg. Co., 64 S. E. 87, 132 Ga. 246, 22 L. R. A. (N. S.) 684 (diversion of water); Batson v. Higginbothem, 68 S. E. 455, 7 Ga. App. 835 (trespass on land).

Iowa: Harvey v. Mason, C. & F. D. R. R., 129 Ia. 465, 105 N. W. 958, 3 L. R. A. (N. S.) 973 (flooding land).

Maine: Munroe v. Stickney, 48 Me. 462 (diversion of water).

Missouri: Hahn v. Cotton, 136 Mo. 216, 37 S. W. 919 (withholding land).

New Hampshire: Tillotson v. Smith, 32 N. H. 90, 64 Am. Dec. 355 (overflowing water course).

New Jersey: Newark v. Chestnut Hill Land Co.,   N. J. Eq.   , 75 Atl. 644 (diversion of water).

New York: New York Rubber Co. v. Rothery, 132 N. Y. 293, 30 N. E. 841 (diversion of water); Slingerland v. International C. Co., 169 N. Y. 60, 61 N. E. 995, 56 L. R. A. 494 (impairment of access to river); Devendorf v. Wert, 42 Barb. 227 (breach of contract).

Vermont: Fullman v. Cummings, 16 Vt. 697 (conversion of written account).

England: Patrick v. Greenaway, 1 Wms. Saunds. 346b, note (unlawfully fishing).

[20] *Connecticut:* Chapman v. Thames Manuf. Co., 13 Conn. 269, 33 Am. Dec. 401.

New Hampshire: Bassett v. Salisbury Manuf. Co., 28 N. H. 438.

[21] Hathorne v. Stinson, 12 Me. 183; Seidensparger v. Spear, 17 Me. 123.

[22] *Pennsylvania:* Pastorius v. Fisher, 1 Rawle, 27; Ripka v. Sergeant, 7 W. & S. 9.

[23] *United States:* Whipple v. Cumberland Manuf. Co., 2 Story, 661.

§ 100. Application of the rule in torts—English cases.

* In an early English case, well known as that of *The Tunbridge Wells Dippers*,[24] an action on the case was brought by the plaintiffs, who were dippers at Tunbridge Wells, against the defendants for dipping without being duly appointed; and on the subject of damage, "there was no proof of the defendants having received any gratuity, other than general evidence that the employment of dipper is attended with profits which arise from the voluntary contribution of company resorting to Tunbridge Wells." The Court of Common Pleas, in noticing the objection, said, "There is a real damage to the dippers in depriving them of some gratuity which they would otherwise have received, perhaps more than they might truly deserve for their labor and pains. Besides, an action upon the case will lie for a *possibility* of a damage and an injury; as for persuading A. not to come and sell his wares at the market of B., the lord of the market may have his action."

So, again, subsequently in an action on the case for a surcharge of common, it was held that the plaintiff need not show that he turned on any cattle of his own at the time of the surcharge, but only that he could not have enjoyed his common so beneficially as he might; and Nares, J., commenting on the Dippers' case, said it was there held that a *"probable"* damage is a sufficient injury on which to ground an action.[25]   And

Alabama: Stein v. Burden, 24 Ala. 130, 60 Am. Dec. 453; Ulbricht v. Eufaula Water Co., 86 Ala. 587, 6 So. 78, 11 Am. St. Rep. 17.

Connecticut: Parker v. Griswold, 17 Conn. 288, 42 Am. Dec. 739.

Illinois: Plumleigh v. Dawson, 6 Ill. 544, 41 Am. Dec. 199.

Maine: Blanchard v. Baker, 8 Me. 253, 23 Am. Dec. 504; Munroe v. Gates, 48 Me. 463.

Massachusetts: Bolivar Manuf. Co. v. Neponset Manuf. Co., 16 Pick. 241; Newhall v. Ireson, 8 Cush. 595, 54 Am. Dec. 790; Stowell v. Lincoln, 11 Gray, 434; Lund v. New Bedford, 121 Mass. 286; Hooten v. Barnard, 137 Mass. 36.

Minnesota: Dorman v. Ames, 12 Minn. 451.

Nevada: Truckee Lodge v. Wood, 14 Nev. 293.

New Hampshire: Amoskeag Manuf. Co. v. Goodale, 46 N. H. 53.

New York: Crooker v. Bragg, 10 Wend. 260, 25 Am. Dec. 555.

North Carolina: Kimel v. Kimel, 4 Jones L. 121.

Pennsylvania: Kemmerer v. Edelman, 23 Pa. 143; Delaware & Hudson Canal Co. v. Torrey, 33 Pa. 143; Graver v. Sholl, 42 Pa. 58.

Vermont: Tuthill v. Scott, 43 Vt. 525.

Canada: Mitchell v. Barry, 26 Up. Can. Q. B. 416; Plumb v. McGannon, 32 Up. Can. Q. B. 8; Warren v. Deslippes, 33 Up. Can. Q. B. 59.

[24] Weller v. Baker, 2 Wils. 414.

[25] Wells v. Watling, 2 W. Black. 1233.

"probable" is, perhaps, the more correct phrase. An invasion of right being shown, the law holds injury to be a *probable* result, and therefore gives judgment against the wrongdoer. In other words, it presumes some damage to have resulted from the wrong. And the principle was adhered to by the King's Bench in an action on the case for injuries to a right of common, the jury having found a verdict of one farthing, and a motion to set aside the verdict and to enter a nonsuit being denied.[26]

But in a suit brought by the owner of a house against a lessee for opening a door without leave, the premises not being in any way injured or weakened by the opening, the court refused to allow nominal damages, and remitted the case to the jury to say whether the plaintiff's reversionary interest had, in point of fact, been prejudiced.[27] This case, however, does not present any exception to the general rule, for the court evidently considered that a verdict for nominal damages would have been right if there had been any proof of the plaintiff's *title* being affected. So, again, in the King's Bench, in an action on the case for the fraudulent imitation of the plaintiff's trademarks; the jury having found a verdict with one farthing damages, a motion was made to enter a nonsuit; but the rule was refused, and Littledale, J., said, "The act of the defendants was a fraud against the plaintiff; and if it occasioned him no specific damage, it was still, to a certain extent, an injury to his right." [28]

And in the same court, in an action on the case brought by a tenant against his landlord, for illegally distraining for more rent than was due, it appearing that the proceeds of the sale were insufficient to satisfy the rent actually in arrears, the jury found a verdict for the plaintiff, with one shilling damages. A motion was made to enter a nonsuit, but it was denied, and

By this decision a dictum of Lord Coke, in Robert Marys's case, was overruled. 9 Co. 111b, 113. "So," says Lord Coke, "that if the trespass *be so small* that the commoner has not any loss, but sufficient in ample manner remains for him, he shall not have any action for it."

[26] Pindar *v.* Wadsworth, 2 East, 154.

We shall hereafter see that this principle does not apply in cases of waste, and that if the damages there be purely nominal, the defendant may enter judgment. Harrow School *v.* Alderton, 2 B. & P. 86.

[27] Young *v.* Spencer, 10 B. & C. 145.

[28] Blofeld *v.* Payne, 4 B. & A. 410.

Denman, C. J., said, "There was a wrongful act of the defendant, and though by reason of the value of the goods taken falling short of the actual rent due, no real damage was sustained, yet there was a legal damage and cause of action, for which the plaintiff was entitled to a verdict."[29] This case carries the principle of the English law to its extreme limit; for so far from the plaintiff's having proved any damage, it was conclusively shown that he could not have suffered any; and on the contrary, the defendant was the real loser.[**]

In an action brought under the statute of Marlbridge (52 Hen. III, c. 4) for excessive distress, the plaintiff was held entitled to nominal damages, although he proved no actual damage.[30]

Thus, also, it has been held by the English Common Pleas, in an action on the case for deceit against the secretary of an insurance company for false representations as to the management and affairs of the company, whereby the plaintiff was induced to effect an insurance with them, though it did not appear that he had sustained any positive loss, that he was entitled to nominal damages.[31]

The principle has been applied to the diversion of watercourses. It has been long held that the riparian proprietor of a stream has a right to the use of its waters, but it has been doubted whether he could recover in an action for its diversion without showing actual damage. It is now, however, well settled, in favor of the right; and if the infringement be established, nominal damages, at least, will in all cases be given.[32]

[29] Taylor v. Henniker, 12 A. & E. 488, which overruled the cases of Avenell v. Croker, Moo. & M. 172, and Wilkinson v. Terry, 1 M. & Rob. 377. See, also, Butts v. Edwards, 2 Denio, 164, where it is said that in case for illegal distress, if no actual damage is sustained, the plaintiff could at most but recover nominal damages.

[30] Chandler v. Doulton, 3 H. & C. 553.

[31] Pontifex v. Bignold, 3 Scott N. R. 390. The text contains the substance of the marginal note, but it should be noticed that the question came up on demurrer to the plea, that the declaration alleged that the policy was of less value to the plaintiff than if the representations complained of had been true, and that Tindal, C. J., said: "This case ranges itself within Pasley v. Freeman, 3 T. R. 51, and Haycraft v. Creasy, 2 East, 92, and that class of cases, where it was held that a false affirmation made by the defendant with intent to defraud the plaintiff, whereby *the plaintiff receives damage*, is the ground of an action upon the case in the nature of a deceit."

[32] Bower v. Hill, 1 Bing. N. C. 549;

So where a reversioner brought trover against his tenant for cutting some branches off the trees growing on the demised close, it was held that the plaintiff was entitled to nominal damages, though no proof of the value was given at the trial.[33]

§ 101. American cases.

The general rule has been recognized by the Supreme Court of New York, in relation to personal actions as well as those affecting real property. In an action of trespass,[34] Bronson, J., said: "If the plaintiff succeeded in showing an unlawful entry upon his land, or that his fences or any portion of them were improperly thrown down and his fields exposed, he was entitled to a verdict for *nominal damages* at the least. It was not necessary for him to prove a *sum*, or that any particular amount of damages had been sustained. Every unauthorized entry upon the land of another is a trespass, and whether the owner suffer much or little, he is entitled to a verdict for some damages.[35] Even if the result of the trespass benefits the plaintiff instead of damnifying him, he is entitled to nominal damages.[36]

The obstruction of a highway gives a right of action to one thereby prevented from passing, against the person who erected the obstruction.[37] So, also, nominal damages may be recovered by a riparian proprietor for a bare infringement of his rights.[38]

Northam *v.* Hurley, 1 E. & B. 665; Embrey *v.* Owen, 6 Ex. 353.

[33] Cotterill *v.* Hobby, 4 B. & C. 465.

[34] Dixon *v.* Clow, 24 Wend. (N. Y.) 188.

[35] The same point has been ruled elsewhere.
North Carolina: White *v.* Griffin, 4 Jones L. 139.
Texas: Carter *v.* Wallace, 2 Tex. 206.

[36] *Maine:* Jewett *v.* Whitney, 43 Me. 242.
Missouri: Jones *v.* Hannovan, 55 Mo. 462.
New Hampshire: Johnson *v.* Conant, 64 N. H. 109, 7 Atl. 116.
New York: Moore *v.* New York E. R. R., 23 N. Y. Supp. 863, 4 Misc. 132, 30 Abb. N. C. 306.

Wisconsin: Murphy *v.* Fond du Lac, 23 Wis. 365, 99 Am. Dec. 181.

[37] Brown *v.* Watson, 47 Me. 161, 74 Am. Dec. 482.

[38] *Alabama:* Ubricht *v.* Eufaula Water Co., 86 Ala. 587, 6 So. 78, 11 Am. St. Rep. 17.
Connecticut: Watson *v.* New Milford Water Co., 71 Conn. 442, 42 Atl. 265.
Maine: Butman *v.* Hussey, 12 Me. 407.
Massachusetts: Newhall *v.* Ireson, 8 Cush. 595; Lund *v.* New Bedford, 121 Mass. 286; Peck *v.* Clark, 142 Mass. 436, 8 N. E. 335.
New Hampshire: Tillotson *v.* Smith, 32 N. H. 90; Blodgett *v.* Stone, 60 N. H. 167.
New York: Shannon *v.* Burr, 1 Hilt.

So in case of unlawful flowage of lands, nominal damages at least will be given.[39]

So in an action of trespass for false imprisonment.[40] The plea containing an allegation that the trespass consisted in arresting the plaintiff on an execution on a judgment in trover, it was replied that the plaintiff had obtained his discharge from imprisonment, and that the defendant had notice of the discharge, to which a demurrer was put in; the court said: "Want of notice may indeed depress the damages to a mere nominal sum, but is never allowed absolutely to excuse a trespass"; and there was judgment for the plaintiff.

In a case where fraud was charged, the same court was equally explicit. They said: "Actual damage is not necessary to an action. A violation of right, with a possibility of damage, forms the ground of an action. . . . Once establish, therefore, that in all matters of pecuniary dealing, in all matters of contract, a man has a legal right to demand that his neighbor shall be honest, and the consequence follows, namely: if he be drawn into a contract by fraud, this is an injury actionable *per se*. Indeed, it would not be difficult, in all such cases, to show the degree of actual damage. The time of the injured party has been consumed in doing a vain thing, or one comparatively vain; and time is money. Fraud is odious to the law; and fraud in a contract can hardly be conceived of without being attended with damage in fact." [41] And it may be said

39; New York Rubber Co. *v.* Rothery, 132 N. Y. 293, 30 N. E. 841, 28 Am. St. Rep. 575.

Pennsylvania: Clark *v.* Pennsylvania R. R., 145 Pa. 438, 22 Atl. 989.

Texas: Champion *v.* Vincent, 20 Tex. 811.

Washington: Shotwell *v.* Dodge, 8 Wash. 337, 36 Pac. 254.

Canada: Mitchell *v.* Barry, 26 Up. Can. Q. B. 416.

But in some States it has been laid down that actual material damage must be shown.

Indiana: Cory *v.* Silcox, 6 Ind. 39.

Ohio: M'Elroy *v.* Goble, 6 Oh. St. 187.

[39] *Alabama:* Eagle & P. M. Co. *v.* Gibson, 62 Ala. 369, 60 Am. Dec. 453.

Illinois: Doud *v.* Guthrie, 13 Ill. App. 653.

Massachusetts: Hooton *v.* Barnard, 137 Mass. 36.

Mississippi: Chapman *v.* Copeland, 55 Miss. 476.

New Hampshire: Gerrish *v.* New Market Manuf. Co., 30 N. H. 478; Amoskeag Manuf. Co. *v.* Goodale, 46 N. H. 53.

North Carolina: Little *v.* Stanback, 63 N. C. 285.

[40] Deyo *v.* Van Valkenburgh, 5 Hill, 242.

[41] *New York:* Allaire *v.* Whitney, 1

generally that wherever there is an actionable wrong, irrespective of damage, nominal damages may be recovered; [42] while,

Hill, 484; Whitney v. Allaire, 4 Denio, 554, 1 N. Y. 305.

[42] *Trespass or other direct injury to land:*

Delaware: Quillen v. Betts, 1 Pennewill, 53, 39 Atl. 595.

Illinois: Kurrus v. Seibert, 11 Ill. App. 319 (unlawful entry of landlord after end of term).

Iowa: Foster v. Elliott, 33 Iowa, 216 (action by tenant).

Maine: Fitzpatrick v. Boston & M. R. R., 84 Me. 33, 24 Atl. 432 (obstruction of private way).

Mississippi: Keirn v. Warfield, 60 Miss. 799.

Missouri: Hahn v. Cotton, 136 Mo. 216, 37 S. W. 919.

New York: Rich v. Rich, 16 Wend. 663; Dixon v. Clow, 24 Wend. 188.

Pennsylvania: Williams v. Esling, 4 Pa. 486, 45 Am. Dec. 710 (obstruction of right of way).

South Carolina: Caruth v. Allen, 2 McCord, 226.

Texas: Champion v. Vincent, 20 Tex. 811.

Wisconsin: Diana Shooting Club v. Lamoreux, 114 Wis. 44, 58, 89 N. W. 880 (trespass on land where plaintiff had exclusive right of hunting).

Trespass or other direct injury to personal property:

North Carolina: Edwards v. Erwin, 62 S. E. 545, 148 N. C. 429 (wrongful stoppage in transitu of goods).

Vermont: Fullman v. Cummings, 16 Vt. 697 (trover for written account); Paul v. Slason, 22 Vt. 231, 54 Am. Dec. 75 (trespass on chattel).

Detention of personal property, in an action of replevin:

Colorado: Hammond v. Solliday, 8 Colo. 610, 9 Pac. 781.

Indiana: Stevens v. McClure, 56 Ind. 384; Robinson v. Shatzley, 75 Ind. 461.

New York: Von Schoening v. Buchanan, 14 Abb. Pr. 185 (court may insert nominal damages in verdict if jury omitted to do so); Segelke v. Finan, 48 Hun 310, 1 N. Y. Supp. 381 (court may insert in verdict).

Assault and battery:

Crosby v. Humphreys, 59 Minn. 92, 60 N. W. 843.

Failure to deliver telegraph message:

Alabama: Kennon v. Western U. T. Co., 92 Ala. 399, 9 So. 200.

Ohio: Sullivan v. Western U. T. Co., 30 Oh. Circ. Ct. 435.

Refusal to receive passenger:

Pleasants v. North Beach & M. R R., 34 Cal. 586.

Personal injury to passenger:

New York: Levine v. Brooklyn, A. C. & S. R. R., 134 App. Div. 606, 119 N. Y. Supp. 315.

Texas: Fiedler v. St. Louis, B. & M. Ry., 51 Tex. Civ. App. 244, 112 S. W. 699.

Unreasonable delay in transporting freight:

Crutcher v. Choctaw & O. G. R. R., 74 Ark. 358, 85 S. W. 770.

Damages for death:

United States: Howard v. Delaware & H. C. Co., 40 Fed. 195, 6 L. R. A. 75.

Alabama: Alabama Mineral R. R. v. Jones, 121 Ala. 113, 25 So. 814.

Kansas: St. Louis & S. F. R. R. v. Blinn, 10 Kan. App. 468, 62 Pac. 427.

New York: McIntyre v. N. Y. Cent. R. R., 43 Barb. 532.

South Carolina: Bradley v. Flewitt, 6 Rich. Law, 69 (death of slave).

Eminent domain:

Chicago, B. & Q. R. R. v. Naperville, 169 Ill. 25, 47 N. E. 734.

But in Morris & E. M. C. Co. v. Delaware, L. & W. R. R., 190 Pa. 448, 42 Atl. 883, it was held that there can be no recovery without actual damages.

of course, in certain actions on the case where damage is the gist of the action, there can be no recovery of nominal damages.[43]

§ 102. In actions upon patents or trade-marks.

The general principle has been also laid down by Mr. Justice Story, in regard to patents. In an action for the infringement of a patent right by making a machine, it was argued for the defendant, that no action lay except for actual damage. "But," said Story, J., "we are of opinion that where the law gives an action for a particular act, the doing of that act imports of itself a damage to the party. Every violation of a right imports some damage; and if none other be proved, the law allows a nominal damage." [44] And so for the infringement of a trade-mark nominal damages may be recovered though no actual damages be proved.[45]

§ 103. In actions against public officers.

It has been so held in Massachusetts, in the case of a sheriff neglecting to return an execution. "The plaintiff is entitled," said Wilde, J., "to nominal damages for the officer's neglect, in not returning the execution till after the return day. No actual damages are proved, but where there is a neglect of duty, the law presumes damages." [46] So where the sheriff does not return a *fi. fa.* after being notified to do so, if the plaintiff has intermeddled with the execution of the writ so as to defeat its operation, he is still entitled to nominal damages.[47] So in an action for breach of duty in the compromise by an at-

Other wrongs:
California: Shanklin v. Gray, 111 Cal. 88, 43 Pac. 399 (statutory action by stockholder against director for failure to make reports).
Iowa: Boardman v. Marshalltown Grocery Co., 105 Iowa, 445, 75 N. W. 343 (action by stockholder for refusal to allow inspection of stock-book).
[43] Craig v. Chambers, 17 Ohio St. 253 (action against surgeon for malpractice).
[44] *United States:* Whittemore v. Cutter, 1 Gall. 429, 478.

Massachusetts: Marsh v. Billings, 7 Cush. 322, 54 Am. Dec. 723.
Rhode Island: Davis v. Kendall, 2 R. I. 566.
[45] Canada Paint Co. v. Johnston, 4 Quebec Super. Ct. 253.
[46] Laflin v. Willard, 16 Pick. (Mass.) 64, 26 Am. Dec. 629; Goodnow v. Willard, 5 Met. (Mass.) 517; Lawrence v. Rice, 12 Met. (Mass.) 535.
[47] Mickles v. Hart, 1 Den. (N. Y.) 548; but in England there can be no recovery without actual damage. Stimson v. Farnham, L. R. 7 Q. B. 175; and acc., State v. Case, 77 Mo. 247.

torney of a suit contrary to his client's express directions, although the compromise was a reasonable one and made in good faith, and there was no positive damage.[48]   And so generally any violation of duty by a public officer is ground for the recovery of nominal damages at least.[49]   We shall have occasion to consider this branch of the subject more at large when treating of damages in suits against sheriffs and other public officers.[50]

In Vermont, an able effort was made to limit nominal damages strictly to cases where some damage is the probable result of the defendant's act, or where the act would be evidence afterwards in favor of the wrongdoer, or where a right is wantonly invaded for the purpose of injury; and it was said, "that no case can be found where damages have been given for a trespass to personal property, when no unlawful intent or disturbance of a right or possession is shown, and where not only all *probable* but all *possible* damage is expressly disproved."[51] But in a later case in the same State, it is held that if, during the pendency of an action against an officer for not keeping property attached so that the execution could be levied on it, the execution be paid and discharged, the plaintiff may recover nominal damages and costs, if he had a good cause of action at the commencement of the action.[52]   And still later it was held that the maxim, *de minimis non curat lex,* is never applied to a wrongful invasion of property from which result damages capable of estimation, however small.[53]

§ 104. General principle in actions of tort.

The general principle in regard to nominal damages in cases

[43] Fray v. Voules, 1 E. & E. 839; acc., Wilcox v. Plummer, 4 Pet. 172, 7 L. ed. 821; M'Leod v. Boulton, 3 Up. Can. Q. B. 84; Doan v. Warren, 11 Up. Can. C. P. 423.

[49] *Missouri:* State ex rel. Armour Packing Co. v. Dickmann, 124 S. W. 29, 146 Mo. App. 396 (failure to return summons); State v. Miles, 149 Mo. App. 638, 129 S. W. 731 (false return).

Nebraska: Head v. Levy, 52 Neb. 456, 72 N. W. 583 (issuing process without receiving undertaking.)

England: Reg. v. Fall, 1 Q. B. 636, 2 G. & D. 803, 13 L. J. Q. B. 187, 41 E. C. L. 706 (refusal by parish officers to produce poor-rate); Clifton v. Hooper, 6 Q. B. 468 (delay in executing process); Williams v. Mostyn, 4 M. & W. 145 (sheriff permitting escape).

[50] *Post,* ch. xxiv.

[51] Paul v. Slason, 22 Vt. 231, 54 Am. Dec. 75, per Poland, J.

[52] Brown v. Richmond, 27 Vt. 583.

[53] Fullam v. Stearns, 30 Vt. 443.

of tort seems to be this: If a trespass is committed, that is, if a right is invaded or interfered with, although without any actual damage resulting, the person to whom the right belongs may maintain an action and recover nominal damages. But where a person is directly using or confines his operations to his own property only, although the doing so may inconvenience another, there is no right of action, and no damages whatever can be recovered, so long as the damage is not appreciable.[54] The maxim, *Sic utere tuo ut alienum non lædas*, does not here apply to the extent of giving a right of action. The law, in such case, no longer distinguishes between no "appreciable damage" and no damage at all.[55]

§ 105. Actions of contract—English cases.

* The rule that the invasion of a right gives a claim in all cases to nominal damages, applies equally to matters of contract; and so it was held by the Court of King's Bench, in an action brought against a banker, for refusing payment of a check although in funds, no actual damage being sustained.[56]

But when the debt was paid, though after maturity, it was held to support a plea that it was paid in full satisfaction of debt and damage, and the plaintiff was not allowed to recover either interest or nominal damages.[57] And so, again, in assumpsit, where the defendant, on being applied to by the plaintiff for payment of interest, stated that he would bring her some on the following *Sunday*, it was held that, though this was an admission that something was due, still as it did not appear what the nature of the debt was, or that it was due to the plaintiff as executrix, or in her own right, or that it was a debt for which assumpsit would lie, the plaintiff was not entitled to recover even nominal damages, and a nonsuit* was entered.[58] **

---

[54] St. Helen's Smelting Co. *v.* Tipping, 11 H. L. C. 642.

[55] Smith *v.* Thackerah, L. R. 1 C. P. 564.

[56] Marzetti *v.* Williams, 1 B. & A. 415. See, also, Winterbottom *v.* Wright, 10 M. & W. 109. See, also, Rolin *v.* Steward, 14 C. B. 595, where actual damages were given—an important case.

[57] Beaumont *v.* Greathead, 2 C. B. 494.

[58] Green *v.* Davies, 4 B. & C. 235; and also Teal *v.* Auty, 2 Bro. & Bing. 99. *Sed vide contra* at *nisi prius*, Dixon *v.* Deveridge, 2 C. & P. 109.

§ 106. American cases.

The same principle in regard to contracts, as well as invasions of right in general, has been recognized in this country. Therefore where a contract has been broken, but no damage has been suffered or proved, the plaintiff is entitled to nominal damages;[59] and his case cannot be withdrawn from the jury because no damages are proved,[60] nor dismissed on demurrer because none are claimed.[61] Even if the breach of contract has actually benefited the plaintiff, he is nevertheless entitled to recover nominal damages.[62]

So in an action on the common money counts,[63] the Supreme Court of New York held that if in assumpsit an issue be joined on a plea of payment, and no evidence be given at the trial by either party, the plaintiff will be entitled to a verdict, but such verdict will be for nominal damages only. When plaintiff in a suit for wages proves services, but fails to prove their value, he is entitled at least to a nominal sum.[64] Where judgment is given by the court on agreed facts, but no damages are agreed by the parties, the judgment for the plaintiff will be for nominal damages only.[65]

In an action of covenant it has been held that the plea of *non est factum* admits a breach on the part of the defendant, and throws on him the onus of showing the contrary, but that

---

[59] *Alabama:* Treadwell *v.* Tillis, 108 Ala. 262, 18 So. 886.

Georgia: Green *v.* Weaver, 63 Ga. 302.

Kansas: Missouri Valley L. Ins. Co. *v.* Kelso, 16 Kan. 481.

Minnesota: Stoggy *v.* Crescent Creamery Co., 72 Minn. 316, 75 N. W. 225.

Missouri: Fulkerson *v.* Eads, 19 Mo. App. 620.

New Jersey: New Jersey School, etc., Furniture Co. *v.* Board of Education, 58 N. J. L. 646, 35 Atl. 397; Van Schoick *v.* Van Schoick, 76 N. J. L. 242, 69 Atl. 1080.

North Carolina: Clinton *v.* Mercer, 3 Murph. 119.

Texas: Miller *v.* Moore, 111 S. W. 750, Tex. Civ. App.

Utah: Stevens *v.* Rogers, 16 Utah, 105, 51 Pac. 261.

[60] *Illinois:* Radloff *v.* Haase, 196 Ill. 365, 63 N. E. 729.

New York: Coppola *v.* Kraushaar, 102 App. Div. 306, 92 N. Y. Supp. 436.

[61] *California:* McCarty *v.* Beach, 10 Cal. 461.

Georgia: Sutton *v.* Southern Ry., 101 Ga. 776, 29 S. E. 53.

[62] *Connecticut:* Excelsior Needle Co. *v.* Smith, 61 Conn. 56, 23 Atl. 693.

New York: Ellsler *v.* Brooks, 54 N. Y. Super. 74.

[63] New York D. D. Co. *v.* M'Intosh, 5 Hill (N. Y.), 290.

[64] Owen *v.* O'Reilly, 20 Mo. 603.

[65] McAneany *v.* Jewett, 10 All. (Mass.) 151.

such admission only entitled the plaintiff to nominal damages.[66] And it is held that in an action upon an instrument under seal, a court of law will give *nominal* damages only, where the presumption of valuable consideration is negatived by something appearing on the face of the paper.[67]

Upon a covenant to an attorney to pay him a reasonable fee for defending the defendant on a criminal charge, nothing more can be recovered than nominal damages, unless it be averred that he did defend, or special damage be shown.[68] So the omission of an administrator to settle his account with the probate court, renders him at all events liable to nominal damages.[69] So the damages in a suit on the covenant against incumbrances are merely nominal, if the plaintiff has paid nothing towards the incumbrance.[70] In such an action nominal damages may be recovered, though the incumbrances are removed before suit is brought.[71]

So in a suit growing out of an attachment, the goods having been delivered to a receiptor, and he having failed to perform his duty, it was said that if there was a good cause of action, at the time of the commencement of the suit, but the right of action is lost by a neglect to take the necessary steps to preserve the attachment, nominal damages may be recovered.[72] So in an action on a bond given to procure the release of a debtor from arrest, there being no evidence of the loss sustained by the plaintiff, it was held that the execution could issue for nominal damages only.[73] In Iowa, in an action on a penal bond under the Code of that State, unless special damage is averred and proved, nominal damages only can be recovered.[74] In an action on a covenant to transfer to the plaintiff the defendant's *title*

---

[66] Goulding *v.* Hewitt, 2 Hill (N. Y.), 644.

[67] Cox *v.* Sprigg, 6 Md. 274.

[68] Wilson *v.* Barnes, 13 B. Mon. (Ky.) 330.

[69] *Maine:* Webb *v.* Gross, 79 Me. 224.

Maryland: State *v.* Bishop, 24 Md. 310, 87 Am. Dec. 608.

Massachusetts: Fay *v.* Haven, 3 Met. 109; McKim *v.* Bartlett, 129 Mass. 226.

Vermont: Probate Court *v.* Slason, 23 Vt. 306.

But *contra,* that no damages at all can be recovered unless actual loss is suffered: Olmstead *v.* Brush, 27 Conn. 530.

[70] Tufts *v.* Adams, 8 Pick. (Mass.) 547.

[71] Smith *v.* Jefts, 44 N. H. 482.

[72] Moulton *v.* Chapin, 28 Me. 505.

[73] Waldron *v.* Berry, 22 Me. 486.

[74] Linder *v.* Lake, 6 Ia. 164.

to a slave, it was held that the measure of damages was not the value of the slave, but of the defendant's title; and that appearing to be defective, it was considered a case for nominal damages.[75] So in Louisiana, in a suit against the sureties on a sequestration bond.[76] And generally, for the technical breach of a bond unattended by actual damages, the obligee is entitled to nominal damages, and no more.[77]

§ 107. Where no loss is inflicted damages must be nominal.

The principles already examined concern the allowance of nominal damages where the question at issue is the right to recover. The question of nominal damages, however, is often raised by the defendant's attempt, not to defeat the action altogether, but to restrict the amount of damages recovered to a nominal sum by proving that the injury itself has not been substantial. The question involved in such cases is really one of compensation purely.

§ 107a. Nominal damages where the amount of damage is not proved.

The amount of loss is as much to be proved by the plaintiff as the fact of loss. Consequently where the injury is proved, but there is no evidence as to the amount of loss, the plaintiff is entitled to nominal damages only.[78] And so where the injury shown is damage to property, no actual damages can be re-

[75] Whitehead v. Ducker, 11 Sm. & M. (Miss.) 98.

[76] Clarke v. Scott, 2 La. Ann. 907.

[77] State v. Reinhardt, 31 Mo. 95.

[78] *United States:* East Moline Co. v. Weir Plow Co., 95 Fed. 250, 37 C. C. A. 62 (contract); Murray v. Pannaci, 130 Fed. 529 (taking sand; no evidence of quantity taken).
Alabama: Seaboard Mfg. Co. v. Woodson, 98 Ala. 378, 11 So. 715 (personal injury).
Arkansas: Scarborough v. State, 24 Ark. 20 (failure of executor to render account).
Connecticut: Havens v. Hartford & N. H. R. R., 28 Conn. 69 (personal injury; after demurrer overruled no evidence of damage offered); Eldridge v. Gorman, 77 Conn. 699, 60 Atl. 643 (trespass on land).
Delaware: Pennington v. Lewis, 4 Pennew. 447, 56 Atl. 378 (trespass on land).
Georgia: Richmond Hosiery Mills v. Western U. T. Co., 123 Ga. 216, 51 S. E. 290 (failure to deliver a telegram; no actual damage proved).
Indiana: Freese v. Crary, 29 Ind. 524; State v. Davis, 117 Ind. 307 (negligent recording of deed).
Iowa: Carl v. Granger Coal Co., 69 Ia. 519; Thorp v. Bradley, 75 Ia. 50; Freeman v. Strobehn, 122 Ia. 157, 97 N. W. 1094 (destruction of check given in payment of debt; no evidence that debtor was not still responsible); Perry v. Howe C. C. Co., 125 Ia. 415, 101

covered unless there is evidence from which the jury will be justified in finding the value of the property.[79]   And so where an action is brought to recover the value of services rendered, if there is no evidence of the value of the services nominal dam-

N. W. 150 (nuisance; fact of annoyance shown but no evidence as to extent of it).

Kentucky: Diers *v.* Edwards, 63 S. W. 276, 23 Ky. L. Rep. 500 (breach of contract; no damage proved).

Michigan: Scongale *v.* Sweet, 125 Mich. 311, 82 N. W. 1061 (libel; no damage shown).

Mississippi: Thompson *v.* New Orleans, J. & G. N. R. R., 50 Miss. 315, 19 Am. Rep. 12 (passenger carried beyond destination).

Missouri: Ross *v.* New H. S. M. Co., 24 Mo. App. 353 (trespass on land); Sheedy *v.* Union Press Brick Works, 25 Mo. App. 527 (shedding water on street so as to obstruct it); Abeles *v.* Western Union Tel. Co., 37 Mo. App. 554 (delay in delivering cipher message); Cravens *v.* Hunter, 87 Mo. App. 456 (agreement to build fence).

Nevada: Richardson *v.* Jones, 1 Nev. 405 (contract naming penalty; no evidence of damage offered).

New Hampshire: Bruce *v.* Pettengill, 12 N. H. 341.

New York: Bates *v.* Loomis, 5 Wend. 134 (personal injury); Rich *v.* Rich, 16 Wend. 663 (trespass; justification fails, no evidence of damage given); Hopkins *v.* Davis, 23 App. Div. 235, 48 N. Y. Supp. 745 (replevin; no evidence as to length of period of detention).

Ohio: Hough *v.* Young, 1 Ohio, 504 (failure to protest note).

South Carolina: Hunt *v.* D'Orval, Dudley, 180.

South Dakota: Roberts *v.* Minneapolis Threshing M. Co., 8 S. D. 579, 67 N. W. 607 (breach of contract; damages uncertain); Hudson *v.* Archer, 9 S. D. 240, 68 N. W. 541 (breach of contract; damages entirely speculative).

West Virginia: Douglass *v.* Ohio R. R. R., 51 W. Va. 523, 41 S. E. 911 (breach of covenant to fence; no use for the fence proved).

England: Marzetti *v.* Williams, 1 B. & Ad. 415 (failure to pay check). Skinner *v.* London M. A. Corp., 14 Q. B. Div. 882 (delay in registering shares).

[79] *Georgia:* Ford *v.* Atlantic C. L. R. R., 68 S. E. 1072,   Ga. App. (use of clothing).

Illinois: Brent *v.* Kimball, 60 Ill. 211, 14 Am. Rep. 35 (dog); Peoria & P. U. Ry. *v.* Peoria & F. U. Ry., 105 Ill. 110 (land).

Iowa: Williams *v.* Brown, 76 Iowa, 643, 41 N. W. 377 (use of land).

Louisiana: Wilde *v.* New Orleans, 12 La. Ann. 15 (use of horse).

Massachusetts: Tufts *v.* Bennett, 163 Mass. 398, 40 N. E. 172 (goods).

Minnesota: Knowles *v.* Steele, 59 Minn. 452, 61 N. W. 557 (rental value of land).

Missouri: Niemetz *v.* St. Louis, A. & M. Assoc., 5 Mo. App. 59 (goods); Haynes *v.* Connelly, 12 Mo. App. 595 (land); Weber *v.* Squier, 51 Mo. App. 601 (goods).

New York: Donohoe *v.* Henry, 4 E. D. Smith, 162 (private letters); Whitmark *v.* Lorton, 15 Daly, 548, 8 N. Y. Supp. 480 (goods); Schwartz *v.* Schendel, 24 N. Y. Misc. 733, 53 N. Y. Supp. 829 (goods); Griggs *v.* Day, 158 N. Y. 1, 52 N. E. 692 (stock); Jelalian *v.* New York, N. H. & H. R. R., 134 App. Div. 381, 119 N. Y. Supp. 136 (clothing).

Ohio: Besuden *v.* Hamilton County, 7 Ohio Cir. Ct. 237 (land).

Texas: Smith *v.* Huizar, 25 Tex. Supp. 205 (use of land).

ages only can be recovered; [80] and in actions for personal injury where loss of time is shown, the plaintiff can recover no more than nominal damages when the value of his time is not shown. [81]

§ 107b. Where the extent of damage is uncertain in its nature.

In some cases by the very character of the injury damages are in their nature uncertain, and no particular amount of damage can be proved by the plaintiff. This happens in the case of contracts so uncertain in their terms that the amount of damage from the breach is not capable of being determined. In such cases nominal damages only can be recovered. [82] So where an agreement is incomplete, one term (as the price) being left to be agreed upon later, the amount of damage is too uncertain. [83] A contract for the sale of the output of a colliery for twenty years provided that the prices should be agreed upon by the parties from month to month. After performance for several years, the parties failed to agree upon a price, and the vendor ceased deliveries. For breach of this contract, the damages were held to be nominal. [84] So where by the negligence of the defendant in transmitting a message the plaintiff lost the benefit of a contract of employment,

[80] Belfour v. Raney, 8 Ark. 479.

[81] Greensboro v. McGibboney, 93 Ga. 672, 20 S. E. 37.

[82] *Colorado:* Patrick v. Colorado Smelting Co., 20 Colo. 268, 38 Pac. 236 (to furnish ore for treatment at agreed price; no agreement on grade of ore, which would determine the cost).

Indiana: Atkins v. Van Buren School Twp., 77 Ind. 447 (contract to employ a teacher at fixed salary; time undetermined); Smith v. Parker, 148 Ind. 127, 45 N. E. 770 (contract to lend money; rate of interest not determined).

Massachusetts: Noble v. Hand, 163 Mass. 289, 39 N. E. 1020 (to solicit orders for goods, receiving a commission on orders not rejected by defendant); Todd v. Keene, 167 Mass. 157, 45

N. E. 172 (contract to perform in a theatre for a share of the proceeds).

New York: United Press v. N. Y. Press Co., 164 N. Y. 406, 58 N. E. 527, 53 L. R. A. 288, affirming 35 N. Y. App. Div. 444, 54 N. Y. Supp. 807 (to receive news from plaintiff and pay not more than $300 a week; exact amount not determined.)

Utah: Ternes v. Dunn, 7 Utah, 497, 27 Pac. 692 (agency for sale of land given to plaintiff; price not fixed).

Washington: Sproul v. Huston, 84 Pac. 631, 42 Wash. 106 (contract to cut and deliver lumber at a certain price per thousand feet; amount undetermined).

[83] Smith v. Loag, 132 Pa. 301, 19 Atl. 137.

[84] Watts v. Weston, 62 Fed. 136, 10 C. C. A. 302, 26 U. S. App. 121.

which, however, was terminable at the will of either party, without notice, it was held that only nominal damages could be recovered.[85]

§ 107c. Where the act is not by its nature calculated to cause loss.

In some cases the defendant's act, though wrongful, was of such a nature that it was in fact not calculated to cause loss to the plaintiff.[86] In such cases the plaintiff can recover nominal damages only.[87]

Thus the defendant, having mortgaged his life interest in certain property to secure a loan of £12,500, which was further secured by a conveyance of the reversion in fee and of a policy for £13,000, payable within three months after the death of the defendant, in case he should "leave issue male by his then present wife living at his death," covenanted that he would during his life, and so long as the £12,500 or any part thereof remained due, continue to pay the premiums on the policy.   The mortgage deed also provided that the plaintiff might pay the premiums if the defendant neglected to do so, and charge such payments against the mortgaged premises, but contained no covenant on the part of the defendant to repay the premiums so paid.   The defendant, after paying the premiums for a time, discontinued doing so, after there was no further possibility of issue by his then wife.   The subsequent premiums

---

[85] Merrill v. Western U. T. Co., 78 Me. 97.

[86] *Massachusetts:* Woods v. Varnum, 21 Pick. 165.

New York: Chamberlain v. Parker, 45 N. Y. 569.

[87] *Connecticut:* Richards v. New York, N. H. & H. R. R., 77 Conn. 501, 60 Atl. 295 (technical obstruction of cove too shallow to be really navigable).

Iowa: Wire v. Foster, 62 Iowa, 114, 17 N. W. 174 (wrongful sale at market price).

New Jersey: Thiel v. Bull's F. L. Co., 58 N. J. L. 212, 33 Atl. 281 (tenant wrongly holding over; illegal trespass on land by landlord).

New York: Horton v. Bauer, 129 N. Y. 148, 29 N. E. 1 (agreement that tracks should be removed before certain date; claim that delay in removal interfered with a sale of the land; court found this impossible in fact and in law, and regarded the alleged sale as merely colorable).

Wisconsin: Benson v. Waukesha, 74 Wis. 31, 41 N. W. 1017 (village having right to build sidewalk on plaintiff's land did the work a few days sooner than it should).

England: Steer v. Crowley, 14 C. B. 337 (abstract of title negligently showed title in two grantors; entire title was in fact in one of them).

were regularly debited year by year by the office to the mortgage account of the defendant, but the defendant had no notice of this course of dealing.   In an action brought against the defendant on his covenant to pay the premiums, it was held, assuming the plaintiffs to have paid the premiums, they were not entitled to more than nominal damages.[88]

And where the assignee of a mortgage had paid the assignor part of the amount, and given his bond conditioned to collect the balance by foreclosure or otherwise, and pay it over, or after foreclosure sell the land by auction and pay the assignor the proceeds, deducting the amount paid and the costs and interest, and afterwards assigned the mortgage to another person, who entered on the land for the purpose of foreclosure, but subsequently instead purchased the equity of redemption and sold the land at auction within three years for $1,500, it was held that, although there was a technical breach of the bond, as the mortgage was not foreclosed, the plaintiff, in the absence of proof of actual damage from the mode of sale, was entitled to nominal damages only.[89]

So where goods were illegally attached, but were immediately replevied by the plaintiff and never taken out of his possession, only nominal damages could be recovered.[90]   And where a deed given into the defendant's possession in escrow was wrongfully recorded by him, the grantor could recover only nominal damages, since the deed was not valid.[91]   So where a plaintiff was imprisoned on two warrants, one legal and the other illegal, the justice issuing them could be held for no more than nominal damages.[92]

§ 107d. Where no loss happened on the facts of the case.

It may often appear on the facts of a case that the defendant's act, though it would naturally cause loss, did not do so in the present instance.[93]   So in an action for breach of covenants

[88] Browne v. Price, 4 C. B. (N. S.) 598.

[89] Pollard v. Porter, 3 Gray (Mass.), 312.

[90] *Massachusetts:* Whitman v. Merrill, 125 Mass. 127.

Michigan: Chicago & W. M. Ry. v. Reid, 74 Mich. 366, 41 N. W. 1083.

[91] McLeod v. Sandell, 26 N. B. 526; Derry v. Derry, 3 P. & B. (N. B.) 621.

[92] Doherty v. Munson, 127 Mass. 495.

[93] *United States:* Dow v. Humbert, 91

in a deed, where it appears that there is a technical defect in the title, but the plaintiff has notwithstanding remained in undisturbed possession, he can recover nominal damages only.[94] In some cases it is held that for breach of an agreement to pay a debt of the plaintiff, the latter, if he has not been called upon to pay the debt, cannot recover more than nominal damages;[95] and although in other jurisdictions a different view has been taken,[96] yet where the debt has in fact been paid, and not by the plaintiff (as, for instance, out of a security which did not belong to the plaintiff) all authorities would agree that the damages are nominal only.[97]

Other applications of the rule are numerous. Thus in Massachusetts, though an officer who takes a bail-bond is liable to an action for not returning it with the writ, yet if he deliver or offer to deliver it to the plaintiff in season for him to prosecute

U. S. 294, 23 L. ed. 368 (refusal to place plaintiff's judgment on tax-list of a town; it was so placed after institution of suit).

California: Empire G. M. Co. v. Bonanza G. M. Co., 67 Cal. 406, 7 Pac. 810 (taking ore; value of the metal in the ore less than the cost of extracting it).

Indiana: Reeves v. Andrews, 7 Ind. 207 (appeal bond; appeal withdrawn by defendant immediately).

Massachusetts: Pond v. Merrifield, 12 Cush. 181 (bond to mortgagee to complete building in certain time; delay caused increased insurance, but was accompanied by extra work which increased value by greater amount); Newcomb v. Wallace, 112 Mass. 25 (covenant against incumbrances; grantee had retained amount out of contract price and agreed to pay it himself).

Michigan: Mitchell v. Shuert, 16 Mich. 444 (conversion of note: maker insolvent); Brady v. Whitney, 24 Mich. 154 (plaintiff in trover had transferred his title immediately after bringing suit).

Missouri: Flynt v. Chicago, B. & Q.

Ry., 38 Mo. App. 94 (soil dug up by mistake and replaced without damage on discovery of mistake).

New Jersey: Marquardt v. Hudson C. G. Co. (N. J. Law), 59 Atl. 1054 (injury by asphyxiation; mere temporary unconciousness caused without any detrimental result).

New York: First National Bank v. Fourth National Bank, 77 N. Y. 320, 33 Am. Rep. 618 (failure to present draft seasonably; draft could still be collected from the drawer).

Wisconsin: Murphy v. Fond du Lac, 23 Wis. 365, 99 Am. Dec. 181 (throwing earth on plaintiff's land: the earth caused no damage to the land).

Canada: Kelty v. Jones, 2 All. (N. B.) 465 (prisoner taken in execution escapes but immediately returns).

[94] *Indiana:* Jones v. Noe, 71 Ind. 368.
Iowa: Norman v. Winch, 65 Iowa, 263, 21 N. W. 598.
Wisconsin: Mecklem v. Blake, 22 Wis. 495.

[95] Schooley v. Stoops, 4 Ind. 130; Rhine v. Morris, 96 Ind. 81.

[96] *Post,* § 789.

[97] Muhlig v. Fiske, 131 Mass. 110.

a *scire facias* against the bail, he is liable for nominal damages only.[98]

So in Connecticut, in an action of slander for charging the plaintiff, a female, with want of chastity, the judge directed the jury "that if they should find that the plaintiff had so destroyed her character by her own lewd and dissolute conduct as to have sustained no injury from the words spoken by the defendant, they might give only nominal damages"; and on review this was held correct.[99]

The plaintiff, a sheriff, attached goods of the defendant and took a delivery bond. The defendant brought an action of replevin against the sheriff, and the latter recovered; the defendant elected to retain the goods, and paid the value of them to the sheriff. In an action by the sheriff on the delivery bond, it was held that he could recover only nominal damages.[100] When the plaintiff's intestate, who was killed by the defendant's negligence, remained unconscious from the time of the injury till his death, and therefore suffered no pain either physical or mental, only nominal damages could be recovered in an action for personal injury.[101]

It is upon this general principle that a plaintiff is allowed to recover nominal damages only when he should have avoided the entire loss,[102] or when the property taken has been restored to him without loss to him;[103] or when the benefit conferred by the wrong was equal to the injury.[104] And so where performance of the obligation would have been absolutely worth-

[98] Glezen v. Rood, 2 Met. (Mass.) 490.

[99] Flint v. Clark, 13 Conn. 361.

[100] Stuart v. Trotter, 75 Ia. 96.

[101] Tully v. F. R. R., 134 Mass. 500.

[102] Ingraham v. Pullman Co., 190 Mass. 33, 76 N. E. 237, 2 L. R. A. (N. S.) 1087 (car company refused to provide plaintiff with drawing-room he had engaged; offered him another equally good).

[103] *Maine:* Jones v. Cobb, 84 Me. 153, 24 Atl. 798.

New York: Simon v. Seide, 24 N. Y. Misc. 186, 52 N. Y. Supp. 629.

[104] *Maine:* Jewett v. Whitney, 43 Me. 242 (old mill torn down and better one erected in its place).

Michigan: Wilson v. Wagar, 26 Mich. 452 (failure to deliver goods; overpayment already made greater than damage by non-delivery).

Mississippi: Clark v. Hart, 3 So. 33 (trees cut but used in fencing land).

Missouri: Mize v. Glenn, 38 Mo. App. 98 (flowing land caused benefit to land).

New Hampshire: Johnson v. Conant, 64 N. H. 109, 7 Atl. 116 (trespass on land materially improving it).

See *ante*, § 63.

less to the plaintiff he is entitled to nominal damages only; [105] as where defendant agreed to give plaintiff stock in a corporation, and at the time for delivery the stock had no value.[106]

§ 108. Nominal damages as affecting costs.

* The importance of the principle of nominal damages is mainly its effect upon the costs.[107] Costs are usually made to depend on the amount recovered, according to the nature of the action.   Thus in Massachusetts, a plaintiff is entitled to full costs in personal actions, in which the title to real estate may be concerned, if he recover any sum less than twenty dollars.[108] The practical results of the principle, therefore, can only be understood by a careful analysis of the statutes of costs, of the details of which, being matters of local legislation, this work cannot properly treat.

Where the action is brought to prevent trespasses, to try titles to land, or to determine rights of any kind, it is very equitable that the party in the wrong should bear the expense of the controversy; but in most other cases the rule of nominal damages, provided they carry costs, only tends to engender litigation.[109] We shall have occasion hereafter to notice this

---

[105] *United States:* Spafford v. Goodell, 3 McLean, 97, 22 Fed. Cas. No. 13197 (escape; prisoner absolutely insolvent).

Maine: Hotchkiss v. Whitten, 71 Me. 577 (escape; prisoner absolutely insolvent).

New Jersey: Gerli v. Poidebard Silk Mfg. Co., 57 N. J. L. 432, 31 Atl. 401, 51 Am. St. Rep. 611, 30 L. R. A. 61.

Ohio: First National Bank v. Western Union Tel. Co., 30 Ohio St. 555, 27 Am. Rep. 485 (failure to deliver worthless message).

[106] *Missouri:* Gibson v. Whip Pub. Co., 28 Mo. App. 450.

New York: Barnes v. Brown, 130 N. Y. 372, 29 N. E. 760 (modifying 55 Hun, 339, 8 N. Y. Supp. 843).

Ohio: Fosdick v. Greene, 27 Ohio St. 484, 22 Am. Rep. 328.

[107] In admiralty, where costs are discretionary, the right to nominal dam-

ages seems to be regarded as less important than in the common-law courts. Thus, in Barnett v. Luther (1 Curtis' C. C. 434), Curtis, J., said: "If it were admitted that in an action at law a seaman could recover nominal damages for a blow inflicted by the master, it does not follow that the Admiralty will award him nominal damages. . . . At the common law, the prevailing party having a legal right to costs, which is of itself a substantial right, it is necessary to decide claims to nominal damages upon strict legal principles, even where nothing but a question of costs is involved. But in the Admiralty the costs are in the discretion of the court."

[108] Pub. Stats. of Mass., ch. 198, §§ 5, 6; Ryder v. Hathaway, 2 Met. 96.

[109] It is provided by statute in England, and generally in the different

more particularly; but it should be borne in mind that the rule of nominal damages, unless carefully limited to cases where a right is necessarily litigated, results in gross injustice.   It is of no consequence whether a claim to real or to personal property is in question; the defendant ought not to be charged with the costs of the proceeding if the suit be either malicious or unnecessary.   The law should hold out no inducement to useless or vindictive litigation.[110] **

§ 109. Error in the disallowance of nominal damages.

A motion for a nonsuit should be denied where the plaintiff is entitled to nominal damages;[111] and a demurrer in such a case should be overruled.[112]   But a new trial will not be granted to the plaintiff where, upon the whole case presented, it appears that he is entitled to nominal damages only,[113] un-

States of the Union, that in actions at law for the recovery of money, a recovery to a certain amount beyond nominal damages shall be necessary to carry costs.   Where a jury, acting on the information of the plaintiff's counsel in a summing up, that a verdict for less than £5 would not carry costs, found that amount for a trifling assault, the court granted a new trial. Poole v. Whitcomb, 12 C. B. (N. S.) 770.

[110] This language is cited with approbation in Vermont, in Paul v. Slason, 22 Vt. 231, per Poland, J.

[111] *California:* Hancock v. Hubbell, 71 Cal. 537.

New York: Quin v. Moore, 15 N. Y. 432.

[112] Gurr v. W. U. T. Co.,   Ga. App.   , 69 S. E. 1085.

[113] *United States:* East Moline Co. v. Weir Plow Co., 95 Fed. 250, 37 C. C. A. 62.

Alabama: New Orleans, M. & T. R. R. v. South. & Atl. Tel. Co., 53 Ala. 211.

Arkansas: Bunch v. Potts, 57 Ark. 257, 21 S. W. 437.

California: Kenyon v. Western U. Tel. Co., 100 Cal. 454, 35 Pac. 75;

Bustamente v. Stewart, 55 Cal. 115; McAllister v. Clement, 75 Cal. 182.

Connecticut: Ely v. Parsons, 55 Conn. 83.

Georgia: Eiswald v. Southern Express Co., 60 Ga. 496.

Illinois: People v. Petrie, 94 Ill. App. 652.

Indiana: Coffin v. State, 144 Ind. 578, 43 N. E. 654, 55 Am. St. Rep. 188; Jennings v. Loring, 5 Ind. 250; Hill v. Forkner, 76 Ind. 115; Platter v. Seymour, 86 Ind. 323.

Iowa: McIntosh v. Lee, 57 Ia. 356; Thorp v. Bradley, 75 Ia. 50; Faulkner v. Closter, 79 Ia. 15; Harwood v. Lee, 85 Iowa, 622, 52 N. E. 521; Boardman v. Marshalltown Grocery Co., 105 Iowa, 445, 75 N. W. 343.

Kentucky: Robertson v. Gentry, 2 Bibb, 542.

Michigan: Hickey v. Baird, 9 Mich. 32; Haven v. Beidler Mfg. Co., 40 Mich. 286; McLean v. Charles Wright Medicine Co., 96 Mich. 479, 56 N. W. 68.

Minnesota: Harris v. Kerr, 37 Minn. 537; U. S. Exp. Co. v. Koerner, 65 Minn. 540, 68 N. W. 181, 33 L. R. A. 600.

less the recovery of nominal damages would have carried costs,[114] or unless the allowance of nominal damages is necessary for the protection of the plaintiff's interest in property.[115]

Mississippi: Clark v. Hart, 3 So. 33.

Nebraska: French v. Ramge, 2 Neb. 254.

New York: Brantingham v. Fay, 1 Johns. Cas. 255; Electric Co. v. Battery Co., 96 App. Div. 344, 80 N. Y. Supp. 325.

Ohio: Chambers v. Frazier, 29 Oh. St. 362.

South Carolina: Watson v. Hamilton, 6 Rich. L. 75.

South Dakota: Roberts v. Minneapolis T. M. Co., 8 S. D. 579, 67 N. W. 607.

Utah: Ternes v. Dunn, 7 Utah, 497, 27 Pac. 692.

Virginia: Briggs v. Cook, 99 Va. 273, 38 S. E. 148.

Wisconsin: Hibbard v. W. U. Tel. Co., 33 Wis. 558, 14 Am. Rep. 775; Middleton v. Jerdee, 73 Wis. 39, 40 N. W. 629; Benson v. Waukesha, 74 Wis. 31, 41 N. W. 1017.

Wyoming: Hecht v. Harrison, 5 Wyo. 279, 40 Pac. 306.

Canada: Haine v. Dunlap, 33 N. B. 556; Beatty v. Oille, 12 Can. 706.

But a new trial was granted for failure to give nominal damages, though without argument of the point, in Woods v. Varnum, 21 Pick. (Mass.) 165; Brown v. Emerson, 18 Mo. 103.

There is an analogous rule, viz.: that trifling damages found on insufficient evidence are not ground for a new trial Maher v. Winona & St. P. R. R., 31 Minn. 401.

Where the court expressly instructed the jury to find for the plaintiff, and in disregard of the instruction the jury found for the defendant, the judgment will in some States be reversed because of the refusal of the jury to follow the instructions.

Indiana: Lewis v. Hoover, 3 Blackf. 407.

Missouri: Bungenstock v. Nishnabotna Drainage Dist., 163 Mo. 198, 64 S. W. 149.

South Carolina: Norvell v. Thompson, 2 Hill, 470.

Wisconsin: Jones v. King, 33 Wis. 422 (semble).

[114] *United States:* East Moline Co. v. Weir Plow Co., 95 Fed. 250, 37 C. C. A. 62.

Michigan: Lewis v. Flint & P. M. Ry., 56 Mich. 638, 23 N. W. 469; Wyatt v. Herring, 90 Mich. 581, 51 N. W. 684.

Nebraska: French v. Ramge, 2 Neb. 254; Heater v. Pearce, 59 Neb. 583, 81 N. W. 615.

New York: Moore v. New York El. R. R., 4 Misc. 132, 23 N. Y. Supp. 863, 30 Abb. N. Cas. 306.

Ohio: Chambers v. Frazier, 29 Oh. St. 362.

Tennessee: Seat v. Moreland, 7 Humph. 575.

Texas: Miller v. Moore, Tex. Civ. App. , 111 S. W. 750.

Wisconsin: Middleton v. Jerdee, 73 Wis. 39, 40 N. W. 629; Sayles v. Bemis, 57 Wis. 315, 15 N. W. 432.

[115] *Connecticut:* Ely v. Parsons, 55 Conn. 83.

Illinois: Merrill v. Dibble, 12 Ill. App. 85 (plea of right of way); Johnson v. Stinger, 39 Ill. App. 180 (plea of title).

Iowa: Harvey v. Mason, C. & F. D. R. R., 129 Ia. 465, 105 N. W. 958, 3 L. R. A. (N. S.) 973 (flooding land by embankment); Wing v. Seske, 109 N. W. 717 (adverse occupation of land).

New York: Skinner v. Allison, 54 App. Div. 47, 66 N. Y. Supp. 288 (restrictive building covenant).

South Carolina: Caruth v. Allen, 2 McCord 226 (plea of title).

But though on the plaintiff's case as presented at the trial a verdict for nominal damages only would have been justified, yet if the court can now see that substantial damages may be proved at another trial they will reverse the judgment and grant a new trial.[116] If the jury finds substantial damages when only nominal damages should have been found, the court cannot give judgment for the defendant *non obstante veredicto*, but must award a new trial.[117] Where nominal damages should be given on the facts as found, but the jury neglected to find any damages, the court may amend the record by awarding a nominal sum as damages.[118]

South Dakota: Olson *v.* Huntimer, 8 S. D. 220, 66 N. W. 313 (plea of title).

Canada: Beatty *v.* Oille, 12 Can. 706.

In a few cases of trespass on land, even though title is not put in issue, the court has reversed the judgment for failure to award nominal damages.

Arkansas: Brock *v.* Smith, 14 Ark. 431.

North Carolina: Harriss *v.* Sneeden, 104 N. C. 369, 10 S. E. 477.

[116] *New Jersey:* Wartman *v.* Swindell, 54 N. J. L. 589, 25 Atl. 356, 18 L. R. A. 44.

New York: Thomson-Houston Electric Co. *v.* Durant Land Imp. Co., 144 N. Y. 34, 39 N. E. 7.

Utah: Stevens *v.* Rogers, 16 Utah, 105, 51 Pac. 261.

[117] Carl *v.* Granger Coal Co., 69 Ia. 519.

[118] *New York:* Segelke *v.* Finan, 48 Hun, 310.

England: Regina *v.* Fall, 1 Q. B. 636.

So where a judgment for the defendant is reversed because nominal damages will carry costs, it has been held that the court will not grant a new trial, but will give judgment for nominal damages and costs. Jones *v.* Telegraph, 101 Tenn. 442, 47 S. W. 699.

CHAPTER VII

PROXIMATE AND REMOTE DAMAGES

§ 110. Not all results of a wrongful act are compensated.

Having in the last chapter stated the measure of damages in cases where nominal damages only are given, we now proceed to consider the general rule which fixes the limit of compensation in cases where compensation is allowed. * That rule is the one which prohíbits any allowance for damages remotely resulting from the principal illegal act. Such damages are frequently termed *remote damages*, and sometimes *consequential damages*. These terms are not, however, necessarily synonymous, or to be indifferently used. All remote damages are consequential, but all consequential damages are by no means remote.**

§ 111. Direct and indirect results of a wrong.

A wrongful act may be followed directly and immediately by certain consequences; and from these may result, more indirectly, other consequences. For instance, an assault and battery may directly result in pain and bruises, and in the aggravation of a pre-existing disease. These are direct results of the battery. It may also result in loss of time, expense of medical attendance, and loss of a business situation. These are, perhaps, direct results of illness caused by the battery, but they are indirect results of the battery itself. A loss which is the immediate result of the wrong is called a direct loss; one that is an indirect result of the wrong is called a consequential loss. Again, a consequential loss may be one step or a dozen in the line of causation from the wrong. If it is sufficiently near the wrong for the law to concern itself with the connection, it is called a proximate loss; if not sufficiently near, it is called a remote loss; both proximate and remote losses being consequential. Still further, a result may be the consequence that might naturally have been expected to follow from the wrong, or it may be quite unexpected. Consequences of the expected sort are called natural consequences. It has been urged with much force by Grove, J., in Smith *v.* Green,[1] that a more correct term would be *normal* consequences. Every consequence in the order of nature must in one sense be natural. But a perfectly natural consequence may be at the same time such as is not generally expected to flow from the act in the normal or usual order. But the term *natural* consequence is, perhaps, too well fixed to be now changed.

Another class of consequences, which it is necessary briefly to refer to here, are those called *avoidable*. These are such consequences as under ordinary circumstances would be ground for recovery, but which are nevertheless excluded from consideration on the ground that the plaintiff should, acting as a person of ordinary prudence under the circumstances, have prevented or avoided them. These will be fully considered in a subsequent chapter. It is only necessary here to point out that in many decided cases elements of avoidable damage have been excluded by the courts as *remote*. Indeed it will further appear that there is much ground for holding all consequences treated by the law as avoidable to be in the strict sense of the word remote, as being the result not of the cause of action, but primarily of the negligence or indifference of the plaintiff. They are the result, in the view of the law, not of the cause of action, but of this combined with the influence of the plaintiff's own will.

§ 111a. Fundamental distinctions.

At the outset of any discussion of direct and consequential loss, proximate and remote damages, and proximate and remote cause, it is necessary to notice some fundamental distinctions often lost sight of. In the case of any action at law the first question to be settled is whether there is any legal liability at all. If there is, then the damages to be recovered may be either (a) nominal or (b) substantial, but with reference to the limits of substantial recovery there are several distinct classes of cases, *e. g.*, the act complained of may be (1) a breach

---

[1] 1 C. P. D. 92. For a further consideration of the rules involving the question of cause and consequence see Sedgwick, El. of Dam. (2d ed.), ch. v.

of contract; (2) it may be some species of wrong consisting of the commission of an act or acts involving the legal notion of tort (*e. g.*, assault, libel, trespass, false imprisonment); (3) it may be that the action is founded on an omission of due care (negligence) causing damage; or (4) it may be that the action is for what is called a nuisance, in which case there must be an illegal act of commission or omission in relation to property of or in some way controlled by the defendant, coupled with damage to the plaintiff arising therefrom; the nuisance being illegal, though the act or omission, in itself, in the absence of ensuing damage, might have been perfectly lawful. It will be observed that the last two cases closely resemble each other. In every one of these cases, special circumstances exist or may exist which distinguish it from each of the other three as to the limits of recovery. In the case of a simple tort, there must be some direct damage though it may be nominal in amount; consequential damages also may be recoverable, but these must be proximate; loss so remote from the wrongful act that this cannot be considered sufficiently active and efficient in the result for the notion of legal liability to attach is never allowed. In this sort of action, the legal proximate cause of all damage allowed must be *the tort*. In the case of a breach of contract, the legal proximate cause is the *breach*, but there is the additional circumstance that here, the wrong being the violation of an agreement *inter partes, the contemplation of the parties* may enlarge the scope of the potential anticipation of loss, and thus let in damages as natural and normal which would not be let in in an ordinary case; the third and fourth cases differ entirely from the other two in the fact that for liability to attach some damage as a consequence of the negligence or act of commission must ensue, *damage* being the gist of the action and negligence or act alone raising none. And here two questions arise: (a) Was the act charged the legal proximate cause of the alleged damage? (b) This being settled, the question arises as to any particular *head* or *element* of damage—is this to be allowed also or is it too remote? When a "wrongful act" is spoken of, it may mean either a simple tort, a breach of contract or negligence causing damage, or an act of commission or omission productive of a nuisance. Negligence with very little direct damage is enough to furnish the legal *proximate cause* of very great indirect but proximate damage, but it cannot be the proximate cause of remote damage.

§ 111b. Proximate and remote cause.

The term *Proximate,* as used in the law, is a relative, not an absolute term; it means *near,* not *nearest.* "Proximate cause" means, in law, no more than a cause which is not so remote in efficiency as to be dismissed from consideration by the court. This of itself explains why it has never been possible to ascertain any general test of proximate cause even for a given class of cases; since in law whatever is not proximate is remote, and *vice versa,* it is equally true that no general test of remoteness exists. A remote cause is simply one which because of its having ceased to be actively efficient, or never having become actively efficient, in the result, is neglected by the court. The legal distinction between what is proximate and what is remote is not a logical one, nor does it depend upon relations of time or space; it is purely practical, the reason for distinguishing between proximate and remote causes being a purely practical one. In the language of Lord Bacon, "It were infinite for the law to judge the causes of causes, and their impulsion one on another. Therefore, it contenteth itself with the immediate cause, and judgeth of acts by that without looking to any further degree."[2] If courts were to employ their time in searching out the infinity of causes leading to the particular result under investigation, doomsday would find their search incomplete, and the general body of suitors left unheard. The courts must for their own protection and entirely in the public interest, without regard to the particular claims of a defendant, set a limit to the inquiry, and rule out all causes beyond this arbitrary limit as remote, while those causes within the limit are accepted as proximate. The limit is set at a point where for the purpose of the law, a particular cause may be said substantially to have spent its force, and to have fallen into the great mass of circumstance which has ceased to be an active force.

[2] Maxims of the Law, Reg. 1.

§ 111c. Tests proposed for the determination of proximate causes.

The various tests actually employed to assist in the decision of cases, when closely examined, themselves show this. It is often said, for instance, that if the damage or loss for which the recovery is asked *might have been foreseen* by the defendant, then the cause for which it is sought to establish or measure liability is proximate: but this is no *test;* for recovery is also quite as often allowed for loss or damage that could not by any possibility have been foreseen; again even where the test of prevision of consequences is adopted, it is not maintained that the *precise form* in which the injury actually resulted must be foreseen. Even where, as in claims for consequential damages in contract, an apparent test exists in the rule that they must have been "within the contemplation of the parties," the rule does not mean that the precise form of damage suffered must have been actually contemplated by the parties, but merely means that had their minds been directed to the question, the contract would have been regarded by them as contemplating such and such damages as within its purview. But this only means that the natural, probable, normal and usual consequences of any breach of contract are to be treated as having been within the potential contemplation of the parties to it. So in cases of ordinary tort, the natural, probable, normal and usual potentialities in the course of nature are looked upon as within the contemplation of the defendant. The same thing is true in cases where the liability arises from negligence coupled with damage, and in cases of nuisance.

§ 111d. Time and distance.

Time and space, though they may throw light on the question of proximateness and remoteness in law, are no tests of them. Their inadequacy in this respect may be illustrated by a case decided by the New York Court of Appeals. A corporation negligently allowed a fire on its own premises to spread over the lands of intervening owners for some two miles to land of plaintiff, causing damage; the evidence being undisputed, it was held as a matter of law, two judges dissenting, that the cause was not proximate. "The limit," according to the opinion of the majority, is *the boundary of the abutter*.[3] Otherwise "where is the line to be drawn? Shall it be one mile, two miles or ten miles distant from the place of the original starting of the fire? Who is to specify the distance? It is suggested that it might be left to the jury; but a jury in one part of the State might answer one mile, and in another . . . ten miles."[4] Vann, J., in dissenting had no difficulty in showing that making liability depend on the distance intervening between the boundary of the person on whose land the fire starts and the boundary of his next neighbor is just as arbitrary as making it dependent on a measured distance. Liability, under such a rule, might extend a hundred miles, if the land were all owned by one person, and on the other hand, stop short at fifty feet if that was the distance of his boundary. In other words, proximateness in law is determined, on principle, neither by a uniform limit of distance nor by an arbitrary limit of extended ownership. At the same time, the intervening space might be too obviously great to allow of even the consideration of a cause of action. No court would listen patiently to an argument that loss of property in Boston was a proximate result of negligence as to fire on premises in San Francisco. For one thing, proof of any connection would be almost inconceivable, while the number of intervening causes, interrupting human agencies, etc., would be incalculable. "It were infinite for the law to judge the causes of causes, and their impulsion one on another."[5] So also of time. The lapse of a great interval of time always involves the interruption of the causal sequence by numerous intervening causes, but on the other hand, a single fatally interrupting cause may break the chain within a moment after the alleged *causa causans* has come into play. The rule of proximate cause "is not to be controlled by time or distance."[6]

[3] Hoffman *v.* King, 160 N. Y. 618, 628, 55 N. E. 401. See Sedgwick, El. of Dam. 58.

[4] 160 N. Y. 618, 628.

[5] Bacon, Maxims of the Law, Reg. 1.

[6] Per Thompson, C. J., in Pennsylvania R. R. *v.* Kerr, 62 Pa. 353, 366;

Haverly *v.* R. R., 135 Pa. 50, 58, 35 Atl. 50. In this case, a fire smouldered from one day to another and a wind having risen, then caused the damage. The lapse of time was held to be no obstacle to a recovery. See also dissenting opinion of Ladd, J., in Gilman *v.* Noyes, 57 N. H. 627.

§ 111e. Probability and rarity; possibility and impossibility.

Neither will any dividing line between probability and rarity or possibility and impossibility serve as a test. If the effect is the probable, natural, usual and normal consequence of the act or omission complained of, it is proximate; but the fact that the consequence is improbable and rare does not necessarily make it remote. There is no such thing as a liability for all *possible* consequences.

§ 111f. Causal sequence.

Nor can a decisive test of proximateness be found in causal sequence. If such a test were decisive, the person legally responsible for the injury would always be the one who immediately caused it. In the squib case, the law would have looked no further than to the last person who threw the squib; such a test would confound the legal liability with causal sequence in nature and almost recall that primitive stage of society in which even things are conceived of as endowed with legal responsibility. In Vandenburgh v. Truax,[7] the immediate cause in natural sequence of the loss of the wine was the boy's accidentally knocking out the faucet in B's store; the efficient cause, proximate in law but more remote in causal sequence, was A's pursuit of the boy with a pickaxe. But for this no loss would have occurred.

§ 112.[a] Causa sine quâ non. The " but for which " rule.

The defendant may have been negligent and the plaintiff may have suffered injury and a causal connection between the two may have been proved; but obviously this is not enough, for there are other causes which have contributed to produce the loss or damage. The essential point in law is that the connection must be proved to be *necessary;* the negligence must be a cause *but for which* the injury would not have been suffered. In the same way, liability once established, the *extent* to which the law will go in allowing specific heads or elements of damage must depend upon their having a necessary connection with the cause of action. In an action by a boarding-house keeper for

---

[7] 4 Den. (N. Y.) 465.   [a] For § 112 of the 8th ed. see § 121b.

an injury caused by negligence, evidence that her house was not as well filled as before is not enough to warrant a recovery. This may be explained by other causes.[8] So in accident cases brought by railway passengers for personal injury, liability having been established, the question whether recovery can be had for a miscarriage depends on whether the injury was *causa sine quâ non* of this particular damage. This "but for" rule, which is frequently mistaken for a decisive test, may be expressed as follows:—The proximate cause to which legal liability attaches must be a cause but for which the loss or damage would not have arisen. But the *causal chain is a legal conception,* abstracted from the infinite web of cause and effect, as it appears and vanishes in nature, formed for the purpose of attaching legal responsibility to a human agent, and in this chain, to say that a cause satisfies the "but for" rule is not to say that it is a proximate cause since it may equally well be a remote cause. Two entirely independent conditions must be satisfied. First, to be proximate and entail legal responsibility, a cause must be one but for which the result would not have happened. Second, not only must this test be satisfied, but also this cause must be active enough in the result for it to be regarded in the law as efficient in responsibility. To say that but for it the result would not have happened is not in any way decisive upon the question whether it was a cause efficient enough in the result for legal responsibility to attach.[9] There being no general test of proximateness or remoteness or in law, we are obliged to fall back upon the general rule or definition that by a proximate cause in law is meant a cause, sufficiently near in ordinary natural sequence, to which legal effect is given, either in establishing liability or in determining the measure of recovery.

But in the decision of a case, before the legal chain with its efficient cause or causes is finally disentangled from the natural *plexus,* many *naturally* proximate causes may come under dis-

---

[8] Wallace *v.* Pennsylvania R. R., 195 Pa. 127, 45 Atl. 485.

[9] For an interesting discussion of this subject, see note, 36 Am. St. Rep. 807–861, on Gibson *v.* Delaware & H. C. Co., 65 Vt. 213, 26 Atl. 70, 36 Am. St. Rep. 802, to the unknown author of which the editors of the present edition are indebted for a great part of the above analysis of *tests.*

cussion, and these are, pending the decision, inevitably all called proximate:—this fact leads to, or rather involves a comparison, which necessarily results in error. Except by constantly bearing in mind that the terms proximate and remote are always ambiguous, no pathway can be found through the maze.

§ 113. Remote consequences not compensated.

It has already been stated that the law does not and cannot give complete compensation for the injury sustained; it refuses to take into consideration any damages remotely resulting from the act complained of.[10]

In the language of the Supreme Court of Pennsylvania, to visit upon the defendant *all* the consequences of his wrongful act "would set society on edge, and fill the courts with useless and injurious litigation. It is impossible to compensate for all losses, and the law therefore aims at a just discrimination, which will impose upon the party causing them, the proportion of them that a proper view of his acts and the attending circumstances would dictate."[11]

And as the Supreme Court of Massachusetts expresses it, "A rule of damages which should embrace within its scope all the consequences which might be shown to have resulted from a failure or omission to perform a stipulated duty or service, would be a serious hindrance to the operations of commerce, and to the transaction of the common business of life. The effect would be to impose a liability wholly disproportionate to the nature of the act or service which a party has bound himself to perform, and to the compensation paid and received therefor."[12] Courts of justice, therefore, allow recovery only

[10] § 38. Where two causes concur to bring about a result, but one only slightly contributes and the other is the predominant cause, the latter only is considered.

United States: Insurance Co. *v.* Transportation Co., 12 Wall. 199, 20 L. ed. 378.

Texas: Ellyson *v.* International & G. N. R. R., 33 Tex. Civ. App. 1, 75 S. W. 868. This does not mean that the cause or condition which is nearest in time or place is necessarily to be deemed the proximate cause. The law does not consider the cause of causes beyond seeking the efficient predominant cause. Freeman *v.* Mercantile M. A. Assoc., 156 Mass. 353, 30 N. E. 1013, 17 L. R. A. 753.

[11] Agnew, J., in Fleming *v.* Beck, 48 Pa. 309, 313.

[12] Bigelow, C. J., in Squire *v.* Western U. T. Co., 98 Mass. 232, 237, 90 Am. Dec. 157.

for such damage as is the proximate consequence of the defendant's wrong, and exclude from consideration consequences which are remote.[13]

§ 114. Consequences of an act complex in nature.

Before examining the decided cases, it should be clearly comprehended that recovery of compensation for remote loss is refused, not because the wrongful act was not in one sense the cause of the loss, but because the loss is so far in causal sequence from the injury that *the law cannot take it into account in fixing liability*. It should be noticed that the effects which flow from the *cause of action* do not form a single chain, but that each effect in this chain is produced in part by one or more other causes. Every effect is the product of numerous causes, and every cause produces in its turn numerous effects. The general result is a network of causes and effects rather than a single causal chain. For example: A fails to pay his note when

---

[13] Chidester *v.* Consolidated People's Ditch Co., 53 Cal. 56; Carter *v.* Towne, 103 Mass. 507.

A question analogous to the one we are now considering arises in cases of tort, where the defendant attempts to show that the entire injury is too remote a result of his act or omission fairly to be attributed to it. It is evident that much the same considerations are involved, whether the attempt is to show that the injury itself is remote, or only certain consequences of the injury. The former question concerns the right to bring an action; the latter involves a discussion of the measure of damages. These classes of cases are, however, often difficult to distinguish in practice; and a case turning upon the right of action may frequently be a precedent for the decision of a case involving the measure of damages. It is impossible, therefore, entirely to exclude from this treatise cases involving the right of action, or, as it is frequently called, proximate cause. The doctrine is founded, or at

least found its first expression, in the maxim, *Cause proxima, non remota, spectatur.* See *ante*, §§ 111a *et seq.*

Other terms have often been employed to distinguish between such consequences as are to be considered and such as are not. The term *special damages* is often employed; but this is rather a matter of pleading and indicates such damages recoverable on general principles of law as must be specially claimed in the declaration, to give notice of the claim to the defendant and thus avoid surprise. The term *natural* is frequently employed in the phrase "natural and proximate." Greenl. on Evid., vol. ii, § 256. See also Donnell *v.* Jones, 13 Ala. 490; Crain *v.* Petrie, 6 Hill (N. Y.), 522, 41 Am. Dec. 765; Vicars *v.* Wilcocks, 8 East, 1; Kelly *v.* Partington, 5 B. & A. 645. In cases in contract (in which the inquiry is whether the damage was within the contemplation of the parties) natural and proximate means within the contemplation of the parties.

due to B. B, in consequence, loses the money, and becomes bankrupt. But this failure was due not only to the lack of this particular money, but to a multitude of co-operating causes, such as a stringency in the money market, which at the time made the loss irreparable. Hence we say that the only direct and proximate consequence was the loss of the money, leav-the effect of the combination of the cause of action with other causes wholly out of view. So, one effect of B's failure is domestic misery and the consequent death of his child. But in this appear the effects of additional co-operating causes, such as exposure, constitutional tendency to disease, etc. As the law stops short at this primary effect, *a fortiori*, it must set these down as remote consequences.

§ 115. Scott v. Shepherd.

In the discussion of the question of proximate cause the famous squib case is often cited.[14] In that case it appeared that the defendant threw a lighted squib into the market-house, which fell on the stall of a ginger-bread seller; he, to save himself, threw it on another stall; the proprietor of the second stall also threw it off, and in so doing struck the plaintiff and put out his eye. The decision was in favor of the plaintiff. The judges differed in opinion.

Nares, J., held that trespass would lie because the natural and probable consequence of the defendant's act was injury to somebody, and therefore the act was unlawful; and being unlawful, the defendant was answerable for its consequences, whether the injury were *mediate* or *immediate*. In this opinion Gould, J., concurred, expressing further the opinion that trespass would lie for the mischievous consequences of another's act, whether lawful or not. Blackstone, J., dissenting, held that the injury being *consequential* only and *not immediate*, the action of trespass could not be maintained, but that case should have been brought. De Grey, C. J., held that the injury was the direct and immediate result of the act of the defendant, and that trespass would lie. It thus appears that the difference between the judges turned upon the form of action; but all agreed that the injury was proximate.

[14] Scott *v.* Shepherd, 2 W. Bl. 892.

Later cases have followed the decision, on the ground that the acts of the others were natural and instinctive; that the injury to the plaintiff was, therefore, the *immediate* result of the defendant's acts, as if the squib had struck against boards, and rebounded instead of having been thrown.

§ 115a. What consequences are remote.

Every consequence may be conceived as a result of two or more concurring causes which by their mutual action bring about the new condition. Each of these causes is in its turn the result of two or more prior causes, and so *ad infinitum*. All prior causes have a part in the final result; but among the infinity of prior causes the greater number play so small a part as to be practically negligible. Each of these prior causes has had an immediate and important effect upon later consequences; but its importance has gradually declined until it finally ceased to be a practically active cause. It is now only remotely the cause of succeeding consequences. Only such causes can be regarded as proximate for the sake of fixing legal responsibility for them, as are still regarded by the law, in view of its own purpose, active in the result in question. *Remoteness* is neither a philosophical, nor merely, as in common speech, a strongly descriptive term, but a practical though not fixed measure.

§ 116. Question of remoteness a question of fact.

The question whether an item of loss is or is not a proximate consequence of the wrong is in each case a question of fact. Only general principles can be laid down, and in applying them much latitude must necessarily be left to the court and jury. If the case is a clear one, the court will direct the jury upon the question; but if the question is a doubtful one it will be left to the jury.[15] In many actions of contract, *e. g.*, in actions on policies, when the question of a breach depends on the cause of action being the *peril insured against*, the question of remoteness is one of the interpretation of the contract, and hence for

[15] *Maryland:* Maryland Steel Co. *v.* Marney, 88 Md. 482, 42 Atl. 60, 42 L. R. A. 842; Carroll Springs Distilling Co. of Baltimore *v.* Schnepfe, 111 Md. 420, 74 Atl. 828.

Massachusetts: Allen *v.* Truesdell, 135 Mass. 75.

Missouri: Clemens *v.* Hannibal & S. J. R. R., 53 Mo. 366, 14 Am. Rep. 460.

the courts.[16] The difficulties inherent in the subject are not lessened by the fact that the distinction between the question of proximate or remote consequences and the question of natural consequences has been so frequently lost sight of; on the other hand, the matter has been further confused with questions of certainty or uncertainty of loss. The line between proximate and natural consequences is in fact a vague one, and an item of damage might often be disallowed either as a remote or as a non-normal consequence of the wrongful act. But the subject will be clearer upon considering remote and unexpected losses separately, and much will be gained by a classification of the cases, so far as that is possible.

§ 117. Instances of proximate and remote consequences.

Every suit at law is likely to involve some novel question of remoteness of damage. So far-reaching and varied are the consequences of what seems the least important act, that every wrong drags after it a chain of more or less disastrous consequences, which the injured party may ascribe with truth to the first wrongful act; and in every suit the plaintiff attempts to shift to the defendant the burden of as many links as possible of this chain. A few simple cases may first be stated.

The plaintiff having been induced to put money into an oil speculation by the defendant's false representations, afterwards, but before he discovered the fraud, put in more money. The loss of the latter money was a proximate consequence of the false representation, and the plaintiff could recover compensation for it.[17] And where by the negligence of the defendant a house was set on fire and the children in it were burned to death, their death was a proximate consequence of the fire.[18] On the other hand, where a train was late and the conductor for that reason sent a female passenger to a hotel to spend the night, agreeing on behalf of the carrier to pay the expenses, and a lamp given her by the innkeeper exploded and she was burned,

---

[16] *Massachusetts:* Lynn Gas & Electric Co. *v.* Meriden F. Ins. Co., 158 Mass. 570, 33 N. E. 690.

Wisconsin: Cary *v.* Preferred Accident Ins. Co., 127 Wis. 67, 106 N. W. 1055. See Sedgwick, El. of Dam. 61.

[17] Crater *v.* Binninger, 33 N. J. L. 513, 97 Am. Dec. 737.

[18] Rajnowski *v.* Detroit, B. C. & A. R. R., 74 Mich. 20, 41 N. W. 847.

this burning was held to be a remote consequence of the delay of the train.[19]

In an action for wrongfully mining the plaintiff's coal it appeared that the defendant left large pillars of coal standing where he had taken out the rest of the coal and the result of this was that the coal was drained of water and rapidly deteriorated; and that the coal so left was less easy to mine. It was held that the damage caused by the deterioration of the coal and the added difficulty of mining was the proximate consequence of the trespass, and might be recovered.[20] The plaintiff, who was suing his debtor, applied to the defendant, a public officer, for a certificate of his age, to be used in the case. Defendant gave him a false certificate, and in consequence it was necessary to continue the case until the next term. Before the next term the debtor died, which necessitated a further continuance. It was held that the first continuance was a proximate consequence of the defendant's error, but the subsequent continuance was remote.[21] In an action for the conversion of plaintiff's carpet bag it appeared that plaintiff was a laborer and the carpet bag contained his working clothes and for lack of the clothes he was obliged to work in better clothes than he needed and they were injured. This was held to be a remote consequence of the taking.[22] Owing to the negligent construction of a bridge, the bridge fell and it was necessary to draw the water off from the canal which it crossed in order to recover the materials and take them out of the canal. Plaintiff was injured by the withdrawing of the water. This was held a proximate consequence of the defect in the bridge, and he could recover.[23]

An entirely harmonious course of decision on such a question is not expected. As the determination is really one of fact, under proper directions, and ordinarily for the jury, the decision may simply be the result of the court's upholding the right of the jury to decide one way or the other; and even if the court

---

[19] Central of G. Ry. *v.* Price, 106 Ga. 176, 32 S. E. 77, 43 L. R. A. 402.

[20] Williams *v.* Raggett, 46 L. J. Ch. 849, 37 L. T. Rep. (N. S.) 96, 25 Wkly. Rep. 874.

[21] Maxwell *v.* Pike, 2 Me. 8.

[22] Saunders *v.* Brosius, 52 Mo. 50.

[23] Dayton *v.* Pease, 4 Ohio St. 80.

itself determine the question, as is not infrequent in practice, it is nevertheless natural to expect differences of opinion upon what are really close questions of fact. Thus where by reason of negligence a railroad locomotive struck a person on the track and threw his body so violently against the plaintiff as to cause injury, this has been held a proximate result of the negligence,[24] while on the other hand it has been held remote.[25]

§ 118. Cause and condition.

The conception of a remote cause as one that is not an active and efficient factor in bringing about the result has led to an important distinction between cause and condition. A circumstance which, though a factor in the result, is a purely passive one, is called a mere condition, and is not a proximate cause. Thus if a man while in his house is struck by lightning, and killed, his act in staying at home at the time is only remotely the cause of his death; and the same is true if he is walking along the road when he is struck and killed.[26] And if one throws anything out of his window, and an unforeseen wind blows it against a man, this is not the act of the thrower, but of the wind;[27] while if the thrower had known of the wind, or had in anyway acted with reference to the wind, he would have been held for the result, not because his act in throwing the thing from his window would have been different, but because he would in that case have made the wind his minister, and would have been responsible for what it did. This principle might perhaps be invoked to solve the difficult questions considered in the following sections.

§ 119. Exposure to risk: negligence concurring with cause for which defendant is not responsible.[28]

Where the defendant's wrongful act or negligence has ex-

---

[24] Western & A. R. R. v. Bailey, 105 Ga. 100, 31 S. E. 547.

[25] *Indiana:* Evansville & T. H. Ry. v. Welch, 25 Ind. App. 308, 58 N. E. 88.

Pennsylvania: Wood v. Pa. R. R., 177 Pa. 306, 35 Atl. 699, 55 Am. St. Rep. 728.

[26] Lewis v. Flint & P. M. Ry., 54 Mich. 55, 19 N. W. 744.

[27] Y. B. 6 Edw. 4, 7, 18; Rex v. Gill, 1 Stra. 190. And see Y. B. Lib. Assis. 287, 17.

[28] The discussion in this and the five following sections represents the views of Mr. A. G. Sedgwick only. Mr. Beale dissents from them in every particular.

posed the plaintiff to the risk of injury from an independent
cause, for which the defendant is not at all responsible, and
from this independent cause the injury actually happened, the
defendant's responsibility for the injury is often difficult to
determine. A common case of this sort is the wrongful delay
by a carrier, whereby the goods he carries are placed in a position where they are destroyed by an act of God, like an extraordinary flood, or by some other cause for which the carrier is
either by some principle of law, or by contract, not responsible.
On one side it is urged that but for the delay the goods would
not have been exposed to the flood; that at the very time of the
flood the effect of the delay was active; that it was therefore
the proximate cause of the loss, and that in an action for delay compensation for the loss should be recovered. Thus stated,
the argument seems unanswerable. But in some cases the
delay as an active force has ceased to exist, the goods continuing
for an appreciable interval of time unharmed in spite of the
delay; in such cases it is urged that the delay is no more active
a cause of the flood overwhelming them than any other antecedent circumstance, such as the act of the shipper in sending
them on a particular train. In the natural *plexus* of causation
it is obvious that when the connection between the delay and
the flood is merely accidental and fortuitous, the loss of the
goods is a remote consequence of the delay; but when the delay
continuously keeps alive the risk of loss, the injury has a direct
relation to the delay, and is in nature a proximate result of it.
Suppose, for instance, a carrier has several rivers to cross, the
mere delay between rivers would be no more likely to cause
than to prevent a destruction of the goods he was carrying by
a flood. Thus if two trains were traversing the route an hour
apart, an hour's delay to both which would cause the first to
be overwhelmed by a flood at one of the rivers might save the
second from the same fate. The connection between the delay
and the loss is merely fortuitous. But if the train had been un-
duly delayed on a bridge in a season of floods, the loss by a flood
would be a proximate result of the delay. We must not, however, overlook the fact that the question is not one simply of
natural causation, but which is the *causa proxima in law:* the
negligence involved in continuous delay, or the concurring flood.

According to what is generally supposed to be the prevailing view, therefore, loss by a cause for which the defendant is not accountable is the remote consequence of a delay which does not increase the risk of loss, and the plaintiff cannot recover damages for it.[29] But where the risk was increased by the delay, as for instance, where the carrier delays in winter and the goods are frozen because of long exposure to the cold, the delay is the proximate cause of the freezing.[30]

[29] *So of loss by flood:*
United States: Railroad Co. v. Reeves, 10 Wall. 176, 19 L. ed. 909; Empire S. C. Co. v. Atchison, T. & S. F. Ry., 135 Fed. 135; Gleeson v. Virginia Midland Ry., 5 Mack. (D. C.) 356.

Massachusetts: Denny v. New York C. R. R., 13 Gray, 481, 74 Am. Dec. 645.

Missouri: Davis v. Wabash, S. L. & P. Ry., 89 Mo. 340, 1 S. W. 327; Grier v. St. Louis, M. B. T. R. R., 108 Mo. App. 565, 84 S. W. 158; Moffatt C. Co. v. Union P. Ry., 113 Mo. App. 544, 88 S. W. 117.

Ohio: Daniels v. Ballantine, 23 Oh. St. 532, 13 Am. Rep. 264.

Pennsylvania: Morrison v. Davis, 20 Pa. 171, 57 Am. Dec. 695.

Texas: Hunt v. Missouri, K. & T. R. R., Tex. Civ. App. , 74 S. W. 69.

Loss by fire:
Massachusetts: Hoadley v. Northern T. Co., 115 Mass. 304, 15 Am. Rep. 106.

Mississippi: Yazoo & M. V. R. R. v. Millsaps, 76 Miss. 855, 25 So. 672, 71 Am. St. Rep. 543.

North Carolina: General F. I. Co. v. Carolina & N. W. Ry., 137 N. C. 278, 47 S. E. 208.

See Merchants' W. B. Assoc. v. Wood, 64 Miss. 661, 2 So. 76.

In McRea v. Hill, 126 Ill. App. 349, this doctrine was wrongly applied in a case where the goods had been placed in the wrong warehouse; see *post*, § 121a.

Loss by severe storm:
Virginia: Herring v. Chesapeake & W. Ry., 101 Va. 778, 45 S. E. 322.

Unless of course there is subsequent negligence on the part of the defendant.
United States: Railroad v. Reeves, 10 Wall. 176, 19 L. ed. 909.

Missouri: Davis v. Wabash, S. L. & P. Ry., 89 Mo. 340, 1 S. W. 327.

On the other hand, many courts hold the contrary view.

Loss by flood:
Illinois: Wald v. Pittsburg, C., C. & St. L. R. R., 162 Ill. 545, 44 N. E. 888, 35 L. R. A. 356, 53 Am. St. Rep. 332.

Iowa: Green-Wheeler Shoe Co. v. Chicago, R. I. & P. Ry., 130 Ia. 123, 106 N. W. 498.

Minnesota: Bibb B. C. Co. v. Atchison, T. & S. F. Ry., 94 Minn. 269, 102 N. W. 709, 69 L. R. A. 509.

New York: Michaels v. New York C. R. R., 30 N. Y. 564, 86 Am. Dec. 415; Read v. Spaulding, 30 N. Y. 630, 86 Am. Dec. 426.

Loss by fire:
Alabama: Louisville & N. R. R. v. Gidley, 119 Ala. 523, 24 So. 753.

Kentucky: Hernsheim v. Newport, N. & M. V. Co., 18 Ky. L. Rep. 227, 35 S. W. 1115.

New York: Condict v. Grand Trunk R. R., 54 N. Y. 500.

In Green-Wheeler Shoe Co. v. Ry., *supra*, McClain, C. J., in a very able opinion collects the authorities and decides in favor of this latter view.

[30] *Loss by freezing:*
Illinois: Michigan C. R. R. v. Curtis, 80 Ill. 324.

Massachusetts: Fox v. Boston & M. R. R., 148 Mass. 220, 19 N. E. 222.

Missouri: Wolf v. Express Co., 43

In accordance with this distinction, it has been held that where a passenger was carried beyond his destination and was obliged to walk back along the track, and was without negligence on his part injured by a passing train, the carrier was liable; [31] but where under similar circumstances he became confused because of smoke from a neighboring fire, mistook the path and fell into a cattle guard which he well knew to be there, the carrier was held not liable,[32] the court saying that it was as if while walking back he had been struck by lightning or accidentally wounded by a gun. Where, by the defendant's neglect to fence its right of way, as required by statute, the plaintiff's horse got into the defendant's premises and there stepped into a small hole and was injured, the hole being such a one as would be found in any field, the consequence was held remote.[33] A customer in a store stumbled and fell into an elevator well left dangerously unprotected; [34] a person on the street, jumping aside to avoid collision with a bicycle, fell off the sidewalk into a hole negligently left unguarded; [35] a foot passenger stepped into a hole in a plank sidewalk caused by a bicycle immediately in front of him throwing out a loose plank: [36] in all these cases the person responsible for the defective condition of the building or sidewalk is liable. But where a person

Mo. 423; Armentrout v. St. Louis, K. E. & N. R. R., 1 Mo. App. 158.

West Virginia: McGraw v. Baltimore & O. R. R., 18 W. Va. 361, 41 Am. Rep. 696.

Contra, however, where the defendant delivered safely to a succeeding carrier, and the goods were frozen while carried by the latter carrier without delay. See Michigan Cent. R. R. v. Burrows, 33 Mich. 6.

Loss by flood, delay being at ford in river:

Campbell v. Morse, Harp. (S. C.) 468.

Loss by failure to arrive, the train being delayed by natural causes after the wrongful delay:

Sutton v. Western U. T. Co., 129 Ky. 166, 110 S. W. 874.

[31] *California:* Benson v. Central P. R. R., 98 Cal. 45, 32 Pac. 809.

[32] Lewis v. Flint & P. M. Ry., 54 Mich. 55, 19 N. W. 744. In Hollenbeck v. Johnson, 79 Hun, 499, 29 N. Y. Supp. 945, the defendant's cow trespassed in plaintiff's barn and broke through the floor, which was rotten, and fell into a cistern and was killed; plaintiff on going into the barn fell through the floor and was injured; it was held that the injury was a remote consequence of the trespass.

[33] Nelson v. Chicago, M. & S. P. Ry., 30 Minn. 74, 14 N. W. 360.

[34] Rosenbaum v. Shoffner, 98 Tenn. 624, 40 S. W. 1086.

[35] Knouff v. Logansport, 26 Ind. App. 202, 59 N. E. 347.

[36] Chacey v. Fargo, 5 N. D. 173, 64 N. W. 932.

on the street is caused to step aside by an obstruction, and a bale of hay is then negligently pushed upon him, the obstruction is only remotely the cause of the injury.[37]   And where defendant wrongfully placed a cable on a fire-boat on which plaintiff was an officer; an alarm of fire sounded, plaintiff ordered the line cast off and started the boat ahead, and his foot was caught and injured, it was held that the intervening act of the plaintiff in starting the boat was the proximate cause of the injury and not the placing of the line on the boat.[38]

Where by reason of delay in constructing a vessel it was crossing the sea to its destination at a later time than was intended and it was caught by a hurricane and lost, this was held a remote consequence of the delay in construction.[39]   And delay in the performance of a contract to thresh grain is not necessarily the proximate cause of a loss of grain by a storm.[40]

In a Pennsylvania case the defendant undertook to carry goods on a canal boat; and by reason of his negligence in starting with a lame horse the transit was delayed, and the goods lost in a flood.   The loss was held too remote from the delay for recovery.[41]   In another case, the defendant by blocking the entrance to a lock kept the plaintiff's boat in a dangerous position outside the lock, exposed to the dangers of the river; by a rise of the river it was swept over the dam.   The plaintiff was allowed to recover, on the ground that the defendant had exposed him to a serious risk of loss; and the court pointed out that so far from the delay increasing the risk in the earlier case, if the horse had been still more lame and unfit and the delay greater, the loss would not have happened.[42]

This general principle was invoked in an action for deceit by a contractor against the president of a railroad company with whom he had made a contract to build a railroad.   The president had represented that the right of way had been obtained. This was not true, and there was considerable delay in obtain-

---

[37] Parmenter v. Marion, 113 Iowa, 297, 85 N. W. 90.

[38] Trapp v. McClellan, 68 App. Div. 362, 74 N. Y. Supp. 130.

[39] De Ford v. Maryland Steel Co., 113 Fed. 72, 51 C. C. A. 59.

[40] Hayes v. Cooley, 13 N. D. 204, 100 N. W. 250.

[41] Morrison v. Davis, 20 Pa. 171, 57 Am. Dec. 695.

[42] Scott v. Hunter, 46 Pa. 192.

ing it, during which the price of rails rose. It was held that no recovery could be had on that ground, since the delay might have caused the price of rails to go down as well as up.[43] The general principle seems to have been lost sight of in a New York case. It appeared that the defendant interposed the plaintiff's body between himself and a bomb which a third person was about to explode, and the plaintiff was injured by the explosion; but it did not appear that the plaintiff would not have been injured in any case. The act of the defendant was an actionable trespass; but the injury caused by the bomb was held not to be a proximate consequence of the defendant's act. It would seem that the defendant by his act increased the risk of damage, and that he should have been held.[44]

§ 119a. Cases against carriers. Comparative exposure to risk. Anticipation of loss.

On the whole array of cases against carriers, the following observations are to be made. They often afford illustrations of the confusion already referred to between the conception of proximate cause in nature and in law, and in them what may be called the doctrine of comparative exposure to risk sometimes seems to complicate the question of proximate cause and remoteness with that of anticipation of loss. Whenever it is held that either liability in the action or, this being ascertained, liability for a particular head of damage depends on reasonable potential anticipation of the consequence or the absence of it, negligence or the absence of due care may depend on the degree of exposure to risk brought into view; if the exposure to risk is reasonable, it is *not negligent;* if it is negligent, it is because it is unreasonable. To expose apples to the risk of freezing is negligent in winter; in summer it is not so. But on principle,

[43] Phelps *v.* George's Creek & C. R. R., 60 Md. 536.

[44] Laidlaw *v.* Sage, 158 N. Y. 73, 52 N. E. 679, 44 L. R. A. 216. The decision seems to uphold the most extreme application of the "but for which" test, adhered to with fanatical tenacity by the New York courts. No plaintiff can always prove that but for defendant's trespass he would not have been injured. In this case he proved a direct causal connection, which led to a necessary *inference.* If the decision had rested on findings for the *defendant* that the injury would have occurred *whether or no* the trespass had been committed, the case would have been different.

where the case itself is decided on the assumption of negligence, the question of comparative exposure to risk does not arise. If one active cause of the loss by the negligence involved is continuous delay (and certainly delay in transportation not made up *en route* must be continuous negligence) and the other concurring cause be one for which the carrier is not responsible, the question of comparative exposure to risk is no longer involved in the case. All that remains is whether the proximate cause is one or the other. If the proximate cause is held to be an act of God or a risk contractually excepted, such as fire not due to defendant's negligence, then the other cause is remote in law and the proximate cause being one for which the carrier is not responsible, the action fails. *Vice versa* if the negligence is held to be the *causa causans* but for which the other cause would not have been effective, then the action lies. This is an illustration of the difference between proximate in law and in natural causation. In the latter, one is as much *causa causans* as the other; in the former, it can only be the negligence. In cases of this sort, where the risk is excepted by the rules of law themselves, as in the case of an act of God, some cases hold that the exception does not apply, because to be an act of God the agency of the defendant must not enter into it in any way. In such a view, it may be technically correct to speak of remoteness in law, any cause which the law excludes being necessarily remote, but it is really a case of legal exclusion of an exception. Under this legal exclusion, no choice between causes being possible, only one *causa causans*, the negligence, is left. If the nomenclature of proximate and remote causation is retained, the negligence may be called the proximate cause and the act of God the remote cause; but it would seem preferable to say that the exception does not apply.[45]

The difficulty comes, perhaps, most completely into view in the cases in which there is no question of an act of God but there is negligent delay without which the loss would not have happened, and concurrent with it an ordinary cause from liability for which, however, the carrier has exempted himself by contract; *e. g.*, fire not due to his negligence. Here as well as in cases involving acts of God, as appears by the cases already

[45] See Michaels *v.* New York C. R. R., 30 N. Y. 564, 66 Am. Dec. 415, 418, 420.

cited, the courts are irreconcilably divided, it being held in some jurisdictions that all negligence is of one sort and that degrees of antecedent exposure to risk are immaterial when once negligence causing loss is established, and that such cases are governed by the rule that when of two concurring causes, one is a cause for which the carrier is not responsible and the other is his negligence, the latter is the proximate cause. In others it is held that the delay is the remote; the cause for which the carrier is not responsible the proximate cause.[46]

§ 119b. Causes of divergence in the cases.

Whatever view may be taken of the divergence in the cases and the nomenclature employed in deciding them, confusion has evidently been introduced by several causes. One of these has been already adverted to. The notion of remoteness being determined by anticipation of risk can have no force when once the fact of negligence and loss caused thereby is established; but besides this, according to the prevailing view, in all actions founded on negligence, ordinary, normal, natural perils of all kinds are within the scope of that potential anticipation which the law takes as the basis of liability, and any reasonable person must foresee that delay extends the time during which casualties may overtake the risk.[47]

The argument often referred to as important in cases of delay that the transportation on time might have exposed the goods to exactly the same or a greater risk can, we think, be shown to be fallacious. The usual illustration is the beginning of the transportation in a canal boat with a lame horse.[48] Owing to the delay caused, the goods carried are caught in an extraordinary flood and damaged or lost. Had the horse been

---

[46] In this discussion it must throughout be borne in mind that *exposure to risk* is not in itself a tort, or a ground of liability. Exposure to risk may tend to show, or clearly prove, negligence, if the risk is sufficiently obvious, if not, it shows nothing, and is entirely neutral or even innocent. It is through potential conscious perception of the consequences that negligence comes into view, which, combined with damage, results in liability. Exposure to risk is merely a fact, which in itself has no necessary legal consequences.

[47] Green-Wheeler Shoe Co. *v.* Chicago, R. I. & P. Ry., 130 Ia. 123, 129, 106 N. W. 498.

[48] Morrison *v.* Davis, 20 Pa. 171; Scott *v.* Hunter, 46 Pa. 192, 195.

still more lame; *i. e.*, had there been greater negligence, the goods would have arrived after the subsidence of the flood and therefore escaped it.   On the other hand, had the horse not been lame at all, the stage of the flood might have been higher and the loss greater.   Or, to resort to an illustration given above: [49] If two trains are traversing a route one hour apart, an hour's delay to both, causing the first to be overwhelmed by a flood, might save the second.   The answer to this is that while the consequences suggested are quite possible, the argument involves throughout the fallacy of confusing a question of natural causation with one of legal proximate cause; had the horse not been lame, there would have been no negligence, and hence the case could not have arisen; while, had the horse been more lame, then the second train would have escaped loss altogether, and there would have been negligence but no damage. Consequently in neither of these cases could there have been a cause of action.   As to the accident to the first train, this merely presents the usual case of negligence followed by damage.   There is no rule better settled than that one who has by his negligence caused a loss cannot *excuse himself* by showing that the natural consequences of greater negligence might have made the loss less, or that due care might have been followed by loss.   Such a speculation is foreign to the whole system of legal responsibility, the object of which is defeated the moment we wander from the pursuit of the incidence of the burden of legal liability.

§ 119c. Analogy in cases of deviation.

The well-known rule in cases of deviation furnishes an analogy.[50]   The rule is that if the carrier transports the goods over some route other than that contracted for, or within the contemplation of the parties, he must answer for any damage occurring during such deviation, though arising from a cause which would not otherwise have rendered him liable.   He cannot set up for a defense the bare possibility that the loss might have happened if there had been no deviation.   To excuse himself,

---

[49] § 119.

[50] Constable *v.* National S. S. Co., 154 U. S. 51, 38 L. ed. 993, 14 Sup. Ct.

1062; Green-Wheeler Shoe Co. *v.* Chicago, R. I. & P. Ry., 130 Ia. 123, 130, 106 N. W. 498.

he must show that the loss *must* have happened in either case. Whether, according to one view, this rule is founded on the theory that deviation is conversion, or not, there is no doubt that an analogy between the two classes of cases exists. Deviation, like delay, involves a continuous exposure to risk of almost every variety, and why there should be different rules in the two cases, it is hard to see.

§ 119d. Leading cases in Massachusetts, New York and Pennsylvania.

Between what has been called the Massachusetts rule and that adopted in New York, there is a fundamental divergence. In the Massachusetts case, the action was to recover for damage to wool delivered to a carrier for carriage from S. to A. Owing to negligent delay, the wool arrived at A. six days late, was delivered, and was afterwards submerged by an extraordinary flood. The wool was intended to go to a further point, and but for the delay, would have gone on and escaped the flood; the opinion of the court was that the delay, through delivery of the goods at the end of the route, "had ceased to operate as an active, efficient and prevailing cause," that the act of God was "a subsequent inevitable accident," and that the negligence of the defendant was remote.[51] The New York courts, which repudiate the so-called Massachusetts rule, make this distinction decisive. In the leading case [52] which is all the more interesting because the loss was the result of the same flood, the Court of Appeals calls attention to it and restates the grounds of decision in the Massachusetts case as follows:

"The decision was put in this case upon the ground that the defendants were responsible only for the proximate and not for the remote consequences of their actions. And the court, arriving at the conclusion that the defendants were not liable, placed much stress upon the fact that the duty of the defendants as carriers *had terminated at the time the injury happened.* They had made the delivery required of them and they were sought to be charged because they had not made it earlier. At the time of the flood, therefore, they were not in charge of the

[51] Denny *v.* New York C. R. R., 13 Gray, 481, 487.   [52] Read *v.* Spaulding, 30 N. Y. 630.

wool as common carriers. All their duties and responsibilities as such had ceased except that they were liable for such damages as the owners had sustained by reason of their delay in the delivery of it. The court says that the rise in the waters of the Hudson which did the mischief to the wool occurred at a period subsequent to this; that is, the termination of their duty as carriers, and consequently was the direct and proximate cause to which that mischief was to be attributed. The negligence of the defendants was remote."

But in the New York case, *the property was yet in the custody, care and control of the carrier,* and on the ground of this fundamental distinction between the two cases, the Court of Appeals held the carrier's negligence the proximate cause of the loss. Adopting the language of the trial court, it lays down the rule, now followed in many jurisdictions, as follows:

"A common carrier in order to claim exemption from liability for damage done to goods in his hands in the course of transportation, though injured by what is deemed the act of God, must be without fault himself; his act or neglect must not concur and contribute to the injury. If he departs from the line of duty and violates his contract, and while thus in fault, and in consequence of the fault, the goods are injured by the act of God, which would not otherwise have caused the injury, he is not protected." [53]

The Massachusetts case is usually referred to as being founded on the Pennsylvania case of Morrison *v.* Davis,[54] but a careful examination of the opinion in the Pennsylvania case and the facts as stated by the court show that it cannot be regarded as furnishing a satisfactory foundation for the Massachusetts decision. The action was against carriers by canal for damage to goods caused by the wrecking of a canal boat occasioned by an extraordinary flood. When the boat started on its voyage one of the horses was lame and by reason of this great delay resulted, but for which the boat would have passed the point where the accident occurred and would have arrived in safety. The case was decided in favor of the defendants on the express ground that the loss was not to have been foreseen "by

[53] Read *v.* Spaulding, 30 N. Y. 630, 635.   [54] 20 Pa. 171.

ordinary forecast," and that the ordinary consequence of the delay in such a case was "loss of time" only. It is expressly *assumed* by the court that *"the proximate cause of the disaster was the flood and the fault of having a lame horse a remote one"* which by concurring with the proximate cause, became fatal. The decision rests upon the simple idea that the carrier in cases of delay with an extraordinary accident as a concurring cause can never be answerable for anything more than the loss of time because extraordinary accidents are not within the scope of anticipation. Further than this, it is clear that in this case, the terms proximate and remote are used in the natural and non-legal sense, because if the terms are taken in their legal sense, the above assumption would of itself have decided the case. No rule embodying this idea exists, and the Massachusetts court did not *follow* the Pennsylvania court, but decided the Massachusetts case on an entirely different fact, *i. e.*, that there was at the time of the loss no concurring negligence. In the New York case, this fact did not exist and the naked question arose of the concurrence of the act of God with continuing negligence on the part of the carrier at the time of loss, or what is sometimes erroneously called continuous exposure to risk, and the New York rule was the necessary result.

§ 119e. Confusion of authorities.

Apparently the fundamental distinctions existing between these early leading cases have been generally lost sight of, with the result that the weight of *authority* is said to be in favor of the rule that in case of delay concurring with the act of God or risk excepted by contract, the negligence is always remote. In the light of this discussion, no such general rule exists; the weight of reason is in favor of the New York rule; and the Massachusetts rule should be followed only in the cases to which it was explicitly restricted,—those in which the delay has, through delivery, ceased to operate as an "active, efficient and prevailing cause." Limited in this way, the two leading cases on the subject are not in conflict but reinforce and confirm one another, and a great deal of the confusion existing in the cases decided ever since may be attributed to the original mistaken idea that the decisions themselves were in conflict—

(an idea which New York judges expressly repudiate), and hence must be the source of two radically opposed rules. In consequence of this, countless cases have been decided since in such a way as to introduce still further confusion. This it is hopeless, here, owing to want of space, to attempt to disentangle; a fact of which the space taken up with the effort just now made to analyze but three cases may perhaps be taken as a sufficient proof.

§ 120. Lack of privity or duty as affecting cause of action.

There is a class of cases in which the refusal of recovery is based not on the remoteness in fact of the consequence, but because the defendant owes the plaintiff no duty whether contractual or arising from the relations of the parties. The plaintiff *is not the person in whose favor the duty*, alleged to have been violated, is imposed on the defendant. These cases deserve closer attention that they may be distinguished from cases involving remoteness of *result*. Thus an insurance company which has been forced to pay a policy on the life of a person killed by the defendant's negligence,[55] or a fire policy on property burned by the defendant,[56] cannot recover because of lack of privity between the parties; and where a searcher prepares an abstract of title which contains an error, he is not liable to a stranger who lends money on faith of the abstract.[57] So where the plaintiff by contract was obliged to maintain certain paupers, and defendant assaulted one of the paupers and so made plaintiff's contract more onerous, the plaintiff could not recover.[58] And where plaintiff's son had contracted to support plaintiff for life, and defendant negligently killed the son, it was held that defendant was not liable to plaintiff.[59] Where plaintiff had a contract with a manufacturing company for a supply of all goods manufactured by them, and defendant by

[55] Connecticut M. L. I. Co. *v.* New York & N. H. R. R., 25 Conn. 265, 65 Am. Dec. 571 (see the underlying principle clearly stated in the opinion of the court, by Storrs, J.).
[56] Rockingham M. F. I. Co. *v.* Bosher, 39 Me. 253, 63 Am. Dec. 618.
[57] National Sav. Bank *v.* Ward, 100 U. S. 195, 25 L. ed. 621; Equitable B. & L. Assoc. *v.* Bank of Commerce, 118 Tenn. 678, 102 S. W. 901.
[58] Anthony *v.* Slaid, 11 Met. (Mass.) 290.
[59] Brink *v.* Wabash Ry., 160 Mo. 87, 60 S. W. 1058, 83 Am. St. Rep. 459, 53 L. R. A. 811.

an injury to the company prevented it from manufacturing any goods, it was held that there was no privity between the parties and the act of the defendant gave no cause of action to the plaintiff.[60]

In non-contractual cases, the principle applies to the whole field of cases in which a right of action is denied, not because the injury is remote, but because the defendant was engaged in the exercise of an absolute right, to which no corresponding duty is annexed. All these are cases of proximate *damnum*, without *injuria*.

It is a well-known rule, on the other hand, that when one is dealing in an article dangerous in itself, like a poisonous drug, he is liable for a negligent mistake by which another than the person to whom he sells it is injured.[61] On this principle a Kentucky case may be supported; [62] defendant wrongly established a smallpox pest house near C's house. Plaintiff was a guest of C. One of C's children contracted smallpox from the pest house and the plaintiff contracted it from the child. It was held that this was a proximate result of the defendant's wrong and recovery could be had. And in all cases where there is an implied warranty of fitness of goods sold, the seller is liable for a defect not only to the purchaser but to other users of the goods. So where defendant sold a folding bed which because of its faulty construction shut up and injured the person in it, he was held liable to the occupant of the bed, though not the purchaser; and the intervening act of the purchaser in supplying it to the plaintiff did not make the result remote, unless he knew of the defect.[63]

§ 120a. Damage supervening from a collateral cause.

It not infrequently happens that after an injury a damage

[60] Dale *v.* Grant, 34 N. J. L. 142.

[61] *Massachusetts:* Norton *v.* Sewall, 106 Mass. 143, 8 Am. Rep. 298.

New York: Thomas *v.* Winchester, 6 N. Y. 397, 57 Am. Dec. 455.

Ohio: Davis *v.* Guarnieri, 45 Ohio St. 470, 15 N. E. 350, 4 Am. St. Rep. 561.

West Virginia: Peters *v.* Johnson, 50 W. Va. 644, 41 S. E. 190, and cases cited.

The distinction is well pointed out in Bank *v.* Ward, 100 U. S. 195, 204, 25 L. ed. 621.

[62] Henderson *v.* O'Haloran, 24 Ky. L. Rep. 995, 70 S. W. 662.

[63] Lewis *v.* Terry, 111 Cal. 39, 43 Pac. 398, 52 Am. St. Rep. 146, 1 L. R. A. 220.

follows, not as a result in any way of the injury but from an entirely independent collateral cause. The apparent connection, due to the immediate sequence in time, is shown not to exist, and the damage not to be a consequence of the injury. In such a case the damage is of course not to be considered.[64]

§ 120b. Proximate and remote results of statutory injuries.

Where a cause of action is created by statute, the form of the statute sometimes restricts the recovery so that not all proximate consequences may be recovered. Thus in an action against a railroad, upon the statute, for killing stock, it is held that the killing must be caused by an actual blow from the train.[65]

§ 121.[a] Louisiana law.

In Louisiana the subject of damages is regulated by the Code of that State, and it is declared in reference to our present subject, "that when the object of the contract is anything but the payment of money, where the debtor has been guilty of no fraud or bad faith, he is liable only for such damages as were contemplated, or may reasonably be supposed to have entered into the contemplation of the parties, at the time of the contract;" and this principle has frequently been carried out by the courts of that State.[66] So, in a case where it might be inferred to be in the contemplation of the parties to a contract that a sugar-mill and engine, which the manufacturer undertook to put up within a given time, was for the purpose of getting a certain crop, it was held that a failure to put it up in

[a] For § 121 of the eighth edition, see § 117.

[64] *Alabama:* Burton v. Henry, 90 Ala. 281, 7 So. 925; Brown v. Floyd, 50 So. 995, 163 Ala. 317.

Delaware: Baldwin v. People's Ry., 76 Atl. 1088, 7 Pennew.

Iowa: Parkinson v. Kortrum, 127 N. W. 205.

Missouri: Smart v. Kansas City, 208 Mo. 168, 105 S. W. 709.

Nebraska: Bahr v. Manke, 77 Neb. 552, 110 N. W. 300.

North Carolina: Phillips v. Durham & C. R. R., 138 N. C. 12, 50 S. E. 462.

Texas: Mayo v. Goldman, 122 S. W. 449,   Tex. Civ. App.

[65] *Indiana:* Jeffersonville, M. & I. R. R. v. Downey, 61 Ind. 287.

New York: Knight v. N. Y., L. E. & W. R. R., 99 N. Y. 25, 1 N. E. 108. [Compare Leggett v. Rome, W. & O. R. R., 41 Hun (N. Y.), 80.]

[66] Williams v. Barton, 13 La. 404.

time entitled the plaintiff to recover for the loss of crop and extra wages caused by the delay.[67] If the contract is violated in bad faith, the plaintiff is entitled to all the consequences which can be traced to the breach of contract, without regard to whether the damages are natural and proximate.[68]

The rule in other jurisdictions where the basis of the law is the Roman law is the same; as in Lower Canada.[69]

§ 121a. Consequences of intermeddling with property.

One class of cases is exceptional, in that the defendant is held responsible for all consequences, even though remote; these are cases where the defendant, having meddled with the plaintiff's property, as by displacing it wrongfully, becomes an insurer of the property, taking the risk of its safe return to the owner. So where the defendant without legal right tied the plaintiff's horse to a post, and the horse escaped and was killed, the defendant was liable;[70] and where defendant induced a slave of plaintiff to ride a race, and the horse threw the slave against a tree and killed him, it was held that plaintiff could recover the value of the slave: there is a difference between a loan and an officious interference with another's property without his consent; in the latter case the defendant is responsible for all damages the owner sustains.[71] The commonest case is that of a bailee who uses the goods bailed in a way not permitted by the bailment. Thus where a gratuitous bailee, instead of holding the goods for the bailor, sent them to him by mail, and they were lost in the mail, the bailee was held liable;[72] and where goods shipped to go by a certain vessel were carried in another, the carrier was liable for their loss though it occurred by an excepted cause.[73] So where defendant received plaintiff's goods to keep them in a certain warehouse, and instead of doing so he put them in a different warehouse, and without negligence on

[67] Goodloe v. Rogers, 10 La. Ann. 631.

[68] Civil Code of Louisiana, § 1934.

[69] Civil Code, § 1054.

[70] So where one who had a right to remove his goods from plaintiff's boat moved the boat to another wharf, and it was there damaged by storm, he was liable for the damage. Bear v. Harriss, 118 N. C. 476, 24 S. E. 364.

[71] Wright v. Gray, 2 Bay (S. C.), 464.

[72] Jenkins v. Bacon, 111 Mass. 373.

[73] Wallace v. Swift, 31 U. C. Q. B. 523.

his part they were burned, he was held responsible for the loss.[74]

§ 121b. Direct consequence always proximate.

The direct consequence of a wrongful act is always proximate, and therefore a subject for compensation, whether it is or is not a natural (*i. e.*, normal), consequence, and though the extent of the injury is greater than the defendant intended or expected.[75] So where the result of an assault was the closing up of the plaintiff's tear-passages, thus weakening his eyes, he was allowed compensation for it.[76] And where an assault rendered the plaintiff subject to fits, he was allowed compensation for the injury.[77] In Eten *v.* Luyster,[78] an action for dispossessing the plaintiff under a New York statute, where the

[74] Lilley *v.* Doubleday, 7 Q. B. D. 510, 44 L. T. Rep. (N. S.) 814, 46 J. P. 708, 51 L. J. Q. B. 167, 66 L. T. Rep. (N. S.) 442. *Contra,* McRea *v.* Hill, 126 Ill. App. 349.

[75] *United States:* Bowas *v.* Pioneer Tow Line, 2 Sawy. 21, 3 Fed. Cas. No. 1,713; Armour & Co. *v.* Kollmeyer, 161 Fed. 78, 88 C. C. A. 242.

Indiana: Louisville, N. A. & C. Ry. *v.* Wood, 113 Ind. 544, 14 N. E. 572, 16 N. E. 197.

Kansas: Walbridge *v.* Walbridge, 80 Kan. 567, 103 Pac. 89.

Missouri: Yeager *v.* Berry, 82 Mo. App. 534.

So where a person injured by the defendant was earning more than an ordinary laborer, the defendant is nevertheless liable for the value of his time, and cannot lessen the damages by claiming that he supposed the injured person to be only an ordinary laborer.

Massachusetts: Braithwaite *v.* Hall, 168 Mass. 38, 46 N. E. 398.

England: Smith *v.* London & S. W. Ry., L. R. 6 C. P. 14, 22.

[76] Blake *v.* Lord, 16 Gray (Mass.), 387.

[77] Sloan *v.* Edwards, 61 Md. 89.

[78] 60 N. Y. 252.

New Hampshire: Jewell *v.* Grand Trunk Ry., 55 N. H. 84.

New Jersey: Haufler *v.* Public Service Ry., 75 Atl. 163, 79 N. J. L. 404.

New Mexico: Roswell *v.* Davenport, 14 N. Mex. 91, 89 Pac. 256.

Oregon: Elliff *v.* Oregon R. & N. Co., 53 Ore. 66, 99 Pac. 76.

Texas: Sawyer *v.* Dulany, 30 Tex. 479; Galveston, H. & S. A. Ry. *v.* Butshek, 34 Tex. Civ. App. 194, 78 S. W. 740; Houston E. Co. *v.* Green, 106 S. W. 463, 48 Tex. Civ. App. 242.

Washington: Jordan *v.* Seattle, 30 Wash. 298, 70 Pac. 743.

Wisconsin: Stewart *v.* Ripon, 38 Wis. 584; Macnamara *v.* Clintonville, 62 Wis. 207, 22 N. W. 472, 51 Am. Rep. 722; Vosburg *v.* Putney, 80 Wis. 523, 50 N. W. 403, 27 Am. St. Rep. 47, 14 L. R. A. 226; Vosburg *v.* Putney, 86 Wis. 278, 56 N. W. 480.

Canada: Loranger *v.* Dominion Transport Co., 15 Quebec Super. Ct. 193 (scrofulous constitution).

It is immaterial that the tendency was caused by the plaintiff's voluntary intemperance.

Maguire *v.* Sheehan, 117 Fed. 819, 59 L. R. A. 496.

proceedings were set aside on appeal as unauthorized by the act, it was held that the plaintiff could recover for the destruction of a building and the loss of his chattels and money which were in the building, even though the money was kept in an unusual place, and the defendants probably did not suspect its presence; Allen, J., saying: "The loss of the money, although the defendants may not have suspected its presence, was the direct and necessary consequence of the acts of the defendants."

In actions of tort, a common case of directly ensuing loss is where a physical injury stimulates a pre-existing disease or morbid tendency,[79] or leads to peculiarly unfortunate results

[79] *United States:* Crane Elevator Co. v. Lippert, 63 Fed. 942, 11 C. C. A. 521.

Alabama: Louisville & N. R. R. v. Jones, 83 Ala. 376, 3 So. 902 (plaintiff suffering from pneumonia).

Arkansas: St. Louis Southwestern Ry. v. Lewis, 121 S. W. 268, 91 Ark. 343 (predisposition to hernia).

California: Sloane v. Southern California Ry., 111 Cal. 668, 44 Pac. 320, 33 L. R. A. 193 (peculiar susceptibility to nervous disease); Campbell v. Los Angeles Traction Co., 137 Cal. 565, 70 Pac. 624.

Colorado: Denver v. Hyatt, 28 Colo. 129, 63 Pac. 403.

Florida: Atlantic Coast Line R. R. v. Dees, 56 Fla. 127, 48 So. 28.

Illinois: Chicago City Ry. v. Saxby, 213 Ill. 274, 72 N. E. 755, 104 Am. St. Rep. 218, 68 L. R. A. 164.

Indiana: Terre Haute & I. R. R. v. Buck, 96 Ind. 346, 49 Am. Rep. 168; Louisville, N. A. & C. Ry. v. Falvey, 104 Ind. 409, 3 N. E. 908 (scrofulous constitution); Louisville, N. A. & C. Ry. v. Jones, 108 Ind. 551; Ohio & M. R. R. v. Hecht, 115 Ind. 443, 17 N. E. 297; Louisville, N. A. & C. Ry. v. Snyder, 117 Ind. 435, 20 N. E. 284, 10 Am. St. Rep. 60, 3 L. R. A. 434.

Louisiana: Lapleine v. R. R. & S. Co., 40 La. Ann. 661, 4 So. 875, 1 L. R. A. 378.

Maryland: Baltimore C. P. Ry. v. Kemp, 61 Md. 74, 48 Am. Rep. 134; Baltimore & L. T. Co. v. Cassell, 66 Md. 419, 59 Am. Rep. 175, n.

Michigan: Elliott v. Van Buren, 33 Mich. 49, 20 Am. Rep. 664; Shumway v. Walworth & N. Manuf. Co., 98 Mich. 411, 57 N. W. 251 (scrofulous constitution); Schwingschlegl v. Monroe, 113 Mich. 683, 72 N. W. 7; Hall v. Cadillac, 114 Mich. 99, 72 N. W. 33 (rheumatism); Beauerle v. Michigan C. Ry., 152 Mich. 345, 116 N. W. 424.

Minnesota: Purcell v. St. Paul City Ry., 48 Minn. 134, 50 N. W. 1034, 16 L. R. A. 203 (feeble state of health); Watson v. Rinderknecht, 82 Minn. 235, 84 N. W. 798; Ross v. Great Northern Ry., 101 Minn. 122, 111 N. W. 951 (diseased bone); Bloomquist v. Minneapolis F. Co., 112 Minn. 143, 127 N. W. 481 (predisposition to tuberculosis).

Missouri: Brown v. Hannibal & St. J. R. R., 66 Mo. 588; Owens v. Railroad, 95 Mo. 182, 8 S. W. 350, 6 Am. St. Rep. 39; Smart v. Kansas City, 208 Mo. 162, 105 S. W. 709, 14 L. R. A. (N. S.) 565; St. Louis Trust Co. v. Murmann, 90 Mo. App. 555; Basham v. Hammond Packing Co., 107 Mo. App. 542, 81 S. W. 1227 (tuberculous condition); Delaplain v. Kansas City, 109 Mo. App. 107, 83 S. W. 71.

owing to a prior injury [80] or to a delicate state of health,[81] or to a peculiar physical condition such as pregnancy.[82]   In all these cases the loss is the direct though unexpected consequence of the injury, and the plaintiff may recover compensation for it.[83] The lapse of time does not interfere with the directness of the result.   Thus where a person was injured by the defendant, and died as a result of the injury sixteen months later, it was held that compensation could be recovered for her death; the criminal-law rule requiring death within a year and a day not applying to a civil action for death.[84]

In cases of breach of contract direct consequences are generally natural.   In some cases, however, principally contracts of carriage, the direct consequence of the breach is unexpected; but compensation for it is allowed.[85]   So where a package of jewels was sent by a carrier, no notice being given of the contents, the carrier having lost the package was required to make compensation for the jewels, though the loss of jewels was an

Nevada: Murphy v. Southern Pac. R. R., 31 Nev. 120, 101 Pac. 322.

New Hampshire: Emery v. Boston & M. R. R., 67 N. H. 434, 36 Atl. 367.

Wisconsin: Woodward v. Boscabel, 84 Wis. 226, 54 N. W. 332.

[80] *Alabama:* Montgomery & E. Ry. v. Mallette, 92 Ala. 209.

Iowa: Allison v. Chicago & N. W. Ry., 42 Ia. 274.

Massachusetts: Coleman v. New York & N. H. R. R., 106 Mass. 160 (hernia).

Michigan: Rawlings v. Clyde, P. & M. R. R., 158 Mich. 143, 122 N. W. 504, 16 Detroit Leg. N. 607.

Texas: Driess v. Frederich, 73 Tex. 460, 11 S. W. 493 (limb previously broken).

[81] *Alabama:* East T., V. & G. R. R. v. Lockhart, 79 Ala. 315.

Georgia: Bray v. Latham, 81 Ga. 640, 8 S. E. 64.

Illinois: Brownback v. Frailey, 78 Ill. App. 262.

Missouri: Neff v. Cameron, 213 Mo. 350, 111 S. W. 1139, 18 L. R. A. (N. S.) 320.

New York: Tice v. Munn, 94 N. Y. 621.

[82] *United States:* Mann B. C. Co. v. Dupre, 54 Fed. 646, 4 C. C. A. 540; Campbell v. Pullman P. C. Co., 42 Fed. 484.

Mississippi: Barbee v. Reese, 60 Miss. 906.

Wisconsin: Oliver v. LaValle, 36 Wis. 592; Brown v. Chicago, M. & St. P. Ry., 54 Wis. 342, 11 N. W. 356, 911, 41 Am. Rep. 41.

[83] In Pullman P. C. Co. v. Barker, 4 Colo. 344, the Supreme Court of Colorado refused to allow such damages where they resulted from the peculiar physical condition of the plaintiff.   The case is opposed to all the other authorities, and has been often criticised.

[84] Purcell v. Lauer, 14 App. Div. 33, 43 N. Y. Supp. 988.

[85] Collins v. Stephens, 58 Ala. 543. Thus for breach of a contract to supply water for domestic purposes, damages for the physical inconvenience of being deprived of water may be recovered. Birmingham W. W. Co. v. Ferguson, 164 Ala. 494, 51 So. 150.

unexpected consequence of the loss of the package.[86]   And where a carrier lost a package containing plans from which it was intended to build a house the owner was allowed to recover the cost of obtaining new plans, though the carrier did not know the contents of the package.[87]   And generally, when the value of the goods is enhanced by special circumstances not known to the carrier, such enhanced value may be recovered.[88]   In an action for breach of contract to indemnify the plaintiff for an injury caused by surrounding his frozen-in canal boat (containing potatoes) with manure as a protection against frost, he can recover for rottenness which was caused to the timber and woodwork of the boat by the manure, the measure of damages being the excess of rottenness of the boat over what would have been produced by the heating of the potatoes, had these been stored in the ordinary way.[89]   And in an action for rescue of a debtor from an officer who had arrested him, the defendant was adjudged to pay the amount of all the executions on which the debtor was held, not simply the one on which he had been arrested.[90]

§ 121c. Classification of cases involving remoteness.

In order to deal with the mass of cases involving the question of remoteness, some method of classification must be adopted; and the most natural method is to classify according to the nature of the intervening cause. This may be either an interposition of a new active cause, or it may be the deprivation of a means to a result, thus bringing about a different result. The active cause interposed may be an act of nature; it may be the act of an animal; or it may be that of the plaintiff himself, either done in the effort to avoid the consequences of the defendant's wrong or done entirely without reference to the wrong; or it may be the act of a third person. We shall therefore proceed to consider the cases in this order: 1. Interposition of natural force. 2. Interposition of act of an animal. 3. Inter-

---

[86] Kenrig v. Eggleston, Aleyn, 93; Little v. Boston & M. R. R., 66 Me. 239.

[87] Mather v. American E. Co., 138 Mass. 55, 52 Am. Rep. 258.

[88] France v. Gaudet, L. R. 6 Q. B. 199; Wilson v. Lancashire & Y. Ry., 9 C. B. (N. S.) 632.

[89] Starbird v. Barrows, 62 N. Y. 615.

[90] Kent v. Kelway, Lane, 70, Beale's Cas. Dam. 78.

position of human agency, (a) of plaintiff, (b) of defendant, (c) of a third party. 4. Deprivation of means to an end.

§ 121d. Interposition of a natural force.

Where a natural force, following the defendant's wrong, and directly connected with it, causes damage, the damage is a proximate consequence of the wrong; but if the natural force is entirely independent, the damage is remote.

The defendant negligently ran against a pier on which the plaintiff was working, though he had not been seen by the defendant. The jar knocked out a brace between two piles, and the piles, coming together, caught the plaintiff and he was injured. It was held that the plaintiff could recover.[91] So where a defective boiler, sold by the defendant to the plaintiff, exploded and injured the plaintiff's mill and machinery, the damage thus done was held not too remote for recovery.[92] Plaintiff purchased paint of the defendant which was warranted as to quality; when used, it faded. The loss thereby caused was proximate.[93] Defendant broke into a blacksmith shop and made a fire which spread, and burned down the blacksmith's house. This was held a proximate consequence.[94] A fire caused a short circuit of a current of electricity the result of which was that machinery was wrecked by the excess of power. The consequence is proximate.[95]

But on the other hand, where a public bridge over a slough became impassable for want of repairs, by reason of which the plaintiff could not transport over it a quantity of wood collected for that purpose, and the wood, while awaiting transportation, was washed away by a freshet, the loss was held too remote for recovery.[96]

---

[91] Hill v. Winsor, 118 Mass. 251. This was a case involving the right of action, and so cannot properly be cited as an authority on the measure of damages; but it affords a striking illustration of a direct but entirely unexpected consequence of a wrongful act.

[92] Page v. Ford, 12 Ind. 46; Erie C. I. W. v. Barber, 106 Pa. 125, 51 Am. Rep. 496.

[93] McCaa v. Elam Drug Co., 114 Ala. 74, 21 So. 479, 62 Am. St. Rep. 88.

[94] Wyant v. Crouse, 127 Mich. 158, 86 N. W. 527, 53 L. R. A. 626.

[95] Lynn, G. & E. Co. v. Meriden F. I. Co., 158 Mass. 570, 33 N. E. 490.

[96] Dubuque W. & C. A. v. Dubuque, 30 Ia. 176.

Where an earthquake destroyed the water mains, and so prevented the extinguishment of a fire which burned plaintiff's building, it was held that the fire was the proximate cause of the loss, and that recovery could be had on an insurance policy against fire which excepted loss by earthquake.[97]

When the defendant's tort causes a flood of water to wash away the land [98] or to cover it so that it cannot be used [99] the defendant is responsible for the result; and the same liability exists where the flood drowns the plaintiff's cattle,[100] or sweeps away his logs,[101] or spreads upon his land the seeds of noxious weeds.[102]

Where defendant's negligently constructed water tower fell, and the water therefrom rushed upon deceased's house, overturning a lighted lamp, whereby deceased was fatally burned, the damages sustained were held to be the proximate result of the wrong; [103] but where by reason of negligent repairs to a vessel by defendant, the vessel leaked and the water reached certain lime which formed part of the cargo, and thereby the vessel was burned, the result was held remote.[104] So it has been held that the loss of crops is not the proximate result of deprivation of an animal by which the owner intended to harvest the crops; consequently in an action for deprivation of the animal no compensation can be recovered for loss of the crop.[105] So where through deprivation of the use of an agricultural machine or through a defect in it the owner loses his crops, such loss is too remote, and he cannot recover compen-

[97] Pacific Union Club v. Commercial Union Assur. Co., 10 Cal. App. 203, 107 Pac. 728.

[98] *Massachusetts:* Dickinson v. Boyle, 17 Pick. 78, 28 Am. Dec. 281.

Rhode Island: Hathaway v. Osborne, 25 R. I. 249, 55 Atl. 700.

[99] *Louisiana:* Bentley v. Fischer Co., 51 La. Ann. 451, 25 So. 262.

Pennsylvania: Douty v. Bird, 60 Pa. 48 (coal mine).

[100] Sabine & E. T. Ry. v. Johnson, 65 Tex. 389.

[101] Auger v. Cook, 39 Up. Can. Q. B. 537.

[102] Illinois C. R. R. v. Heisner, 45 Ill. App. 143.

[103] Rigdon v. Temple W. W. Co., 11 Tex. Civ. App. 542, 32 S. W. 828. So of a windmill negligently constructed by defendant on plaintiff's premises. Flint & Walling Mfg. Co. v. Beckett, 167 Ind. 491, 79 N. E. 503, 12 L. R. A. (N. S.) 924.

[104] Bell v. Mut. Mach. Co., 150 N. C. 111, 63 S. E. 680.

[105] *North Carolina:* Sledge v. Reid, 73 N. C. 440; Jackson v. Hall, 84 N. C. 489.

Vermont: Luce v. Hoisington, 54 Vt. 428, 56 Vt. 436.

sation for it.[106]   And loss of crops from loss of service of a servant or slave is too remote to be compensated in an action
founded on the loss of service.[107]   It has, however, been held
that where no other assistance can be procured the plaintiff
may recover compensation for the loss.[108]

§ 122. Loss by exposure to the weather.

Where because of defendant's wrong the plaintiff is exposed
to the weather and personally injured by it, the consequence
is not remote.[109]   And where plaintiff's building is unroofed
by an explosion, damage resulting from water passing through
the roof is proximate.[110]   So where the defendant wrongly
marked ties cut by plaintiff and placed beside a railroad track
for carriage, as claimed by the defendant, and as a consequence
the railroad refused to carry them, loss caused by exposure of
the ties to the weather was held proximate.[111]

But where defendant wrongfully built a bridge without a
draw, and this delayed the transportation of a cargo of cotton
seed, and during the delay the seed deteriorated by reason of
exposure, this was held remote.[112]   And where defendant delayed the delivery of materials for a building as a consequence
of which the roof was not completed and rain got in and
flooded the basement with water, causing the foundations to
sink, this was held a remote consequence of the delay.[113]

[106] *Indiana:* Fuller *v.* Curtis, 100 Ind. 237, 50 Am. Rep. 786.

Iowa: McCormick *v.* Vanatta, 43 Ia. 389.

Minnesota: Osborne *v.* Poket, 33 Minn. 10, 21 N. W. 752.

Wisconsin: Brayton *v.* Chase, 3 Wis. 456.

It is held in Louisiana that on failure to deliver a sugar mill the purchaser may recover compensation for the crop *necessarily* lost. Goodloe *v.* Rogers, 10 La. Ann. 631.

[107] *Iowa:* Prosser *v.* Jones, 41 Ia. 674.

Kansas: Usher *v.* Hiatt, 18 Kan. 195.

Maryland: Johnson *v.* Courts, 3 H. & Mc. H. 510.

New York: Peters *v.* Whitney, 23 Barb. 24.

[108] *Georgia:* Hobbs *v.* Davis, 30 Ga. 423.

Kansas: Houser *v.* Pearce, 13 Kan. 104.

[109] Ehrgott *v.* New York, 96 N. Y. 264.

[110] Scott *v.* Bay, 3 Md. 431.   So where the building remained without roof by reason of defendant's delay in supplying materials. Bridges *v.* Holt, 99 Mich. 606, 58 N. W. 623.

[111] Alabama Co. *v.* Slaton, 120 Ala. 259, 24 So. 720.

[112] Farmers' C. M. Co. *v.* Albermale R. R., 117 N. C. 579, 23 S. E. 43.

[113] Bridges *v.* Holt, 99 Mich. 606, 58 N. W. 623.

§ 123.[a] Injury by supervening disease or accident.

When a physical injury inflicted by defendant results in a disease, the defendant is liable for the death.[114] And where it later resulted in a miscarriage and afterwards in a second miscarriage, the defendant was held for both.[115] Illness resulting from failure to repair a house is remote.[116] But illness from flooding lands is proximate.[117]

Where the plaintiff suffered a fracture of a limb and as a result of the weakening of the limb a second fracture was afterwards suffered, it is not remote from the first injury. In such a case it appeared that the plaintiff's leg had been broken by the injury and had healed, when it was again broken by an accident, which was not chargeable in any way to the plaintiff. If the leg had not been weakened by the first fracture, it would not have been broken by the accident. It was held that the second fracture was a proximate consequence of the first injury, and that his damages should include compensation for it.[118] So where plaintiff's shoulder was dislocated, and this resulted in a tendency to dislocation and to subsequent dislocations, this could be considered.[119] But in such a case where the plaintiff after recovery fell again, because the broken leg, though fully knit, was so stiff that he could not save himself when he accidentally slipped, and the result of the fall was a second fracture, this was held a remote consequence of the first;[120] and where the plaintiff as a result of the first injury

[a] For § 123 of the eighth edition, see § 114.

[114] *Kentucky:* Louisville Ry. *v.* Steubing, Ky. , 136 S. W. 634 (cancer).

Pennsylvania: Brashear *v.* Phila. Tr. Co., 180 Pa. 392, 36 Atl. 914 (tetanus).

Texas: Equitable Life Assur. Soc. *v.* Lester, Tex. Civ. App. , 110 S. W. 499 (pneumonia).

[115] Rapid Tr. Ry. *v.* Smith, (Tex. Civ. App.) 82 S. W. 788; *acc.,* Chicago U. T. Co. *v.* Ertrachter, 228 Ill. 114, 81 N. E. 816.

[116] Collins *v.* Karatopsky, 36 Ark. 316.

[117] Woodstock Hardwood & Spool Mfg. Co. *v.* Charleston Light & Water Co., 84 S. C. 306, 66 S. E. 194.

[118] *Alabama:* Postal T. C. Co. *v.* Hulsey, 132 Ala. 444, 31 So. 527.

Missouri: Conner *v.* Nevada, 188 Mo. 148, 86 S. W. 256, 107 Am. St. Rep. 314.

Wisconsin: Weiting *v.* Millston, 77 Wis. 523, 46 N. W. 879. In Lincoln *v.* Saratoga & S. R. R., 23 Wend. (N. Y.) 425, the possibility of such a second fracture is held too remote for consideration.

[119] Donnelly *v.* Chicago C. Ry., 235 Ill. 35, 85 N. E. 233.

[120] Wineberg *v.* DuBois, 209 Pa. 430, 58 Atl. 807.

was obliged to use a crutch, which slipped and caused a fall and a second injury, the plaintiff was not allowed in an action for the first injury to recover compensation for the second.[121] Where as a result of defendant's carelessness a sponge was left in the wound after an operation on the plaintiff, and this resulted in ulceration and disease, plaintiff could recover for the resulting damage.[122]

§ 124.[a] Interposition of the act of an animal.

Where the defendant frightens an animal negligently and the animal in his fright kicks or runs, the defendant is responsible for the immediate result. So where the defendant drove against the plaintiff's carriage, and by the shock the plaintiff's friend was thrown off the seat on to the dashboard, and the dashboard falling on the horse, he kicked and broke it; it was held that all the damage so sustained was recoverable in trespass.[123] So where the defendant's injury caused a horse to kick and he afterwards as a result became a kicking horse, and was worth much less on that account, the impairment of value could be recovered.[124] And where a horse, in fright by reason of defendant's negligence, ran away and was injured, the defendant is responsible for the injury.[125] Even where a horse was frightened by the act of a third party, and in running was injured by falling through a defective railing on a turnpike, the turnpike company was held liable.[126]

[a] For § 124 of the eighth edition, see § 111.

[121] Vander Velde v. Leroy, 140 Mich. 359, 103 N. W. 812. The decision appears to have turned on a question of pleading rather than on the remoteness of the second injury.

[122] Samuels v. Willis, 133 Ky. 459, 118 S. W. 339.

[123] Gilbertson v. Richardson, 5 C. B. 502, 17 L. J. C. P. 112, 12 Jur. 292.

[124] English v. Missouri Pac. Ry., 73 Mo. App. 232; acc., Gillam v. Hogue, 39 Pa. Super. Ct. 547 (fright diminished value of horse for driving).

[125] *Kansas:* Topeka v. Tuttle, 5 Kan. 311.

North Dakota: Ouverson v. Grafton, 5 N. D. 281, 65 N. W. 676.

England: Randall v. Newson, 2 Q. B. Div. 102 (question for the jury).

[126] Baldwin v. Greenwoods Turnpike Co., 40 Conn. 238, 16 Am. Rep. 33.

One case which seems to be contrary to this decision was really decided on a different ground. The suit was brought under the statute for injury caused by defect in the way; and the lack of railing was held not to be a defect in the way. Moulton v. Sanford, 51 Me. 127. In Brown v. Laurens County, 38 S. C. 282, 17 S. E. 21, however, the court in such a case held that the lack of railing was not a cause of the injury.

Defendant negligently ran his train so as to divide into two parts a herd of cattle which were being driven across the railway. Plaintiff diligently tried to collect his cattle together after the train had passed, but some succeeded in escaping and could not be recovered. They afterwards wandered on the line of the railroad and were killed. It was held that this was a proximate result of the defendant's wrong.[127]

Where land which was used as a pasture for cattle was wrongfully overflowed by the defendant, and while wet was trampled by cattle, greatly injuring it, the flooding was held a proximate cause of the injury.[128] A stagnant pool, wrongfully caused by defendant, communicated malaria to plaintiff and his family. Malaria was communicated by mosquitoes bred in the stagnant water, but could not be communicated unless the mosquitoes had first bitten a person who was suffering with malaria. It was held that this did not render the injury remote.[129]

The defendant is liable for all damages not remote, whether he committed the injury intentionally, wantonly or negligently. So where defendant wantonly shot a dog in front of plaintiff's house, knowing that she was alone there, the dog sprang up, rushed wildly toward the house, ran violently against the plaintiff, knocked her down and injured her, the court held that since by his wanton act the dog was set wildly in motion and the motion continued until plaintiff was injured thereby, defendant was responsible.[130] And where the defendant wilfully turned water from a hose on horses and caused them to run away, he was liable for the injury thereby caused to plaintiff's wagon.[131]

§ 125.[a] Infectious disease.

Where animals sold have an infectious disease, known to the seller, but not to the purchaser, which is communicated to

[a] For § 125 of the eighth edition, see § 117.

[127] Sneesby v. Lancashire & Y. Ry., L. R. 9 Q. B. 263.

[128] St. Louis B. & M. Ry. v. West, Tex. Civ. App.   , 131 S. W. 839.

[129] Towaliga Falls Power Co. v. Sims, 65 S. E. 844, 6 Ga. App. 749.

[130] Isham v. Dow, 70 Vt. 588, 41 Atl. 585, 67 Am. St. Rep. 691, 45 L. R. A. 87.

[131] Forney v. Geldmacher, 75 Mo. 113, 42 Am. Rep. 388.

other animals of the purchaser, the latter may recover compensation for the damage done to his other animals.[132]   The same rule applies where the defendant's sheep trespass on the plaintiff's land and communicate disease.[133]   And where the defendant's rams trespassed on the plaintiff's land and got his ewes with lamb out of season, so that the lambs died soon after birth, the plaintiff was allowed to recover the diminution in value of the ewes for breeding and other purposes.[134]

Where the plaintiff's horse was injured by the defendant's wrongful act, and as a result was rendered timid, unsound, and unkind, loss from this source was not too remote from the injury.[135]   So damages from the non-thriving of cattle in consequence of the construction of a railroad through their pasture were held not too remote.[136]

§ 125a.   Defects in fences and gates.   Straying cattle.

Trespass by cattle and injury to crops is a natural consequence of a defect in a fence, and damages therefor are accordingly recoverable.[137]   Through the defendant's failure to keep

---

[132] *Illinois:* Wheeler *v.* Randall, 48 Ill. 182.

Iowa: Sherrod *v.* Langdon, 21 Ia. 518; Joy *v.* Bitzer, 77 Ia. 73.

Kansas: Broquet *v.* Tripp, 36 Kan. 700.

Kentucky: Faris *v.* Lewis, 2 B. Mon. 375.

Massachusetts: Bradley *v.* Rea, 14 All. 20.

Michigan: Skinn *v.* Reutter, 135 Mich. 57, 97 N. W. 152, 63 L. R. A. 743.

Nebraska: Long *v.* Clapp, 15 Neb. 417.

New York: Jeffrey *v.* Bigelow, 13 Wend. 518, 28 Am. Dec. 476.

Texas: Wintz *v.* Morrison, 17 Tex. 372, 67 Am. Dec. 658; Routh *v.* Caron, 64 Tex. 289.

Vermont: Packard *v.* Slack, 32 Vt. 9.

England: Mullett *v.* Mason, L. R. 1 C. P. 559; Smith *v.* Green, 1 C. P. D. 92; Knowles *v.* Nunns, 14 L. T. R. 592.

[133] Barnum *v.* Vandusen, 16 Conn. 200.

[134] Stearns *v.* McGinty, 55 Hun, 101.

[135] Whiteley *v.* China, 61 Me. 199.

[136] Baltimore & O. R. R. *v.* Thompson, 10 Md. 76.

[137] *Alabama:* Garrett *v.* Sewell, 108 Ala. 521, 18 So. 737 (wrongful removal of fence).

Illinois: Gray *v.* Waterman, 40 Ill. 522 (wrongful removal of fence); Scott *v.* Kenton, 81 Ill. 96.

Kentucky: Illinois C. R. R. *v.* Doss, 137 Ky. 659, 126 S. W. 349.

Missouri: Miller *v.* St. Louis, I. M. & S. Ry., 90 Mo. 389, 2 S. W. 439 (fence burned by defendant's negligence).

North Carolina: Bridgers *v.* Dill, 97 N. C. 222, 1 S. E. 767 (repeated wrongful removals of fence).

South Carolina: Hardin *v.* Kennedy, 2 McCord, 277.

Texas: St. Louis Cattle Co. *v.* Gholson (Tex. Civ. App.), 30 S. W. 269.

a fence in repair, his calf strayed into the plaintiff's premises. It was held that the plaintiff in an action of trespass for the entry (alleged as defendant's trespass), could show, in aggravation of damages, that the calf bit off some limbs of one of the plaintiff's trees and broke another tree, although it was shown that this was not an injury which cattle are by nature wont to commit.[138]

And where, through the defect of a gate which the defendant was bound to repair, his horse, which was not shown to be vicious, strayed into the plaintiff's field and there kicked the plaintiff's horse, the damage was held not too remote.[139]

So where the plaintiff's cattle wander out of the field by reason of a defective fence or a gate wrongfully left open and are lost, the loss is usually held to be proximate.[140] Where the plaintiff's sheep wandered out of their pasture because of defendant's failure to put up the bars, and were eventually killed by bears, it was held that the jury should determine whether this was the proximate consequence of defendant's wrong.[141]

Where the defendant had not repaired his fence, by reason of which the plaintiff's horses escaped into the defendant's close and were there killed by the falling of a hay-stack, the court considered that such damage was not too remote.[142] And where, on account of the disrepair of a fence which defendant was required to maintain, the plaintiff's cattle strayed into a field, ate branches of a yew-tree, and were thereby poisoned, the defendant was held liable for the loss of the cattle.[143] And so where the statute provided that a party neglecting to keep in repair his part of a fence should "be liable for all damages done to or suffered by the opposite party in consequence of such neglect," and in consequence of the defective condition of the defendant's fence, the plaintiff's horses escaped into the defendant's pasture, where they were

---

Contra, in an action for breach of contract to build a good fence. Turner v. Gibbs, 50 Mo. 556.

[138] Keenan v. Cavanaugh, 44 Vt. 268.

[139] Lee v. Riley, 34 L. J. C. P. 212; Lyons v. Merrick, 105 Mass. 71.

[140] North Carolina: Welch v. Piercy, 29 N. C. 365.

Tennessee: Damron v. Roach, 4 Humph. 134.

[141] Gilman v. Noyes, 57 N. H. 627.

[142] Powell v. Salisbury, 2 Y. & J. 391.

[143] Lawrence v. Jenkins, L. R. 8 Q. B. 274.

gored by a vicious bull of the defendant, the damage was held not too remote, the court considering the defendant's liability very much that of a party at common law—"bound to do an act, from the omission to do which an injury results to others," and not regarding it as indispensable to the maintenance of the action that the vicious habits of the bull should have been known to the defendant.[144]

The same doctrine applies where a railroad fails to provide the cattle guards required by law; it is responsible for the resulting injury to the land.[145]   A railroad so arranged its cotton seed house that seed got on the tracks. Cattle went on the track to eat the seed and threw off the train in which plaintiff was riding and injured him. It was held that this was not a remote consequence of defendant's carelessness in allowing cotton seed to be on the track, since it was the nature of cattle to be fond of cotton seed.[146] On the other hand, where a person walking on a railroad track turned to get off when a train was coming and at that moment an animal coming through an opening in the fence pushed him on the track and he was injured, it was held that the failure to fence was not a proximate cause of the injury, since it was entirely unforeseeable.[147]

§ 126.[a] Intervention of human agency.

It is often said that the intervention of a human agency makes further results of a preceding cause remote. This, however, cannot be accepted as a statement of a general principle, even as a principle subject to numerous exceptions. So long as the act of the defendant still concurs with the new human act it remains a proximate cause of any further loss. It is therefore necessary to examine in detail the cases of this class.   There are three possible cases: intervention of the plaintiff, intervention of the defendant, and intervention of a third party. Intervention of the defendant causing further loss it is not necessary to consider since he is of course respon-

[a] For § 126 of the eighth edition, see § 117.

[144] Saxton v. Bacon, 31 Vt. 540.

[145] Atlanta & B. A. L. Ry. v. Brown, 158 Ala. 607, 48 So. 73.

[146] Ill. Cent. R. R. v. Seamans, 79 Miss. 106, 31 So. 546.

[147] Schreiner v. Great Northern Ry. 86 Minn. 245, 90 N. W. 400.

sible for the further loss caused by his own subsequent act; intervention of the defendant in reduction of loss, or diminution of injury, e. g., in case of benefits accepted, gives rise to questions discussed elsewhere. Intervention of the plaintiff and intervention of a third party remain to be considered.

§ 126a. Interposition of plaintiff.

One of the simplest cases of such intervening agency on the part of the plaintiff is presented where he makes an effort to avoid the loss caused by the defendant's wrong and in such effort causes further damage to himself. As will be seen on a fuller examination of the question in a later chapter,[148] any further loss caused by a reasonable and *bona fide* effort on the part of the plaintiff to avoid the loss inflicted by the defendant can be recovered from the defendant. But there are many other cases.

Where defendant supplies defective articles for use, and the plaintiff is injured in using them, the injury is a proximate consequence of the defendant's fault;[149] but if the article is dangerous only when used in connection with another article, and such use is made, the defendant is only remotely the cause of the loss where he did not supply the defective article for such use.[150] Where the plaintiff is requested to act by the defendant, and does so to his harm, the loss is proximate.[151] So where defendant, in shutting off gas from plaintiff's house, had carelessly allowed it to escape but assured plaintiff that no gas was escaping, and plaintiff smelt gas and went to the door of the cellar with a lighted candle, as a result of which gas exploded and she was injured, it was held that defendant was liable for the explosion.[152]

[148] *Post*, §§ 215 *et seq.*

[149] Moriarty *v.* Porter, 22 N. Y. Misc. 536, 49 N. Y. Supp. 1107 (bicycle supplied by defendant broke while plaintiff was riding and injured him).

[150] Davidson *v.* Nichols, 11 Allen (Mass.), 514.

Where defendant negligently shipped on a railroad train, fireworks which were liable to explode by concussion and an explosion caused a fire, and a fireman engaged in an effort to put out the fire was injured by another explosion, this was held not to be a remote result of defendant's wrong. Houston, B. & T. Ry. *v.* O'Leary (Tex. Civ. App.), 136 S. W. 601.

[151] Pacific P. T. C. Co. *v.* Bank of Palo Alto, 109 Fed. 369, 48 C. C. A. 413, 54 L. R. A. 711.

[152] Louisville Gas Co. *v.* Gutenkuntz, 82 Ky. 432.

On the other hand, where the plaintiff acted entirely on his own account, deliberately and in a way not required by the defendant's wrong, he cannot recover for the result of his own act. So where the plaintiff sent a message by the defendant telegraph company to one person, and the company negligently delivered it to the wrong person, whereupon plaintiff entered into business relations with the person to whom the message was delivered and suffered loss, the company was not chargeable with the loss.[153]

Plaintiff was in possession of land; defendant wrongfully claimed the title and brought suit against him. Plaintiff intended to use the place for a store, and was about to build a cellar to hold potatoes. By reason of the claim he delayed building the cellar, and the potatoes were frozen. This was too remote.[154] In an action for the wrongful escape of gas, it appeared that plaintiff was a florist. Some of the flowers were injured, but the injury to them did not at once appear, and they were sold to customers. Plaintiff claimed damages for injury to his business reputation caused by the flowers fading after the customers got them. This was too remote.[155] As a result of an unlawful obstruction of a street by a railroad plaintiff could not get home in the direct way, and had to walk round and go into another street, where she slipped on some ice and fell. This was a remote result of blocking the street, and plaintiff could not recover damages from railroad.[156] In an action for wrongfully tearing down plaintiff's barn it appeared that plaintiff could get no other barn because he did not have money, and he therefore sold his horses at a sacrifice. It was held that this was not the proximate consequence of the barn being torn down.[157]

A personal injury resulted after some weeks in insanity; while insane the injured person committed suicide. This was

[153] Western U. T. Co. v. Barlow, 51 Fla. 351, 40 So. 491, 4 L. R. A. (N. S.) 262.

[154] Cormier v. Bourque, 32 N. B. 283.

[155] Dow v. Winnipesaukee Gas & Electric Co., 69 N. H. 312, 41 Atl. 288, 42 L. R. A. 569.

[156] Pittsburgh, C. & S. L. Ry. v. Staley, 41 Ohio St. 118, 52 Am. Rep. 754. Nor could he recover where, being drunk, he walked along the railroad track and was struck by a train. Seaboard Air Line Ry. v. Smith, 59 S. E. 199, 3 Ga. App. 1.

[157] Chandler v. Smith, 70 Ill. App. 658.

held not to be a proximate result of the injury.[158] The suicide was a voluntary act—a new and independent act—breaking the chain of causation. But where a servant of a railroad company was put in charge of a passenger who could not take care of himself, and the passenger was allowed to wander off and strayed on the road and was killed by a train, the company was held liable.[159]

Wool imported by the plaintiff was wet by the defendant's tort, and the plaintiff was obliged to open the original packages in order to dry it. Congress afterwards allowed importers a drawback on wool in the original packages. It was held that the loss of this drawback was too remote a consequence of the defendant's tort to be compensated.[160]

The defendant, a master of a vessel, wrongfully imprisoned a passenger; the passenger left the vessel at the next port, and took passage in another vessel. The payment of the passage money on the second vessel was a remote consequence of the imprisonment.[161] The defendant wrongfully gave the plaintiff several blows, and in consequence the plaintiff felt obliged to give up his business and remove to another city; the consequence was remote.[162] Defendant without authority sold a ticket over plaintiff's railroad. Plaintiff refused to honor the ticket, and ejected the person who presented it; whereupon the latter sued for assault and battery and recovered a judgment. In a suit by the railroad from which he recovered it against the other, the illegal ejection is remote from the defendant's wrong.[163] Where a passenger, having been unjustifiably ordered out of a railway carriage, left a pair of race-glasses on his seat, and lost them in consequence, the loss was held not to be the result of the wrongful act, and the passenger could not recover for it.[164]

---

[158] Daniels v. New York, N. H. & H. R. R., 183 Mass. 393, 67 N. E. 424, 62 L. R. A. 751. Cf. Scheffer v. Washington, C. V. M. & C. S. R. R., 105 U. S. 249, 26 L. ed. 1070.

[159] Wells v. New York C. & H. R. R. R., 25 App. Div. 365, 49 N. Y. Supp. 510.

[160] Stone v. Codman, 15 Pick. (Mass.) 297.

[161] Boyce v. Bayliffe, 1 Camp. 58.

[162] Moore v. Adam, 2 Chit. 198.

[163] Pennsylvania R. R. v. Wabash, S. L. & P. Ry., 157 U. S. 225, 39 L. ed. 682, 15 Sup. Ct. 576.

[164] Glover v. London & S. W. Ry., L. R. 3 Q. B. 25.

Where by fault of defendant a woman was left at the wrong station at night and she went to a hotel, where she was placed in a cold room and staid in it all night without a fire, thereby contracting a severe cold, the cold was held to be only a remote result of defendant's wrong.[165]

§ 126b. Damage resulting to feelings of the injured party.

Where the result of an intentional trespass upon a person's land or chattels is mental suffering, this is not too remote for compensation.[166] So the plaintiff in such a case may recover damages for shame and humiliation,[167] inconvenience,[168] and invasion of privacy.[169] But where the plaintiff suffered a miscarriage through the defendant's wrong, her grief at the loss of the child is too remote to be compensated.[170]

§ 126c. Loss through a forced sale of property.

Where through the defendant's default the plaintiff is obliged to raise money, and in order to raise it his goods are sold at a loss, this loss is too remote from the injury to be compensated.

So in New York, the plaintiff sued the defendant on a contract, by which the defendant, in consideration of $5 paid him,

---

[165] Cincinnati, N. O. & T. P. Ry. v. Raine, 130 Ky. 454, 113 S. W. 495.

[166] *Alabama:* Snedecor v. Pope, 143 Ala. 275, 39 So. 318.

Indiana: Moyer v. Gordon, 113 Ind. 282.

Massachusetts: Fillebrown v. Hoar, 124 Mass. 580.

Mississippi: Bonelli v. Brown, 70 Miss. 142, 11 So. 791.

Missouri: Hickey v. Welch, 91 Mo. App. 4.

Texas: Fort Worth Ry. v. Smith (Tex. Civ. App.), 25 S. W. 1032.

Contra, where there are no circumstances of aggravation.

Nebraska: Murray v. Mace, 41 Neb. 60, 59 N. W. 387, 43 Am. St. Rep. 664.

Texas: Williams v. Yoe (Tex. Civ. App.), 46 S. W. 659 (but see McCarthy v. Miller, (Tex. Civ. App.), 57 S. W. 973).

Wisconsin: Ford v. Schliessman, 107 Wis. 479, 83 N. W. 761.

See *ante,* § 43j.

[167] Moyer v. Gordon, 113 Ind. 282.

[168] *Alabama:* Snedecor v. Pope, 143 Ala. 275, 39 So. 318.

Indiana: Moyer v. Gordon, 113 Ind. 282.

New York: Ives v. Humphreys, 1 E. D. Smith, 196.

Canada: Benson v. Connor, 6 Up. Can. C. P. 356.

[169] Ives v. Humphreys, 1 E. D. Smith, 196.

[170] *Texas:* Western U. T. Co. v. Cooper, 71 Tex. 507, 9 S. W. 598, 10 Am. St. Rep. 772, *n.*

Vermont: Bovee v. Danville, 53 Vt. 183.

agreed to take a note executed by the plaintiff and a surety, payable the first of May, and to forbear prosecution of the note for nine months; and it was alleged that the defendant did not forbear, but sued on the note, by which the plaintiff lost $500. The plaintiff offered to prove, to enhance the damages, that when he was sued he was engaged in his harvest, and that for the purpose of raising money to satisfy the demand he was obliged to quit his work and thresh his grain, and that he was put to great trouble in raising the money. But on certiorari to the Supreme Court, Woodworth, J., said, "It appears to me that this could not form a ground of damage, although the plaintiff might have suffered inconvenience and loss by the failure to fulfil the contract. Such remote consequences cannot be taken into consideration in estimating the damages"; which was qualified by this remark, "Besides, there does not appear any necessity that the plaintiff, at the moment the writ was served, should quit his harvest and make sacrifices to raise the money." [171]

So in Alabama, in a case for malicious prosecution whereby the plaintiffs were driven to an assignment, the loss in the sale of the goods made under the assignment is not a proximate or natural consequence of the malicious prosecution.[172] So in an action for failure to accept drafts, a loss on pork which the plaintiff was obliged to sell in order to raise money was held too remote for compensation.[173] So in Texas, where the defendant had sued the plaintiff in his absence from the State, by publication, and the plaintiff's agent, seeing the advertisement in the paper, got the defendant to promise to discontinue the suit, which he failed to do, and judgment having been obtained in it, a tract of the plaintiff's land, worth about $5,000, was sold, under an execution on the judgment, to a purchaser in good faith, without notice, for $150—it was held that if the defendant were liable for his failure to dismiss the

[171] Deyo v. Waggoner, 19 Johns. 241; acc., Carland v. Cunningham, 37 Pa. 228.

[172] Donnell v. Jones, 13 Ala. 490, 48 Am. Dec. 59; acc., Fitzjohn v. Mackinder, 9 C. B. (N. S.) 505, 2 L. T. (N. S.) 374. And the same decision was reached where the assignment was caused by a wrongful attachment. Cochrane v. Quackenbush, 29 Minn. 376.

[173] Larios v. Bonany y Gurety, L. R. 5 P. C. 346.

suit, the loss of the tract of land, if a consequence at all of such failure, was too remote to make him responsible for it.[174]

The plaintiff built a railroad for the defendant. The contract price not being paid by the defendant at the proper time, the plaintiff was unable to pay his workmen, and the plaintiff's tools and carts were seized and sold for debt at a sacrifice. It was held that this loss was too remote a consequence of the breach of contract.[175]

And where by reason of a wrongful attachment the plaintiff lost business, and as a result was obliged to sell out his stock in trade at a loss, this was a remote consequence of the attachment.[176]

§ 126d. Interposition of act of a third person.

The interposition of the absolutely independent act of a third party, where such act is itself the active cause of the loss complained of, will ordinarily make the original cause remote. Thus in an English case the defendant engaged the plaintiff as a seaman for a voyage to Peru; the vessel proved to be a privateer. In Peru the plaintiff went ashore to consult the consul, and was arrested and imprisoned by the Peruvian authorities as a deserter from the Peruvian army. It was held that this consequence of the defendant's fraud was too remote for compensation.[177] So where plaintiff and defendant were fighting, and during the fight defendant's son, who had not been engaged in the quarrel, without knowledge of defendant cut plaintiff, this was not the proximate result of the original fight.[178]

In an action against the master of a vessel for breach of contract in leaving the vessel during the voyage it appeared that the mate left at the same time because the master did, though the master took no steps to procure him to leave. It was held that the loss caused by the mate leaving was a too remote consequence of the master's breach of contract to be recovered.[179]

[174] Travis *v.* Duffau, 20 Tex. 49.
[175] Smith *v.* O'Donnell, 8 Lea (Tenn.), 468.
[176] Casper *v.* Klippen, 61 Minn. 353, 63 N. W. 737.

[177] Burton *v.* Pinkerton, L. R. 2 Ex. 340.
[178] White *v.* Conly, 14 Lea (Tenn.), 51.
[179] Smith *v.* Osborn, 143 Mass. 185, 9 N. E. 558.

Defendant enticed plaintiff's daughter from home to serve in his family. While there the daughter was seduced by defendant's son. It was held that this was not a proximate result of the defendant's act, and plaintiff could not recover.[180] Defendant negligently placed a gas meter on plaintiff's premises as a result of which they took fire. Some of his goods were burned, others were thrown out into the street and carried away by strangers. It was held that defendant was liable for goods that were burned, but not for the goods that were stolen by strangers, for that loss was too remote.[181] In an action of slander, charging plaintiff, a married man, with the crime of adultery, he claimed special damages because of the expense of defending an action for divorce and also because his wife deserted him. It was held that these could not be recovered, on the ground that they were neither natural nor proximate consequences of the slander.[182] Defendant agreed to furnish centres for masonry arches which X was to build. He did not furnish all the centres called for by the contract. There not being enough arches, the defendant's foreman took down one of the used centres before the masonry had sufficiently set and it fell and injured plaintiff's intestate. It was held that this was not the proximate result of defendant's breach of contract.[183] Defendant wrongfully left a barrel of quicklime in the street. A child took some of the lime and threw it into a vessel of water held by plaintiff; an explosion resulted, and plaintiff's eyes were injured by it. This was held not to be a proximate result of defendant's act.[184] Action against sheriff for escape of a prisoner under indictment for assault on plaintiff. When the prisoner escaped he made another assault and the plaintiff for his own safety was compelled to have him bound over to keep the peace. It was held that the second assault and the expense of binding him over to keep the peace were not chargeable to the sheriff.[185] Defendant entered plaintiff's house and murdered a servant in it. Plaintiff's family

---

[180] Stewart *v.* Strong, 20 Ind. App. 44, 50 N. E. 95.

[181] Klein *v.* Equitable Gaslight Co., 13 N. Y. St. 736.

[182] Georgia *v.* Kepford, 45 Iowa, 48.

[183] Hofnagle *v.* New York C. & H. R. R. R., 55 N. Y. 608.

[184] Beetz *v.* Brooklyn, 10 N. Y. App. Div. 382, 41 N. Y. Supp. 1009.

[185] Hullinger *v.* Worrell, 83 Ill. 220.

thereupon refused to live longer in the house nor would anyone else live in it. It was held that plaintiff was not entitled to recover for the loss thereby caused.[186] Where because of defendant's wrongful delay in transporting goods a drayman who had agreed to haul them wrongfully refused to do so, this was held not chargeable to defendant.[187] And so where defendant wrongfully claimed as his own and seized a dredge which plaintiff was operating and as a result plaintiff's employees in violation of their contracts left his service, this was held to be the act of the employees alone, and not a proximate result of defendant's wrong.[188]

Where, however, the act of the third party is intentionally caused by the defendant, the result is not remote. So where defendant maliciously and tortiously ordered X not to discharge his cargo at plaintiff's wharf (claiming to be a public official, having the right to do so), and X thereupon left plaintiff's wharf and plaintiff lost the profit from having his wharf used, it was held that he could recover as in this case it was a proximate result.[189] So where the plaintiff was wrongfully arrested by the defendant and delivered to the authorities, who imprisoned him, compensation for the imprisonment was allowed against the defendant.[190] And the same result is sometimes reached, where the intervening act is negligent, where the defendant himself acted in such a way that he should have foreseen the negligence of the third party. So where defendant wrongfully sold a young son of plaintiff a toy pistol loaded with powder and ball, and the child left it on the floor and a younger child picked it up and fired it and killed the other child, it was held that the fact that an agency intervened between the original wrong and the injury did not necessarily make the injury remote. If it was the natural and probable result of the wrong, then it was not remote. It is a probable result of selling such dangerous explosives to a child

[186] Clark v. Gray, 112 Ala. 777, 38 S. E. 81.

[187] Texas C. R. R. v. Shropshire (Tex. Civ. App.), 125 S. W. 369.

[188] Brown v. Pillow, 174 Fed. 967, 98 C. C. A. 579.

[189] Gregory v. Brooks, 35 Conn. 437, 95 Am. Dec. 278.

[190] Tyler v. Pomeroy, 8 All. (Mass.) 480.

that they will be used by any children among whom it is natural to expect they will be taken so as to injure bystanders.[191] Where the act of the third party is induced directly and naturally by the defendant's act, it will ordinarily be proximate. So where the defendant maliciously attached the plaintiff's property, the damages caused by other attachments being immediately placed on the property is a proximate consequence.[192] And where the defendant should have guarded against the act the rule is the same. On this principle, where the defendant negligently recommended a broker to the plaintiff, who gave the broker money for investment, and the broker embezzled it, defendant was held liable.[193]

§ 126e. Concurring negligence of third person.

If the act of the third person does not actively cause the loss complained of, but is merely a negligent failure to prevent the loss, the defendant's act is nevertheless a proximate cause. So where the defendant injured the plaintiff, a child, and death ensued, the fact that the plaintiff's parents were negligent in nursing her, was held no defense to the action.[194] Defendant, a physician, had carelessly made out a prescription wrongly. The druggist who put up the prescription was negligent in not noticing the mistake. The person for whom it was intended took it and died. Defendant was held liable in spite of the concurrent negligence of the druggist.[195] Defendant wrongfully allowed gas to escape into plaintiff's premises. A gas fitter employed to mend the pipe negligently used a lighted candle while trying to discover the leak, and there was an explosion which injured plaintiff's property in the house. It was held that the explosion, though the consequence of the negligence in a third party, was nevertheless chargeable to the defendant.[196] And where the defendant railroad negligently

[191] Binford v. Johnston, 82 Ind. 426, 42 Am. Rep. 508.

[192] Crimes v. Bowerman, 92 Mich. 258, 52 N. W. 751.

[193] De la Bere v. Pearson, [1907] 1 K. B. 483, 76 L. J. K. B. 309, 96 L. T. Rep. 425, 23 T. L. R. 264.

[194] Bradshaw v. Frazier, 113 Iowa, 579, 85 N. W. 752, 55 L. R. A. 258.

[195] Murdock v. Walker, 43 Ill. App. 590.

[196] Burrows v. March Gas, etc., Co., L. R. 7 Exch. 96, 41 L. J. Exch. 96, 26 L. T. Rep. (N. S.) 318, 20 Wkly. Rep. 493.

kindled a fire on land and the owner of the land on which it was kindled by culpable negligence allowed it to increase and escape and it spread to plaintiff's land, the defendant was liable to the plaintiff for the consequent loss.[197]

§ 127. Loss of credit.

Loss of credit or custom generally involves the intervention of the will of strangers, and is therefore generally remote. Thus, in case of a wrongful attachment, no compensation is allowed for loss of credit,[198] and the same result was reached where the defendant wrongly sued out a writ of *ne exeat*.[199] So, in Alexander *v.* Jacoby,[200] it was held that a plaintiff, whose goods had been attached, could not recover damages for their diminished market value by their reputation being affected, the court saying, "The injury is too vague and uncertain, and the damage too remote." So where the defendant failed to assign to the plaintiff (according to agreement) a judgment against him, in consequence of which property of the plaintiff was seized and sold to satisfy the judgment, it was held that loss of credit arising therefrom was too remote to be compensated.[201] And loss of business credit by reason of the failure of the defendant to supply the plaintiff with money to buy tobacco, according to agreement, is remote.[202]

Where the defendant's wrong has no direct connection with the business carried on, a damage to the business, being caused directly by the acts of the customers, is remote. So in an action for delay in furnishing a cider-press, loss of custom is too remote.[203] And where the defendant negligently allowed oil to drip from his tenement above the plaintiff down on the

---

[197] Wiley *v.* West Jersey R. R., 44 N. J. L. 247.

[198] *Iowa:* Lowenstein *v.* Monroe, 55 Ia. 82, 7 N. W. 406.

Mississippi: Marqueze *v.* Sontheimer, 59 Miss. 430.

Vermont: Weeks *v.* Prescott, 53 Vt. 57.

In Pollock *v.* Gannt, 69 Ala. 373, the court seems to have assumed that compensation in such a case may be recovered for loss of credit; but the point was not involved in the decision. In MacVeagh *v.* Bailey, 29 Ill. App. 606, compensation was allowed for injury to credit.

[199] Burnap *v.* Wight, 14 Ill. 301.

[200] 23 Oh. St. 358.

[201] Gilbert *v.* Campbell, 1 Hannay (N. B.), 471.

[202] Carsay *v.* Farmer, 117 Ky. 826, 79 S. W. 245, 25 Ky. L. R. 1905.

[203] Dennis *v.* Stoughton, 55 Vt. 371.

plaintiff's goods, it was held that loss of custom to the plaintiff through the injury to his goods was too remote for compensation.[204] And on breach of a contract by the landlord to keep in repair premises used for a dentist's office, loss of custom by reason of plumbing out of repair was held remote.[205]

§ 127a. Loss of business.

Where the defendant trespasses upon the business premises or the stock in trade of the plaintiff, a loss of business is a proximate consequence of the trespass, and compensation for it may be recovered.[206] And so where any direct injury is done to the business, the loss of business is proximate. Thus, where the defendant, agent of the plaintiff in G., broke his contract to keep a cash account of £500 to meet drafts of the plaintiff, and in consequence a draft was returned dishonored, he was held liable for the loss of trade in G., which was consequently suspended, and for loss in the general business of the plaintiff because of his impaired credit.[207] In a case at Nisi Prius,[208] Lord Kenyon held that an action lay for firing on negroes on the coast of Africa, and thereby deterring them from trading with the plaintiff, so that the plaintiff lost their trade. So where defendant loosened shoes which plaintiff, a blacksmith, had put on a horse, in order that the owner of the horse might think the work badly done, and as a result

[204] Stopenhorst v. American M. Co., 36 N. Y. Super. Ct. 392.

[205] Chadwick v. Woodward, 12 Daly (N. Y.), 399.

[206] *California:* Hawthorne v. Siegel, 88 Cal. 159, 25 Pac. 1114, 22 Am. St. Rep. 291.

Colorado: Georgetown, B. & L. Ry. v. Eagles, 9 Colo. 544, 13 Pac. 696; Georgetown, B. & L. Ry. v. Doyle, 9 Colo. 549, 13 Pac. 699.

Georgia: Bass v. West, 110 Ga. 698, 36 S. E. 244.

Maryland: Moore v. Schultz, 31 Md. 418 (trespass d. b. a.).

Massachusetts: White v. Moseley, 8 Pick. 356.

Michigan: Chandler v. Allison, 10 Mich. 460; Allison v. Chandler, 11 Mich. 542.

Missouri: Freidenheit v. Edmundson, 36 Mo. 226, 88 Am. Dec. 141; Allred v. Bray, 41 Mo. 484, 97 Am. Dec. 283.

New Jersey: Luse v. Jones, 10 Vr. (39 N. J. L.) 707 (trespass d. b. a.).

New York: Schile v. Brokhahus, 80 N. Y. 620; O'Horo v. Kelsey, 60 App. Div. 604, 70 N. Y. Supp. 14.

[207] Boyd v. Fitt, 14 Ir. C. L. 43; *acc.,* Larios v. Bonany y Gurety, L. R. 5 P. C. 346.

[208] Tarleton v. McGawley, Peake, N. P. 205.

the plaintiff lost trade, he was allowed to recover.[209] So for fraud in selling to a dealer goods which were not as represented, the buyer may recover damages for loss of trade resulting from his selling the inferior goods to his customers.[210] And in an action for wrongful communication of contagious disease plaintiff may recover for loss of business, owing to patrons being kept away by fear of the disease.[211] And where the defendant himself threatens customers if they trade with plaintiff, he is obviously liable for the loss of business.[212]

§ 128. Loss caused by a crowd attracted.

Whether a trespasser who draws a crowd after him is responsible for the injury done by it depends upon whether his act was of a nature to attract a destructive crowd. Where the defendant made a harangue in the street, and a crowd collecting to hear him broke a pile of paving stones belonging to the plaintiff, the question whether or not the loss was proximate to the defendant's act was held to depend upon whether it was to be expected to result.[213] Where the defendant went up in a balloon which descended into the plaintiff's garden and attracted a crowd, who trod down the plaintiff's vegetables and flowers, the original wrongdoer was held answerable for the injury done by the crowd as well as by himself.[214] And where the defendant led a body of men upon the plaintiff's premises

[209] Hughes v. McDonough, 43 N. J. L. 459, 39 Am. Rep. 603.

[210] American Pure Food Co. v. G. W. Elliott & Co., 66 S. E. 451, 151 N. C. 393 (spurious baking powder).

But in Crain v. Petrie, 6 Hill (N. Y.), 522, 41 Am. Dec. 765, an action for deceit in the sale of sheep, where it was alleged that defendant sold diseased sheep as healthy sheep, so that a butcher who had contracted to purchase mutton from plaintiff refused to fulfil his bargain on account of the report that plaintiff had purchased diseased sheep from the defendant, it was held that plaintiff could not recover any damages for the failure of this butcher to fulfil his contract, nor for the loss of

the custom of other persons in the neighborhood, owing to the sale by defendant to plaintiff of the diseased sheep.

[211] *United States:* Smith v. Baker, 20 Fed. 79.

Texas: Missouri, K. & T. Ry. v. Raney, 99 S. W. 589, 44 Tex. Civ. App. 517.

[212] Sparks v. McCrary, 156 Ala. 382, 47 So. 332, 22 L. R. A. (N. S.) 1224.

[213] Fairbanks v. Kerr, 70 Pa. 86, 10 Am. Rep. 664.

[214] Guille v. Swan, 19 Johns. (N. Y.) 381, 10 Am. Dec. 234; acc., Scott v. Moss, 17 Scotch Sess. Cas. (4th Ser.) 32.

to ascertain whether plaintiff's workmen were satisfied with their hours, he was held liable for acts of violence done by them.[215]

In an action on the stat. 1 Geo. I, st. 2, c. 5, § 6, against the hundred for reparation in damages on account of rioters having pulled down in part the plaintiff's dwelling house, it appeared that the plaintiff was a baker, and that the mob compelled the plaintiff to sell a quantity of flour at a price much below its value; that they then began to break the windows of the bake-house, and of his dwelling-house. Besides this, they burst open the lock of a warehouse belonging to the plaintiff on the other side of the street, and threw some flour into the street. It was held that the damage done the warehouse was an act not consequential to the other, and that the flour which the mob compelled the plaintiff to sell was not a damage recoverable against the hundred.[216] And the same point was held in another action brought against the hundred, as to flour taken away or stolen by a mob.[217] These cases turn on the construction of the statute.

But where the defendant did not himself incite or accompany the crowd, the case is different. So where defendant wrongfully built a levee on plaintiff's land, and a mob was collected and destroyed the levee, doing damage to plaintiff's land, it was not a proximate consequence of defendant's act.[218]

§ 129. Loss of employment.

Loss of employment which is closely resultant on the defendant's wrong will be regarded as a proximate consequence of it. So where the plaintiff was wrongfully expelled from a protective union, whereby he lost employment in his trade, he was allowed to recover compensation for the loss of employment.[219] And in an action for false arrest the plaintiff may recover for loss of employment consequent on the arrest.[220]

[215] Webber v. Barry, 66 Mich. 127, 33 N. W. 289, 11 Am. St. R. 466.

[216] Burrows v. Wright, 1 East, 615.

[217] Greasley v. Higginbottom, 1 East, 636.

[218] Bentley v. Fischer Co., 51 La. Ann. 451, 25 So. 262.

[219] People v. Musical M. P. Union, 118 N. Y. 101, 23 N. E. 129. So of loss of employment caused by a libel. Sunley v. Met. L. Ins. Co., 109 N. W. 463, 132 Ia. 123.

[220] Thompson v. Ellsworth, 39 Mich. 719.

In one such case it was held that the plaintiff could not recover compensation for loss of an employment for which he had applied, but had not received, and the decision was put on the ground that the loss of employment was too remote; [221] but it would seem that it should have been based on the uncertainty and speculative nature of the loss. In a similar case, where the plaintiff offered to prove as special damage, that having been imprisoned till after 2 o'clock P. M., and become unwell from his imprisonment, he did not go to a certain place where he would have obtained a situation if he had appeared at 2 o'clock, the alleged damage was held too remote. [222] And a loss of nine months' salary is not the natural or probable result of one night's imprisonment, preventing plaintiff from keeping an appointment. [223]

§ 130.[a] Loss of a dependent contract.

The defendant had agreed to let the plaintiff have the carrying of passengers from its station at D. to G. by stage. The plaintiff had also had the carriage of them by steamboat from G. to K., but not under any contract with the defendant. It was held [224] (1) that the plaintiff was not confined to the difference between what he was to receive for each passenger and what it would have cost him to carry the passengers; that he was also entitled to profits he would have made on way passengers, express, mail, etc., by being so situated (by his contract with the defendant) that he could have carried more cheaply than any one else. It was further held (2) that the plaintiff could not recover for loss of profits on the route from G. to K., for that loss did not arise, "according to the usual course of things, from the breach of the contract itself, nor was such as might reasonably be supposed to have been in the contemplation of both parties at the time they made the contract, as the probable result of a breach of it." They were

[a] For § 130 of the eighth edition, see § 126c.

[221] Brown *v.* Cummings, 7 All. (Mass.) 507.

[222] Hoey *v.* Felton, 11 C. B. (N. S.) 142. So in an action for wrongful expulsion from a railroad train. Carsten *v.* Northern P. Ry., 44 Minn. 454, 47 N. W. 49.

[223] Carpenter *v.* Pennsylvania R. R., 43 N. Y. Supp. 203.

[224] Frye *v.* Maine C. R. R., 37 Me. 414.

excluded, it was said, as in Fox *v.* Harding,[225] as profits arising from another independent and collateral undertaking, and, therefore, too uncertain and remote to be taken into consideration as part of the damages occasioned by the breach of the contract in question.

In Mandia *v.* M'Mahon [226] the plaintiff contracted to supply laborers to the defendant at $1.25 per day. He procured the laborers, but the defendant refused to hire them. It was held that the plaintiff could recover nothing for loss of commissions from the laborers. In an action against a physician for negligence in examining plaintiff and reporting wrongly his state of health, as a result of which he lost the opportunity to marry, it was held that the breaking of the marriage engagement was not too remote.[227] And where the plaintiff's property was wrongly seized and sold by a sheriff, he was held entitled to damages for loss of an advantageous contract for the sale of it.[228]

§ 131.[a] Judicial or other official action.

When a defendant wrongly sets in motion some official action, he is liable for the continuance of the action in the ordinary course of business. So one who causes a wrongful attachment is answerable for a subsequent sale of the goods; [229] and where a sheriff made a false return of service of process, judgment and execution are the proximate result of the return.[230] One who directs an attachment of specific goods is liable for their detention, even after he ordered a return of them.[231] One who falsely represented that no steerage passengers were carried on a steamship is liable for detention in quarantine caused by cholera among such passengers.[232]

On the other hand, where the supervening official act was itself illegal the defendant will not be held responsible for it. So in an old case where one party appealed another of robbery and the appellee was finally acquitted, it was held that his dam-

---

[a] For § 131 of the eighth edition, see § 125.

[225] 7 Cush. (Mass.) 516, 522.

[226] 17 Ont. App. 34.

[227] Harriott *v.* Plimpton, 166 Mass. 585, 44 N. E. 992.

[228] First Nat. Bank *v.* Thomas, Tex. Civ. App. , 118 S. W. 221.

[229] Jacobs *v.* Robb, 10 Up. Can. Q. B. 276.

[230] State *v.* Finn, 87 Mo. 310.

[231] Henry *v.* Mitchell, 37 Up. Can. Q. B. 217 (*semble*).

[232] Beers *v.* Hamburg-American Packet Co., 62 Fed. 469.

ages should not include compensation for being kept in prison after the judges should have heard his case.[233]   And where the plaintiff was detained in quarantine by reason of the defendant's wrong he could not recover for ill treatment while in quarantine.[234]

| Where the defendant's act had no relation to any official action, this being instituted independently of his act, it will usually be only remotely the cause of such action. So where a bank wrongfully refused to honor plaintiff's check, and plaintiff was arrested for the crime of obtaining property by false pretences by giving the check, this was held a remote consequence of the failure to honor the check.[235]

§ 132.[a] Deprivation of means to an end.

Where the defendant wrongfully deprives the plaintiff of something to which he has a right, the plaintiff may recover compensation for the proximate consequence of not having the thing to use. So where defendant broke his contract to rebuild a sea-wall, and upon the matter being called to his attention, promised to build it, but continued to delay doing so, it was held reasonable to rely on his promise to rebuild, and plaintiff could recover loss of rent of the land to be protected and made rentable by the wall.[236]   And in an action for damages for failing to furnish water to a flour mill to run it, where as a result wheat which had been bought by plaintiff to make into flour deteriorated, and it appeared that plaintiff had contracts for all the flour he could make out of this wheat and could have saved the loss if the water had been turned on, it was held that this could be recovered.[237]   And where the defendant negligently killed plaintiff's mare, the increased expense of taking care of her colt was recoverable.[238]

[a] For § 132 of the eighth edition, see § 125a.

[233] Anon., 42 Lib. Assis., pl. 19, Beale's Cas. Dam. 78.

[234] Beers v. H a m b u r g-American Packet Co., 62 Fed. 469.

[235] Bank of Commerce v. Goos, 39 Neb. 437, 58 N. W. 84, 23 L. R. A. 190.

[236] Willey v. Fredericks, 10 Gray (Mass.), 357.

[237] Gordon v. Constantine Hydraulic Co., 117 Mich. 620, 76 N. W. 142.   In an action for obstructing a watercourse by reason of which plaintiff was prevented from floating logs, which caused loss of use of engine and increase of cost of labor, these items of loss were not remote.   Creech v. Humptulips B. & R. G. Co., 37 Wash. 172, 79 Pac. 633.

[238] Morrison v. Darling, 47 Vt. 67.

On the other hand, in an action for breach of a contract to convey an undivided share of certain land, the other share of which was owned by the plaintiff, it was held that the expense of proceedings for partition of the land was too remote.[239] And in an action for diversion of a stream, where by reason of the diversion the defendant, being unable to use the water of it in drinking, was obliged to use well water and his wife became ill therefrom, it was held that the illness was not the proximate result of the diversion.[240] So in an action for personal injury it appeared that the plaintiff dealt in gold, which he kept locked in a safe, and that no one but himself knew the combination. As a consequence, no gold could be sold during the absence caused by the injury. This consequence, however, was held to result from "his abnormal and peculiar mode of doing his business," and to be too remote.[241]

In an action for injury to a mare, it was held that damage to her colt from loss of milk could not be recovered; but this turned on a question of pleading.[242]

§ 133.[a] Deprivation of property.

The same general principles apply where plaintiff has been deprived of property. So where plaintiff brought replevin for a chest of tools which had wrongfully been taken by the defendant, and claimed as damages for loss of tools the wages that he might have made by his labor and was unable to make on account of the loss of tools, it was held that he could not recover.[243] And in an action for trespass in wrongfully carrying away plaintiff's mule and mare while he was engaged in farming, damages resulting to his farming operations therefrom are too remote to be recovered.[244] Where defendant

[a] For § 133 of the eighth edition, see §§ 134, 134a.

[239] Woodstock Iron Works v. Stockdale, 143 Ala. 550, 39 So. 335.

[240] Phyfe v. Manhattan Ry., 30 Hun (N. Y.), 377.

[241] McDonnell v. Minneapolis, S. P. & S. S. M. Ry., 17 N. D. 604, 118 N. W. 819.

[242] *Indiana:* Teargarden v. Hetfield, 11 Ind. 522.

Iowa: Gamble v. Mullin, 74 Ia. 99, 36 N. W. 909.

[243] Kelly v. Altemus, 34 Ark. 184, 36 Am. Rep. 6.

[244] Street v. Sinclair, 70 Ala. 110. Where defendant destroyed legal papers, the consequent delay and expense in prosecuting a claim was too remote. Bourke v. Whiting, 19 Colo. 1, 34 Pac. 172.

injured a race horse, loss sustained through inability to keep racing engagements cannot be recovered.[245] But on the other hand, upon breach of warranty of the quality of paris green, sold to kill potato bugs, the loss of labor in using it and the loss of the crop are proximate consequences;[246] and for breach of contract to furnish a fertilizer for raising a crop the diminution in the yield of the land is proximate.[247] Defendant wrongfully cut off the gas by which plaintiff's room was heated. Plaintiff's husband was convalescent from typhoid fever at the time, and because of the cold resulting he contracted pneumonia and died. It was held that the pneumonia was the proximate result of cutting off the gas.[248]

§ 134.[a] Deprivation of business premises.

For deprivation of premises used in business, the injured party may recover damages for the value to him of the use of the premises.[249] A railroad contractor built houses for shelter of his workmen. The defendant wrongfully took possession of the premises. The contractor was allowed to recover compensation for loss by reason of his men leaving him for lack of shelter.[250] In an action on an injunction bond, where the injunction prevented the erection of a stable, the plaintiff may recover for the exposure of his cow to the weather and the diminution of her milk.[251]

Upon eviction from the premises, plaintiff may recover damages for depreciation in value of the stock [252] and for injury to his business.[253] But for a mere temporary interrup-

---

[a] For § 134 of the eighth edition, see § 135.

[245] Louisville & N. R. R. v. Gormley, 33 Ky. L. Rep. 802, 111 S. W. 289.

[246] *Rhode Island:* Kent v. Halliday, 23 R. I. 182, 49 Atl. 700; *Texas:* Jones v. George, 56 Tex. 149, 42 Am. Rep. 689.

[247] Herring v. Armwood, 130 N. C. 177, 41 S. E. 96.

[248] Hoehle v. Allegheny Heating Co., 5 Pa. Super. Ct. 21.

[249] Moore v. Davis, 49 N. H. 45, 6 Am. Rep. 460.

[250] Carlisle v. Callahan, 78 Ga. 320.

[251] Lange v. Wagner, 52 Md. 310. But where a wagon, by means of which the plaintiff was moving his goods over frozen roads, was wrongfully seized by the plaintiff and detained until spring, when the bad condition of the roads increased the expense of moving the property, it was held that this increased expense was too remote to be compensated. Vedder v. Hildreth, 2 Wis. 427.

[252] Snow v. Pulitzer, 142 N. Y. 263, 36 N. E. 1059.

[253] Gildersleeve v. Overstolz, 90 Mo.

tion of possession, like forcible entry of the premises and an attempt to expel the plaintiff, injury to business is too remote.[254]

Where the injury consists in the breach of an obligation to provide the plaintiff with a building for business purposes, mere incidental losses are often too remote for recovery. So upon failure to provide plaintiff with a building for part of his department store at the time agreed, the loss by not being able to get in merchandise ordered and prepare it for sale and by extra work caused by the failure to get the building was too remote.[255] And where plaintiff, who was keeping a boarding house, decided to enter upon mercantile business and leased premises from defendant, and the premises were not furnished, whereupon plaintiff claimed damages resulting from the loss of the boarders dismissed in expectation o f entering upon the other business, this was held too remote.[256]

§ 134a. Deprivation of machinery.

Where the plaintiff has been deprived of machinery or other means of carrying on his business, he may recover for loss of business, if such loss naturally follows. Thus, for deprivation of machinery evidently to be used in a mill, the owner may recover damages caused by the loss of use of the mill; for instance, wages paid the hands in excess of the work they were able to do,[257] or loss of stock on hand rendered useless for lack of the machine.[258] Where a machine is broken, the amount

App. 518; Price *v.* Murray, 10 Bosw. (N. Y.) 243. Unless too speculative. Doyle *v.* Days, 94 Ga. 633, 20 S. E. 133.

Where the business could not be carried on without a license, damages are limited to the term of the existing license; the probability of the license being renewed cannot be considered. Porter *v.* Johnson, 96 Ga. 145, 23 S. E. 123.

[254] Beidler *v.* Fish, 14 Ill. App. 623.

[255] Dwyer *v.* Tulane Educational Fund, 47 La. Ann. 1232, 17 So. 796.

[256] Greer *v.* Varnell, 27 Tex. Civ. App. 255, 65 S. W. 196.

[257] *United States:* New York & C. M.

S. *v.* Fraser, 130 U. S. 611, 9 Sup. Ct. 665.

Michigan: John Hutchinson Mfg. Co. *v.* Pinch, 91 Mich. 156, 51 N. W. 930.

Wisconsin: Jolly *v.* Single, 16 Wis. 280.

England: Waters *v.* Towers, 8 Ex. 401.

Contra, Ruthven W. Co. *v.* Great W. Ry., 18 Up. Can. C. P. 316.

[258] *Georgia:* Savannah, F. & W. Ry. *v.* Pritchard, 77 Ga. 412, 1 S. E. 261, 4 Am. St. Rep. 92; Van Winkle *v.* Wilkins, 81 Ga. 93, 7 S. E. 644, 12 Am. St. Rep. 299.

paid for having the work of the machine done elsewhere, before repairs can be made, is an element of damage.[259]

§ 135.[a] Deprivation of means of protection to person or property.

When the plaintiff has provided shelter for his person or protection for his property and he is deprived of it by the defendant's wrong, the injury to the person or property caused by the lack of the shelter or protection is the proximate consequence of the defendant's wrong. So where the defendant, either by tort or by breach of contract, deprives plaintiff of a tight roof, plaintiff may recover compensation for personal injury caused by exposure to the elements on account of the defect.[260]

Where the defendant wrongfully took possession of a place of safety behind a sea-wall to which the plaintiff was exclusively entitled, and thereby prevented the plaintiff's vessels from being protected from the weather, it was held that the plaintiff could recover for the loss of his vessels;[261] and where, by the result of a collision for which the defendant was liable, the masts of the plaintiff's vessel were carried away, and she was wrecked in a storm which immediately arose, the defendant was required to pay compensation for the loss of the vessel.[262]   In an English case it appeared that in pursuance of the defendants' agreement to admit the plaintiffs' ship into the dock at a certain time, and of notice to the plaintiffs to bring her at that time, they did so; but on the arrival of the ship she could not be admitted, owing to the dock chain being out of order. The day was stormy and the captain was ignorant of the river. After a discussion as to what should be done, with the pilot, who thought he might take the ship into a place of safety, the captain anchored her immediately outside the dock, where she grounded, and in consequence was much

[a] For § 135 of the eighth edition, see § 136.

South Carolina: Sitton v. MacDonald, 25 S. C. 68, 60 Am. Rep. 484.

[259] Jackson A. I. Works v. Hurlbut, 36 N. Y. Supp. 808.

[260] *New York:* Stephen v. Woodruff, 18 App. Div. 625, 45 N. Y. Supp. 712.

North Carolina: Hatchell v. Kimbrough, 49 N. C. 163.

[261] Derry v. Flitner, 118 Mass. 131.

[262] The George and Richard, L. R. 3 Adm. 466.

damaged. The jury found neither the captain nor pilot in fault, but disagreed as to whether the vessel might in fact have been taken to a place of safety. It was held that the finding of the jury did not enable the court to say whether the defendants should be liable or not, and that the jury must come to an agreement on the points on which they had failed to agree; for the question whether the damage was too remote was not yet ripe for the decision of the court, but depended on the issue not yet found by the jury.[263]

Where an action was brought on the warranty of a chain-cable, that it should last two years, as a substitute for a rope cable of sixteen inches, and it was alleged that within the two years the cable broke, and that thereby an anchor, to which the cable was affixed, was lost, the loss was held not too remote.[264]

The defendant wrongfully entered plaintiff's house and left it open; the plaintiff's goods were taken from the house, it did not appear by whom. The defendant was held responsible.[265] Defendant wrongfully filled in land between plaintiff and a river and placed a building thereon. Plaintiff's buildings got on fire, and the fire company was unable to get quickly to the river and get water and put out the fire because of defendant's building. This was held a remote consequence of the wrongful building.[266]

§ 136. Detention of property.

In an action against a carrier for delay in delivering goods, the plaintiff may recover compensation for decline in market value during the time of delay.[267] So where the defendant detained the plaintiff's logs by placing a boom across the stream, the plaintiff was allowed to recover for depreciation

---

[263] Wilson v. Newport Dock Co., L. R. 1 Ex. 177.

[264] Borradaile v. Brunton, 8 Taunton, 535; s. c. 2 J. B. Moore, 582.

[265] Jesse French P. & O. Co. v. Phelps, 47 Tex. Civ. App. 385, 105 S. W. 225.

[266] Bosch v. Burlington & M. R. R. R., 44 Iowa, 402, 24 Am. Rep. 171, 42 L. R. A. 302.

[267] Collard v. Southeastern Ry., 7 H. & N. 79.

Georgia: Columbus & W. Ry. v. Flournoy, 75 Ga. 745.

Massachusetts: Cutting v. Grand T. Ry., 13 All. 381; Scott v. Boston & N. O. S. S. Co., 106 Mass. 468.

North Carolina: Lindley v. Richmond & D. R. R., 88 N. C. 547.

in the market while detained.[268] And where the defendant, by obstructing a river, delayed the plaintiff's logs until the annual dry season, when the plaintiff was put to additional expense in getting the logs to market, it was held that he might recover compensation for such increase of expense,[269] and for wages necessarily paid workmen for a reasonable time while waiting for the obstruction to be removed.[270]

The plaintiff, a cap manufacturer, ordered cloth of a certain style to be sent by the defendant, a common carrier. The defendant negligently delayed delivery of the cloth until the season for it was passed, and it was therefore less valuable. It was held that the plaintiff might recover compensation for loss in value of the cloth.[271]

In an action for wrongful attachment, the plaintiff may recover compensation for the deterioration in value of the goods while attached.[272]

Where the plaintiff's vessel is injured by collision, he may recover the amount paid out to the crew in wages during the period of detention.[273] And where through repairs improperly made a sea-going steamship was detained, the owner may recover the expense of the detention.[274]

§ 137. Loss of service.

Where the defendant, by the malicious arrest of the plaintiff's engineer while in the performance of his duties, deprived the plaintiff of the latter's services, it was held that the damage caused the plaintiff by the stoppage of its train was not

[268] *Maine:* Plummer v. Penobscot L. A., 67 Me. 363.

Minnesota: Mississippi & R. R. B. Co. v. Prince, 34 Minn. 71, 24 N. W. 344.

Pennsylvania: Dubois v. Glaub, 52 Pa. 238.

[269] Gates v. Northern P. R. R., 64 Wis. 64, 24 N. W. 494.

[270] McPheters v. Moose R. L. D. Co., 78 Me. 329.

[271] Wilson v. Lancashire & Y. Ry., 9 C. B. (N. S.) 632.

[272] *Illinois:* MacVeagh v. Bailey, 29 Ill. App. 606.

Iowa: Knapp v. Barnard, 78 Ia. 347.

Not, however, for deterioration in value of real estate pending the attachment of it, since the attachment did not cause the deterioration. Tisdale v. Major, 106 Iowa, 1, 75 N. W. 663.

[273] New Haven S. B. Co. v. Mayor, 36 Fed. 716.

[274] Wilson v. General I. S. C. Co., 47 L. J. Q. B. 239.

too remote for compensation.[275]   And where an operative in a
mill had left the owner's employment without giving a fourteen days' notice as required in the agreement, it was held that
the owner could recover loss suffered by the stoppage of the
looms, caused by the fact that a jack ceased running which it
was the operative's duty to attend to.   He was allowed to
recover for the three days' loss of the use of the looms, during
which he was unable to get other workmen.[276]

Where the jury found that in consequence.of the wrongful
abduction of all the plaintiff's slaves, the cattle of the neigh-
bors destroyed his corn, and a flood in the river swept away a
quantity of his wood, it was held that it was not erroneous
to tell the jury that they might take all these circumstances
into consideration, in the damages, in an action of trespass for
carrying away the slaves, nor to allow compensation for corn
eaten by hogs through lack of the slaves to guard it.[277]   But
where the plaintiff, in an action for abduction of part of his
slaves, had prepared a larger tract of land for cultivation than
his other negroes could cultivate and had procured horses and
by reason of loss of the service of his abducted slaves some
horses were absent during part of the year and the land remained uncultivated, all this loss was held a remote consequence of the abduction.[278]   And where a farm hand wrongfully left plaintiff's employment during the harvest, loss of
crops by failure to get them harvested was too remote for recovery.[279]

[275] St. Johnsbury & L. C. R. R. v.
Hunt, 55 Vt. 570, 45 Am. Rep. 639.
[276] Satchwell v. Williams, 40 Conn.
371.
[277] McAfee v. Crofford, 13 How. 447,
14 L. ed. 217.

[278] Burton v. Holley, 29 Ala. 318, 65
Am. Dec. 401.
[279] Macy v. Peach, 2 Kan. App. 575,
44 Pac. 687.

CHAPTER VIII.

NATURAL CONSEQUENCES

§ 138.[a] Natural Consequences, meaning of the term.

A consequence, however proximately it follows the defendant's act, may nevertheless not result in accordance with the

---

[a] For § 138 of the eighth edition, see § 130.

usual course of things; or, as it is generally expressed, may not be a natural consequence. In one sense every result naturally follows its cause; everything happens subject to the laws of nature. But only such a consequential injury as according to common experience and the usual course of events could reasonably have been anticipated is called a natural consequence. If, for instance, the defendant fails to provide shelter for cattle, injury to the cattle from exposure to the weather is a natural consequence of the breach; but failure to win a prize at an agricultural fair because of the resulting poor condition of the cattle, though following of course in the order of nature, could not have been anticipated and is not a natural consequence in law.

§ 139. Unnatural or unexpected consequences how far actionable.

It is often said that the plaintiff may recover only for proximate and *natural* consequences.[1] But it is only when this phrase is used with reference to *the existence of a cause of action* founded on negligence that it is accurate. In all other cases, where the cause of action is not based on the failure to use the care necessary to avoid a harmful consequence, the element of naturalness in determining the existence of a cause of action is immaterial; an action being allowed because of the doing of the act itself, or because of malice or some other condition of which care is not an element. Negligence means the absence of such care as would be expected of a prudent man under all the circumstances. If the wrong done, therefore, is alleged to have been done through negligence, the question whether the defendant was in fact negligent must depend upon how far the risk of injury in general existed according to common experience and the usual course of events, that is, whether it was natural. Thus, for instance, if the defendant is charged with *negligently* maintaining a structure which causes damage to the plaintiff, and the damage is directly effected by an opera-

---

[1] *Massachusetts:* Hoadley v. Northern Transp. Co., 115 Mass. 304.

New Jersey: Warwick v. Hutchinson, 45 N. J. L. 61.

North Carolina: Chalk v. Charlotte, C. & A. R. R., 85 N. C. 423.

tion of nature, the defendant's liability will depend upon whether the injury occurred in the usual course of events;[2] and this is the general doctrine.[3]

§ 140. Damages for unexpected consequences of a legal injury.

Where, however, a cause of action is established, the question whether the wrongdoer can be held for certain consequences involves different considerations. If his act was in itself a legal wrong, he is held for all the consequences which are not remote. "The measure of the defendant's duty in determining whether a wrong has been committed is one thing, the measure of liability when a wrong has been committed is another."[4]

§ 141. Difference between tort and breach of contract.

The difference becomes still clearer when the duty to act was voluntarily assumed by the defendant by entering into a contract. The duty to refrain from a tort is a duty which no one can avoid; it is imposed upon him by the law, and no act of his can increase or diminish it. But in entering into a contract he is undertaking a duty which the law does not require of him; its assumption is purely voluntary, and fairness requires that he should be able to understand the extent of the obligation he undertakes. A just rule, therefore, would put upon a person who commits a tort the risk of all proximate consequences of his wrong, but upon one who breaks a contract such risk as he could have foreseen when he undertook the duty: and this appears to be the conclusion of the law.

§ 142. General conclusion as to natural consequences.

The principles governing recovery for natural consequences may be summarized as follows:

---

[2] *Missouri:* Flori *v.* St. Louis, 69 Mo. 341, 33 Am. Rep. 504 (roof of market-house blown off by cyclone; city not liable because not foreseeable).

Wisconsin: Borchardt *v.* Wausau Boom Co., 54 Wis. 107, 11 N. W. 440, 41 Am. Rep. 12 (dam flooded plaintiff's land: but only in case of extraordinary flood; not liable for such unforeseeable result).

[3] *Massachusetts:* Hill *v.* Winsor, 118 Mass. 251.

England: Smith *v.* London & S. W. Ry., L. R. 6 C. P. 14.

[4] Holmes, J., in Spade *v.* Lynn & B. R. R., 172 Mass. 488, 491, 52 N. E. 747.

1st. In ascertaining whether there is a *cause of action* for negligence the test of natural consequences is to be applied and no action is to be allowed for consequences of the negligence which are not regarded as natural. They must be both natural and proximate.

2d. In determining *the amount of damages* which may be recovered for an admitted tort, whether the tort was based on negligence or on some other wrong, the test is only that of proximateness and not of naturalness. If the damage is, under the rules previously considered, a proximate result of the tort, then it is recoverable whether it is or is not a natural result. It may be proximate only.

3d. In determining *the amount of damages* due for breach of contract or for other assumed obligation, the test is whether the damage is natural, or within the actual or potential contemplation of the parties at the time the obligation was assumed. If the damage in question was not natural, then there can be no recovery for it. To justify recovery, it must be both natural and proximate.

A consideration of the cases follows.

§ 143. Natural consequences in actions of tort.

In actions of tort, where the wrongdoer voluntarily or negligently did an act which in itself was illegal, he is responsible for all the proximate consequences of the wrongful act, whether the consequences are natural or not.[5] And even when the tort is accomplished through a failure to perform a specific duty, as by the failure of a public service company to supply guards or furnish police protection, the rule is the same.[6] Where, how-

[5] *Kansas:* Enlow v. Hawkins, 71 Kan. 633, 81 Pac. 189.

Kentucky: Kentucky Heating Co. v. Hood, 133 Ky. 383, 118 S. W. 337.

North Dakota: McDonnell v. Minneapolis, St. P. & S. S. M. Ry., 17 N. D. 606, 118 N. W. 819.

Wisconsin: Oleson v. Brown, 41 Wis. 413.

[6] *District of Columbia:* Washington, A. & M. V. Ry. v. Lukens, 32 App. D. C. 442 (exposure of passenger to cold).

Indiana: Coy v. Indianapolis Gas Co., 146 Ind. 655, 46 N. E. 17, 36 L. R. A. 535 (failure to furnish gas for heating).

Minnesota: Schumaker v. St. Paul & D. R. R., 46 Minn. 39, 48 N. W. 559, 12 L. R. A. 257 (ejection from train).

Pennsylvania: Hilsdale C. & C. Co. v. Pa. R. R., 229 Pa. 61, 78 Atl. 28 (discrimination).

ever, an action, though in form based on a tort, really amounts to an action for breach of a contract, the rule in this respect is the same as in case of breach of contract; [7] as for instance in case of an action against a carrier for delay in the delivery of goods.[8]

§ 144. The rule in Hadley v. Baxendale.

The application of the rule in actions of contract is governed by a series of decisions founded on the leading case of Hadley v. Baxendale.[9]

The plaintiffs were owners of a steam mill. The shaft was broken, and they gave it to the defendant, a carrier, to take to an engineer, to serve as a model for a new one. On making the contract, the defendant's clerk was informed that the mill was stopped, and that the shaft must be sent immediately. He delayed its delivery; the shaft was kept back in consequence; and in an action for breach of contract, they claimed, as specific damages, the loss of profits while the mill was kept idle. It was held that if the carrier had been made aware that a loss of profits would result from delay on his part, he would have been answerable. But as it did not appear he knew that the want of the shaft was the only thing which was keeping the mill idle, he could not be made responsible to such an extent. The court said:

"We think the proper rule in such a case as the present is this: Where two parties have made a contract which one of them has broken, the damages which the other party ought to receive in respect of such breach of contract should be such as may fairly and reasonably be considered either arising naturally, i. e., according to the usual course of things, from such breach of contract itself, or such as may reasonably be supposed to have been in the contemplation of both parties at the time they made the contract, as the probable result of the breach of it. Now, if the special circumstances under which the

[7] Webster v. Woolford, 81 Md. 329, 32 Atl. 319 (action against one who professed to be plaintiff's agent in sale of property).

[8] See infra, § 152.

[9] 9 Ex. 341, 23 L. J. Ex. 179; 18 Jur. 358; 26 Eng. L. & Eq. 398. So entirely is the later law founded on this case, that the great body of cases since decided involving the measure of damages for breach of contract, resolve themselves into a continuous commentary upon it.

contract was actually made were communicated by the plaintiff to the defendant, and thus known to both parties, the damages resulting from the breach of such a contract which they would reasonably contemplate, would be the amount of injury which would ordinarily follow from a breach of contract under these special circumstances so known and communicated. But, on the other hand, if these special circumstances were wholly unknown to the party breaking the contract, he, at the most, could only be supposed to have had in his contemplation the amount of injury which would arise generally, and in the great multitude of cases, not affected by any special circumstances, from such a breach of contract. For had the special circumstances been known, the parties might have specially provided for the breach of contract by special terms as to the damages in that case, and of this advantage it would be very unjust to deprive them. The above principles are those by which we think the jury ought to be guided in estimating the damages arising out of any breach of contract."

§ 145. Griffin v. Colver.

The leading case in this country was decided in New York on somewhat similar facts.[10]

The plaintiff agreed to build and deliver to the defendant, on a certain day, a steam engine which he knew the defendant intended to use to drive certain machinery for sawing and planing lumber. In an action for the price, the defendant recouped damages for the plaintiff's delay in delivering the engine. It was held that the measure of damages was not, as claimed by the defendant, the net average value of the use at the place where it was located for the purpose for which it was intended and in connection with defendant's machinery, and it was said that the proper method of measuring the damages was to ascertain what would have been a fair price to pay for the use of the machinery, in view of all the hazards and chances of the business. In the course of the opinion the court said: [11]

"The broad, general rule in such cases is, that the party in-

[10] Griffin v. Colver, 16 N. Y. 489, 69 Am. Dec. 718, n.   [11] Selden, J., at p. 494.

jured is entitled to recover all his damages, including gains prevented as well as losses sustained; and this rule is subject to but two conditions. The damages must be such as may fairly be supposed to have entered into the contemplation of the parties when they made the contract, that is, must be such as might naturally be expected to follow its violation; and they must be certain, both in their nature and in respect to the cause from which they proceed. The familiar rules on the subject are all subordinate to these. For instance: That the damages must flow directly and naturally from the breach of contract, is a mere mode of expressing the first; and that they must be not the remote but proximate consequence of such breach, and must be not speculative or contingent, are different modifications of the last."

Selden, J., cited Blanchard v. Ely,[12] as an instance of profits which were the direct consequence, but were too uncertain. He continued:

"So they may be definite and certain, and clearly consequent upon the breach of contract, and yet if such as would not naturally flow from such breach, but for some special circumstances, collateral to the contract itself or foreign to its apparent object, they cannot be recovered; as in the case of the loss by the clergyman of his tithes by reason of the failure to deliver the horse."

The decision in this case was that profits could be recovered, since the defendant had notice of the consequence of his delay.

§ 146. Meaning of the rule in Hadley v. Baxendale.

The rule in Hadley v. Baxendale would seem to mean that the plaintiff may recover such damages as normally result from the breach of contract; or he may in addition, allege and show certain special facts to have been known to the defendant at the time of the contract, which would give notice to him that a breach of the contract would result in an otherwise unexpected loss, and in such case the plaintiff may also recover his special loss.[13] The decision in the case was clearly that loss of profits

---

[12] 21 Wend. 342, 34 Am. Dec. 250, n.

[13] It was intimated in the case of Wilson v. Newport Dock Co., L. R. 1 Ex.

177, that the rule in Hadley v. Baxendale applies only to profits; and in Gee v. Lancashire & Y. Ry., 6 H. & N. 211,

of a mill was not a natural consequence of a carrier's delay in delivering machinery; but the court added that if the special circumstances had been known at the time of the contract of bailment, the damages claimed might have been recovered.

The New York court, in Griffin v. Colver, took substantially the same view of the decision. The court says, as quoted above, "The damages must be such as may fairly be supposed to have entered into the contemplation of the parties when they made the contract, *that is*, must be such as might naturally be expected to follow its violation. . . . That the damages must flow directly and naturally from the breach of contract, is a mere mode of expressing" the former principle.[14]

§ 147. Cory v. Thames I. W. & S. B. Co.

In Cory v. Thames I. W. & S. B. Co.[15] the defendants had agreed to sell and deliver to the plaintiffs, within a certain time, the hull of a floating boom derrick, supposing the plain-

Mr. Baron Wilde observed that while in Hadley v. Baxendale an excellent attempt was made to lay down a rule, yet the rule is not capable of meeting all cases; and that it would probably turn out that there could be no such thing as a rule applicable in all cases. But these suggestions have not been followed. Explanations of the case as laying down a general rule have been made in Hobbs v. London & S. W. Ry., L. R. 10 Q. B. 111; Cory v. Thames I. W. & S. B. Co., L. R. 3 Q. B. 181, 188; Hammond v. Bussey, 20 Q. B. D. 79, 88; Welch v. Anderson, 61 L. J. (N. S.) Q. B. 167.

[14] Other New York cases in which the same view was taken are Baldwin v. United States Tel. Co., 45 N. Y. 744, 750; Ward v. New York C. R. R., 47 N. Y. 29, 32; Booth v. Spuyten Duyvel R. M. Co., 60 N. Y. 487, 492; Devlin v. Mayor of New York, 63 N. Y. 8, 25.

In New York, however, the language used in Hadley v. Baxendale, the "usual course of things," is seldom adopted as a guide. Instead of it, as we have seen, the courts have adopted the expression, "such as may fairly be supposed to have been in the contemplation of the parties." The New York form of the rule is sometimes misleading. See Little v. Boston & Maine R. R., 66 Me. 239; Collard v. S. E. Ry., 7 H. & N. 79; Gee v. Lancashire & Yorkshire Ry., 6 H. & N. 211; Wilson v. Lancashire & Yorkshire Ry., 9 C. B. (N. S.) 632; Wilson v. Newport Dock Co., L. R. 1 Ex. 177. It is possible to say, with some definiteness, what will follow in the usual course of things; but what the contemplation of the parties *probably* was, is often a very difficult matter to arrive at. The criticism of Alderson, B., in Wilson v. Newport Dock Co., L. R. 1 Ex. 177, seems also very just, viz., that parties usually contemplate the performance and not the breach of contracts. The rule in the commoner form must therefore mean, not within the actual contemplation but within the possible, natural or normal contemplation of the parties, in view of all the circumstances.

[15] L. R. 3 Q. B. 181.

tiffs intended to use it as a coal store. The plaintiffs, in fact, intended to apply it to the purpose of transhipping coal directly from colliers to barges without the necessity of an intermediate landing, a purpose which was unusual and unknown to the defendants. It was held that the plaintiffs could recover damages to the extent of the profits which would have resulted from its use as a coal store. They, in fact, suffered a much greater damage, for they would have derived a much larger profit from the use they intended than from its use as a coal store.

In reply to the argument of the defendant, that damages for loss of use of the derrick for a store were not within the contemplation of the parties, Cockburn, C. J., said (p. 187):

"The two parties certainly had not in their common contemplation the application of this vessel to any one specific purpose. The plaintiffs intended to apply it in their trade, but to the special purpose of transhipping coals; the defendants believed that the plaintiffs would apply it to the purpose of their trade, but as a coal store. I cannot, however, assent to the proposition that, because the seller does not know the purpose to which the buyer intends to apply the thing bought, but believes that the buyer is going to apply it to some other and different purpose, if the buyer sustains damage from the non-delivery of the thing, he is to be shut out from recovering any damages in respect of the loss he may have sustained. I take the true proposition to be this. If the special purpose from which the larger profit may be obtained is known to the seller, he may be made responsible to the full extent. But if the two parties are not *ad idem quoad* the use to which the article is to be applied, then you can only take as the measure of damages the profit which would result from the ordinary use of the article for the purpose for which the seller supposed it was bought."

§ 147a. General results of Hadley v. Baxendale.

The rule in Hadley *v.* Baxendale has been discussed in a multitude of cases, and on the whole, it will be found that the general tendency of judicial opinion in the United States as well as in England is that no new rule of damages has been introduced; that the plaintiff recovers such damages as are proximate and natural, and that in ascertaining what are natural consequences, we must take into the account all the circumstances of the case, including all facts bearing on the question which were in the knowledge of both parties, even though these be such as would not necessarily, without such knowledge, enter into it. It is on this principle that the plaintiff is allowed to charge the defendant with loss on subcontracts, sales, etc., on proving *notice*, which, in the absence of such notice, would not be treated as natural or expected consequences.

§ 148. Natural consequences of breach of contract.

The general principle being thus established, the difficulty in dealing with the subject becomes one of applying the principle to the facts of cases. To learn how the courts have applied the principle it is desirable to examine the facts of many cases.

Where an agent, authorized to sell a flock of sheep, sold a portion of them with knowledge that they were diseased, and the diseased sheep were mixed with another flock, it was held that the claim of the purchaser against the principal was not limited to the loss of the sheep purchased, but extended to that of the others to which the distemper was communicated; and the court said, "This damage was the natural consequence of the fraudulent act of the defendant's agent." [16]

The defendant undertook to pasture plaintiff's mare in a field which was separated by a wire fence from a cricket field. Defendant wrongfully left the gate open between the fields and the mare got into the cricket field. The cricketers tried to drive the mare back, but only frightened her, and she ran against the fence and was injured. It was held natural that the occupants should try to drive her out and it is natural that a horse should not go back through the gate, but should run. The injury to the mare was therefore the natural consequence of leaving the gate open, and defendant was responsible.[17] A. purchased jute, put it in a warehouse and received weight

---

[16] Jeffrey *v.* Bigelow, 13 Wend. (N. Y.) 518, 28 Am. Dec. 476.

[17] Halestrap *v.* Gregory, [1895], 1 Q. B. 561, 64 L. J. Q. B. 415, 72 L. T. Rep. (N. S.) 292, 15 Reports, 306, 43 Wkly. Rep. 507.

notes for it. He then got advances on the jute from C., depositing with B. the weight notes as security. The jute having been destroyed by fire, A. without right got the notes from B. and then got from the vendor of the jute the deposit which A. had made with him upon purchase. By the agreement of purchase, the risk of the jute was to remain on the seller until full payment. A. became insolvent and failed to pay C. his advances. C. sued B. for breach of contract in delivering the weight notes to A. It was held that C. was entitled to recover the amount of his advances.[18]

A question sometimes arises where the breach of contract subjected plaintiff to a fine or forfeiture. Thus in one case it appeared that the importation of certain goods was forbidden under a fine unless a certain document was furnished by the importer. Defendants contracted to furnish such document but failed, and as a result the importer was obliged to pay the fine. It was held that the imposition of the fine was within the contemplation of the parties, and the defendant was responsible for it.[19] Defendant was employed by plaintiff to do a piece of work in digging a street, which involved obtaining a proper license. Defendant did the work without obtaining the license, and as a result plaintiff was sued and had to pay damages. He was allowed to recover from defendant the amount which he was thus obliged to pay.[20] In a somewhat similar case plaintiff contracted to build a canal. Defendant failed to procure a right of way at the proper time and so delayed plaintiff's construction. The plaintiff was allowed to recover the rental value of the machinery which he had prepared for use in building the canal.[21]

In the case of real covenants a question is sometimes presented. Where land is sold with covenants of title, and a claimant is in possession, and the grantee brings a suit to oust him, the expense of the suit is a natural consequence of the breach, whether the suit is successful [22] or unsuccessful.[23]

[18] Matthews v. Discount Corp., L. R. 4 C. P. 228.
[19] Hecla Powder Co. v. Sigua Iron Co., 157 N. Y. 437, 52 N. E. 650.
[20] Baynard v. Harity, 1 Houst. (Del.) 200.
[21] Sanitary Dist. v. McMahon & M. Co., 110 Ill. App. 510.
[22] Coleman v. Clark, 80 Mo. App. 339.
[23] Pitkin v. Leavitt, 13 Vt. 379.

Defendant broke his covenant not to assign his lease; the sub-lessee carried on a dangerous business on the premises, as a result of which they were destroyed by fire. This loss was within the contemplation of the parties.[24] A lease contained covenants against sub-letting, with an agreement on the part of the lessee to allow the premises to be shown and a "to let" sign to be posted. Posting was refused; and the house after expiration of the lease remained unoccupied for some time. It was held that plaintiff could recover for loss of rent caused by the refusal.[25]

§ 149.[a] Unnatural consequences of breach of contract.

On the other side are the cases in which recovery has been refused on the ground that the loss was not a natural consequence of the breach. In an action upon a contract by plaintiff to build a railroad for defendant, defendant in recoupment claimed to show that because the plaintiff delayed in building the road, it had been necessary for him to haul coal by teams; and it had cost very much more than it would have done to haul them over the road if it had been completed. It was held that damages could not be recovered for this loss.[26] Plaintiff, while in Europe being educated, entered into a contract to teach school in the United States and came home for that purpose. She intended to return to the United States eventually. In an action for refusal to employ her it was held that the expense of her journey home in order to accept the employment was not within the contemplation of the parties, and she could not recover.[27] Defendant contracted to carry the mail; he broke his contract, and the government brought a man from another State and paid his expenses and hotel bills to carry out the contract. It was held that this expense was not within the contemplation of the parties, but that whatever reasonable and natural expenditures were made in getting another man would be chargeable to the defendant.[28] De-

---

a For § 149 of the eighth ed., see § 147*a*.

[24] Lepla *v.* Rogers, [1893] 1 Q. B. 31.

[25] U. S. Trust Co. *v.* O'Brien, 143 N. Y. 284, 38 N. E. 266.

[26] Williams *v.* Case, 79 Ill. 356.

[27] Benziger *v.* Miller, 50 Ala. 206.

[28] Brown *v.* Cowles, 72 Neb. 896, 101 N. W. 1020.

§ 149 UNNATURAL CONSEQUENCES 271

fendant agreed, if plaintiff would erect a banking house, to erect a large building opposite. Plaintiff erected a banking house, but defendant did not erect the large building. Plaintiff claimed to recover the increased cost of his building incurred in view of the defendant's expected building. It was held that this was not shown to be within the contemplation of the parties.[29]

In a case in Tennessee, it appeared that the State leased convicts to the defendant, and agreed to keep a guard over them. It failed to keep the guard. The defendant's shop was burned by a fire set by one of the convicts, and in an action by the State for the hire the defendant set up his loss in recoupment. The court held that the loss was not the natural consequence of the State's breach of contract.[30]

In the case of a claim for damages by reason of defendant's delay in preparing an abstract of title to plaintiffs' land, plaintiffs intended to borrow money on the land and therewith purchase other lands for which they had been negotiating. The lands they intended to buy had already increased in value by the amount of six thousand dollars. These damages were held too remote.[31] In an action for breach of covenant in a deed it appeared that defendant had conveyed land to plaintiffs subject to a mortgage of eight hundred dollars, with covenant of warranty. Defendant had accidentally omitted to put one of the deeds in his chain of title on record, as a result of which the plaintiff was unable to raise money on a mortgage to pay off the eight hundred dollar mortgage, and that was foreclosed and he lost the land. Defendant afterwards put the missing deed on record. It was held that the loss of the land by foreclosure was too remote.[32] Plaintiff sold paint to defendant for his own use in painting his

[29] First Nat. Bank v. Thurman, 69 Iowa, 693, 25 N. W. 909.

Defendant sold land to plaintiff but failed to give immediate possession. In anticipation of getting the land plaintiff had dismantled his power plant on other land in order to erect it on defendant's land. In the absence of notice, this was not within the contemplation of the parties. Bantel v. Amer. Mach. Co. (Ky.), 137 S. W. 799.

[30] State v. Ward, 9 Heisk. (Tenn.) 100.

[31] Pendleton v. Cline, 85 Cal. 142, 24 Pac. 659.

[32] Lamb v. Buker, 34 Neb. 485, 52 N. W. 285.

house. Defendant demanded recoupment for breach of warranty, and proved that he had sold the paint to other parties and, because of its quality, lost their custom. It was held that since defendant bought for his own use, plaintiff could not anticipate this other loss.[33] A seller of lumber did not follow his shipping instructions, but sent the lumber to the wrong place. The plaintiff claimed compensation because the consignee, a manufacturing company, had his foreman idle while waiting for the lumber and for the detention of a barge at the place to which the goods should have been sent. But it was held that these items were not within the contemplation of the parties.[34] The plaintiff brought suit for wrongful failure to deliver a bill of lading, by which plaintiff was hindered in getting clothing. For lack of the clothing he suffered from cold. It was held that this was not the natural result, within the contemplation of the parties; and in the absence of notice that plaintiff had no other clothing and would suffer, the damages could not be recovered.[35] In an action for failure of a mine owner to supply sufficient fresh air in a mine, it appeared that plaintiff was driving a mule which suddenly stopped, his light went out for lack of fresh air, and he slipped and fell between the mule and the car, and was seriously injured. It was held that this was not the ordinary and natural result of imperfect ventilation; the accident was not reasonably to be anticipated as a result of omission to supply fresh air, and therefore was not the natural result of such omission, and no damages could be recovered for the accident.[36] For failure to supply sufficient heat in a house rented with heat, the occupant cannot recover for illness.[37]

§ 150. Action against carrier of passengers.

The theory at one time held by some judges that the rule

[33] Detroit White Lead Works v. Knaszak, 13 N. Y. Misc. 619, 34 N. Y. Supp. 924.

[34] Billmeyer v. Wagner, 91 Pa. 92.

So where the seller falsely notified the buyer of the shipment of goods, the buyer may recover the expense of sending teams to the station to get the goods: Brownfield v. Dudley E. Jones Co. (Ark.), 136 S. W. 664.

[35] St. Louis S. W. Ry. v. May (Tex. Civ. App.), 44 S. W. 408.

[36] Rosan v. Big Muddy Coal & Iron Co., 128 Ill. App. 128.

[37] Sargent v. Mason, 101 Minn. 319, 112 N. W. 255.

in Hadley *v*. Baxendale changed the law, had its effect in the decision of an English case which must here be noticed. Hobbs *v*. London & South Western Railway [38] was an action for breach of contract. The plaintiff, with his wife and two children, took tickets to H. on the defendants' railway. They were set down at E. It being late at night, the plaintiff could not get a wagon or accommodation at an inn. They had, therefore, to walk five or six miles on a rainy night, and the wife caught cold, was laid up in bed for some time, and was unable to assist her husband. Expenses were incurred for medical attendance. The jury found £8 for inconvenience suffered by having to walk home, and £20 for the wife's illness and its consequences. The Queen's Bench held the plaintiff could recover the £8, but not the £20. Cockburn, C. J., said, that the item of £20 was too remote, and on that question he said: "I think that the nearest approach to anything like a fixed rule is this: That, to entitle a person to damages by reason of a breach of contract, the injury for which compensation is asked should be one that may be fairly taken to have been contemplated by the parties as the possible result of the breach of contract. Therefore you must have something immediately flowing out of the breach of contract complained of, something immediately connected with it, and not merely connected with it through a series of causes intervening between the immediate consequence of the breach of contract and the damage or injury complained of." Blackburn, J., agreed with these remarks of the Lord Chief Justice.

This case was considered later in McMahon *v*. Field.[39] In the latter case the defendant contracted with the plaintiff to furnish stabling for his horses during a fair, but instead of doing so he let his stable to a third party, who turned out the plaintiff's horses in the middle of the night without their blankets. It was held that the defendant, in an action of contract, must compensate the plaintiff for a loss caused by his horses taking cold. Brett, L. J., said, "it was not the necessary consequence of the breach of contract, but I have no doubt that it was the probable consequence, and if so, it follows that it was in the contemplation of the parties within

[38] L. R. 10 Q. B. 111.   [39] 7 Q. B. Div. 591.

18

the meaning of the third rule." In the later case of Pounder *v.* Northeastern Railway [40] Hobbs' case was followed. A "scab" workman became a passenger; the carriage in which he rode was allowed to become overcrowded, against his protest, and after the train started he was assaulted by strikers, who had crowded into the carriage, and was injured. Recovery was denied, on the ground that this was not contemplated by the railway at the time he was received as a passenger. But this case and Hobbs' case were seriously shaken by doubts expressed in the opinions delivered in the House of Lords in a later case. [41] Hobbs' case has been doubted also by the Supreme Court of Canada. The plaintiff, having become heated by an altercation with the defendant's conductor, was wrongfully put off the car on a cold night, caught cold, and contracted rheumatism. It was held that he might recover compensation for the illness. [42]

In this country Hobbs' case has been followed in Massachusetts, where a distinction is made between actions sounding in contract and actions of tort for the same injury. In Murdock *v.* Boston & Albany Railroad [43] the plaintiff was wrongfully ejected from the train and delivered to a police officer, who detained him over night. It was held that in an action for breach of the contract of carriage the plaintiff could not recover for the indignity of his imprisonment, mental suffering, and sickness produced by a cold caught. The court said: "Without inquiring whether all the elements of damage admitted by the court would be competent, if this had been an action of tort for an assault and false imprisonment, we are of opinion that too broad a rule was adopted in this case. Damages for the breach of a contract are limited to such as are the natural and proximate consequences of the breach, such as may fairly be supposed to enter into the contemplation of the parties when they made the contract, and such as might naturally be expected to result from its violation."

This decision is rested on the ground that the action was not tort. The conductor who ejected the passenger was him-

[40] [1892] 1 Q. B. 385.
[41] Cobb *v.* Great Western Ry., [1894] A. C. 419.

[42] Toronto Ry. *v.* Grinsted, 24 Can. 570.
[43] 133 Mass. 15, 43 Am. Rep. 480, *n.*

self a railroad police officer, and delivered the passenger into the hands of the local police; the act by which the contract was broken was therefore a tort, and in those jurisdictions in which all forms of action have been abolished, it would probably have been impossible to tell whether the action sounded in tort or contract, or both. The measure of damages should not depend on a distinction so difficult of application.

In the case of Williams v. Vanderbilt [44] the defendant agreed to transport the plaintiff to California by the way of the Isthmus of Panama; but failed to furnish transportation across the Isthmus. After waiting some time in the unhealthy climate of the Isthmus, the plaintiff was taken back to his starting-point; but meanwhile he had contracted a sickness through remaining on the Isthmus. It was held that he could recover compensation for loss of time and expense caused by the sickness. The form of action was tort.

There can be little doubt that the decisions in McMahon v. Field and Williams v. Vanderbilt are sound. The contrary opinion rests on a mistaken understanding of one of the forms of the rule in Hadley v. Baxendale, that is, that such damages only can be recovered as the parties may be supposed to have had present in mind at the time of the contract. Most of the American authorities accept the doctrine of Williams v. Vanderbilt.[45]

It is of course to be noticed that the question whether the result is natural depends to some extent upon the reasonableness of the plaintiff's behavior in view of the wrong done. The defendant cannot be held responsible for any result which is due to the plaintiff's needless exposure of himself to

[44] 28 N. Y. 217, 84 Am. Dec. 333.

[45] *District of Columbia:* Washington, A. & M. V. Ry. v. Lukens, 32 App. D. C. 442.

Indiana: Cincinnati, H. & I. R. R. v. Eaton, 94 Ind. 474.

Kentucky: Louisville & N. R. R. v. Daugherty, 32 Ky. L. Rep. 1392, 108 S. W. 336.

Maryland: Baltimore C. P. R. R. v. Kemp, 61 Md. 74.

Minnesota: Serwe v. Northern Pac. R. R., 48 Minn. 78, 50 N. W. 1021.

Missouri: Evans v. St. Louis, I. M. & S. Ry., 11 Mo. App. 463.

Nebraska: Chicago, B. & Q. R. R. v. Spirk, 51 Neb. 167, 70 N. W. 926.

Texas: St. Louis S. W. Ry. v. Ferguson, 26 Tex. Civ. App. 460, 64 S. W. 797.

Wisconsin: Brown v. Chicago, M. & S. P. Ry., 54 Wis. 342.

And see *post,* § 867 *ff.*

the risk of damage.[46] It was perhaps on this ground that in Virginia recovery was denied in a case of this sort. A ticket agent assured the plaintiff when she bought her ticket that a certain train connected with another that she must take. The agent was in error and plaintiff failed to make the connection, and hired a carriage to take her to her destination. The road was rough, and she was jolted about, and wet through by showers. It was held that the damages caused by taking the conveyance were not foreseeable.[47]

§ 151.[a] Loss caused by unexpected natural causes supervening on the defendant's act.

When the act of the defendant brings property into such a situation that it is afterwards injured or destroyed by unexpected natural causes, the injury is too unnatural a consequence of the defendant's wrong to be compensated. So where the defendant had contracted to beat the plaintiff's rice before any other, but did not do so, as a result of which it remained over night in the mill and was burned with the mill, it was held that the loss of the rice was too remote a result of the breach of contract to be recovered.[48] And where a farm laborer leaves before his time has expired, loss of crops for lack of his services is not a natural result of his breach of contract.[49] Upon breach of a contract to put a harvester in order, loss of crops is not a natural consequence.[50] And the same thing is held upon breach of a contract to thresh grain.[51] In an action for delay in performance of contract to transport wood it appeared that the wood was washed away by a freshet

a For § 151 of the eighth edition, see § 147.

[46] *Georgia:* Georgia Cent. R. R. v. Dorsey, 116 Ga. 719, 42 S. E. 1024.

Missouri: Corrister v. Kansas City, S. J. & C. B. Ry., 25 Mo. App. 619.

[47] Fowlkes v. Southern Ry., 96 Va. 742, 32 S. E. 464.

[48] Ashe v. De Rossett, 5 Jones (N. C.) L. 299, 72 Am. Dec. 552.

[49] *Iowa:* Riech v. Bolch, 68 Ia. 526, 27 N. W. 507.

New York: Peters v. Whitney, 23 Barb. 24.

[50] *Indiana:* Fuller v. Curtis, 100 Ind. 237, 50 Am. Rep. 786.

Minnesota: Wilson v. Reedy, 32 Minn. 256, 20 N. W. 153; Osborn v. Poket, 33 Minn. 10, 21 N. W. 752.

Nebraska: Sycamore M. H. Co. v. Sturm, 13 Neb. 210, 13 N. W. 202.

[51] *Iowa:* Prosser v. Jones, 41 Ia. 674.

North Dakota: Hayes v. Cooley, 13 N. Dak. 204, 100 N. W. 250.

But see Baldwin v. Blanchard, 15 Minn. 489.

and plaintiff suffered damages in recovering the wood. This was held not to be within the contemplation of the parties.[52]

So where the defendant contracted to pay damages caused by cutting away a dam and allowing a river to flow in and out of a basin previously protected by it, and the river, a year later, became dammed up by ice, and the water rushed into the basin with such unusual velocity as to injure plaintiff's property there, the loss was held not to be in contemplation of the parties, and compensation was not allowed for it.[53]

On the other hand, if the supervening natural cause is expected the loss from it will be regarded as natural.

The defendant failed to furnish a tug as agreed for carrying stones to protect an ocean bulkhead. Owing to the delay only a small part of the bulkhead could be protected before a certain day, on which a great storm wrecked the bulkhead, except that part which had been protected by stones. Defendant knew that storms were likely to arise, and, probably, loss in case of delay. It was held that plaintiff could recover.[54] Defendant agreed to go and tow off a vessel which was ashore at a dangerous place at a season of the year when gales are usual. Defendant delayed in going to tow the vessel off, and as a result she was destroyed by a storm. This was held within the contemplation of the parties, and defendant was liable.[55]

§ 152.[a] Carrier's delay in transportation of, or loss of machinery or supplies.

It is not the natural consequence of the failure or delay of a carrier to deliver machinery that the use of a mill should be lost; consequently, in the absence of notice or of facts in the knowledge of the carrier indicating that such would be the case, the owner cannot recover damages for loss of use of the mill.[56] And the stoppage of a mill not being a normal conse-

a For § 152 of the eighth edition, see § 151.

[52] Slaughter v. Denmead, 88 Va. 1019, 14 S. E. 833.

[53] People v. Albany, 5 Lans. (N. Y.) 524.

[54] Mott v. Chew, 137 Fed. 197.

[55] Boutin v. Rudd, 82 Fed. 685, 27 C. C. A. 526.

[56] *Alabama:* Reed Lumber Co. v. Lewis, 94 Ala. 626, 10 So. 333.

Georgia: Oxford Knitting Mills v. American Wringer Co., 16 Ga. App. 301, 65 S. E. 791.

Kentucky: Louisville & N. R. R. v. Mink, 126 Ky. 337, 103 S. W. 294, 31 Ky. L. Rep. 833.

Mississippi: Vicksburg & M. R. R.

quence of delay in transporting material for manufacture or for packing and shipping, the mill owner in an action against the carrier for delay cannot, in the absence of notice, recover compensation for the loss of use of his mill.[57] For the same reason, in an action against a carrier for delay in delivering fuel, a mill owner cannot recover compensation for the loss of use of his mill.[58] And in an action for delay in sending goods from plaintiff to his travelling salesman, by reason of which the salesman left the place of destination before the goods arrived there and profits expected from his sales were lost, the loss was not within the contemplation of the parties.[59]

A delay in delivering goods does not normally result in loss of business; consequently the owner cannot, in an action for the delay, recover compensation for such loss.[60] So where the

v. Ragsdale, 46 Miss. 458; American Exp. Co. *v.* Jennings, 86 Miss. 329, 333, 38 So. 374.

New York: Bracco *v.* Merchants' Depatch Transp. Co., 113 N. Y. Supp. 131, 61 N. Y. Misc. 60.

North Carolina: Sharpe *v.* Southern Ry., 130 N. C. 613, 41 S. E. 799.

South Carolina: Moore *v.* Atlantic C. L. R. R., 85 S. C. 19, 67 S. E. 11.

Texas: Pacific E. Co. *v.* Darnell, 62 Tex. 639.

Wisconsin: Thomas B. & W. M. Co. *v.* Wabash, St. L. & P. Ry., 62 Wis. 642, 51 Am. Rep. 725.

England: Hadley *v.* Baxendale, 9 Ex. 341.

Nor can recovery be had for loss of the profit of manufacture. Goodin *v.* Southern Ry., 125 Ga. 630, 54 S. E. 720, 6 L. R. A. (N. S.) 1054.

[57] *Alabama:* Southern Ry. *v.* Moody, 53 So. 1016 (cases for packing and transporting eggs).

Florida: Williams *v.* Atlantic C. L. R. R., 56 Fla. 735, 48 So. 209, 24 L. R. A. (N. S.) 134 (boxes for packing fruit).

Kentucky: Patterson *v.* Illinois Cent. R. R., 123 Ky. 783, 97 S. W. 426 (cotton seed for feeding cattle); Illinois Cent. R. R. *v.* Nelson, 97 S. W. 757, 30 Ky. L. Rep. 114 (cotton seed for feeding cattle); Illinois Cent. R. R. *v.* Hopkinsville Canning Co., 132 Ky. 578, 116 S. W. 758 (cans for tomatoes).

North Carolina: Davidson Development Co. *v.* Southern Ry., 147 N. C. 503, 61 S. E. 381 (brick for building); Asheboro W. & M. Co. *v.* Southern Ry., 149 N. C. 261, 62 S. E. 1091 (iron for manufacture).

England: Gee *v.* London & Y. Ry., 6 H. & N. 211 (cotton for manufacture).

[58] *Georgia:* Cooper *v.* Young, 22 Ga. 269, 68 Am. Dec. 502 (coal).

Texas: Haberzettle *v.* Trinity & B. V. Ry., 46 Tex. Civ. App. 527, 103 S. W. 219 (oil).

[59] Great Western Ry. *v.* Redmayne, L. R. 1 C. P. 329, 12 Jur. (N. S.) 692, 35 L. J. C. P. 123.

[60] *Maryland:* Baltimore & O. Ry. *v.* Pumphrey, 59 Md. 390.

Wisconsin: Buffalo B. W. C. *v.* Phillips, 64 Wis. 338, 64 N. W. 338.

England: Anderson *v.* Northeastern Ry., 4 L. T. R. (N. S.) 216.

So of delay of goods intended for sale: Franklin *v.* Louisville & N. R. R., 116 S. W. 765, 34 Ky. L. Rep.   . Of tools of trade: Milhous *v.* Atlantic C. L. R. R., 75 S. C. 351, 55 S. E. 764. Of

owner used the goods to hire out as regalia for processions, he cannot recover compensation for the hire he would have obtained for them.[61]

The same principle applies when the carrier loses or destroys the thing carried. So where a piece of machinery is destroyed in transit, loss of business was not within the contemplation of the parties.[62] A dentist cannot recover against a carrier, in an action for the loss of a set of dentist's instruments, the profits and earnings he might have made if the loss had not occurred,[63] unless the carrier had notice of the special use. And in an action against a carrier for the loss of a package containing plans, the carrier having no notice of the contents of the package, the owner cannot recover damages for the delay in constructing the house, caused by the loss of the plans.[64]

§ 153. Breach of contract to supply machinery or materials for trade or manufacture.

Upon failure to supply machinery for manufacturing, in the absence of some notice that the manufacture cannot be carried on without the machinery, loss caused by failure to carry on the business cannot be recovered.[65] In a few cases, however,

medicine: Wells, Fargo & Co. Exp. v. Thompson (Tex. Civ. App.), 116 S. W. 607.

So where a shipment of buggies was delayed, and as a result of the delay the owner was unable to store them on arrival and was therefore obliged to sell them at forced sale, the carrier, not being aware of the circumstances, was not responsible for the loss. Rutland v. Southern Ry., 81 S. C. 448, 62 S. E. 865.

[61] Hales v. London & N. W. Ry., 4 B. & S. 66.

[62] Thomas B. & W. Manuf. Co. v. Wabash, S. L. & P. Ry., 62 Wis. 642, 51 Am. Rep. 725, 22 N. W. 827.

So of injury to machinery: Stone v. Adams Exp. Co., 122 S. W. 200, 34 Ky. L. Rep.   .

[63] Brock v. Gale, 14 Fla. 523, 14 Am. Rep. 356.

[64] Mather v. American Ex. Co., 138 Mass. 55.

[65] *United States:* Howard v. Stilwell & B. M. Co., 139 U. S. 199, 35 L. ed. 147, 11 Sup. Ct. 500 (loss of profits); Central Trust Co. v. Clark, 92 Fed. 293, 34 C. C. A. 354 (machinery for cable road: without it cars could not be run at high speed; not within contemplation).

Indiana: Acme Cycle Co. v. Clarke, 157 Ind. 271, 61 N. E. 561 (loss of profits).

Kansas: Johnson v. Mathews, 5 Kan. 118 (wages of idle hands).

South Dakota: Simpson Brick-Press Co. v. Marshall, 5 S. D. 528, 59 N. W. 728 (loss of profits).

Texas: Tompkins Co. v. Galveston St. Ry., 4 Tex. Civ. App. 1, 23 S. W. 25 (machinery for generating electricity to propel cars; fewer cars could be run; not within contemplation).

where the peculiar nature of the machine indicated its necessity, a consequential loss resulting from failure to furnish it was regarded as within the contemplation of the parties.[66] Thus where defendant sold flues for curing tobacco, to be delivered in July, and it was well known that tobacco must be harvested and cured at about that time, it was held that damage to the crop caused by delay in delivering the flues was within the contemplation of the parties.[67]

In the same way, when the defendant fails to supply materials for trade or manufacture, a loss by injury to the business or other merely consequential loss is not usually within the contemplation of the parties.[68] So upon a delay of one day by the defendant, a warehouseman, in delivering cotton, the plaintiff cannot recover compensation for the payment of an unusually high rate of interest on money borrowed (as the custom was) on security of the cotton.[69] And in an action for failure to furnish the fire box for an engine, the plaintiff cannot recover damages he was obliged to pay to a third party for failure to deliver the engine to him at an agreed time.[70] So where an editor, by not receiving some "plate paper," on which to print a frontispiece for his magazine, suffered damage in loss of circulation and of credit, and in having a number of copies left on his hands, such damages could not be recovered.[71]

Canada: Ruthven W. Co. *v.* Great W. Ry., 18 Up. Can. C. P. 316 (wages of idle hands).

But in Kenyon *v.* Goodall, 3 Cal. 257, loss of time of idle hands was allowed.

[66] *Illinois:* Benton *v.* Fay, 64 Ill. 417 (planing machine bought to set up in new mill; loss of rent of building and machinery within contemplation).

Missouri: Chalice *v.* Witte, 81 Mo. App. 84 (engine to be used in grinding corn for fodder; increased cost of other fodder necessarily bought is within contemplation).

New York: Rochester Lantern Co. *v.* Stiles & P. Press Co., 16 N. Y. Supp. 781 (dies for manufacture of lanterns; loss of use of factory and of wages are within contemplation).

[67] Neal *v.* Pender-Hyman Hardware Co., 122 N. C. 104, 29 S. E. 96, 65 Am. St. Rep. 697.

[68] *United States:* Peace River Phosphate Co. *v.* Grafflin, 58 Fed. 550 (phosphate rock).

Indiana: Connersville W. Co. *v.* McFarlan C. Co., 166 Ind. 123, 76 N. E. 294, 3 L. R. A. (N. S.) 709 (wagon wheels).

Iowa: Bushnell *v.* Geo. E. King Bridge Co., 140 Ia. 405, 118 N. W. 407.

Wisconsin: Malneg *v.* Hatten Lumber Co., 140 Wis. 381, 122 N. W. 1057.

[69] Swift *v.* Eastern W. Co., 86 Ala. 294.

[70] Portman *v.* Middleton, 4 C. B. (N. S.) 322.

[71] Parsons *v.* Sutton, 66 N. Y. 92.

And in an action for failure to deliver hogs bought of the defendant, the plaintiff cannot recover compensation for the loss he suffered by having hired cars to transport the hogs.[72]

But on the other hand, where the goods are to be delivered for a certain purpose, the natural and direct result of the failure to have them to use for this purpose is within the contemplation of the parties. So where, upon breach of a contract to deliver timber for a bridge, it was necessary for plaintiff to get timber elsewhere, and the only practicable way was to manufacture it by hand on the spot, it was held that defendant must pay the difference between the cost of manufacturing the timber in this way and the contract price.[73] Upon this principle, if the defendant contracted to deliver raw material to the plaintiff, a manufacturer, and failed to do so, and no other material of the sort could be procured, the defendant is liable for the resulting loss. "If an article of the same quality cannot be procured in the market, its market price cannot be ascertained and we are without the necessary data for the application of the general rule. This is a contingency which must be considered to have been within the contemplation of the parties, for they must be presumed to know whether such articles are of limited production or not. In such a case the true measure is the actual loss which the vendee sustains in his own manufacture, by having to use an inferior article, or not receiving the advance on his contract price upon any contract which he had himself made in reliance upon the fulfilment of the contract by the vendor."[74]

§ 153a. Breach of contract to supply money.

For failure to perform a contract to lend money to the plaintiff, he cannot recover the amount of the loan; the damage usually cannot be greater than interest on the amount,[75] and if interest was to be paid on the loan the difference, if

---

[72] Cuddy v. Major, 12 Mich. 368.

[73] Paine v. Sherwood, 21 Minn. 225.

[74] Sharswood, J., in McHose v. Fulmer, 73 Pa. 365; acc., Carroll-Porter B. & T. Co. v. Columbus Mach. Co., 55 Fed. 451, 5 C. C. A. 190.

[75] Arnott v. Spokane, 6 Wash. 442, 33 Pac. 1063.

See infra, § 622.

The plaintiff of course cannot recover the amount which the defendant agreed to loan. Turpie v. Lowe, 114 Ind. 37, 54, 15 N. E. 834.

any, between such interest and the current rate is the measure of it.[76] No recovery can be had for the loss of a bargain that might have been obtained by use of the money.[77] *A fortiori* the defendant cannot be held responsible for a contingent loss from which the plaintiff might have been saved by having the money. So where because of failure to get the money plaintiff's workmen demanded he was obliged to pay higher wages, this loss could not be recovered;[78] and where plaintiff in order to get the money was obliged to borrow it and pledge personal property as collateral, which he eventually lost by failure to pay the loan, this loss was not within the contemplation of the parties.[79] Where plaintiff had a contract by the terms of which his creditors might enter judgment for a large sum if the amount of money he was to receive was not paid to them, and by reason of defendant's default they entered judgment, levied on his stock and fixtures, and ruined his business, this loss was held to be outside the contemplation of the parties.[80] In another case plaintiff was agent of X., who owed defendant money. Plaintiff paid a large sum of X.'s money to defendant, upon defendant's agreement to apply part of it to the payment of the debt and to accept drafts of X. for the remainder. Instead of doing so he refused to accept the drafts, and applied all the cash received to the payment of his debts. Plaintiff had made an arrangement with other creditors of X. by which they were to receive X.'s drafts in payment, and upon the drafts being accepted by defendant were to pay plaintiff ten per cent. commission. It was held that the loss of this commission by defendant's failure to accept the drafts could not be recovered.[81]

The allowance of consequential damages is often claimed in actions against a bank for refusal to pay checks or drafts. Such a refusal leads, in the case of a business man,[82] naturally

[76] Smith *v.* Parker, 148 Ind. 127, 45 N. E. 770.

[77] *California:* Pendleton *v.* Cline, 85 Cal. 142, 24 Pac. 659.

Indiana: Lewis *v.* Lee, 15 Ind. 499.

[78] Fox *v.* Poor Ridge & Sugar Creek Turnpike Road Co., 8 Ky. L. Rep. 427.

[79] *United States:* Kelly *v.* Fahrney, 97 Fed. 176, 38 C. C. A. 103.

California: Savings Bank *v.* Asbury, 117 Cal. 96, 48 Pac. 1081.

[80] Brooke *v.* Tradesmen's Nat. Bank, 69 Hun, 202, 23 N. Y. Supp. 802.

[81] Gerson *v.* Slemons, 30 Ark. 50.

[82] *Tennessee:* J. M. James Co. *v.*

to loss of credit; but not in the case of one who is not in trade.[83] Other consequential damages are outside the contemplation of the parties, as for arrest for obtaining property by false pretences,[84] or nervous shock.[85] Where the failure to pay the check of a stockbroker caused his being suspended from the stock exchange, damage to him as a speculator, and also in respect to his business and credit as a broker, was held recoverable.[86]

§ 154. Telegraph and messenger companies.[87]

Where a message is delayed by a telegraph company, no consequential damages can be recovered unless the sender or the language of the message itself gives an indication of its special importance.[88] So in the absence of notice no consequential damages can be recovered for delay in transmitting a cipher message.[89] So where plaintiff telegraphed for money and by negligence of defendant the message was delayed, and he was left among strangers without money, and suffered mortification because he could not pay his board bill, it was held that this was not within the contemplation of the parties,

Continental Nat. Bank, 105 Tenn. 1, 58 S. W. 261, 51 L. R. A. 255.

England: Dean v. Melbourne, S. E. A. & B. Co., 16 Vict. L. R. 403.

[83] *Canada:* Henderson v. Bank of Hamilton, 25 Ont. 641 (clergyman).

Australia: Bank of New South Wales v. Milvain, 10 Vict. L. R. 3 (farmer).

[84] Bank of Commerce v. Goos, 39 Neb. 437, 58 N. W. 84, 23 L. R. A. 90.

[85] American Nat. Bank v. Morey, 24 Ky. L. Rep. 658, 69 S. W. 759, 58 L. R. A. 956.

[86] Dean v. Melbourne Stock Exchange Agency & Banking Corporation, 16 Vict. L. R. 403.

[87] The special questions that arise in connection with telegraph companies will be considered at large in a later chapter.

[88] *United States:* Western U. T. Co. v. Hall, 124 U. S. 444, 31 L. ed. 479, 8

Sup. Ct. 577; Primrose v. W. U. T. Co., 154 U. S. 1, 38 L. ed. 883, 14 Sup. Ct. 1098.

Louisiana: Deslottes v. Baltimore & O. T. Co., 40 La. Ann. 183.

New York: Curtin v. W. U. T. Co., 36 N. Y. Supp. 1111.

England: Sanders v. Stuart, 1 C. P. D. 326.

But a contrary rule now prevails in some jurisdictions: see chapter on Telegraph Companies.

[89] *Nevada:* Mackay v. Western U. T. Co., 16 Nev. 222.

North Carolina: Cannon v. Western U. T. Co., 100 N. C. 300, 6 S. E. 731, 6 Am. St. Rep. 590.

Pennsylvania: Fergusson v. Anglo-Amer. T. Co., 178 Pa. 377, 35 Atl. 979.

Texas: Daniel v. Western U. T. Co., 61 Tex. 452, 48 Am. Rep. 305.

Wisconsin: Candee v. Western U. T. Co., 34 Wis. 471.

and plaintiff could not recover.[90]   And where a messenger company failed to deliver a letter to plaintiff's wife, stating that he had been called out of town, the company was not liable for the plaintiff's loss of his wife's services due to nervous prostration because she did not know where the plaintiff was.[91]

§ 155. Agreement to repair.

Loss of rent and injuries caused by the stench are natural consequences of a failure to keep the drains of premises in repair.[92]   On the breach of a covenant to repair contained in the lease of a hotel, the lessee may recover compensation for the loss of use of rooms rendered useless by the disrepair; [93] but on breach of covenant to repair in a lease loss of custom by plaintiff as dentist and illness of members of the plaintiff's family, resulting from the plumbing not being repaired, are not in the absence of special circumstances within the contemplation of the parties.   In such cases, the ordinary measure of damages is what it costs the tenant to make the repairs, or the loss of the use of the premises for the time.[94]   Where repairs were so unskilfully made that the rain leaked in and damaged property in the house, this was within contemplation.[95]   For delay in the repair of machinery loss of use of the mill is not within the contemplation of the parties,[96] unless the defendant knew that the machine was necessary for the use of the mill.[97]   A suit was brought for breach of obligation to fence.   A gate in the fence was allowed to fall into disrepair, as a result of which it was troublesome to shut, and so a person passing through usually left it open.   The gate was left open, probably by some third person passing through it in the night, and damages resulted.   The court held that

[90] Voegler v. Western U. T. Co., 10 Tex. Civ. App. 229, 30 S. W. 1107.

[91] Hadden v. Southern Messenger Service (Ga.), 69 S. E. 480.

[92] Jutte v. Hughes, 67 N. Y. 267.

[93] Myers v. Burns, 35 N. Y. 269.

[94] Chadwick v. Woodward, 12 Daly (N. Y.), 399.   And so where a tenant contracted pneumonia by reason of a leaky roof, the damage was not recoverable.   Eschbach v. Hughes, 7 Misc. 172, 27 N. Y. Supp. 320.

[95] Krebs Mfg. Co. v. Brown, 108 Ala. 508, 18 So. 659, 54 Am. St. Rep. 188.

[96] Iron Wks. v. Boling, 75 Ark. 469, 88 S. W. 306.

[97] Muller v. Ocala F. & M. Works, 49 Fla. 189, 38 So. 64.

under ordinary circumstances the railway was not obliged to see that the gate was kept closed, but here, since under the circumstances it was likely that one passing through this gate would fail to shut it because of the defect, this probable action should have been anticipated by the railroad and it was liable.[98]

§ 156. Loss of a sub-contract.

The loss suffered on a sub-contract (either through the necessity of paying damages on it or through loss of the benefit of it) in the absence of notice is not a normal result of a breach of contract and will not be compensated.[99] There is, however, an exception in certain cases where the contract contemplates a sub-contract. A building contract, for instance, contemplates the purchase of materials, and on breach of it the builder may recover compensation for the damages he is compelled to pay on a contract to furnish certain necessary materials.[100] So the purchase of coal, warranted to be of a certain quality by a coal dealer, contemplates a resale of it as of that quality: and if there is a recovery against the purchaser, on account of the inferior quality of the coal, he may recover, in an action on the warranty, the damages and costs of that action.[101] In the absence of a custom for re-

[98] Morrison v. Kansas City, S. J. & C. B. Ry., 27 Mo. App. 418.

[99] *United States:* Loewer v. Harris, 57 Fed. 368, 6 C. C. A. 394; The A. Denicke, 138 Fed. 645, 71 C. C. A. 95.

Alabama: Reed Lumber Co. v. Lewis, 94 Ala. 626, 10 So. 389.

California: Wallace v. Ah Sam, 71 Cal. 197.

Georgia: Sanderlin v. Willis, 94 Ga. 171, 21 S. E. 291.

Indiana: Rahm v. Deig, 121 Ind. 283.

Iowa: Brown v. Allen, 35 Ia. 306; Mihills M. Co. v. Day, 50 Ia. 250.

Michigan: Wetmore v. Pattison, 45 Mich. 439, 60 Am. Rep. 534, 8 N. W. 67; Henry v. Hobbs, 130 N. W. 616.

New York: Devlin v. Mayor, 63 N. Y. 8; Horner v. Wood, 16 Barb. 386; Zippert v. Acme A. E. & P. Co., 113 N. Y. Supp. 998.

North Carolina: Lindley v. Richmond & D. R. R., 88 N. C. 547.

Pennsylvania: Clyde Coal Co. v. Pittsburgh & L. E. R. R., 226 Pa. 391, 75 Atl. 596.

Texas: Parks v. O'Connor, 70 Tex. 377.

England: Caledonian Ry. v. Colt, 3 Macq. 833, 3 L. T. R. (N. S.) 252 (H. of L.); Thol v. Henderson, 8 Q. B. D. 457.

Nova Scotia: Bruhm v. Ford, 33 Nova Sco. 323.

[100] Smith v. Flanders, 129 Mass. 322.

[101] *United States:* Nashua, I. & S. Co. v. Brush, 91 Fed. 213.

Illinois: Thorne v. McVeagh, 75 Ill. 81.

selling at once, a resale before delivery cannot be shown for any purpose. Thus, in England, a resale of land before the deeds are passed, cannot be shown to fix damage on failure to convey.[102] And in general, in the absence of notice, a resale of land is not the use of the land naturally to be expected, and damages cannot be recovered for loss of a resale of it.[103] The defendant made a mistake in date of printing notice of judicial sale. As a result of the mistake, which was not discovered until the date of the sale, the purchaser refused to take a deed of the land. It was too late to readvertise the sale, as the six months after judgment had expired, and the land was seized by another creditor. The plaintiff, the sheriff, was obliged to pay damages because of the defect in the sale, and now sued the printer. It was held that this was not a natural result of the advertisement, and he could not recover.[104] And in an action for delay in completing the printing and binding of books, the publisher offered to show that there would have been a demand for the books at a certain time if they had been ready as they ought to have been. The plaintiff was not allowed to recover.[105]

In a number of cases, however, recovery has been allowed for loss of a resale. Where there is no market value, the price for which goods could be resold might be taken as the value, and the profit of the resale recovered on that ground.[106] And in other cases it must be taken that there was notice of the contemplated resale, either expressly or by reason of the circumstances.[107]

England: Hammond v. Bussey, 20 Q. B. D. 79.

[102] *United States:* Tincley v. Jennison, 74 Fed. 177, 20 C. C. A. 37.
England: Walker v. Moore, 10 B. & C. 416.
[103] *Georgia:* Sanderlin v. Willis, 94 Ga. 171, 21 S. E. 291.
Massachusetts: Batchelder v. Sturgis, 3 Cush. 201.
Nebraska: Violet v. Rose, 39 Neb. 661, 58 N. W. 216.
[104] Jackson v. Adams, 9 Mass. 484, 6 Am. Dec. 94.
[105] Hill v. Parsons, 110 Ill. 107. The

court placed its decision principally on the ground that no sales had actually been made.
[106] *Pennsylvania:* Culin v. Woodbury Glass Works, 108 Pa. 220.
Virginia: Trigg v. Clay, 88 Va. 330, 13 S. E. 434, 29 Am. St. Rep. 723.
[107] *United States:* Bell v. Cunningham, 3 Pet. 69, 7 L. ed. 606.
Georgia: Fontaine v. Baxley, 90 Ga. 416, 17 S. E. 1015.
Texas: A. J. Anderson Electric Co. v. Cleburne, W. I. & L. Co. (Tex. Civ. App.), 44 S. W. 929.

NOTICE

§ 157. Notice—General rule.

The effect of notice, under the rule in Hadley *v.* Baxendale, is to enlarge the boundaries of natural consequences. The general rule is, that the notice must be such as to inform the defendant of any extraordinary damages which will be suffered.[108] Only for the natural and proximate consequences of the facts made known can plaintiff recover. Thus, where the defendant had notice that goods were bought by the plaintiff for the purpose of fulfilling a sub-contract, the plaintiff cannot recover for loss of the sub-contract, unless he shows that the goods could not be elsewhere procured.[109] A delay in the work for which the goods were bought would be a natural result of their non-delivery, and the consequences of delay may be recovered; but an entire cessation of the work is not a natural result.[110] Where the defendant contracted to supply rigging for a vessel and failed to do so, and the plaintiff was unable to procure rigging in the market, it was held that he could not recover for the loss of use of the vessel. Notwithstanding the notice of the object, an abnormal factor intervened—the peculiar state of the market; consequently, the notice given in this case was not sufficient to inform the defendant of the danger of extraordinary loss.[111]

A defendant has notice of what will occur in the ordinary course of business; for instance, that goods bought by a dealer in them will be resold,[112] but not that a failure to deliver

[108] Horne *v.* Midland Ry., L. R. 7 C. P. 583, 8 C. P. 131.

It is not enough to give notice that it is very important that the matter should be rushed: Fitch *v.* Western U. T. Co., 150 Mo. App. 149, 130 S. W. 44; or that the goods shipped are badly needed: Kolb *v.* Southern Ry., 81 S. C. 536, 62 S. E. 872; or that the consignee requires the goods urgently: Harris *v.* Fargo, 113 N. Y. Supp. 577.

[109] *United States:* Carroll-Porter, B. & T. Co. *v.* Columbus Machine Co., 55 Fed. 451, 5 C. C. A. 190.

If they cannot, he may recover compensation for the loss of a subcontract. McHose *v.* Fulmer, 73 Pa. 365.

[110] *California:* Friend & T. L. Co. *v.* Miller, 67 Cal. 464, 8 Pac. 40.

Maine: Bridges *v.* Stickney, 38 Me. 361.

[111] Clark *v.* Moore, 3 Mich. 55.

[112] Hammond *v.* Bussey, 20 Q. B. D. 79. But see H. G. Holloway & Bro. *v.* White-Dunham Shoe Co., 151 Fed. 216, 80 C. C. A. 568, 10 L. R. A. (N. S.) 704.

goods to a manufacturer will cause a stoppage of his mill,[113] nor that on a contract to sell goods the goods will be resold before delivery.[114]

Notice to an agent must be given to the agent with whom the contract is made.[115]

§ 158. Notice of consequences of a breach of contract.

The theory that mere notice of an unusual consequence likely to follow a breach of contract given before breach gives a right to recover compensation for such consequence was suggested by the able opinion of Bramwell, B., in Gee v. London & Yorkshire Railway: [116] "I am not sure that another qualification might not be added which would be in favor of the plaintiff in this case, viz.: that in the course of the performance of the contract one party may give notice to the other of any particular consequences which will result from the breaking of the contract, and then have a right to say, 'If, after that notice, you persist in breaking the contract, I shall claim the damages which will result from the breach.' " The majority of the court, however, took a different view. And however reasonable the view may be in itself, another rule is firmly established. Hadley v. Baxendale, as we have seen, held that damages for breach of contract were limited to such as were either normal or communicated *at the time of the contract*.

§ 159. Notice must form the basis of a contract.

It appears that the notice must be more than knowledge on the defendant's part of the special circumstances. It must be of such a nature that the contract was to some extent based upon the special circumstances. This appears from the language of the courts in many cases where the subject is discussed. In Smeed v. Foord,[117] Campbell, C. J., doubted whether notice could have any effect in changing the rule of damages, unless it formed part of the contract. In British

---

[113] Gee v. Yorkshire & L. Ry., 6 H. & N. 211.

[114] Williams v. Reynolds, 6 B. & S. 495.

[115] *Kentucky:* Louisville & N. R. R. v. Mink, 103 S. W. 294, 31 Ky. Law Rep. 833, 126 Ky. 337.

Texas: Pacific Exp. Co. v. Jones, (Tex. Civ. App.), 113 S. W. 952.

[116] 6 H. & N. 211.

[117] 1 E. & E. 602, 608.

Columbia S. M. Co. *v.* Nettleship,[118] Willes, J., said: "The mere fact of knowledge cannot increase the liability. The knowledge must be brought home to the party sought to be charged under such circumstances that he must know that the person he contracts with reasonably believes that he accepts the contract with the special condition attached to it." In Booth *v.* Spuyten Duyvil Rolling Mill Co.,[119] Church, C. J., stated, as his opinion, that notice of the object of the contract would not, of itself, change the measure of damages, "unless it formed the basis of an agreement." Proof of notice, of course, cannot be received to *vary* the contract, which always speaks for itself; it is merely an attendant circumstance, which, like any other matter in evidence, affects the consequences of the breach and the measure of recovery.

Hadley *v.* Baxendale lays no stress on the question whether the contract was founded upon or influenced by the notice; but the weight of recent authority seems to be in accordance with these opinions, to the effect that the notice must be such as that the contract was in some degree founded on it. The defendant sold goods to rig a vessel, and damages were claimed for loss of use of the vessel. The Supreme Court of Michigan said: "To create such extraordinary liability, there must in every case be something in the terms of the contract, read in the light of the surrounding circumstances, which show an intention on the part of the vendor to assume an enlarged engagement, a wider responsibility than is assumed by the vendor in ordinary contracts for the sale and delivery of merchandise."[120]

The notice must, as stated above, be given at the time the contract is made. Notice given after the making of the contract, as at the time for performance, will not vary the amount of liability,[121] But where goods were lost by a carrier, and

[118] L. R. 3 C. P. 499, 509.

[119] 60 N. Y. 487.

[120] *United States:* Southern Ry. *v.* Myers, 87 Fed. 149, 32 C. C. A. 19.

Maryland: Winslow, E. & M. Co. *v.* Hoffman, 107 Md. 621, 69 Atl. 394.

Michigan: Clark *v.* Moore, 3 Mich. 55, 61.

[121] *Alabama:* Dickerson *v.* Finley, 158 Ala. 149, 48 So. 548.

Connecticut: Jordan *v.* Patterson, 67 Conn. 473, 35 Atl. 521.

Kentucky: Patterson *v.* Ill. Cent. R. R., 97 S. W. 426, 30 Ky. Law Rep. 78, 123 Ky. 783.

Missouri: Fitch *v.* Western U. T.

notice of special damages was given after the loss, such notice was sufficient to inform the carrier of such special damages from delay in transporting goods shipped to take the place of those lost.[122]

The purchase price of goods, as compared with the large amount of the special damage, is often regarded by the courts as material in deciding the question of notice. So in a case in Illinois,[123] the plaintiff sued for the price due him for building a railroad. The defendant claimed to recoup damages for delay in the construction. It appeared that bonds were to be issued, with agreement that interest should be waived for the time the road was completed before July 1st, and this agreement was known to the plaintiff at the time his contract was made. The plaintiff's work was to have been completed six months before the time named in the sub-contract. It was held that the plaintiff should not be charged with the interest which the defendant was obliged to pay from January 1st to the completion of the work. The court laid special stress on the fact that the interest rebated was enormously disproportionate to the contract price of the work. If the case can be supported on this ground, it must be because the disproportion showed that the contract was not based upon the special circumstances.

§ 160. But need not be part of the contract.

In Horne *v.* Midland Railway,[124] Blackburn, J., went further,

Co., 150 Mo. App. 149, 130 S. W. 44.

South Carolina: McMeekin *v.* Southern Ry., 82 S. C. 468, 64 S. E. 413.

Texas: Missouri, K. & T. R. R. *v.* Belcher, 89 Tex. 428, 35 S. W. 6.

Wisconsin: Bradley *v.* Chicago, M. & S. P. Ry., 94 Wis. 44, 68 N. W. 410.

It has however been held in Texas that when notice of special circumstances which indicate a loss by non-delivery is given to a carrier after the goods have arrived at their destination and are ready for delivery, the consignee upon failure of the carrier to deliver may recover the special damages. Bourland *v.* Choctaw, O. & G.

R. R., 99 Tex. 407, 90 S. W. 483, 3 L. R. A. (N. S.) 1111.

And in a case in North Carolina, where a carrier delayed delivery, the majority of the court held that the action might be treated as one sounding in tort, and therefore notice of the consequences given after shipment, but before time for delivery would be sufficient. Virginia-Carolina Peanut Co. *v.* Atlantic C. L. R. R. (N. C.), 71 S. E. 71.

[122] McMeekin *v.* Southern Ry., 82 S. C. 468, 64 S. E. 413.

[123] Snell *v.* Cottingham, 72 Ill. 161.

[124] L. R. 8 C. P. 131.

and said that in his opinion notice did not change the rule of damages unless it were such as to create a special contract. It is to be observed that if this opinion is sound, it does away at once with the whole doctrine of notice. For if the notice of special circumstances is incorporated into the contract, that is, if the contract provides against the special loss, the loss, if it happens, is not a consequential but a direct result of a breach of the contract, and as such is of course recoverable. The opinion of Lord Blackburn has not been supported by any decided case; and the weight of authority is against it.[125] So a verbal notice has been allowed to change the rule of damages, although the contract was in writing. The defendant had failed to carry out a contract to deliver a piece of machinery. The plaintiffs required this machinery in order to carry out a contract with one J. The contract with J., though made subsequently to the contract with the defendant, was the subject of a conversation between the parties before they entered into any agreement. It was held in the Court of Appeal that the plaintiff could recover the profits he would have derived from his contract with J., and also the expenses to which he had been put in making part of an engine for J., which had been thrown away.[126]

§ 161. Notice of a sub-contract.

Where the plaintiff makes the contract in order to fulfil another contract with a stranger, and so informs the defendant, he may recover such damages as the information given would indicate as likely to happen.[127]

[125] Baldwin v. U. S. T. Co., 45 N. Y. 744, 6 Am. Rep. 165 (semble); Cory v. Thames I. W. & S. B. Co., L. R. 3 Q. B. 181.

[126] Hydraulic Eng. Co. v. M'Haffie, 4 Q. B. Div. 670; acc., Am. Bridge Co. v. American Dist. Steam Co., 107 Minn. 140, 119 N. W. 783.

[127] United States: Iowa Mfg. Co. v. B. F. Sturtyvant Co., 162 Fed. 560, 89 C. C. A. 346, 18 L. R. A. (N. S.) 575.

Georgia: Carolina Portland Cement Co. v. Columbia Imp. Co., 3 Ga. App. 99, 60 S. E. 279.

Illinois: Hagan v. Rawle, 143 Ill. App. 543.

Kentucky: Feland v. Berry 130 Ky. 328, 113 S. W. 425.

Michigan: Industrial Works v. Mitchell, 114 Mich. 29, 72 N. W. 25.

New York: Meyer Bros. Drug Co. v. McKinney, 121 N. Y. Supp. 845, 137 App. Div. 541.

See Maryland C. & C. Co. v. Quemahoning Coal Co., 176 Fed. 303, 99 C. C. A. 641, where the court appears to have held that such damages could not be recovered until they had actually been suffered.

In Borries *v.* Hutchinson [128] the plaintiffs bought caustic soda of the defendant, part to be shipped in June, part in July, and the rest in August, and the defendant knew at the time of the sale that the plaintiffs bought it for shipment and resale abroad, but not that it was for Russia, although he learned this also before the end of August. He neglected to deliver any of the soda until September, in which month and in October he delivered a portion. There was then no market for the soda, and the plaintiffs, who had contracted for the resale to one Heitman, in Russia, lost the profit of the resale on what was not delivered, and by reason of the approach of winter in the Baltic, were obliged to pay increased rates of freight and insurance for what was delivered. In this case there was no market value for the caustic soda. It was held that the plaintiff could recover the profits he would have made on his resale to Heitman, and could also recover the increased rates of freight and insurance. It was further held that the plaintiff could not recover money which he had paid to reimburse Heitman for damages which Heitman had been obliged to pay to a sub-vendee, Heimburger, for failure to perform a contract with him.

Elbinger Actien-Gesellschaft *v.* Armstrong [129] was an action for the defendant's breach of a contract to furnish the plaintiffs with 666 sets of wheels and axles. The plaintiffs were under a contract to supply wagons to the Russian Government by a certain date. They informed the defendants that they were under a contract to deliver wagons to the Russian Government under a penalty, but did not state the date of delivery or the amount of the penalty. By reason of the defendant's delay the plaintiffs had to pay £100 on their sub-contract. Although the market price had kept the same, it was held that the plaintiffs could recover substantial damages, and it was said that it would have been proper to instruct the jury, "that the plaintiffs were entitled to such damage as, in their opinion, would be fair compensation for the loss which would naturally arise from the delay, including therein the probable liability of the plaintiffs to damages by reason of the breach of that contract, to which, as both parties knew, the defend-

[128] 18 C. B. (N. S.) 445, 463.   [129] L. R. 9 Q. B. 473, 479.

ant's contract with the plaintiffs was subsidiary," for, said the court, the direction would not, at all events, have been too unfavorable to the defendants.

The distinction between these cases seems to be that in the former case, the sub-contract by the sub-vendee, Heitman, was not brought to the defendant's notice.

In Hinde v. Liddell [130] the defendant contracted to supply the plaintiff with shirtings of a certain quality to fill a contract. The defendant broke his contract, and the plaintiff, being unable to procure shirtings of the same quality in the market, was obliged to fulfil his sub-contract by delivering more valuable shirtings. It was held that he could recover the excess of price.

The leading case on the subject is Grébert-Borgnis v. Nugent. [131] The defendant agreed to furnish the plaintiff with goods of a certain sort, not procurable in the market, knowing that the plaintiff required them to fulfil a contract with a French customer, but not knowing the price named in the latter contract. It was held that the plaintiff could recover, in addition to ordinary damages, compensation on account of his enforced breach of the French contract; that the amount recovered by the French customer against the plaintiff in an action on the other contract might be shown, not as a measure of the compensation, but as evidence of what a reasonable compensation for forcing the plaintiff to break the contract would be.

In Messmore v. New York Shot & Lead Co. [132] it was held that the plaintiff could recover, for the vendor's failure to supply bullets, the profits he would have made on a contract of resale, the defendant having notice of the contract. Mason, J., delivered the opinion of the court. He stated that usually the difference between the market and the contract price determined the measure of damages, because the vendee could go into the market and supply himself. He said the rule, however, was different where notice was given, because in such a case the profits of the resale might be said to be in the contemplation of the parties. He continued (p. 428): "It

[130] L. R. 10 Q. B. 265.　　　　[132] 40 N. Y. 422.
[131] 15 Q. B. D. 85.

(the notice) showed that these profits to this plaintiff were in the contemplation of the parties in entering into this contract, and as the evidence showed such to be the fact, these profits that would have accrued to the plaintiff, had the contract been performed by the defendants, are in no sense speculative or uncertain profits." He pointed out that in this case the plaintiff could not have supplied himself in the market.

Where a carrier has notice that plaintiff is being carried in order to fill an engagement as actor, the carrier is liable, in case of unreasonable delay, for such loss of compensation as can be proved with reasonable certainty.[133] For breach of contract to carry to his destination at a certain time the plaintiff claimed loss of profits on engagements for the two evenings and on a breaking up of the troupe due to failure to pay the performers, which could have been done from the profits of those two evenings. It was held that, since defendant knew the troupe was going to give performances, the loss from the two performances could be recovered, though not the loss from failure to pay the troupe.[134] And where a defendant was informed that delay would subject the plaintiff to a penalty contract, it is liable in case of unreasonable delay to the amount of the penalty.[135] And for delay to furnish a car to ship grain the carrier, who had notice of a contract for the sale of it, was held liable for loss of the resale.[136]

The question arose in an action for breach of a contract for furnishing materials for constructing a street in the city of New York. One party was already under a contract with the city to build the street and the other was making a sub-contract with him. The contract between the parties recited the principal contract. It was held, since the defendant knew at the time he made his contract, that it was made

[133] Liman v. Pa. R. R., 4 N. Y. Misc. 539, 24 N. Y. Supp. 824.

In Southern Ry. v. Myers, 32 C. C. A. 19, 87 Fed. 149, the plaintiff had no guarantee, and was to be paid a share of the profits; and recovery was impossible because of the uncertainty.

[134] Foster v. Cleveland, C., C. & S. L. Ry., 56 Fed. 434.

[135] United States: Northwestern S. B. & M. Co. v. Great Lakes Engineering Works, 181 Fed. 38.

Tennessee: Railroad v. Southern S. & C. Co., 104 Tenn. 568, 58 S. W. 303.

[136] Gulf, C. & S. F. Ry. v. Hodge (Tex. Civ. App.), 39 S. W. 986.

in order to fulfil the principal contract, that he was liable for failure to fulfil it, and the principal contractor might recover the damages caused to him by his failure to fulfil the principal contract; though damages claimed by reason of the fact that he was unable to get other contracts, this one not having been fulfilled, are too remote.[137] So in an action for failure to furnish dredges for use in dredging a canal under a government contract of which the defendant had notice the plaintiff, who could obtain no other dredges, was allowed to recover the profits he would have made by performance of the contract.[138]

§ 162. Notice of a contemplated resale.

In Mann v. Taylor [139] the defendant contracted to deliver to the plaintiff certain goods for the purpose of resale, knowing that certain expenses were necessary in preparation for resale. Upon failure to deliver the goods, the plaintiff was allowed compensation for such expenses.

In Hammond v. Bussey [140] the defendant sold the plaintiff coal as of a certain quality, knowing he was buying it to resell as coal of that sort. It was not of the quality named, but the difference could be discovered only when the coal was used. The plaintiff, having sold some of the coal, was sued by the purchaser on account of the inferiority of the quality; he gave notice of the suit to the defendant, who declined to defend it. It was held that the plaintiff might include in his damages the damages and costs in the action against him by the purchaser. The court held that the rule as to sub-contracts extended to contracts not made at the time of the original contract, but in the ordinary course of business sure to be made.

In Harvey v. Connecticut & Passumpsic Railroad [141] the carrier to whom goods were given to carry was informed that they were to be resold; but it was held that if they were lost, profits of a resale were not the natural result of the loss. On

---

[137] Dillon v. Masterson, 42 N. Y. Super. Ct. 176.

[138] Watkins v. Junker, 4 Tex. Civ. App. 629, 23 S. W. 802.

[139] 78 Ia. 355, 43 N. W. 220; acc.,

Hanson & Parker v. Wittenberg, 205 Mass. 319, 91 N. E. 383.

[140] 20 Q. B. Div. 79, 93, 99.

[141] 124 Mass. 421.

the other hand, where goods were bought for the purpose of resale the ordinary profits of a resale, lost by non-delivery, may be recovered.[142] The true distinction seems to be:— if besides notice of contemplated resale, the defendant also had notice that other goods could not be obtained to supply the place of those not delivered—then the profits of a resale may be recovered; if there was no such notice it would be held that loss of profits of a resale was not within the contemplation of the parties.[143] If there was such notice,[144] or if the defendant asserted his intention to keep the contract until it was too late to obtain other goods,[145] the lost profits may be recovered.

§ 163. Notice of a sub-contract, but not of the price.

In Horne v. Midland Railway [146] the plaintiffs were under a contract to supply a quantity of military shoes to H., in London, for the use of the French army, at 4s. per pair, an unusually high price. On the day on which the shoes were to be delivered they sent them to the defendants' station at K., in time to be delivered in the usual course of business, in the evening of that day, when they would have been accepted. Notice was given that the plaintiffs had a contract,

---

[142] Jordan v. Patterson, 67 Conn. 473.

[143] Marshall v. Clark, 78 Conn. 9 (S. C. Righter v. Clark, 60 Atl. 741); Gulf, C. & S. F. Ry. v. Barber, 127 S. W. 258 (Tex. Civ. App.).

[144] *Connecticut:* Jordan v. Patterson, 67 Conn. 473, 35 Atl. 521.

Florida: Robinson v. Hyer, 35 Fla. 544, 17 So. 745.

Illinois: Illinois C. R. R. v. Cobb, 64 Ill. 128; Van Arsdale v. Rundel, 82 Ill. 63.

Iowa: Cobb v. Illinois C. R. R., 38 Ia. 601.

Kentucky: Pulaski Stave Co. v. Miller's Creek Lumber Co., 138 Ky. 372, 128 S. W. 96.

Minnesota: Emerson v. Pacific C. & N. P. Co., 96 Minn. 1, 104 N. W. 573, 1 L. R. A. (N. S.) 445, 113 Am. St. Rep.

603; Independent Brewing Ass'n v. Burt, 109 Minn. 323, 123 N. W. 932.

New Jersey: Lissberger v. Kellogg, 73 Atl. 67, 78 N. J. L. 85.

New York: Goldston v. Wade, 123 N. Y. Supp. 114, 68 Misc.   ; Delafield v. J. K. Armsby Co., 131 App. Div. 572, 116 N. Y. Supp. 71.

Oregon: Hockersmith v. Hanley, 29 Ore. 27, 44 Pac. 497.

Virginia: Trigg v. Clay, 88 Va. 330, 13 S. E. 434, 29 Am. St. Rep. 723.

Washington: Sedro Veneer Co. v. Kwapil, 113 Pac. 1100.

Of course if the resale is not reasonably certain there can be no recovery. Loeb v. Kamak, 1 Mont. 152; Allison v. Tennessee, C. I. & R. R. Co. (Tenn. Ch.), 46 S. W. 348.

[145] Hamilton v. Magill, L. R. 12 Ir. 186, 202.

[146] L. R. 7 C. P. 583.

and unless they were delivered on that day they would be thrown on their hands, but not of the price stated in the contract. The market price was 2s. 9d. It was held that the plaintiffs could not recover the difference between 4s. and 2s. 9d. per pair. Willes, J., said: "The damages are to be limited to those that are the natural and ordinary consequences which may be supposed to have been in the contemplation of the parties at the time of making the contract." This decision was affirmed in the Exchequer Chamber.[147] Mellor, J., distinguished France v. Gaudet,[148] on the ground that in that case champagne of a similar quality was not procurable in the market, and therefore the resale was the only test of the value of the goods. Kelly, C. B., referred to the fact that the defendant was a common carrier, and bound to accept, even if notice had been given. He continued: "But in the absence of any such contract expressly entered into, there being no power on the part of the company to refuse to accept the goods, or to compel payment of an extraordinary rate of carriage by the consignor, it does not appear to me any contract to be liable to more than the ordinary amount of damages can be implied from the mere receipt of the goods after such a notice as before mentioned." He then pointed out that there was no notice here of the exceptional nature of the contract and of the unusual loss that would result; that here the defendants would only expect a contract at the market price. Pigott, B., dissented from the decision, saying that the company could decline to carry goods except at the ordinary risks, and if they accepted goods after such a notice, they became liable for the special value. He continued: "Such loss being actually the result of the defendants' breach of contract, why are the plaintiffs not to recover it? It can only be by reason of some artificial rule established by the decisions or some ground of public policy, that makes the measure of damages which may be recovered less than that which is actually sustained." He said that here the consignee had notice and should have made further inquiries.

The decision properly rests upon the same principle that excludes unexpected consequences in general. The defendant

[147] L. R. 8 C. P. 131.   [148] L. R. 6 Q. B. 199.

knew of the sub-contract of sale, and was prepared to take the risk of it; but no notice had been given that the sub-contract was for an extraordinary price.[149]

On the other hand, where the sub-contract is at the market price, or for a reasonable advance over the contract sued on, and the defendant is notified of the sub-contract, but not of the price, the plaintiff upon default may recover the profit of the sub-contract.[150]

In an action for breach of a contract to deliver steel caps for rails, it appeared that the plaintiffs were under a contract to deliver a quantity of steel-capped rails to the Hudson River Railroad Company at $315 per ton, and the defendant was informed of the contract, but not of the price. This contract they could not perform, owing to the defendant's failure. There was no market value for either steel caps or steel-capped rails. It was held that the plaintiff could recover the profits of his contract with the Hudson River Railroad Company. Church, C. J., said that the damages recoverable in breach of contract, were such "as ordinarily and naturally flow from the non-performance." He approved of the principle of Hadley v. Baxendale, that the damages must be such as were in the contemplation of the parties. As to the damages in this case, he said that the plaintiff's recovery could not be objected to on the ground that the plaintiff had not suffered loss, for he had lost his sub-contract; nor on the ground of uncertainty, since the damages were fixed and definite. As to the notice of the object of the contract, he said: "If the article is one which has a market-price, although the sub-contract is contemplated, there is some reason for only imputing to the vendor the contemplation of a sub-contract at that price, and that he should not be held for extravagant or exceptional damages provided for in the sub-contract."[151]

The same rule applies where the defendant has no actual

<hr />

[149] *Iowa:* Morgan & Wright v. Sutlive Bros., 126 N. W. 175.

New York: Collins v. A. Luban Co., 127 N. Y. Supp. 461.

Wisconsin: Goetzkow Bros. Co. v. Andrews, 92 Wis. 214, 66 N. W. 119, 52 L. R. A. 209.

[150] *Ante,* § 162. But *contra*, Harper v. Miller, 27 Ind. 277 (*semble*).

[151] Booth v. Spuyten Duyvil R. M. Co., 60 N. Y. 487.

notice of the sub-contract, but it is made in the regular course of trade, of which he was cognizant.[152]

Where the defendant had notice that in preparation for performance the plaintiff must make a contract of sale, but he did in fact sell at an extraordinary low price, this loss was held not to be a contemplated result of the breach.[153]

§ 164. Notice of a special use for goods.

When one who has undertaken to deliver goods knows of a special purpose for which they are needed, the ordinary consequences of failure to have the goods for the intended use are within his contemplation. So where one undertakes to furnish water for use (among other things) in putting out fires, and because of his failure to furnish sufficient water a fire cannot be put out, the loss of the property burned was within his contemplation.[154] And where a natural gas company, having been notified of the illness of plaintiff's child, wrongfully failed to furnish gas for fuel, it was responsible for the consequent death of the child.[155] Upon breach of a contract to furnish distillery slops for feeding cattle, the plaintiff may recover the loss on the cattle, so far as it could not be prevented by obtaining other food; [156] and if the slops as furnished contained a deleterious substance, he is responsible for the injury to the cattle caused by eating it.[157] For breach of an agreement by a landlord to furnish fertilizer for the crops it was held that the

[152] *United States:* Carroll-Porter, B. & T. Co. *v.* Columbus Machine Co., 55 Fed. 451, 5 C. C. A. 190.

Pennsylvania: McHose *v.* Fulmer, 73 Pa. 365.

This case was followed in Murdock *v.* Jones, 38 N. Y. Supp. 461: for delay in completing a building caused by a sub-contractor's delay in furnishing materials, the contractor was allowed to recover from the sub-contractor the damages which the owner recovered from the former.

[153] Bennett *v.* Dyer, 102 Me. 361, 66 Atl. 725.

[154] *Kentucky:* Paducah Lumber Co. *v.* Paducah Water Supply Co., 89 Ky.

340, 25 Am. St. 536, 12 S. W. 554, 7 L. R. A. 77.

Maine: Milford *v.* Bangor, R. & E. Co., 104 Me. 233, 71 Atl. 759.

Tennessee: Harris *v.* Columbia, W. & L. Co., 114 Tenn. 328, 85 S. W. 897.

England: Atkinson *v.* Newcastle & G. W. W. Co., L. R. 6 Ex. 404.

[155] Coy *v.* Indianapolis Gas Co., 146 Ind. 655, 46 N. E. 17, 36 L. R. A. 535.

[156] *United States:* Lillard *v.* Distilleries, etc., 134 Fed. 168, 177, 67 C. C. A. 74.

Kentucky: New Market Co. *v.* Embry, 20 Ky. L. Rep. 1130, 48 S. W. 980.

[157] Wilson *v.* Dunville, 6 L. R. Ire. 210.

tenant could recover the loss to the crops.[158] For failure of a boom company to turn out the plaintiff's logs, where the company knew that the plaintiff needed the logs to operate his mill and could get no more, it was held that the plaintiff could recover the profit he would have made by manufacturing them into lumber.[159]

In Smeed v. Foord [160] the defendant had contracted to deliver a threshing machine to a farmer within three weeks, knowing that it was the plaintiff's practice to thresh his wheat in the field, and send it off at once to the market. The defendant failed to deliver it in time. The farmer made some attempts to hire another machine, but not any very active ones, as he was continually receiving letters from the defendant leading him to expect the arrival of the machine. He stacked the wheat, but being unable to hire thatchers, it was injured by the rain. On this account it became necessary to kiln-dry it. The plaintiff claimed damages: First, for the expense of stacking and drying the wheat, and for loss arising from its deterioration in value by the rain. Second, for the fall in the market value between the time when it would have been ready and when it actually was. It was held that the parties must reasonably have contemplated injury by the weather if the wheat was not threshed at once, and therefore the first claim was sustained; but the court refused to allow damages for a fall in the market value, holding that that was not within the contemplation of the parties.

The same doctrine applies where a carrier delays the transportation of goods which he knows are needed for a special use. So upon failure to transport scenery which, as defendant knew, was to be used for theatrical purposes every day for a considerable time, this was held to be notice which would indicate to defendant that failure to transport would mean failure to give a performance; and plaintiff was entitled to recover the gross returns that he would have been likely to receive from the

---

[158] Herring v. Armwood, 130 N. C. 177, 41 S. E. 96, 57 L. R. A. 958.

[159] Mississippi & R. R. B. Co. v. Prince, 34 Minn. 71, 24 N. W. 344. On the other hand, in the absence of notice of special facts, the necessity of closing a logging camp because a boom company allowed plaintiff's logs to escape is not a natural consequence of the wrong. Skagit R. & L. Co. v. Cole, 1 Wash. St. 330, 26 Pac. 535.

[160] 1 E. & E. 602.

performance, less the cost.[161] The discussion here appears to have been confined to the question of special notice and contemplation and did not take up the question of certainty.

In Simpson *v.* London & North Western Railway [162] the plaintiff had been exhibiting his wares at a show at B. He usually sold some, but his chief object was to exhibit them as an advertisement to procure custom. He delivered them to the defendant to take to *the show ground* at N., and indorsed on the consignment note that they must be there by a certain day. They did not arrive there till the show was over. It was held that the plaintiffs could recover damages which had been given for either loss of profit or of time. It was said that the defendant had sufficient notice of the special circumstances, and therefore it must be deemed to have been in the contemplation of the parties that the damage would include whatever loss the plaintiff suffered by missing the show.[163] In Hamilton *v.* Western North Carolina Railroad [164] the defendant company failed to furnish freight cars to the plaintiff on a certain day, according to agreement. The company had notice that by shipment of his goods on that day the plaintiff could get the advantage of a favorable market. The company was held liable for the loss of the favorable market. The defendant contracted with the plaintiff, a butcher, to furnish the ice required for his ice-box, knowing the use which the plaintiff had for it. In an action for failure to supply the ice, it was held that the plaintiff could recover compensation for meat spoiled for lack of ice.[165]

In a case which immediately followed Hadley *v.* Baxendale, the defendant had contracted to build a ship, which was to be delivered to the plaintiff on the 1st of August, 1854. It was not delivered till March, 1855. The vessel was intended by the plaintiffs—and from the nature of her fittings the defendants must have known the fact—for a passenger ship in the Australian trade. Evidence was given that freights to Aus-

[161] Weston *v.* Boston & M. R. R., 190 Mass. 298, 76 N. E. 1050, 4 L. R. A. (N. S.) 569, 112 Am. St. Rep. 330.

[162] 1 Q. B. D. 274.

[163] *Acc.,* Richardson *v.* Chynoweth, 26 Wis. 656.

[164] 96 N. C. 398, 3 S. E. 164; *acc.,* Deming *v.* Grand T. R. R., 48 N. H. 455, 2 Am. Rep. 267.

[165] Hammer *v.* Schoenfelder, 47 Wis. 455.

tralia were very high in July, August, and September, but fell in October, and continued low till May, when the vessel sailed; and that, had she been delivered on the day named, she could have earned £2,750 more than she did. On the other hand, it was shown that the plaintiffs would have extended the time for delivery till the first of October, if the defendants would have bound themselves to that day under a demurrage (which, however, was refused), and that they had stated as their reason for wishing to have the ship then, "that after that time the days would be shortening so fast that they would be seriously inconvenienced and prejudiced in fitting the vessel out." The judge charged in the words of Hadley v. Baxendale, and the jury found a verdict of £2,750. An attempt was made to set aside the verdict for excess of damages, on the ground that if the plaintiff's offer had been complied with, the loss of freight would not have been suffered, and that the damages should be measured rather by the species of loss which they had themselves pointed out, than by that which they afterwards set up. The rule was refused.[166]

In Schilze v. Great Eastern Railway [167] the plaintiff sued the defendant, a common carrier, for failure to deliver a package containing samples. The defendant had notice of the contents of the package. The plaintiff having lost a season's trade by the non-delivery of the samples was allowed to recover damages on that account.[168] In Fox v. Boston & Maine Railroad [169] the plaintiff made a special arrangement with the defendant, a common carrier, with a view to the mildness of the weather, to deliver apples which were shipped to a connecting railroad at a certain time. The defendant delayed the delivery, and as a consequence the apples were frozen while

---

[166] Fletcher v. Tayleur, 17 C. B. 21.
[167] 19 Q. B. D. 30.
[168] Acc., Gledhill W. P. Co. v. Baltimore & O. R. R., 119 N. Y. Supp. 623; Strange v. Atlantic C. L. R. R., 77 S. C. 182, 57 S. E. 724. So where defendant broke its contract to furnish trading stamps to a grocer, and it was shown that his sales, which had greatly increased while the trading stamps were

furnished, suddenly and as greatly fell off upon defendant's failure to furnish them longer, it was held that the loss of profits by reason of the breach of contract was within the contemplation of the parties. Gagnon v. Sperry & Hutchinson Co., 206 Mass. 547, 92 N. E. 761
[169] 148 Mass. 220, 19 N. E. 222, 1 L. R. A. 702.

in transit on the connecting line. The defendant was held liable for the loss of the apples.

Where there was notice that lumber was bought for a building to be constructed at a distance, and inferior lumber was furnished by the defendant, the increased cost of building and the cost of getting other lumber were within the contemplation of the parties, and could be recovered.[170] And where iron bands were bought for the purpose of binding wooden pipes for an aqueduct, and inferior bands were furnished, the cost of putting the bands on the pipes and removing them could be recovered.[171]

§ 164a. Breach of warranty of fitness for purpose.

Where goods are expressly or impliedly warranted fit for a purpose, the warrantor necessarily has notice that they will be used for the purpose; and any damage which results from so using them is within the contemplation of the parties. Thus in an English case it appeared that the defendant furnished a chain to be used by plaintiffs in delivering goods to defendant. There was an implied warranty that the chain would be sufficient. It broke, and one of plaintiff's workmen was injured; and the workman thereupon brought an action for compensation and recovered damages. It was held that this was within the contemplation of the parties at the time the chain was delivered, and that plaintiff was entitled to recover the amount he had been obliged to pay. It was admitted that the plaintiff acted reasonably with regard to the action for compensation.[172] So where defendant warranted a safe burglar-proof, and burglars opened the safe and stole money, it was held that the loss of such a sum of money as might reasonably be expected to be put in the safe was within the contemplation of the parties; though the court intimated that recovery would be limited to a reasonable amount.[173] Where a stallion was sold for breeding purposes, and proved unfit, the expense of keep-

[170] Canton Lumber Co. v. Lieler, 112 Md. 258, 76 Atl. 415.

[171] McDonald v. Kansas City, B. & N. Co., 149 Fed. 360, 79 C. C. A. 298, 8 L. R. A. (N. S.) 1110.

[172] Mowbray v. Merryweather, [1895] 2 Q. B. 640, 59 J. P. 804, 65 L. J. Q. B. 50, 73 L. T. Rep. (N. S.) 459, 14 Reports, 767, 44 Wkly. Rep. 49.

[173] Deane v. Michigan Stove Co., 69 Ill. App. 106.

ing him a reasonable time to test him was within the contemplation of the parties;[174] and it has also been held that loss of profits during the season which could be proved with reasonable certainty might be recovered.[175] Where coal dust was sold to be made into brick, with a warranty that it contained no soft coal dust, and there was notice that if there was soft coal dust it would destroy the bricks that were to be made, and there was soft coal dust, it was held that plaintiff was entitled to recover the damage caused by the bricks being destroyed.[176] So where plaintiff bought carriage springs to be used by him in manufacturing carriages, and the springs were defective and had to be taken out of the carriages after they were built, the plaintiff may recover the cost of removing the springs from the carriages.[177] Where defendant contracted to carry a sick person to a certain place in a hack, injury to the passenger's health by being obliged to leave the hack before reaching his destination was within the contemplation of the parties.[178] The defendant sold salmon with a warranty that it was fit for food. Plaintiff's wife died from eating the salmon, and a consequence was he had to hire other persons to perform the services in the care of the house, etc., that she had performed. It was held that plaintiff could recover damages for loss of her services.[179] Defendant supplied a pole for a carriage. By reason of a defect it broke while being used, the carriage was forced on to the horses, one of them kicked, and injured the other and the carriage. It was left to the jury to say whether this was a natural consequence of a defect in the pole.[180] Plaintiff, a manufacturer of ice cream, purchased the defendants' coloring matter manufactured by them, which they represented as pure and harmless, knowing the purpose for

[174] Peak v. Frost, 162 Mass. 298, 38 N. E. 518.

[175] Stewart v. Patton, 65 Mo. App. 21. But see Connoble v. Clark, 38 Mo. App. 476, where profits were not allowed in such a case.

[176] Milburn v. Belloni, 39 N. Y. 53, 100 Am. Dec. 403.

[177] Thoms v. Dingley, 70 Me. 100, 35 Am. Rep. 310.

[178] Trout v. Watkins L. & U. Co., 148 Mo. App. 621, 130 S. W. 136.

[179] Jackson v. Watson & Sons, [1909] 2 K. B. 193, 78 L. J. K. B. 587, 100 L. T. 799, 25 T. L. R. 454, 53 Sol. Jo. 447.

[180] Randall v. Newson, 2 Q. B. D. 102, 46 L. J. Q. B. 259, 36 L. T. Rep. (N. S.) 164, 25 Wkly. Rep. 313.

which it was to be used. Persons who used ice cream colored with this material were made ill; and plaintiff then destroyed all the ice cream which had been made containing the coloring matter. He was held entitled to recover the value of the goods so destroyed, and also the loss of custom caused by the sale of the poisonous ice cream.[181] On the other hand, in an action for breach of warranty in the sale of grease, the plaintiff claimed that because of inferior quality he could not sell the grease in Cincinnati, but had to reship it to Chicago for sale. It was held that the cost of reshipment was not within the contemplation of the parties.[182]

The general principle seems to have been lost sight of in a few cases. Thus where the defendant sold milk to the plaintiff for resale as good milk, and it was in fact skimmed milk, though the defendant did not know it, and the plaintiff was prosecuted for selling it to his customers and had to pay a fine, it was held that the amount of this fine could not be recovered, since it was not a result which the defendant reasonably contemplated because he sold it innocently.[183] And in a Massachusetts case, in an action for falsely representing that a horse was kind in harness, the plaintiff was held not entitled to recover the value of a wagon and harness broken by the horse.[184]

For the loss to be within the contemplation of the parties in such a case the plaintiff must have used reasonable diligence in avoiding it. So in an action for breach of warranty of a harvester the plaintiff may recover for depreciation in the value of his crop while experimenting with the machine for a reasonable time, but not for too long a time; [185] nor may he recover for loss of the crop unless at the time of the warranty there was notice that no other way of harvesting the grain was open to the plaintiff.[186] On this ground, where defendant sold

[181] Swain v. Schieffelin, 134 N. Y. 471, 31 N. E. 1025, 18 L. R. A. 385.

[182] Goodkind v. Rogan, 8 Ill. App. 413.

[183] Sloggy v. Crescent Creamery Co., 72 Minn. 316, 75 N. W. 225.

[184] Case v. Stevens, 137 Mass. 551. But in Sharon v. Mosher, 17 Barb. (N. Y.) 518, it was held to be a question for the jury whether such injury was a natural consequence of the breach of warranty.

[185] Wilson v. Reedy, 32 Minn. 256, 20 N. W. 153.

[186] Frohreich v. Gammon, 28 Minn. 476, 11 N. W. 88.

plaintiff a computing scale with a warranty, the scale under-weighed, and plaintiff claimed as damages losses suffered in selling by the scale for four months before he discovered the defect, it was held that he should have had the scale examined, in accordance with the city ordinance, before using it, and he could not recover for the loss.[187]

Part of the loss may be contemplated, but not the whole. Thus in an action for breach of warranty on sale of a locomotive for use on a private railway, the cost of giving it a reasonable test could be recovered, but not damages from stoppage of plaintiff's sawmill because logs could not be hauled to it over the railway.[188]

In Ontario a distinction in the allowance of such damages appears to be made between express and implied warranties; such damages being allowed for breach of an express but not for breach of an implied warranty.[189]

§ 165. Notice of use for machinery.

Where notice is given that machinery is to be used in running a mill, loss caused by stoppage of the mill, such as loss of use of the mill or the machine, deterioration in stock, loss from idle hands, etc., may be recovered, whether the action is against a seller of the machinery for failure to deliver it [190] or against a carrier for delay in transporting it.[191]

[187] Wright v. Computing Scale Co., 47 Wash. 107, 91 Pac. 571.

[188] Marbury Lumber Co. v. Stearns Mfg. Co., 107 S. W. 200, 32 Ky. L. Rep. 739.

[189] McMullen v. Free, 13 Ont. 57; Stewart v. Sculthorp, 25 Ont. 544.

[190] *United States:* D. A. Tompkins & Co. v. Monticello C. O. Co., 153 Fed. 817.

Georgia: Van Winkle v. Wilkins, 81 Ga. 93, 7 S. E. 644, 12 Am. St. Rep. 299.

Kentucky: Bates Machine Co. v. Norton Iron Works, 113 Ky. 372, 68 S. W. 423; American Bridge Co. v. Glenmore Distilleries Co., 107 S. W. 279, 32 Ky. L. Rep. 873.

Ohio: Champion I. M. & C. S. Co. v. Pennsylvania I. W. Co., 68 Ohio St. 228, 67 N. E. 486; Cleveland, P. & S. W. Co. v. Consumers' Carbon Co., 75 Ohio St. 153, 78 N. E. 1007.

Oregon: Mine Supply Co. v. Columbia Min. Co., 48 Or. 391, 86 Pac. 789.

South Carolina: Standard Supply Co. v. Carter & Harris, 81 S. C. 181, 62 S. E. 150.

[191] *Georgia:* Savannah, F. & W. Ry. v. Pritchard, 77 Ga. 412, 1 S. E. 261, 4 Am. St. Rep. 92.

Illinois: Priestly v. Northern I. & C. R. R., 26 Ill. 205, 79 Am. Dec. 369.

Iowa: Elzy v. Adams Express Co., 141 Ia. 407, 119 N. W. 705.

Missouri: Morrow v. Missouri Pac.

In British Columbia S. M. Co. *v.* Nettleship [192] it appeared
that several cases containing machinery intended for the erection of a mill at Vancouver's Island were delivered to the
defendant's servants at Glasgow for transportation to that
place, and the defendant knew generally of what the shipment
consisted, but did not know for what purpose it was intended.
The measure of damages for the loss of one of the cases was
held to be the cost of replacing the missing articles at the
Island, the plaintiff having been obliged to send to England
for it, as none similar could be procured at Vancouver's Island.
It was further held that the plaintiff could recover interest on
the amount for the delay in sending to England, but not
profits he might have made if the mill had been erected. The
rule of Hadley *v.* Baxendale was distinctly affirmed on the
ground that some limitation must be put on a defendant's
liability, and that seemed the most proper limitation. Willes,
J., also pointed out that the damages claimed here were speculative in the extreme. As to the effect of notice of the object
of the contract, he said (p. 509): "To my mind, that leads to
the inevitable conclusion that the mere fact of knowledge
cannot increase the liability. The knowledge must be brought
home to the party sought to be charged, under such circumstances that he must know that the person he contracts with
reasonably believes that he accepts the contract with the
special condition attached to it."

In Hydraulic E. Co. *v.* M'Haffie [193] it appeared that the
defendant had failed to carry out a contract to deliver a piece
of machinery. The plaintiffs required this machinery in order
to carry out a contract with one J. The contract with J.,
though made subsequently to the contract with the defendant,
was the subject of a conversation between the parties before
they entered into any agreement. It was held in the Court of
Appeal that the plaintiff could recover the profits he would
have derived from his contract with J., and also the expenses

Ry., 140 Mo. App. 200, 123 S. W.
1034.

North Carolina: Harper Furniture
Co. *v.* Southern Express Co., 148 N. C.
87, 62 S. E. 145; Story Lumber Co. *v.*

Southern Ry., 151 N. C. 23, 65 S. E.
460.

[192] L. R. 3 C. P. 499.
[193] 4 Q. B. D. 670.

to which he had been put in making part of an engine for J., which had been thrown away.

In an action for failure to furnish proper heating apparatus according to contract, the defendant knew that the building to be heated was a greenhouse; he was held responsible for the destruction of plants in the greenhouse by reason of the low temperature.[194] For failure to furnish machinery which formed a part of a compress, special notice that this would be the result having been given, the plaintiff could recover damages for the loss of use of the compress, equal to its rental value.[195] In an action for breach of contract to furnish part of machinery for manufacturing crates, it appeared that defendants were informed that orders had been received for a certain number of crates, and that plaintiff had no machinery to make them. This brought the loss of profits on the orders for crates within the contemplation of the parties; and the cost of manufacturing and the contract price being shown, the profits could be determined.[196]

§ 166. Notice of a special use for material.

When notice is given of a special use for material, the defendant who fails to deliver or delays delivery is liable for the special damages thereby caused, whether the material was needed for construction or manufacture,[197] for packing,[198] or for fuel.[199]

In Gee v. Lancashire & Yorkshire Railway,[200] the plaintiffs, who were cotton spinners, having rented a new mill which was in readiness to begin working, and engaged a number of hands for it, caused to be delivered to the defendants, to be carried

---

[194] Kramer v. Messner, 101 Iowa, 88, 69 N. W. 1142.

[195] Livermore F. & M. Co. v. Union S. & C. Co., 105 Tenn. 187, 58 S. W. 270.

[196] Pender Lumber Co. v. Wilmington Iron Works, 130 N. C. 584, 41 S. E. 797.

[197] *United States:* Taber Lumber Co. v. O'Neal, 160 Fed. 596, 87 C. C. A. 498 (logs for manufacture).

Illinois: Ledgerwood v. Bushnell, 128 Ill. App. 555 (lumber for constructing a building).

New York: Julius Jonson's Sons v. Buellesbach, 119 N. Y. Supp. 839 (iron columns for building).

[198] Pacific S. M. Works v. California Canneries Co., 164 Fed. 980, 90 C. C. A. 108 (cans for canning fruit and vegetables).

[199] Texarkana & Ft. S. Ry. v. Neches Iron Works, 122 S. W. 64, (Tex. Civ. App.) (coke).

[200] 6 H. & N. 211.

from Liverpool to Oldham, some bales of cotton, which were, through the negligence of the carriers, delayed in the delivery for some days beyond the usual time. In consequence of the delay, the plaintiffs having no other cotton to work with, the mill was kept idle, and the work-people were unemployed. The necessity of cotton to enable the plaintiff to work this mill was not communicated to the defendants at the time of its delivery for freight, but was so communicated immediately on its non-arrival at the proper time, after which there was still an unreasonable delay in the delivery on the part of the carrier. The county judge had charged that the plaintiff could recover as legal damage such loss as arose from the stoppage of the mill, and that the jury should give the amount of wages and other actual loss. This was held to be error. The court said that the stoppage of the mill was not a necessary consequence of the non-delivery of the cotton, for the fact that the plaintiff had no other cotton was the more immediate cause. Pollock, C. B., thought that the company could not be held liable, unless it had special notice of the object of the contract at the time of sending the goods. Bramwell, B., pointed out that the decision was not to the effect that the plaintiff could not, in any event, recover the wages and the loss of profit. He said that they could, if it were the custom for mills to have so little supply of cotton on hand, and that therefore it should have been left to the jury to say whether the stoppage was the natural consequence of the non-delivery.

In Jones *v.* National Printing Co.[201] the defendant contracted to furnish paper of a peculiar size at a certain day. The defendant was told that if the paper was not furnished the presses would stand idle. As a matter of fact the plaintiff was under contract with a third party to do certain printing, for which the paper ordered of the defendant was required; but the defendant was not notified of the latter contract. The delivery of the paper was delayed, and the plaintiff was required to do extra night presswork in order to fulfil his contract for printing. It was held that the plaintiff might recover compensation for his presses remaining idle during the period of delay, but not for the expense of the night presswork. In Vickery *v.* McCor-

[201] 13 Daly, 92.

mick [202] the defendant agreed to deliver timber to be used for special work, and had notice that delay in delivery would stop the work. In an action for delay in delivery, it was held that the plaintiff might recover compensation for his loss through stoppage of the work. Defendant contracted to supply ironwork for a building. The ironwork was not delivered at proper time. As a result of the delay a brick wall was blown down, a certain amount was expended in removing the débris, plaintiff was prevented from completing his contract in time and therefore lost interest on the money retained until the completion of contract, and he was obliged to do a large portion of the work during the winter season at an increased expense. It was held that all these damages were within the contemplation of the parties and were sufficiently proximate for recovery.[203] But if no notice is given that failure to furnish the material will stop work, no recovery can be had for its being stopped.[204]

§ 167. Notice of special use for premises.

The rental value of a building will be the measure of damages in an action for delay in delivering possession; but if the contract be to furnish a building for a particular purpose, the rental value of a building used in that way will be the measure of damages.[205] Townsend v. Nickerson Wharf Co.[206] was an action by a lessee against his lessor for failure to deliver all the demised premises. The plaintiff had entered upon part of the premises, and had paid the rent in full for the whole term. It was held that the plaintiff could only recover the diminished value of the lease from its not giving him all the premises; that he could not recover for expenses put on the building, nor for injury to his business on account of the fact that the lease was only of use to him if he had the whole building. The court said, however, that if the lessor had special

[202] 117 Ind. 594, 20 N. E. 495.

[203] Meyer v. Haven, 70 N. Y. App. Div. 529, 75 N. Y. Supp. 261.

[204] *Iowa:* Laporte Imp. Co. v. Brock, 99 Iowa, 485, 61 Am. St. 245, 68 N. W. 810 (no notice that other material could not be had).

Minnesota: Paine v. Sherwood, 19 Minn. 315 (no notice that contract must be completed at a fixed time).

See Hickok v. Adams Co., 18 O. D. 14, 99 N. W. 77.

[205] Hexter v. Knox, 63 N. Y. 561.

[206] 117 Mass. 501.

notice of the lessee's object in hiring the premises, the plaintiff could have recovered the damage to his business. The defendant failed to perform his contract to build a building for the plaintiff to store his corn in. The plaintiff was allowed compensation for loss of his corn, caused by lack of shelter for it.[207]

Where a building is rented for a dwelling, and the defendant fails to give possession, it has been held that the cost of moving the tenant's furniture from another town is not within the contemplation of the parties.[208] And where premises are leased for business purposes, it has been held that the loss caused by the abandonment by the tenant of a former situation in anticipation of the new business was not a natural result of the failure to give possession.[209] On the other hand, a plaintiff was allowed to recover compensation for being obliged to discharge hands hired for the new business,[210] and for loss on fixtures made for use on the premises, but not for loss on a stock of goods bought, since it was deemed unnecessary to buy the stock before getting possession.[211] Where the lease of an opera house is put an end to wrongfully the tenant may recover the expense of advertising.[212] Loss of profits of a new business have been said not to be within the contemplation of the parties;[213] but where the profits are reasonably certain they may be recovered. So in an action for breach of contract by which a mortgagee agreed not to foreclose the mortgage on a farm for three years, the farm being used for a milk farm, as defendant knew, and plaintiff selling an average number of cans a day, recovery was allowed for loss of profits of the farm.[214] Plaintiff, lessee of an opera house, was behind in the rent, and a new agreement was made by which he was to be allowed to hold under the new lease

[207] Haven v. Wakefield, 39 Ill. 509.

[208] Serfling v. Andrews, 106 Wis. 78, 81 N. W. 991.

[209] O'Connor v. Nolan, 64 Ill. App. 357.

[210] Lawrence v. Wardwell, 6 Barb. (N. Y.) 423.

[211] Friedland v. Myers, 139 N. Y. 432, 34 N. E. 1058.

[212] New York Academy of Music v. Hackett, 2 Hilt. (N. Y.) 217.

[213] Serfling v. Andrews, 106 Wis. 78, 81 N. W. 991. Query whether the true reason for refusing recovery was not the uncertainty of the profits.

[214] Manning v. Fitch, 138 Mass. 273.

and as soon as his profits under the new lease were enough to pay the back rent, he was to be restored to all his rights under the old lease. Defendant, the lessor, withheld possession under the new lease, and plaintiff claimed as part of his damages the loss of the advantages of the old lease which he expected to regain from the profits of the new lease. This was held too remote; not, it is clear, from lack of notice of the consequences of a breach of contract, but because the profits of the new lease were uncertain.[215]

§ 168. Notice of special use for funds.

Mere notice of the purpose for which money is to be used is not enough to bring a consequential loss within the contemplation of the parties, since it is ordinarily possible to get money elsewhere.[216] So where the defendant agreed to pay a creditor of the plaintiff, and on his default the creditor attached the plaintiff's property and sold it at a sacrifice, it was held that the loss was too remote and the plaintiff could not recover damages for the sale.[217] And for breach of an agreement to pay off incumbrances, a loss of the property by foreclosure is not ordinarily recoverable.[218] But where the purpose is made known to the defendant and he has notice of facts showing the impossibility of getting the money elsewhere, the plaintiff may recover any loss which he can prove with sufficient certainty to have resulted from failure to have the money.[219] So where the defendant constantly assured plaintiff that the money needed to buy a coal mine would be forthcoming, but finally failed to furnish it, plaintiff may recover the value of his contract for buying the mine.[220] So where the defendant, a common carrier, neglected to deliver in time some money which was to pay the premium on an

[215] Wilson v. Weil, 67 Mo. 399.

[216] *North Carolina:* C. B. Coles & Sons Co. v. Standard L. Co., 150 N. C. 183, 63 S. E. 736 (loss of profits).

Texas: Western Nat. Bank v. White, Tex. Civ. App.   , 131 S. W. 828 (arrest for swindling as a result of dishonor of check).

[217] Mitchell v. Clarke, 71 Cal. 163, 60 Am. Rep. 529.

[218] *Indiana:* Lowe v. Turpie, 147 Ind. 652, 675, 44 N. E. 24, 37 L. R. A. 233.

Michigan: Dean v. Radford, 141 Mich. 36, 104 N. W. 329.

[219] Equitable Mort. Co. v. Thorn (Tex. Civ. App.), 26 S. W. 276.

[220] Manchester & O. Bank v. Cook, 49 L. T. Rep. (N. S.) 674.

endowment policy, and the policy consequently lapsed, the defendant having had notice of the object for which the money was intended, it was held that the plaintiff could recover the value of the policy when it lapsed.[221]   And where a telephone company neglected to transmit money for expense of preparing the body of plaintiff's daughter for shipment, as a result of which the funeral was delayed, plaintiff was allowed to recover for his mental suffering thereby caused.[222]

§ 169. Notice of special use for information.[223]

In the case of delay in delivery or failure to deliver a message by a telegraph company, the company may, if it had express notice of special circumstances, be held responsible for consequences not otherwise within the contemplation of the parties.   A telegraph company failed to deliver a telegram from plaintiff to a person accused of crime, saying "come at once."   The company knew that plaintiff was expecting to capture the accused; and though he did not know that a reward would be offered or had been offered, he had reason to suppose that one would be.   By reason of non-delivery of the message plaintiff did not capture the accused.   It was held that in view of notice of these facts the damage was within the contemplation of the parties.[224]

Usually such notice as the company receives is derived from the nature of the message itself.   When a message is sent, apparently in connection with a business transaction, and containing a statement of terms, even though it is not in a form intelligible to the company, a business loss as a result of failure to deliver the message is within the contemplation of the parties.   So in a case in Maine, in an action for failure to send a message accepting an offer to sell the plaintiffs some corn, the message was, "Ship cargo named at ninety if you can secure freight at ten."   It was held that the measure of damages was the difference between the price

---

[221] Grindle v. Eastern Exp. Co., 67 Me. 317, 24 Am. Rep. 31.

[222] Cumberland T. & T. Co. v. Quigley, 129 Ky. 788, 112 S. W. 897.

[223] The cases on this subject are more fully considered in the chapter on Telegraph and Telephone Companies, post, ch. xxxix.

[224] McPeek v. Western U. Tel. Co., 107 Iowa, 356, 78 N. W. 63, 70 Am. St. Rep. 205, 43 L. R. A. 214.

named and that which the plaintiff would have been obliged to pay at the same place, in order by due and reasonable diligence, after notice of the failure of the telegram, to purchase the like quantity and quality of the same species of merchandise.[225] If, however, the terms of the message are so vague as not necessarily to indicate a business transaction, a business loss is not brought within the contemplation of the parties. So in an action for failure to deliver a telegram instructing the plaintiff's correspondents in Nebraska City to "ship oil as soon as possible at the very best rates you can," it was held that the plaintiff could recover what he paid for the transmission of the message and the increased price of freight on the oil, but not profits that he might have made on the oil if the message had been delivered and the oil sent in time.[226] Cases must be distinguished where recovery is refused, not because the loss was not within the contemplation of the parties, but because it was too uncertain. So in Baldwin v. The United States Telegraph Co.[227] the plaintiff had received an offer by telegram for his interest in an oil well. He at once telegraphed, by defendant's and a connecting company, to an agent, inquiring how much the well was producing, telling the operator of the connecting company that he would sell his interest unless he received an answer promptly. The delivery of the message was delayed by defendant's carelessness. The plaintiff accordingly sold his interest. Very soon afterward he received a message from his agent, informing him that the interest was much more valuable than the price for which he had sold it, and offering him $1,200 more than he had received from the sale. The market price was found to be even greater than this. On the trial he recovered $1,200 damages, but on appeal this was held to be error. The court to be sure recited the requirement that the damages should have been in the contemplation of the parties; but added that these damages were too remote, and depended upon too many contingencies; that if the message had been received, the agent might not have answered;

[225] True v. International T. Co., 60 Me. 9, 11 Am. Rep. 156, n.

[226] Western U. Tel. Co. v. Graham, 1 Colo. 230.

[227] 45 N. Y. 744.

if he had, it was doubtful what he would have answered; and the answer might not have been received.

In another class of cases the message may in itself convey notice of necessary facts. In those jurisdictions where one may recover damages for mental suffering for the non-delivery of a message conveying the intelligence of the illness or death of a near relative, the near relationship may be indicated to the company by the terms of the message.[228]   And where a message was sent calling a physician and was not delivered, the sender may recover for the physical effects of his failure to secure the physician.[229]

§ 169a. Notice of special need for promptness.

Where notice is given of facts which show the special need of promptness in the delivery of goods, damages may be recovered for a loss consequent upon actionable slowness. Thus where goods are bought for sale at a special season, and the seller or carrier, knowing the facts, delays the delivery, compensation may be recovered for loss of the season's sale.[230] So where a carrier is notified of any other special reason for prompt delivery, he may be charged with the loss caused by delay.[231]   And where plaintiff engaged a moving picture machine for use on election night for advertising his special edition, as the defendant had notice, plaintiff's expenses in preparing the edition could be recovered where defendant by failing to deliver the machine made the expense useless.[232]

---

[228] W. U. Tel. Co. v. Adams, 75 Tex. 531, 16 Am. St. 920, 12 S. W. 857, 6 L. R. A. 844 ("Come quick, Ruth is dying"); W. U. Tel. Co. v. Feegles, 75 Tex. 537, 12 S. W. 860 ("Lee is dangerously wounded"); W. U. Tel. Co. v. Moore, 76 Tex. 66, 18 Am. St. 25, 12 S. W. 949 ("Bill is very low, come at once"); W. U. Tel. Co. v. Kirkpatrick, 76 Tex. 217, 18 Am. St. 37, 13 S. W. 70 ("father is very low, come at once")

Except in the last case, it is difficult to see how the words conveyed any notice of relationship.

[229] Western U. T. Co. v. Ford, (Ga. App.), 70 S. E. 65.

[230] *New York:* Wolfe v. Weir, 112 N. Y. Supp. 1078, 61 Misc. 57 (fall trade).

Texas: Pittman v. Bloch Queensware Co., 106 S. W. 724, 48 Tex. Civ. App. 320 (holiday trade).

[231] *Michigan:* Hayes v. Wabash R. R., 163 Mich. 174, 128 N. W. 217.

Texas: Waugh v. Gulf, C. & S. F. Ry. (Tex. Civ. App.), 131 S. W. 843.

[232] American-Hungarian Pub. Co. v. Miles Bros., 123 N. Y. Supp. 879, 68 Misc. 334.

But if in such a case the defendant has no knowledge of the necessity for haste such consequences are not natural.[233]   On this ground it has been held that where defendant unreasonably delayed the installation of a fire hydrant loss by fire during the period of delay was not a natural consequence of the delay.[234]

[233] *Kentucky:* Brand *v.* Illinois C. R. R., 32 Ky. Law Rep. 1335, 108 S. W. 356.

New York: J. H. Lichtenstein & Co. *v.* Fargo, 121 N. Y. Supp. 327, 66 Misc. 149.

But see Lambert-Murray Co. *v.* Southern Express Co., 146 N. C. 321, 59 S. E. 991, where the court appears to have taken the view that the carrier is put upon his inquiry as to the need of haste. The case, however, may be supported on the ground that the market value of the goods, which apparently were needed for a special occasion, had fallen to nothing before delivery.

[234] Hunt Bros. Co. *v.* San Lorenzo Water Co., 150 Cal. 51, 87 Pac. 1093, 7 L. R. A. (N. S.) 913.   Since protection from fire was the purpose of the installation, the correctness of this decision may perhaps be questioned.

CHAPTER IX

CERTAIN AND UNCERAIN DAMAGES: PROFITS

§ 170. Fact of loss must be shown with reasonable certainty.

A party who claims compensation for a legal injury must show, as part of his case, that he has suffered a loss through the injury; and the burden of proving what loss he has suffered is upon him. He is to show, with that reasonable certainty required by the law, the nature and extent of the loss for which he is entitled to compensation; and no recovery can be had for any damage which is not satisfactorily proved by the evidence. "It must not be supposed that under the principle of Hadley v. Baxendale mere speculative profits, such as might be conjectured to have been the probable results of an adventure which was defeated by the breach of the contract sued on, the gains from which are entirely conjectural, with respect to which no means exist of ascertaining, even approximately, the probable results, can, under any circumstances, be brought within the range of damages recoverable. The cardinal principle in relation to the damages to be compensated for on the breach of a contract, that the plaintiff must establish the quantum of his loss by evidence from which the jury will be able to estimate the extent of his injury, will exclude all such elements of injury as are incapable of being ascertained by the usual rules of evidence to a reasonable degree of certainty."[1]

On this ground no recovery can be had upon a loss which is insufficiently proved to have been actually suffered. So in an action where it appeared that defendant destroyed a hose connected with a fire engine by means of which an attempt was being made to put out a fire on plaintiff's premises, plaintiff claimed to recover the value of his property burned, on the ground that if the hose had not been destroyed the fire would have been extinguished; but this was held too conjectural.[2] So where a performance of the duty would have given the plaintiff an opportunity to make a contract, or special use of property, without any certainty that he would have chosen to do so, no loss is sufficiently proved.[3] And wherever the fact of

---

[1] Depue, J., in Wolcott v. Mount, 36 N. J. L. 262, 271, 13 Am. Rep. 438. Complete indefiniteness of proof is fatal to the recovery of substantial damages. The Oscoda, 70 Fed. 110. See Harrison v. Redden, 53 Kan. 265, 36 Pac. 325 (plaintiff wrongfully caused to change his residence).

[2] Mott v. Hudson R. R. R., 1 Robert. (N. Y.), 585.

[3] *Mississippi:* Johnson v. Western U. Tel. Co., 79 Miss. 58, 29 So. 787, 89

Am. St. Rep. 584 (defendant failed to transmit offer of a contract).

West Virginia: Douglass v. Ohio River R. R., 51 W. Va. 523, 41 S. E. 911 (failure to fence; plaintiff claimed that he might have changed his practice and used the land for grazing). But see Barker v. Western U. Tel. Co., 134 Wis. 147, 114 N. W. 439, where defendant failed to transmit a message calling plaintiff, a physican, to a case in Chicago. Plaintiff was trying to

loss depends upon whether defendant would have chosen or will in future choose to act in a certain way, it is not sufficiently proved.[4] A fortiori if the occurrence of the loss depends upon a future exercise of choice by a third party, it is not usually provable with sufficient certainty. So upon failure to deliver a telegram asking plaintiff whether he would accept receivership of a bank, signed by an officer of the government, it was held that plaintiff could recover only nominal damages, since there is no reasonable certainty that if he had accepted he would have been appointed.[5] And in an action by a stockholder against a director for negligence, it was held that plaintiff could not recover for the chance of being called upon to pay money under his stockholder's liability, no such liability having as yet been claimed or enforced.[6] So where a railroad company contracted with the plaintiff that if plaintiff would erect a first-class hotel near the station and entertain its employees at half price it would support the hotel by passenger business, and plaintiff erected the hotel but defendant did not furnish enough passengers to support it, it was held that the contract was too indefinite to recover damages on.[7] And where defendant wrongfully used proxies in the election of bank officers, by which means plaintiff was deprived of his office as president of the bank, plaintiff's recovery was confined to the loss of the office for a single year; he could not recover compensation for a loss of the office in subsequent years.[8] On this ground one cannot usually recover compensa-

build up a practice in Chicago. He was allowed to recover damages for loss of the opportunity.

[4] *Maine:* Chase v. Cochran, 67 Atl. 320, 102 Me. 431 (plaintiff might have used water power to run a factory).

Massachusetts: Noble v. Hand, 163 Mass. 289, 39 N. E. 1020 (breach of contract to allow plaintiff to obtain orders for goods for defendant, defendant having the right to reject any order).

Minnesota: Doud v. Duluth Milling Co., 55 Minn. 53, 56 N. W. 463 (breach of contract by defendant to take such

barrels as he might need in his business).

New York: Katz v. Wolf, 16 Misc. 82, 37 N. Y. Supp. 648 (contract to deposit money on purchase of furniture to be bought when defendant should marry).

[5] Walser v. W. U. Tel. Co., 114 N. C. 440, 19 S. E. 366.

[6] Bloom v. National U. Benefit Savings & L. Co., 152 N. Y. 114, 46 N. E. 166.

[7] Hart v. Georgia R. R., 101 Ga. 188, 28 S. E. 637.

[8] Witham v. Cohen, 100 Ga. 670, 676, 28 S. E. 505.

tion for the loss of specific sales which he hoped to make, whether of goods [9] or of land,[10] nor for the loss of expected leases of real estate.[11] And future injuries which are possible results of the defendant's wrong, but are not established as reasonably certain to occur, cannot be considered.[12] In an action for delay by a theatrical troupe in beginning an entertainment plaintiff, for whom it was given, sought to recover damages because of loss of sale of tickets. It was held, however, that this loss was not sufficiently certain to form a ground of recovery.[13]

§ 170a. Absolute certainty not required as to amount of loss.

But where the existence of a loss is established, absolute certainty in proving its quantum is not required. The true rule on the subject is announced by the Supreme Court of Michigan in a well-reasoned case.[14] "Shall the injured party . . .

---

[9] *Georgia:* Bradstreet Co. v. Oswald, 96 Ga. 396, 23 S. E. 423.

Maryland: Western U. Tel. Co. v. N. Lehman & Bro., 106 Md. 318, 67 Atl. 241.

Michigan: Dowagiac Manuf. Co. v. Corbit, 127 Mich. 473, 86 N. W. 954, 87 N. W. 886.

Nebraska: Silurian Mineral Spring Co. v. Kuhn, 65 Neb. 646, 91 N. W. 508.

[10] Coos Bay, K. & E. R. R. & N. Co. v. Nosler, 30 Ore. 547, 48 Pac. 361.

But see Bannatyne v. Florence Milling & Mining Co., 77 Hun, 289, 28 N. Y. Supp. 334, where plaintiff was allowed to show the great probability of the sale.

[11] *Pennsylvania:* McConaghy v. Pemberton, 168 Pa. 121, 31 Atl. 996.

Texas: Clifford v. Leroux, 14 Tex. Civ. App. 340, 37 S. W. 172, 254.

[12] *Michigan:* Brininstool v. Michigan United Rys., 157 Mich. 172, 121 N. W. 728, 16 Detroit Leg. N. 340 (possible nervous breakdown).

New York: Johnson v. State, 116 N. Y. Supp. 253, 62 Misc. 15 (possible flooding of land); Osterhout v. Delaware, L. & W. R. R., 122 N. Y. Supp.

692, 138 App. Div. 625 (possible miscarriage).

[13] Alkahest Lyceum System v. Curry, 6 Ga. App. 625, 65 S. E. 580.

[14] Christiancy, J., in Allison v. Chandler, 11 Mich. 542, 555.

See to the same effect the following cases:

United States: Hetzel v. Baltimore & O. R. R., 169 U. S. 26, 42 L. ed. 648, 18 Sup. Ct. 255.

California: Holt Mfg. Co. v. Thornton, 136 Cal. 232, 68 Pac. 708.

Illinois: Baltimore & O. S. W. Ry. v. Then, 159 Ill. 535, 42 N. E. 971, affirming 59 Ill. App. 561; North Chicago St. R. R. v. Fitzgibbons, 180 Ill. 466, 54 N. E. 483.

Minnesota: First Nat. Bank v. St. Cloud, 73 Minn. 219, 75 N. W. 1054.

New York: Leach v. N. Y., N. H. & H. R. R., 89 Hun, 377, 35 N. Y. Supp. 305; Schriver v. Johnstown, 24 N. Y. Supp. 1083; Smalling v. Jackson, 133 App. Div. 382, 117 N. Y. Supp. 268.

Tennessee: East Tennessee, V. & G. R. R. v. Staub, 7 Lea, 397.

Washington: Jemo v. Tourist Hotel Co., 55 Wash. 595, 104 Pac. 820.

be allowed to recover no damages (or merely nominal) because he cannot show the exact amount with certainty, though he is ready to show, to the satisfaction of the jury, that he has suffered large damages by the injury? Certainty, it is true, would be thus attained; but it would be the certainty of injustice. . . . Juries are allowed to act upon probable and inferential, as well as direct and positive proof. And when, from the nature of the case, the amount of the damages cannot be estimated with certainty, or only a part of them can be so estimated, we can see no objection to placing before the jury all the facts and circumstances of the case, having any tendency to show damages, or their probable amount; so as to enable them to make the most intelligible and probable estimate which the nature of the case will permit." In Satchwell v. Williams,[15] Phelps, J., said that it was no objection that the defendant could only state his damage proximately, though it would be to show that his evidence was so vague and uncertain that the court could not deduce from it that the defendant had sustained any particular amount of damage.

Thus, in the extreme case, where the defendant has by his own wrong put it out of the plaintiff's power to prove the quantum of damage exactly, the presumption is against the defendant, and the burden is upon him to reduce the amount from the greatest possible amount.[16]

In an action for wrongful expulsion of plaintiff from the Brotherhood of Locomotive Engineers it appeared that by reason of the expulsion the plaintiff would probably lose the benefit of a policy of insurance in the order; and that each mem-

---

[15] 40 Conn. 371.

[16] *United States:* Montana Mining Co. v. St. Louis, M. & N. Co., 183 Fed. 51.

Indiana: Tea v. Gates, 10 Ind. 164; Kavanaugh v. Taylor, 2 Ind. App. 502, 28 N. E. 553 (potatoes).

England: Armory v. Delamirie, 1 Stra. 504 (jewel). So where goods having no market value are consigned to a broker for sale at a certain price, and he sells at a lower price, the plaintiff can recover the amount which he had instructed the broker to obtain, since there is no way of proving that the value of the goods was less. Blot v. Boiceau, 3 N. Y. 78, 51 Am. Dec. 345, n.

In Goltra v. Penland, 42 Ore. 18, 69 Pac. 925, an action for the conversion of sheep, where no evidence could be given as to the value of the individual sheep converted, plaintiff was allowed to show the value of ordinary sheep; acc., Fletcher v. Jacob Dodd Packing Co., 41 App. Div. 30, 58 N. Y. Supp. 612.

ber had, and by his expulsion he was deprived of, a "travelling card" which by the courtesy of all railroads in the United States and Canada would enable him to travel free. The value of these things was difficult of estimation; but the plaintiff was none the less entitled to compensation for their loss.[17] So in an action for injury to the good will of a business, the court said that in proving the value of the good will it was impossible to expect the certainty of proof that could be had in case of ordinary property, the best evidence the nature of the case admits is all that can be required.[18] And in a case where a woman suffered injuries which, according to the testimony, if she afterwards married, might affect her, the court said, it is true that she might never be married; but it is to be assumed that every physical endowment, function and capacity is of importance to the life of every man or woman and that occasion will arise for its exercise. When any function is destroyed or its discharge rendered painful or dangerous, the party is entitled to some damages.[19] In an action for a continuing nuisance the fact that part of the damage was suffered so long before the action as to be barred by the statute of limitations, and that it was very difficult to determine what portion had accrued within the period, did not bar recovery.[20]

§ 171. Best proof possible must be given.

But on the other hand where the amount of damage is susceptible of proof, proof must be offered; and if in such a case no proof of the quantum of damages is offered, recovery can be had for a nominal amount only.[21] Thus in Duke v.

---

[17] St. Louis S. W. Ry. v. Thompson, (Tex. Civ. App.), 108 S. W. 453.

[18] Burckhardt v. Burckhardt, 42 Ohio St. 474, 498, 51 Am. Rep. 842.

[19] Alabama Great Southern Ry. v. Hill, 93 Ala. 514, 9 So. 722, 30 Am. St. Rep. 65.

[20] Park v. Northport S. & R. Co, 47 Wash. 597, 92 Pac. 442.

[21] No recovery was allowed without evidence of value in these cases:

Injury to property:

Alabama: Birmingham R. L. & P. Co. v. Camp, 161 Ala. 456, 49 So. 846, (harness).

California: Johnson v. Levy, 86 Pac. 810, 3 Cal. App. 591 (rental value of livery stable).

Illinois: Joliet v. Fox, 135 Ill. App. 444 (nuisance to real estate).

Kansas: Brown v. Morris, 3 Kan. App. 86, 45 Pac. 98 (use of horses).

Pennsylvania: Forrest v. Buchanan, 203 Pa. 454, 52 Atl. 267.

Missouri Pacific Railway,[22] an action for personal injuries, nothing had been paid by the plaintiff on account of medical expenses, and no evidence was offered as to the value of the services rendered. The court said: "When such damages are susceptible of proof with approximate accuracy, and may be measured with some degree of certainty, they should not be left to the guess of the jury, even in actions *ex delicto*." In a similar case in New York,[23] where the plaintiff failed to prove the value of the time lost, the court said: "Where loss is pecuniary and is present and actual and can be measured, but no evidence is given showing its extent or from which it can be inferred, the jury can allow nominal damages only. For pain and suffering or injuries to the feelings there can be no measure of compensation save the arbitrary judgment of a jury. But that is a rule of necessity. Where actual pecuniary damages are sought some evidence must be given showing their existence and extent. If that is not done the jury cannot indulge in an arbitrary estimate of their own." And a general statement of loss, such as evidence that because of defendant's wrong plaintiff "had to pay more for goods than before and was unable to compete with other dealers" is insufficient.[24] But a minimum amount of damage may be sufficiently proved, and compensation for it recovered, though other damage is alleged but not proved definitely enough for recovery.[25]

Wisconsin: Anderson *v.* Savoy, 137 Wis. 44, 118 N. W. 217 (ice).

Loss of time:
Missouri: Shanahan *v.* Transit Co., 109 Mo. App. 228, 83 S. W. 783.

Pennsylvania: Olin *v.* Bradford, 24 Pa. Sup. Ct. 7.

Texas: Dallas Consol. Electric St. Ry. *v.* Motwiller, 109 S. W. 918, 101 Tex. 515 (stenographer).

Medical expenses:
Iowa: Reed *v.* Chicago, R. I. & P. R. R., 57 Iowa, 23, 10 N. W. 285; Eckerd *v.* Chicago & N. W. Ry., 70 Iowa, 353, 30 N. W. 615.

Texas: Fry *v.* Hillan, (Tex. Civ. App.), 37 S. W. 359; Gulf, C. & S. F. Ry. *v.* Craft, (Tex. Civ.

App.), 102 S. W. 170. See § 171 *a*, note.

For insufficient proof of damages for breach of contract, see § 610.

[22] 99 Mo. 347, 351.

[23] Leeds *v.* Metropolitan G. L. Co., 90 N. Y. 26; Danforth and Tracy, JJ., diss. And see *acc.*, Wood *v.* Watertown, 11 N.Y. Supp. 864; Page *v.* Delaware & H. C. Co., 54 N. Y. Supp. 442; Mabrey *v.* Cape Girardeau & J. G. R. R., 42 Mo. App. 596.

[24] Ziegenheim *v.* Baltimore Wholesale Grocery Co., 108 Md. 515, 69 Atl. 1071.

[25] Hitson *v.* Hurt, 45 Tex. Civ. App. 360, 101 S. W. 292.

§ 171a. **Value found by jury without evidence.**
But while this is the doctrine generally accepted, there are nevertheless many cases (often from the same jurisdiction where the stricter rule has been laid down) in which, no evidence of value having been offered, the jury is allowed to find the value upon their general knowledge. This is of course necessarily so in cases where no evidence of value can be given, as in the case of pain and suffering, physical or mental;[26] inconvenience,[27] or loss of society,[28] but it has been extended to cover cases of purely pecuniary injury.[29] So in Feeney v. Long Island Railroad[30] where the number of times a physician had visited the plaintiff was shown, but not the value of his services, it was held that the jury must give at least a nominal amount on account of medical expenses, and if no instruction was asked by the defendant on the subject the latter could not object to a reasonable amount found by the jury on account of medical expenses; and in many cases the jury have

[26] *Idaho:* Tarr v. Oregon Short Line Ry., 14 Ida. 192, 93 Pac. 957.
Illinois: Pratt v. Davis, 224 Ill. 300, 79 N. E. 562, 7 L. R. A. (N. S.) 609.
Michigan: Rice v. Rice, 104 Mich. 371, 62 N. W. 833.
Texas: Galveston, H. & S. A. Ry. v. Garrett, 44 Tex. Civ. App. 406, 98 S. W. 932; Missouri, K. & T. Ry. v. Linton, (Tex. Civ. App.), 109 S. W. 942; Houston & T. C. Ry. v. Maxwell, (Tex. Civ. App.), 128 S. W. 160.
In Rice v. Rice, *supra*, Grant, J., said:
"They are not capable of accurate measurement, and it is not necessary to introduce any evidence of value. When the jury have before them the social standing and character of the parties, and the circumstances surrounding the wrong done, they have all that is proper and necessary upon which to find a verdict."
[27] International & G. N. R. R. v. Stewart, (Tex. Civ. App.), 101 S. W. 282.

[28] Northern Tex. Traction Co. v. Mullins, 44 Tex. Civ. App. 556, 99 S. W. 433.
[29] *Georgia:* Atlantic C. L. R. R. v. Moore, (Ga. App.), 68 S. E. 875 (expectancy of life).
Illinois: Schaffner v. Ehrman, 139 Ill. 109, 28 N. E. 917, 32 Am. St. Rep. 192 (injury to business reputation).
New York: Ward v. Vanderbilt, 4 Abb. Dec. 521 (time).
Pennsylvania: J. Schlitz Brewing Co. v. McCann, 118 Pa. 314, 12 Atl. 445 (loss of custom); Hartman v. Pittsburgh Incline Co., 159 Pa. 442, 28 Atl. 145 (cost of repairing damage to house).
In Post v. Munn, 4 N. J. L. 61, 7 Am. Dec. 570, an action for interference with plaintiff's right of fishery by direct trespass on the net, where by reason of loss of use of the net the plaintiff lost the run of fish, it was held that he could recover damages for loss of the run of the shad, though no evidence appears to have been offered as to the value of the run.
[30] 116 N. Y. 375.

been allowed to place a value on services from their own general knowledge.[31] How far the courts may differ as to what matters may properly be left to a jury is illustrated by the course of decision on the question whether a jury may without evidence place a value on medical services.[32]

[31] *California:* Washington v. Pacific E. R. R., 11 Cal. App. 589, 112 Pac. 904 (woman physician).

Georgia: Augusta v. Owens, 111 Ga. 464, 36 S. E. 830 (laborer).

Illinois: Chicago Wire Chair Co. v. Kennedy & Wright Co., 141 Ill. App. 196 (solicitor).

Missouri: Murray v.   R. R., 101 Mo. 236 (nurse); Loe v. Chicago, R. I. & P. Ry., 57 Mo. App. 350; Drogmund v. Metropolitan St. Ry., 122 Mo. App. 154, 98 S. W. 1091 (nurse).

Texas: Gulf, C. & S. F. Ry. v. Booth, 97 S. W. 128, (Tex. Civ. App.) (wife).

Washington: Curtley v. Security Sav. Soc., 51 Wash. 242, 98 Pac. 667 (attorney).

So the jury in the following cases was allowed to estimate the loss caused by permanent diminution of capacity to labor.

Georgia: Atlanta & W. P. R. R. v. Haralson, 133 Ga. 231, 65 S. E. 437; Southern Ry. v. Petway, 7 Ga. App. 659, 67 S. E. 886.

Kansas: Missouri, K. & T. Ry. v. Fowler, 61 Kan. 320, 59 Pac. 648.

In Ihl v. Forty-second St. & G. S. F. R. R., 47 N. Y. 317, 7 Am. Rep. 450, the jury having seen the parents and been informed of their position in life was allowed to find the value of the life of their child killed by defendant's negligence.

On the other hand, the jury was not allowed to find damages without specific evidence of value in the following cases:

Michigan: Britton v. Street Ry., 90 Mich. 159, 51 N. W. 276 (impairment of capacity to labor).

Missouri: Woodward v. Donnell, 146 Mo. App. 119, 123 S. W. 1004 (services of dentist's assistant); Brake v. Kansas City, (Mo. App.), 75 S. W. 191 (time of married woman).

New York: Friedman v. Horn, 104 N. Y. Supp. 745 (services of wife).

West Virginia: Rodgers v. Bailey, (W. Va.), 69 S. E. 698 (value of support of husband).

See ante, § 171, note.

[32] In some jurisdictions it has been held that, the character of the services being shown, the jury may on their own knowledge, without evidence, find the value of such services.

Arkansas: St. Louis, I. M. & S. R. R. v. Stell, 87 Ark. 308, 112 S. W. 876.

Kentucky: Frankfort & V. T. Co. v. Hulette, 32 Ky. L. Rep. 732, 106 S. W. 1193.

Massachusetts: Scullane v. Kellogg, 169 Mass. 544, 48 N. E. 622; McGarrahan v. New York, N. H. & H. R. R., 171 Mass. 211, 50 N. E. 610.

New Hampshire: Moran v. Dover, S. & R. S. Ry., 74 N. H. 500, 69 Atl. 884, 19 L. R. A. (N. S.) 920.

New York: Feeney v. Long Island R. R., 116 N. Y. 375, 22 N. E. 402, 5 L. R. A. 544; but see Carter v. Nunda, 55 App. Div. 501, 66 N. Y. Supp. 1059.

South Carolina: Farley v. Charleston, B. & V. Co., 51 S. C. 222, 28 S. E. 193.

In most jurisdictions, however, evidence of the value of the services must be given; and in the absence of such evidence no recovery can be had on account of loss of the services.

Illinois: Joliet v. Henry, 11 Ill. App. 154.

Indiana: Chicago, S. L. & P. R. R. v. Butler, 10 Ind. App. 244, 38 N. E. 1.

The true doctrine would seem to lie between the extreme views expressed. A certain minimum of loss must inevitably follow from certain injuries, and a jury upon its own knowledge might well find a loss equal to this minimum; but beyond that amount no verdict should be found without the production of the best evidence possible under the circumstances.

In one class of cases the court gives substantial damages without proof, in a matter not particularly within the knowledge of a jury. Where a bank refuses wrongfully to honor the check of a depositor substantial damages are given to a trader without any proof of actual damage,[33] because in many cases it is impossible to prove the actual extent of the damage. The case is analogous to that of slander when the words affect the plaintiff in his trade or profession; for they always *import* injury, and in many cases it is impossible to show any actual *special* damage. In exactly the same way, if the plaintiff is a trader or merchant, the theory of the law is that dishonoring his check or draft imports damage; and therefore a substantial verdict may be recovered without further proof. They seem to constitute an exceptional class of cases; for the trial court itself will reduce the damages if they are not reasonably within bounds as to amount; and hence courts

Iowa: Reed v. Chicago, R. I. & P. R. R., 57 Ia. 23, 10 N. W. 285; Bowsher v. Chicago, B. & Q. R. R., 113 Ia. 16, 84 N. W. 958.

Kansas: Cudahy Packing Co. v. Broadbent, 70 Kan. 535, 79 Pac. 126.

Missouri: Duke v. Missouri Pac. R. R., 99 Mo. 347, 12 S. W. 636; Smith v. Chicago & A. R. R., 108 Mo. 243, 18 S. W. 971; Gibler v. Terminal R. R. Assoc., 203 Mo. 208, 101 S. W. 37; Nelson v. Metropolitan S. R. R., 113 Mo. App. 659, 88 S. W. 781; Grattan v. Suedmeyer, 144 Mo. App. 719, 129 S. W. 1038.

Pennsylvania: Brown v. White, 202 Pa. 297, 51 Atl. 962, 58 L. R. A. 321.

Texas: Wheeler v. Tyler S. W. R. R., 91 Tex. 356, 43 S. W. 876; Houston & T. C. R. R. v. Cheatham (Tex. Civ. App.), 113 S. W. 777.

Washington: Olson v. Erickson, 53 Wash. 458, 102 Pac. 400.

[33] *Georgia:* Atlanta Nat. Bank v. Davis, 96 Ga. 334, 23 S. E. 190; Hilton v. Jesup Banking Co., 128 Ga. 30, 57 S. E. 78, 11 L. R. A. (N. S.) 224.

Illinois: Schaffner v. Ehrman, 139 Ill. 109, 28 N. E. 917.

Pennsylvania: Patterson v. Marine Nat. Bank, 130 Pa. 419, 18 Atl. 632, 17 Am. St. Rep. 779.

Tennessee: J. M. James Co. v. Continental Nat. Bank, 105 Tenn. 1, 58 S. W. 261, 51 L. R. A. 255.

England: Marzetti v. Williams, 1 B. & A. 415; Rolin v. Steward, 14 C. B. 595; Prehn v. Royal Bank, L. R. 5 Ex. 92; Fleming v. Bank of New Zealand, [1900] A. C. 577.

have adopted the rule in dealing with the jury that they must be "temperate." This doctrine is confined to actions against a bank; it cannot be invoked in an action against a telegraph company for failure to deliver a telegram calling for the payment of money by the company.[34]

§ 171b. Alternative rules of damages.

It may often happen that there are alternative methods of estimating the amount of a particular loss, of which one must be discarded as too uncertain, while the other may be accepted as sufficiently certain to be allowed. Thus the loss occasioned by lack of money might be measured by the loss of profits that might have been made by its use, or by the current rate of interest; the former is usually too uncertain, and the latter is the normal rule.[35] So for the loss of use of land, the rental value is recovered rather than the expected profits from the use; [36] and for the use of a machine, the value of its use rather than the value of the expected product.[37] But in all these cases the alternative rule may come into play where the objection of uncertainty in view of the particular facts of the case disappears. In the cases referred to in this chapter numerous illustrations of this principle will be found; and the elasticity of the law in respect to the measure of damages disclosed by it deserves careful attention, because it is one of the features which strikingly discriminates any survey of the whole law of compensation as it exists to-day, from the same law as it existed before the differences between the old common-law forms of action lost their importance, owing to the introduction of modern reformed procedure. Before that time the effort of the courts was to find for each *separate form of action* an appropriate measure of damages. This was inevitable, for each form suited only one particular state of facts, and if the facts developed on the trial were not adapted to the form the appropriate rule could not be applied and there was no other; but now that the rule applied is merely that one which is adapted to the facts as developed by the

---

[34] Smith *v.* Western U. Tel. Co., 150 Pa. 561, 24 Atl. 1049.

[35] *Post,* § 179.

[36] *Post,* § 184.

[37] *Post,* § 190.

proof, there is obviously a frequent choice between two or three different rules according as one measure or another is capable or not of being proved with certainty.

There are in fact, as the proof develops, different rules of damages for the same species of injury. "Cases not unfrequently occur in which . . . it is certain that some loss has been sustained, or damage incurred, and that such loss or damage is the direct, immediate, and natural consequence of the breach of contract, but where the amount of the damages may be estimated in a variety of ways. In all such cases the law, in strict conformity to the principles already advanced, uniformly adopts that mode of estimating the damages which is most definite and certain."[38]

Illustrations will be found in every branch of the law. For the breach of a contract the alternative may be profits on the one hand, or the value of the plaintiff's time;[39] or instead of the value of the plaintiff's time, the hire of a chattel of which he has been deprived may be given him. Again, he may recover rent or on the other hand interest. When the value of the use of a thing fails interest may be substituted as more capable of proof; or the difference between actual and contract value may be resorted to in one case, where in another the net value of a contract, less expenses of performance, may be awarded.[40]

And finally on a survey of the whole subject, the ultimate alternative, which first found definition in the Roman law comes into view—the alternative which exhausts the law of compensation—*Lucrum Cessans, Damnum Emergens*—loss suffered; gain prevented.

§ 172. Prospective loss.

Where the injury is in the nature of a loss inflicted, the amount may generally be proved without any uncertainty. The chief difficulty experienced is in cases of prospective loss. When the plaintiff claims compensation for consequences of

---

[38] Per Seldon, J., in Griffin *v.* Colver, 16 N. Y. 489, 495, 69 Am. Dec. 718, *n.*
[39] Howe S. M. Co. *v.* Bryson, 44 Ia. 159, 163, 24 Am. Rep. 735.

[40] For further illustrations, see Sedg. El. Dam. 21.

the injury which he has not yet experienced, he must prove with reasonable certainty that such consequences are to happen; [41] and compensation is not to be given where there is a mere conjectural probability of future loss. [42] The jury has no right to allow damages for mere possibilities. [43]

"Future consequences, which are reasonably to be expected to follow an injury, may be given in evidence for the purpose of enhancing the damages to be awarded. But to entitle such apprehended consequences to be considered by the jury, they must be such as in the ordinary course of nature are reasonably certain to ensue. Consequences which are contingent, speculative, or merely possible, are not proper to be considered in ascertaining the damages. . . . To entitle a plaintiff to recover present damages for apprehended future consequences, there must be such a degree of probability of their occurring, as amounts to a reasonable certainty that they will result from the original injury." [44]

So in an action on the case against a railroad company, for injuries resulting from a collision, the plaintiff proved that his leg was broken, and that the oblique character of

[41] *California:* De Costa v. Massachusetts F. W. & M. Co., 17 Cal. 613.

Iowa: Fry v. Dubuque & S. Ry., 45 Ia. 416.

New York: Lincoln v. Saratoga & S. R. R., 23 Wend. 425; Staal v. Grand St. & N. R. R., 107 N. Y. 625, 13 N. E. 624.

Texas: Houston, E. & W. T. Ry. v. Richards, 20 Tex. Civ. App. 203, 49 S. W. 687.

[42] *United States:* Chicago & N. W. Ry. v. De Clow, 124 Fed. 142, 61 C. C. A. 34; Chicago, M. & St. P. Ry. v. Lindeman, 143 Fed. 946, 75 C. C. A. 18; Daigneau v. Grand Trunk Ry., 153 Fed. 593; Chicago, M. & St. P. Ry. v. Newsome, 154 Fed. 665, 83 C. C. A. 422.

Alabama: Rutledge v. Rowland, 161 Ala. 114, 49 So. 461.

California: Cordiner v. Los Angeles Tr. Co., 5 Cal. App. 400, 91 Pac. 436.

Illinois: Chicago C. Ry. v. Henry, 62 Ill. 142; Amann v. Chicago Consol. Traction Co., 243 Ill. 263, 90 N. E. 673; Knickerbocker Ice Co. v. Leyda, 128 Ill. App. 66.

Massachusetts: Pullen v. Boston E. Ry. (Mass.), 94 N. E. 469.

Nebraska: Carlile v. Bentley, 81 Neb. 715, 116 N. W. 772.

Texas: Rapid Transit Ry. v. Allen, (Tex. Civ. App.), 117 S. W. 486.

Washington: Ongaro v. Twohy, 49 Wash. 93, 94 Pac. 916.

Wisconsin: Block v. Milwaukee St. Ry., 89 Wis. 371, 61 N. W. 1101; Raymond v. Keseberg, 91 Wis. 191, 64 N. W. 861.

[43] Fry v. Dubuque & S. Ry., 45 Ia. 416.

[44] Rapallo, J., in Strohm v. New York, L. E. & W. R. R., 96 N. Y. 305, 306; Blate v. Third Ave. R. R., 44 N. Y. Supp. 615; Savage v. Third Ave. R. R., 54 N. Y. Supp. 932.

the fracture rendered it very probable that a second fracture would take place; but this the Supreme Court of New York held too remote. The present and probable future condition of the limb were proper matters for inquiry; but the consequences of an hypothetical second fracture were obviously beyond the range of it, and calculated to draw the minds of the jury into fanciful conjectures.[45]   So where the plaintiff was bitten by defendant's dog, and received a wound which would leave a scar and cause disfigurement, it was held that the plaintiff, who was a girl five years old, could not recover compensation for loss of the opportunity of marriage, as the matter was too uncertain.[46]   And where a switchman on a railroad was injured, it was held that the jury could not consider, in estimating his loss, the probability of future promotion, as the matter was too uncertain.[47]   The reasonable certainty required, however, does not mean absolute certainty, but reasonable probability.[48]

§ 172a. Future effects of personal injury.

Where no evidence appeared as to the circumstances and condition in life of the plaintiff, his earning power, skill or capacity, no damages could be awarded for future pecuniary loss.[49]   But the fact and amount of future loss is a question for the jury,[50] which has discretion in estimating it,[51] and in cases of personal injury will give damages for future pain and suffering and for impairment of physical or mental power

---

[45] Lincoln v. Saratoga & S. R. R., 23 Wend. (N. Y.) 425.

[46] Price v. Wright, 35 N. Brunsw. 26.

[47] Richmond & D. R. R. v. Elliott, 149 U. S. 266, 37 L. ed. 728, 13 Sup. Ct. 837.

[48] *Iowa:* Huggard v. Glucose Sugar Refining Co., 132 Ia. 724, 109 N. W. 475; Witt v. Town of Latimer, 139 Ia. 273, 117 N. W. 680.

New York: Griswold v. New York C. & H. R. R. R., 115 N. Y. 61, 21 N. E. 726, 12 Am. St. Rep. 775 (explaining Strohm v. Ry.); Feeney v. Long Island R. R., 116 N. Y. 375, 22 N. E. 402.

Washington: Rowe v. Whatcom County Ry. & Light Co., 44 Wash. 458, 87 Pac. 921.

[49] Staal v. Grand St. & N. R. R., 107 N. Y. 627, 13 N. E. 624

[50] Colby v. Wiscasset, 61 Me. 304.

[51] Union P. Ry. v. Dunden, 37 Kan. 1. If the evidence shows that the disabilities have lasted up to the time of trial, the necessary inference is that they will last some time longer, and expert testimony is not indispensable to the determination of the question by the jury. Union Pac. Ry. v. Jones, 4 U. S. App. 115, 49 Fed. 343.

which are proved with reasonable probability.[52] So the value of loss of future support and earning capacity can be estimated in a statutory action for causing death of a husband,[53] parent,[54] or child.[55] It is, however, held in actions for defamation that prospective damages for injury to reputation cannot be recovered,[56] for the verdict heals the reputation.[57]

§ 173. Gain prevented—Profits.

Where an injured party claims compensation for gain prevented, the amount of loss is always to some extent conjectural; for there is no way of proving that what might have been, would have been. Thus, when the claim is made for compensation for a deprivation of property, it may be that if the property had remained in the owner's control it would have brought no gain. When the compensation claimed is for loss of earnings through a personal injury, it might have been impossible for the injured party, if uninjured, to earn anything. The question of certainty of loss, therefore, arises in all cases of gain prevented (the *lucrum cessans* of the civil law). The word *profits* is often loosely used in the sense of gain prevented; and this use of the word has caused confusion in the cases. Much would be gained by restricting the use of the word to the gains of business ventures; but so firmly fixed is the looser use that both meanings are to be borne in mind. In speaking of profits as damages a court may mean either the wages a man could earn, the rent or value of use of property, the advantages of a contract, or the true profits of a business.

---

[52] *Illinois:* Donk Bros. Coal & Coke Co. *v.* Thil, 81 N. E. 857, 228 Ill. 233 (affirming 128 Ill. App. 249).

Missouri: Rosenkranz *v.* Lindell Ry., 108 Mo. 9, 18 S. W. 890; Wilkerson *v.* Met. St. Ry., 126 Mo. App. 613, 105 S. W. 24; Frazier *v.* St. Louis Smelting & Refining Co., 150 Mo. App. 419, 130 S. W. 485.

New York: Ayres *v.* Delaware, L. & W. R. R., 158 N. Y. 254, 35 N. E. 22.

South Carolina: Green *v.* Catawba Power Co., 55 S. E. 125, 75 S. C. 102.

Texas: Indust. L. Co. *v.* Bivens, 47 Tex. Civ. App. 396, 105 S. W. 831.

[53] Lawson *v.* Chicago, St. P., M. & O. Ry., 64 Wis. 447, 24 N. W. 618, 54 Am. Rep. 634.

[54] Eames *v.* Brattleboro, 54 Vt. 471.

[55] Houghkirk *v.* Delaware & H. C. Co., 92 N. Y. 219, 44 Am. Rep. 370; Hoppe *v.* Chicago, M. & St. P. Ry., 61 Wis. 357; Johnson *v.* Chicago & N. W. Ry., 64 Wis. 425.

[56] Bradley *v.* Cramer, 66 Wis. 297.

[57] Halstead *v.* Nelson, 24 Hun, 395.

§ 174. Allowance of profits, how regulated.

The allowance of profits, when not excluded as unnatural or remote, is wholly a question of the certainty of proof. Wherever there is an interference with, or withholding of property, or breach of contract, or commission of a tort, the gain prevented, if provable, may be recovered. As a general rule, the *expected* profits of a business cannot be proved and therefore cannot be recovered. They might have been made, and they might not. Instead of profits there might have been losses. Hence in such cases the measure of damages is, not the expected profits, but the average value of the use of the land, property, or business, and to ascertain this, evidence of actual past profits must be admissible.[58] This bears a close analogy to the ordinary rule with regard to money. Expected profits from the use of money cannot be recovered. The measure of damages is the average value of the use, or in other words, interest. Going a step further, we shall find that whenever expected profits become capable of certain proof, then they can be recovered.

Thus in all actions for breach of contract in which the value of a sub-contract is allowed, and in all actions against carriers for the loss of specific personal property when the market value at the time and place of destination is given, and in all actions by the vendee for failure to deliver property sold, where the difference between price and market value is allowed, the plaintiff really recovers the specific profit lost, or gain prevented. In cases in which the plaintiff does not recover gain prevented or profits, or the value of the use, he should be allowed at all events the expenses to which he has been put by the tort of breach of contract.

§ 175. Early cases.

The early cases, in both the English and American courts, generally concurred in denying profits as any part of the damages to be compensated, and that, whether in cases of contract or of tort. So in a case of illegal capture, Mr. Justice Story rejected the item of profits on the voyage, and held this gen-

---

[58] John Hutchinson Mfg. Co. *v.* Pinch, 91 Mich. 156, 51 N. W. 930, 30 Am. St. Rep. 463.

eral language: "Independent, however, of all authority, I am satisfied upon principle that an allowance of damages upon the basis of a calculation of profits is inadmissible. The rule would be in the highest degree unfavorable to the interests of the community. The subject would be involved in utter uncertainty. The calculation would proceed upon contingencies, and would require a knowledge of foreign markets to an exactness, in point of time and value, which would sometimes present embarrassing obstacles. Much would depend upon the length of the voyage and the season of the arrival, much upon the vigilance and activity of the master, and much upon the momentary demand. After all, it would be a calculation upon conjecture, and not upon facts. Such a rule, therefore, has been rejected by courts of law in ordinary cases; and instead of deciding upon the gains or losses of parties in particular cases, an uniform interest has been applied as the measure of damages for the detention of property." [59]

So where a privateer had improperly detained a merchant vessel, and taken out her crew, in consequence of which she was lost, it was held by the Supreme Court of the United States, that the owners of the privateer were liable only for the value of the vessel, the prime cost of the cargo, with all charges, and the premium of insurance.[60]

So in the same court, where a privateer had improperly boarded a vessel and taken away her papers, in consequence of which her voyage was broken up, it was held that the owners were not liable for the loss of profits on the intended voyage, nor for loss by deterioration of the cargo which was not caused by the improper conduct of the captors.[61] And in a similar case,[62] the same principle was applied to a claim for damages for loss of a market.

So in Massachusetts, in an action of trespass against a deputy sheriff, for taking a schooner of the plaintiff under an attachment against a third party, there being some evi-

[59] The Schooner Lively, 1 Gall. 315.
[60] The Anna Maria, 2 Wheat. 327, 4 L. ed. 252.

[61] The Amiable Nancy, 3 Wheat. 546, 4 L. ed. 456.
[62] La Amistad de Rues, 5 Wheat. 385, 5 L. ed. 44.

dence that she was preparing for a voyage, and there being no malice on the part of the defendant, the jury were instructed to estimate her value at the time of taking, and "the additional damage sustained, if any." But it was held by the Supreme Court, that this would not justify the jury in assessing damages for the breaking up of the voyage.[63]

So in a case of collision between vessels, it has been held that the owner of the injured vessel cannot recover for profits on the voyage broken up by the accident.[64]

These cases were at one time cited as of general authority in cases involving the allowance of profits. But they probably should not be so considered. With the exception of the Massachusetts case, where profits were properly disallowed as conjectural, they are cases where a voyage was interrupted, and the court refused to allow expected profits upon the cargo. The loss having occurred on the high seas, the value of the cargo at that place was taken; and as the most certain basis of value, the prime cost was shown, and the freight and charges added to it.[65] Moreover, at that time every mercantile voyage was more or less a speculative venture, and hence profits were as a matter of fact conjectural, where through the introduction of steam and the telegraph, they have now become almost a matter of certainty. The preceding cases are therefore not to be regarded as authorities upon the allowance of profits generally.

§ 176. Profits recoverable if proximate, natural, and certain.

The plaintiff may now, in all proper cases, show a gain

[63] Boyd v. Brown, 17 Pick. (Mass.) 453.

[64] Smith v. Condry, 1 How. 28, 11 L. ed. 219; acc., Minor v. Steamboat Picayune No. 2, 13 La. Ann. 564. In the original text of this work, the author said of these cases: "It may well be doubted whether the language of some of the earlier American cases which I have cited has not pushed the rule beyond the true line. The analogies of the law have certainly not been regarded. If on a contract to deliver goods at a distant point, their value at the place of delivery is the true criterion; if on a contract for the sale of chattels, the market price on the day fixed for delivery is the true measure of damage, it is difficult to assign a reason why the same rule should not be applied to the breaking up of a voyage actually commenced, nor why the victim of an illegal capture should be limited to the prime cost of his cargo."

[65] See the chapters on Insurance and Torts in Admiralty.

prevented as a ground for compensation. It must, of course as has been seen in the last chapter, be a natural and proximate consequence of the injury; it must also, as will be seen in this chapter, be a certain consequence of the injury. But if a plaintiff is not allowed to recover compensation for a gain prevented, it must be either because the failure to realize the gain is too remote and unlooked-for a consequence of the injury, or because it is uncertain whether the gain would have been realized; and not because the gain was in the nature of an expected profit.

In the leading case on the subject,[66] Selden, J., said of the supposed rule that profits could not be a basis for recovery:

"It is not a primary rule, but is a mere deduction from that more general and fundamental rule which requires that the damages claimed should in all cases be shown, by clear and satisfactory evidence, to have been actually sustained. It is a well-established rule of the common law, that the damages to be recovered for a breach of contract must be shown with certainty, and not left to speculation or conjecture; and it is under this rule that profits are excluded from the estimate of damages in such cases, and not because there is anything in their nature which should *per se* prevent their allowance. Profits which would certainly have been realized but for the defendant's default, are recoverable; those which are speculative and contingent are not."

He cited, as instances of profits being allowed, cases where a common carrier or a vendor fails to deliver goods, in which case their market value at the place of delivery determines the damages, though that is an allowance of profits. He again said (p. 492):

"Indeed, it is clear that whenever profits are rejected as an item of damages, it is because they are subject to too many contingencies, and are too dependent upon the fluctuations of markets and the chances of business to constitute a safe criterion for an estimate of damages."

And a few pages later (p. 494):

"The broad, general rule in such cases is, that the party injured is entitled to recover all his damages, including gains

[66] Griffin *v.* Colver, 16 N. Y. 489, 491, 69 Am. Dec. 718, *n.*

prevented as well as losses sustained; and this rule is subject to but two conditions: the damages must be such as may fairly be supposed to have entered into the contemplation of the parties when they made the contract, that is, must be such as might naturally be expected to follow its violation; and they must be certain, both in their nature and in respect to the cause from which they proceed."

In Brigham *v.* Carlisle[67] the court said: "Profits are not excluded from recovery because they are *profits;* but, when excluded, it is on the ground that there are no *criteria* by which to estimate the amount with the certainty on which the adjudications of courts, and the findings of juries, should be based."

§ 177. General rule.

The general rule is, then, that a plaintiff may recover compensation for any gain which he can make it appear with reasonable certainty the defendant's wrongful act prevented him from acquiring; subject, of course, to the general principles as to remoteness, compensation, etc., already stated. His compensation will be measured by the most liberal scale which he can show to be a proper one. Damages for interruption of the business of a manufacturer, for instance, may be measured either by the rental value of the property kept unproductive, or by profits of manufacture lost if the plaintiff can show that they would have been greater than the rental value. The questions that arise in the cases are therefore questions of sufficiency of proof, and it is to be expected that the courts will not in all cases agree in their interpretation of facts; but the decisions show, under the circumstances, a surprising degree of harmony.

§ 178. Cases of entire loss do not fall within the rule.

It is important to observe that actions brought for the immediate destruction of property do not involve any question of gain prevented. If compensation is asked for destruction, that is, for the whole value of the property, it is upon the theory that the plaintiff's entire interest in the property

[67] 78 Ala. 243, 249, 56 Am. Rep. 28, per Clopton, J.

ceased at the time of the injury, and was replaced by a right to have the value of the property in money. Since, therefore, the plaintiff no longer has title to the property, he can no longer claim that he might make a future gain from it; and his recovery is limited to the value of the property at the time and place of destruction, with interest.[68] If the injury does not extinguish the plaintiff's title, he has a right to compensation for the loss of any use he might rightfully make of the property, subject to the other general principles of the law of damages.[69] The probable aggregate value of such uses, that is, the gain prevented, is therefore a subject for compensation only when the injury leaves the title to the thing injured in the plaintiff.

A misapprehension of the true distinction has led to a few decisions that must be pointed out as unsound. Thus, in an action on a contract to build a steamboat, where the breach was delay in delivering the vessel, the court allowed interest on the value of the vessel at the time and place it should have been delivered, from that time until the delivery actually took place.[70] Where through a defect a boiler manufactured by the defendant exploded and injured the plaintiff's mill, it was held that interest on the money expended in repairs (that is, on the *loss sustained*) was all that could be recovered on account of gains prevented.[71]

An example of the proper application of this principle is found in a Wisconsin case. A machine was destroyed in transit. The owner was allowed to recover the value of the machine; but no compensation for being out of the use of it, which he would have had if the action had been for delay in delivery.[72] So where the plaintiff's horse was drowned in consequence of a collision of canal boats, it was held wrong to allow, besides the value of the horse and interest on that value, the expense of hiring another horse to tow the plaintiff's boat to its place

[68] McKnight *v.* Ratcliff, 44 Pa. 156; Erie C. I. W. *v.* Barber, 106 Pa. 125.

[69] Choctaw, O. & G. R. R. *v.* Alexander, 7 Okla. 579, 52 Pac. 944.

[70] Taylor *v.* Maguire, 12 Mo. 313.

[71] Erie C. I. W. *v.* Barber, 102 Pa. 156, 51 Am. Rep. 508; but on a later consideration of the same case, damages for loss of use were allowed; 106 Pa. 125.

[72] Thomas B. & W. M. Co. *v.* Wabash, St. L. & P. Ry., 62 Wis. 642, 51 Am. Rep. 725.

of destination.[73] But although in this class of actions the value of property destroyed, with interest for the time the owner was deprived of it, will compensate him for the loss if no special or extraordinary damage occurred, yet if the injury not only caused a loss of property, but also other proximate loss, further compensation should be given to that extent.

§ 179. Gain expected from the use of money.

Where an injury consists of a deprivation of money, the compensation established by the business practice of many generations is the current rate of interest; and such is the measure of damages adopted by the law. The profits which might have been made by the use of the money are too conjectural to be considered.[74]

In an action for the non-payment of money, in which the plaintiffs claimed damages for profits they expected to realize from the use of the money, the Supreme Court of Massachusetts said:[75] "In the use of money, instead of realizing great profits, they [the plaintiffs] might have encountered difficulties and sustained injuries unforeseen at the time, and have suffered, like thousands of others. Theirs is not a loss, in the just sense of the term, but the deprivation of an opportunity for making money, which might have proved beneficial, or might have been ruinous; and it is of that uncertain character, which is not to be weighed in the even balances of the law, nor to be ascertained by well-established rules of computation among merchants."

The principles governing the allowance of interest as damages for non-payment of money will be considered later.[76]

---

[73] Edwards v. Beebe, 48 Barb. 106.

[74] *United States:* Levinski v. Middlesex Banking Co., 92 Fed. 449, 34 C. C. A. 452 (contract to loan money for building house; expected profits from renting cannot be recovered).

Illinois: Hoblit v. Bloomington, 71 Ill. App. 204.

Kentucky: Carsey v. Farmer, 117 Ky. 826, 79 S. W. 245, 25 Ky. L. R. 1965 (breach of contract to advance money to buy tobacco; expected profits of purchase cannot be recovered).

New York: Goldsmith v. Holland Trust Co., 5 App. Div. 104, 38 N. Y. Supp. 1032 (breach of contract to loan money for buying land; cannot recover expected profits of purchase).

Pennsylvania: Delp v. Edlis, 190 Pa. 25, 42 Atl. 462 (failure of partner to advance capital).

[75] Greene v. Goddard, 9 Met. (Mass.) 212, 232, per Hubbard, J.

[76] Chapter XV.

§ 180. Loss through injury to capacity for labor.

When a person is so injured as to interrupt his earnings, he is entitled to recover compensation for his loss of time;[77] that is, for the income which he would have received from his labor during the time lost. The safest way of estimating the loss, adopted in ordinary cases, is to give him the market value of his labor; that is, the average earnings of such a person expressed in wages or salary. If the plaintiff is an ordinary workman, whose labor has an established value in the market, he may, for loss of opportunity to labor, recover the amount a workman in his line of employment would have received.[78] So in a suit for freedom a negro has been held entitled to

[77] *United States:* Wade v. Leroy, 20 How. 34, 15 L. ed. 813; Carpenter v. Mexican N. R. R., 39 Fed. 315.

Alabama: South & N. A. R. R. v. McLendon, 63 Ala. 266.

District of Columbia: Larmon v. District, 16 D. C. 5 Mackey) 330.

Illinois: Pierce v. Millay, 44 Ill. 189; Chicago & A. R. R. v. Wilson, 63 Ill. 167; Chicago v. Jones, 66 Ill. 349; Chicago v. Langlass, 66 Ill. 361; Chicago v. Elzeman, 71 Ill. 131; Sheridan v. Hibbard, 119 Ill. 307; Joliet v. Conway, 119 Ill. 489; Amann v. Chicago Consol. Tract. Co., 148 Ill. App. 151.

Indiana: Indianapolis v. Gaston, 58 Ind. 224.

Iowa: McKinley v. Chicago & N. W. Ry., 44 Ia. 314; Stafford v. Oskaloosa, 64 Ia. 251.

Kansas: Tefft v. Wilcox, 6 Kan. 46; Kansas P. Ry. v. Pointer, 9 Kan. 620; Missouri, K. & T. Ry. v. Weaver, 16 Kan. 456.

Kentucky: Kentucky C. R. R. v. Ackley, 87 Ky. 278, 8 S. W. 691, 12 Am. St. Rep. 480.

Louisiana: Rutherford v. Shreveport & H. R. R., 41 La. Ann. 793.

Massachusetts: Jordan v. Middlesex R. R., 138 Mass. 425; Stynes v. Boston E. Ry., 206 Mass. 75, 91 N. E. 998.

Mississippi: Memphis & C. R. R. v. Whitfield, 44 Miss. 466, 7 Am. Rep. 699, n.

Missouri: Stephens v. Hannibal & S. J. R. R., 96 Mo. 207, 9 S. W. 589, 9 Am. St. Rep. 336, n.

Nevada: Cohen v. Eureka & P. R. R., 14 Nev. 376.

New York: Sheehan v. Edgar, 58 N. Y. 631; Clifford v. Dam, 44 N. Y. Super. Ct. 391; Brignoli v. Chicago & G. E. Ry., 4 Daly, 182.

North Carolina: Wallace v. Western N. C. R. R., 104 N. C. 442.

Oregon: Oliver v. Northern P. T. Co., 3 Ore. 84.

Pennsylvania: Pennsylvania & O. C. Co. v. Graham, 63 Pa. 290, 3 Am. Rep. 549; Scott v. Montgomery, 95 Pa. 444; Lake Shore & M. S. Ry. v. Frantz, 127 Pa. 297, 18 Atl. 22.

Texas: Houston & T. C. Ry. v. Boehm, 57 Tex. 152.

Wisconsin: Goodno v. Oshkosh, 28 Wis. 300.

England: Phillips v. Southwestern Ry., 4 Q. B. D. 406.

[78] *Alabama:* Alabama G. S. R. R. v. Yarbrough, 83 Ala. 238, 3 So. 447, 3 Am. St. Rep. 715.

Nebraska: Wittenberg v. Mollyneaux, 55 Neb. 429, 75 N. W. 835.

South Carolina: Bridger v. Asheville & S. R. R., 27 S. C. 456, 3 S. E. 860, 13 Am. St. Rep. 653.

recover damages in the nature of hire for the period of the restraint.[79]

In a very large class of cases the earnings of the injured party have depended entirely on his individual abilities, as in the case of professional men and teachers, and travelling salesmen who are paid by a percentage on their sales. In the case of most professional men, there can be no way of fixing a general scale of remuneration. The exclusive services of such men cannot be measured by any pecuniary scale common to a whole class. The most trustworthy basis of damages in such a case is the amount which the injured party has earned in the past. This is, however, only evidence, from which the jury will be enabled to say what the services of such a man as the plaintiff are worth, and the jury should distinctly understand that it is not to be taken as the necessary and legal measure of damages.[80]   In an action for injury by collision,[81] it was held that evidence was admissible that the plaintiff's business was dealing in land, and also of the value of his business and the profits arising from it. The court below had charged that the plaintiff could recover profits which might reasonably be anticipated, but if the business was uncertain and speculative, and not attended with

[79] Moore v. Minerva, 17 Tex. 20.

[80] We give a few examples—*Actor:* Ware v. Welch, 32 Mich. 77. *Architect:* New Jersey Ex. Co. v. Nichols, 33 N. J. L. 434, 97 Am. Dec. 722. *Clergyman:* Parshall v. M. & St. L. Ry., 35 Fed. 649. *Dentist:* Nash v. Sharpe, 19 Hun (N. Y.), 365. *Lawyer:* Walker v. Erie Ry., 63 Barb. (N. Y.) 260. *Midwife:* Luck v. Ripon, 52 Wis. 196. *Music teacher:* Baker v. Manh. Ry., 54 N. Y. Super. Ct. 394. *Owner of junk shop:* Wayne v. Atlantic Ave. R. R., 35 N. Y. Supp. 1034. *Peddler:* Hanover R. R. v. Coyle, 55 Pa. 396.
Physician:
Indiana: Indianapolis v. Gaston, 58 Ind. 224; Logansport v. Justice, 74 Ind. 378, 39 Am. Rep. 79, *n.*
Maine: Holmes v. Halde, 74 Me. 28.

New York: Metcalf v. Baker, 57 N. Y. 662.
Wisconsin: McNamara v. Clintonville, 62 Wis. 207, 22 N. W. 472, 51 Am. Rep. 722.
England: Phillips v. London & S. W. Ry., 5 C. P. Div. 280.
Professional man: Collins v. Dodge, 37 Minn. 503. *School teacher:* Bloomington v. Chamberlain, 104 Ill. 268. *Selling agent:* Illinois C. R. R. v. Davidson, 76 Fed. 517, 22 C. C. A. 306.
The dictum of Grover, J., in Masterton v. Mt. Vernon, 58 N. Y. 391, is in conflict with the current of authorities.
See this subject fully examined, *post,* § 482.

[81] Pennsylvania R. R. v. Dale, 76 Pa. 47.

any reasonable certainty of profits, that none could be recovered. This charge was approved on appeal.

Since the recovery in this case is measured not by the value of any contract or contracts lost, but by the value of the services of such a person as the plaintiff, it is not material whether or not the plaintiff is entitled, as a matter of law, to such payment. The question is one not of legal right to the earnings, but of the customary receipt of them. Thus a physician, paid by fees which are regarded as *honoraria*, may recover compensation for interruption of his professional labor.[82] A physician or midwife who, not having received a diploma from a regular medical college, cannot sue for a fee, may recover for interruption of professional labor.[83] But one who is forbidden by law to practice,—for instance, an unlicensed midwife,—can recover nothing.[84]

§ 180a. Probable future increase of capacity.

The amount of recovery is not necessarily based on the plaintiff's earnings at the time of the injury. Thus an unskilled engineer, who was learning his profession, may recover compensation based on the probable skill he would have acquired if the defendant had not put it out of his power to attend to his work.[85] And one not engaged in business at the time of the injury may recover compensation for being prevented in future from engaging in business in which he might reasonably expect success, though he was not entirely certain of it. [86] It has been held that a person becoming expert in various branches of the railroad business may be compensated for the loss of a reasonable prospect of more lucrative employment in future.[87] But in other jurisdictions the court

---

[82] Phillips *v.* London & S. W. Ry., 5 C. P. Div. 280.

[83] *Maine:* Holmes *v.* Halde, 74 Me. 28.

Wisconsin: Luck *v.* Ripon, 52 Wis. 196; McNamara *v.* Clintonville, 62 Wis. 207, 22 N. W. 472, 51 Am. Rep. 722.

[84] *Connecticut:* Jacques *v.* Bridgeport H. R. R., 41 Conn. 61, 19 Am. Rep. 483.

Illinois: Chicago W. D. Ry. *v.* Lambert, 119 Ill. 255.

[85] Howard Oil Co. *v.* Davis, 76 Tex. 630.

[86] Fisher *v.* Jansen, 128 Ill. 549.

[87] *Arkansas:* A. L. Clark Lumber Co. *v.* St. Coner, (Ark.), 133 S. W. 1132 (plaintiff had been promised a better position when vacancy occurred).

Georgia: Schaufele *v.* Central of Geor-

has taken a more conservative attitude, and held that any mere hope of promotion is too speculative for consideration.[88]

§ 181. Personal injury resulting in loss of business.

Cases have already been examined where a personal injury results in a loss of the professional income of the plaintiff, which is, in a sense, a loss of the profits of a business. In many cases, where the injured party was at the head of an ordinary mercantile business, compensation is claimed for the loss of the profits of such business. In such a case there might enter into the profits of the business several sources of profit: interest on the capital employed, the value of the personal services of the plaintiff, the value of the good will of the business, and receipts from the employment of special property, like patents, trade-marks, or franchises, which have a special and peculiar value. The first, third, and last of these items would not be affected by the injury. The value of the plaintiff's personal services would therefore alone be left as fixing the amount to be recovered, and such value is to be estimated upon the principles just stated. It is well settled, therefore, that even if a personal injury results in a loss of profits of the plaintiff's business, no compensation can be recovered on account of such loss of profits; the recovery is limited to the value of the plaintiff's lost time.[89]

But though the profits of the business cannot be recovered as such, it is evidently impossible to arrive with any degree

gia Ry., 6 Ga. App. 660, 65 S. E. 708.

Texas: Galveston, H. & S. A. Ry. *v.* Still, 45 Tex. Civ. App. 169, 100 S. W. 176.

[88] *United States:* Richmond & D. R. R. *v.* Elliott, 149 U. S. 266, 37 L. ed. 728, 13 Sup. Ct. 837.

Indiana: Ohio Valley Trust Co. *v.* Wernke, 42 Ind. App. 326, 84 N. E. 999.

Iowa: Brown *v.* Chicago, R. I. & P. Ry., 64 Ia. 652, 21 N. W. 193.

Ohio: Hesse *v.* Columbus, S. & H. B. Co., 58 Ohio St. 167, 50 N. E. 354.

[89] *Iowa:* Homan *v.* Franklin Co., 90

Ia. 185, 57 N. W. 703; Jordan *v.* Cedar Rapids & M. C. Ry., 124 Iowa, 180, 99 N. W. 693.

Michigan: Silsby *v.* Mich. Car Co., 95 Mich. 204, 54 N. W. 761.

New York: Marks *v.* Long Island R. R., 14 Daly, 61.

Pennsylvania: Goodhart *v.* Pennsylvania R. R., 177 Pa. 1, 35 Atl. 191, 55 Am. St. Rep. 705.

Wisconsin: Bierbach *v.* Goodyear R. Co., 54 Wis. 208, 11 N. W. 514, 41 Am. Rep. 19.

See this subject fully examined, *post,* § 482*a.*

of certainty at the value of the time of a business man without knowing the extent and profits of his business; and it ought not to be too difficult in a given case, where the business is established and the profits uniform, or reasonably so, to determine what portion of them is due to the individual talents and exertions of the person who is carrying on the business. And by the better view where the personal exertions of the owner of a business enter in a considerable degree into the success of it, the earnings in the past may be shown not as a measure of the damage or an item of recovery, but as evidence from which the jury may estimate the value of the owner's time.[90] The true rule has been well stated by the Court of Appeals of New York: "Where the facts disclose such a preponderance of the business element over the personal equation, or such an admixture of the two, that the question of personal earnings could not be safely or properly segregated from returns upon capital invested, the income or profits from a business should not be considered in determining the amount of the damages to which the plaintiff is entitled." [91]

Where, however, the profits of a business are in their nature speculative and uncertain they cannot be proved even as evidence of the value of the lost time.[92]

[90] *Iowa:* Mitchell *v.* Chicago, R. I. & P. Ry., 138 Ia. 283, 114 N. W. 622.

Kansas: Chicago, R. I. & P. R. R. *v.* Posten, 59 Kan. 449, 53 Pac. 465.

New Jersey: New Jersey Express Co. *v.* Nichols, 33 N. J. Law, 434, 97 Am. Dec. 722.

Pennsylvania: Wallace *v.* Pennsylvania R. R., 195 Pa. 127, 45 Atl. 685, 52 L. R. A. 33.

Wisconsin: Heer *v.* Warren Scharf Asphalt Paving Co., 118 Wis. 57, 94 N. W. 789.

Upon this principle evidence of profits has been allowed in the following cases:

Illinois: Chicago Union Traction Co. *v.* Brethauer, 79 N. E. 287, 223 Ill. 521, affirming 125 Ill. App. 204 (jobber of jewelry).

Iowa: Lund *v.* Tyler, 115 Iowa, 236, 88 N. W. 333 (fisher); Jordan *v.* Cedar Rapids & M. C. Ry., 124 Iowa, 177, 99 N. W. 693 (cattle dealer).

New York: Kronold *v.* City of New York, 186 N. Y. 40, 78 N. E. 572 (importer of embroideries).

Pennsylvania: Pennsylvania R. R. *v.* Dale, 76 Pa. 47 (dealer in land).

On the other hand, proof of profits has been refused in the following cases:

Illinois: Chicago City Ry. *v.* Flynn, 131 Ill. App. 502 (coal dealer).

Missouri: York *v.* City of Everton, 97 S. W. 604, 121 Mo. App. 640 (milliner).

[91] Weir *v.* Union Ry., 188 N. Y. 416, 81 N. E. 168.

[92] Evidence of profits was excluded on the ground that the business was too speculative in the following cases:

So in Masterson *v.* Mount Vernon[93] it was held error to allow evidence of the profits of the plaintiff as a tea merchant, for several years previous, to be given as evidence of the loss sustained, by showing the falling-off in the year after the accident, in consequence of the injury. The plaintiff had testified that he was engaged in the tea-importing business, buying and selling teas; that it was his duty to buy the teas for the firm, but that in consequence of the injury he could not make purchases, and there was a great falling-off in the business. Grover, J., said: "Where, in such a case, the plaintiff has received a fixed compensation for his services, or his earnings can be shown with reasonable certainty, the proof is competent. . . . In none of these cases is any intimation given that proof may be given as to the uncertain future profits of commercial business; or, that the amount of past profits derived therefrom may be shown to enable the jury to *conjecture* what the future might probably be. These profits depend upon too many contingencies, and are altogether too uncertain to furnish any safe guide in fixing the amount of damages." He continued: "But the profits of importing and selling teas are still more uncertain. In some years they may be large, and in others attended with loss. The plaintiff had the right to prove the business in which he was engaged, its extent, and the particular part transacted by him, and, if he could, the compensation usually paid persons doing such business for others. These are circumstances the jury have a right to consider in fixing the value of his time. But they ought not to be permitted to speculate as to uncertain profits of commercial ventures, in which the plaintiff, if uninjured, would have been engaged."

§ 182. Profits of an established business.

Where it clearly appears that the defendant has interrupted an established business from which the plaintiff expected to realize profits, the plaintiff should recover compensation for

New York: Weir *v.* Union Ry., 188 N. Y. 416, 81 N. E. 168 (lunch counter).

Washington: Kirk *v.* Seattle Electric Co., 58 Wash. 283, 108 Pac. 604 (getting out special editions of newspapers).
[93] 58 N. Y. 391.

whatever profit he makes it reasonably certain he would have realized. Here as elsewhere the question is one of fact: whether the profit can be proved with reasonable certainty.[94] In an Illinois case the court said:[95]

"We all know that in many, if not all, professions and callings, years of effort, skill and toil are necessary to establish a profitable business, and that when established it is worth more than capital. Can it then be said, that a party deprived of it has no remedy, and can recover nothing for its loss, when produced by another? It has long been well-recognized law, that when deprived of such business by slander, compensation for its loss may be recovered in this form of action. And why not for its loss by this more direct means? And of what

[94] *United States:* Sonneborn v. Stewart, 2 Woods, 599; Central Coal Co. v. Hartman, 111 Fed. 96, 49 C. C. A. 244.

California: Selden v. Cashman, 20 Cal. 56, 81 Am. Dec. 93; Lambert v. Haskell, 80 Cal. 611.

Georgia: Sturgis v. Frost, 56 Ga. 188; Smith v. Eubanks, 72 Ga. 280; Stewart v. Lanier H. Co., 75 Ga. 582.

Illinois: Chapman v. Kirby, 49 Ill. 211; Lawrence v. Hagerman, 56 Ill. 68, 8 Am. Rep. 674; Dobbins v. Duquid, 65 Ill. 464; Smith v. Wunderlich, 70 Ill. 426.

Indiana: Terre Haute v. Hudnut, 112 Ind. 542, 13 N. E. 686.

Kentucky: Pettit v. Mercer, 8 B. Mon. 51.

Louisiana: Dennery v. Bisa, 6 La. Ann. 365.

Maryland: Moore v. Schultz, 31 Md. 418; Shafer v. Wilson, 44 Md. 268; Lawson v. Price, 45 Md. 123; Evans v. Murphy, 87 Md. 498, 40 Atl. 109.

Massachusetts: White v. Moseley, 8 Pick. 356; French v. Connecticut R. L. Co., 145 Mass. 261, 14 N. E. 113.

Michigan: Chandler v. Allison, 10 Mich. 460; Allison v. Chandler, 11 Mich. 542.

Minnesota: Goebel v. Hough, 26 Minn. 252; Cushing v. Seymour, 30 Minn. 301.

Mississippi: Marqueze v. Sontheimer, 59 Miss. 430.

New Hampshire: Holden v. Lake Co., 53 N. H. 552.

New Jersey: Luse v. Jones, 39 N. J. L. 707; East Jersey W. Co. v. Bigelow, 60 N. J. L. 201, 38 Atl. 631.

New York: Lacour v. New York, 3 Duer, 406; St. John v. New York, 6 Duer, 315; Walter v. Post, 6 Duer, 363.

Ohio: Alexander v. Jacoby, 23 Oh. St. 358.

Oregon: Willer v. Ore. Ry. & Nav. Co., 15 Ore. 153.

Pennsylvania: Pennsylvania R. R. v. Dale, 76 Pa. 47; Stofflet v. Stofflet, 160 Pa. 529, 28 Atl. 857; Keber v. Mahoney City Gas Co., 143 Pa. 276, 22 Atl. 759.

Rhode Island: Simmons v. Brown, 5 R. I. 299, 73 Am. Dec. 66; Trafford v. Hubbard, 15 R. I. 326.

Wisconsin: Shepard v. Wilwaukee Gas Light Co., 15 Wis. 318.

England: Lancashire & Y. Ry. v. Gidlow, L. R. 7 H. L. 517; Simpson v. London & N. W. Ry., 1 Q. B. D. 274; Gunter v. Astor, 4 Moore, 12; Ingram v. Lawson, 6 Bing. N. C. 212; Llewellyn v. Rutherford, L. R. 10 C. P. 456.

[95] Walker, J., in Chapman v. Kirby, 49 Ill. 211, 219.

does this loss consist, but the profits that would have been made had the act not been performed by appellants? And to measure such damages, the jury must have some basis for an estimate, and what more reasonable than to take the profits for a reasonable period next preceding the time when the injury was inflicted, leaving the other party to show, that by depression in trade, or other causes, they would have been less? Nor can we expect that in actions of this character, the precise extent of the damages can be shown by demonstration. By this means they can be ascertained with a reasonable degree of certainty."

Allison v. Chandler,[96] the leading case on this subject, was a case where the defendant, a landlord, wrongfully ejected the plaintiff, his tenant, from premises where he was established as a jeweller. In an able opinion the court held that the plaintiff was entitled to damages for injury to his business.

This principle applies to injuries of every sort where an item of damage is interference with an established business.[97]

[96] 11 Mich. 542.

[97] *United States:* Engine Co. v. Du Bois, 130 Fed. 834, 65 C. C. A. 172 (breach of contract to supply gasoline engines for sale by plaintiff).

Arkansas: Border City Ice, &c., Co. v. Adams, 69 Ark. 219, 62 S. W. 591 (failure to supply ice to carry on established ice business).

California: Barnes v. Berendes, 139 Cal. 32, 72 Pac. 406 (prevention of erection of building to carry on established business).

Connecticut: Lawton v. Herrick (Conn.), 76 Atl. 986 (polluting stream so as to destroy ice business).

Illinois: Illinois & S. L. R. R. & C. Co. v. Decker, 3 Ill. App. 135 (eviction from business premises); Keegan v. Harlan, 134 Ill. App. 363 (illegal distraint).

Indiana: Jackson v. Stanfield, 137 Ind. 592, 36 N. E. 345 (unlawful conspiracy to injure established business).

Maine: National Fibre Board Co. v. Lewiston & A. Electric Light Co., 95 Me. 318, 49 Atl. 1095 (interruption of business at flour mill by wrongfully raising a stream).

Maryland: Brown v. Werner, 40 Md. 15 (injury to business premises).

Michigan: Oliver v. Perkins, 92 Mich. 304, 52 N. W. 609 (failure to supply machines for sale by plaintiff, who had carried on the business for two years); McCausey v. Hoek, 124 N. W. 570, 159 Mich. 570 (conversion of stock in trade).

Missouri: Wolff Shirt Co. v. Frankenthal, 96 Mo. App. 307, 70 S. W. 378 (wrongfully disabling engine necessary to carry on established business).

Nebraska: Kyd v. Cook, 56 Neb. 71, 71 Am. St. 661, 76 N. W. 524 (wrongful attachment of business stock; profits of preceding year shown); Kitchen Bros. Hotel Co. v. Philbin, 2 Neb. (Unof.) 340, 96 N. W. 487 (eviction from premises where plaintiff was carrying on established business as broker).

So where the defendant, wishing the plaintiff to come into a town and there carry on a business which he had established at another place, guaranteed that a railroad would come to the town and plaintiff broke up his business and came to the town, and the railroad not having come there plaintiff was unsuccessful, it was held that he could show the profits of the established business he had given up to prove his damages.[98] So where the defendant broke his contract not to compete with the plaintiff's business, it was held that the plaintiff might recover compensation for the profit he had lost, to be ascertained by comparing the amount his business actually fell short of what he might have done, with the business done by the defendant.[99] Where the injury complained of was, that the defendants had invited the plaintiff's servants to dinner, and induced them to leave him, and the injurious consequence complained of was, that the plaintiff had lost the profits of the sales of pianos for two years; this was held not to be too remote, although the servants were not hired by the plaintiff for any definite period, but worked by the piece.   Richardson, J., remarked: "The measure of damages he is entitled to receive from the defendants is not necessarily to be confined to those servants he might have in his employ at the time they were so enticed, or for the part of the day on which they absented themselves from his service;

New Jersey: Standard Amusement & Mfg. Co. *v.* Champion, 72 Atl. 92, 78 N. J. L. 000 (ejection from premises used as skating rink).

New Mexico: De Palma *v.* Weinman, 103 Pac. 782, 13 N. Mex. 266 (causing wall of shop to fall).

New York: Dickinson *v.* Hart, 142 N. Y. 183, 36 N. E. 801 (exclusion from premises where business had been carried on two years); Menard *v.* Stevens, 44 N. Y. Super. Ct. 515 (eviction from premises used in established restaurant business); Langan *v.* Potter, 8 N. Y. Misc. 541, 28 N. Y. Supp. 752 (wrongful exclusion from business premises); Laufer *v.* Boynton Furnace Co., 84 Hun, 311, 32 N. Y. Supp. 362 (destruction of greenhouse stock; sales for preceding year shown); Swain *v.* Schieffelin, 12 N. Y. Supp. 155 (injury to established ice-cream business by supplying poisonous coloring matter); Ebenreiter *v.* Dahlman, 19 Misc. 9, 42 N. Y. Supp. 867 (wrongful attachment).

Wisconsin: Raynor *v.* Valentin Blatz Brewing Co., 100 Wis. 414, 76 N. W. 343 (failure to keep in repair building leased for business; recovery for loss of profits pending repairs).

[98] Arkansas Valley Town & L. Co. *v.* Lincoln, 56 Kan. 145, 42 Pac. 706.

[99] *United States:* Hitchcock *v.* Anthony, 28 C. C. A. 80, 83 Fed. 779.

Missouri: Peltz *v.* Eichele, 62 Mo, 171.

but he is entitled to recover damages for the loss he sustained by their leaving him at that critical period." [100]

The defendant raised an embankment, by which he cut off the plaintiff's access to a river. The plaintiff used the river to get the products of his farm to market. It was held that he could recover the loss of profits of his farm due to loss of market.[101] The defendant obstructed a river, as a consequence of which the plaintiff lost custom at his hotel on the bank. It was held that he could recover compensation for the diminution in his business and profits.[102]

The rule may result in evidence of professional earnings. Thus, when a physician abandoned his profession to become sole agent for the sale of a patented article, giving his entire time to it, and the contract to furnish him with the article was broken by defendants, it was held that he could recover not only the amounts he expended in the business, but the professional earnings which he would otherwise have made.[103]

While the nature and extent of the business for a considerable time in the past may be shown, it is not enough to prove the weekly profits for a few weeks before the loss, as the time is not long enough to show a safe average profit.[104]

§ 182a. Uncertain profits of an established business.

The business may be of such an uncertain nature that its profits never become established.[105] For instance, where the

---

[100] Gunter v. Astor, 4 Moore, 12; acc., Smith v. Goodman, 75 Ga. 198.

[101] Willer v. Oregon Ry. & N. Co., 15 Ore. 153.

[102] French v. Connecticut R. L. Co., 145 Mass. 261.

[103] Meylert v. Gas Consumers' Benefit Co., 14 N. Y. Supp. 148.

[104] Kostopolos v. Pezzetti, 207 Mass. 277, 93 N. E. 571. In Gagnon v. Sperry & Hutchinson Co., 206 Mass. 547, 92 N. E. 761, the plaintiff was allowed to show an increase in his business while he was supplied with trading stamps by the defendant, and a sudden falling off when he was no longer so supplied.

[105] Examples of business the profits of which have been held sufficiently certain for consideration are the following:

Cattle raising: Arkansas Land & Cattle Co. v. Mann, 130 U. S. 69, 9 Sup. Ct. 458, 32 L. ed. 854. *Theatrical entertainment:* Chappell v. Western Ry., (Ga. App.), 70 S. E. 208; Weston v. Boston & M. R. R., 190 Mass. 298, 76 N. E. 1050, 4 L. R. A. (N. S.) 569, 112 Am. St. Rep. 330. *Ice supply:* Border City Ice, etc., Co. v. Adams, 69 Ark. 219, 62 S. W. 591. *Ice cutting:* Lawton v. Herrick, (Conn.), 76 Atl. 986. *Sheep growing:* Schrandt v. Young, 2 Neb. (Unof.) 546, 89 N. W. 607. *Green-*

defendant wrongfully took the fixtures from the plaintiff's premises, which the plaintiff let from time to time for entertainments, it was held that profits expected were too speculative.[106] Where a river boat lost a trip through a collision, it was held that the profits expected from the return trip were too conjectural for recovery.[107] This would hardly be true in the ordinary case. It was held in North Carolina that where the plaintiff had been in the business of manufacturing patented machines and the business was broken up, he could recover profits only so far as he could show orders for machines; profits based on his sales for the year before were too uncertain.[108] The decision is questionable. It might, however, be supported if the demand for the machine, being a patented one and so presumably novel, were ephemeral. On this general principle must be rested the case of Martin v. Deetz.[109] This was an action for breach of contract to organize a corporation in order to carry on the mill business in which the plaintiff had been engaged and was on the point of failure. Plaintiff claimed that if defendants had acted, money could have been raised to meet the obligations and the business could have been carried on at a profit. But it was held that profits were too uncertain and speculative to form a basis for measuring damages.[110]

house: Laufer v. Boynton Furnace Co., 84 Hun, 311, 32 N. Y. Supp. 362. *Mining:* Paul v. Cragnaz, 25 Nev. 293, 60 Pac. 983, 47 L. R. A. 540. *Fishing:* Pacific Steam Whaling Co. v. Alaska Packers, 138 Cal. 632, 72 Pac. 161; *contra,* Wright v. Mulvaney, 78 Wis. 89, 46 N. W. 1045. *Toll-bridge:* West v. Martin, 51 Wash. 85, 97 Pac. 1102, 21 L. R. A. (N. S.) 324.

The following have been held too uncertain for consideration: ·

Horse-racing: Cain v. Vollmer, (Ida.), 112 Pac. 686; Western Union Tel. Co. v. Crall, 39 Kan. 580, 18 Pac. 719. *Sale of Liquor:* Selden v. Cashman, 20 Cal. 56, 81 Am. Dec. 93. *Sale of wallpaper:* Lehman v. McQuown, 31 Fed. 138.

In Bates v. Warrick, 77 N. J. L. 387, 69 Atl. 185, the "normal Christmas trade" was held too uncertain and speculative to be the basis of recovery.

Profits may of course be too uncertain for recovery not because of the nature of the business, but because sufficient proof of them is not produced. Lehman v. Amsterdam Coffee Co., (Wis.), 131 N. W. 362.

[106] Willis v. Branch, 94 N. C. 142.

[107] Hunt v. Hoboken L. I. Co., 3 E. D. Smith (N. Y.), 144.

[108] Jones v. Call, 96 N. C. 337, 60 Am. Rep. 416.

[109] 102 Cal. 55, 36 Pac. 368, 41 Am. St. Rep. 151.

[110] In Casper v. Klippen, 61 Minn. 353, 63 N. W. 737, 52 Am. Rep. 604, the court said that cases where the profits of a mercantile business could

§ 182b. Profits of an unlawful business.

No damages can be recovered for injury to an unlawful business, such as gambling,[111] or the illegal sale of liquor.[112] And where a business had been carried on for several years every day in the week, including Sunday, when the doing of such business was illegal, it was held that the profits which had been derived from business done on Sunday must be omitted from the computation.[113]

§ 183. Of a new business.

Where the plaintiff was about to embark on a new business venture, which was wrongfully prevented by the defendant, he can recover nothing on account of the expected profits: for there is nothing to prove that a profit would have been made.[114]   Where the defendant fails to furnish machinery for a new use, he cannot be held to compensate the plaintiff for the profits he might have made.[115]   The measure of damages is the ordinary value of the use of the machine.   So, in Cory v. Thames I. W. & S. B. Co.,[116] the plaintiff intended to use the machine ordered for a novel purpose, by which he claimed that he could make large profits; but the court held that the measure of damages was the value of the use of the machine for the purpose it was ordinarily used for.   So where the defendant destroys a building in course of erection by the plaintiff, prospective profits which the plaintiff might have

be regarded as sufficiently established to be considered are rare. The court's view is certainly different from that usually taken.

[111] Kauffman v. Babcock, 67 Tex. 241. Or "ticket scalping," Sherman House Hotel Co. v. Cirkle, 136 Ill. App. 381.

[112] *Louisiana:* Prude v. Sebastian, 107 La. 64, 31 So. 764.

New York: Kane v. Johnston, 9 Bosw. 154.

[113] Raynor v. Valentin Blatz Brewing Co., 100 Wis. 414, 76 N. W. 343.

[114] *United States:* Central Coal Co. v. Hartman, 111 Fed. 96, 49 C. C. A. 244.

Georgia: Red v. Augusta, 25 Ga. 386; Kenny v. Collier, 79 Ga. 743.

Illinois: Green v. Williams, 45 Ill. 206; Hair v. Barnes, 26 Ill. App. 580.

Kansas: States v. Durkin, 65 Kan. 101, 68 Pac. 1091.

Maryland: Winslow Elevator & Machine Co. v. Hoffman, 69 Atl. 394, 107 Md. 621, 17 L. R. A. (N. S.) 1130.

Montana: First Nat. Bank v. Carroll, 35 Mont. 302, 88 Pac. 1012.

New York: Morey v. Metropolitan G. L. Co., 38 N. Y. Super. Ct. 185.

[115] Coweta F. M. Co. v. Rogers, 19 Ga. 416, 65 Am. Dec. 602; Crabbs v. Koontz, 69 Md. 59, 13 Atl. 591.

[116] L. R. 3 Q. B. 181.

made by renting the building are not recoverable.[117]   A publisher of a paper who merely by mistake neglects to insert an advertisement of the sale of real estate, is liable only for the amount paid for the advertisement, not for speculative damages.[118]   In an action of replevin for a boat which was taken from the plaintiff at a time when he was about to use it in getting oats from a stranded vessel, the profits which he expected in that way to gain cannot be considered.[119]   When defendant leased to plaintiff a stand at a fair and agreed not to permit rivals within certain limits, on a breach of this agreement it was held that profits which might have been made but for the presence of the rivals were too uncertain. The measure of damages was the difference between the rental value of the premises with and without the rival stands.[120] So in the case of fraudulent representations by means of which plaintiff is induced to purchase an existing business, he cannot recover profits which he might have made had a corporation taken over the company, by the aid of an underwriting syndicate.[121]

In a few cases the courts have been very liberal in allowing evidence of profits to be shown where the business had hardly become an established one. So where plaintiff, being in the messenger business, hired a telephone for a year, and the telephone was taken out in three months, it was held that plaintiff might recover for loss of profits of his business during the remainder of the contract time. They were contemplated by the parties and could easily be proved, though not with entire certainty; the business had been carried on for a short time but was increasing, and the jury might assume that the increase would continue.[122]

The rule by which the profits of a new business are excluded is equally applicable to a case where an old business had been

[117] Bingham v. Walla Walla, 3 Wash. 68.

[118] Eisenlohr v. Swain, 35 Pa. 107, 78 Am. Dec. 328.

[119] Aber v. Bratton, 60 Mich. 357.

[120] Montgomery County Union Agricultural Soc. v. Harwood, 126 Ind. 440, 26 N. E. 182, 10 L. R. A. 532 (selling candy at agricultural fair).

[121] Loewer v. Harris, 57 Fed. 369, 14 U. S. App. 615, 6 C. C. A. 394.

[122] Owensboro-Harrison Telephone Co. v. Wisdom, 23 Ky. L. Rep. 97, 62 S. W. 529.

given up, and a renewal of it was contemplated.[123] The view taken by the law of the status of an established business, as to the possibility of estimating its normal capacity to produce an ascertainable annual quantum of profit, usually follows the ordinary commercial practice, by which an established business of any kind, commercial or professional, is every day bought and sold in the market on this basis. It may also be leased, in which case the rental has a close analogy to the value, for hire, of chattels.

§ 184. Damages for obstructing the use of land.

Where an owner of land is wrongfully prevented from occupying it, the measure of his damages is the value of the use of the land,—that is, its rental value. So where the plaintiff's farming land was wrongfully overflowed by the defendant, the measure of damages is the use of the land, not the value of the crops that might have been raised on it; [124] where a mine was flooded and thereby rendered useless, the measure of damages was not the profits that might have been made from the mine, but the actual value of the mine; [125] and where access to plaintiff's land was obstructed, he could not recover the profits he might have made by selling clay from it; [126] or by selling the land itself.[127] The rule is the same in all actions for injury to business premises [128] or for obstructing access thereto.[129] In the case of a stream, the tollage, or reasonable value of the use for the purpose of floating logs, may be recovered.[130] But since the rental value depends upon the nature of the land, that may be shown; and as the net profits realized

---

[123] Boston & A. R. R. v. O'Reilly, 158 U. S. 334, 39 L. ed. 1006, 15 Sup. Ct. 830.

[124] *Illinois:* Chicago v. Huenerbein, 85 Ill. 594, 28 Am. Rep. 626.

Iowa: Drake v. Chicago, R. I. & P. Ry., 63 Ia. 302, 50 Am. Rep. 746, 19 N. W. 215.

[125] McKnight v. Ratcliff, 44 Pa. 156.

[126] Garitee v. Baltimore, 53 Md. 422.

[127] San Antonio v. Mullaly, 11 Tex. Civ. App. 596, 33 S. W. 256.

[128] *Minnesota:* Todd v. Minneapolis

& S. L. Ry., 39 Minn. 186, 39 N. W. 318.

Pennsylvania: McNeil v. Crucible Steel Co., 207 Pa. 493, 56 Atl. 1067.

See Capel v. Lyons, 3 Misc. (N. Y.) 73, 22 N. Y. Supp. 378, where plaintiff was allowed the profits he had lost on orders actually received.

[129] Park v. C. & S. R. Co., 43 Iowa, 636.

[130] De Camp v. Bullard, 159 N. Y. 450, 54 N. E. 26.

from the use of it afford the best indication of the value of its use, they may be shown if they can be proved with reasonable certainty.[131] Thus where the defendant by a malicious and unfounded injunction prevented the plaintiff from using its coal lands for a year, it was held that not only the nature and extent of the coal beds, but also the profit on possible sales of coal, might be shown, "not in order to be allowed by the jury as profits, but to be treated as one of the facts that throw light upon the value of the rights taken."[132] And where the plaintiff was excluded from his mine, it was held that he might show the profits of working the mine, not to recover prospective profits, but to show the amount of the actual loss; and the fact that before and after the period in question large profits had been made from working the mine showed with sufficient certainty loss of profits by plaintiff.[133] And where the defendant, by wrongfully blasting in the neighborhood of the plaintiff's factory, caused the plaintiff's workmen to leave the building at each blast, under a reasonable apprehension of danger, it was held that the plaintiff might recover the value *to him* of the time thus lost; not necessarily measured by the wages paid.[134] But uncertain profits, such as profits which the plaintiff claims he might have made by a use of the land to which in fact he has never put it, cannot be shown.[135]

§ 185. Failure to give possession of real estate.

Where a vendor or a lessor fails to give possession of the premises, the measure of damages is the difference between the value and the contract price, or in case of a lease, the

[131] *Maryland:* Washington County Water Co. v. Garver, 91 Md. 398, 46 Atl. 979.

Michigan: Taylor v. Cooper, 104 Mich. 72, 62 N. W. 157.

Rhode Island: Simons v. Brown, 5 R. I. 299, 73 Am. Dec. 66.

[132] Newark Coal Co. v. Upson, 40 Oh. St. 17.

[133] Hunter v. Farren, 127 Mass. 481, 34 Am. Rep. 423.

But in other cases the profits of mining have been held too uncertain for recovery. Coosaw Min. Co. v. Carolina Min. Co., 75 Fed. 860; M'Cormick v. United States Min. Co., 185 Fed. 748.

[134] *California:* Giaccomini v. Bulkeley, 51 Cal. 260 (profits of large dairy when plaintiff never had more than three cows).

West Virginia: Douglass v. Ohio R. R. R., 51 W. Va. 523, 41 S. E. 911 (profits of grazing; land always used for cropping).

[135] Paul v. Cragnaz, 25 Nev. 293, 59 Pac. 857, 60 Pac. 983, 47 L. R. A. 540.

actual rental value and the rent reserved. The rule is the same, whether the leased property is a farm,[136] a dwelling-house or hotel,[137] or business premises,[138] or land intended for sale.[139] If, however, the premises were necessary to the plaintiff for carrying on an established business, and that fact were known to the defendant at the time the lease was made, the plaintiff might on principles elsewhere discussed recover further damages. The measure of damages would be the difference between the rent and the value for the plaintiff's business, which would involve an allowance of profits.[140] If the business were a new one, since there could be no basis on which to estimate profits, the plaintiff must be content to recover according to the general rule.[141] The profits expected from a singer's performance are not certain enough to be recovered in an action by the lessee of an opera-house against the lessor for breach of a contract to furnish it by a certain time for the lessee's use.[142]

§ 186. Failure to put a structure on land.

When the defendant undertakes himself to put a structure on his own land, or that some one else shall build a structure, the effect of which would benefit the plaintiff's land, the

[136] *Alabama:* Snodgrass v. Reynolds, 79 Ala. 452.

Arkansas: Rose v. Wynn, 42 Ark. 257.

Illinois: Olmstead v. Burke, 25 Ill. 86; Cilley v. Hawkins, 48 Ill. 308.

West Virginia: Robrecht v. Marling, 29 W. Va. 765.

Contra, Indiana: Aven v. Frey, 69 Ind. 91, where the court allowed the plaintiff to show the value of the crops that could have been raised on the land during the period of the lease, "with a view to laying grounds for damages." There was no argument nor citation of authorities.

[137] *New York:* Hexter v. Knox, 63 N. Y. 561.

Virginia: Burruss v. Hines, 94 Va. 413, 26 S. E. 875.

[138] *Iowa:* Alexander v. Bishop, 59 Ia. 572, 13 N. W. 714.

Kentucky: Koch v. Godshaw, 12 Bush, 318.

Massachusetts: Townsend v. Nickerson Wharf Co., 117 Mass. 501.

New York: Giles v. O'Toole, 4 Barb. 261; Fondavila v. Jourgensen, 52 N. Y. Super. Ct. 403.

[139] *California:* Muldrow v. Norris, 2 Cal. 74, 56 Am. Dec. 313.

New York: Hexter v. Knox, 63 N. Y. 561.

Wisconsin: Poposkey v. Munkwitz, 68 Wis. 322.

England: Ward v. Smith, 11 Price, 19.

[140] Carbondale Invest. Co. v. Burdick, 58 Kan. 517, 50 Pac. 442.

[141] Hodges v. Fries, 34 Fla. 63, 15 So. 682.

[142] New York Academy of Music v. Hackett, 2 Hilt. (N. Y.) 217.

measure of damages for breach is not the anticipated profits, but the difference in value of the plaintiff's land as it would have been with the structure built and as it is without the structure.[143]

The rule is the same in case of failure to put a structure on plaintiff's land. So where the defendant agreed to put a new mill on the plaintiff's land, but failed to do so, the plaintiff can recover nothing on account of loss of profits.[144] If the mill was built, but the completion of it was wrongfully delayed, rent of the mill for the period of delay may be recovered, but not expected profits from the use of it.[145] A plaintiff cannot recover on defendant's failure to make improvements on a lot, the profits which he would have made by erecting a distillery on the lot, as he intended to do.[146] But upon failure to repair an established mill the plaintiff may recover the profit he would have made by sawing the logs ready for manufacture at the mill.[147]

In a case where the defendant attempted to recoup, in an action on a building contract, the rent which he might have obtained from the store if it had been finished at the agreed time, it was held that the plaintiff could reduce the recovery to nominal damages by showing that the building if finished at the agreed time could not have been rented.[148] In a somewhat similar case in Michigan, where a mill remained idle through non-delivery of machinery, Cooley, J., went further, and intimated that the plaintiff, as part of his case, should show that the mill might have been rented, or else he should

[143] So for breach of contract to construct a street railway near plaintiff's land: Smith v. Los Angeles & P. Ry., 98 Cal. 210, 33 Pac. 53.

False representation, on sale of land, that railroad station was to be built near the land: Wilson v. Yocum, 77 Iowa, 569, 42 N. W. 446.

Contract to erect and operate a steel plant on land conveyed: Ironton Land Co. v. Butchart, 73 Minn. 39, 75 N. W. 749.

Contract to erect and maintain a store: Iowa-Minnesota Land Co. v. Conner, 136 Ia. 674, 112 N. W. 820.

But in Cincinnati, I. & W. Ry. v. Baker, 130 Ill. App. 414, breach of contract to erect a station on land, the plaintiff was allowed no more than the value of the land which had been conveyed as consideration for the contract.

[144] Jones v. Nathrop, 7 Colo. 1.

[145] Abbott v. Gatch, 13 Md. 314, 71 Am. Dec. 635.

[146] Hahn v. Horstman, 12 Bush (Ky.), 249.

[147] Hinckley v. Beckwith, 13 Wis. 31.

[148] Wagner v. Corkhill, 40 Barb. (N. Y.) 175.

be allowed to recover no damages.[149]   The latter case has been overruled;[150] and even the former case seems very questionable.   Rent is given, not as specific damage, but as a fair average measure of compensation for interfering with the owner's use of property: and no inquiry should be permitted as to the likelihood in the particular case of rent having been obtained. In fact, how can it be proved with reasonable certainty that rent could not have been obtained?   In an action for mesne profits the plaintiff recovers the fair rental value, irrespective of the actual yield or income, and this case is analogous.[151]

But while the rental value lost by the delay should be allowed, there is no way in the ordinary case of proving the loss of any particular sum of money which would have been received; and no recovery can be had therefore on account of the anticipated rentals of the particular building.[152]   In other words, here also we recover the general average return, *i. e.*, the rental value, and not the anticipated profits.

§ 187. Loss of use of a road or bridge.

Where the defendant failed to complete and deliver to the plaintiff a line of railroad at the agreed time, the measure of damages is the value of the use of the road during the time of delay.   Expected profits from the use of the road cannot be recovered.[153]   The defendant failed to finish a turnpike at the time prescribed by the contract; in an action the plaintiff claimed compensation on account of the loss of tolls during the period of delay.   It was held, however, that the loss was too uncertain and conjectural.[154]   But where the plaintiff's toll-bridge, which had been in use for some time, was carried away, through the fault of the defendants, it was held that the plaintiff could recover compensation for loss of the tolls

[149] Allis *v.* McLean, 48 Mich. 428.
[150] John Hutchinson Mfg. Co. *v.* Pinch, 91 Mich. 156, 51 N. W. 930, 30 Am. St. Rep. 463.
[151] *United States:* Campbell *v.* Brown, 2 Woods, 349.
Virginia: Bolling *v.* Lersner, 26 Gratt. 36.
[152] *Iowa:* Schillinger Bros. *v.* Bosch-Ryan Grain Co. (Ia.), 116 N. W. 132.

Washington: Jones *v.* Nelson, 112 Pac. 88.
[153] *United States:* Phillips & C. C. Co. *v.* Seymour, 91 U. S. 646; Hunt *v.* Oregon P. Ry., 13 Sawy. 516, 1 L. R. A. 842, 36 Fed. 481.
Illinois: Snell *v.* Cottingham, 72 Ill. 161.
[154] Western G. R. Co. *v.* Cox, 39 Ind. 260.

during the time reasonably necessary to rebuild.[155] In this case, the business being an established one, the profits of it were not conjectural.

§ 188. Damages for wrongful eviction.

Where an occupant of real estate has been wrongfully evicted, the general measure of damages would be the value of the lease. In a case in Ohio, the defendant had agreed to make to the plaintiff, for the term of ten years, a lease of certain lands on which to plant and cultivate a peach orchard. The plaintiff took possession of the land, but the defendant failed to make the lease, and within two years from the time of the plaintiff's occupation of the premises caused him to be evicted. Evidence of the probable future profits of the land was held incompetent in determining the plaintiff's damages. To the extent that they depended on the loss of use of the land, its market value at the time of· the eviction, subject to the performance of the contract on the plaintiff's part, furnished the standard of their assessment. If it had no general market value, its value should be ascertained from the opinions of qualified witnesses, in view of the hazards of the business.[156] If, however, the natural result of the eviction would be injury to an established business, the plaintiff should also recover compensation for the injury to his business.[157] This has been said to be an allowance of compensation for the *good will* of the premises.[158] If there is no safe criterion by which to estimate profits, no compensation for the loss of them can be recovered.

Where the defendant prevails in an action for forcible

[155] *New Hampshire:* Sewall's F. B. Co. *v.* Fisk, 23 N. H. 171.

Washington: West *v.* Martin, 51 Wash. 85, 97 Pac. 1102, 21 L. R. A. (N. S.) 324.

[156] Rhodes *v.* Baird, 16 Oh. St. 573.

[157] *Michigan:* Shaw *v.* Hoffman, 25 Mich. 163.

Pennsylvania: Seyfert *v.* Bean, 83 Pa. 450.

Rhode Island: Collins *v.* Lavelle, 19 R. I. 45, 31 Atl. 434.

It was held in Denison *v.* Ford, 10 Daly, 412, that such damages could not be recovered; this decision must be rested on the ground of remoteness, not of uncertainty. In Louisiana, under the code, there can be no recovery of profits in such cases: Redon *v.* Caffin, 11 La. Ann. 695.

[158] Llewellyn *v.* Rutherford, L. R. 10 C. P. 456.

entry and detainer, and is allowed by the statute damages for the eviction, it is doubtful whether he can in any case recover more than the value of the use of the property taken possession of.[159] In every decided case of the sort, however, the decision has been rested on other grounds, and no intimation has been given of the court's opinion upon the point.

§ 189. Loss of the use of business premises.

When the wrongful act of the defendant deprives the plaintiff of the use of business premises, the measure of damages would ordinarily be the value of the use of the premises, that is, their rental value.[160] If, however, the business is an established one, and the interruption of business not remote, the plaintiff may recover the value of the use of the premises to him in his business.[161] This has been held in an action for direct injury to business premises,[162] for diversion or obstruction of water from a mill,[163] and for destruction of a mill dam[164] or failure to keep it in repair.[165] The profits previously made may be shown in order that the jury may estimate the

[159] *Michigan:* Howser *v.* Melcher, 40 Mich. 185.

New York: Hayden *v.* Florence S. M. Co., 54 N. Y. 221.

[160] *Illinois:* Favar *v.* Riverview Park, 144 Ill. App. 86 (location for show at amusement park).

Indiana: Sinker *v.* Kidder, 123 Ind. 528, 24 N. E. 341.

Iowa: Leick *v.* Tritz, 94 Ia. 322, 62 N. W. 855.

New York: Witherbee *v.* Meyer, 155 N. Y. 446, 50 N. E. 85.

Virginia: Newbrough *v.* Walker, 8 Gratt. 16, 56 Am. Dec. 127.

[161] *New York:* Ebenreiter *v.* Dahlman, 42 N. Y. Supp. 867, 19 Misc. 9.

Texas: Orange Hotel Co. *v.* Townsend (Tex. Civ. App.), 130 S. W. 701.

[162] *California:* Hawthorne *v.* Siegel, 88 Cal. 159, 25 Pac. 1114.

Michigan: Allison *v.* Chandler, 11 Mich. 542.

New York: Schile *v.* Brokhaus, 80

N. Y. 614; Snow *v.* Pulitzer, 142 N. Y. 263, 36 N. E. 1059; Capel *v.* Lyons, 20 N. Y. Supp. 49; Sositti *v.* Valente, 127 N. Y. Supp. 319.

[163] *Iowa:* Gibson *v.* Fischer, 68 Ia. 29.

Michigan: Woodin *v.* Wentworth, 57 Mich. 278.

New York: Colrick *v.* Swinburne, 105 N. Y. 503; Pollitt *v.* Long, 58 Barb. 20; Lakeside Paper Co. *v.* State, 45 App. Div. 112, 60 N. Y. Supp. 1081.

[164] *Massachusetts:* White *v.* Moseley, 8 Pick. 356.

Rhode Island: Simmons *v.* Brown, 5 R. I. 299, 73 Am. Dec. 66.

[165] *Iowa:* Winne *v.* Kelley, 34 Ia. 339.

Michigan: Bostwick *v.* Losey, 67 Mich. 554.

Minnesota: Cargill *v.* Thompson, 57 Minn. 534, 59 N. W. 638.

Oregon: Williams *v.* Island City Milling Co., 25 Ore. 574, 37 Pac. 49.

Wisconsin: Raynor *v.* Blatz Brewing Co., 100 Wis. 414, 76 N. W. 343.

value of such use.[166]   But the plaintiff cannot recover compensation for the loss of expected specific profits; the earning of such profits is too conjectural, and depends upon too many contingencies.[167]   In a Canadian case, an action for detention of the plaintiff's logs by the defendant, it was held that "the loss of use of the plaintiff's mill was too uncertain, and its ascertainment too much dependent on contingencies and conjectures, and too remote."[168]   The true ground on which to rest the decision seems to be the remoteness and not the uncertainty of the loss.

The same rule applies where the loss of use of the premises results from failure to supply machinery or power.[169]   Thus, when a mill was prevented from being run by reason of a steam-engine not being furnished for it according to contract, the loss of use of the mill during the time of its being stopped was held to be rightly included in the damages.   The court said: "When a contractor undertakes to perform a contract to erect a building or put a mill or other machinery in operation, he ought to be holden to indemnify the other party against the loss of the use of the building, mill, or other machinery, after the expiration of the time for performance of the

---

[166] *Illinois:* Carter v. Cairo, V. & C. Ry., 145 Ill. App. 653, affirmed 240 Ill. 152, 88 N. E. 493 (mine).

Iowa: Willis v. Perry, 92 Iowa, 297, 60 N. W. 727, 26 L. R. A. 124 (bath business).

Michigan: Barrett v. Grand Rapids Veneer Works, 110 Mich. 6, 67 N. W. 976.

New Hampshire: Crawford v. Parsons, 63 N. H. 438.

New York: Dickinson v. Hart, 142 N. Y. 183, 36 N. E. 801; Snow v. Pulitzer, 142 N. Y. 263, 36 N. E. 1059. And see § 944.

So it may be shown that the business had been operated at a loss: Phœnix J. C. Co. v. Grant, 136 Ky. 751, 125 S. W. 165 (mine).

[167] *Illinois:* Green v. Williams, 45 Ill. 206.

Michigan: Talcott v. Crippen, 52 Mich. 633, 18 N. W. 392; John Hutchinson Manuf. Co. v. Pinch, 91 Mich. 156, 51 N. W. 930, 30 Am. St. Rep. 463.

New York: Dodds v. Hakes, 114 N. Y. 260; Pollitt v. Long, 58 Barb. 20; Witherbee v. Meyer, 155 N. Y. 446, 50 N. E. 58 (reversing 84 Hun, 146, 32 N. Y. Supp. 537); Sossitti v. Valente, 127 N. Y. Supp. 319.

North Carolina: Sharpe v. Southern Ry., 130 N. C. 613, 41 S. E. 799.

Ohio: Cincinnati v. Evans, 5 Oh. St. 594.

Virginia: Newbrough v. Walker, 8 Gratt. 16, 56 Am. Dec. 127; Atlantic & D. Ry. v. Delaware Construction Co., 98 Va. 503, 37 S. E. 13.

Canada: Marrin v. Graver, 8 Ont. 39.

[168] Godard v. Fredericton Boom Co., 6 All. (N. B.) 448.

[169] W. P. Callahan & Co. v. Chickasha Cotton Oil Co., 87 Pac. 331, 17 Okla. 544.

contract. And in case it was defectively made, he should indemnify the party for the loss of the use of the property for the time necessarily required to repair it and put it in order."[170] And in an action for failure to supply a sufficient amount of water power for a grist mill, the measure of damages was held to be the difference between the rental value of the mill with the power contracted for and its rental value with the power actually furnished, the reasons given for excluding profits being (1) that in most cases they are too dependent on numerous and changing contingencies; (2) that they are ordinarily remote; (3) that such damages cannot generally be considered within the contemplation of the parties.[171] The first reason alone is enough, and will exclude profits when the cause of action is not breach of contract but tortious interference. The second reason is questionable. It is not because the loss is remote, but because there is a more certain and direct way of measuring it, that profits are excluded.

§ 190. Injury to machinery.

When machinery is not furnished according to agreement, or is wrongfully injured, the measure of damages is the value of the use of it. This is not an allowance of the profits which in the particular case might have been made, but of the average sum, represented by rent, which such property is worth. Expected profits, in such a case, are entirely too contingent; but rent is sufficiently certain to be allowed. The distinction is well shown by two New York cases, in the first of which profits were not, and in the other the value of the use was, allowed to be recovered. The first case was an action brought for the price of a steamboat. The defendant showed that part of the machinery was unsound, and proved other imperfections by which considerable delay was caused; and claimed to deduct from the contract price of the boat not only the sum necessary to remedy the actual defects, but also loss of profits upon the trips that might have been run during the time the

---

[170] *New York:* Taggart, P. J., in Davis *v.* Talcott, 14 Barb. 611, 628.

South Carolina: Standard Supply Co.

v. Carter, 81 S. C. 181, 62 S. E. 150, 19 L. R. A. (N. S.) 155.

[171] Witherbee *v.* Meyer, 155 N. Y. 446, 50 N. E. 58.

vessel was delayed on account of the imperfections in the construction, having proved that each trip would bring one hundred dollars net profits. But it was disallowed; and the court, citing the language of Pothier, said: "In short, it will be seen that on the subject in question our courts are more and more falling into the track of the civil law." [172]

The other was an action for the non-delivery of certain machinery which was to be used in the plaintiff's mill. The court allowed the plaintiff to recover not only the value of the machinery, but also the rent which might have been obtained from the use of the machinery.[173]

Selden, J., delivering the opinion of the court, said:

"Had the defendants, in the case of Blanchard v. Ely, taken the ground that they were entitled to recoup, not the uncertain and contingent profits of the trips lost, but such sum as they could have realized by chartering the boat for those trips, I think their claim must have been sustained. The loss of the trips which had certainly occurred, was not only the direct but the immediate and necessary result of the breach of the plaintiff's contract. . . . The rent of a mill or other similar property, the price which should be paid for the charter of a steamboat, or the use of machinery, etc., etc., are not only susceptible of more exact and definite proof, but in a majority of cases would, I think, be found to be a more accurate measure of the damages actually sustained in the class of cases referred to, considering the contingencies and hazards attending the prosecution of most kinds of business, than any estimate of anticipated profits; just as the ordinary rate of interest is upon the whole a more accurate measure of the damages sustained in consequence of the non-payment of a debt than any speculative profit which the creditor might expect to realize from the use of the money. It is no answer to this to say that, in estimating what would be the fair rent of a mill, we must take into consideration all the risks of the business in which it is to be used. Rents are graduated according to the value of the property and to an average of profits arrived at by very extended observation;

---

[172] Blanchard v. Ely, 21 Wend. (N. Y.) 342, 34 Am. Dec. 250, n.

[173] Griffin v. Colver, 16 N. Y. 486, 496, 69 Am. Dec. 718, n.

and so accurate are the results of experience in this respect that rents are rendered nearly if not quite as certain as the market value of commodities at a particular time and place."

Where, then, the defendant's wrongful act resulted in the stoppage of machinery, the measure of damages is the value of the use, that is, the rental value of the machinery; [174] so in an action against a carrier for delay in delivering the machinery; [175] against a manufacturer of machinery for failure to furnish it according to contract;[176] against one who broke a contract to keep machinery in repair.[177]

But profits expected from the use of the machinery cannot be recovered as such.[178] The defendant agreed to build a foundation for a mill which the plaintiff had bought and was to move to the foundation; it was held that the plaintiff, in an action for breach of the agreement, could recover the rental value of the mill, but could not recover compensation for the loss of expected profits.[179]

[174] *Connecticut:* Satchwell v. Williams, 40 Conn. 371.

Illinois: Strawn v. Cogswell, 28 Ill. 457; Benton v. Fay, 64 Ill. 417.

New York: Griffin v. Colver, 16 N. Y. 489, 69 Am. Dec. 718, *n.;* Cassidy v. Lefevre, 45 N. Y. 562; Freeman v. Clute, 3 Barb. 424; Davis v. Talcott, 14 Barb. 611.

North Carolina: Brown v. East Carolina R. R., 70 S. E. 625.

Pennsylvania: Pittsburgh Coal Co. v. Foster, 59 Pa. 365.

Tennessee: Pettee v. Tennessee M. Co., 1 Sneed, 381.

Wisconsin: Hinckley v. Beckwith, 13 Wis. 31.

England: Cory v. Thames I. W. & S. B. Co., L. R. 3 Q. B. 181.

[175] Priestley v. Northern I. & C. R. R., 26 Ill. 205.

[176] Green v. Mann, 11 Ill. 613.

[177] Middlekauff v. Smith, 1 Md. 329.

[178] *Georgia:* Willingham v. Hooven, 74 Ga. 233, 58 Am. Rep. 435.

Indiana: Connersville Wagon Co. v.

McFarlan Carriage Co., 166 Ind. 123, 76 N. E. 294, 297.

Michigan: McKinnon v. McEwan, 48 Mich. 106; Allis v. McLean, 48 Mich. 428.

New York: Krom v. Levy, 48 N. Y. 679.

North Carolina: Sharpe v. Southern Ry., 130 N. C. 613, 41 S. E. 799.

Ohio: Davis v. Cincinnati, H. & D. R. R., 1 Disney, 23.

Oregon: Hoskins v. Scott, 96 Pac. 1112, 52 Ore. 271.

Pennsylvania: Pennypacker v. Jones, 106 Pa. 237; Dixon Woods Co. v. Phillips Glass Co., 169 Pa. 147, 32 Atl. 432.

South Carolina: McMeekin v. Southern Ry., 82 S. C. 468, 64 S. E. 413.

Texas: Fraser v. Echo, M. & S. Co., 9 Tex. Civ. App. 210, 28 S. W. 714.

So, in an action for the price of milling machinery, defendant cannot set off loss of profits arising from delay in delivery. Howard v. S. & B. Mfg. Co., 139 U. S. 199, 35 L. ed. 148, 11 Sup. Ct. 500.

[179] Rogers v. Bemus, 69 Pa. 432. But in an action for breach of a similar con-

§ 191. Injury to crop—Warranty of seed.

A farmer cannot in general recover damages for the loss of profit he expected from a crop destroyed before maturity. The value of the mature crop is too uncertain.[180] Thus, where the defendant wrongfully seized the plaintiff's negroes, the profits of a crop he expected to plant and cultivate by means of the negroes are too uncertain to afford ground for recovery.[181] The defendant wrongfully seized the plaintiff's mule, which he intended to use to cultivate his crop; the loss of his crop was held both too uncertain and too remote for compensation.[182] If the mule were intended to use for the harvesting of a crop already matured, the loss would not be too uncertain. The defendant sold a drug which he warranted to kill cotton-worm; but it failed to do so. It was held that the loss of the crop was too uncertain to afford ground for recovery.[183] If the crop is partially grown at the time it is destroyed, it may already have a value as a growing crop; and in that case such value may be recovered.[184]

Under some circumstances the value of the mature crop may be shown with sufficient certainty to be allowed. So where defendant overflowed part of plaintiff's land and prevented his making a crop of sugar cane on such land, but the yield of other portions of plaintiff's land for the season was shown, and it was shown to be an unusually good season

tract, where the plaintiff, instead of moving an old mill to the foundation was to build a new mill upon it, the loss of use of the mill was too uncertain and conjectural for compensation. Bridges v. Lanham, 14 Neb. 369, 15 N. W. 704, 45 Am. Rep. 121.

[180] *Alabama:* Gresham v. Taylor, 51 Ala. 505.

Illinois: Young v. West, 130 Ill. App. 216.

K a n s a s: Missouri Pac. Ry. v. Haynes, (Kan. App.), 42 Pac. 259.

New York: Richardson v. Northrup, 66 Barb. 85.

North Carolina: Roberts v. Cole, 82 N. C. 229.

Texas: Texas & S. L. R. R. v. Young, 60 Tex. 201.

[181] McDaniel v. Crabtree, 21 Ark. 431.

[182] Sledge v. Reid, 73 N. C. 440.

[183] Jones v. George, 56 Tex. 149, 42 Am. Rep. 689.

[184] *Michigan:* People's Ice Co. v. Steamer Excelsior, 44 Mich. 229, 6 N. W. 636 (ice crop; get value of ice formed, allowing for all contingencies of harvest).

T e x a s: Sabine & E. T. Ry. v. Joachimi, 58 Tex. 456; Freeman v. Field (Tex. Civ. App.), 135 S. W. 1073 (immature cotton crop; get value of complete crop less expenses of maturing, harvesting and marketing).

for cane, it was held that the damages might include the value of the crop which it was reasonably shown could have been raised on the land, though no crop in fact came up.[185] In an Alabama case a contract was made for the sale of fertilizer, "with notice that it was intended for use on defendant's cotton crop" on a certain place. The fertilizer could not be purchased elsewhere, and the difference between that portion of the crop on which the fertilizer was used and that on which it was not was plainly visible and easily estimated. The plaintiff was allowed to recover the value of this difference.[186]

In a few cases the courts have gone further, and allowed the crops raised in other seasons or on other land to be shown.[187] So where gas from defendant's coke ovens injured plaintiff's crops it was said that a comparison of the crops with those raised before the ovens were built would afford some basis for an estimate of the damage sustained.[188] In California the same decision has been reached, in a case where the defendant broke a contract to lease a farm to the plaintiff: the court allowed the plaintiff to recover compensation based on the crop the average farmer would have raised with such tools, teams, etc., as the plaintiff had.[189] In cases such as the last two, the true measure of damages, in the light of principle, would seem to be the value of the use of the land, evidence of the average value of the crop of that or other years being admissible.

Where seed is warranted good and does not grow, expected profits from the crop to be raised are too uncertain. The rent of the land and the wasted labor and expense furnish all the compensation that are certain enough to base recovery upon.[190] If, however, a crop is raised, but is of inferior qual-

---

[185] Payne v. Morgan's Louisiana & T. R. R. & S. S. Co., 38 La. Ann. 164, 58 Am. Rep. 174. So in Texas the reasonable market value of peanuts which might have been raised on the premises, deducting cost of cultivating and marketing, was allowed. Cockrell v. Ellison (Tex. Civ. App.), 137 S. W. 150.

[186] Bell v. Reynolds, 78 Ala. 511, 56 Am. Rep. 52.

[187] *Illinois:* Chicago & R. I. R. R. v. Ward, 16 Ill. 522.

Texas: Dunbar v. Montgomery, (Tex. Civ. App.), 119 S. W. 907.

[188] Robb v. Carnegie Bros. & Co., 145 Pa. 324, 22 Atl. 649.

[189] Rice v. Whitmore, 74 Cal. 619, 16 Pac. 501, 5 Am. St. Rep. 479.

[190] *Connecticut:* Ferris v. Comstock, 33 Conn. 513.

ity, the element of uncertainty is removed. The value of the crop, if it had been of the quality warranted, can be ascertained with exactness; and the measure of damages is the difference between the value of the crop raised, and the value of the same crop from the seed ordered.[191] So in the case of unproductive hop roots warranted by the defendant, the plaintiff was allowed to recover the profit he would have made on the plants that grew if they had been productive.[192]

It will be noticed that there are three classes of cases arising out of the breach of warranty of seed. In the first class of cases, the seed is of such a quality that nothing grows from it. In such cases there is no basis for the estimation of expected profits, and they are therefore disallowed as uncertain. In the second class of cases the plants grow and the crop matures, but is of inferior quality. Here there is a reasonable basis on which to estimate the profit that would have been made if the seed had been of the quality called for by the contract; for the court has only to estimate the difference in value between the crop actually raised and the same crop of the proper quality. An allowance in these cases is therefore

---

Georgia: Butler *v.* Moore, 68 Ga. 780, 45 Am. Rep. 508.

Kansas: Shaw *v.* Smith, 45 Kan. 334, 25 Pac. 886, 11 L. R. A. 681.

North Carolina: Reiger *v.* Worth, 127 N. C. 230, 37 S. E. 217, 52 L. R. A. 362, 80 Am. St. Rep. 798.

Ohio: Phelps *v.* Eyria Milling Co., 12 Ohio Dec. 692.

An intimation to the contrary in England, Page *v.* Pavey, 8 C. & P. 769, is a bare intimation at *nisi prius.*

[191] *Florida:* Vaughan's Seed Store *v.* Stringfellow, 56 Fla. 708, 48 So. 410.

Illinois: Baltimore & O. S. W. R. R. *v.* Stewart, 128 Ill. App. 270.

Missouri: Anderson *v.* St. Louis, I. M. & S. Ry., 129 Mo. App. 384, 108 S. W. 605 (corn crop nearly mature).

New Jersey: Wolcott *v.* Mount, 36 N. J. L. 262, 13 Am. Rep. 438.

New York: Passinger *v.* Thorburn, 34 N. Y. 634, 90 Am. Dec. 753; White *v.*

Miller, 7 Hun, 427, 71 N. Y. 118, 27 Am. Rep. 13; Landreth *v.* Wyckoff, 67 App. Div. 145, 73 N. Y. Supp. 388; Depew *v.* Peck Hardware Co., 121 App. Div. 28, 105 N. Y. Supp. 390.

Wisconsin: Flick *v.* Wetherbee, 20 Wis. 392; Folsom *v.* Apple River Log Driving Co., 41 Wis. 602 (grass partly grown).

England: Randall *v.* Raper, E. B. & E. 84.

In Van Wyck *v.* Allen, 69 N. Y. 61, 25 Am. Rep. 136, there was an intimation that the decision on this point in the case of Passinger *v.* Thorburn was still open for revision. And Hurley *v.* Buchi, 10 Lea (Tenn.), 346, holds that even where the crop from the inferior seed matured, no compensation can be recovered for loss of crop.

[192] Schutt *v.* Baker, 9 Hun (N. Y.), 556.

made for loss of profits. The third class of cases lies between the first two. The plants grow, but are of such a sort that no crop matures at all. Here the expected profit is less conjectural than in the first class of cases, for the possible extent of the crop is limited by the number of plants which grow. On the other hand, the profit is more conjectural than in the second class of cases, for there is no matu.ed crop as a basis for estimating the profit.[193]

§ 192. Profits of a contract.

The benefits which would have accrued to the plaintiff from a contract broken by the defendant may be recovered, though they are in a certain sense contingent. The plaintiff, as has been seen, must prove that the benefit would have been secured. "The jury cannot be asked to guess. They are to try the case upon evidence, not upon conjecture."[194] But having made it appear reasonably certain that he would have obtained a benefit, the plaintiff is entitled to recover it.[195]

The leading case on this subject is Masterton v. Mayor of Brooklyn,[196] which will be more fully considered later. In that case it appeared that in January, 1836, an agreement was entered into between the defendants and the plaintiffs, by which the latter agreed to furnish and deliver marble to build a City Hall in Brooklyn, from Kain & Morgan's quarry, in Eastchester. The defendants were to pay $271,600 in different sums, as the work proceeded. The plaintiffs proved the delivery of the marble under their contract with the defendants, till July, 1837; when the latter refused to receive any more marble, although the plaintiffs were ready to proceed. The entire quantity of marble necessary to fulfil the plaintiff's contract was 88,819 feet. At the time the work

[193] See further, § 768.

[194] Strong, J., in Lentz v. Choteau, 42 Pa. 435.

[195] *United States:* Philadelphia, W. & B. R. R. v. Howard, 13 How. 305, 14 L. ed. 157; United States v. Behan, 110 U. S. 338, 28 L. ed. 168, 4 Sup. Ct. 81; Anvil Min. Co. v. Humble, 153 U. S. 540, 14 S. Ct. 876, 38 L. ed. 814.

But if the contract involves an option which the plaintiff might now have exercised, only nominal damages can be recovered on breach. Troy L. M. Co. v. Dolph, 138 U. S. 617, 34 L. ed. 1083, 11 Sup. Ct. 412.

[196] 7 Hill, 61.

was suspended, the plaintiffs had delivered 14,779 feet, for which the contract price had been paid. The defendant claimed that the profits expected from a full performance of the contract were too contingent and speculative to be allowed. The court, however, held otherwise. So where defendant agreed to make part payment for services in preferred stock of a corporation, and such stock was never issued, though the company was prosperous, it was held that the profits of the contract were not too uncertain for recovery.[197] Defendant agreed to buy two thousand cows at a certain price per thousand pounds. Plaintiff had bought 863 cows, and could buy the remainder in the same locality, when defendant defaulted. It was claimed that no amount of damages could be certainly proved, because it was impossible to estimate the weight of the unbought cows. But it was held that the cows which had been bought could be used as a standard of weight for all the cows.[198] And similarly, where defendant agreed to employ plaintiff to sink wells at a certain price per foot, and broke his agreement, on proof that wells in the neighborhood averaged five hundred feet deep the jury was allowed to give damages based on the profit of sinking wells of not greater depth than five hundred feet.[199]

§ 193. Contracts for a share in the profits of a business.

In that class of contracts, however, where the benefit secured is *a share in the profits of a business*, there is, as we have seen, difficulty. In Bagley *v.* Smith,[200] which was an action for the wrongful dissolution of a partnership, it was insisted by the defendant's counsel that the making of either the prospective or the past profits of a partnership the basis of a rule of damages was contrary to principle; that the inquiry into past profits involved the taking of an account which was impracticable in a trial at law, and that there was no basis for the jury to measure the fluctuations of trade, the danger

[197] Crichfield *v.* Julia, 147 Fed. 65, 77 C. C. A. 297.

[198] Fletcher *v.* Jacob Dold Packing Co., 41 App. Div. 30, 58 N. Y. Supp. 612.

[199] Sanford *v.* East R. I. District, 101 Cal. 275, 35 Pac. 865.

[200] 10 N. Y. 489, 61 Am. Dec. 756.

of losses, and the effects of competition, which were all involved in a calculation of future profits. Moreover, as the profitable prosecution of the business of the firm depended on the mutual confidence and harmonious co-operation of its members, its dissolution under circumstances which precluded these conditions, could not subject the withdrawing partner to damages on the basis of prospective profits.

But the court held that no rule of law required that the breach of a covenant contained in partnership articles should be compensated by nominal damages only; that as the object of commercial partnerships was profit, the most direct and legitimate injury which could be occasioned by an unauthorized dissolution of a firm was the loss of profits; that although there was great inherent difficulty in accurately estimating future gains, this difficulty would not be lessened by shutting out the light from the past, and that as no one out of a court of justice could undertake to judge of the future profits of a business without informing himself, if practicable, as to those in the past, there appeared to be no reason why a legal tribunal should not do so. The court also refused to limit the plaintiff's claim for profits to the period between the dissolution and his subsequent entry into business.

The question is still one of certainty. Where a profit has actually been made, this may be proved as very pertinent to the question what the future profits would probably have been had not the business been interrupted, and as a material aid to the jury in the solution of this question;[201] but where no profit has ever been realized, the mere loss of an opportunity to try to make a profit is of too uncertain value to be compensated.

Where an action was brought for breach of an agreement to form a partnership, and it was proved that the plaintiff had given up an East India voyage, as was well known to the defendant, he was allowed to show the value of the voyage, not as special damage, but as an ingredient for estimating the value which each of the parties set on the contract in dis-

---

[201] *New York:* Dart v. Laimbeer, 107 N. Y. 664; Bathrick v. Coffin, 13 App. Div. 101, 43 N. Y. Supp. 313.

Pennsylvania: Reiter v. Morton, 96 Pa. 229.

England: Gale v. Leckie, 2 Stark. 107.

pute.[202]   Where, however, the partnership was terminable at any time upon notice, no recovery can be had on account of expected future profits.[203]

In Dennis *v.* Maxfield [204] the plaintiff was hired for a whaling voyage, and was to receive a certain "lay" or percentage of the profits, and additional compensation if the cargo reached a certain amount.   Being wrongfully dismissed, it was held he could recover compensation for both items of loss, the voyage having ended and the profits of the voyage being known.   The court (Bigelow, C. J.) said: "The parties have expressly stipulated that profits should be the basis on which a portion of the plaintiff's compensation for services should be reckoned.   These earnings or profits were therefore within the direct contemplation of the parties, when the contract was entered into.   They are undoubtedly in their nature contingent and speculative and difficult of estimation; but, being made by express agreement of the parties of the essence of the contract, we do not see how they can be excluded in ascertaining the compensation to which the plaintiff is entitled." The court then cited contracts of partnership and of insurance of profits, and continued: "In such cases the parties, having by their contract adopted a contingent, uncertain, and speculative measure of damages, must abide by it, and courts and juries must approximate as nearly as possible to the truth in endeavoring to ascertain the amount which a party may be entitled to recover on such a contract in the event of a breach. If this is not the rule of law, we do not see that there is any alternative short of declaring that where parties negotiate for compensation or indemnity in the form of an agreement for profits or a share of them, no recovery can be had on such a contract in a court of law—a proposition which is manifestly absurd."

This, it must be noted, is a contract where the profits are those of a business, not the profits of the plaintiff's individual exertions.   He may in such a case wait until the business is completed and the profit realized, and then recover his pro-

---

[202] M'Neill *v.* Reid, 9 Bing. 68.

[203] *New York:* Skinner *v.* Tinker, 34 Barb. 333.

Texas: Ball *v.* Britton, 58 Tex. 57.

[204] 10 All. (Mass.) 138.

portion, as he did in the case just cited; [205] or if the business has been so long established that he can reasonably prove that a profit will be realized, he may recover at once upon the breach. [206]   But if it is a new enterprise, and there is no proof that profit will be made, the plaintiff can prove no loss and should recover no damages on account of the loss of profits; the burden of proving a profit is upon him. [207]   Thus, where the plaintiff had a contract by which he was to have half the wood standing on a certain lot for cutting and cording it, and the standing wood was negligently destroyed by the defendant, it was held that the plaintiff could recover no compensation for the profit he might have made, for it was too uncertain. [208]

On this principle the profits of a theatrical performance are so uncertain that where the profits are to be shared between the manager of the company and the owner of the house neither can recover anticipated profits upon breach by the other; and therefore when the manager fails to bring the play to the theatre the owner can recover no damages. [209]

On the other hand, the profit may be sufficiently certain for recovery.   Thus in the case of a contract to mine ore from defendant's mine (the contract having been arbitrarily terminated by defendants) [210] if there is reasonable certainty of proof, the plaintiff may recover for prospective profits; and in an action upon a contract for working a farm on shares for five years, which contained a provision that the defendant should pay the damages suffered by the plaintiff if the farm was sold before the end of the term, and it appeared that it was sold after one year, it was held that plaintiff might recover

[205] Tygart v. Albritton, 5 Ga. App. 412, 63 S. E. 521.

[206] Wakeman v. Wheeler & W. M. Co., 101 N. Y. 205, 4 N. E. 264, 54 Am. Rep. 676; Crittenden v. Johnston, 7 App. Div. 258, 40 N. Y. Supp. 87; Lavens v. Lieb, 12 App. Div. 487, 42 N. Y. Supp. 901.

[207] United States: Curran v. Smith, 149 Fed. 945, 81 C. C. A. 537.

Maine: Winslow v. Lane, 63 Me. 161.

Pennsylvania: Delp v. Edlis, 190 Pa. 25, 42 Atl. 462.

[208] Barnard v. Poor, 21 Pick. (Mass.) 378.

[209] Missouri: Hughes v. Robinson, 60 Mo. App. 194.

New York: Moss v. Tompkins, 69 Hun, 288, 23 N. Y. Supp. 623; Cutting v. Miner, 30 App. Div. 457, 52 N. Y. Supp. 288.

[210] Anvil Mining Co. v. Humble, 153 U. S. 540, 38 L. ed. 814, 14 Sup. Ct. 876.

the loss of profits on the four remaining years; and the profit of the year already gone by could be shown, not as a measure, but to help the jury fix the profit of succeeding years.[211]

§ 193a. Agency commission contracts.

Contracts by which agents secure compensation for extending a business, payable by commission on business obtained, are very common. In such cases, loss of profits may be recovered, upon wrongful discharge of the agent, if they can be proved with reasonable certainty.[212]

§ 193b. Contracts in restraint of trade or competition.

On the same principle, in the case of lawful contracts in restraint of trade, a breach often makes an inquiry into profits necessary. Thus in an action by the vendor of certain property to recover damages for breach of an agreement by the vendee not to use it in conflict with the vendor's business, loss of profits may be shown, and evidence of plaintiff's profits before and after breach is competent.[213] And in an action for breach of a contract by which defendant was to sell ice through plaintiff, giving plaintiff half profits and contracting not to sell himself within the territory, and he did sell other ice within the territory, it was held that the measure of damages was the profits on the ice sold within the territory which would otherwise

---

[211] Depew v. Ketchum, 75 Hun, 227, 27 N. Y. Supp. 8.

[212] *United States:* Wells v. National Life Assoc., 99 Fed. 222, 39 C. C. A. 476.

Iowa: Hickhorn v. Bradley, 117 Iowa, 130, 90 N. W. 592 (evidence of sales made by others after breach).

Maryland: Stern v. Rosenheim, 67 Md. 503, 10 Atl. 221, 307 (of sales for four months before breach).

Michigan: Mueller v. B e t h e s d a Spring Co., 88 Mich. 390, 50 N. W. 319 (of sales made by plaintiff's successor).

New York: Wakeman v. Wheeler & W. M. Co., 101 N. Y. 205, 4 N. E. 264, 54 Am. Rep. 676 (of sales by plaintiff's

successor); De Leon v. McKernan, 25 N. Y. Misc. 182, 54 N. Y. Supp. 167 (sales for preceding year shown).

South Dakota: Cranmer v. Kohn, 7 S. D. 247, 64 N. W. 125 (sales for two preceding years shown).

Wisconsin: Richey v. Union Cent. Life Ins. Co., 140 Wis. 486, 122 N. W. 1030 (business of preceding years shown).

Contra, California: Parke v. Frank, 75 Cal. 364, 17 Pac. 427 (recovery restricted to commissions on orders sent in).

See *post*, § 669.

[213] Hitchcock v. Anthony, 83 Fed. 779, 54 U. S. App. 439, 28 C. C. A. 80.

have been sold by the plaintiff, not including, however, sales made where ice was not delivered.[214]

On the other hand, in an action for breach of a contract not to sell a patented article in plaintiff's territory, it was held that it could not be proved that the plaintiff would have made the sale which the defendant made, or would have made any particular profit; but he was allowed to recover the amount of profit made by the defendant on the sale.[215]

§ 194. Collateral profits.

Profits which the plaintiff might have made in any other transactions if the defendant had performed his contract, even though the loss of them is a natural consequence of the wrong, are frequently disallowed, on the ground that they are more or less speculative and contingent. He is able only to show that he *might* have made those profits. He is not able to prove that he certainly could or would have made them if the defendant had not committed any wrong. In Fox v. Harding [216] the court said that "If the profits are such as would have accrued and grown out of the contract itself, as the direct and immediate result of its fulfilment," then they should be allowed. "But if they are such as would have been realized by the party from other independent and collateral undertakings, although entered into in consequence and on the faith of the principal contract, then they are too uncertain and remote to be taken into consideration as a part of the damages occasioned by the breach of the contract in suit." When that is the objection, the plaintiff is usually given the average of profits, as being what he would probably have made. On a contract to furnish a boat to ferry excursionists who were to arrive at a certain time, the measure of damages was held to be the ordinary earnings of such a boat at such a time.[217] But where the boat was to be used as an excursion boat on an entirely new route, anticipated profits

---

[214] Hall v. Stewart, 58 Iowa, 681, 12 N. W. 741.

Acc., Russell v. Horn B. & F. Mfg. Co., 41 Neb. 567, 59 N. W. 901.

[215] Cincinnati Siemens-Lungren Gas Illuminating Co. v. Western Siemens Lungren Co., 152 U. S. 200, 14 S. Ct. 523, 38 L. ed. 411.

[216] 7 Cush. (Mass.) 516; *acc.*, Smith v. Flanders, 129 Mass. 322.

[217] Mace v. Ramsey, 74 N. C. 11.

are too uncertain, and nothing can be recovered on account of the loss of use of the boat.[218] So on a breach of contract to furnish an excursion train to the plaintiff, the profit he would have made on tickets already sold may be recovered; but profit he might have made by a sale of tickets after the breach of the defendant's agreement are too uncertain.[219]

It was attempted in a New York case [220] (which is not sustained by later authorities) to apply this same rule in a case of partnership. The distinction is plain. In the latter case the plaintiff is attempting to recover the benefit conferred on him by the contract; here the profit is claimed, not as promised by the defendant, but as likely to arise collaterally out of the performance of the contract.

An exposition company agreed to allow plaintiff to exhibit his cigarette machine; on breach of this agreement, the profits he might have made by sales of the machine are too uncertain for recovery.

A railroad company agreed to build houses for its hands near the plaintiff's land. It was held that possible loss of profits at his store and mill was too speculative.[221] Where a railroad company failed to perform its agreement to make the city of Fort Scott the terminus of one division of its line, and erect machine-shops, etc., there, it was held that an inquiry into the value of real estate and amount of business, in order to show what profits would have been made, was improper; such profits were too speculative. But the city might show the value of the buildings to it as taxable property, damages to be estimated on the principle of annuity, on the average rate of taxation during past years.[222] On a contract by the defendant to erect a factory or establish a business in a place where the plaintiff owned land, it has been held that profits which might have been made by the plaintiff through a rise in the value of his land are too uncertain.[223]

[218] Mitchell v. Cornell, 44 N. Y. Super. Ct. 401.

[219] Houston & T. C. Ry. v. Hill, 63 Tex. 381, 51 Am. Rep. 342.

[220] New York: Van Ness v. Fisher, 5 Lans. 236.

North Carolina: Winston C. M. Co. v. Wells, W. T. Co., 141 N. C. 284, 53 S. E. 885, 8 L. R. A. (N. S.) 255.

[221] Evans v. Cincinnati, S. & M. Ry., 78 Ala. 341.

[222] Missouri, K. & T. Ry. v. Fort Scott, 15 Kan. 435.

[223] Michigan: Shaw v. Hoffman, 25

But in Watterson v. Allegheny Valley Railroad,[224] an action for the defendant's breach of contract to construct a depot on land sold the plaintiff by the defendant, it was held that the plaintiff could recover the additional value which would accrue to the plaintiff's other land by the erection of such a depot, the court saying that the profits of the plaintiff's business could not be added to his damages, for they were too speculative and uncertain.

Where it can be made reasonably certain that a gain would have resulted, and there is no other objection to its allowance, the mere fact that the amount is to some extent conjectural will not prevent its allowance. In the case of Frye v. Maine Central Railroad [225] it was held, in an action for breach of an agreement to allow plaintiff the carriage of passengers from D. to G., that the plaintiff could not only recover the profits he would have made on the carriage from D. to G., but also what he would have made on way passengers, on express, and on the mail, by being so situated that he could carry more cheaply than any one else.

So where the object of a contract, known to the defendant, is to enable the plaintiff to perform another contract already made, the profits of such already existing contract may be proved with sufficient certainty to be recovered.[226]

§ 195. Loss of use of personal property.

Where the defendant wrongfully injured or withheld the plaintiff's chattel, the measure of damages is the average or usual value of the use of the chattel during the time the plaintiff lost the use of it, and not the profits hoped for from its use.[227] If the owner had an established custom of letting the chattel for hire, so that the jury could determine what

Mich. 162; Fitzsimmons v. Chapman, 37 Mich. 139, 26 Am. Rep. 508.

Pennsylvania: McConaghy v. Pemberton, 168 Pa. 121, 31 Atl. 996.

Canada: Dullea v. Taylor, 35 Up. Can. Q. B. 395.

[224] 74 Pa. 208; acc., Louisville, S. L. & T. Ry. v. Neafes, 93 Ky. 53, 18 S. W. 1030.

[225] 67 Me. 414.

[226] *Michigan:* Industrial Works v. Mitchell, 114 Mich. 29, 72 N. W. 25.

Virginia: Consumers' Ice Co. v. Jennings, 100 Va. 719, 42 S. E. 879.

[227] *Connecticut:* Fritts v. New York & N. E. R. R., 62 Conn. 503, 26 Atl. 347 (horse).

income he had from it, he may recover that income, which is analogous to the profit of an established business.[228] Thus where the plaintiff's stallion was injured by the defendant, it was held that the profits he would probably have made during the season could be shown, "not as the measure of damages, but as a guide to the exercise of that discretion which must always, to a certain extent, rest with the jury." [229] In an action for a fraudulent representation as to the age of a female slave, it was held not to be an element of the damage that she might have borne several children if she had been as young as represented. This is too uncertain.[230] So where a travelling salesman, whose compensation is based on commissions on such orders secured by him as his employer approves, shipped his trunks of samples over the line of a common carrier, and they were unreasonably delayed, he cannot, in a suit for breach of the contract to convey, recover as damages for such delay the profits from orders which, tested by past experience, he would have secured during the period he was without his trunks.[231]

§ 196. Loss of use of a vessel.

In adjusting the damages against the official liquidator of a ship-building company for delaying the repairs of a ship beyond the time agreed, the Lord Chancellor observed that "he had proceeded on the principle that if a profit would arise from a chattel, and it is left with the tradesman to repair, and detained by him beyond a stipulated time, the measure of damages is *prima facie* the sum which would have

District of Columbia: Washington & G. R. R. *v.* American Car Co., 5 App. D. C. 524 (cars for street railway).

Illinois: Benton *v.* Fay, 64 Ill. 417.

Indiana: Shelbyville L. B. R. R. *v.* Lewark, 4 Ind. 471.

Kansas: Monroe *v.* Lattin, 25 Kan. 351; Brown *v.* Hadley, 43 Kan. 267.

Massachusetts: Johnson *v.* Holyoke, 105 Mass. 80.

Minnesota: Williams *v.* Wood, 55 Minn. 323, 56 N. W. 1066 (threshing machine).

Vermont: Luce *v.* Hoisington, 56 Vt. 436.

Wisconsin: Wright *v.* Mulvaney, 78 Wis. 89, 46 N. W. 1045.

But *contra,* McLaughlin *v.* Bangor, 58 Me. 398.

[228] Cushing *v.* Seymour, 30 Minn. 301.

[229] Fultz *v.* Wycoff, 25 Ind. 321.

[230] Whitson *v.* Gray, 3 Head (Tenn.) 441.

[231] Seaboard Air Line Ry. *v.* Harris, 121 Ga. 707, 49 S. E. 703.

been earned in the ordinary course of employment of the chattel in the time."[232]   And the same rule was applied where the defendant, the builder, delayed the delivery of a vessel beyond the stipulated time.[233]   But where, in an action on a bond given to obtain the discharge of a vessel attached under a lien for repairs, the defendants sought to recoup the damages sustained by them from the plaintiff's delay in completing the contract, it was held that the probable earnings or profits of the vessel were too uncertain to form a rule of damages.   The true measure of damages was the price which would have to be paid for the charter of a similar boat during the period of unnecessary detention, less all expenses which would necessarily have been incurred by the owner.[234]   Where a vessel was injured by a collision, the measure of damages was held to be the loss of freight during the period she was laid up; in other words, the loss of use of the vessel.[235]   But expected specific profits cannot be recovered for the loss of use of a vessel.[236]

[232] *In re* Trent and Humber Co., L. R. 4 Ch. 112, 117, affirming L. R. 6 Eq. 396.

[233] *United States:* De Ford v. Maryland Steel Co., 113 Fed. 72, 51 C. C. A. 59.

Pennsylvania: Brown v. Foster, 51 Pa. 165.

Bohn v. Cleaver, 25 La. Ann. 419, was an action for breach of an agreement to furnish the plaintiff, on a certain day, with a steamer for a full cargo to Liverpool or Havre, at a stipulated rate. The ship was not ready, but on that day freights to Liverpool were higher than the agreed rate. The plaintiff was not allowed to recover any damages, the court holding that they would be too speculative. Two judges, however, dissented, holding that the measure of damages was the difference between the contract and the ruling rate on a full cargo. This latter seems the correct view.

[234] *New York:* Rogers v. Beard, 36 Barb. 31, s. c. 20 How. Pr. 98.

Pennsylvania: Brown v. Foster, 51 Pa. 165.

[235] *United States:* Williamson v. Barrett, 13 How. 101, 14 L. ed. 68; The Potomac, 105 U. S. 630, 26 L. ed. 1194; The Mayflower, 1 Bro. Adm. 376, 388; The Narragansett, Olcott, 388; The M. J. Sanford, 37 Fed. 148.

Connecticut: New Haven S. B. Co. v. Vanderbilt, 16 Conn. 420.

New York: Mailler v. Express P. L., 61 N. Y. 312.

England: Heard v. Holman, 19 C. B. (N. S.) 1; The Clarence, 3 Rob. Adm. 283; The Argentino, 14 App. Cas. 519.

But see Smyrna, L. & P. S. B. Co. v. Whillden, 4 Harr. (Del.) 228. In Brown v. Beatty, 35 Up. Can. Q. B. 328, it was held that the loss of freight could not be compensated in an action at law, but only in a proceeding in admiralty; but the court in this seems to have been mistaken.

[236] *United States:* De Ford v. Mary-

The same rule applies in an action on a charter party for the detention of a vessel; the measure of damages is her probable net earnings, that is, the value of the use, during the period of detention.[237]

In case of loss of use of a yacht there is some difficulty in arriving at the value of the use, since the boat is used for pleasure, not for profit. If evidence can be given of what the yacht could have been chartered for, this may be shown.[238]

§ 197. Profits expected from a sale of goods.

The profits expected upon a sale of goods at retail cannot usually be recovered, for two reasons. In the first place, the value of the goods is their actual wholesale market price; in the second place, such profits are too contingent.[239]

The case of Wehle v. Haviland [240] is an important decision on this point. The action was for seizing the stock in trade of the plaintiff under an attachment. The court below, on the authority of an opinion previously expressed by the Commission of Appeals in the same case,[241] had allowed the plaintiff to recover the fair *retail* value of her goods. In the Court of Appeals this was held to have been an error, Allen, J., saying: "The retail value or the price at which goods are sold at retail, includes the expected and contingent profits, the earning of which involves labor, loss of time and expenses, supposes no damage to or depreciation in the value of the goods, and is dependent upon the contingency of finding purchasers for cash, and not upon credit, within a reasonable time, the sale of the entire stock without the loss by unsalable remnants, and the closing out of a stock of goods as none

land Steel Co., 113 Fed. 72, 51 C. C. A. 59.

Delaware: Smyrna, L. & P. S. B. Co. v. Whillden, 4 Harr. 228.

Massachusetts: Brown v. Smith, 12 Cush. 366.

Michigan: Aber v. Bratton, 60 Mich. 357.

Missouri: Callaway M. & M. Co. v. Clark, 32 Mo. 305.

[237] Huron Barge Co. v. Turney, 79 Fed. 109.

[238] The Walter W. Pharo, 1 Lowell, 437; The Sagonda, 44 Fed. 367; The Conqueror, 166 U. S. 110, 41 L. ed. 937, 17 Sup. Ct. 510. In this case the allowance of $15,000 as demurrage, on a yacht which cost $75,000, for a little over five months of autumn and winter, was held to be obviously excessive.

[239] Young v. Cureton, 87 Ala. 727.

[240] 69 N. Y. 448.

[241] Reported as Wehle v. Butler, 61 N. Y. 245.

ever was or ever will be closed out, by sales at retail at full prices. . . . The plaintiff was entitled to compensation, and that consisted of the market value of the goods, their cost, or what they would have cost in the market, and interest thereon, and nothing more. The retail profit was not included in the compensation to which she was entitled." If, however, no more goods of the sort are to be procured at wholesale, the retail price, if proved with reasonable certainty, may be recovered.[242]

If as often happens a sale by plaintiff was only possible, not certain, the profits of sale would be too uncertain for recovery. Thus where in an action for breach of contract by which defendant agreed to advertise her patent remedies as on sale at plaintiff's store, plaintiff claimed loss of profits by failure of the advertisement, it was held that they were merely conjectural and there could be no recovery.[243] And for failure to print plaintiff's book, on which she was to receive a royalty only after the sales had exceeded 2,000 copies, she could not show a loss with sufficient certainty to be entitled to damages for loss of royalty.[244]

§ 198. Profits included in the market price.

On the other hand, the owner of goods, or the purchaser of goods which are not delivered, may always recover the market price at the place where he should have had the goods; this often includes profits. So in trover, where the plaintiff recovers the value of the goods at the place of conversion, without taking into account their cost in some distant market, and the expenses of their carriage, he may really obtain profits.[245] So in an action against a carrier for failure to deliver goods, the owner recovers the market value of the goods at the time and place of delivery.[246] And in an action for failure to deliver goods bought, the purchaser's recovery is based upon the market value at the time and place of delivery.[247]

---

[242] Alabama I. W. *v.* Hurley, 86 Ala. 217. There being no wholesale market, the real value would be that at retail.

[243] Stevens *v.* Yale, 113 Mich. 680, 72 N. W. 5.

[244] Bean *v.* Carleton, 12 N. Y. Supp. 519.

[245] Blum *v.* Merchant, 58 Tex. 400.

[246] See chapter on Carriers.

[247] See chapter on Sales.

France *v.* Gaudet [248] rests upon this principle. The plaintiff had purchased champagne lying at defendant's wharf at 14*s.* per dozen, and resold it at 24*s.;* defendant refused to deliver the wine. The plaintiff could not fulfil his contract, as similar wine was not procurable in the market. The defendant had no notice of the resale. It was held that the plaintiff could recover the price at which he had resold the champagne, since that was its actual value at the time and place of delivery. Other cases rest upon the same principle. So where by the defendant's fault the plaintiff's cattle are poorly pastured, he may recover compensation for the weight which they should have gained, that is, for the additional value they should have had in the market. [249]

§ 199. Profits expected from the manufacture of raw material.
Where raw material warranted by the defendant to be of a certain quality is manufactured by the plaintiff, and after being manufactured is discovered to be of inferior quality, the measure of damages is not the lessened value of the material, but of the product: provided, of course, the inferiority could not be discovered before manufacture. In Parks *v.* Morris A. & T. Co. [250] a plaintiff was allowed, in an action for breach of warranty as to the quality of steel, to recover the difference between the value of axes he had manufactured with the steel and the value of such axes if they had been manufactured of steel of the quality warranted. Where the plaintiff bought dust warranted to be of hard coal for use in making bricks, and it proved to contain soft coal dust, the measure of damages was the lessened value of the bricks. [251] Such cases seem to amount to an indirect allowance of profits, which form part of the *value* which the plaintiff has lost.

But where goods were purchased for manufacture, and were not supplied, the plaintiff cannot recover the expected profit of manufacture and sale of the manufactured goods where such profits are speculative. [252]

---

[248] L. R. 6 Q. B. 199.
[249] Hoge *v.* Norton, 22 Kan. 374; Gilbert *v.* Kennedy, 22 Mich. 117.
[250] 54 N. Y. 586.

[251] Milburn *v.* Belloni, 39 N. Y. 53, 100 Am. Dec. 403.
[252] *Alabama:* Byrne Mill Co. *v.* Robertson, 149 Ala. 273, 42 So. 1008; Dick-

The same general rule applies, and profits anticipated from the manufacture of raw material are denied, in cases where the failure to complete the manufacture is due to failure to supply machinery[253] or delay in transporting the material,[254] or failure to furnish one of the processes of manufacture,[255] or destruction of material.[256]

On the other hand, where the defendant agreed to take the entire output of plaintiff's factory for a year at an agreed price, and failed to do so, it was held that the amount of profits that would have been realized from the manufacture was not too uncertain for recovery.[257]   And where the elements of the profit are certain, and the loss of it was necessarily caused by the defendant's wrong, as where the manufacturer was unable to procure other material, recovery for loss of profits may be had.   So where the defendant converted logs which the plaintiff was about to saw in his mill, and the plaintiff was unable to get other logs, it was held that the profits he would have made, i. e., the full value of the lumber less the expense of sawing, could be recovered.[258]   Where it appeared that the logs were afterwards delivered to the plaintiff, sawed, and sold, but that during the period of delay the price of lumber had fallen, such profits were measured by the difference between the price of lumber at the time of sale and at the time it would have been sold but for the defendant's delay.[259]

§ 200. From competition or speculation. Value of a chance.

Profits expected from a competition or a speculation are too uncertain for compensation.   In a case in England, where

erson v. Finley, 158 Ala. 149, 48 So. 548.

Kentucky: Asher v. Stacey, 23 Ky. L. Rep. 1586, 65 S. W. 603.

Nebraska: French v. Ramge, 2 Neb. 254.

[253] Acme Cycle Co. v. Clarke, 157 Ind. 271, 61 N. E. 561.

[254] Reading v. Donovan, 6 La. Ann. 491.

[255] Amsden v. Atwood, 69 Vt. 527, 38 Atl. 263.

[256] Quay v. Duluth, S. & A. Ry., 153 Mich. 567, 116 N. W. 1101.

[257] *Iowa:* Taft v. Tiede, 55 Iowa, 370, 7 N. W. 617.

Massachusetts: Speirs v. Union Drop Forge Co., 180 Mass. 87, 61 N. E. 825.

[258] Auger v. Cook, 39 Up. Can. Q. B. 537; Cockburn v. Muskoka, M. & L. Co., 13 Ont. 343.

[259] Mississippi & R. R. B. Co. v. Prince, 34 Minn. 71.

a prize had been offered for the best plan and model of a machine, and plans and models were to be sent by a certain day, the plaintiff sent a plan and model accordingly, by a railway, but through the negligence of their agents it did not arrive at its destination till after the time appointed; it was considered that the proper measure of damages was the value of the labor and materials expended on the plan and model, and that the chance of obtaining the prize was too remote to be estimated.[260] In a similar case in Pennsylvania this opinion was disapproved, the court holding that the value of the opportunity to compete for the premium furnished the measure of the plaintiff's damages. If the company were informed of the object of the transmission, the loss of the privilege of the competition was in view of both parties when they entered into the contract, and if not, the loss was still the result of the carrier's negligent breach. But it appearing from the evidence of one of the committee by whom the prizes were awarded, that the plaintiff must at any rate have failed to obtain the prize, he was held entitled to nominal damages only.[261] The rule laid down by the English court seems most in accordance with principle.

It has been held that in an action for the wrongful transmission of a telegraph message, whereby the plaintiff was prevented from entering his horse in a race, no damages could be recovered on account of the chance of winning a prize.[262] And in an action for injuring a horse, the owner could recover nothing for the loss of the chance of winning prizes in races.[263]

On the other hand, where a carrier has notice that goods are intended for exhibition at a show, and delays carriage so that they cannot be shown, it has been held that the plaintiff may recover the profits he would have made from exhibiting the goods and selling them at the stores,[264] or from the increase in his business which he can with reasonable certainty show would have resulted.[265]

[260] Watson v. Ambergate, N. & B. Ry., 15 Jur. 448.

[261] Adams Express Co. v. Egbert, 36 Pa. 360, 78 Am. Dec. 382.

[262] Western U. T. Co. v. Crall, 39 Kan. 580.

[263] Mizner v. Frazier, 40 Mich. 592, 29 Am. Rep. 262.

[264] Jameson v. Midland Ry., 50 L. T. Rep. (N. S.) 426.

[265] Kennedy v. American Express Co., 22 Ont. App. 278.

It has been held that the chance of obtaining employment in a particular situation, for which the plaintiff intended to apply, is too uncertain;[266] but the chance that a father would pay a son's debt to release him from custody can be estimated.[267]

A telegram ordering the purchase of oil at a certain price was delayed, until the next day, when the price had risen, and no oil was bought. It was held that no damages could be recovered of the telegraph company for loss of possible profit on a purchase and sale of oil; for the sale might not have been made, and the chance of gain was too contingent.[268]

Where the defendant agreed to pool his stock with the plaintiff's until it could be sold together, but broke the contract by selling to a stranger, who thereby obtained control of the corporation, it was held that the chance of realizing a profit by the pool was too contingent to be compensated.[269] In organizing new companies, agreements to pay for assistance in the stock of the company when formed are common. In such a case, suit was brought to recover the par value of 2,000 shares in a new corporation, the formation of which was alleged to have been prevented by the defendant. There was no evidence that the stock would have been worth more than 50, and a verdict for the full amount claimed was set aside.[270] Where a contract called for the sale of treasury stock, and private stock was conveyed instead, the difference was a mere matter of speculation and could not be considered in damages.[271] Defendant, operating a public telephone, received a message for a constable that a murderer, for whom $200 reward had been offered, was in a certain place. Instead of informing the constable, defendant himself went and captured the murderer and got the reward. It was held that while nominal damages could be recovered for not delivering the

---

[266] Hoey v. Felton, 11 C. B. (N. S.) 142; Brown v. Cummings, 7 All. (Mass.) 507 (application withdrawn after injury before it had been acted upon).

[267] Macrae v. Clark, L. R. 1 C. P. 403.

[268] Western U. T. Co. v. Hall, 124 U. S. 444, 31 L. ed. 479, 8 Sup. Ct. 577.

[269] Havemeyer v. Havemeyer, 45 N. Y. Super. Ct. 464.

[270] Pitt v. Kellogg, 11 N. Y. Supp. 526.

[271] Findlater v. Dorland, 152 Mich. 301, 116 N. W. 410, 15 Detroit Leg. N. 285.

message, the chance of capturing the murderer was not one for which the constable could recover. Until the reward was earned he had no proprietary rights in it. All he was deprived of was an opportunity to make an attempt to earn the reward before some one else should do so. The court remarked that human law has never proved adequate to meet all varieties of human meanness.[272]

The question sometimes arises whether the run of fish on a particular fishing ground can be proved with sufficient certainty to form the basis of recovery. Thus where a net was destroyed by the defendant, resulting in delay in fishing, it was held that the anticipated catch was too uncertain to form the basis of recovery.[273] But in another case where the cause of action was wrongful exclusion from the fishing grounds it was held that the amount of fish which would probably have been taken could be shown.[274] In an action for breach of a contract by which plantiff was given the right to sell 80 per cent. of defendant's pack of fish, it was shown that defendant refused to sell through plaintiff, and it was held that plaintiff could recover the amount of profits. Deep-sea fishing is not more speculative than mining, for instance; there was no uncertainty as to the existence, but only as to the extent of profits; and the defendant having by his misconduct made it impossible to prove the exact amount, is not entitled to set up uncertainty. Evidence of sales by other agents after the breach could be received to show the probable amount of profit.[275]

Drilling an oil-well is a speculative venture; and for breach of contract to drill a well no damages can be recovered, where the plaintiff has made no expenditures on faith of the contract.[276]

Two recent English cases are worth comparing on this point.

[272] Smith a v. Gentry, 45 S. W. 515, 20 Ky. L. Rep. 171, 42 L. R. A. 302.

[273] Wright v. Mulvaney, 78 Wis. 89, 46 N. W. 1045. The same decision was reached in an action for dumping refuse into the water near plaintiff's fishweir, thus causing him to lose the run of fish. Lamond v. Sea Coast Canning Co., (Me.), 79 Atl. 385.

[274] Pacific Steam Whaling Co. v. Alaska Packers' Assoc., 128 Cal. 632, 72 Pac. 161.

Acc., New York: Smalling v. Jackson, 117 N. Y. Supp. 268, 133 App. Div. 382.

[275] Emerson v. Pacific C. & N. Co., 96 Minn. 1, 104 N. W. 573.

[276] Gayton v. Day, 178 Fed. 249.

In the first of them defendant agreed to furnish his stallion for plaintiff's brood mare, but instead of doing so he sold his stallion; but another stallion served plaintiff's mare. Plaintiff offered evidence of the profit he had made from the sale of foals by the same stallion and claimed damages based on loss of value of the foal from this mare. It was held that such damage was too contingent, and plaintiff was entitled to nominal damages only. The court enumerated nine contingencies on which depended his hoped-for profit.[277]

In the other case, the defendant contracted to give fifty ladies, selected by the votes of readers of a newspaper, a chance of presenting themselves before him for the choice of twelve of them for engagements at varying remunerations. The plaintiff was one of the fifty ladies chosen, but was not given a reasonable chance of presenting herself for the final selection. It was held in the Divisional Court that she could recover substantial damages for the loss of the promised chance, and the jury allowed her £100. The court admitted that the chance was a speculative one, and depended largely on the personalty of the defendant.[278] The decision was affirmed in the Court of Appeal.[279] The earlier case was distinguished on the ground that in it the number of contingencies was greater.

[277] Sapwell v. Bass, [1910] 2 K. B. 486.

[278] Chaplin v. Hicks, 27 T. L. R. 244.
[279] 27 T. L. R. 458.

CHAPTER X

AVOIDABLE CONSEQUENCES

I.—Avoidable Consequences not Recoverable

II.—Limitations

III.—Recovery of Expense of Avoiding Loss

I.—AVOIDABLE CONSEQUENCES NOT RECOVERABLE

§ 201. Plaintiff cannot recover for avoidable consequences.

* The same principle which refuses to take into consideration any but the direct consequences of the illegal act, is applied to limit the damages where the plaintiff, by using reasonable precautions, could have reduced them.**

So in Maine, in an action of assumpsit for a quantity of limestone, the court said:

"In general, the delinquent party is holden to make good the loss occasioned by the delinquency. But his liability is limited to direct damages which, according to the nature of the subject, may be contemplated or presumed to result from his failure. Remote or speculative damages, although susceptible of proof and deducible from the non-performance, are not allowed; and if the party injured has it in his power to take measures by which his loss may be less aggravated, this will be expected of him. If the party entitled to the benefit of a contract can protect himself from a loss arising from a breach, at a trifling expense or with reasonable exertions,— he fails in social duty if he omits to do so. For example, a party contracts for a quantity of bricks to build a house, to be delivered at a given time, and engages masons and carpenters to go on with the work. The bricks are not delivered. If other bricks, of an equal quality and for the stipulated price, can be at once purchased on the spot, it would be unreasonable, by neglecting to make the purchase, to claim and receive of the delinquent party damages for the workmen, and the amount of rent which might be obtained for the house if it had been built." [1]

[1] Miller *v.* Mariner's Church, 7 Me. 51, 20 Am. Dec. 341. The same language is held in Iowa, Davis *v.* Fish, 1 Greene (Ia.), 406, 48 Am. Dec. 387.

So in trespass in Massachusetts, it appearing that the defendant had broken down the plaintiff's fence in November, but that the plaintiff did not repair the breach till May, in consequence of which cattle got in and destroyed the crop of the next year, and the claim being for the loss of the subsequent year's crop, as well as the expense of repairing the fence, the Supreme Court said: [2]

"In assessing damages, the direct and immediate consequences of the injurious act are to be regarded, and not remote, speculative, and contingent consequences, which the party injured might easily have avoided by his own act. Suppose a man should enter his neighbor's field unlawfully, and leave the gate open; if, before the owner knows it, cattle enter and destroy the crop, the trespasser is responsible. But if the owner sees the gate open, and passes it frequently, and wilfully and obstinately, or through gross negligence, leaves it open all summer, and cattle get in, it is his own folly. So, if one throw a stone and break a window, the cost of repairing the window is the ordinary measure of damage. But if the owner suffers the window to remain without repairing a great length of time after notice of the fact, and his furniture, or pictures, or other valuable articles, sustain damage, or the rain beats in and rots the window, this damage would be too remote. We think the jury were rightly instructed, that, as the trespass consisted in removing a few rods of fence, the proper measure of damages was the cost of repairing it, and not the loss of a subsequent year's crop, arising from the want of such fence." [3]

And the rule is applied in equity as well as at law.[4]

§ 202. Reason of the rule.

It is frequently said that it is the *duty* [5] of the plaintiff to

---

[2] Loker v. Damon, 17 Pick. 284, per Shaw, C. J.

[3] *Acc.*, Thompson v. Shattuck, 2 Met. (Mass.) 615; Gulf, C. & S. F. Ry. v. Simonton, 2 Tex. Civ. App. 558, 22 S. W. 285.

[4] Taylor v. Read, 4 Paige (N. Y.), 561.

So, also, in Admiralty. Pettie v. Boston Tow Boat Co., 49 Fed. 464, 1 U. S. App. 57; The Timor, 61 Fed. 633.

[5] The use of the word *duty* is common in the cases, and it is almost impossible to avoid it; but it should be clearly understood that its use is loose; there being no corresponding *right* in the defendant to require the plaintiff to avoid the consequences.

reduce the damages as far as possible. It is more correct to say that by consequences which the plaintiff, acting as prudent men ordinarily do, can avoid, he is not legally damaged. Such consequences can hardly be the direct or natural consequence of the defendant's wrong, since it is at the plaintiff's option to suffer them. They are really excluded from the recovery as *remote*. In this view the doctrine would rest on the intervention of the plaintiff's will as an independent cause. *Ad hoc* he is not damaged by the defendant's act, but by his own negligence or indifference to consequences. Thus, in a case in New Jersey, the cause of action was the taking by the defendant of the plaintiff's flat from his ferry, whereby the plaintiff was prevented from crossing a river, and obliged to leave his horses and wagon on the bank to go in search of the flat. In his absence the horses ran into the river and were drowned; but it was held that the plaintiff could not recover for their loss, which was caused by his own negligence in leaving them unsecured.[6] And the rule applies in every case where the damages are increased by the negligence of the plaintiff,[7] since the increased damages are in that case chargeable to him and not to the defendant.[8]

§ 203.[a] Different from the rule of contributory negligence.

The application of the doctrine of contributory negligence and of that of avoidable consequences often produce results that closely resemble each other; but there is a distinction

[a] For former § 203, see § 226a.

[6] Gordon v. Butts, 2 N. J. L. 333.

[7] *Massachusetts:* Cavanagh v. Durgin, 156 Mass. 466, 31 N. E. 643.

New Jersey: Lord v. Carbon I. M. Co., 42 N. J. Eq. 157, 6 Atl. 812.

New York: Clark v. Marsiglia, 1 Denio, 317.

Texas: Williams v. Yoe, 19 Tex. Civ. App. 281, 46 S. W. 659.

[8] *United States:* Texas & P. Ry. v. White, 101 Fed. 928, 42 C. C. A. 86, 62 L. R. A. 90 (plaintiff injured by defendant; instead of attending to the injury he takes a long journey).

Illinois: Moss v. Pardridge, 9 Ill.

App. 490 (plaintiff injured by defendant's dog; he employed an improper person to look after the injury).

Michigan: Talley v. Courter, 93 Mich. 473, 53 N. W. 621 (fire set by defendant on plaintiff's land; plaintiff discovers it, but fails to put it out).

New York: Wood v. New York C. & H. R. R. R., 184 N. Y. 290, 77 N. E. 27 (hole dug in plaintiff's land by defendant; plaintiff falls into it. It was plaintiff's duty as employee of defendant to examine the premises. He cannot recover for the personal injury, only for the trespass to the land).

between the two.   Contributory negligence defeats the action itself.   The rule of avoidable consequences can never produce this result, as it cannot be applied until a cause of action, which in any event will entitle the party injured to nominal damages, has arisen.[9]   The rule, therefore, is really a rule of limitation upon the plaintiff's recovery.   Nor is it properly to be regarded as a species of mitigation of damages.   This relates to the defendant and generally to the character of his acts; e. g., that a tort was not malicious; that, after committing a trespass, he repaired the wrong as far as possible.   But a reduction of the *plaintiff's* damages by any such particulars as flow from his own imprudent act or omission to act *after the wrong has been committed*, constitute a distinct class of remote damages in the strict sense of the word; of damages which flow from the illegal act, but for which the law gives no redress.

There are cases in which contributory negligence comes into play to defeat the action, not after the wrong has been committed and the cause of action arisen, but after the *negligence* of the defendant has occurred, e. g., when a signal is omitted by an approaching train, and the person to be warned might have protected himself, but failed to do so, he cannot maintain an action.   There is, however, no lack of harmony between this and the general principle.   The negligence which

---

[9] Lawson *v.* Price, 45 Md. 123, 137; Baltimore & S. P. R. R. *v.* Hackett, 87 Md. 224, 39 Atl. 510.   This distinction is made very clear by the fact that in such a case as that of personal service, a plea *in bar of the action* that by reasonable diligence plaintiff might have procured employment at a compensation equal to that agreed to be paid him, is bad.   Armfield *v.* Marsh, 31 Miss. 361.   He is entitled to nominal damages, at any rate.   It is true that in the case of Franklin *v.* Smith, 21 Wend. (N. Y.) 624, it was held that, in an action against a notary for omission of notice of protest, where it appeared that the plaintiff need not have sustained any loss with ordinary atten-tions to the case, the notary was not liable.   On the other hand, in Williams *v.* Yoe, 19 Tex. Civ. App. 281, 46 S. W. 659, in an action of trespass *q. c. f.*, it was held error to refuse to charge the jury "that if plaintiff could have avoided the damages had he acted as a prudent and reasonable man would have done under the circumstances and that the damages he may have sustained were the result of plaintiff's carelessness or negligence they should find for the defendant."   Nominal damages should have been allowed as the action was trespass *q. c. f.* but in Franklin *v.* Smith, damage was the gist of the action.

contributes to defeat the action may obviously be prior to, simultaneous with, or subsequent to the defendant's negligence.[10]

§ 204.[a] The rule of general application.

The rule applies, both in contract and tort, and illustrations may be drawn from every branch of the law.[11] Thus in an ordinary contract for manufacture and delivery of chattels, when a vendor fails to deliver, the usual rule is the difference between the contract and market price, and this, says Sharswood, J.,[12] is "for the evident reason that the vendee can go into the market and obtain the article contracted for at that price." This would be an application of the rule of avoidable consequences, and it follows that when it appears that an article of the same quality cannot be procured in the same market, the true measure is the actual loss in manufacture by having to use an inferior article, or the loss on any sub-contract. But even here, the rule of avoidable consequences cannot be lost sight of.

§ 205.[b] Application of the rule to contracts generally.

The rule may be applicable in any case of breach of contract. Where damages are claimed, not for the direct injury, that is, the loss of the value of the contract itself, but for a consequential loss, the plaintiff cannot recover for such loss if he might reasonably have avoided it. So for breach of contract to insure plaintiff's property the plaintiff, who learned of the breach, could not recover the value of the property which was some time afterwards destroyed by fire, since he might himself have insured the property within a reasonable time.[13] In an action for breach of contract to furnish steam power to plaintiff, no recovery can be had for damages caused by an attempt to run the machines with insufficient power.[14]

---

[a] For former § 204, see § 203.

[10] Cf. Southern Ry. v. Smith, 86 Fed. 292.

And see Chaves v. Torlina, 99 Pac. 690, (N. Mex.).

[11] Loomer v. Thomas, 38 Neb. 277, 56 N. W. 973.

[b] For former § 205, see § 204.

[12] McHose v. Fulmer, 73 Pa. 365.

[13] Brant v. Gallup, 111 Ill. 487, 53 Am. Rep. 638.

[14] Russell v. Giblin, 16 Daly, 258, 10 N. Y. Supp. 315 (affirming 5 N. Y. Supp. 545).

In an action for breach of contract to repair a mill-dam the miller cannot recover for loss of use of the mill, since he might have repaired the dam himself.[15]　For breach of contract to maintain a fence plaintiff cannot recover for loss of crops from lack of the fence, since he could have built it himself.[16]　For breach of contract by defendant to serve as overseer of a plantation, plaintiff cannot recover for loss of crop, since he might have employed another overseer.[17]　In an action for breach of covenant of warranty, where the plaintiff lost his land because of a tax sale before plaintiff received his deed, it appeared that the plaintiff had notice of the tax sale one year before the time for redemption expired.　It was held that he could not recover damages for the loss of the land.[18] And the rule has been applied generally.[19]　Some particular classes of contracts will now be considered.

§ 206. Contracts for personal services.

When a servant, or other employee, is discharged without

[15] Thompson v. Shattuck, 2 Met. (Mass.) 615.

[16] Lake Erie & W. R. R. v. Power, 15 Ind. App. 179, 43 N. E. 959.

[17] Dryer v. Lewis, 57 Ala. 551.

[18] McCollum v. Davis, 8 U. C. Q. B. 150.

[19] *United States:* Warren v. Stoddart, 105 U. S. 224, 26 L. ed. 1117 (failure to supply books sold by plaintiff, an agent).

California: Mabb v. Stewart, 147 Cal. 413, 81 Pac. 1073 (failure to supply water for irrigation).

Georgia: Oxford Knitting Mills v. American Wringer Co., 6 Ga. App. 642, 65 S. E. 791 (failure to deliver machinery for mill).

Indiana: Heavilon v. Kramer, 31 Ind. 241 (wrongful discharge).

Iowa: Beymer v. McBride, 37 Ia. 114 (failure to deliver goods sold); Kimball Bros. Co. v. Citizens' Gas & Electric Co., 141 Ia. 632, 118 N. W. 891 (failure to furnish electric power).

Kansas: Sherman Center Town Co.

v. Leonard, 46 Kan. 354, 26 Pac. 717, 26 Am. St. Rep. 101 (failure to move a building for use as a hotel).

Nebraska: Loomer v. Thomas, 38 Neb. 277, 56 N. W. 973 (failure to pasture plaintiff's cattle).

New Jersey: Ramsey v. Perth Amboy S. & E. Co., 65 Atl. 461, 72 N. J. Eq. 165 (contract to build vessels left partly completed).

New York: Wilson v. Martin, 1 Den. 602; Spencer v. Halstead, Ib. 606 (failure to furnish board and lodging); Dillon v. Anderson, 43 N. Y. 231 (failure to construct boilers for steamboat); Pierce v. Cornell, 102 N. Y. Supp. 102, 117 App. Div. 66 (failure to furnish iron work for building).

Pennsylvania: Hoffman v. Delaware, L. & W. R. R., 39 Pa. Super. Ct. 47 (failure to deliver machine for cutting fodder for cattle).

Wisconsin: Anderson v. Savoy, 124 N. W. 1053, 142 Wis. 127 (failure to supply ice).

lawful cause, he will, acting with ordinary prudence, seek other employment, and the amount which he earns in this way, or which he might have earned had he used reasonable efforts, will be allowed in reduction of the damages given for his discharge.[20] And a plaintiff who receives as much in the new employment as he would have received in the old one, is, on the principles already stated, still entitled to nominal damages.[21] The rule does not mean that the party injured is bound to take any employment that offers, nor to abandon his home and place of residence to seek other employment, but only to use reasonable diligence in procuring employment of the same or similar kind.[22]

§ 207. Employment of different kind.

It is well established that the plaintiff is not compelled to accept employment of an entirely different sort.[23] "The defendants had agreed to employ the plaintiff in superintending a railroad from Albany to Schenectady, and they cannot insist that he should, in order to relieve their pockets, take up the business of a farmer or a merchant. Nor could they require him to leave his home and place of residence to engage in business of the same character with that in which he had

[20] *Arkansas:* Walworth v. Pool, 9 Ark. 394; McDaniel v. Parks, 19 Ark. 671.

Maine: Sutherland v. Wyer, 67 Me. 64.

New York: Hoyt v. Wildfire, 3 Johns. 518; Shannon v. Comstock, 21 Wend. 457, 34 Am. Dec. 262, *n.*; Howard v. Daly, 61 N. Y. 362, 19 Am. Rep. 285.

North Carolina: Hendrickson v. Anderson, 5 Jones L. 246.

Pennsylvania: King v. Steiren, 44 Pa. 99, 84 Am. Dec. 419.

Wisconsin: Gordon v. Brewster, 7 Wis. 355.

And as the plaintiff cannot enhance his damages by lying idle, so it has been said he cannot make a claim for services by performing his side of the contract after breach by defendant. Thus, in a case of employment to do work and labor in cleaning and repairing paintings, when defendant notified

plaintiff not to go on, but the latter nevertheless completed the work, it was held by the Supreme Court of New York that he had no right to increase his claim in this way. Clark v. Marsiglia, 1 Denio, 317.

[21] Williams v. Chicago Coal Co., 60 Ill. 149.

[22] Williams v. Chicago Coal Co., 60 Ill. 149; Costigan v. Mohawk & H. R. R., 2 Den. 609, 43 Am. Dec. 758, *n.;* Howard v. Daly, 61 N. Y. 362, 19 Am. Rep. 285; Fuchs v. Koerner, 107 N. Y. 529. The case of Huntington v. Ogdensburgh & L. C. R. R., 33 How. Pr. 416, seems in conflict with this general limitation of the rule.

[23] *United States:* Leatherberry v Odell, 7 Fed. 641;

New York: Fuchs v. Koerner, 107 N. Y. 529.

been employed by the defendants." [24]   So in a case where
the manager of a bank was wrongfully discharged, the court
said: "No doubt the position of manager of a bank was not
to be got every day, and that was to be considered." [25]   Nor
is a discharged agent or servant bound to accept employment
of greatly inferior sort than that from which he was discharged.
Thus, where a mate was wrongfully discharged, and was able
to get employment only before the mast, it was held that he
was not bound to accept such employment; and what he had
in fact earned before the mast was not deducted from the
wages due him by his contract. [26]   And the plaintiff may in
certain cases have a right to reject employment suitable in
kind but defective in some other essential respect.   Thus, the
plaintiff's minor son having been wrongfully discharged by the
defendant, it was held that the father was not bound to accept for his son the first employment that was offered, but
had a right to look for other things than mere wages, namely,
for the material and moral welfare of his son. [27]

§ 208. Duty to seek employment does not arise in all con-
tracts.

The duty to seek employment, too, is dependent upon the
original contract being one of employment or hiring.   It is
not applicable to every species of contract.   This question has
been considered by the Supreme Court of Pennsylvania [28] in
the case of the lease of a farm when possession was refused.
In an action by the lessee the lessor was permitted to prove
that the lessee had engaged in a totally different occupation
from farming, which had been more profitable to him.   The
Supreme Court of Pennsylvania held this to be error, on the
ground that ordinary contracts of hiring and contracts for
the performance of some specific undertaking cannot be governed by the same rule; that in the one case the party can

---

[24] Costigan v. Mohawk & H. R. R., 2 Den. (N. Y.) 609, 43 Am. Dec. 758, n.

[25] Hartland v. General Exchange Bank, 14 L. T. Rep. 863.

[26] Sheffield v. Page, 1 Sprague, 285; but quære, as to the last point: if he ac- tually earned it, since what he recovers is the value of the contract, i. e., the value of his whole time, must not all actual earnings be deducted?

[27] Strauss v. Meertief, 64 Ala. 299, 38 Am. Rep. 8.

[28] Wolf v. Studebaker, 65 Pa. 459.

earn no more than the wages, and if he gets that his loss will be but nominal; whereas, in the other case, the loss of the party is the loss of the benefit of the contract. To apply the doctrine of avoidable consequences to such cases would "involve proof of everything, great and small, no matter how various the items done by the plaintiff during the period of the contract might be, and how much he made in the meantime." Besides this, in analogy with the principle of proximate cause, it was said that whatever is to have the effect of lessening the plaintiff's damages should have some proximate relation to the contract itself.[29] The value of such contracts as these does not lie in the value of plaintiff's time, as they are usually capable of performance through sub-contracts.

§ 208a. Replacement in the market.

If the breach of contract results in depriving the plaintiff or in preventing the acquisition by the plaintiff of something, the rule of avoidable consequences may cast upon him the practical necessity of deciding, as a reasonable man, whether or not to replace the property of which he is thus deprived. It must be noticed at the outset that since the rule has to do with consequential loss only, the plaintiff can never be called upon to replace property of which he has been deprived in

[29] *Acc., Florida:* Sullivan v. McMillan, 37 Fla. 134, 19 So. 340, 56 Am. St. Rep. 239 (contract to haul logs).

Kentucky: Horn v. Carroll, 90 S. W. 559, 28 Ky. L. Rep. 839 (contract to manufacture cross-ties).

New York: Simon v. Levinson, (N. Y. Misc.), 126 N. Y. Supp. 659. In this case plaintiffs were employed to manufacture coats for defendants at a certain price per coat, defendants to supply cloth and material. Defendants cannot reduce damages by showing plaintiff's earnings on other contracts; distinguishing Levine v. Rosenschein, 134 App. Div. 157, 118 N. Y. Supp. 890, because by construction of that contract it involved the rendition of personal services by plaintiffs to the full extent of their time, though they might be assisted in such service by others. Here, a certain result was to be obtained for defendants irrespective of personal services by the plaintiffs.

See also Richey v. Union C. L. I. Co., 140 Wis. 486, 122 N. W. 1030. Plaintiff employed as defendant's district agent had built up a business, and was then wrongfully discharged. He was allowed to recover the value of the business, from which nothing should be deducted on account of plaintiff's subsequent earnings in other business. The court said: "When appellee terminated the agreement and destroyed the business, its liability became fixed. It was responsible for the value of the agency business as it then existed, and which went out of existence by its illegal act."

order to avoid a direct loss. Thus upon breach of a contract
to deliver goods to the plaintiff, the latter cannot be called
upon to procure other goods in order to gain the advantage
of a subsequent rise in price; and this for two reasons: first,
it would not affect the direct loss, *i. e.*, the loss of the profit
of the contract, since that is determined by deducting the
contract price from the value of the goods at the time for
performance; second, if goods were bought by the plaintiff
at the time of the breach and this purchase, because of a subsequent rise in the value of the goods, proved profitable, the
plaintiff and not the defendant should be entitled to the benefit of the profit, since it is the result of his good judgment in
buying and the compensation for his risk.[30]

If, however, the plaintiff is claiming damages, not for loss
of the direct profits of the contract, but because of some consequential loss, and this loss might have been prevented if
he had with reasonable prudence replaced himself in the
market by procuring the thing elsewhere, the general rule
of avoidable consequences will prevent his recovering the
consequential loss which he might thus have avoided.[31] So a
purchaser (giving notice of the intended use) can, for failure
to deliver machinery, recover for damages for his mill being
kept idle only till he could replace himself in the market.[32]
In Hinde *v.* Liddell,[33] an action for breach of contract to deliver shirtings, it appeared that the plaintiff had bought the
best substitute he could get after the defendant's breach, so
as to comply with a sub-contract he had entered into. Although this substitute was more expensive and of better
quality, it was held that he could recover the difference between the contract price and the price he had paid for these
shirtings, Blackburn, J., saying: "But there was no market
for this particular description of shirtings, and therefore no
market price; in such a case the measure of damages is the
value of the thing at the time of the breach of the contract,
and that must be the price of the best substitute procurable."
And so upon breach of a contract to supply plaintiff with ice

[30] See *post,* § 641a.
[31] Barnett *v.* Elwood Grain Co., (Mo.
App.), 133 S. W. 856 (*semble*).

[32] Benton *v.* Fay, 64 Ill. 417.
[33] L. R. 10 Q. B. 265.

he will as a reasonable man procure ice elsewhere as cheaply as possible in order to mitigate the consequential loss.[34]

Scott *v.* Boston & N. O. S. S. Co.[35] was a case against a carrier for non-delivery, where the plaintiff lost a sub-contract at an increased price. The case seems to be rested by the court on the absence of notice, but it is also said that "it would ordinarily be unjust" to make loss of profits in such a case a basis of damages, because the plaintiff can generally protect himself from loss by a purchase of the commodity at the market. "He cannot be permitted to recover of the defendant for losses which by reasonable effort he might have avoided."

This principle often finds an application in the case of error in transmission of or failure to transmit a telegram, the result being a failure by the sender to acquire property. The loss of the property being a consequential result of the breach of the telegraph company's obligation, it must be avoided, if possible, by acquiring the property elsewhere after notice of the breach. So in True *v.* International Telegraph Company,[36] an action against a telegraph company for failure to deliver a message which accepted an offer to sell plaintiffs some corn, the measure of damages was held to be the difference between the price named and that which the plaintiff would have been obliged to pay at the same place, in order, *by due and reasonable diligence after notice of the failure* of the telegram, to purchase the like quantity and quality of the same species of merchandise. And where plaintiff telegraphed an acceptance of an offer to buy cotton of him, on finding that the message had not been sent, it was held that he should have taken, within a reasonable time, steps to prevent unnecessary loss. "If he had the cotton to deliver, or had arranged to procure it for delivery, he should have made an effort to sell it; and if he made future contracts for its purchase, for the purpose of fulfilling his contract of sale, he was not authorized to extend them from month to month on a declining market, and fasten the loss on defendant."[37]

---

[34] Creve Cœur Lake Ice Co. *v.* Tamm, 90 Mo. App. 189.

[35] 106 Mass. 468.

[36] 60 Me. 9.

[37] Western Union Telegraph Co. *v.* Way, 83 Ala. 542.

So where, by reason of a mistake in the transmission of a telegram, plaintiff through his agent bought cotton which he did not want, and on learning of the mistake next morning he ordered a sale of it, and it was sold at a loss, the court held that in ordering the sale he was acting properly; if he had held the cotton for a speculation he would have done so at his own risk. The plaintiff was therefore allowed to recover the loss caused by the sale, which was in effect a step to put a stop to further loss.[38]

§ 209. Landlord's agreement to repair.

In a suit by tenant against landlord for breach of agreement to repair, the general rule is that the measure of damages is the expense of the repairs; for these the plaintiff, being in possession of the premises, may and should make. And therefore, if a landlord fails to make repairs as agreed before a certain date, the damages are to be assessed as of that date. The tenant cannot recover a claim paid by him to another party for damages subsequently caused by the defective condition of the premises.[39] When the landlord agrees to furnish timber to keep old fences in repair and pay the tenant for any new rails made and put up necessary for repairs, and the tenant could have made the fences good and at trifling expenditure, it was held that he should have done so, and not having taken the proper steps, could not recover for subsequent injury therefor owing to want of fences.[40] And so where the landlord covenanted to repair a mill-dam, and failed to do so, it was the place of the tenant to repair it, and he could not neglect to do so and then recover for injury to the machinery caused by its inactivity and for loss of custom.[41] In a case in

[38] Heath v. Postal T. C. Co., (S. C.), 69 S. E. 283.

[39] Sparks v. Bassett, 49 N. Y. Super. Ct. 270.

[40] Parker v. Meadows, 86 Tenn. 181.

[41] Fort v. Orndorff, 7 Heisk. (Tenn.) 167. In this case, as well as the preceding, a right to repair was reserved to the tenant by contract, but the cases were decided upon the general principle under discussion. In the case of a mill-dam where the ownership on the two banks of a stream is in different persons, an express stipulation may (as in Fort v. Orndorff, supra) give the tenant a right to make repairs on premises outside the lease which he would otherwise not have. In such a case as Parker v. Meadows, above, the stipulation would oblige the landlord to pay under the contract what otherwise the tenant might compel him to pay out-

Missouri [42] the lessor covenanted to build a wall on leased premises, and it was held by the Supreme Court of that State that the lessee's measure of damages in such a case was not the difference in rental value, but the cost of rebuilding the wall and damages for the period of delay. The tenant cannot abandon the premises and then claim damages for the whole loss. And such is the general rule.[43] Nor can the tenant recover compensation for injury to his own property on the premises caused by the lack of repairs,[44] at least where it is not prudent to keep property on the premises while they are unrepaired.[45] So where, in a lease of a dairy farm for five years, the lessor agreed to put the barns on the premises in a good state of repair, but neglected to do so; it was held that the lessee could recover the amount it would cost to put the barns in repair, but not the damage sustained by injuries to the cows and young cattle, the increase of food required and the decrease of produce resulting from the state of the barns; these damages being "altogether too remote and contingent."[46] And so in an action brought on a covenant to keep one-half of a mill-dam in repair it was held in Massachusetts that the plaintiff, whose duty it was to repair the other half, could not recover the loss of profits in his business through the dam falling out of repair.[47] The lessor of a mill covenanted to repair a dam, and if he did not the lessee had the right to make

side the contract by way of damages for its breach.

[42] Fisher v. Goebel, 40 Mo. 475.

[43] *Maryland:* Middlekauff v. Smith, 1 Md. 329.

Massachusetts: Flynn v. Trask, 11 All. 550.

New York: Walker v. Swayzee, 3 Abb. Pr. 136.

Vermont: Keyes v. Western Vt. Slate Co., 34 Vt. 81.

England: Penley v. Watts, 7 M. & W. 601.

[44] *Nebraska:* Caves v. Bartek, 85 Neb. 511, 123 N. W. 1031 (non-repair of plastering; goods injured by mice).

New York: Rose v. Butler, 69 Hun, 140. 23 N. Y. Supp. 375 (goods injured by non-repair of premises).

Wisconsin: Muth v. Frost, 68 Wis. 425, 32 N. W. 231 (machinery injured by non-repair of roof).

In Miller v. Smythe, 22 S. E. 532, in an action against a landlord for failure to repair some shelves, it was said that the plaintiff's negligence in having her goods upon them would not defeat the action unless it amounted to a want of ordinary care, the exercise of which would have prevented the injury, though it should be considered by the jury in reducing the damages.

[45] Cook v. Soule, 56 N. Y. 420 (affirming 1 T. & C. 116).

[46] Dorwin v. Potter, 5 Denio (N. Y.), 306.

[47] Thompson v. Shattuck, 2 Met. (Mass.) 615.

repairs at the expense of the lessor.   In an action by the lessee
for breach of the covenant of repair it was held that loss of
profits caused by the disrepair of the dam was too remote.[48]
If the repairs are so extensive that it would not pay the
tenant to make them, he is entitled to recover the difference
in rental value of the premises with and without the repairs.[49]

It is to be noticed, however, that the general rule appears
to be departed from in a few cases.   Thus in the case of a covenant by a landlord to repair it has been held by the New
York Court of Appeals that the tenant has an option either
to make the repairs and charge the expense to the landlord,
or to hold the latter for the full amount of the damage.[50]   In
a subsequent case [51] the court (Grover, J.) approved this rule,
but said: "There may be exceptions to this rule.   In cases
where the requisite repairs are trifling, and the damage by
not making them is large, I think it is the duty of the tenant
to make them and charge the landlord with the cost." [52]   This
would make the doctrine of avoidable consequences the exception, while the general rule governing covenants to repair
would be that the tenant had a choice whether to repair or
not.

Two Alabama cases seem at variance with each other on
the subject of the general rule that where a landlord, who is
under obligation to repair fences, fails to do so, it is the tenant's place to make them, and that if he fails he cannot hold
the landlord responsible for consequential damages, such as
the depredations of cattle.[53]   In the first of these cases the decision is expressly rested on the ground that the labor and
expense which the repairs would have required were of an
extraordinary character, and that the diligence required "did
not extend so far," which seems to recognize the rule of avoidable consequences.   But in the second case the court held that
the tenant had the right to rely on the promise of the landlord

---

[48] Fort v. Orndorff, 7 Heisk. (Tenn.)
167.

[49] Biggs v. McCurley, 76 Md. 409, 25
Atl. 466.

[50] Myers v. Burns, 35 N. Y. 269; Hexter v. Knox, 63 N. Y. 561.

[51] Cook v. Soule, 56 N. Y. 420.

[52] Citing Miller v. Mariners' Church,
7 Me. 51, 20 Am. Dec. 341; Loker v.
Damon, 17 Pick. 284.

[53] Vandegrift v. Abbott, 75 Ala. 487;
Culver v. Hill, 68 Ala. 66, 44 Am. Rep.
134.

to make the repairs, and that on a breach the landlord was liable for damages by depredations.

§ 210. Tenant's agreement to make repairs.

The case of a breach by a tenant presents a different question. The landlord is out of possession, and therefore in general is not in a position to make repairs himself. Usually his measure of damages will be the injury to the reversion, and the rule of avoidable consequences will not apply.[54]

§ 211. Failure to furnish freight or cargo.

For failure to furnish cargo, the measure of damages is the contract price, less the net earnings of the vessel, during the period of the charter.[55]

And so when defendant agreed to hire a barge for freighting, and subsequently abandoned it, the plaintiff notified him that unless he used the barge he would do so himself, and credit him with all net earnings. The barge having been used in this way, it was held that plaintiff was entitled to recover the contract price, less such net earnings.[56] And the rule is the same in cases of land-carriage.[57]

§ 212. Contracts of carriage.

The general rule applies to contracts of carriage.[58] Hamilton v. McPherson [59] was a case against a carrier for injury

[54] Turner v. Lamb, 14 M. & W. 412; Payne v. Haine, 16 Id. 541; Smith v. Peat, 9 Ex. 161; Doe v. Rowlands, 9 C. & P. 734.

[55] *Alabama:* Murrell v. Whiting, 32 Ala. 54.

California: Utter v. Chapman, 38 Cal. 659.

Massachusetts: Bailey v. Damon, 3 Gray, 92.

Missouri: Dean v. Ritter, 18 Mo. 182.

New York: Shannon v. Comstock, 21 Wend. 457, 34 Am. Dec. 262, n.; Heckscher v. McCrea, 24 Wend. 304; Ashburner v. Balchen, 7 N. Y. 262.

England: Smith v. McGuire, 3 H. & N. 554.

[56] Johnson v. Meeker, 96 N. Y. 93, 48 Am. Rep. 609.

[57] Dunn v. Daly, 78 Cal. 640.

[58] *Indiana:* Cincinnati & C. A. L. R. R. v. Rodgers, 24 Ind. 103.

Massachusetts: Sullivan v. Old Colony St. Ry., 200 Mass. 303, 86 N. E. 511.

So where goods were sent from New York to London instead of to Paris, they should be shipped to Paris from London, not returned to New York. Spiero v. New York C. & H. R. R. R., 64 Misc. 53, 117 N. Y. Supp. 1039.

[59] 28 N. Y. 72.

Acc., Harrison v. Weir, 71 App. Div. 248, 75 N. Y. Supp. 909.

to goods through delay. It was held in accordance with the general rule that the plaintiffs could not recover for the injury, if it were caused by the neglect on their part to take ordinary precautions to prevent damages from the breach of defendant's contract. In a case, where, through the negligence of an express company, an endowment policy lapsed, it was said to be the plaintiff's duty to use proper care and to adopt all reasonable means to prevent further damage, either by reinstating himself with the company, or by reinsuring, and that the defendant would not be liable for loss the plaintiff could have prevented, the court saying: "But the law makes it incumbent upon a person for whose injury another is responsible, to use ordinary care and take all reasonable measures within his knowledge and power to avoid the loss and render the consequences as light as may be; and it will not permit him to recover for such losses as by such care and means might have been prevented." The court, however, pointed out that the plaintiff could show a good excuse for not reinsuring.[60] Where the shipment of cattle was delayed, the owner should take care of them during the delay to prevent injury.[61] So in an action for delay in carrying cattle, when defendant stopped shipping cattle, but then began again, as the plaintiff knew, it was held that the plaintiff should have offered his cattle for shipment again as soon as the defendant had begun to carry, but he should not have shipped them before they had rested from their former drive to the station, as that would have been imprudent.[62]

The same rule applies in the case of the carriage of passengers.[63] And so it has been decided that a passenger should

[60] Grindle v. Eastern Express Co., 67 Me. 317.

[61] Vencill v. Quincy, O. & K. C. R. R., 132 Mo. App. 722, 112 S. W. 1030.

[62] Shelby v. Missouri Pac. Ry., 77 Mo. App. 205.

[63] *Alabama:* Central of Georgia Ry. v. Morgan, 161 Ala. 483, 49 So. 865 (carriage beyond station; passenger must not stand in cold if could get shelter, *semble*).

Georgia: Georgia R. E. Co. v. McAl-

lister, 126 Ga. 447, 54 S. E. 957, 7 L. R. A. (N. S.) 1177 (passenger put off short of station; must take reasonable means to prevent injury from exposure); Cent. of Ga. Ry. v. White, (Ga.), 69 S. E. 818 (failure to stop for passenger; should not stand in cold beside track, but should seek shelter).

Kentucky: Southern Ry. v. Miller, 129 Ky. 98, 110 S. W. 351 (delay in reaching station; cannot recover for injury from exposure in walking to it);

procure another conveyance on a railroad's failure to perform the contract of carriage;[64] and he cannot recover damages for the discomfort or illness caused by walking, when a conveyance could reasonably and cheaply be procured.[65] Where plaintiff was wrongfully expelled from a station, when he went to take a train to go to see his sick wife, and claimed damages for being unable to see his wife, it was held that he could not recover, because his expulsion from the station did not prevent his taking the train that was due half an hour later.[66] The question whether a passenger must pay the fare illegally demanded and so avoid ejection will be considered later.[67]

§ 212a. Telegraph companies.

The same principle is applied in actions against telegraph companies for failure to deliver or error in delivering telegrams.[68] Thus in Baldwin v. U. S. Tel. Co.[69] plaintiff delivered a message to a telegraph company, requesting his agent to telegraph back information as to petroleum wells, the property of the plaintiff. Plaintiff informed the operator that unless an answer was received he would sell at a certain price. Receiving no reply, he sold at the offer. It was held that he could not hold the telegraph company for the difference between this price and a higher market value, the court,

Cincinnati, N. O. & T. P. Ry. v. Rose, 115 S. W. 830, 34 Ky. L. Rep. (failure to provide berth; cannot recover for injury from exposure in driving home at night, if proper accommodation could be found near station); Illinois Cent. R. R. v. Poston, (Ky.), 125 S. W. 253 (failure to stop train; cannot recover for injury by exposure in walking a long distance if proper shelter could be found near at hand).

New York: Norton v. Union Ry., 109 N. Y. Supp. 73, 58 Misc. 188 (passenger required to change cars; should do so, not insist on sitting in first car).

South Carolina: Carter v. Southern Ry., 75 S. C. 355, 55 S. E. 771 (failure to stop at station; should get out at

station before destination and take next train, not ride beyond and walk back).

[64] Indianapolis, B. & W. Ry. v. Birney, 71 Ill. 391.

[65] Louisville & N. R. R. v. Spinks, 104 Ga. 692, 30 S. E. 968.

[66] St. Louis, I. M. & S. R. R. v. Stroud, 67 Ark. 112, 56 S. W. 870.

[67] *Post,* § 222.

[68] *North Carolina:* Hocutt v. W. U. Tel. Co., 147 N. C. 186, 60 S. E. 980.

South Carolina: Dempsey v. W. U. Tel. Co., 77 S. C. 399, 58 S. E. 9.

Texas: Western Union Tel. Co. v. Williams, (Tex. Civ. App.), 122 S. W. 280.

[69] 45 N. Y. 744, 6 Am. Rep. 165.

among other reasons, calling attention to the fact that the notice to the operator did not relieve the plaintiff of the ordinary duty to take all reasonable measures to diminish damages.

§ 212b. Defects in goods supplied or work done.

Where defendant breaks his contract to supply property or to do work not by altogether failing to do the thing contracted, but by doing it improperly, the plaintiff can recover no more than the cost of remedying the defect. So upon the sale of a machine which contained defects, where the defects could have been remedied by a small expenditure, it was held that this must be done; and plaintiff could not recover damages based on a continuance of the injury.[70] In an action to recover damages for breach of contract for the manufacture and sale of certain milk-coolers, it appeared that the defect complained of was simply in the pans used; it was held that the measure of damages was simply the expense of substitution of perfect pans.[71] Mather v. Butler County[72] was an action for furnishing materials and work and labor on defendant's courthouse. The defendant had a counterclaim for damages caused by defective work. It was held that an instruction should have been given to the effect that if defendant could have protected itself from such damages, at a moderate expense and by ordinary efforts, it was bound to do so, and could charge the plaintiff only for such expense and efforts, and for damages which would not be prevented by such efforts and at such expense. In Campbell v. Miltenberger[73] the court refused to allow large damages for injuries resulting from the defendant's having put up a fence improperly, holding that the plaintiff, who had stood by for seven years seeing the fence slowly go to ruin, could only recover the amount which it would have cost to put the fence in a proper condition when the discovery of the defect was first made.

If instead of remedying the defect the plaintiff uses goods in their bad condition, the defendant is not responsible for

---

[70] Frick Co. v. Falk, 50 Kan. 644, 32 Pac. 360.

[71] N. Y. State Monitor Milk Pan Co. (Limited) v. Remington, 109 N. Y. 143, 16 N. E. 48.

[72] 28 Ia. 253.

[73] 26 La. Ann. 72.

the resulting injury.[74] So where the plaintiff bought of the defendant potatoes which were rotten, and he claimed damages for the loss of old potatoes destroyed by decay communicated from those bought, it was held that he could not recover for the loss of his old potatoes, since he should have removed the new ones as soon as he found they were rotten.[75] And where a lease contained a covenant to furnish a certain amount of power, and less was furnished, it was held that loss caused by an attempt to manufacture with inadequate power was remote.[76] Where on a contract for the delivery of 50 pound beams the seller delivered 40 pound beams, and the buyer could at a glance tell the difference, he was not allowed to recover the loss caused by putting the beams into the building and then taking them out again.[77]

Where the breach of warranty of machinery makes it impossible to get something necessary for use, the purchaser must minimize damages by procuring it elsewhere. So where a steam pump to be used to pump water for a greenhouse fell short of the warranted capacity, the purchaser must avoid loss by procuring water elsewhere.[78]

§ 213.[a] Use of property or materials left on hand.

Where the breach of a contract causes materials or property of any kind, supplied by the plaintiff for the performance of the contract, to be left on his hands, he cannot abandon the property and allow the material to waste. If the property is the direct subject of the contract, the very thing which

[a] For former § 213, see § 222.

[74] *Connecticut:* Hitchcock v. Hunt, 28 Conn. 343 (leaky barrels; contents spoiled).

District of Columbia: Armour v. Gundersheimer, 23 D. C. App. 210 (bad eggs; cake spoiled).

Illinois: Graham v. Eiszner, 28 Ill. App. 269 (leaky barrels; contents lost); Ford v. Illinois Refrigerating Constr. Co., 40 Ill. App. 222 (defective refrigerator; contents spoiled).

Missouri: Mark v. H. D. Williams Cooperage Co., 204 Mo. 242, 103 S. W.

20 (defective steam pipe: factory often shut down).

Nebraska: Uhlig v. Barnum, 43 Neb. 584, 61 N. W. 749 (defective furnace; house burned).

[75] Northern Supply Co. v. Wangard, 123 Wis. 1, 100 N. W. 1066.

[76] Manhattan S. W. v. Koehler, 45 Hun (N. Y.), 150.

[77] Hawkins v. Deitz, 27 N. Y. Misc. 200, 57 N. Y. Supp. 751.

[78] Ralph B. Carter Co. v. Fischer, 121 N. Y. Supp. 614.

the defendant had contracted to take and give compensation for, the plaintiff is charged with the value of the thing so left because his direct loss, the profits of his contract, is found by deducting the value of the thing from the amount of his compensation.[79]

And so in an action against a railroad company for breach of contract to take water from a water-station to be constructed by plaintiff, it was held that the plaintiff could not, because the railroad had abandoned the contract, suffer the property to go to decay and become utterly useless, so as to hold the defendant for the original cost and value. The plaintiff's course was to sell the materials for the best price obtainable, or to put them to some use to which they were adapted.[80] In Grau v. McVicker,[81] a case of a lease of a theatre to commence at a future time, where, before the time came, the lessor notified the lessee that he would not take the theatre, it was held that this refusal was a breach,[82] entitling the lessor to sue at once, and that the measure of his damages would be the stipulated rental, less anything which he might have made or did make by letting the premises meantime. Where, however, the materials left on the plaintiff's hands were not the very things which were to be delivered to the defendants in performance of the contract, but were provided by the plaintiff to enable him to perform, and he claims to have suffered the loss of them, this is consequential damage, and the rule of avoidable consequences applies; if he might reasonably have avoided the loss he cannot recover compensation for it. So in an action for breach of contract, where the plaintiff had materials left on his hands, the court said that damages should not be allowed the claimant for loss or injury to his materials, which he might have prevented by the exercise of reasonable care and prudence.[83]

§ 214. Actions of tort.

The rule is of frequent application in actions of tort. So

[79] Post, §§ 613ff.
[80] New Orleans, J. & G. N. R. R. v. Echols, 54 Miss. 264.
[81] 8 Biss. 13.
[82] Following Hochster v. De la Tour, 2 E. & B. 678.
[83] U. S. v. Smith, 94 U. S. 214.

where the defendant wrongfully removed to another place
the plaintiff's boat, which was wrongfully on his premises,
and the plaintiff, who knew of the removal, did nothing about
it and it was abandoned and swept away by the stream and
sunk, it was held that it was the plaintiff's duty to take the
boat and prevent further damage, and he could recover no
damages except those that were suffered immediately upon
the defendant's act.[84] And where defendant wrongfully turned
plaintiff's cattle out of their enclosure onto the public land,
where they starved to death for lack of food, and the plaintiff
was notified but did not take care of them, it was held he could
not recover.[85] In an action in admiralty to recover damages
for a collision a boatman who after the collision unnecessarily
exposed himself to injury cannot make the injury thus incurred
an item of the damages caused by the collision.[86] Among
the numerous other cases of tort, in which the rule has been
applied, may be mentioned the following: trespass by landowner against railroad for digging ditches;[87] action of deceit
for sale of an impotent bull;[88] action for seizure of furniture;[89]
for obstruction of mill-race;[90] for interference with water-
power;[91] for setting fire to a prairie,[92] or to woods;[93] for trespass by cattle;[94] for injury to vessel by negligent collision;[95]
for wrongful libel placed upon a vessel;[96] for negligence of a
telegraph company;[97] against a public officer.[98] The rule

[84] Mark v. Hudson River Bridge Co.,
56 How. Pr. (N. Y.) 108.
But see Runnells v. Pentwater, 109
Mich. 512, 67 N. W. 558.

[85] Story v. Robinson, 32 Cal. 205.

[86] The Brinton, 50 Fed. 581.

[87] Kansas Pacific Ry. v. Mihlman, 17
Kan. 224.

[88] Maynard v. Maynard, 49 Vt. 297.

[89] *New Jersey:* Luse v. Jones, 39 N. J.
707.
Texas: Williams v. Yoe, 19 Tex. Civ.
App. 281, 46 S. W. 659.

[90] Lawson v. Price, 45 Md. 123.

[91] Decorah Woolen Mill Co. v. Greer,
49 Ia. 490.

[92] Waters v. Brown, 44 Mo. 302.

[93] Bevier v. Delaware & H. C. Co., 13

Hun, 254; Hogle v. New York Central
& H. R. R. R., 28 Hun, 363.

[94] Little v. McGuire, 38 Ia. 560, 43
Ia. 447. See Story v. Robinson, 32 Cal.
205.

[95] Grant v. Egyptian, [1910] A. C.
400.

[96] Niagara Falls Paper Co. v. Lee, 20
N. Y. App. Div. 217, 47 N. Y. Supp. 1.

[97] Marr v. Western U. T. Co., 85
Tenn. 529.

[98] *Massachusetts:* Priest v. Nichols,
116 Mass. 401.
Missouri: State v. Powell, 44 Mo.
430.
New York: Baker v. Freeman, 9
Wend. 36; Clark v. Hallock, 16 Wend.
607; Terry v. The Mayor, 8 Bos. 504.

has been applied in New York, in actions for the conversion of goods of fluctuating value, to the ascertainment of the proper time at which the value should be estimated; limiting that time to a reasonable time after notice of the conversion.[99] Some particular classes of torts will now be considered.

§ 214a. Actions for personal injury.

In all cases of personal injury, the party injured will in the exercise of ordinary prudence take reasonable precautions to avoid the consequences of the injury, by the employment of medical aid, etc. Where he omits to take such steps, he cannot recover for the consequences which come from his own omission.[100] And where a husband sues for loss of services of his wife by personal injury, he cannot recover damages which she should have avoided by reasonable prudence.[101]

As has been seen, the loss to be avoided is the consequential loss; the direct loss cannot be avoided. Where a personal injury causes loss of earning power, full compensation for such loss may be recovered. If the injured party was not wholly prevented from earning money he can recover only for a partial loss of earning power, and to that extent his ability to work is to be considered; but such loss as has actually been inflicted cannot be avoided, and the injured party cannot be called upon to show that he has gone to work and earned what he could.[102]

§ 214b. For injury to real estate.

Damages consequential upon an injury to real estate are

[99] Baker v. Drake, 53 N. Y. 211, 13 Am. Rep. 507. See post, Chap. XXI.

[100] United States: Smith v. Baker, 22 Blatch. 240; Texas & P. Ry. v. White, 101 Fed. 928, 42 C. C. A. 86.

Illinois: Chicago City Ry. v. Saxby, 213 Ill. 274, 72 N. E. 755, 104 Am. St. Rep. 218, 68 L. R. A. 164.

Iowa: Allender v. Chicago, R. I. & P. R. R., 37 Ia. 264; White v. Chicago & N. W. Ry., 145 Ia. 408, 124 N. W. 309.

Massachusetts: French v. Vining, 102 Mass. 132, 3 Am. Rep. 440; Dooley v. Boston Elevated Ry., 201 Mass. 429, 87 N. E. 586.

Missouri: Fullerton v. Fordyce, 144 Mo. 519, 44 S. W. 1053; Glasgow v. Metropolitan St. Ry., 191 Mo. 347, 89 S. W. 915.

Vermont: Bardwell v. Jamaica, 15 Vt. 438.

[101] Gulf, C. & S. F. Ry. v. Bagby, (Tex. Civ. App.), 127 S. W. 254.

[102] Missouri, K. & T. Ry. v. Flood (Tex. Civ. App.), 70 S. W. 331.

recoverable only up to the time when plaintiff has a reasonable opportunity to put a stop to them.[103]   So where defendant wrongfully piled bushes on plaintiff's land, causing danger from fire, the plaintiff should remove the bushes; and the danger of fire is therefore not an element of damage recoverable in an action for the trespass.[104]   And where defendant wrongfully makes an opening into plaintiff's building, plaintiff must close it or suffer the consequential damage.[105]

The rule is often invoked in cases of injury by water.   So where plaintiff's premises were injured by flood, it was his duty to put the premises in repair as soon as possible; and he could not recover damages caused by their continuing to be out of repair.[106]   So in an action for flooding plaintiff's land above defendant's dam, if plaintiff could at small expense avoid the consequences by building a gate across the outlet of his ditch, he cannot recover for flooding.[107]   And in an action for wrongful diversion of water, which overflowed in a new channel and injured plaintiff's mine, and by an expenditure of a hundred dollars in rip-rapping the bank of the new channel this could have been avoided, the plaintiff cannot recover the damages caused by the overflow.[108]   And generally where a landowner is injured by water wrongfully cast upon his land, he must take reasonable steps to avoid loss.[109]

§ 214c. For destruction of fences.

Another application of the rule is to the case where the

---

[103] *Minnesota:* Karst v. St. Paul, S. & T. F. R. R., 22 Minn. 118.

Missouri: Knight v. Chicago, R. I. & P. Ry., 122 Mo. App. 38, 98 S. W. 81 (meadow burned, must reseed).

[104] Chase v. Clearfield Co., 209 Pa. 422, 58 Atl. 813.   And where defendant actually sets a fire, the owner should put it out.   Aune v. Austin-Williams Timber Co., 52 Wash. 356, 100 Pac. 746.

[105] *Illinois:* Hartford Deposit Co. v. Calkins, 186 Ill. 104, 57 N. E. 863.

Maine: Davis v. Poland, 102 Me. 192, 66 Atl. 380, 10 L. R. A. (N. S.) 212.

[106] German Theological School v. Dubuque, 64 Iowa, 736, 17 N. W. 153.

[107] Gniadck v. Northwestern Imp. & Boom Co., 73 Minn. 87, 75 N. W. 894.

[108] Sweeny v. Montana Central Ry., 19 Mont. 163, 47 Pac. 791.

[109] *Alabama:* Sloss-Sheffield Steel & Iron Co. v. Mitchell, 161 Ala. 278, 49 So. 851.

Indiana: Cromer v. City of Logansport, 78 N. E. 1045, 38 Ind. App. 661; Gaerrett v. Winterich, 84 N. E. 1006, (Ind. App.).

Kentucky: Louisville & N. R. R. v. Moore, 101 S. W. 934, 31 Ky. Law Rep. 141, 10 L. R. A. (N. S.) 579.

New York: Stevens v. State, 121 N. Y. Supp. 402, 65 Misc. 240.

plaintiff's fences are broken by the defendant or his animals. The plaintiff cannot lie by and allow his land to be injured or his crops destroyed for lack of a fence to protect them, but must seasonably rebuild the fence; if he does not do so, he cannot recover for the resulting loss.[110] And therefore in an action for destroying plaintiff's fences the plaintiff cannot recover for injury to his grain caused by the cattle of a third person some time after the original trespass.[111] And for the same reason, that plaintiff should repair the fence, it was rightly held, in an action for pulling down the plaintiff's fence, that the expense of keeping intruders out of the plaintiff's unfenced enclosure was "too remote." [112]

§ 215.[a] For obstruction of ways.

Defendant wrongfully closes a wagon road used by plaintiff in feeding his cattle; his natural course is not to leave the cattle to starve, but to feed them by a more circuitous way; [113] and where the road was used by the plaintiff to get in his crops, he must use the most practicable way left.[114] If the defendant opens another way plaintiff must use it.[115]

§ 216.[b] Actions of replevin.

The same general principle applies in actions of replevin. Thus in replevin for ice, where the defendant is liable on outstanding contracts for ice, which he is obliged to fulfil, he cannot recover any extraordinary damages he has had to pay for a breach of these contracts, for "it would be easy for him to replace the ice taken, by ice to be purchased, for which he would be obliged to pay only the fair value, which will be precisely what he will receive." [116]

---

[a] For former § 215, see § 226b.

[110] *Massachusetts:* Loker *v.* Damon, 17 Pick. 284.

Pennsylvania: Smith *v.* Johnson, 76 Pa. 191.

Texas: Gulf, C. & S. F. Ry. *v.* McMurrough, 41 Tex. Civ. App. 216, 91 S. W. 320.

Vermont: Watkins *v.* Rist, 67 Vt. 284, 31 Atl. 418.

[111] Berry *v.* San Francisco & N. P. R. R., 50 Cal. 435.

[b] For former § 216, see § 226c.

[112] Krueger *v.* Le Blanc, 62 Mich. 70, 28 N. W. 757.

[113] Texas & P. Ry. *v.* Newton, (Tex. Civ. App.), 30 S. W. 475.

[114] Ohio & M. Ry. *v.* McGhee, 47 Ill. App. 348.

[115] Fitzpatrick *v.* Boston & M. R. R., 84 Me. 33, 24 Atl. 432.

[116] Washington Ice Co. *v.* Webster, 62 Me. 341, 16 Am. Rep. 462; *acc.,* Bowen *v.* Harris, 146 N. C. 385, 59 S. E. 1044.

§ 217.[a] Statutory damages—Eminent domain.

The general rule applies as well where the damages are statutory. So in cases of injuries inflicted through the exercise of the power of eminent domain, it is to be expected that the owner will use reasonable and proper precautions to prevent or diminish the injury, and expenses incurred in this way are a part of his measure of damages.[117]   And where a city is liable for damages through changing the grade of the street, it has been held that the measure is the expense of changing the grade of the house and lot to conform.[118]

Where part of the plaintiff's sea wall was appropriated, but the wall still served its former use, it was held that the measure of damages was what would make the plaintiff whole for the occupation of the wall, and not what the wall cost, for this might be more or less than the actual damages.[119]   On the other hand, where the defendant cut through another railroad's embankment, it was held that the measure of damages was the cost of building a bridge and keeping it in repair.[120] So, in estimating damages caused by laying a railroad illegally in a highway without making compensation, it has been held that the measure of damages may be the cost of removing the obstruction and restoring the highway to its former condition.[121]   And it has been said that where the damage is to an easement of access, the measure of damages may be the expense of making the access as good as it had been before.[122]

II.—LIMITATIONS

§ 218.[b] Limits of the rule.

We have seen that the plaintiff is always limited in his recovery by the boundary of ordinary care and of reasonable expense.   So there are many other limitations, which are really

[a] For former § 217, see § 226d.

[117] *Maryland:* Gregg v. The Mayor, 56 Md. 256.

Missouri: In re Wyandotte & C. Sts. 23 S. W. 127.

[118] McCarthy v. St. Paul, 22 Minn. 527.   But see *contra*, Fort Worth v. Howard, 3 Tex. Civ. App. 537, 22 S. W. 1059.

[b] For former § 218, see § 226j.

[119] Gear v. C. C. & D. R. R., 39 Ia. 23.

[120] Chicago & A. R. R. v. Springfield & N. W. R. R., 67 Ill. 142.

[121] Lawrence R. R. v. Mahoning County, 35 Oh. St. 1.

[122] *In re* N. Y., W. S. & B. Ry., 29 Hun, 646.

involved in the rule itself, but the statement of which con-
duces to a clearer apprehension of the reason upon which it is
founded. Thus it has been decided that it does not relate
to the performance of the primary obligations of the contract and the party whose duty it is to perform, cannot, while
the contract is in force, be heard to say that the plaintiff
might have performed for him.[123] And so the mere fact
that the plaintiff might by some acts of his have avoided the
consequences, will not prevent the plaintiff's recovery. There
must be a want of ordinary diligence. Thus in Clark v. Miller,[124] an action for failure on the part of a town supervisor
to present to supervisors of a county a reassessment of damages in the plaintiff's favor, the plaintiff was allowed to recover
the amount of the reassessment, and he was not limited in
his recovery of interest to the period when he might have
had his claim presented to another board of supervisors (perhaps because what the result would have been was not certain).
And in an action against a register of deeds for a false return
in omitting a mortgage, it was held that plaintiff was not
bound to tell the defendant of the mortgage when he heard
of it, so that the defendant could buy it up before foreclosure, the court saying: "It is undoubtedly true that the
plaintiff was under obligation to make reasonable exertions to
prevent the increase of damages likely to fall upon himself,
and thus incidentally to protect the defendant; but it was not
his duty to go one step further," or "to do an act which will
not affect his own damages, though it would be of service to
the wrongdoer."[125] And in a similar case the plaintiff brought
an action for damages for failure to get the certificate of the
manufacturer in the United States of certain boxes sent to
Mexico, by reason of which upon their return goods in the
boxes were seized as dutiable. The defendant claimed that
the plaintiff should have made further efforts before the
Treasury Department to get the boxes through; but it was

[123] *Indiana:* Louisville, N. A. & C. Ry. v. Sumner, 106 Ind. 55, 55 Am. Rep. 719; Same v. Moore, 106 Ind. 600.

Minnesota: Cargill v. Thompson, 57 Minn. 534, 59 N. W. 638.

Oregon: Haas v. Dudley, 30 Ore. 355, 48 Pac. 168.

Wisconsin: Pewaukee M. Co. v. Howitt, 86 Wis. 270, 56 N. W. 784.

[124] 54 N. Y. 528.

[125] Van Schaick v. Sigel, 9 Daly, 383.

held that while he should have made reasonable efforts, he was not required to institute or prosecute proceedings of doubtful result in the Treasury Department.[126]

The plaintiff cannot be called upon to accept a substitute of an entirely different sort. Thus in case of breach of covenant for quiet enjoyment, where the lessee is prevented from obtaining possession of a store, in which to carry on his business, he will, as a prudent man procure a new store; but he is not bound to remove to a remote part of the city, and thus lose to some extent the good will of his business, which had been carried on in the vicinity of the premises leased; nor would he be required to take another store not reasonably well adapted to his business.[127] Nor can he be called upon to incur personal danger, as, in a case of personal injury, to submit to a dangerous and doubtful surgical operation.[128]

In some cases of injury to property, where the plaintiff has the right to regard the injury as a total one, he cannot be called upon to reduce the damages by salvage of the fragments of the property which remain; as in actions of trover he is not obliged to take back the property, even though it is tendered to him in good condition.[129] So in an action against a railroad for wrongfully killing cattle, plaintiff cannot be called upon to take and dispose of the dead and mangled bodies of the cattle so as to lessen the damage.[130] Where defendant wrongfully ejects plaintiff from his premises, scattering about his personal property, this constitutes a conversion of the personal property, and plaintiff cannot be called upon to collect and take care of such portions of his personal property as he may find.[131] And where defendant sank plaintiff's vessel so that she was a total wreck plaintiff was not obliged to reduce

[126] Pierpont Mfg. Co. v. Goodman Produce Co. (Tex. Civ. App.), 60 S. W. 347.

[127] Roposky v. Munkwitz, 68 Wis. 322.

[128] Kehoe v. Allentown & L. V. Traction Co., 187 Pa. 474, 41 Atl. 310; Mattis v. Philadelphia Traction Co., 6 Pa. Dist. 94, 19 Pa. Co. Ct. Rep. 65. The fact that an injury may be cured by an operation may, however, always be shown, as bearing on the actual amount of damages caused by the injury. Joseph Schlitz Brewing Co. v. Duncan, 6 Kan. App. 178, 51 Pac. 310.

[129] Ante, § 53.

[130] Rockford, R. I. & S. L. R. R. v. Lynch, 67 Ill. 149.

[131] United States: Eisele v. Oddie, 128 Fed. 941.

New York: Eten v. Luyster, 60 N. Y. 253.

damages by raising the wreck.[132]   Some of the more usual limitations will now be considered.

§ 219.[a] Plaintiff not called upon to take unreasonable steps to avoid loss.

The defendant cannot complain that the plaintiff did not go to unreasonable expense or take steps not reasonably necessary to avoid the loss.[133]   So in an action for a personal injury which had seemed to be a slight one, defendant claimed that because plaintiff did not at once call in a physician he could not recover for the consequences of his injury; but the court held that the plaintiff is called upon to take only such steps as appear to be reasonable and necessary to avoid the loss.[134]   And so it has been held in Maryland that for breach of contract to furnish freight and employment to plaintiff's boat, it was not the duty of the plaintiff to get rid of expense by keeping his boat and horses unemployed and dismissing his hands.[135]

§ 220.[b] Rule does not require impossibilities.

In an action against a carrier for non-delivery of corn, where the plaintiff claimed to recover for a sub-contract, and defendant urged that the plaintiff might have bought the corn in the market to fill the contract, and that not having done so

---

[a] For former § 219, see § 220.

[132] O'Reilly v. New Brunswick, A. & N. Y. S. B. Co., 26 N. Y. Misc. 195, 55 N. Y. Supp. 1133.

[133] *Kentucky:* Illinois Cent. R. R. v. Poston, 125 S. W. 253 (woman left at flag station not obliged to remain during night for shelter in house near station of which the only occupant was a strange man); Madisonville, H. & E. R. R. v. Cates, 138 Ky. 257, 127 S. W. 988 (not called on to dig ditches at great expense); T. J. Moss Tie Co. v. Phelps, 137 S. W. 516 (not called on to sell goods left on hand to man of doubtful credit).

Texas: International & G. N. R. R. v. Duncan, (Tex. Civ. App.), 121 S. W. 362 (personal injury, can be called on to take only ordinary care to avoid aggravation).

[b] For former § 220, see § 217.

[134] *Illinois:* Galesburg v. Rahn, 45 Ill. App. 351.

Michigan: Moore v. Kalamazoo, 109 Mich. 176, 66 N. W. 1089.

Missouri: Wise v. Wabash R. R., 135 Mo. App. 230, 115 S. W. 452; Webb v. Metropolitan St. Ry., 89 Mo. App. 604.

Pennsylvania: Vallo v. U. S. Exp. Co., 147 Pa. 404, 23 Atl. 594, 30 Am. St. Rep. 741, 14 L. R. A. 743.

Washington: Kuhnis v. Lewis R. B. & L. Co., 51 Wash. 196, 98 Pac. 655.

[135] Benson v. Atwood, 13 Md. 20; Borden Mining Co. v. Barry, 17 Md. 419. But this must not be taken as an invariable rule of law, as circumstances might show that the expense was plainly useless, and in such a case, to incur it would be a wilful act on the part of the plaintiff, and no part of the ordinary conduct of a prudent man.

the measure of damages was merely the market price, the Supreme Court of Illinois said: "However this might be, *if they had not already invested their money in the corn in controversy*, we cannot so hold in the present case. It would be very unreasonable to require one who has bought and paid for an article, to have the money in his pocket with which to buy a second, in case of non-delivery of the first."[136]

And so in Startup v. Cortazzi,[137] Alderson, B., said: "It appears that the price at that time was not the proper criterion for estimating the damages; for as the plaintiffs had already parted with their money they were not then in a situation to purchase other seed." So in Wilcox v. Campbell,[138] where the plaintiff, in order to save land from foreclosure, would have had to raise money in excess of the value of the land, and it did not appear that he could have raised it, it was held by the New York Supreme Court that the rule did not apply, although, if he had raised it, he would have been entitled to recover it back; and on appeal the judgment was affirmed.[139] Upon the same principle the plaintiff will not be barred of recovery because of failure to avoid the consequences of defendant's wrong if the plaintiff's illness prevented his doing so; [140] or if he failed to avoid loss by procuring other goods when there were none in the market.[141]

[136] Illinois Cent. R. R. v. Cobb, 64 Ill. 128. This would, as stated, seem to make the rule applicable only where no consideration had passed, but the court probably did not mean to go so far. The onus is on the defendant to prove that plaintiff might have procured the corn. If the plaintiff had no more money, nor credit, this would be a matter for him to prove in reply. See Middlekauff v. Smith, 1 Md. 329, where the Maryland Court of Appeals, speaking of a covenant by landlord to repair, and the rule of avoidable consequences as applicable to the lessee, says: "Many repairs may have been needed which *his peculiar situation or circumstances* would not have permitted him to have made, and thus one of the very purposes he may have had in view

in requiring from his landlord a covenant to repair, might have been defeated." There would seem to be no way of escaping the conclusion that in all such cases the party injured may prove his pecuniary incapacity to make expenditures of the magnitude required. And this limitation upon the rule appears to have been applied in Wilcox v. Campbell, 35 Hun, 234, 106 N. Y. 325, *infra*, note (138).

[137] 2 C. M. & R. 165.

[138] 35 Hun, 234.

[139] S. C. on appeal, 106 N. Y. 325.

[140] Gulf, C. & S. F. Ry. v. McMurrough, 41 Tex. Civ. App. 216, 91 S. W. 320.

[141] Southern I. & E. Co. v. Holmes Lumber Co., 164 Ala. 517, 51 So. 531.

§ 221. Amount of care required.

As the rule allows only reasonable expenses, so it requires the party injured to use ordinary efforts,[142] neither greater nor less than a prudent man would be likely to use; and consequently where the jury were told that they must find for the plaintiffs unless a *slight expense* and *slight effort* would have prevented the injury, this was held to be error.[143] And, on the other hand, the party injured is not under any obligation to use *more* than ordinary diligence.[144] Prudent action is required, but "not that action which the defendant, upon after-thought, may be able to show would have been more advantageous to him." [145] The amount of care required is not to be measured by "*ex post facto* wisdom"; and the plaintiff is not bound at his peril to know the best thing to do.[146] The assurances of the defendant that he will repair the injury will justify the plaintiff in failing to take steps to avoid loss.[147]

§ 221a. What care is reasonable.

The amount of effort must be determined by all the circumstances of the case. If great expense would be required to prevent the loss, it might be reasonable to decline to incur it. So in an action against a railroad for failure to erect cattle-guards, in compliance with statute, it appeared that injury to the crops might have been prevented by keeping a constant watch day and night for four or five months, at a cost of two

---

[142] Parker *v.* Meadows, 86 Tenn. 181.

[143] *Iowa:* Simpson *v.* Keokuk, 34 Ia. 568; Allender *v.* Chicago, R. I. & P. R. R., 37 Ia. 264.

Texas: Gulf, C. & S. F. Ry. *v.* Dunham (Tex. Civ. App.), 31 S. W. 1070.

In Chase *v.* New York Central R. R., 24 Barb. 273, an action brought for damage done to plaintiff's premises by water which got into her cellar, the trial judge charged that she was bound to use "ordinary care and diligence" to prevent the house being injured thereby, and *only ordinary* "care and diligence." The General Term held this erroneous, for reasons which the opinion of Mullett, J., does not make clear. The decision seems to be con-

trary to the current of authority. So also does the language of the Supreme Court of Illinois (Green *v.* Mann, 11 Ill. 613), to the effect that the rule only requires the performance of "trifling acts."

[144] *Indiana:* Louisville, N. A. & C. Ry. *v.* Falvey, 104 Ind. 409, 425, 3 N. E. 908.

New York: Leonard *v.* New York, A. & B. E. M. T. Co., 41 N. Y. 544. He is required only to exercise "good faith and fair dealing." Gilbert *v.* Kennedy, 22 Mich. 117.

[145] The Thomas P. Sheldon, 113 Fed. 779.

[146] Waco A. W. Co. *v.* Cauble, 19 Tex. Civ. App. 417, 47 S. W. 538.

[147] *Post,* § 226.

or three dollars a day for a man alone; but it was held that to require this would be to call for unreasonable efforts and great expense.[148] But the mere fact that the expense is greater than the plaintiff thinks it ought to be will not justify refusal to incur it. So in an action for wrongfully sinking plaintiff's canal boat, plaintiff attempted to raise the boat before the tide should reach it, and damage the goods; but he could not hire help except for double wages, and refused to do so, and the goods were injured. It was held that it was his reasonable duty to hire men to help him at such price as he had to pay, and that he could not recover for injury to the cargo that could have been avoided by employing men at the high rate.[149] A remedy recently discovered and not generally known cannot reasonably be required. So in an action for deceiving plaintiff by selling him a vineyard which was affected by black rot, defendant urged that by the use of a certain spray the rot could be killed. The remedy was very recent and it was not in general use at the time the plaintiff was in occupation of the land, and it was useful only if used with great skill and judgment, and was very expensive. It was held that plaintiff could not be charged with negligence for not using it.[150] If the use of the remedy is a mere matter of judgment, plaintiff cannot be held responsible for exercising his judgment wrongly. By overflow of plaintiff's land pasturage of his cattle was injured. It was claimed that he should have put his cattle on the market at that time and sold in order to avoid further loss; but it was held that he was not obliged to do so. If in his judgment the market would have been better in a short time, he could exercise discretion in the matter; but he should not allow his cattle to depreciate if he could avoid it.[151]

Plaintiff may in some cases be held responsible for his ignorance, though under ordinary circumstances he would not.

[148] Smith v. Chicago, C. & D. R. R., 38 Ia. 518.

And it has been held that the plaintiff is under no obligation himself to erect the cattle guards under such circumstances. San Antonio & A. P. Ry. v. Knoepfli, 82 Tex. 270, 17 S. W. 1052; City Ry. v. Adams, 63 Tex. 200.

[149] Pennsylvania R. R. v. Washburn, 50 Fed. 335.

[150] Lurch v. Holder (N. J. Eq.), 27 Atl. 81.

[151] McCleneghan v. Omaha, etc., R. R., 25 Neb. 523, 41 N. W. 350, 13 Am. St. Rep. 508.

Where defendant closed a right of way of plaintiff, but put in place of it another right of way, and plaintiff refused to travel on it, under the mistaken impression that if he did, he would ratify the change, it was held that he could not recover damages for loss of use of the way because it was his duty to reduce the damages by using the substituted way.[152]   But in an action for failure to furnish water to cattle, where plaintiff might have got water from another water company, but he did not know this, and instead used river water which injured the cattle, it was held that he could recover, as he was not bound at his peril to know the best thing he could do; if he acted reasonably, he was not barred of recovery.[153]

In Bradley v. Denton [154] it is held to be well settled and founded on the clearest principles of equity that if the freighter fails to furnish return freight, it is the duty of the master to seek for and obtain other freight, if possible. But where, on a contract to furnish several cargoes, after one has been furnished, the shipper notifies the carrier that he will not furnish any more, this is a breach, and the freighter cannot enhance the damages by returning empty, and claiming full freight. His natural course is to seek other employment; whether in the port of destination only, or in other ports as well, must depend on all the circumstances of the case, such as insurance, the weather, or the condition of the vessel.

In an action against a railroad company for wrongfully selling plaintiff a ticket over the wrong route, plaintiff upon being carried off his route procured a ticket to his destination which took him over a line where the discomfort of travel was greater than it would have been over a different line. It was held that if he selected his route with reasonable care he could recover for the discomfort.[155]

§ 221b. Reasonable care in case of personal injury.

The doctrine that only reasonable care is required of the plaintiff finds a common application in actions for personal

[152] Fitzpatrick v. Boston & M. R. R., 84 Me. 33, 24 Atl. 432.

[153] Waco Artesian Water Co. v. Cauble, 19 Tex. Civ. App. 417, 47 S. W. 538.

[154] 3 Wis. 557.

[155] Texas & P. Ry. v. Armstrong (Tex. Civ. App.), 41 S. W. 833.

injury, where a physician employed by plaintiff is charged by the defendant with really aggravating the injury by malpractice. For this, however, the plaintiff, if he selected his physician with reasonable care, is not responsible; the defendant and not the plaintiff is chargeable with the result of the physician's acts.[156] It has even been held possible for the plaintiff to disregard his physician's advice reasonably and without thereby becoming responsible for the result.[157] And where the plaintiff, without actually taking medical advice, had done what would have been advised by a proper physician, it was held that plaintiff was not bound to get the most skilful physician in the country, but had done enough when he did what would be advised by a reasonably skilful physician.[158] On the other hand, if the plaintiff employed a physician whom he knew to be incompetent, he cannot charge the defendant with the result.[159]

[156] *Illinois:* Pullman Palace Car Co. v. Bluhm, 109 Ill. 20, 50 Am. Rep. 601; Chicago City Ry. v. Saxby, 213 Ill. 274, 72 N. E. 755, 104 Am. St. Rep. 218, 68 L. R. A. 164; Sandwich v. Dolar, 34 Ill. App. 199; Mt. Sterling v. Crummy, 73 Ill. App. 572; Chicago City Ry. v. Cooney, 95 Ill. App. 471; Joliet v. Le Pla, 109 Ill. App. 336.

Maine: Hooper v. Bacon, 64 Atl. 950, 101 Me. 533.

Massachusetts: McGarrahan v. New York, N. H. & H. R. R., 171 Mass. 211, 50 N. E. 610.

Michigan: Reed v. Detroit, 106 Mich. 224, 65 N. W. 567.

Minnesota: Goss v. Goss, 102 Minn. 346, 113 N. W. 690.

Nevada: Murphy v. Southern Pac. Co., 31 Nev. 120, 101 Pac. 322.

New York: Sauter v. New York C. & H. R. R. R., 66 N. Y. 50, 23 Am. Rep. 18; Foels v. Tonawanda, 59 Hun, 567, 14 N. Y. Supp. 46.

Rhode Island: O'Donnell v. Rhode Island Co., 28 R. I. 245, 66 Atl. 578.

South Carolina: Berry v. Greenville, 84 S. C. 122, 65 S. E. 1030.

Texas: Houston & T. C. R. R. v.

Hanks, (Tex. Civ. App.), 124 S. W. 136; Texas & P. Ry. v. Mosley, (Tex. Civ. App.), 124 S. W. 485.

Washington: Hoseth v. Preston Mill Co., 49 Wash. 682, 96 Pac. 423.

Wisconsin: Selleck v. Janesville, 100 Wis. 157, 75 N. W. 975, 69 Am. St. Rep. 906, 41 L. R. A. 563.

But in Crete v. Childs, 11 Neb. 252, it was held that an instruction that if the plaintiff employed such persons to attend her "as she *thought* competent, and in good faith," she would not be responsible for contributing to the damages, was erroneous.

The aggravation of an injury by subsequent pregnancy, at least when no warning against it had been given by a physician, will not bar recovery for the whole injury. Salladay v. Dodgeville, 85 Wis. 318, 55 N. W. 696.

See *post,* § 228, note 304.

[157] Williams v. Brooklyn, 33 App. Div. 539, 53 N. Y. Supp. 1007 (advice to submit to an operation).

[158] Arkansas River Packet Co. v. Hobbs, 105 Tenn. 29, 58 S. W. 278.

[159] Baldwin v. Lincoln County, 29 Wash. 509, 69 Pac. 1081.

§ 222. Reparation offered by defendant.

The question has arisen in the case of contracts for personal services, whether after a breach the duty of the plaintiff to seek new employment obliges him to accept employment if offered by the employer who has discharged him. In Bigelow v. The American Forcite Powder Manufacturing Company [160] the New York Supreme Court held (Daniels, J., dissenting) that the plaintiff must reduce damages in this way; in another case,[161] however, where the defendant offered to continue the employment *at a less rate*, it was held that this did not go to reduce the damages, on the very questionable ground that if the plaintiff had accepted the new offer, it would have been a modification of the original contract by consent, which would have precluded him from recovering any damages at all.[162] Where the injury complained of was the breach of a contract to make plaintiff sole agent for the sale of machinery, and evidence was offered to the effect that the agent of those having control of the machines offered after the breach to let the plaintiff sell them, it was held that this tended to show that plaintiff was not damaged at all.[163] And where plaintiff became agent for the sale of defendant's books and made sales to customers, and defendant refused to supply the books except for cash, it was held that plaintiff could not claim damages caused by failure to get the books, since he should have paid cash to get them.[164] The same difference of view appears in other cases. So in case of failure to comply with the terms of a contract of sale, authorities are divided as to the obligation of the plaintiff to accept defendant's offer to deliver at a higher price. Thus in Havemeyer v. Cunningham,[165] a case between vendor and vendee, where, after failure to deliver, the defendant offered to sell to plaintiffs at a price below the market value on the day fixed for delivery, the same court said, "The defendants could not relieve themselves from the consequences of their refusal to deliver, by an offer to sell at a higher price, although less than the subsequent

---

[160] 39 Hun (N. Y.), 599.

[161] Whitmarsh v. Littlefield, 46 Hun (N. Y.), 418.

[162] Parsons v. Sutton, 66 N. Y. 92.

[163] Beymer v. McBride, 37 Ia. 114.

[164] Warren v. Stoddart, 105 U. S. 224, 26 L. ed. 1117.

[165] 35 Barb. 515.

market value. Such an offer, if accepted by the plaintiffs before the time of performance arrived, might have exposed them to the charge of having abandoned the first contract." In another case already cited,[166] the question came before the New York Court of Appeals in a different way. There, after a failure to deliver, the vendor offered to let the vendee have the goods, and it was held that while the vendee might refuse to receive them, he could not refuse and then claim special damages because he could not get them. So in the converse case of refusal of the buyer to take at the agreed price, coupled with an offer to pay a lower price, it has been held that the plaintiff need not accept the lower price for the purpose of reducing the damages.[167] In an action for failure to furnish premises according to a lease [168] or for eviction from leased premises [169] it has been held that a lessor can show that he has offered other premises, in lieu of those he had agreed to lease, on discovering his inability to give possession. Where defendant wrongfully took out a telephone from plaintiff's premises, but afterwards offered to replace the telephone at a higher rate, it was held that plaintiff could not recover consequential damages for loss of the telephone, since he should have accepted the offer and avoided the loss at the expense of the additional charge demanded.[170] Where plaintiff owned land and irrigation stock which he pledged, but failed to pay the assessment on the stock and the pledgee paid it and had the water cut off wrongfully, and trees were injured, it was held that he could not recover for the injury to the trees, since he might have paid the assessment and so had the water turned on.[171] But where defendant induced a third party to break his contract for supplying plaintiff with a machine, the court would not reduce damages upon evidence that plaintiff might have bought a similar machine of defendant, since

[166] Parsons v. Sutton, 66 N. Y. 92.

[167] Brazell v. Cohn, 32 Mont. 556, 81 Pac. 339.

[168] Fodges v. Fries, 34 Fla. 63, 15 So. 682. And so where he offered the same premises later. Huntington Easy Payment Co. v. Parsons, 62 W. Va. 26, 57 S. E. 253, 9 L. R. A. (N. S.) 1130.

[169] Dobbins v. Duquid, 65 Ill. 464.

[170] Ashley v. Rocky Mountain Bell Tel. Co., 25 Mont. 286, 296, 64 Pac. 765.

[171] Mabb v. Stewart, 147 Cal. 413, 81 Pac. 1073.

that would result in accomplishing defendant's unlawful purpose.[172]

The conflict of authority is especially apparent in the case of contracts of carriage. Where a carrier wrongfully refuses to carry a passenger without the payment of an additional fare it is said in many cases that he need not pay the additional fare, but may stand on his rights and recover for all damages suffered as a consequence.[173] In other cases it is held that he must pay the additional fare, and if he refuses to do so he must himself suffer the consequences.[174]

In a case in Texas,[175] where plaintiff agreed to furnish transportation with wagons and trains, but on finding that there

---

[172] See Willis v. Perry, 92 Ia. 297, 60 N. W. 727, 26 L. R. A. 124; Tubular Rivet & Stud Co. v. Exeter Boot & Shoe Co., 159 Fed. 824, 88 C. C. A. 648.

[173] *California:* Elser v. Southern Pac. Co., 7 Cal. App. 493, 94 Pac. 852.

Mississippi: Ill. Cent. R. R. v. Gortikov, 90 Miss. 787, 45 So. 363.

Texas: St. Louis, etc., R. R. v. Mackie, 71 Tex. 491, 10 Am. St. 766, 9 S. W. 451, 1 L. R. A. 667; Galveston, H. & S. A. Ry. v. Wiseman, (Tex. Civ. App.), 136 S. W. 793.

Wisconsin: Yorton v. Milwaukee, L. S. & W. Ry., 62 Wis. 367.

[174] *Arkansas:* St. Louis, I. M. & S. Ry. v. Cates, 87 Ark. 162, 112 S. W. 202.

Georgia: Louisville & N. R. R. v. Spinks, 104 Ga. 692, 30 S. E. 968.

Michigan: Brown v. Rapid Ry., 134 Mich. 591, 96 N. W. 925.

So it has been held that he must not enhance the damages by resisting ejectment.

Kansas: Arnold v. Atchison, T. & S. F. Ry., 81 Kan. 400, 105 Pac. 541.

Minnesota: Morrill v. Minneapolis St. Ry., 103 Minn. 362, 115 N. W. 395.

At any rate, the passenger cannot recover for the humiliation of ejectment if he really sought ejectment for the purpose of acquiring a damage suit against the carrier.

Arkansas: Brenner v. Jonesboro L. C. & E. R. R., 82 Ark. 128, 100 S. W. 893, 9 L. R. A. (N. S.) 1060.

Georgia: Southern Ry. v. Barlow, 104 Ga. 213, 30 S. E. 732, 69 Am. St. Rep. 166.

North Carolina: Holmes v. Carolina C. R. R., 94 N. C. 318.

Ohio: Cincinnati, H. & D. R. R. v. Cole, 29 Oh. St. 126, 23 Am. Rep. 729.

But the passenger need not go about among his friends in the car and try to borrow money to pay his fare. Light v. Detroit & M. Ry., 130 Mich. 1125.

In the analogous case of refusal to give plaintiff a seat in a theatre which he had bought, the same rule applies. If he is offered an equally good seat and refuses to take it, he can get nominal damages only. Horney v. Nixon, 213 Pa. 20, 61 Atl. 1088, 1 L. R. A. (N. S.) 1184, 110 Am. St. Rep. 520. So where plaintiff was refused admission to a theatre while he wore the uniform of a private soldier, but was promised admission if he would wear civilian dress, which he might have done, it was held that he could not recover damages for the humiliation of being excluded. Buenzle v. Newport Amusement Assoc., 29 R. I. 23, 68 Atl. 721, 14 L. R. A. (N. S.) 1242.

[175] Heilbroner v. Hancock, 33 Tex. 714.

were no goods of defendant's to transport, refused to take other goods offered him by defendant's agent, it was held on demurrer that he could not maintain an action for the entire amount of *dead* freight.

The same considerations apply in actions of tort. In an action for false imprisonment it has been held that the fact that plaintiff after an illegal conviction 'might have paid the fine imposed and thus have escaped imprisonment is immaterial.[176]

This conflict is irreconcilable; but it will appear that the distinct weight of authority is in favor of the application of the rule of avoidable consequences in this class of cases. No offer of reparation by the defendant can affect his liability for the direct loss; but when its acceptance would prevent the occurrence of consequential damages, such damages must be avoided by the plaintiff.

§ 223. Plaintiff's knowledge—Notice.

Notwithstanding that a wrong has been committed, the plaintiff may be in ignorance of the fact, and so long as he remains in ignorance, the duty to avoid the consequences cannot arise. Thus in Loker *v.* Damon [177] the learned Chief-Justice Shaw said: "Suppose a man should enter his neighbor's field unlawfully, and leave the gate open, if, *before the owner knows it*, cattle enter and destroy the crop, the trespasser is responsible. But if the owner sees the gate open, and passes it frequently, and wilfully and obstinately or through gross negligence leaves it open all summer, and cattle get in, it is his own folly." And so in case of a sale, if the vendor has *reason to suppose* that the article does not correspond with a warranty or description, he cannot be permitted to shut his eyes to the probable consequences, and then hold the defendant for them.[178]

In most cases, there is probably little doubt as to what is the most proper course for the plaintiff to pursue; but this does not always happen. Thus in a case in Texas, where the

---

[176] Barker *v.* Anderson, 81 Mich. 508, 45 N. W. 1108.

[177] 17 Pick. 284.

[178] Bagley *v.* Cleveland Rolling Mill Co., 22 Blatchf. 342.

plaintiff sued to recover for personal injuries, it appeared that the injuries had been aggravated by his own conduct in neglecting to refrain from all exertion while under treatment; but it not appearing clearly that he knew of the importance of this, or that he had been seriously advised as to the proper course to pursue, it was held that he was not precluded from recovering for the entire loss.[179]

In Sherman v. Fall River Iron Works Co.,[180] where a lessee, a livery-stable keeper, had a right of action against defendant for an escape of gas through the ground and into a well used by him for his livery-stable, it was held that he might recover for expenses incurred in reasonable and proper attempts to exclude the gas, but not for injury caused by allowing his horses to drink the water after he knew that it was corrupted. Hoar, J., said: "He can recover only for the natural and direct consequences of the wrongful act of the defendants, and not for consequential damages which might have been avoided by ordinary care on his own part." And so where cotton stored with defendants as warehousemen, was thrown into the street by military authority, it was held that the owner, if *he was chargeable with knowledge of the facts*, should have taken reasonable steps to protect his property.[181]

§ 224. Plaintiff need not anticipate wrong.

The duty to prevent damages, or to lessen the loss which will ultimately fall on plaintiff, cannot possibly arise until a wrong or breach of contract has actually been committed. And so, in proceedings under the eminent domain statute, it has been held that before the *taking*, the landowner is under no duty to avoid improving his property merely because he has notice of proceedings to condemn. Such proceedings may be abandoned, and until they are consummated his position is that of any owner.[182] On the same principle, where a cargo

---

[179] Gulf, Col. & S. F. Ry. v. McMannewitz, 70 Tex. 73.

[180] 2 All. (Mass.) 524.

[181] Smith v. Frost, 51 Ga. 336.

[182] Driver v. Western Union R. R., 32 Wis. 569, 14 Am. Rep. 726. The court in this case says: "There is no ground for saying that the plaintiff proceeded in bad faith, and made an expensive improvement merely for the purpose of enhancing the damages." But if the plaintiff with knowledge that the State is likely to take the land places improvements upon it merely in order to

of fruit was injured through a fumigation wrongfully made by a member of a Board of Health, and it appeared that plaintiff might have unloaded, and was advised so to do, and might thus have avoided loss, the defendant was, after full consideration, held responsible by the Supreme Court of Louisiana, on the ground that a threat of the commission of a trespass does not raise a duty in the person threatened to take any steps to avoid the consequences of such a wrong.[183]   And in an action to recover damages for injury to plaintiff's hay through the building of a dam, where the jury found that by the expenditure of $60 above what was usual and necessary before the dam was erected, the hay might have been secured, it was held that the plaintiff's damages were not to be reduced on this account, as it did not appear that he had any good reason to anticipate the injury.   It would seem as if this decision might be rested explicitly on the principle that it is never the duty of the plaintiff to attempt to reduce the loss which may flow from anticipated wrong.[184]   And so a plaintiff need not exercise any care of logs to prevent their being lost by the defendant's wrong in putting a boom across a stream, unless he had notice that they were in danger; and it seems that he need do nothing, even when he heard of the defendant's intention of swinging the boom, the court saying that it is enough if he exercises ordinary care for the preservation of the logs after he knows that the wrong is done.[185]   So where a trespasser turns his cattle into plaintiff's field and goes on doing so as fast as plaintiff turns them out, plaintiff can recover in trespass for injury to his own cattle from lack of feed caused by the overstocking of the pasture, and good

enhance damages, he is not entitled to compensation for the improvements. Champlain S. & S. Co. v. State, 66 Misc. 434, 123 N. Y. Supp. 546.

[183] Beers v. Board of Health, 35 La. Ann. 1132, 48 Am. Rep. 256.

[184] *Connecticut:* Lawton v. Herrick, 76 Atl. 986.

Indiana: Garrett v. Winterich, 44 Ind. App. 322, 87 N. E. 161, 88 N. E. 308.

Maine: Reynolds v. Chandler R. Co., 43 Me. 513.

So where defendant daily detains water above plaintiff's mill, though by building a larger dam plaintiff could hold water enough for his use during the period of detainer, he need not in this way anticipate wrong in the future. Price v. High S. M. Co., 132 Ga. 246, 64 S. E. 87, 22 L. R. A. (N. S.) 684.

[185] Plummer v. Pen. Lumber Assoc., 67 Me. 363.

faith and fair dealing do not require him to take his own cattle elsewhere to prevent this damage.[186]

In an action for delay in the completion of a building, brought against a surety on the contract, the defendant claimed that the plaintiff, when delay seemed likely, should have taken charge of the building operations and completed the building, so as to prevent the delay. The court held, however, that so long as the contractor was continuing to do work the plaintiff was under no obligation to take charge in anticipation of delay; though it might be otherwise if there had been a total abandonment of the work by the contractor.[187] And one who owns land alongside a railroad is entitled to use it in the ordinary way, and is not bound to keep his property away from the railroad or to stand guard over it in order to prevent loss from fire communicated by sparks from locomotives.[188]

This general principle applies even though legal means are given for guarding against anticipated injury. Thus, in a Montana case, the defendant built a dam which seemed insecure. A statute provided that persons who lived on a stream below a dam might institute proceedings to have the dam declared dangerous, and if it was so declared the owner must either make it secure or let out the water. Plaintiff did not avail himself of this statutory provision. The dam burst, and plaintiff's property was injured. The defendant urged that no damages could be recovered, because the plaintiff might have avoided the loss by instituting the statutory proceedings. But the court held that his failure to do so would not bar recovery; saying that the statutory provisions never were intended to shield those who were careless from liability in damages for the consequences of negligently maintaining a fearful danger to those lawfully occupying their homes below the point of such danger.[189]

§ 225. Plaintiff cannot be called on to commit a wrong.

The rule never can be pushed to the extent of requiring

[186] Gilbert v. Kennedy, 22 Mich. 117.
[187] Leghorn v. Nydell, 39 Wash. 17, 80 Pac. 833.
[188] Jacksonville, T. & K. W. Ry. v. Peninsular L. T. & M. Co., 27 Fla. 1, 9 So. 661, 17 L. R. A. 33.
[189] Hollenback v. Dingwell, 16 Mont. 335, 40 Pac. 863.

the plaintiff to commit a wrong himself; *e. g.*, where the cause of original wrong is on land of defendant, plaintiff cannot be under any obligation to trespass on that land to abate it.[190] So in an action for overflowing mining claims, although by pulling off a board from the flume the plaintiff might have stopped the damage, he was held not to be bound to reduce the loss in this way, because in order to accomplish it, he would have been obliged to commit a trespass.[191]   And so, probably for the same reason, in an action against a city for injuries caused to abuttors by accumulations of water, in consequence of the construction of gutters and drains, the court, in laying down the usual rule, was careful to qualify it by adding: "We do not intimate that it would have been the duty of plaintiff to interfere with the streets or gutters, so as to change the construction of them." [192]   And so, generally, the plaintiff is not required to take any measures to reduce the damages which are not within his legal rights; [193] *e. g.*, he could not be called upon to violate a contract with a third party,[194] or to trespass on the land of a third party,[195] or to commit a criminal offence.[196]

§ 226. Defendant prevents plaintiff from avoiding consequences.

But the plaintiff may be prevented by the defendant himself from preventing avoidable consequences. It may happen that when there is a breach of contract by defendant, as in the case of an obligation to keep leased premises in repair, the plaintiff is prevented from taking the necessary steps to

---

[190] *California:* Wolf *v.* St. L. I. W. Co., 15 Cal. 319.

Illinois: Chicago, R. I. & P. R. R. *v.* Carey, 90 Ill. 514.

New York: Walrath *v.* Redfield, 11 Barb. 368.

Texas: Gulf, C. & S. F. R. R. *v.* Reed (Tex. Civ. App.), 22 S. W. 283.

See also Baltimore & S. P. R. R. *v.* Hackett, 87 Md. 224, 39 Atl. 510, which can best be supported on this ground.

[191] Wolf *v.* St. Louis Independent Water Co., 15 Cal. 319.

[192] Simpson *v.* Keokuk, 34 Ia. 568.

[193] Kankakee & S. R. R. *v.* Horan, 23 Ill. App. 259.

[194] Earl, Ch. J., in Leonard *v.* New York, etc., Tel. Co., 41 N. Y. 544, 566.

[195] Fromm *v.* Ide, 144 N. Y. 630, 39 N. E. 493, affirming 68 Hun, 310, 23 N. Y. Supp. 56.

[196] Wabash R. R. *v.* Campbell, 219 Ill. 313, 76 N. E. 346, 3 L. R. A. (N. S.) 1092.

render the damage as light as possible by the dilatory action of the defendant himself; *e. g.*, where the defendants, after notice to repair, promise from time to time, but fail to do so. In such a case, where through such a prolongation of the period of loss it finally extended the cost of the repairs, it was held in Vermont that the loss was caused by and should fall on the defendants.[197] But as soon as it is apparent that the defendant will not perform, the plaintiff should act to avoid further loss. Thus in another case in the same State, the complainants had purchased of defendants, in 1868, a patent stone channelling machine for $6,000, the defendants agreeing to indemnify them against the consequences of infringement. In 1870 complainants were enjoined for infringement of another patent, and set the machine aside. They might then have bought an equally valuable machine at the same price, but did not do so, as defendants from time to time promised to furnish another. They therefore hired their channelling done at regular prices, and at an expense, down to the spring of 1872, of $1,749.80 more than the work done by their own machine would have cost them. By this time it became understood that defendants would not furnish another machine, but the complainants went on hiring the work done as before, until the increased cost amounted to $9,243.45, for which sum they brought suit. It was held, however, that the complainants should have purchased another machine, as soon as they knew that the defendants would not furnish one, and that their increase of damages was: 1st, the actual cost of the work, $1,749.80, with interest from May 1st, 1872, also the cost of another machine ($6,000), with interest from the same date; subject to the right of the defendants to take back the old machine or apply its value in reduction of damages.[198] The same view has been taken by the Supreme Court of Massachusetts in an action for breach of agreement, in

[197] Keyes v. Western Vt. Slate Co., 34 Vt. 81.

Acc., Alabama: Southern I. & E. Co. v. Holmes Lumber Co., 164 Ala. 517, 51 So. 531.

Georgia: Hardwood Lumber Co. v. Adam, 134 Ga. 821, 68 S. E. 725.

Kentucky: Illinois Cent. R. R. v. Doss, 137 Ky. 659, 126 S. W. 349; T. J. Moss Tie Co. v. Phelps, 137 S. W. 516.

[198] Eureka Marble Co. v. Windsor Mfg. Co., 51 Vt. 170.

making a sale of a house, to assign the policy of insurance.[199] Defendant, though often requested, did not assign, but continued to promise, and it was held that plaintiff was not entitled to recover the value of the building upon its destruction by fire, although the policy had become void by the failure to assign, and the insurance was thus lost, and could recover only the cost of insurance for the unexpired term of policy, the reason being that after the defendant's default had become evident, she should have insured herself.

A fortiori where the defendant by active steps prevents the plaintiff from avoiding consequences, he cannot set up in mitigation the plaintiff's failure to do so. So where defendant company had insured plaintiff against liability from injury to employees, and upon suit being brought against plaintiff by an employee defendant had advised him not to settle, in an action on the policy defendant could not claim that plaintiff ought to have settled the case.[200] And in an action for unlawfully ejecting plaintiff from her home, whereby she was compelled to remain in the street all night, where defendant claimed that plaintiff should have sought shelter and not remained in the street, this claim was answered by showing that plaintiff had repeatedly tried to re-enter her home, but each time was prevented by defendant from doing so.[201]

III.—RECOVERY OF EXPENSE OF AVOIDING LOSS

§ 226a. Rule sometimes results in enhancing damages.

The observance of the rule by the plaintiff will not always have the effect of reducing the damages; it may even enhance them. Accordingly, where an animal is injured by defendant's wrong, the owner may recover the expense reasonably incurred in an attempt to cure the animal, whether or not the attempt was unsuccessful.[202] Thus, where one has hired a horse, and

---

[199] Dodd v. Jones, 137 Mass. 322.

[200] Fidelity & Casualty Co. v. Southern Ry. News Co., 101 S. W. 900, 31 Ky. Law Rep. 55 (rehearing denied, 103 S. W. 297, 31 Ky. Law Rep. 725).

[201] McCartney v. Smith, 10 Kan. App. 580, 62 Pac. 540.

[202] *Alabama:* Southern H. & S. Co. v. Standard E. Co., 158 Ala. 596, 48 So. 357.

Indiana: Summers v. Tarney, 123 Ind. 560, 24 N. E. 678.

Louisiana: Jones v. Texas & P. Ry., 125 La. Ann. 542, 51 So. 582.

Maine: Watson v. Lisbon Bridge Co., 14 Me. 201, 31 Am. Dec. 49.

by improper treatment returns him in an injured condition, and the owner employs a proper veterinary surgeon, who treats the animal according to his best judgment, but is unable to cure him, the hirer will be liable for the full value, although such treatment was in fact improper and contributed to the horse's death.[203] And so, if a passenger in a coach, by reason of a peril arising from an accident for which the proprietors are liable, is in so dangerous a situation as to render his leaping from the coach an act of reasonable precaution, and he leaps therefrom, and thereby injuries himself, the proprietors are responsible in damages, though he might have retained his seat in safety.[204]

§ 226b. Expense of avoiding consequences recoverable.

The reasonable expenses of avoiding the consequences of the defendant's wrong are recoverable, and when the plaintiff fails to take proper steps, he is limited in his recovery on this head to what the cost of such steps would have been.[205]

Massachusetts: Eastman v. Sanborn, 3 All. 594.

Michigan: Ellis v. Hilton, 78 Mich. 150, 43 N. W. 1048, 6 L. R. A. 454, 18 Am. St. Rep. 438.

Texas: Railway Co. v. Keith, 74 Tex. 289, 11 S. W. 1117; Ulit v. Biggs, (Tex. Civ. App.), 116 S. W. 126.

In a few jurisdictions the recovery cannot in any case exceed the entire value of the animal.

Georgia: Telfair County v. Webb, 119 Ga. 916, 47 S. E. 218; Southern Ry. v. Stearnes, 68 S. E. 623, (Ga. App.).

Minnesota: Keyes v. Minneapolis & St. Louis Ry., 36 Minn. 290, 30 N. W. 888.

Washington: Wilson v. Seattle, R. & S. Ry., 55 Wash. 656, 104 Pac. 1114.

This doctrine seems to leave out of sight the real principle involved, namely, that the necessity of taking reasonable steps to avoid loss caused an additional expenditure, the result of the wrong but not a part of it, for which the defendant should be held responsible.

A different view was taken in U. S. v. Pine R. L. & I. Co., 89 Fed. 909, an action of trover, in which case it was held that in that form of action the expenses of following the property are only recoverable where the property is in fact regained and that fact is pleaded in mitigation; the plaintiff then recoups his expenses against the mitigation. Where there is no recovery of the property, the plaintiff is limited to the market value and interest.

This apparent conflict must be referred to the peculiarity of the form of action.

[203] Eastman v. Sanborn, 3 All. (Mass.) 594.

[204] *Massachusetts:* Ingalls v. Bills, 9 Met. 1.

England: Jones v. Boyce, 1 Stark. 493. See for an interesting discussion of the principles involved, Wilson v. Newport Dock Co., 4 H. & C. 232.

[205] *Illinois:* Indianapolis, B. & W. Ry. v. Birney, 71 Ill. 391.

Kansas: Kansas Pacific Ry. v. Mihlman, 17 Kan. 224.

Thus in an action against an officer for a false return, in certifying that he had left a true copy of a notice to appear for examination, that the person served might thereby avoid the issuing of an execution against his body (under the poor debtor's act), when in fact the place of examination was omitted in the copy, it was held that the plaintiff could recover an adequate remuneration for the inconvenience of making inquiries of the justice or the officer, and ascertaining the place.[206] When a railroad is under a statutory duty to erect cattle-guards, plaintiff recovers not only for damages to crop destroyed by cattle, but the expenses of a reasonable effort to protect his crop.[207] On a contract to furnish machinery for a mill, the owner may, if the machinery proves defective, recover a sum of money sufficient to remedy the defects, together with a reasonable compensation for the loss of its use during the period of delay.[208] And on breach of a contract by a railroad company with an owner of lots to build a bridge over its road, the measure of damages is not the difference between the value of the lots when sold and their value had the bridge been constructed, but the cost of making such a bridge, including reasonable compensation for time and labor, and perhaps whatever damages might have been incurred during the time required to build it.[209] Where the defendant, by the wrongful construction of a water-pipe, caused water to flow into the plaintiff's cellar, the expense of a reasonable attempt to keep it out may be recovered.[210] And the rule is of general

Massachusetts: Shaw v. Cummiskey, 7 Pick. 76; Sherman v. Fall River Iron Works Co., 2 All. 524; Emery v. Lowell, 109 Mass. 197.

New York: Jutte v. Hughes, 67 N. Y. 267; Hoffman v. Union Ferry Co., 68 N. Y. 385; Worth v. Edmonds, 52 Barb. 40; Comstock v. New York C. & H. R. R. R., 48 Hun, 225; Robertson v. National S. S. Co., 17 N. Y. Supp. 459.

Texas: Southern K. Ry. v. Isaacs, 20 Tex. Civ. App. 466, 49 S. W. 690; Texas & P. Ry. v. Newton (Tex. Civ. App.), 30 S. W. 475.

Vermont: Lloyd v. Lloyd, 60 Vt. 288.

England: Borries v. Hutchinson, 18 C. B. (N. S.) 445.

[206] Wright v. Keith, 24 Me. 158.

[207] St. Louis & S. F. Ry. v. Ritz, 33 Kan. 404.

[208] Strawn v. Cogswell, 28 Ill. 457; Phelan v. Andrews, 52 Ill. 486.

[209] St. Louis, J. & C. R. R. v. Lurton, 72 Ill. 118.

[210] Comstock v. New York C. & H. R. R. R., 48 Hun (N. Y.), 225. See also Nashville v. Sutherland, 94 Tenn. 356, 29 S. W. 228.

application; [211] but is of course subject to the general rules as to remoteness.[212]

§ 226c. Expense of following and recovering property.

The plaintiff may recover the reasonable expense of attempting to find and retake property of which he has been wrongfully deprived.[213] Such a decision was reached in a case where the defendant had taken a horse and wagon belonging to the plaintiffs. They spent four days in searching for the horse and wagon, and incurred other expenses in the search. A verdict was given for the time spent, and expenses incurred in the pursuit. It was objected that the damages were too remote; but the verdict was retained by the Supreme Court of New York; and considerable stress was laid on the circumstance that the damages were occasioned by the wrongful act of the defendant.[214] So where the owner of property is obliged to pay money to the holder of it to get it back, he may recover the amount from the one who illegally took it.[215]

[211] *Alabama:* W. K. Syson Lumber Co. *v.* Dickens, 146 Ala. 471, 40 So. 753 (breaking boom and taking logs).

Kansas: First Nat. Bank *v.* Williams, 62 Kan. 431. 63 Pac. 744 (expense of stopping payment on false draft).

Texas: Hughes *v.* Austin, 12 Tex. Civ. App. 178, 33 S. W. 607 (wrongful flooding of pasture; expense of caring for stock recoverable).

[212] It is not admissible, in an action of trespass for taking corn, for the plaintiff to prove, for the purpose of enhancing the damages, that in consequence of the trespass he was compelled to work as a day laborer to procure other corn. Sims *v.* Glazener, 14 Ala. 695, 48 Am. Dec. 120.

Where defendant levied an illegal distress upon plaintiff's corn, whereby plaintiff was obliged to sell some stock to obtain corn for his hogs, and for his family, the damages were held to be too remote. Burger *v.* Rhiney (Tex. Civ. App.), 42 S. W. 590.

[213] *Connecticut:* Dennison *v.* Hyde, 6 Conn. 508.

Georgia: Grier *v.* Ward, 23 Ga. 145; Savannah, F. & W. Ry. *v.* Pritchard, 77 Ga. 412, 1 S. E. 261, 4 Am. St. Rep. 492.

Illinois: Coffman *v.* Buckhalter, 98 Ill. App. 304.

Maine: Merrill *v.* How, 24 Me. 126.

New York: Parmalee *v.* Wilks, 22 Barb. 539; Sprague *v.* McKinzie, 63 Barb. 60; Hough *v.* Bowe, 51 N. Y. Super. Ct. 208; Miller *v.* Garling, 12 How. Pr. 203.

Vermont: Chase *v.* Snow, 52 Vt. 525.

England: Hales *v.* London & N. W. Ry., 4 B. & S. 66.

Contra in *California*, under the Code: Kelly *v.* McKibben, 54 Cal. 192; Redington *v.* Nunan, 60 Cal. 632.

In *South Carolina* it was held that a passenger could not recover the expense of following lost baggage, in the absence of notice to the carrier that such would be the result of loss. Turner *v.* Southern Ry., 75 S. C. 58, 54 S. E. 825.

[214] Bennett *v.* Lockwood, 20 Wend. (N. Y.) 223.

[215] *New York:* Ford *v.* Williams, 4 N. Y. 359.

Upon this principle it is sometimes possible to recover the costs of another action undertaken to recover possession of the property, as an action of replevin; even though in that action the plaintiff failed to recover the goods.[216] But generally the expense of collateral actions cannot be recovered.[217]

§ 226d. Expense of repairing or redressing the injury.

The expense of repairing or redressing an injury may be recovered. So in an action for wrongful arrest (on the bond given at the time of suing out the writ), the expense of procuring release from arrest may be recovered.[218] Where a defective boiler was sold by the defendant and exploded, the owner may recover the expense of repairing the injury it caused.[219] Where a machine was delivered in an unfit condition to do the work it was purchased for, the purchaser was allowed to recover the expense of a reasonable but unsuccessful attempt to adapt it to the contemplated purpose; [220] and so, of course, of a successful attempt.[221] Where a vessel is injured by a collision, the expense of surveying the injuries [222] or of

England: Keene v. Dilke, 4 Ex. 388, 18 L. J. Ex. 440.

[216] *Connecticut:* Bird v. Clark, 3 Day, 272, 3 Am. Dec. 269.

Massachusetts: Berry v. Ingalls, 199 Mass. 77, 85 N. E. 191 (attorney's services for securing redemption of chattel mortgage wrongly foreclosed).

Michigan: Haviland v. Parker, 11 Mich. 103.

New York: Wooden v. Davis, 195 N. Y. 391, 88 N. E. 745 (expense of securing discharge from false arrest).

[217] *United States:* Murray v. Pannaci, 130 Fed. 529 (expense of chancery action to determine ownership of land, still pending, cannot be recovered in action for trespass upon it).

Louisiana: Bendich v. Scobel, 107 La. 242, 31 So. 703 (expense of criminal proceedings for the same trespass cannot be recovered; but see *contra,* Pettit v. Mills, 6 Ont. Prac. 297, *semble*).

England: Holloway v. Turner, 6 Q. B. 928, 14 L. J. Q. B. 143, 9 Jur. 160 (expense of setting aside judgment under which goods were wrongfully seized).

Canada: Wilson v. Ellis, Ber. (N. Brun.) 325 [497] (expense of inquiry by sheriff as to ownership of goods wrongfully seized).

[218] Burnap v. Wight, 14 Ill. 301. But where the defendant suffered a wrongful distress for rent, he cannot recover the expense of setting aside the distress on certain parts of the property as exempt by law. Sturgis v. Frost, 56 Ga. 188.

[219] Phelan v. Andrews, 52 Ill. 486.

[220] Whitehead & A. M. Co. v. Ryder, 139 Mass. 366.

[221] *New York:* Jackson A. I. Works v. Hurlbut, 158 N. Y. 34, 52 N. E. 665.

Vermont: Clifford v. Richardson, 18 Vt. 620.

[222] New Haven S. B. Co. v. Mayor, 36 Fed. 716.

raising and repairing the vessel [223] may be recovered; and where the defendant obstructed a river, and the plaintiff's vessel grounded upon the obstruction, the expense of getting off from and over the obstruction may be recovered. [224] Where defendant's wrongful act sunk the plaintiff's vessel, the expense of an attempt to raise her may be recovered from the defendant. [225] Where fire escaped through the defendant's negligence and burned the plaintiff's meadow, the expense of reseeding the meadow may be recovered. [226]

In an action for injury to land, the cost of restoring it to its original condition may be recovered. [227] For closing up a way, the cost of using a more circuitous way may be recovered. [228] In an action for a wrongful attachment the plaintiff may be compensated for the trouble and expense of procuring a bond to dissolve the attachment. [229] In an action for selling decayed potatoes the cost of sorting out and removing the rotten potatoes on discovering their condition is an item of damage. [230] And in an action for injury to a domestic animal, the owner may recover the expense of curing it, [231] and of keeping it until its recovery. [232]

[223] *United States:* Williamson v. Barrett, 13 How. 101, 14 L. ed. 101.

New York: Mailler v. Express P. Line, 61 N. Y. 312.

[224] Benson v. Malden & M. G. L. Co., 6 All. (Mass.) 149.

[225] Sweeney v. Pt. Burwell H. Co., 17 Up. Can. C. P. 574.

[226] Pittsburgh, C. & St. L. Ry. v. Hixen, 110 Ind. 225. And so where the turf was destroyed by cattle straying in. Illinois Cent. R. R. v. Doss, (Ky.), 126 S. W. 349.

[227] *Illinois:* Coffman v. Burkhalter, 98 Ill. App. 304 (rebuilding fence).

Michigan: Chandler v. Allison, 10 Mich. 460 (repairing building).

New York: O'Riley v. McChesney, 3 Lans. 278 (removing dirt); Parish v. Baird, 160 N. Y. 302, 54 N. E. 724 (repairing sidewalk).

Tennessee: Nashville v. Sutherland, 94 Tenn. 356, 29 S. W. 228 (pumping off water).

[228] *Illinois:* Ohio & M. Ry. v. McGhee, 47 Ill. App. 48.

Texas: Texas & P. Ry. v. Newton (Tex. Civ. App.), 30 S. W. 475.

[229] Tullis v. McClary, 128 Iowa, 493, 104 N. W. 505.

[230] Northern Supply Co. v. Wangard, 123 Wis. 1, 100 N. W. 1066.

[231] *Georgia:* Atlanta S. C. O. Mills v. Coffey, 80 Ga. 145; Telfair County v. Webb, 119 Ga. 916, 47 S. E. 218; Southern Ry. v. Stearnes, (Ga. App.), 68 S. E. 623.

Indiana: Sullivan County v. Arnett, 116 Ind. 438, 19 N. E. 299; Summers v. Tarney, 123 Ind. 560, 24 N. E. 678.

Kentucky: Louisville & N. R. R. v. Gormley, 111 S. W. 289, 34 Ky. L. Rep.

Missouri: Hox v. Quincy, O. & K. C.

[232] Taylor v. Hayes, 63 Vt. 475, 21 Atl. 610.

Where the plaintiff is wrongfully discharged from the defendant's employment, he may recover the expense incurred in obtaining another employment;[233] so a farmer can recover the reasonable expense of trying to save his crops from destruction where they had been injured by defendant's failure to deliver a threshing machine;[234] and the purchaser of a horse with warranty as a foal-getter, the reasonable expense of testing him, but not any expenses subsequent to this.[235]

§ 226e. Expense of perfecting title.

So the expense of perfecting the title of land may be recovered by the grantee in an action for breach of covenant of warranty.[236] In Kelsey v. Remer,[237] an action on a covenant against incumbrances, an attaching creditor recovered judgment, but levied his execution improperly. The plaintiff, having paid off the judgment in good faith, believing, and having reason to believe, that otherwise execution would issue, it was held that he acted with reasonable prudence and care in regard to the interests of the defendant, and the amount paid should be the measure of damages, there being no claim that it was greater than the value of the land. So a plaintiff can show what he has had to pay a third person to do work the defendant agreed to do.[238] In James v. Hodsden [239] it was held that the plaintiff, in assumspit to recover back the consideration paid for an interest in a patent-right fraudulently sold him by defendant, could recover what he paid to compromise certain notes which he had given the defendant, although he could have defended them on the ground of failure of consideration. It was said that he was not obliged to follow them about to different courts and spend his time and fortune, and that the court would presume he did the best he could.

R. R., 100 S. W. 693, 123 Mo. App. 172; Smith v. Chicago & A. Ry., 105 S. W. 10, 127 Mo. App. 160.

South Carolina: Sullivan v. Anderson, 81 S. C. 478, 62 S. E. 862.

[233] Dickinson v. Talmage, 138 Mass. 249.

[234] Smeed v. Foord, 1 E. & E. 602.

[235] Newberry v. Bennett, 38 Fed. 308.

[236] See the chapter upon Real Covenants.

[237] 43 Conn. 129, 21 Am. Rep. 638.

[238] Clark v. Russell, 110 Mass. 133; City of Goldsboro v. Moffett, 49 Fed. 253.

[239] 47 Vt. 127.

§ 226f. Expense of medical and surgical attendance.

In an action for a personal injury, the plaintiff may recover the expense of nursing and medical attendance.[240]   This includes the expense of such future medical or surgical attendance as may be necessary.[241]   The plaintiff, however, cannot recover compensation for this expenditure if he has not himself paid or become responsible for the expense, and if another person is responsible for it and can recover the amount.[242]

---

[240] *United States:* Vicksburg & M. R. R. *v.* Putnam, 118 U. S. 554, 7 Sup. Ct. 2, 30 L. ed. 257; Denver & R. G. R. R. *v.* Lorentzen, 79 Fed. 291; Wade *v.* Leroy, 20 How. 34, 15 L. ed. 813; Beardsley *v.* Swann, 4 McLean, 333; Hanson *v.* Fowle, 1 Sawy. 539.

Alabama: Forbes *v.* Loftin, 50 Ala. 396; South & N. A. R. R. *v.* McLendon, 63 Ala. 266.

Arkansas: St. Louis, I. M. & S. R. R. *v.* Cantrall, 37 Ark. 519, 40 Am. Rep. 105.

District of Columbia: Larmon *v.* District, 16 D. C. (5 Mackey) 330.

Illinois: Pierce *v.* Millay, 44 Ill. 189; Chicago & A. R. R. *v.* Wilson, 63 Ill. 167; Chicago *v.* Jones, 66 Ill. 349; Chicago *v.* Langlass, 66 Ill. 361; Sheridan *v.* Hibbard, 119 Ill. 307.

Indiana: Indianapolis *v.* Gaston, 58 Ind. 224.

Iowa: Muldowney *v.* Illinois C. Ry., 36 Ia. 462; McKinley *v.* Chicago & N. W. Ry., 44 Ia. 314, 24 Am. Rep. 748; Kendall *v.* Albia, 73 Ia. 241.

Kansas: Tefft *v.* Wilcox, 6 Kan. 46; Kansas P. Ry. *v.* Pointer, 9 Kan. 620; Missouri, K. & T. Ry. *v.* Weaver, 16 Kan. 456.

Kentucky: Kentucky C. R. R. *v.* Ackley, 87 Ky. 278, 8 S. W. 691, 12 Am. St. Rep. 480.

Maryland: McMahon *v.* Northern C. Ry., 39 Md. 438.

Michigan: Priebe *v.* Moorland, 162 Mich. 110, 127 N. W. 19, 17 Det. L. N. 500.

Mississippi: Memphis & C. R. R. *v.* Whitfield, 44 Miss. 466, 7 Am. Rep. 699, *n.*

Missouri: Stephens *v.* Hannibal & S. J. R. R., 96 Mo. 207, 9 S. W. 589, 9 Am. St. Rep. 336, *n.*

New Jersey: New Jersey Exp. Co. *v.* Nichols, 32 N. J. L. 166, 33 N. J. L. 434, 97 Am. Dec. 722.

Nevada: Cohen *v.* Eureka & P. R. R., 14 Nev. 376.

New York: Metcalf *v.* Baker, 57 N. Y. 662; Sheehan *v.* Edgar, 58 N. Y. 631; Brignoli *v.* Chicago & G. E. Ry., 4 Daly, 182.

North Carolina: Allen *v.* Durham Traction Co., 144 N. C. 288, 56 S. E. 942; Wallace *v.* Western N. C. R. R., 104 N. C. 442.

Oklahoma: Choctaw, O. & F. R. R. *v.* Burgess, 21 Okla. 653, 97 Pac. 271.

Oregon: Oliver *v.* Northern P. T. Co., 3 Ore. 84.

Pennsylvania: Pennsylvania & O. C. Co. *v.* Graham, 63 Pa. 290, 3 Am. Rep. 549; Scott *v.* Montgomery, 95 Pa. 444; Lake Shore & M. S. Ry. *v.* Frantz, 127 Pa. 297; Brown *v.* White, 202 Pa. 297, 51 Atl. 962.

Utah: Giblin *v.* McIntyre, 2 Utah, 384.

Wisconsin: Goodno *v.* Oshkosh, 28 Wis. 300.

England: Phillips *v.* Southwestern Ry., 4 Q. B. D. 406.

[241] *Michigan:* Beattie *v.* Detroit, 137 Mich. 319, 100 N. W. 475 (future surgical operation).

Missouri: Hickey *v.* Welch, 91 Mo. App. 4 (future medical attendance).

[242] If the services of physician or

So if the plaintiff is a married woman, whose husband is legally bound to pay the expenses of her illness and has an action against the defendant in which he may recover such expenses, the woman cannot recover them in her action,[243] unless she has herself paid them or become responsible for them,[244] as is often the case as a result of married women property acts.[245] So where a minor is injured, no recovery can be had for medical expenses in an action brought in his name if he has a parent alive who has paid or is responsible for the expenses and has an action in which he may recover them;[246] but if the

nurse were rendered as a gratuity, or by one who was under obligation to render them, as for instance by the plaintiff's wife, the plaintiff is the proper person to recover their value. *Ante,* § 67; *post,* § 483.

[243] *Indiana:* Ohio, etc., R. R. *v.* Cosby, 107 Ind. 32, 7 N. E. 373.

Michigan: Rogers *v.* Orion, 116 Mich. 324, 74 N. W. 463.

Minnesota: Belyea *v.* Minneapolis S. P. & S. S. M. Ry., 61 Minn. 224, 63 N. W. 627.

Missouri: Ross *v.* Kansas City, 48 Mo. App. 440; Engelman *v.* Metropolitan St. R. R., 133 Mo. App. 514, 113 S. W. 700.

Nebraska: Pomerine Co. *v.* White, 70 Neb. 177, 98 N. W. 1040.

New York: Burnham *v.* Webster, 54 N. Y. Super. Ct. 30.

The husband is the proper party to recover:

Alabama: Southern Ry. *v.* Crowder, 135 Ala. 417, 33 So. 335.

Texas: Citizens' Ry. & L. Co. *v.* Johns, 52 Tex. Civ. App. 489, 116 S. W. 62.

If the woman was sole at the time of the injury, but married after the services were rendered and before the trial, she is the proper party to recover. Reading *v.* Pennsylvania R. R., 52 N. J. L. 264, 19 Atl. 321.

[244] *Illinois:* Chicago *v.* Gurrell, 137 Ill. App. 377.

Indiana: Indianapolis T. & T. Co. *v.* Kidd, 167 Ind. 402, 79 N. E. 347, 7 L. R. A. (N. S.) 143.

Michigan: Lucas *v.* Detroit City Ry., 92 Mich. 412, 52 N. W. 745; Lammiman *v.* Detroit C. S. Ry., 112 Mich. 602, 71 N. W. 153; Boyle *v.* Saginaw, 124 Mich. 348, 82 N. W. 1057.

Missouri: Tinkle *v.* St. Louis & S. F. R. R., 212 Mo. 445, 110 S. W. 1086.

Nebraska: Pomerine Co. *v.* White, 70 Neb. 177, 98 N. W. 1040.

In *Iowa,* however, it is held that though the wife is jointly liable with her husband she cannot recover. Kellar *v.* Lewis, 116 Ia. 369, 89 N. W. 1102.

[245] *Alabama:* Elba *v.* Bullard, 152 Ala. 237, 44 So. 412.

Illinois: West Chicago R. R. *v.* Carr, 170 Ill. 478, 48 N. E. 992.

Missouri: Tinkle *v.* St. Louis & S. F. R. R., 212 Mo. 445, 110 S. W. 1086.

[246] *Illinois:* Heimsworth *v.* Anderson, 16 Ill. App. 151.

Iowa: Newbury *v.* Getchel & Martin, etc., Mfg. Co., 100 Iowa, 441, 69 N. W. 743, 62 Am. St. Rep. 582.

South Carolina: Tucker *v.* Buffalo Cotton Mills, 57 S. E. 626, 76 S. C. 539.

Wisconsin: Peppercorn *v.* Black River Falls, 89 Wis. 38, 61 N. W. 79, 46 Am. St. Rep. 818.

infant is under guardianship, so that his estate is liable for the expenses, he may recover the amount of them.[247]

§ 226g. Expense of procuring a substitute.

Where the injury is incapable of reparation, but the plaintiff may avoid the effect of it by procuring a substitute to take the place of what has been lost, the expense of procuring the substitute is recoverable. So where the defendant wrongfully caused a highway of the plaintiff to be washed out and destroyed, the cost of maintaining a new road to take the place of the highway washed out may be recovered.[248]   Where the defendant wrongfully refused to allow the plaintiff's vessel to proceed through a certain channel, the only practicable means of reaching its port of destination, it was held that the plaintiff might recover the expense of unloading the cargo by lighters.[249]   Where defendant wrongfully cut plaintiff's water pipe, and refused to permit it to be relaid through defendant's land, plaintiff may recover the cost of constructing a new system of supply from a different source.[250]   And where the plaintiff sold goods for delivery at a distant market on a certain date and shipped them by the defendant, which unreasonably delayed delivery, it was held that the plaintiff could recover the expense of a journey to the place of delivery to get the time of delivery extended, if that was a reasonable and necessary step for the purpose.[251]   Where defendant sold goods to plaintiff which could not be procured in the market, plaintiff can show what he has had to pay for the best subsitute he could procure for what the defendant had neglected to furnish.[252]   And when

[247] Stotler v. Chicago & A. Ry., 98 S. W. 509, 200 Mo. 107.

In *Wisconsin* this doctrine appears to extend to every case where the expenses have not been actually paid by another, on the ground that the services are necessaries and the infant is therefore liable for them; but this should it seems be restricted to cases where the infant himself employed the physician or nurse. Berg v. U. S. Leather Co., 125 Wis. 262, 104 N. W. 60.

[248] Monroe v. Connecticut River Lumber Co., 68 N. H. 89, 39 Atl. 1019.

[249] Buffalo B. S. C. Co. v. Milby, 63 Tex. 492, 51 Am. Rep. 668.

[250] Reynolds v. Braithwaite, 131 Pa. 416, 18 Atl. 1110, 25 W. N. C. 269.

[251] Ohio & M. R. R. v. Dunbar, 20 Ill. 623, 71 Am. Dec. 291, *n*.

[252] *Louisiana:* C. W. Robinson Lumber Co. v. Burton, 128 La. 000, 54 So. 582.

England: Hinde v. Liddell, L. R. 10 Q. B. 265.

the defendant failed to repair the plaintiff's saw-mill according to contract, the expense of hauling his logs to another mill to be sawed may be recovered.[253]   On breach of a contract to furnish dies to be used in the manufacture of lanterns, the ordinary measure of damages is the increased cost of procuring dies elsewhere, and if the contract has been assigned before breach, the assignee can ordinarily recover no more.[254]

Upon a wrongful eviction of the plaintiff from leased premises it would seem that on this principle the cost of removal to other premises should be recovered.[255]

Here as elsewhere the limitation of reasonableness exists; thus where the seller of an automobile agreed to paint it a certain shade, and it was painted differently, it was held that the expense of hiring another car while the car delivered was being repainted could not be recovered; for the color of the car was a mere matter of taste, the car delivered was just as valuable for use without repainting, and loss of use in order to have it repainted would be unreasonable.[256]

§ 226h. Substitute better than original.

In a recent English case [257] the defendants agreed to supply eight steam turbines to the plaintiffs with a certain warranty as to economy of use. The machines as delivered did not comply with the warranty, but the plaintiffs accepted them and used them for a while. Finding, however, that no improvement could bring the machines up to the warranty, they reasonably purchased eight turbines of a different make to take the place of the defendants' machines. This resulted in preventing further loss by operating the uneconomical machine, and the entire purchase price of the new machines was less than the loss would have been by a continued operation of the defendants' machines during the probable period

---

[253] Hinckley v. Beckwith, 13 Wis. 31.

[254] Rochester Lantern Co. v. Stiles & P. P. Co., 135 N. Y. 209, 31 N. E. 1018.

[255] Hawthorne v. Siegel, 88 Cal. 159, 25 Pac. 1114, 22 Am. St. Rep. 291.

But see *contra* Tobin v. French, 93 Ill. App. 18. In a suit for collision it was intimated that the cost of supplying papers lost by the collision could not be recovered. Jacobsen v. Dalles P. & A. N. Co., 93 Fed. 974.

[256] Woodward v. George N. Pierce Co., 147 Ill. App. 339.

[257] British W. E. & M. Co. v. Underground E. R. Co., 104 L. T. R. 105.

of use of the defective machines. It appeared that the new machines were so much better than the old ones would have been even if they had corresponded with the warranty, that good business judgment would have led to the purchase of the new machines and the discarding of the old ones, even if they had not been defective.

On these facts the defendants urged that the damages should be limited to the amount of loss from use of the defective machines up to the time when good business judgment would have dictated the purchase of the new machines. The court, however, held that the new machines were purchased for the purpose of avoiding loss on account of the defective condition of the old machines, that it was a reasonable purchase for this purpose, and that the entire amount paid for the new machines could be recovered. It is submitted that this decision overlooked the fact that by the purchase of the new machines the plaintiff was put in a far better position than he would have been in if the defendants' warranty had been fulfilled, and that therefore the entire expense of the new machines should not have been allowed. If, as argued by the defendants, the placing of the new machines on the market would have put the old machines into the scrap heap as valueless, then the purchase of the new machines was not merely a reasonable means of avoiding loss from breach of warranty, but was an ordinary business expenditure undertaken by the plaintiffs in the ordinary course of business, quite independently of the breach of warranty; and if, as a matter of fact, they were led to investigate such machines by the defendants' breach of warranty and were thereby enabled to buy a much more economical machine, the breach was in fact a benefit rather than an expense to the plaintiffs. The case was in fact not one of avoiding the loss from the breach of warranty, but of avoiding loss because of the purchase of a machine eventually found to be an inferior one.

Another recent English case seems to be inconsistent with the decision just considered, and to be based upon the correct principle.

Plaintiffs sold to defendant companies certain gas properties, reserving gas enough to supply their own plant; defendants cut off the gas. Plaintiffs then procured means of independent supply, of which, however, they disposed in the end at a profit; it was held by the Privy Council, that they were entitled only to nominal damages,[258] and that they could not recover the expense of purchasing the independent supply since the purchase had proved profitable.

§ 226i. Personal efforts to avoid.

It would seem on general principles that the plaintiff should be allowed the value of his time spent in an effort to avoid the loss. And this is allowed in some cases. Thus in actions on attachment and injunction bonds the plaintiff may recover the value of his time spent in securing a dissolution of the attachment or injunction.[259] And in an action against defendant for failure to erect cattle-guards whereby cattle got in and injured the crops, it was held that plaintiff could recover the value of his services in preventing additional damage by driving out the intruding cattle.[260] But such expenses are frequently not allowed. Thus in an action for breach of contract to rent a house to plaintiff it has been held that he cannot recover the value of his time spent in looking up other premises;[261] where fire escaped though defendant's negligence, the plaintiff was refused compensation for the value of his services in fighting the fire;[262] and in an action of trespass a plaintiff was not allowed to recover the value of his services in hunting up the trespassers.[263] The divergence between those cases has not been explained by the courts which have decided against such expenses.

§ 226j. Injury suffered in attempt to avoid.

When in the reasonable effort to avoid the consequences of defendant's wrong the plaintiff injures his own property, he should be allowed compensation for such injury. Thus

[258] Erie Co. N. G. & F. Co., Ld., v. Carroll, [1911] A. C. 105.

[259] See post, § 685a.

[260] St. Louis & S. F. Ry. v. Sharp, 27 Kan. 134.

[261] Schultz v. Brenner, 24 N. Y. Misc. 522, 53 N. Y. Supp. 972.

[262] Spencer v. Murphy, 6 Colo. 453, 41 Pac. 841.

[263] Longfellow v. Quimby, 29 Me. 196, 48 Am. Dec. 525.

where defendant wrongfully set a fire which threatened plaintiff's property, and plaintiff set a back fire to save it, but it was burned by the back fire, it was held that since the back fire was set in the course of a lawful attempt to protect the plaintiff's property, defendant was responsible for the damage it did.[264] Upon a somewhat similar principle, where the defendant illegally attempted to chastise plaintiff's slave, and in his effort to escape the slave broke his leg, the defendant was held responsible for the injury.[265]

The same principle applies where the plaintiff in his effort to lessen the damages suffers a personal injury.[266] So where by reason of a defect in a road or bridge an accident happens to the plaintiff's team, and in trying to repair it plaintiff is kicked by his horse, he may recover compensation for the injury thereby caused;[267] and where defendant negligently set fire to plaintiff's property, and in trying to put it out plaintiff was burned, he is entitled to compensation for the burns.[268] And where defendant illegally imprisoned plaintiff in a freight car, and plaintiff fell and was injured in the attempt to escape, he may recover damages for it.[269] In an action for carrying plaintiff past her station, where as a result she was obliged to travel back in a cold car, it was held that the cold caught by riding back in the cold car during the night was an injury for which she could recover.[270] Upon the same principle, where the plaintiff is obliged to walk for a distance by

[264] McKenna v. Baessler, 86 Iowa, 197, 53 N. W. 103, 17 L. R. A. 310.

[265] Johnson v. Perry, 2 Humph. (Tenn.) 569.

[266] Rexter v. Starin, 73 N. Y. 601. So where narcotics were properly administered to deaden pain, defendant is liable for the mental anguish and expense caused to the sufferer by the use of the narcotics. Sumner v. Kinney (Tex. Civ. App.), 136 S. W. 1192.

[267] Maine: Page v. Bucksport, 64 Me. 51.

Vermont: Stickney v. Maidstone, 30 Vt. 738.

Wisconsin: Oliver v. La Valle, 36 Wis. 592.

Canada: McKelvin v. London, 22 Ont. 70.

[268] Georgia: Wilson v. Cent. of Ga. Ry., 132 Ga. 215, 63 S. E. 1121.

Minnesota: Berg v. Great Northern Ry., 70 Minn. 272, 73 N. W. 648, 68 Am. St. 524.

[269] Emmons v. Quaid, 176 Mo. 22, 75 S. W. 103.

[270] Texas: Missouri, K. & T. Ry. v. Hennesey, 20 Tex. Civ. App. 316, 49 S. W. 917.

Virginia: Fowlks v. Southern Ry., 96 Va. 742, 32 S. E. 464.

Contra, Pickens v. South Carolina & G. R. R., 54 S. C. 498, 32 S. E. 567.

the defendant's fault the defendant should be held liable for any physical injury that results. So where a young boy was put by force in a car and carried five miles from home, he walked back home, and illness resulted, it was held that he could recover compensation for the illness.[271] Where a passenger was carried in the nighttime beyond his destination, and it was necessary to walk back along a path containing a dangerous obstruction, and he was injured by the obstruction, he was allowed to recover for the injury in an action against the carrier.[272] In an action for wrongfully setting fire to plaintiff's house, damages were allowed for the physical injury suffered by plaintiff and his family in fleeing from the house thinly clad.[273] And upon failure to deliver a telegram which would have resulted in giving plaintiff a ticket to travel to a distant city, plaintiff, who had no money, was allowed to recover for the exposure suffered in walking to his destination.[274] In some cases, however, damages which were the result of exposure from being forced to walk have been disallowed as too remote.[275]

§ 226k. Only reasonable expense recoverable.

But a plaintiff can only recover the reasonable expenses under the circumstances. Therefore a delayed passenger cannot recover the expense of a special train to avoid a slight delay. In Le Blanche v. London & North West Railway [276] the plaintiff took a train on the defendants' railway, by which he should, according to the time-table, have reached York in time to catch a train which would have brought him to his destination at half-past seven. The defendants' train arrived in York too late to allow him to catch that train, and by the

---

[271] Drake v. Kiely, 93 Pa. 492.

[272] Yazoo & M. V. R. R. v. Aden, 77 Miss. 382, 27 So. 385.

[273] Serafina v. Galveston H. & S. A. Ry. (Tex Civ. App.), 42 S. W. 142. Damages from sleeping on the cold floor of a neighbor's house were held too remote.

[274] Barnes v. Tel. Co., 76 Pac. 931, 65 L. R. A. 666, 27 Nev. 438.

[275] *Massachusetts:* Fillebrown v. Hoar, 124 Mass. 580 (wrongful eviction; cannot recover for injury to health in being obliged to walk to another house).

North Carolina: Hinson v. Smith, 118 N. C. 503, 24 S. E. 541 (wrongful seizure of horse while plaintiff was riding him; plaintiff cannot recover for catching cold while walking home).

[276] LeBlanche v. London & N. W. Ry., 1 C. P. Div. 286.

next one he would not have reached his destination till 10. He took a special train, by which he arrived there at 9. He had no special engagements which required his presence. In the Court of Appeal it was held that he could not recover the expense of the special train, on the ground that it was not reasonable. The court suggested that any expenditure which, according to the ordinary habits of society, a person who is delayed in his journey would naturally incur at his own cost, if he had no company to look to, he ought to be allowed to incur at the cost of the company, if he has been delayed through a breach of contract on the part of the company; but that it is unreasonable to allow a passenger to put the company to an expense to which he would not think of putting himself if he had no company to look to.

§ 2261. Reasonableness of the expense.

The question turns, in each case, upon the reasonableness of the expense incurred.[277] Thus expenses incurred by the plaintiffs in altering the works of their mill, in consequence of their apprehensions, founded on a trespass of the defendant, which in fact caused nominal damages only, but was accompanied by threats on his part, the carrying out of which would render them necessary, were held too remote.[278] In an action for false imprisonment on board a ship, the plaintiff cannot recover as special damage the expense he incurred in leaving the ship and taking his passage on board another, unless the imprisonment continued to the moment of his transshipment, and was the immediate cause thereof; [279] as if he acted to save his life, or from a reasonable regard to his safety. So an allowance for repairing a vessel will be limited to an offer of a responsible firm, known to the owner, he having unnecessarily increased the damages by disregarding it.[280]

When a tenant makes repairs to avoid the consequences of a breach of a covenant to repair, he can only charge the landlord with a reasonable expense, but he is not compelled

[277] *Missouri:* Dietrich *v.* Hannibal & S. J. R. R., 89 Mo. App. 36.

Texas: Cooper *v.* Dallas, 18 S. W. 565; Galveston H. & S. A. Ry. *v.* Borksy, 21 S. W. 1011.

[278] Sibley *v.* Hoar, 4 Gray, 222.

[279] Boyce *v.* Bayliffe, 1 Campb. 58.

[280] The M. Kalbfleisch, 59 Fed. 198.

to select precisely the same kind of materials, or to be precise to take care that the expense is "not a farthing greater than had before been expended on the same spot." Thus a tenant has been allowed to recover the expense of repainting with zinc paint, which was about fifteen per cent. more expensive than common lead paint—the original style of painting— it appearing that the zinc paint was a more desirable and better material. The whole question is, in fact, one of reasonable expense in view of all the circumstances of the case.[281] So in the common case of medical expenses, it must be shown that the expenses are reasonable before any recovery can be had.[282]

§ 226m. Reasonableness of the means selected.

Not only must the actual expense incurred be reasonable in itself, but the means selected to avoid the loss must be reasonable under the circumstances. So where a passenger is put off a train at a wrong station, he may take necessary steps for self-protection; and if he acts reasonably he may recover compensation of the wrongdoer for all evil results, or for any expense to which he is put. If he can procure another conveyance at reasonable expense, he cannot recover for injury caused by a long or difficult journey on foot.[283] If it is night, and there are houses near by which he sees or should see, he cannot recover for injury caused by walking home unless he tried to obtain admission at the houses and was refused.[284] So where a railroad crossing is obstructed it is not reasonable to drive across the rails at another place, and where plaintiff did so and was thrown out of his wagon the defendant was not responsible;[285] where a bridge was washed away, and plaintiff tried to ford the stream, defendant could not be charged with the resulting injury;[286] and when, the highway being obstructed, plaintiff went onto private land and

---

[281] Myers v. Burns, 35 N. Y. 269.

[282] *Illinois:* Amann v. Chicago C. T. Co., 243 Ill. 263, 90 N. E. 673.

Montana: Storm v. City of Butte, 35 Mont. 385, 89 Pac. 726.

Texas: Missouri, K. & T. Ry. v. Willis (Tex. Civ. App.), 117 S. W. 170; Texas & P. Ry. v. Hemphill, 125 S. W. 340 (Tex. Civ. App.).

[283] Indianapolis, B. & W. Ry. v. Birney, 71 Ill. 391.

[284] Louisville, N. & G. S. R. R. v. Fleming, 14 Lea (Tenn.), 128. See St. Louis, I. M. & S. Ry. v. Evans, 126 S. W. 1058 (Ark.).

[285] Jackson v. Nashville, C. & S. L. Ry., 13 Lea (Tenn.), 491.

[286] Hyde v. Jamaica, 27 Vt. 443.

got stuck in a pond, the town was not responsible.[287] And where defendant obstructed plaintiff's private way, and plaintiff thereupon secured it to be laid out as a public way, on condition of his paying $70 as land damages to the defendant, it was held that this was not the direct and natural way to get rid of the obstruction, which could have been removed more cheaply, and therefore plaintiff could not recover.[288] Where defendant killed some of plaintiff's hogs, and owing to fear that he would kill other hogs the plaintiff expended money in finding his hogs and in shutting them up and feeding them after they were shut up, he was not allowed to recover the expense.[289]

In Northern Supply Company v. Wangard,[290] an action for the sale of potatoes, defendant sought to recoup damages because the potatoes were decaying when delivered. He placed the potatoes with others; and after he discovered their condition, instead of removing them at once, he left all the potatoes in the cellar, occasionally sorting them, in order to get some to sell at retail. It was held that he could not get the expense of this, as it was not a reasonable way of doing. So in an action for failure to deliver lumber for a building the plaintiff instead of procuring other lumber used material for temporary supports for his building, at considerable expense, fitting in the lumber later when it arrived. It was held that he could not recover this unreasonable expense.[291]

§ 226n. Repairs not worth while.

In some cases it may not be worth while to repair the injury to property; the reasonable plan may be to leave the property unrepaired, and recover the diminution in value as the less loss. In Green v. Mann[292] it is laid down that unless the expense of making repairs is "trifling" the defendant cannot

---

[287] Tisdale v. Norton, 8 Met. (Mass.) 388. This case was decided upon the ground that the statute making the town liable for defects in the highway did not cover such a loss.

[288] Holmes v. Fuller, 68 Vt. 207, 34 Atl. 699.

[289] Harmon v. Callahan (Tex. Civ. App.), 35 S. W. 705.

[290] 123 Wis. 1, 100 N. W. 1066.

[291] C. W. Robinson Lumber Co. v. Burton, 128 La. 000, 54 So. 582.

[292] 11 Ill. 613. See also Pewaukee M. Co. v. Howitt, 86 Wis. 270, 56 N. W. 784.

insist that it constitutes the sole measure of damages. But the rule seems to be grounded not on the question whether the expense is trifling, but whether, under all the circumstances of the case, it is such an expense as a prudent man would reasonably incur. And thus, where one had wrongfully delayed delivering a conveyance of land on which was a barn, but afterward conveyed the premises, the expense incurred by the plaintiff in preparing to build another barn on his own ground during the period of the defendant's refusal was held not recoverable.[293] And so where plaintiff's land was threatened with injury by a leak in defendant's canal, and he could have avoided the injury by a ditch, but the ditch would have cost more than the value of the land, it was held that it was not his duty to avoid the loss by the construction of such a ditch.[294]

§ 226o. Necessity of payment before recovery.

It has often been urged that the plaintiff cannot recover compensation for the expense of avoiding loss unless the expense has actually been paid by him before suit, or at least before verdict. But it is clear that such expense need not actually be paid; it is enough that liability to pay has been incurred.[295] Even if the liability itself had not yet been incurred, the probable cost may furnish the measure of damages. Thus where defendant wrongfully allowed dirt to be carried down into plaintiff's mill plant, it was held that the expense of removing could be recovered although it had not been removed, that being the amount by which the value was

---

[293] Warner v. Bacon, 8 Gray (Mass.), 397.

[294] Welliver v. Pennsylvania Canal Co., 23 Pa. Super. Ct. 79.

[295] *Medical expenses:*

Illinois: Chicago, etc., R. R. v. Cleminger, 178 Ill. 536, 53 N. E. 320 (affirming 77 Ill. App. 186); Schmitt v. Jurrus, 234 Ill. 578, 85 N. E. 261; McCarthy v. Spring Valley Coal Co., 243 Ill. 185, 90 N. E. 372.

Missouri: Stoebier v. St. Louis Transit Co., 203 Mo. 702, 102 S. W. 651.

Washington: Cole v. Seattle, R. & S. R. R., 42 Wash. 462, 85 Pac. 3.

Cases are to be distinguished where the recovery of such expenses is refused because of a defect in pleading: Simeon v. Lindsay, 6 Pennew. (Del.) 224, 65 Atl. 778; and of cases refusing recovery because no liability is shown: Nelson v. Western Steam Nav. Co., 52 Wash. 177, 100 Pac. 325. See *ante,* § 67.

For cases involving the recovery of litigation expenses incurred but not paid, see *post,* § 685, *n.*

diminished.[296] In an action against a railway company for breach of contract to fence in land in consideration of right of way granted to it, the measure of damages is the cost of erecting the fences, and it is no defence to such an action that the plaintiff has not erected the fences. On this point the Supreme Court of Indiana said: [297] "The position assumed by counsel that the plaintiff in such a case cannot recover unless he has done the acts which the defendant agreed to do, cannot be correct. Suppose the defendant has agreed to erect a house for the plaintiff, has received the consideration for which he agreed to do the work, but failed to perform the contract on his part, and the plaintiff seeks to recover damages for the breach of the contract, is it the law that he cannot recover unless he has himself first erected the house? We think not." [298]

Even if the injury cannot now be avoided, the cost which would have attended the attempt to avoid may nevertheless be an element of damage as constituting the limit of recovery. Thus in an action for a personal injury of such a nature that the plaintiff ought as a reasonable man to have had a surgical operation, it was held that if he failed to have the operation he could not recover for the injuries which could have been avoided; but in determining that question the jury would include damages for the danger and suffering that would have attended the operation if he had submitted to it.[299]

IV.—Proof of Avoidable Consequences

§ 227. Burden of proof.

It has been repeatedly held that the burden of proof is always on the defendant to prove that the plaintiff might have reduced damages.[300] So a vendee cannot in an action for

[296] O'Riley *v.* McChesney, 3 Lans. (N. Y.) 278.

[297] Logansport, Crawfordsville & S. Ry. *v.* Wray, 52 Ind. 578.

[298] Citing Lawton *v.* Fitchburg R. R., 8 Cush. (Mass.) 230; Chicago & R. I. R. R. *v.* Ward, 16 Ill. 522.

[299] Missouri, K. & T. Ry. *v.* Hagan, 42 Tex. Civ. App. 133, 93 S. W. 1014.

[300] *Alabama:* Birmingham R. L. & P. Co. *v.* Anderson, 163 Ala. 72, 50 So. 1021.

Indiana: Citizens' St. R. R. *v.* Hobbs, 15 Ind. App. 610, 43 N. E. 479, 44 N. E. 377.

New York: Hamilton *v.* McPherson, 28 N. Y. 72.

vendor's failure to deliver logs, recover damages because his mill remained idle, if he could have bought other logs, but the burden of proving that he could is, it seems, on the vendor.[301] "But first of all the defence set up should be proved by the one who sets it up. He seeks to be benefited by a particular matter of fact, and he should, therefore, prove the matter alleged by him. The rule requires him to prove an affirmative fact, whereas the opposite rule would call upon the plaintiff to prove a negative, and therefore the proof should come from the defendant. He is the wrongdoer, and presumptions between him and the person wronged should be made in favor of the latter. For this reason, therefore, the onus must in all such cases be upon the defendant." [302] "*Prima facie,* the plaintiff is damaged to the extent of the amount stipulated to be paid. The burden of proof is on the defendant to show either that the plaintiff has found employment elsewhere, or that other similar employment has been offered and declined, or at least that such employment might have been found." [303]

On the other hand, when the plaintiff desires to recover the *expense* of an attempt to avoid loss, it is *prima facie* sufficient for him to establish the fact of payment; and the burden of introducing evidence that the expense was unnecessary or unreasonable is on the defendant. In consequence of these two related rules the plaintiff should introduce evidence of the amount expended by him for such a purpose, without showing that the expense was necessary or the amount reasonable.[304]

[301] Hopkins v. Sanford, 41 Mich. 243.

[302] Costigan v. Mohawk & H. R. R., 2 Den. 609. See to the same effect:

Alabama: Murrell v. Whiting, 32 Ala. 54.

Indiana: Dunn v. Johnson, 33 Ind. 54, 5 Am. Rep. 177.

New York: Hamilton v. McPherson, 28 N. Y. 72, 84 Am. Dec. 330; Leonard v. New York A. & B. E. M. T. Co., 41 N. Y. 544, 1 Am. Rep. 480; Greene v. Waggoner, 2 Hilt. 297.

Pennsylvania: King v. Steiren, 44 Pa. 99, 84 Am. Dec. 419.

England: Roper v. Johnson, L. R. 8 C. P. 167.

[303] Howard v. Daly, 61 N. Y. 362, 371, 19 Am. Rep. 285; consequently plaintiff need not allege that he has tried to make the damages as light as possible. Merrill v. Blanchard, 40 N. Y. Supp. 48.

When an employee obtains other employment the presumption is said to be that he gets the best wages he can. Hunt v. Crane, 33 Miss. 669, 69 Am. Dec. 381.

[304] Williams v. Newberry, 32 Miss. 256.

§ 228. Court and jury.

Whether the party injured has used ordinary care to make the consequences of the injury as light as possible, is usually a question of fact, depending upon all the circumstances of the case. Thus in the common case of injury to the person, the plaintiff is required to show that he employed a competent physician, but if the physician makes mistakes in his treatment, this is not the fault of the plaintiff.[305] The question whether moderate expense and ordinary effort would have prevented the damages, is for the jury.[306]

In Parker v. Meadows [307] it was held that the court was to determine in each case what was a reasonable expenditure, regard being had to all the circumstances.[308] But whether the plaintiff should have reduced damages, is substantially the same as the question whether he has been negligent; and this is usually for the jury under proper instructions.[309]

[305] *Iowa:* Collins v. Council Bluffs, 32 Ia. 324, 7 Am. Rep. 200, *n.;* Rice v. Des Moines, 40 Ia. 638.

Maine: Page v. Bucksport, 64 Me. 51, 18 Am. Rep. 239.

Massachusetts: Eastman v. Sanborn, 3 Allen, 594.

Missouri: Stover v. Bluehill, 51 Mo. 439.

New Hampshire: Tuttle v. Farmington, 58 N. H. 13.

New York: Lyons v. Erie Ry., 57 N. Y. 489.

Ohio: Loeser v. Humphrey, 41 Ohio St. 378, 52 Am. Rep. 86.

Vermont: Bardwell v. Jamaica, 15 Vt. 438.

See *ante,* § 221*b*, note 156.

[306] *Iowa:* Little v. McGuire, 38 Ia. 560; Smith v. Chicago, C. & D. R. R., 38 Ia. 518.

Minnesota: Cargill v. Thompson, 57 Minn. 534, 59 N. W. 638.

New York: Leonard v. New York, etc., Tel. Co., 41 N. Y. 544.

[307] 86 Tenn. 181.

[308] Citing *Alabama:* Martin v. Hill, 42 Ala. 275.

New York: Hester v. Knox, 63 N. Y. 561.

Wisconsin: Hinckley v. Beckwith, 13 Wis. 31.

[309] Bevier v. Delaware & H. C. Co., 13 Hun, 254.

CHAPTER XI

§ 228a. Connection of replacement with the rule of avoidable consequences.

In the foregoing chapter we have seen that the doctrine of avoidable consequences is not generally considered as founded upon any *duty* resting on the plaintiff to reduce damages as far as possible, but that it springs from the idea that by consequences of a wrong which the plaintiff, acting as rational and prudent men normally do, can avoid, he is not legally damaged.[1] In a number of cases the steps taken by the plaintiff to avoid in his own interest the consequences of the wrong, take the form of *replacement in the market*. The most common instances are cases in which the vendor has broken a contract for the delivery of goods sold, cases involving the purchase and sale of securities or contracts to carry stocks, cases of conversion and replevin, and generally all cases involving the non-delivery or conversion of property by the defendant.[2] The simplest of all instances is the ordinary case of a sale in the market where the vendee, failing to receive the thing bought, immediately replaces himself by the purchase of other goods of the same sort at the market price.

§ 228b. Replacement not a duty.

There can be no duty of replacement in ordinary mercantile contracts nor in any of the other cases above referred to.

[1] See *ante*, § 202.

[2] See Sedgwick on Damages, §§ 507– 525, 735, 745–749, 855; Sedgwick's Elements of Damages, pp. 262, 263, 310.

That is to say, the plaintiff, by the mere fact of a breach of a contract or tort of this sort by the defendant, cannot be placed under a duty to make a contract with a third person to supply himself with that of which he has been deprived. The difference between such cases and those of the ordinary breach of contract of service, where the defendant can always show that the plaintiff is in default if he has not *employed his time* so as to reduce damages, is that in these cases the suit is based entirely on the loss of the value of time, and the failure of the plaintiff to employ his time so as to reduce damages is obviously a voluntary failure to act as a prudent and rational man normally would in his own interest; and his interest coincides to this extent with that of the defendant, so that the analogy here between his natural course of action in his own interest, and what would be his course of action if he were acting under a duty toward the defendant, is very nearly complete. But in the case of breach of ordinary mercantile contracts and of torts involving the conversion or non-delivery of property, it very rarely happens that the idea of duty to the defendant can properly be invoked, and we think it may be said broadly, notwithstanding many *dicta* in the cases to the contrary, that in these cases, the plaintiff is *under no duty* to replace himself in the market. The matter will be found treated in different portions of this work under the various classes of cases in which it arises. Our object here is chiefly to show the causes of the confusion on the subject of replacement which abound in the decisions, and how that confusion may perhaps be cleared up.

§ 228c. Possible cases of replacement.

A wrong sounding either in tort or contract, or both, having been done, there are two possible cases of replacement. The person injured may replace himself, or he may be replaced by the wrongdoer. In the latter case, the question raised is that of the allowance of *benefits*, in which the rules of avoidable consequences have no place. The case which concerns us here is that of replacement by the party injured. The origin of the confusion on the subject is to be found in the fact that in many of the most familiar transactions of business, and wrongs connected with them, in which *market value* at the time of the wrong done furnishes the normal measure of damages, this measure is, owing to this very fact, the same as the cost of replacement. Whenever the plaintiff is deprived of property, or rights, through negligence, trespass, conversion, or non-delivery, the normal measure of damages is the value of the property or rights at the time of the breach of contract or tort. Whenever there is a market, the value is determined by it. But since the plaintiff, if he replaces himself, must do so by a purchase at the market value, the cost of replacement, and the market value, are one and the same.[3] Hence, by a natural confusion, it is easy to fall into the error of laying it down that the cost of replacement is the measure of damages; and from this it is but a step to imagine that a *duty rests upon the plaintiff to fix the measure of damages* by replacing himself in the market. The substitution of the conception of a duty to replace for that of a resort to the cost of replacement as a measure, has led, and is still leading, to the formulation of anomalous rules quite at variance with the underlying principles on which the law of compensatory relief rests—indemnity and certainty.[4]

Perhaps the best reason for the use of replacement as a test is that wherever property or property rights are taken, destroyed, or injured, the person to whom they belong is entitled immediately to an amount of money representing the value *for all lawful purposes;* one of these being enjoyment and use, and another, sale, he is entitled at least either to the opportunity of replacement, or its value; *i. e.,* the sum for which he could have either bought or sold in the market, in other words, the market value.[5]

---

[3] A common case is that of directions to an agent to buy or sell, changed by error of an intermediate agent in transmission, *e. g.,* by a telegraph company. Rittenhouse *v.* Ind. L. of Telegraph, 1 Daly, 474, 44 N. Y. 263; Tylor *v.* W. U. Tel. Co., 60 Ill. 421; De Rutte *v.* N. Y. A. & B. T. Co., 1 Daly, 547.

[4] Suydam *v.* Jenkins, 3 Sand. 614. The opinion of Duer, J., in this re-

plevin case is to-day the best guide that we know of through the whole labyrinth of cases which, since the abolition of the old forms of action, have endeavored to find some new rule of damages in actions for conversion or non-delivery of personal property beyond that of the value lost, increased by consequential damages, and limited by the rule of avoidable consequences.

[5] Sedgwick's Elements .of Damages,

Were replacement a duty there would. be some corresponding right in the wrongdoer. The cases, however, are totally silent on the subject of such a right. In the case of breach of contracts to carry stocks on margin, we hear of the plaintiff's right to call upon the defendant to replace him, and the plaintiff's duty to replace himself. The former is usually merely the right of the pledgor of stocks against money borrowed to call upon the pledgee if the latter has sold them without notice or converted them, to restore the pledgor to the original position of which the defendant's wrong has deprived him; the latter is not a duty at all, but is suggestive of one by analogy in its involving an act on the part of the plaintiff which results in benefiting the defendant by arresting the consequences of his act, though actually a voluntary act dictated by self-interest.[6]

§ 228d. Contracts for carrying stocks on a margin.

The cases which have caused most difficulty and have been productive of most confusion are those involving speculative contracts for carrying stocks. A broker, with whom a margin, i. e., a certain percentage of the par value of the stocks purchased is deposited, buys for the account of a customer a number of shares of stock to be held subject to the latter's order. The broker may call for more margin if the stock declines in value; in other words, the percentage of margin must be "kept good." Such a contract is usually regarded as involving a purchase of stock, the customer becoming the owner and the broker the pledgee with a power to sell if the margin is not kept good, but not without notice. But it is also something else—a continuing speculative venture with borrowed money secured by the collateral of the stock and terminable at will, according to its terms, by either party, but on notice only. If the broker converts the stock to his own use by sale, the customer on discovery of the fact may disaffirm the sale and call upon the broker to replace, or may replace himself. The

p. 129; Smith *v.* Griffith, 3 Hill, 333, 337.

[6] See ch. vi, § 208a. The metaphor is so close that in all cases, to exclude the use of the word "duty" without cumbrous circumlocution, is not easy.

measure of damages for conversion by the broker (which will be discussed hereafter in detail) has been held at different times and in different jurisdictions to be, first, the highest value of the stock in the market down to the time of trial; second, the highest intermediate value within a reasonable time after notice of the fact of conversion, and third, in accordance with the usual rule in conversion, the value at the time of the conversion.

§ 228e. The measure of damages in stock-carrying contracts.

The first measure of damages is founded upon the idea that as the customer *might* have replaced himself in the market if he had had notice, and so might have got the benefit of any subsequent rise in price, he is entitled to whatever profit he might have realized down to the trial. But this theory of the damages has been generally abandoned and it is wholly speculative and uncertain. He might *not* have replaced himself at all, and there is no possible way of proving that he would have replaced himself, if at all, at the right moment. There is here no suggestion that replacement is a duty.

The second measure of damages was established in New York by the leading case of Baker *v.* Drake.[7] Before the case of Baker *v.* Drake, the rule in New York, as established by Markham *v.* Jaudon [8] had been that of the *highest intermediate value,* and although Baker *v.* Drake has been often misquoted or misapplied, the authority of the decision and of the opinion of the court, delivered by Rapallo, J., have never been shaken. This fact justifies a close examination of the case at this early stage of our inquiry.

The facts involved were those of an ordinary contract to carry stocks on margin, as described above. The court in laying down the rule of damages did not treat the matter as one involving any distinction between tort and contract, but decided the case as one in which the rule was equally applicable whether the action was regarded as brought for a breach of

[7] 53 N. Y. 211, 13 Am. Rep. 507. *Cf.* Gruman *v.* Smith, 81 N. Y. 25; Colt *v.* Owens, 90 id. 398.   [8] 41 N. Y. 235.

a special continuing contract to carry stocks on a margin, or as an action of trover in which the plaintiff as owner sued for the conversion of goods pledged.   In either case there is room for consequential damages—in the case of a contract, the loss of "probable profits," [9] in that of conversion, the actual enhancement of the value of the stock converted down to a reasonable time within which the plaintiff might, had he not been kept in ignorance of the sale, have fixed the amount of the loss.   The decision and rule seem to involve the following conclusion: whenever the action is held to be conversion, it is because the contract of purchase is held to vest the *title* in the customer; the broker becomes the selling agent for the customer, and consequently commits a double wrong in selling without notice; he not only converts the property, but converts it without notice to the owner, his principal, and as between principal and agent this is an independent wrong,[10] which consists in the breach of a contract not to sell without notice; and unless the plaintiff is compensated for this wrong, which necessarily lasts until the expiration of a reasonable time after actual notice to replace himself, he loses part of the value of his right of redress.   This seems to justify the New York rule in the case of an ordinary broker's contract to carry stocks, and to show the point of divergence which separates this class of cases from those of simple conversion, and also from sales, etc., etc.   It also shows how mistaken is the idea that the rule of damages is dependent upon the notion that the plaintiff is under a *duty to replace*.   The damages recoverable were said to be merely such as "a *proper degree of prudence* on the part of the complainant would not have averted." In other words, consequences not avoidable by the complainant acting with ordinary prudence, *i. e.*, from self-interest.

The third rule of damages given above is merely the ordinary rule in all cases of conversion or non-delivery of personal property—the value of the property at the time and place of conversion, or failure to deliver.   This in itself does not invoke any duty to replace at all, and is merely the rule in the old action of trover or trespass *d. b. a.*   But it is not a hard and

[9] 53 N. Y. 216.

[10] Brown *v.* McGran, 14 Pet. 479, 496,   10 L. ed. 550; Sedgwick's Elements of Damages, p. 293.

fast rule, as will be seen when we come to deal with the subjects of conversion, trespass, sales, etc.[11]

In this class of cases *consequential damages* are always admitted so far as provable, and as limited by the rule of avoidable consequences. Now the rule of the value at the time and place of conversion, modified in proper cases by the allowance of *consequential damages*, is merely Rapallo, J.'s rule of the actual enhancement down to the reasonable time within which plaintiff *might*, had he not been kept in ignorance of the sale, have fixed the amount of the loss (avoidable consequences); or of "probable profits" if the action be regarded as contractual.

A comparison of the three rules given above, therefore, shows that the only fixed measure is the value at the time of conversion or non-delivery; that the circumstances of the case may let in "reasonable profits"; an enhancement of damages (consequential) growing out of the loss of a reasonable opportunity for replacement due to deprivation of notice, or growing out of such other circumstances as may appear. Therefore, finally, the only general rule of damages in all such stock contracts is the value of the property or property rights lost (direct), enhanced by consequential damages within the limits fixed by the rule of avoidable consequences.

§ 228f. Non-speculative stock contracts.

There is no essential difference on principle in the rule of damages between cases in which stocks are carried on margin and those in which they are bought for investment.[12] The measure is the value of what is lost. The facts are always the same, first, a conversion or failure to deliver with or without notice; second, a reasonable interval of time after notice, during which the natural, normal impulse of one who is the owner of property for any purpose may be to replace. At what price within this period would he naturally replace himself? This, in a proper case, is the value of *what he has lost* and therefore measures it. If the contract to carry is a continuing contract of the sort described above, he may demand

---

[11] Wallingford v. Kaiser, 191 N. Y. 393, 84 N. E. 295.

[12] Wright v. Bank of Metropolis, 110 N. Y. 237, 18 N. E. 79.

that the defendant shall replace *him*, and it is not until this demand is refused that he is obliged to decide whether he will replace himself. Consequently, there may be a considerable interval of time before the moment arrives at which, as a reasonably prudent man, he will be called upon to determine whether to replace himself or not. That reasonable moment is determined by the jury and the value of what has been lost is fixed.

In cases of conversion of stocks without notice the interval is usually considerable; in those of failure to deliver goods under mercantile contracts, very brief; indeed the failure to deliver is usually known on the spot. In the former cases, any damages allowed over and above the difference in value at the instant of conversion, may be considered a species of consequential damages caused by the interval of time between the actual conversion and the reasonable time after discovery, for the privilege of replacement to be exercised. In margin contracts, the measure of damages is the difference between the price obtained by the broker and the highest price reached between the time the customer learned of it, and a reasonable time thereafter.[13] If no time is required for decision, there is no interval.[14]

Unfortunately some courts, especially those of New York, have mistaken the rule properly *applied* in Baker *v.* Drake for a general rule of damages applicable to all stock-carrying contracts, and have substituted for the right of the plaintiff to have an opportunity to replace himself in case of deprivation of notice, a *duty* of replacement on his part. This duty is spoken of in Wright *v.* Bank of the Metropolis as "the duty of the plaintiff to make the damages as light as he reasonably may"; and the rule, it is said, "requires a repurchase within a reasonable time." [15] A recent New York case [16] shows to what confusion this rule, if blindly followed, would lead, and also how impossible it is to part company permanently with the fundamental measure of the value at the time of conver-

[13] Burnham *v.* Lawson, 118 App. Div. 389, 103 N. Y. Supp. 482.

[14] Hurt *v.* Miller, 120 App. Div. 833, 105 N. Y. Supp. 775.

[15] 110 N. Y. 237, 246.

[16] McIntyre *v.* Whitney, 139 App. Div. 557, 124 N. Y. Supp. 234, affirmed, 201 N. Y. 16.

sion. Brokers convert stock purchased for a customer, but after the conversion and without knowledge of it the latter advances additional margin. *Held* that the brokers are responsible for the value of the stock at the time of the conversion, although the stock *declines* later and the customer *would not have realized so much on the stock by replacing himself within a reasonable time after discovery of the conversion.* Treating the rule in Baker *v.* Drake as a rule of *duty to replace,* would have given the plaintiff about one-third of what he had paid out in cash, most of it after the conversion, and the defendants would have gained as profits the total amount of the decline in the stock. On this point the court said:

"I think it may be confidently asserted that the Court of Appeals have never decided or suggested that one guilty of conversion could profit by the decline in the market value of the thing converted between the time of conversion and the discovery of it by the party injured. *The general rule of damage of course is the value of the thing converted at the time and place of the conversion, together with interest thereon from the time of the conversion, and that rule should be adopted in the absence of special circumstances whereby it will not afford complete indemnity to the injured party.*

"The early cases made a distinction in case the property converted was of fluctuating value, so as to give the party injured the advantage of a rising market. The distinction was not confined to speculative stock transactions, and we perceive no reason for treating such transactions as *sui generis.* It was finally decided in Markham *v.* Jaudon [17] in the case of a speculative stock transaction, that the customer was entitled to the highest market price of the property between the time of the conversion and the trial. The rule was limited in Baker *v.* Drake, in which it was held that upon discovering the conversion the customer could not lie by and mulct the defendant for a conjectural loss, based upon the highest value which the stock might attain over an indefinite period thereafter, but that if he wished to continue the venture and to charge his broker for the loss of speculative profits it was his duty within a reasonable time to replace the stock, thus avert-

[17] 41 N. Y. 235.

ing further damage. Judge Rapallo discussed the earlier cases, and it is therefore unnecessary to extend this opinion by reference to them. From his discussion it is apparent that he was considering solely *the right* of the injured party to recover speculative profits in addition to what was realized by the broker from the unlawful sales."

Ingraham, P. J., dissented on the ground that the action was "strictly for conversion," and that consequently plaintiff was limited to the damages sustained by him on the day of conversion. But this leaves out of view the possibility of consequential damages. The decision evidently depends upon replacement being a privilege and not a duty. Plaintiff is under no obligation to replace himself, in case of a decline, in order that the defendant may profit by his own wrong,[18] but he may recover the consequential, in addition to the direct damages.

The latest case in the New York Court of Appeals contains a dictum developing a startling extension of the idea of the so-called *duty* of replacement. In Weld *v.* Postal Telegraph Cable Co.[19] the action was for negligence in the transmission of a message sent in December, directing plaintiff's agent to sell cotton deliverable in March, *March cotton*, at 12.70. As received, the message read "12.07." This error was acted on and the cotton sold at a loss. The case went off on another point, but the court, on the subject of the avoidance of consequences through replacement in the market, says that it was not only "the duty of the plaintiffs to exercise reasonable diligence to minimize their damages," but that "it was equally their duty to annihilate them if they could." We have here a distinctly novel conception which completes the transformation of the doctrine of avoidable consequences. Instead of its being founded on the idea that consequences, which plaintiff in the natural and normal effort to save himself from loss, can avoid, are *remote*, it is that the plaintiff is under a duty to the defendant to reduce his own damages; that the measure of this duty is reasonable care. In this view it would seem to be inevitable that in every action, the normal measure of damages having been ascertained, the next question would

[18] Taussig *v.* Hart, 58 N. Y. 425.   [19] 199 N. Y. 88, 92 N. E. 415.

be, Has the plaintiff used due care to reduce them, as far as possible, by replacing himself by means of making a contract with a third person—a duty which, as we have attempted to show, does not exist.

§ 228g. Contracts for purchase and sale of chattels.

As already explained, the duty, if it exists at all, must exist in all classes of cases, whether sounding in tort or contract or both. It seems to be a necessary consequence that *plaintiff* should prove that he has discharged it, before he can recover. But on the contrary, the rule is that defendant must always show that the plaintiff lost a reasonable opportunity to replace himself, that is, unreasonably enhanced the damages, or failed to reduce them. The English courts have examined the matter carefully in cases of contracts for the purchase and sale of chattels, and have held practically that there is no such thing as a general duty resting upon the plaintiff to make a "forward contract." The following extract from the opinion of Kelly, C. B., in Brown *v.* Muller [20] puts the matter in its true light, and has been generally followed as sound law:

"It has been argued with much ingenuity that the damages ought to be estimated at a lower figure if it appear that when the defendant announced his intention of not delivering, or at all events when the first breach took place, and it became apparent that the contract could never be performed at all, the plaintiff might have entered into a new contract to the same effect as the old one for the months of October and November on as favourable terms; and if the plaintiff, on hearing he would never get delivery, was bound to go and obtain, if he could, the new contract suggested, then, no doubt, assuming that he might have made such a contract, the damages ought to be limited to his loss at that time. But there was, in my opinion, no such obligation. He is not bound to enter into such a contract, which might be either to his advantage or detriment, according as the market might fall or rise. If it fell, the defendants might fairly say that the plaintiff had no right to enter into a speculative contract, and

[20] L. R. 7 Ex. 319, 322 (a breach of contract to deliver goods).

insist that he was not called upon to pay a greater difference than would have existed had the plaintiff held his hand. Or again, by such a course, the plaintiff might be seriously injured and yet have no remedy. Suppose, for example, his new contract was with a person who proved insolvent. He would, in that case, be without redress; he would have lost his former contract, and his new one would turn out worthless. In either event, therefore, I do not think the plaintiff could be called upon to enter into a fresh contract. If he did, and thus obtained an advantage, he no doubt might save the defendant from some damages. But if he should suffer a loss, as by the insolvency of the new contractor, he could not make the defendant answer for it. And if it should happen that he might have done better for the defendant by waiting and making no speculative contract, the defendant would in his turn have a fair right to complain that his loss had not been mitigated as far as possible." [21]

§ 228h. Connection of this subject with the rule of higher intermediate value.

It may be well, in conclusion, to refer to a case which is sometimes erroneously thought to support the idea of a duty to replace. Startup v. Cortazzi [22] was *assumpsit* for non-delivery of linseed pursuant to a contract of sale. Plaintiffs contended that as they had paid a portion of the purchase money in advance they were entitled to damages according to the price at the time of trial. But the rule sustained was the price at the time fixed for delivery. There was no proof of any special damages or loss of speculative profits, nor that the plaintiffs had not the means of replacing themselves, but it seems to have been thought by the judges that had there been circumstances of this sort, the fact that the plaintiffs had parted with the money in advance would have enabled them to have the benefit of the higher rule of damages.

The case therefore is merely one of those which shows that

---

[21] *Cf.* Roper v. Johnson, L. R. 8 C. P. 167; Michael v. Hart, [1902] 1 K. B. 482; Burnham v. Lawson, 103 N. Y. Supp. 482, 118 App. Div. 389; Hart v. Miller, 105 N. Y. Supp. 775, 120 App. Div. 833.

[22] 2 C. M. & R. 165.

consequential damages may in the case of sales be recovered, and that the plaintiff is not always confined to value at the time and place of delivery. It shows also that there is a connection between claiming the profits of a speculation and replacement. But there is nothing to show that the plaintiff is under a duty to replace himself in the market.

§ 228i. Proof of replacement.

Replacement not being a duty, proof of it cannot be part of the plaintiff's case; the proof that plaintiff might have replaced himself, or did replace himself must come, if not admitted by him, from the defendant. In all such cases, it is an application of the rule of avoidable consequences.

CHAPTER XII

EXPENSES OF LITIGATION

§ 229. Expense of carrying on a suit not compensated.

We have seen that in order to recover complete compensation, the plaintiff should, in case he is successful, be allowed the expenses of litigation. Nevertheless, the general rule is, that counsel fees are not recoverable as damages. The law awards to the successful party his taxable costs, but the fees which he pays to counsel are not taken into consideration.[1] "In general the law considers the taxed costs as the only damage which a party sustains by the defence of a suit against him, and these he recovers by the judgment in his favor." [2]

[1] *United States:* Oelrichs v. Spain, 15 Wall. 211, 21 L. ed. 43.

Massachusetts: Henry v. Davis, 123 Mass. 345.

Michigan: Warren v. Cole, 15 Mich. 265.

Pennsylvania: Haverstick v. Erie Gas Co., 29 Pa. 254.

Nor can he recover for his expense and time in attending court. Jacobson v. Poindexter, 42 Ark. 97.

[2] Young v. Courtney, 13 La. Ann. 193. This rule applies also in the analogous case of witness fees. Thus where a physician's charge for attending the plaintiff included compensation for the expense of attending as a witness, that part of the charge which covered this expense was not allowed. Gulf, C. & S. F. Ry. v. Campbell, 76 Tex. 174.

So in an action of assumpsit,[3] the Supreme Court of Massachusetts said, that "the expenditure for counsel fees is an item ordinarily to be borne by the suitor, except so far as it may be remunerated by the taxable costs for the travel and attendance of the party, and the allowance of an attorney's fee." "In actions of debt, covenant, and assumpsit, the plaintiff can recover but legal costs as compensation for his expenditure in the suit, and as punishment to the defendant for his unjust detention of the debt." [4]

And so far was the principle carried in Massachusetts, that a trustee (or garnishee), in whose hands the funds of the debtor are found, could (in the absence of a statute permitting it) retain nothing to meet the expenses of litigation.[5]

This rule of the common law is in some jurisdictions changed by statute. Thus in Georgia [6] counsel fees are included in the damages where the defendant acted in bad faith, or was stubbornly litigious, whether the action is contract or tort.

§ 230. Reason of the rule.

It has been intimated [7] that the reason of this rule disallowing counsel fees is that they are a remote loss. But this would be very difficult to maintain. The expenses of a litigation to obtain compensation would seem to be, though not a direct, certainly a natural and proximate consequence of the injury, and hence to belong to that class of consequential losses which can be recovered. The true foundation of the rule we take to be that the common law has arbitrarily fixed taxable costs as the limit of remuneration for expenses of litigation. That counsel fees are not regarded as in themselves a re-

[3] Guild v. Guild, 2 Met. (Mass.) 229.

[4] Stimpson v. Railroads, 1 Wall, Jr., 164, 169, per Grier, J.

[5] Adams v. Cordis, 8 Pick. (Mass.) 260.

[6] Code, § 3796; Chambers v. Harper, 83 Ga. 382, 9 S. E. 717; Carhart v. Wainman, 114 Ga. 632, 40 S. E. 781, 88 Am. St. Rep. 45.

So in California, under Civil Code, § 3336, which provides that damages for conversion include "a fair compensation for the time and money properly expended in pursuit of the property," the Federal court held that counsel fees incurred in the action of trover might be recovered. Palo Alto Bank v. Pacific Postal Tel. Cable Co., 103 Fed. 841.

See Greenbaum v. Martinez, 86 Cal. 459, 25 Pac. 12.

[7] Pacific Ins. Co. v. Conard, 1 Bald. 138, Fed. Cas. No. 946.

mote loss, is shown in that class of cases where the expenses of a former suit are recovered.

§ 231. Civil and old common law.

* Under the Roman law the successful party was not restricted to a suit for malicious prosecution, and the party justly chargeable with making a totally ungrounded claim or defence was punished with a pecuniary mulct. And this, at one time, seems to have been adopted into the jurisprudence of modern Europe. Francis the First, by his ordinance of 1539, Art. 88, authorized the judge to inflict damages proportioned to the "temerity" of the losing party.[8] And so, too, in England, originally it seems that the plaintiff, in all cases of unsuccessful litigation, might be amerced *pro falso clamore*, and the amerciament [*a merci*, Fr.] was affeered [*affier*, Fr.], or assessed, by the court or its officers.

§ 232. Rule in actions of contract.

This power, however, no longer exists, and in cases of contract no redress is given beyond the taxable costs. Even in cases the most frivolous and vexatious, in no case is any independent redress given, *i. e.*, by a recriminatory action, unless the first suit or proceeding be malicious. This principle is rigorously applied to counsel fees in all cases of contract, and, without discrimination, to both parties to the litigation.** So in an action on an attachment or injunction bond, the expenses of prosecuting the suit on the bond cannot be recovered.[9]

§ 233. General rule in actions of tort.

In cases of tort it has once or twice been intimated that the plaintiff may recover his counsel fees. Thus, in an action on the case for flowing back the water of a river in Maine on the plaintiff's lands, although no malice was proved, Judge Story

[8] Merlin; *Repertoire*, in voc. *Dommages-Intérêts*.

[9] *Arkansas:* Goodbar *v.* Lindsley, 51 Ark. 380, 14 Am. St. Rep. 54.
Iowa: Vorse *v.* Phillips, 37 Ia. 428.

Louisiana: Offutt *v.* Edwards, 9 Rob. 90.

This is a different question from the recovery of the expense of prior litigation on such a bond; *post*, § 237.

told the jury, that for the purpose of giving a full indemnity, they might take into consideration such expenses of fees to counsel, and such other necessary expenses, as they might think were properly and fairly incurred; and on a motion made for a new trial, on the ground that the damages were excessive, the court refused to interfere.[10] And similar suggestions have been made in early cases in a few other jurisdictions.[11]

It is, however, firmly established that counsel fees cannot be included in compensatory damages, at least where there was no malice or oppression.[12] So in Massachusetts, the Supreme Court refused to allow counsel fees in an action on the case for setting a fire on the defendant's own land, whereby the plaintiff's wood was consumed, holding that it was immaterial with reference to the damages, whether the accident resulted from *gross negligence*, or merely the want of *ordinary care*.[13] "It is now well settled," said the court, "that even in an action of trespass or other action sounding in damages, the counsel fees and other expenses of prosecuting the suit, not included in the taxed costs, cannot be taken into consideration in assessing damages." And the Supreme Court of New York have laid down the same rule in an action on the case for negligence, against a railroad, for injuries to the person, which we have already noticed.[14]

In an action of trespass against the marshal of the United

[10] Whipple *v.* Cumberland M. Co., 2 Story, 661.

[11] *Connecticut:* Platt *v.* Brown, 30 Conn. 336; Welch *v.* Durand, 36 Conn. 182, 4 Am. Rep. 55.

Iowa: Armstrong *v.* Pierson, 8 Ia. 29.

Ohio: Finney *v.* Smith, 31 Oh. St. 529, 27 Am. Rep. 524, *n.*

Canada: Rose *v.* Belyea, 1 Han. (N. B.) 109.

[12] *United States:* Flanders *v.* Tweed, 15 Wall. 450, 21 L. ed. 203.

California: Howell *v.* Scoggins, 48 Cal. 355.

Kansas: Winstead *v.* Hulme, 32 Kan. 568.

Michigan: Warren *v.* Ray, 155 Mich. 91, 118 N. W. 741, 15 Detroit Leg. N. 935.

Minnesota: Kelly *v.* Rogers, 21 Minn. 146.

Nebraska: Winkler *v.* Roeder, 23 Neb. 706, 8 Am. St. Rep. 155, *n.*, 37 N. W. 607; Atkins *v.* Gladwish, 25 Neb. 390, 41 N. W. 347.

New York: Hicks *v.* Foster, 13 Barb. 663.

South Carolina: Welch *v.* Northeastern R. R., 12 Rich. 290.

Texas: Landa *v.* Obert, 45 Tex. 539.

Virginia: Burruss *v.* Hines, 94 Va. 413, 26 S. E. 875.

[13] Barnard *v.* Poor, 21 Pick. (Mass.) 378.

[14] Lincoln *v.* Saratoga & S. R. R., 23 Wend. (N. Y.) 425.

States, for making an illegal levy on certain teas, no circumstances of aggravation being shown, Mr. Justice Baldwin held that the jury could not allow the plaintiff his counsel fees by way of damages. He said:

"It may be thought a hardship that the plaintiffs shall not be allowed their actual disbursements in recovering this property; but the hardship is equally great in a suit for money lent, or to recover possession of land; they are deemed in law losses without injury, for which no legal remedy is afforded. I am, therefore, of opinion that you cannot, in assessing damages in this case, allow any of the items claimed by the plaintiffs for disbursements, they being consequent losses only, and not the actual or direct injury to their property which they have sustained by its seizure and detention, for which alone they are entitled to recover damages in this case, it not being attended with any circumstances of aggravation on the part of the defendant. Had there been any such, a very different rule would have been applied, by reimbursing the plaintiffs to the full extent of all their expenses and consequential losses." [15]

In Oelrichs v. Spain [16] Swayne, J., said: "In actions of trespass, where there are no circumstances of aggravation, only compensatory damages can be recovered, and they do not include the fees of counsel. The plaintiff is no more entitled to them, if he succeed, than is the defendant if the plaintiff be defeated." [17] And so generally, in actions for wrongful injury to property where there are no circumstances of aggravation, expenses of litigation cannot be recovered.[18]

---

[15] Pacific Ins. Co. v. Conard, 1 Bald. 138, 146.

[16] 15 Wall. 211, 230, 21 L. ed. 43.

[17] The following cases are to the same effect:

United States: Day v. Woodworth, 13 How. 363, 14 L. ed. 181.

California: Falk v. Waterman, 49 Cal. 224.

Connecticut: St. Peter's Church v. Beach, 26 Conn. 355; Dibble v. Morris, 26 Conn. 416.

Georgia: Georgia R. & B. Co. v. Gardner, 118 Ga. 723, 45 S. E. 600.

Indiana: Young v. Tustin, 4 Blackf. 277.

Louisiana: Knott v. Gough, 10 La. Ann. 562.

Maine: Longfellow v. Quimby, 29 Me. 196, 48 Am. Dec. 525.

[18] Bentley v. Fischer Co., 51 La. Ann. 451, 25 So. 262 (erecting structure on plaintiff's land); Bishop v. Hendrick, 82 Hun (N. Y.), 323, 31 N. Y. Supp. 502 (wrongfully retaining property).

§ 234. In cases of aggravation—Exemplary damages.

In some States it is held that facts which justify the infliction of exemplary damages will also justify the jury in adding the amount of the counsel fees to the verdict, not as part of the exemplary damages, but as compensatory damages.

In an action on the case brought in Connecticut, after stating the rule allowing vindictive or exemplary damages, the court proceeded to use this language:

"The argument in opposition to the doctrine of the charge is substantially founded upon the assumed principle, that the defendant cannot be subjected to a greater sum in damages than the plaintiff has actually sustained. But every case in which the recovery of vindictive damages has been justified, stands opposed to this argument. And we cannot comprehend the force of the reasoning which will admit the right of a plaintiff to recover as vindictive damages, beyond the amount of injury confessedly incurred, and in case of an act and injury equally wanton and wilfully committed or permitted, will deny to him a right to recover an actual indemnity for the expense to which the defendant's misconduct has subjected him. In the cases to which we have been referred in other States, as deciding a different principle, the courts seem to have assumed that the taxable costs of the plaintiff are his only legitimate compensation for the expense incurred. If taxable costs are presumed to be equivalent to actual necessary charges as a matter of law, every client knows as a matter of fact they are not. And legal fictions should never be permitted to work injustice." [19]

In Bennett v. Gibbons [20] Loomis, J., said: "It is not usual to introduce evidence to show specifically the amount of such expenses, yet, inasmuch as it is a legitimate element of damage, we do not see why relevant evidence is not as proper as in relation to any other item of damage, it being understood of course that it is discretionary with the jury to include this or not; but it seems to us that it cannot be erroneous to furnish the jury with some sure basis for such an addition, instead of leaving the whole matter to guesswork." And it is well settled

[19] Linsley v. Bushnell, 15 Conn. 225,   [20] 55 Conn. 450, 452.
38 Am. Dec. 79.

in Connecticut that in such actions counsel fees may be allowed.[21] In a still stronger case in that State, in an action of assault and battery, where, in consequence of the death of a juror, a second trial became necessary, it was held that the jury, in estimating the damages, might take into consideration the expenses of the first trial.[22] The same rule seems to prevail in other jurisdictions.[23] The Supreme Court of Ohio uses the following language: "The authorities are not uniform; but the better opinion now seems to be that in actions *ex contractu* and in cases nominally in tort, but where no wrong in the moral sense of the term is complained of, the fees of counsel ought not to be included; but in cases where the act complained of is tainted by fraud, or involves an ingredient of malice or insult, the jury which has power to punish has necessarily the right to include the consideration of proper and reasonable counsel fees in their estimate of damages." [24] And in Nevada, where a libel had been published, and a libel suit was necessary to vindicate the plaintiff's character, it was held that the plaintiff might recover the expense of litigation.[25] And while this doctrine does not prevail generally, in many States it has been held that the jury in assessing exemplary damages have a right to know and consider the expense of litigation.[26] Thus in Alabama, in an action for malicious

[21] Huntley v. Bacon, 15 Conn. 267; Ives v. Carter, 24 Conn. 392; Beecher v. Derby Bridge Co., 24 Conn. 491; St. Peter's Church v. Beach, 26 Conn. 355; Dibble v. Morris, 26 Conn. 416; Platt v. Brown, 30 Conn. 336; Welch v. Durand, 36 Conn. 182, 4 Am. Rep. 55; Dalton v. Beers, 38 Conn. 529; Wilson v. Granby, 47 Conn. 59, 36 Am. Rep. 51; Mason v. Hawes, 52 Conn. 12, 52 Am. Rep. 552; Wynne v. Parsons, 57 Conn. 73. Taxable costs are to be deducted from the amount so allowed. Maisenbacker v. Society Concordia, 71 Conn. 369, 42 Atl. 67, 71 Am. St. Rep. 312.

[22] Noyes v. Ward, 19 Conn. 250.

[23] Finney v. Smith, 31 Oh. St. 529, 27 Am. Rep. 524, *n.;* Stevenson v. Morris, 37 Oh. St. 10, 41 Am. Rep. 481; Peckham Iron Co. v. Harper, 41 Oh. St. 100.

[24] *United States:* Winters v. Cowen, 90 Fed. 99.
Indiana: Zeigler v. Powell, 54 Ind. 173.
Ohio: Roberts v. Mason, 10 Oh. St. 277.

[25] Thompson v. Powning, 15 Nev. 195.

[26] *Arkansas:* Patton v. Garrett, 37 Ark. 605 (*semble*).
Kansas: Titus v. Corkins, 21 Kan. 722; Winstead v. Hulme, 32 Kan. 568.
Louisiana: Eatman v. New Orleans P. Ry., 35 La. Ann. 1018.
Mississippi: New Orleans, J. & G. N. R. R. v. Allbritton, 38 Miss. 242, 75 Am. Dec. 98; Cowden v. Lockridge, 60 Miss. 385; Taylor v. Morton, 61 Miss. 24.
Texas: Landa v. Obert, 45 Tex. 539;

prosecution, the Supreme Court has said, while recognizing the conflict of authority, "We can readily perceive the justice and good sense of the rule which requires a party who wantonly and maliciously abuses the process of the court, or sues out an attachment for the purpose of worrying and harassing the defendant, without probable cause, to make good his losses, and to furnish complete reparation and indemnity for the injury his malice has occasioned"; and the defendant's counsel fees for defending the original suit were allowed to be "proven and taken into consideration by the jury." [27]

But it is difficult to see why such expenses should be allowed under the head of exemplary damage· The plaintiff's counsel fees are an expense incurred by him, and their reimbursement to him brings the measure of damages back toward the standard of compensation. It is an item of compensation, indeed, not usually allowed; but, nevertheless, it is really compensation. There is nothing especially punitory as regards the defendant in the fact that the sum in which he is mulcted happens, in whole or in part, to represent the counsel fees paid or incurred by his injured adversary. His payment to the plaintiff of a considerable sum is equally a punishment, whether the plaintiff have paid a like or less sum as counsel fees or not. Indeed, when the jury are permitted to break beyond the bounds which the law, having compensation only in view, prescribes, it will be found on analysis, we think, that every attempt to introduce other standards for their guidance will be futile. And accordingly, by the better opinion, no inquiry into counsel fees should be allowed, even in those actions of tort in which the jury may give exemplary damages.[28] Swayne, J., in Oelrichs v. Spain, a case considered in the preceding sec-

and by the codes of California and Georgia: Beckman v. Skaggs, 61 Cal. 362; Savannah v. Waldner, 49 Ga. 316; Guernsey v. Shellman, 9 Ga. 797; Mosely v. Sanders, 76 Ga. 293.

See post, § 359.

[27] Marshall v. Betner, 17 Ala. 832.

[28] California: Howell v. Scoggins, 48 Cal. 355; Falk v. Waterman, 49 Cal. 224.

Minnesota: Kelly v. Rogers, 21 Minn. 146.

New York: Halstead v. Nelson, 24 Hun, 395.

South Carolina: Welch v. Southeastern R. R., 12 Rich. 290.

Texas: Salado College v. Davis, 47 Tex. 131.

Vermont: Hoadley v. Watson, 45 Vt. 289, 12 Am. Rep. 197; Earl v. Tupper, 45 Vt. 275.

tion, in reference to counsel fees in such cases, cites with approval the remarks of the court in Day v. Woodworth: [29] "The punishment of the defendant's delinquency cannot be measured by the expenses of the plaintiff in prosecuting his suit. It is true that damages assessed by way of example may thus indirectly compensate the plaintiff for money expended in counsel fees, *but the amount of these fees cannot be taken as the measure of punishment, or a necessary element in its infliction.*" To the same effect see Fairbanks v. Witter,[30] where the court said that counsel fees could no more be allowed in actions where punitory damages can be given than in others, and that if they could be assessed by the jury, it must be on the principle "that they are consequential damages, and relate to the amount of compensation, rather than refer to damages which may be inflicted by way of penalty or punishment for aggravated misconduct." So in an action of assault and battery, it has been held that, although that was a case in which exemplary damages were allowable, a jury could not take into consideration counsel fees and expenses, for the legislature has fixed the taxable costs as full indemnity. And in New York it has been held error for the judge, in an action of slander, to charge the jury that, in awarding the damages, they might take into consideration the expenses to which the plaintiff had been put, by being compelled to come into court to vindicate her character.[31]

§ 235. Patent and admiralty cases.

In an early case [32] in the Supreme Court of the United States, of a libel filed by the Spanish consul, for restitution of a Spanish vessel captured by a French vessel, it appeared that a charge of sixteen hundred dollars for counsel fees in the courts below had been admitted; and the court said: "We do not think that this charge ought to be allowed. The general practice of the United States is in opposition to it." The authority of this case was for a time shaken by later decisions; [33]

[29] 13 How. 363, 371, 14 L. ed. 181.

[30] 18 Wis. 287, 290, 86 Am. Dec. 765.

[31] Hicks v. Foster, 13 Barb. (N. Y.) 663.

[32] Arcambel v. Wiseman, 3 Dall. 306, 1 L. ed. 613.

[33] The Apollon, 9 Wheat. 362, 6 L. ed. 111; Canter v. American & O. I. Co., 3 Pet. 307, 7 L. ed. 688.

but in the case of The Margaret v. The Connestoga,[34] Grier, J., while apparently admitting the discretionary power of the Admiralty Court to allow counsel fees, expressed his strong repugnance to its exercise, saying that the principle seemed to belong rather to the Hall of the Cadi than the judgment-seat of the court; and counsel fees are no longer allowed in admiralty.[35] The history of counsel fees in patent suits has been similar. It was a favorite doctrine of Mr. Justice Story that counsel fees should be allowed in patent suits;[36] though at first he denied recovery [37] on the authority of Arcambel v. Wiseman. But it is now well established that counsel fees cannot be recovered as "actual damages" in patent suits.[38]

§ 235a. Other actions.

In other actions the same view is usually taken; and it is held that no recovery can be had for any expenses of litigation beyond taxable costs. Thus it has been held that counsel fees cannot be recovered in actions of replevin,[39] or upon bills in equity,[40] or on a writ of mandamus.[41] And in actions based on statute no counsel fees can be recovered unless the statute provides for such recovery.[42] So in a suit to set aside a judgment by confession, no counsel fees can be recovered if no statute allows it.[43]

[34] 2 Wall. Jr., 116.

[35] The Baltimore, 8 Wall. 377, 19 L. ed. 463; Swayne, J., in Oelrichs v. Spain, 15 Wall. 230, 21 L. ed. 43.

[36] Boston M. Co. v. Fiske, 2 Mason, 119; Pierson v. Eagle Screw Co., 3 Story, 402; and so, too, held by Judge Woodbury, in the same circuit, Allen v. Blunt, 2 Woodb. & M. 121.

[37] Whittemore v. Cutter, 1 Gall. 429.

[38] Blanchard's G. T. F. v. Warner, 1 Blatchf. 258; Stimpson v. The Railroads, 1 Wall. Jr., 164.

[39] *Mississippi:* Cowden v. Lockridge, 60 Miss. 385; Taylor v. Morton, 61 Miss. 24.

New York: Hampton & B. R. & L. Co. v. Sizer, 71 N. Y. Supp. 990, 35 Misc. 391.

Canada: Davis v. Cushing, 5 All. (N. B.) 383.

[40] Knefel v. Ahern, 57 Ill. App. 568.

[41] People v. Deutscher Krieger Bund (App. Div.), 113 N. Y. Supp. 367.

[42] Spencer v. Murphy, 6 Colo. App. 453, 41 Pac. 841.

In Missouri it is held that counsel fees can be recovered on the dismissal of condemnation proceedings. St. Louis R. Co. v. Southern Ry., 138 Mo. 591, 39 S. W. 471.

See R. R. v. Lackland, 25 Mo. 515; City of St. Joseph v. Hamilton, 43 Mo. 288; State v. Hug, 44 Mo. 117; City of St. Louis v. Meintz, 107 Mo. 611, 18 S. W. 30; Simpson v. Kansas City, 111 Mo. 240, 20 S. W. 38.

[43] Bull v. Keenan, 100 Iowa, 144, 69 N. W. 433.

§ 236. Expenses of a prior litigation.

Where the plaintiff has defended an action for the benefit or on account of the wrongful act of the defendant, two questions arise: first, whether the costs of defending the first action are recoverable; secondly, whether, if recoverable, counsel fees can be included. Some decisions seem to be to the effect that counsel fees are never recoverable. They are apparently founded on a fiction of law, that the costs are a full indemnity for all expenses incurred in the defence of a suit.[44] But it is very doubtful whether that ever applies except as between the parties to the suit, for the reason seems to be, that it is a fixed sum awarded by law to be paid by the prevailing to the losing party. Where a plaintiff has become involved in another suit by the defendant's acts, he should recover the amount of the reasonable expenses in which he has become involved, and there seems to be no reason for the existence of the fiction in such a case. A distinction has sometimes been made to the effect that if the plaintiff is successful in the prior litigation he cannot recover counsel fees, for he has been fully indemnified by receiving the taxed costs, though the rule is otherwise if he is not successful; but the better view is that counsel fees also are recoverable as well when he was successful as when he failed.[45]

Where the prior litigation was unnecessary, the plaintiff can recover neither the costs nor the counsel fees.[46] So an indorser cannot recover against the maker the costs of the action against him, for he should have paid the note. Very frequently the plaintiff is allowed to recover costs and not counsel fees, where a defence of the prior suit was not proper, for it may have been necessary for him to allow judgment to be entered.

Wherever the prior litigation is a natural consequence of the wrong, and is necessary to determine the amount of damages, or the plaintiff has reasonable grounds to suppose

[44] Leffingwell v. Elliott, 10 Pick. 204; Reggio v. Braggiotti, 7 Cush. 166.

[45] Seitz v. People's Sav. Bank, 140 Mich. 106, 103 N. W. 545.

[46] *Illinois:* Lunt v. Wrenn, 113 Ill. 168.

New York: Gallo v. Brooklyn Sav. Bank, 114 N. Y. Supp. 78, 129 App. Div. 698.

that it is for the interest of the defendant that he should contest the claim, and he does so for the defendant's benefit, the costs and counsel fees are, by the better opinion, recoverable.[47] In New York the "expenses" are recoverable if the litigation is necessary in order to determine the amount of damages.[48] In Hughes v. Graeme,[49] an action for the defendant's misrepresentation of his authority as agent, Blackburn, J., stated one of the grounds on which such expenses are recoverable, as follows: "That if a person takes a particular course, reasonably, naturally, and *bona fide*, resulting from the assertion of the authority, then the results of that course would be a reasonable and natural consequence of the warranty, and the costs of it would be part of the reasonable and natural damages."

There has been some question whether counsel fees can be recovered if they have not been actually paid. The better opinion is that liability to pay them is enough.[50] But if the fee has not actually been paid, interest will of course not be allowed on the amount.[51] The fee must have been a reasonable one; and the reasonableness is a question for the jury.[52]

§ 237. Expense of dissolving injunction or discharging attachment.[53]

On a bond given to indemnify the plaintiff for any expense

[47] Baxendale v. London, C. & D. Ry., L. R. 10 Ex. 35.

[48] Dubois v. Hermance, 56 N. Y. 673.

[49] 33 L. J. Q. B. 335.

[50] *Alabama:* Garrett v. Logan, 19 Ala. 344; Miller v. Garrett, 35 Ala. 96.

Florida: Wittich v. O'Neal, 22 Fla. 592.

Indiana: Lytton v. Baird, 95 Ind. 349.

Louisiana: McRae v. Brown, 12 La. Ann. 181.

Ohio: Noble v. Arnold, 23 Oh. St. 264.

Wisconsin: Bonesteel v. Bonesteel, 30 Wis. 511. The opposite view, however, prevails in California. Willson v. McEvoy, 25 Cal. 169; Prader v. Grimm, 28 Cal. 11.

An allegation of payment is, of course, not sustained by proof of a debt having been incurred. Pritchet v. Boevey, 1

C. & M. 775; Jones v. Lewis, 9 Dowl. P. C. 143; Ward v. Haws, 5 Minn. 440. And if the statute of limitations has run against the claim for counsel fees in the former action, the plaintiff, being no longer liable for fees, cannot recover the amount of them. Cullity v. Dorffel, 18 Wash. 122, 50 Pac. 932.

See, however, the analogous case of bill for medical expenses against which the statute of limitations has run, *post,* § 483.

[51] Walton v. Campbell, 51 Neb. 788, 71 N. W. 737.

[52] *Georgia:* Allen v. Harris, 113 Ga. 107, 38 S. E. 322.

Illinois: Spring v. Olney, 78 Ill 101.

Kansas: Tyler v. Safford, 31 Kan. 608.

England: Pow v. Davis, 1 B. & S. 220.

[53] For a full treatment of this ques-

caused by the wrongfulness of judicial proceedings (such as an injunction or attachment bond), the counsel fees expended in obtaining a dissolution of the injunction, or discharge of the attachment, are recoverable if they can be separated from those which would have been incurred in any event in the defence of the action.[54] In some States the counsel fees incurred in the reference to ascertain the damages suffered by the injunction are also allowed.[55] But no recovery can be had for the general expense of litigating the principal suit,[56] even though the attachment for which the bond was given alone gave the court jurisdiction, and it was found to be wrongful.[57]

tion, with other authorities, see *post*, §§ 682*a*, 685*k*.

[54] *Alabama:* Holmes *v.* Weaver, 52 Ala. 516; Bolling *v.* Tate, 65 Ala. 417.

California: Graves *v.* Moore, 58 Cal. 435.

Florida: Wittich *v.* O'Neal, 22 Fla. 592.

Illinois: Cummings *v.* Burleson, 78 Ill. 281.

Indiana: Morris *v.* Price, 2 Blackf. 457; Raupman *v.* Evansville, 44 Ind. 392; Swan *v.* Timmons, 81 Ind. 243.

Kansas: Sanford *v.* Willets, 29 Kan. 647; Tyler *v.* Safford, 31 Kan. 608.

Kentucky: Trapnall *v.* McAfee, 3 Met. 34, 77 Am. Dec. 152, *n.*

Louisiana: Littlejohn *v.* Wilcox, 2 La. Ann. 620; White *v.* Givens, 29 La. Ann. 571; Adam *v.* Gomila, 37 La. Ann. 479; Aiken *v.* Leathers, 40 La. Ann. 23.

Michigan: Swift *v.* Plessner, 39 Mich. 178.

Montana: Miles *v.* Edwards, 6 Mont. 180.

Nebraska: Raymond *v.* Green, 12 Neb. 215, 41 Am. Rep. 763.

Nevada: Brown *v.* Jones, 5 Nev. 374.

New York: Corcoran *v.* Judson, 24 N. Y. 106; Andrews *v.* Glenville Woolen Co., 50 N. Y. 282; Rose *v.* Post, 56 N. Y. 603; Lyon *v.* Hersey, 32 Hun, 253; Crounse *v.* Syracuse, C. & N. Y. R. R., 32 Hun, 497.

Ohio: Alexander *v.* Jacoby, 23 Oh. St. 358.

Vermont: Lillie *v.* Lillie, 55 Vt. 470.

But *contra*, *Arkansas:* Oliphint *v.* Mansfield, 36 Ark. 191; Patton *v.* Garrett, 37 Ark. 605, 42 Am. Rep. 5.

Iowa: Wallace *v.* York, 45 Ia. 81; Lowenstein *v.* Monroe, 55 Ia. 82, 7 N. W. 406.

[55] *New York:* Disbrow *v.* Garcia, 52 N. Y. 654. But not where no damages were shown. Randall *v.* Carpenter, 88 N. Y. 293.

[56] *United States:* Jacobus *v.* Monongahela Nat. Bank, 35 Fed. 395.

Alabama: Copeland *v.* Cunningham, 63 Ala. 394.

California: Bustamente *v.* Stewart, 55 Cal. 115.

Iowa: Vorse *v.* Phillips, 37 Ia. 428.

Louisiana: Cretin *v.* Levy, 37 La. Ann. 182; Adam *v.* Gomila, 37 La. Ann. 479.

Mississippi: Brinker *v.* Leinkauff, 64 Miss. 236 (but *contra* of an injunction bond in Mississippi: Baggett *v.* Beard, 43 Miss. 120).

Montana: Parker *v.* Bond, 5 Mont. 1.

New York: Randall *v.* Carpenter, 88 N. Y. 293; Northampton Nat. Bank *v.* Wylie, 52 Hun, 146.

Ohio: Alexander *v.* Jacoby, 23 Oh. St. 358.

Vermont: Lillie *v.* Lillie, 55 Vt. 470.

[57] Frost *v.* Jordan, 37 Minn. 544.

Thus in an action on an injunction bond the plaintiff has been allowed to recover counsel fees in obtaining a dissolution of the injunction, the court, however, saying it would be otherwise if the counsel fees were paid in defending the action, and the dissolution of the injunction was only incidental to a successful defence.[58] So, on such a bond, counsel fees were not allowed, it appearing that the services had been rendered in defending the action, and not merely in obtaining a dissolution of the injunction, although that was the result of the decree.[59] It has been held, where the action and injunction or attachment were both defeated, that no distinction could be made between them, and a reasonable attorney's fee for defending both was allowed.[60] But in other States it has been held that where there is nothing to show that the expense of the defence was increased by the fact that an injunction was granted, the cost of defending the action could not be recovered.[61]

This distinction is often taken: if the injunction is ancillary to the principal relief, counsel fees may be recovered; but if it is the principal relief sought, no counsel fees can generally be recovered on the bond, for they were only such fees as would have been incurred in the case if no temporary injunction had been granted.[62] But if extra expense in the way of

[58] *Ohio:* Noble v. Arnold, 23 Oh. St. 264.

South Carolina: Livingston v. Exum, 19 S. C. 223.

[59] *United States:* Oelrichs v. Spain, 15 Wall. 211.

Illinois: Blair v. Reading, 99 Ill. 600.

Louisiana: Cretin v. Levy, 37 La. Ann. 182.

[60] *Alabama:* Dothard v. Sheid, 69 Ala. 135.

Indiana: Wilson v. Root, 43 Ind. 486; Trentman v. Wiley, 85 Ind. 33.

Missouri: Hammerslough v. Kansas City B. L. & S. Assoc., 79 Mo. 80.

New Hampshire: Solomon v. Chesley, 59 N. H. 24.

But not a fee paid for defending the garnishee, when the attachment was a foreign one. Flournoy v. Lyon, 70 Ala. 308.

[61] *Arkansas:* Patton v. Garrett, 37 Ark. 605.

California: Bustamente v. Stewart, 55 Cal. 115; Mitchell v. Hawley, 79 Cal. 301.

New York: Hovey v. Rubber T. P. Co., 50 N. Y. 335; Disbrow v. Garcia, 52 N. Y. 654; Allen v. Brown, 5 Lans. 511; McDonald v. James, 38 N. Y. Super. Ct. 76.

Ohio: Noble v. Arnold, 23 Oh. St. 264.

[62] *Kentucky:* New National Turnpike Co. v. Dulaney, 86 Ky. 516.

Maine: Thurston v. Haskell, 81 Me. 303.

Oregon: Olds v. Carey, 13 Ore. 362.

counsel was required by a temporary injunction, that may be recovered.[63]

The expense of preparing a motion to dissolve an injunction, although the motion was not actually made, has been allowed where the preparation was made in good faith.[64] A reasonable solicitor's fee, in opposing the granting of the injunction, is allowed in Illinois.[65] In a case where the injunction must be dissolved at once or great damage would ensue, and in order to obtain a dissolution it was necessary to procure a special train for the place where the court was in session, it was held that the expense of the train as well as the counsel fee might be recovered in an action on the injunction bond.[66]

If the injunction is dissolved only in part, while the motion was to dissolve it entirely, *all* the counsel fees paid out cannot be recovered.[67]

These expenses can be recovered only where a bond has been given. The expenses of obtaining a dissolution of an injunction cannot be recovered in the injunction suit.[68]

§ 238. Covenants and contracts of warranty or indemnity.

In an action for breach of the covenants of seizin or of warranty, the costs and, if reasonably defended, the counsel fees in the eviction suit are recoverable.[69]

[63] Olds v. Carey, 13 Ore. 362.

[64] Wallace v. York, 45 Ia. 81.

[65] *Illinois:* Cummings v. Burleson, 78 Ill. 281.

But *contra, New York:* Randall v. Carpenter, 88 N. Y. 293; Newton v. Russell, 24 Hun, 40.

[66] Crouse v. Syracuse, C. & N. Y. R. R., 32 Hun, 497.

[67] Ford v. Loomis, 62 Ia. 586.

[68] Galveston, H. & S. A. Ry. v. Ware, 74 Tex. 47; Davis v. Rosedale S. Ry., 75 Tex. 381.

[69] *California:* Levitzky v. Canning, 33 Cal. 299.

Illinois: Harding v. Larkin, 41 Ill. 413.

Kentucky: Robertson v. Lemon, 2 Bush, 301.

Maine: Ryerson v. Chapman, 66 Me. 557.

Michigan: Seitz v. People's Sav. Bank, 140 Mich. 106, 103 N. W. 545.

Minnesota: Allis v. Nininger, 25 Minn. 525.

Missouri: Mackenzie v. Clement, 144 Mo. App. 114, 129 S. W. 730.

Nevada: Dalton v. Bowker, 8 Nev. 190.

New Hampshire: Kennison v. Taylor, 18 N. H. 220.

Vermont: Keeler v. Wood, 30 Vt. 242; Smith v. Sprague, 40 Vt. 43.

England: Williams v. Burrell, 1 C. B. 402; Rolph v. Crouch, L. R. 3 Ex. 44.

Contra, South Carolina: Jeter v. Glenn, 9 Rich. 374.

Texas: Clark v. Mumford, 62 Tex. 531.

In Massachusetts the costs but not the counsel fees may be recovered.

The plaintiff in this action must, however, have been the one on whom the defence necessarily fell. If the litigation was in any degree voluntary on his part he cannot recover counsel fees. Thus, where a suit in equity to try the title was brought against a remote grantor, and the plaintiff, not being a party, undertook the defence at the request of his grantee, he cannot, in an action on the covenant of warranty, recover from his own grantor the counsel fees in that suit.[70] And where a grantor was sued for trespass on a piece of land which both he and his grantor erroneously supposed was included in the conveyance, and after being defeated he brought suit to have the conveyance reformed so as to include this parcel, and for damages on the covenant of warranty, it was held that he could not recover the counsel fees in the action of trespass, as he was not defending for his grantor's benefit but against his own wrong and could not as matters then stood have vouched in his grantor to defend.[71]

In an action for the breach of covenant of quiet enjoyment, the plaintiff may recover the expenses of a suit for ejectment which he defended against the owner of the paramount title,[72] or even of an unfounded suit brought by the lessor himself to recover possession.[73]

Where the defendant sold the plaintiff goods to be resold by him, and warranted them of a certain quality, it was held that the plaintiff might recover the costs of an action brought against him by a purchaser on account of the inferior quality of the goods, which could be discovered only by use;[74] and so in an action upon an implied warranty of title of goods the buyer may recover reasonable counsel fees expended in defending his title.[75]

The same rule that applies in actions upon covenants and

Leffingwell v. Elliott, 10 Pick. 204; Reggio v. Braggiotti, 7 Cush. 166.

[70] Harding v. Larkin, 41 Ill. 413.

[71] Butler v. Barnes, 61 Conn. 399, 24 Atl. 328.

[72] McAlpin v. Woodruff, 11 Oh. St. 120.

[73] California: Levitzky v. Canning, 33 Cal. 299.

Pennsylvania: Mellor v. Philadelphia, 160 Pa. 614, 28 Atl. 991.

[74] Hammond v. Bussey, 20 Q. B. Div. 79; Lewis v. Peake, 7 Taunt. 153; Pennell v. Woodburn, 7 C. & P. 117.

[75] St. Anthony & D. E. Co. v. Dawson, (N. D.), 126 N. W. 1013.

contracts of warranty applies in actions upon covenants of indemnity. Thus on a bond of indemnity against the consequences of an act done by the plaintiff at the direction of the defendant, the plaintiff may recover counsel fees and other expenses of defending an action brought against him for the act.[76] In an action on an indemnity bond against liens, to defend suits and pay the judgments, the owner recovers expenses, attorney's fees, and costs, on account of the sale and in the proceedings to redeem.[77] In an action on an indemnity bond given to the sheriff on his delivery of certain chattels which various persons claimed, he can recover counsel fees paid in defending the actions by other claimants.[78]

Upon the same general principle, where the agent of an undisclosed principal is sued and defends the action, he may recover his litigation expenses from his principal.[79]

§ 239. Notice of prior suit.

The warrantor is entitled to notice of the prior suit brought against his grantees, and to an opportunity to defend it; he should not be subjected against his will to the expense of two suits. Consequently counsel fees and expenses of the prior litigation cannot be recovered as a matter of course, without independent proof of all the facts, unless the defendant was notified of the existence of that suit and given an opportunity to come in and defend it.[80] And if the warrantor after such notice came in to defend, the plaintiff cannot recover expenses of the former suit incurred thereafter.[81] If proper notice is duly given to the defendant the former judgment is conclusive of the facts;[82] and while it is not conclusive that the amount is reasonable, the burden is thrown upon the defendant to prove the amount unreasonable.[83] On the other hand, failure to give notice does not preclude the plaintiff from his

[76] Hadsell v. Hancock, 3 Gray (Mass.), 526. But if the plaintiff had a right to demand a bond of indemnity and failed to do so, he cannot recover the costs and expenses. Russell v. Walker, 150 Mass. 531, 23 N. E. 383.

[77] Kansas City H. Co. v. Sauer, 65 Mo. 279; but contra, McDaniel v. Crabtree, 21 Ark. 431.

[78] Graves v. Moore, 58 Cal. 435.

[79] Legaré v. Frazer, 3 Strob. (S. C.) 377.

[80] Iowa: Yokum v. Thomas, 15 Ia. 67. Rhode Island: Point St. I. W. v. Turner, 14 R. I. 122.

[81] Kennison v. Taylor, 18 N. H. 220.

[82] Thurston v. Spratt, 52 Me. 202.

[83] Ryerson v. Chapman, 66 Me. 557.

present suit; but it leaves upon him the burden of proving all the facts of the case, including the necessity and the reasonableness of the cost of litigation.[84]

§ 239a. Implied warranty of authority.

If the defendant has misrepresented his authority, the person with whom he deals can recover against him the costs of an action against the supposed principal, or the alleged principal who has been subjected to suit may recover the expense of it.[85] So where a defendant, pretending to be the agent of the plaintiff, sold land of the plaintiff, and the plaintiff consequently had to defend a suit for specific performance, it was held, in Illinois, that he could recover damages for the expense and trouble in the defence of that suit.[86] And where the plaintiff had delivered to the defendant a quantity of stone on the false and fraudulent representation of the latter that it was ordered by A., and had failed in an action against A. for the price, it was held that the plaintiff was entitled to recover from the defendant, not only the value of the stone, but also the costs incurred in the former action.[87]

§ 240. Plaintiff subjected to suit through defendant's breach of contract.

Where the plaintiff is forced, by reason of the defendant's breach of contract, to maintain or defend a suit, he may recover, in an action on the contract, the reasonable expenses of the former suit,[88] and this is so held even in Massachusetts, though generally, in that State, the counsel fees in a former suit are not recoverable. In New Haven & Northern Co. v.

[84] *Illinois:* Lunt v. Wrenn, 113 Ill. 168.

Maine: Ryerson v. Chapman, 66 Me. 557.

[85] Godwin v. Francis, L. R. 5 C. P. 295; Collen v. Wright, 7 E. & B. 301, *per* Wightman, J.; Hughes v. Graeme, 33 L. J. Q. B. 335.

[86] Philpot v. Taylor, 75 Ill. 309.

[87] Randell v. Trimen, 18 C. B. 786.

[88] *New York:* Dubois v. Hermance, 56 N. Y. 673.

South Dakota: Rectenbaugh v. North-western Port Huron Co., 22 S. D. 410, 118 N. W. 697.

Such cases must be carefully distinguished from those in which the primary obligation rests on the plaintiff. When a consignee agreed to pay to the plaintiff a sum equal to the amount of wharfage, but did not make himself primarily liable for the wharfage, he was not liable for expenses incurred through its non-payment. Compton v. Heissenbuttal, 16 N. Y. Supp. 524 (reversing s. c. 13 id. 594).

Hayden,[89] the action was for breach of contract to secure the plaintiffs a right of way. The plaintiffs subsequently acquired the right of way by the customary statutory proceedings. The plaintiffs were allowed to recover the costs and expenses of settling the damages for taking the land, which included not only the ordinary legal costs and witness fees, but also attorney and counsel fees, in procuring the settlement. The cases of Leffingwell v. Elliott and Reggio v. Braggiotti [90] were distinguished on the ground that in those cases the employment of counsel was not "a direct and necessary consequence of the breach of contract by the defendants," while here the proceedings were necessary in order to ascertain the damages. In an action for breach of contract to withdraw another suit, the expenses of the defendant in that suit may be recovered.[91] Pond v. Harris [92] was for breach of contract to submit the plaintiff's claims to arbitrators. Although the plaintiff in fact had no valid claims, he was allowed to recover substantial damages, which included "the expenses to which he has been subjected by reason of his necessary preparation for a trial before the arbitrators, on account of his own loss of time and trouble, and of employing counsel, taking depositions," etc., so far only, however, as these things *were not available* for the trial of his cause before the ordinary tribunals. The counsel fees were recoverable, it was said, for they were suitable and therefore properly incurred, and the plaintiff was deprived of the benefit of them by the wrongful act of the defendant.[93] In an action on a contract to deliver up possession, the expenses of dispossessing an under-tenant of the defendant are recoverable.[94] In Proprietors of Locks and Canals v. Lowell Horse Railroad [95] the defendant neglected to repair a bridge which he was bound to repair. The plaintiffs, however, were also bound, as against the city, to repair the bridge. The plaintiffs were allowed to recover against the defendant the amount of damages recovered by the city against them, but

---

[89] 117 Mass. 433.

[90] *Supra*, § 238.

[91] Hagan v. Riley, 13 Gray, 515 (*semble*).

[92] 113 Mass. 114.

[93] *Acc.*, Call v. Hagar, 69 Me. 521.

[94] Henderson v. Squire, L. R. 4 Q. B. 170. But *contra*, Morrison v. Darling, 47 Vt. 67.

[95] 109 Mass. 221.

not the expenses, in the absence of evidence that it was defended at the request of the defendants, or for their benefit, after notice and refusal on their part to come in and defend. In Iowa the costs of such a suit are recoverable where the party liable over aided in the defence of the suit, but not the expenses of an appeal taken without his request.[96]

The general principle applies to a breach of the agent's duty to his principal, whereby the principal is subjected to a suit. Thus where defendant, who was plaintiff's agent to procure a lease, took the lease in his own name instead of plaintiff's, and upon being called upon to assign it failed to procure the assent of the landlord to the assignment, as a result of which plaintiff was involved in litigation, it was held that he might recover the expense of such litigation from his agent.[97]

The suit in which the expense was incurred must have been the proximate result of the defendant's act. Where the mayor and council of Macon, Ga., under discretionary power given in their charter, removed the marshal from office, which removal was subsequently found to be improper, they were bound to pay his salary for the whole year; but not the money expended by him in defending the charges preferred. His damages were defined to be such as necessarily resulted from his amotion from office.[98] So where the plaintiff had agreed with the owner of a threshing-machine to repair it before harvest time, and employed and paid the defendant to make a firebox needed for the repairs, which the defendant agreed to have done in about a fortnight, but failed to do, and the plaintiff had to procure one elsewhere (which he might have done in time to fulfil his contract with the owner, but did not), and having been sued by the owner, paid £20 to settle the suit, it was held that he could recover the amount he had paid the defendant for the fire-box and his additional expense in procuring another, but not the amount paid in settlement of the suit.[99]

In Baxendale v. London, Chatham & Dover Railway [100]

[96] Ottumwa v. Parks, 43 Ia. 119.

[97] McGaw v. Acker M. & C. Co., 111 Md. 153, 73 Atl. 731.

[98] Shaw v. Macon, 19 Ga. 468.

[99] Portman v. Middleton, 4 C. B. (N. S.) 322; Acc., Henderson v. Sevey, 2 Me. 139.

[100] L. R. 10 Ex. 35.

the plaintiff agreed to deliver certain pictures to one H. at Paris; the plaintiff contracted with the defendant as to part of the journey. They were lost through the defendant's negligence. It was held, reversing the judgment of the Common Pleas, that the plaintiff could not recover either the costs incurred by him, or the costs taxed against him in defending an action brought by H. against him, Lord Coleridge, C. J., saying: "It seems to me that the whole of the costs were incurred for the plaintiff's own benefit, and were not in any sense the natural and proximate result of the defendant's breach of duty"; Keating, J., also putting the decision on the ground that they were "not the proximate consequence of the defendant's breach of duty." All the judges expressed their disapproval of Mors-le-Blanch v. Wilson,[101] except Lush, J., who distinguished it on the ground that, in that case, the defence was reasonable, while in the case at bar it was not. This decision was followed with reluctance in Fisher v. Val de Travers Asphalte Co.[102] The plaintiff, Fisher, had contracted with a certain T. to construct a tramway for him on a public road. The plaintiff then made a sub-contract with the defendant, who agreed to construct it and keep it in repair. A party who had been injured brought an action against T., which the plaintiff compromised for £70, paying, in addition, to the attorney of that party, £40 and £18 costs of action. The jury found that it was reasonable to compromise. The plaintiff in this action, brought for the defendant's failure to construct properly and keep in repair, was allowed to recover the £70, for the payment was a natural consequence of the failure to perform, but not the other items; Brett, J., however, saying: "But for the case referred to (Baxendale v. London, Chatham & Dover Railway), I must confess I should have been unable to see any distinction between the damages and the reasonable costs of ascertaining their proper amount."

In Marvin v. Prentice [103] the plaintiff had brought a bill in equity to have a conveyance declared a mortgage, and redemption decreed; and a decree had been given accordingly.

---

[101] L. R. 8 C. P. 227, where upon similar facts counsel fees had been allowed.

[102] 1 C. P. D. 511.

[103] 94 N. Y. 295.

He then brought .the present suit on the agreement to recon-
vey, and claimed as part of his damages his expenses in the
equity suit. But the court said that he might have brought
a single action which would have settled the entire dispute,
and therefore refused a recovery of the expenses of the prior
litigation.

§ 241. Plaintiff subjected to suit through defendant's tort.

And in the same way where the plaintiff is liable to the
injured party for a tort actually committed by the defendant, he may recover from the defendant the expense of a
suit brought against him by the injured party. Westfield *v.*
Mayo [104] was an action brought against the plaintiff at bar
(a town) for an injury, by an obstruction in a highway created
by the negligence of the defendant. It was held that if the
town had properly notified the defendant of the action, and
had requested him to defend it, it could recover reasonable
expenses incurred in defending, including counsel fees. Lord,
J., said: "As a general rule, when a party is called upon to
defend a suit founded upon a wrong, for which he is held responsible in law without misfeasance on his part, but because
of the wrongful act of another against whom he has a remedy
over, counsel fees are the natural and reasonably necessary
consequence of the wrongful act of the other, if he has notified
the other to appear and defend the suit." The learned judge
then proceeded to distinguish Reggio *v.* Braggiotti,[105] Baxendale *v.* London, Chatham and Dover Railway,[106] and Fisher
v. Val de Travers Asphalte Co.,[107] as follows: "When, however, the claim against him is upon his own contract, or for
his own misfeasance, though he may have a remedy against
another, and the damages recoverable may be the same as
the amount of the judgment recovered against himself, counsel
fees paid in defence of the suit against himself are not recoverable." As to the cases above cited he said: "In each of
these cases it will be observed that the counsel fees were paid
in defending a suit upon the party's own contract. In the
present case the plaintiff was not compelled to incur the coun-

[104] 122 Mass. 100, 23 Am. Rep. 292.   [106] L. R. 10 Ex. 35.
[105] 7 Cush. 166.   [107] 1 C. P. D. 511.

sel fees by reason of any misfeasance or of any contract of its own, but was made immediately liable by reason of the wrongdoing of the defendant." He stated the principle to be: "If a party is obliged to defend against the act of another, against whom he has a remedy over, and defends solely and exclusively the act of such other party, and is compelled to defend no misfeasance of his own, he may notify such party of the pendency of the suit, and may call upon him to defend it; if he fails to defend, then, if liable over, he is liable not only for the amount of damages recovered, but for all reasonable and necessary expenses incurred in such defence." [108] It is to be noticed that, in Reggio v. Braggiotti, the amount of the taxable costs were allowed, though not counsel fees. In cases where it is criticised it seems to be looked upon as a decision to the effect that counsel fees can never be allowed; but it merely represents the peculiar Massachusetts doctrine as to counsel fees. In another Massachusetts case, where a sheriff had been sued for the escape of a prisoner, he was allowed to recover his costs from the debtor, though not his counsel fees.[109] So for refusal to place a judgment on the tax list, a plaintiff can recover expenses incurred in the employment of counsel.[110]

The rule is the same with respect to other classes of torts. In actions for fraud or false representations, the plaintiff may recover expenses of former litigation to which he was naturally subjected.[111] So where the defendant wrongfully sold a promissory note made by the plaintiff and given to the defendant to use in a certain way, the plaintiff's expense of defending an action on the note in the bona fide belief that the holder had notice of the fraud, and the expense of effecting a settlement,

[108] Acc., Iowa: Ottumwa v. Parks, 43 Ia. 119.

Maryland: Chesapeake v. O. C. Co. v. Allegany County, 57 Md. 201, 40 Am. Rep. 430.

New York: Rochester v. Montgomery, 72 N. Y. 65.

In all such cases the principle seems to be one of indemnity, closely analogous to, if not identical with, that which governs in the case of contracts to indemnify or save harmless. Oceanic Steam Nav. Co. v. Compania T. E., 134 N. Y. 461, 31 N. E. 987. See § 791.

[109] Griffin v. Brown, 2 Pick. 304.

[110] Newark S. I. v. Parhorst, 7 Biss. 99.

[111] Curtley v. Security Sav. Soc., 46 Wash. 50, 89 Pac. 180.

may be recovered from the defendant.[112] And where defendant fraudulently procured a draft from plaintiff, and plaintiff was obliged to employ counsel to prevent its being cashed, he may recover the counsel fees in an action for the fraud.[113]

So in an action for malicious prosecution or other malicious suit the plaintiff may recover the costs and counsel fees in defending the suit against him; [114] and in an action for false imprisonment the expenses incurred in procuring a discharge from imprisonment are recoverable; [115] and in an action for slander of title, the expenses of a bill to remove the cloud on the title are recoverable.[116]

So where the tort is one of negligence. Thus where a bank lost certain unrecorded transfers of land certificates belonging to the plaintiff, and in order to get duplicates it was necessary for the plaintiff to institute legal proceedings and obtain judgment, the expenses of such proceedings are recoverable in an action against the bank.[117] So where it was defendant's duty to maintain the fence between his land and plaintiff's, and he negligently allowed it to fall out of repair, and a third person's horse, placed by plaintiff's consent in his pasture, was injured by reason of the defect, whereupon the owner sued plaintiff and recovered, plaintiff was allowed to recover from defendant the reasonable expenses of the former action.[118]

---

[112] *Kansas:* Osborne *v.* Ehrhard, 37 Kan. 413.

New York: Hynes *v.* Patterson, 95 N. Y. 1.

[113] Hutchinson First Nat. Bank *v.* Williams, 62 Kan. 431, 63 Pac. 744.

[114] *Illinois:* Lawrence *v.* Hagerman, 56 Ill. 68, 8 Am. Rep. 674; Krug *v.* Ward, 77 Ill. 603.

Indiana: Ziegler *v.* Powell, 54 Ind. 173; McCardle *v.* McGinley, 86 Ind. 538; Lytton *v.* Baird, 95 Ind. 349.

Missouri: Gregory *v.* Chambers, 78 Mo. 294.

Wisconsin: Magmer *v.* Renk, 65 Wis. 364.

But in Georgia, in an action for *malicious distress proceedings,* the tenant cannot recover expenses incurred in procuring his stock to be declared exempt under Georgia laws. Sturgis *v.* Frost, 56 Ga. 188.

[115] *New York:* Blythe *v.* Tompkins, 2 Abb. Pr. 468.

Virginia: Parsons *v.* Harper, 16 Gratt. 64.

Wisconsin: Bonesteel *v.* Bonesteel, 30 Wis. 511.

England: Pritchett *v.* Boevey, 1 Cr. & M. 775; Foxall *v.* Barnett, 2 E. & B. 928; Bradlaugh *v.* Edwards, 11 C. B. (N. S.) 377.

[116] Chesebro *v.* Powers, 78 Mich. 472, 44 N. W. 290.

[117] Birmingham Nat. Bank *v.* Newport Nat. Bank, 116 Ala. 520, 22 So. 976.

[118] Hubbard *v.* Gould, 74 N. H. 25, 64 Atl. 668.

§ 241a. Former litigation must have been reasonable.

As in all cases, the plaintiff's conduct must appear to have been reasonable throughout. A vessel bound to Valparaiso, with liberty to touch at the Falkland Islands, had on board goods consigned to those islands and several hundred barrels of gunpowder for Valparaiso. At the islands, it having been necessary for her to unload the gunpowder before entering the harbor, the defendants furnished a vessel on which the powder was stowed, but afterward removed the powder to another vessel unfit for the purpose, which went down with it. The captain, after his arrival at Valparaiso, having been sued by the consignees, defended the action unsuccessfully. It was held that the defendants, although liable for the value of the gunpowder, were not liable for the costs of defending the action at Valparaiso, it not appearing that the conduct of the captain was prudent in so doing.[119] So where a carrier sued a sheriff for the wrongful attachment of goods which he had been carrying, and claimed to recover the expenses of litigating an action brought against him by the consignee, it was held that he should not have resisted the claim of the consignee, and recovery was not allowed.[120] And where the purchaser of a machine gave his note in payment, and afterwards brought suit for a false representation in the sale of it, he could not recover his expenses in litigating an action brought on the note by a holder known to have acquired the note *bona fide*.[121] And so where the defendant falsely represented that he was informed by the keeper of a public-house that it produced certain average daily returns, and the plaintiff, after having bought the good will of the house on the faith of such representation, discovered that its value was much less than was thus pretended, and without further inquiry sued the vendor for false representations, and failed in the action because, as it proved, no such representation had been made by him, it was held, in an action by the purchaser against the defendant for his false representa-

---

[119] Ronneberg *v.* Falkland I. Co., 17 C. B. (N. S.) 1. Erle, C. J., also expressed the opinion that these damages were too remote.

[120] Holmes *v.* Balcom, 84 Me. 226, 24 Atl. 821.

[121] Walter A. Wood M. & R. M. Co. *v.* Hancock, 4 Tex. Civ. App. 302, 23 S. W. 384.

tion as to what the vendor had said, that the plaintiff could not recover the costs of the action against the innkeeper, as they were not the natural or proximate consequence of the representation.[122]

Where it is reasonably necessary defendant must have been given notice of the prior litigation.[123] Notice should be given to hold the defendant bound by the result of such litigation.[124] In a New Hampshire case the defendant, a city clerk, failed to note in his index the record of a chattel mortgage, and the plaintiff having examined the index and supposing the property to be unimcumbered, loaned money upon it, but afterwards learned of the prior mortgage, and still later the prior mortgagee brought suit to recover the chattels. The plaintiff now sought to recover his expenses in defending that suit but it was held that the defendant, not having been notified of the suit, could not now be charged.[125]

§ 241b. Expenses incurred in other forms of litigation.

In certain cases the former litigation, while in one sense connected with the present suit or even the cause of it, was not of a sort to permit of the expense of it being recovered. This is the case in probate or matrimonial proceedings, where the litigation is not technically contentious. Thus in an action by an executor against the agent of the testator for an accounting, the executor cannot charge the agent with his counsel fees incurred in resisting a petition by the agent to be appointed administrator.[126] And in an action for the unlawful detention of a child the person to whose custody the child was previously awarded on *habeas corpus* proceedings cannot recover his expenses of litigation in those proceedings.[127]

[122] Richardson *v.* Dunn, 8 C. B. (N. S.) 655; Merritt *v.* Nevin, 20 Up. Can. Q. B. 540.
[123] *Ante*, § 239.
[124] Lowell *v.* Boston & L. R. R., 23 Pick. (Mass.) 24.

[125] Chase *v.* Bennett, 59 N. H. 394.
[126] Dorris *v.* Miller, 105 Iowa, 564, 75 N. W. 482.
[127] Lovell *v.* House of the Good Shepherd, 14 Wash. 211, 44 Pac. 253.

CHAPTER XIII

THE MEASURE AND ELEMENTS OF VALUE

§ 242. Value in general.

In almost all cases in which damages are recoverable, the measure of compensation involves an inquiry into the question of value. The plaintiff is to be compensated for some article of property lost, appropriated, destroyed, or injured, for the breach of some contract to be measured in terms of the value of property, or for some tort affecting the value of property. When his damages involve the consideration of time, labor, or services, it is the pecuniary value of these which must be analyzed; and even when the recovery is based on personal injury, a part of the damages at least must be made up of pecuniary elements, such as the value of his time and labor lost, the value of the time and labor expended in surgical aid, the value of the medicine administered, etc. It is in fact only when we attempt to estimate the damages for pain

489

and suffering or to assess what are called exemplary damages that we pass beyond the region of value in its true pecuniary sense. It will accordingly be found that one of the questions with which the courts are most constantly occupied in cases involving the measure of damages is how to arrive at and measure the value involved.

Value in law is generally founded upon the idea of exchange.[1] In the case of the market value of anything, it is the sum of money which the buyers and sellers in the market are willing to give and take for it. It does not inhere in the thing itself, but is a "subjective" conception, a matter of belief concluded by the identity of the conception as *fact* in the minds of all concerned. But when a court determines the value of a thing without reference to the market, as it is frequently obliged to—there being no ascertainable market value, there is nothing logically conclusive about it, because there is no test of exchange or identity of belief, and it has to be accepted as the best approximation that can be made. It is subjective, but not conclusive. One judge may find one value to be correct; another, another. When we go one step further, and undertake to value property arbitrarily, for this or that purpose, we get into a still vaguer region. For purposes of taxation, property may be "valued" at such a sum as is necessary in connection with the annual rate and the valuation of other property, to produce the owner's quota of the whole levy. In street openings or other improvements the value of betterments may be fixed so as to offset the cost of the improvement, including the damages allowed for land taken or injured. Again, the value of property may mean what it will cost to reproduce it, which is usually something entirely different from what it actually cost to produce. For purpose of purchase and sale in the market, a railroad or a bank is worth, like any other business, what it will bring; but the "physical valuation" of a railroad or bank may produce surprisingly different results. In all these cases, the conception of value is wholly subjective, but there being no market, it is arbitrary, and is arbitrarily *imposed* by political power upon those to whose property it is applied. Courts never resort to it except

[1] Nat. Bank of Commerce *v.* New Bedford, 155 Mass. 313, 29 N. E. 532.

when compelled to, and because there is no market or exchange-able value to resort to. In the case just cited, which involved the taxation of bank shares at their "fair cash value," the assessors undertook to get at this value by a computation based upon capital stock, the surplus fund, and undivided profits; but the Supreme Court of Massachusetts held that the cash value of a thing is the amount of cash for which it will exchange in fact, that this meant the market value of the shares.

§ 243. Fundamental rule of value.

Wherever the measure of damages involves the question of value, however much the market may be resorted to to deter-mine what the value is, this resort is had as furnishing usually the best *evidence* of value. What plaintiff is entitled to recover is the real value of the article of property, the time, the labor, or the services, as they would be if unaffected by the defend-ant's tort or if the defendant's contract had been performed. If these things are bought and sold in the market, the mar-ket price shows conclusively what it would cost the plaintiff to be put in as good a position as if the tort had not been com-mitted or as if the contract had been performed. To take the most familiar of all illustrations, in the case of failure to de-liver an ordinary article of commerce sold, the vendee can replace himself by buying the article in the market. Hence his measure of damages is invariably said to be the market value. But as the cases now to be examined will show, the rule, more exactly stated, would be that his measure of dam-ages is the *value* of the article. When there is no market value, the value must be got at by the best proof to be had.

By value, however, we do not mean any ideal value, based on the intrinsic though unknown excellence of the thing for purposes of use. The value of a thing at any particular time, so far as it is important in determining the amount of com-pensation, is based upon such of its qualities as are generally known or knowable, and therefore enter into the estimation in which it is held by people generally: "the opinion of the public of possible buyers." [2]

[2] Holmes, J. in National Bank of   Commerce *v.* New Bedford, 155 Mass.
313, 29 N. E. 532.

For this reason it would seem that the value of a thing at a particular time could not be affected by a later event; though of course evidence of a later event, as for instance a subsequent sale of the property itself or of similar property, might be introduced as evidence of its value at the earlier time. This principle seems to have been lost sight of in an Arkansas case.[3] The question at issue was the value of growing crops at a certain time when they were destroyed by defendant. It appeared that the crops would have been destroyed by a later flood if they had not been destroyed by defendant; and it was held that this fact should be taken into account in arriving at the value of the crops at the time of destruction. It is submitted that this decision is erroneous. It is true that a *liability* to destruction by flood would affect the value of crops, if that liability were understood and thus entered into the calculations of those interested in the crops; but the subsequent fact of an actual destruction could not do so.

In an Alabama case[4] plaintiff claimed damages by reason of changes in a street. The proposed changes at first greatly enhanced the value of land in the neighborhood; but upon discovery of the fact that the change really increased the inconvenience of use the value dropped. It was held that in estimating plaintiff's damage the temporary inflation could not be considered. The court said that "he had no right to the benefit of a common estimate of value which was based upon expectations demonstrated at the time of the trial, and by the very constructions of which he complained, to have been groundless." This decision also seems open to question.

§ 243a. Value not dependent on intended user or price.

The fact that the owner of a thing does not actually use nor enjoy it does not affect its value. Its value lies in the value of the assemblage of rights to use, enjoy, dispose of it, which constitutes it property. If a man whose principles do not allow him to engage in horse-racing owns a valuable race-horse, the value of the horse is not diminished by the fact

---

[3] St. Louis, I. M. & S. Ry. *v.* Yarborough, 56 Ark. 612, 619, 20 S. W. 515.

[4] Meighan *v.* Birmingham T. Co. (Ala.), 51 So. 775.

that the owner uses him for a saddle-horse; or, to employ the illustration used by the House of Lords, if a person takes away my chair, he cannot diminish the damages by showing that I did not usually sit in that chair, or that there were plenty of other chairs in the room.[5] And where goods were lost by a carrier the fact that plaintiff had sold the goods to arrive at a price below the market value would not alter their value for the purpose of recovery.[6]

In The H. H. Dimock[7] the question was as to the value of a steam yacht lost by collision. The vessel was built for her owner at a cost of from \$380,000 to \$400,000, was five years old, and had no market value. The owner was allowed \$190,000. The court classified the cases as follows: First, those in which the property is of such a nature that it cannot be replaced, like a family portrait.[8] Second, those as to which the basis of valuation is that of property as property, which again is subdivided into, *a*, cases when the rule is strictly the cost of replacing;[9] *b*, cases in which an established market value applies; *c*, cases of property not properly marketable, such as a yacht or other vessel adapted only to a special use. To determine the value of such property as this last, the court will call to its aid any circumstances which may assist it to form a correct estimate, such as the original cost, its condition at the time of the loss, the sum for which it might be replaced, what amount a person desiring such a thing might reasonably be expected to be willing to pay, rather than incur the cost of constructing a new one.

§ 243b. Value of use of vessel or vehicle.

So where a vessel is injured, and the use of it lost, the value of the use ought not to be the mere value of the use intended

---

[5] The Steamship Mediana *v.* The Lightship Comet [1900] A. C. 113. Followed, C. W. Hunt Co. *v.* Boston El. Ry., 199 Mass. 220, 85 N. E. 446.

[6] Rodocanachi *v.* Milburn, 18 Q. B. D. 67.

[7] 77 Fed. 226, 23 C. C. A. 123.

[8] See § 251.

[9] Topsham *v.* Lisbon, 65 Me. 449, an action for the destruction of an abutment of a bridge built by the town of Topsham, and which it was bound by law to renew. *Cf.* Stickney *v.* Allen, 10 Gray, 352, an action in which the jury were allowed to consider the cost of replacing stereotype plates having a special value, belonging to the owner, and The Granite State, 3 Wall. 310, 314, 18 L. ed. 179 (cost of repairs).

by the owner, but the value of the possible use. The wrong-doer has no right to consider what use was in fact to be made by the owner. In the important case of The Mediana [10] the House of Lords took this view. In that case it appeared that defendant negligently ran down a lightship. The government kept in commission, at a considerable expense annually, a spare lightship to meet such emergencies, and this was put into commission and used in place of the lightship which the defendant ran down. It was held, notwithstanding, that the defendant was responsible for the value of the use of the lightship. This decision was followed in the case of The Astrachan. [11] By a collision a Danish war vessel, which was just finishing a cruise, was injured and had to be repaired. It appeared that she would have had been laid up for repairs at any rate, that she was not to be used again for three months, and was repaired within that time. But it was held not necessary to show that the owner would have used it; since it was in his power to use it, he was entitled to the value of the use.

This principle seems to have been overlooked in two cases in a lower court in New York, [12] where upon an injury to an automobile the court refused the rental value of such a vehicle to be shown without evidence that it had been used for a business purpose, or that another machine was hired in its place. In a later case, however, [13] the court held that the value of the use lost may be recovered though the use may have been for pleasure only; [14] and appears to have distinguished the earlier cases on the ground that no value of use was there proved. The distinction is unsatisfactory; and there can be no doubt that the doctrine of the later case is correct.

§ 243c. Value of land subject to easement or other hindrance to use.

A thing may have a value, though there is some natural or

---

[10] The Steamship Mediana v. The Lightship Comet, [1900] A. C. 113, 9 Aspin. 41, 69 L. J. P. 35, 82 L. T. Rep. (N. S.) 95, 48 Wkly. Rep. 398.

[11] [1910] P. 172.

[12] Foley v. Forty-Second St. M. & S. N. A. Ry., 101 N. Y. Supp. 780, 52 Misc. 183; Bondy v. N. Y. City Ry., 56 Misc. 602, 107 N. Y. Supp. 31.

[13] Murphy v. New York City Ry., 108 N. Y. Supp. 1021, 58 Misc. 237.

[14] Citing Wellman v. Miner, 19 Misc. 644, 44 N. Y. Supp. 417.

legal obstruction to its use. So land covered by water, in which other persons have natural rights, may be of value.[15] And so where land laid out as a private way is taken for a public way the owner may establish a value in the land taken, though it was already subject to easements of way.[16]

§ 244. Market value.

As just stated, where one is entitled, in any form of action, to compensation based on the value of an article of property, the measure of recovery, where such property can be procured in the market, is the value of it in the market and not the cost; [17] for the owner of property is fully compensated for it by a sum of money which will enable him to replace it. The market value must be ascertained by a money standard based on evidence. It cannot be assessed on conjecture.[18] It is the actual cash market value, not what the property would sell for under special or extraordinary circumstances.[19] Proof of a single sale is not enough to establish a market value.[20] The "market value" of an article requires the investigation of the actual condition of the market, and does not warrant the consideration of the conjectural consequences of a state of things which did not exist, e. g., a probable fall in the price of the article in question, which would have resulted had the defendant delivered the quantity specified in the contract to

---

[15] *In re* Monroe, 131 App. Div. 872, 116 N. Y. Supp. 334.

[16] Beale *v.* Boston, 166 Mass. 53, 43 N. E. 1029.

Contra, however, in New York, where nominal damages only are allowed in such a case. Matter of Decatur St., 196 N. Y. 286, 89 N. E. 829; *In re* Opening of Beverley Rd., 131 App. Div. 147, 115 N. Y. Supp. 208; *In re* West One Hundred and Seventy-Seventh St., 135 App. Div. 520, 120 N. Y. Supp. 354; *In re* Johnson Ave., 120 N. Y. Supp. 798, 135 App. Div. 630; *In re* Schneider, 121 N. Y. Supp. 9, 136 App. Div. 444; *In re* Carroll St., 121 N. Y. Supp. 435, 137 App. Div. 39.

[1.] *Massachusetts:* Coolidge *v.* Choate,

11 Met. 79; Gardner *v.* Field, 1 Gray, 151.

Mississippi: New Orleans, J. & G. N. R. R. *v.* Moore, 40 Miss. 39.

New Jersey: Hopple *v.* Higbee, 3 Zab. (23 N. J. L.) 342.

New York: Campbell *v.* Woodworth, 26 Barb. 648; King *v.* Orser, 4 Duer, 431; Gunn *v.* Burghart, 47 N. Y. Super. Ct. 370.

[18] Fraloff *v.* New York C. & H. R. R. R., 10 Blatch. 16.

[19] *Illinois:* Brown *v.* Calumet R. Ry., 125 Ill. 600.

Canada: McCuaig *v.* Quaker City Ins. Co., 18 Up. Can. Q. B. 130; McMartin *v.* Hurlburt, 2 Ont. App. 146.

[20] Graham *v.* Maitland, 1 Sweeny (N. Y.), 149.

the plaintiff, and had the plaintiff offered it for sale in the market. The principle on which the rule rests is the indemnification of the injured party for the injury which he has sustained. A complete indemnity requires that the vendee should receive the sum which, with the price he had agreed to pay, would enable him to buy the article which the vendor had failed to deliver. The value in the market on the day forms the readiest and most direct method of ascertaining the measure of this indemnity in both cases; and accordingly, where a market value for the article exists, the law has adopted that standard.

§ 245. Market value, how determined.

The question, what determines market value, was much discussed in a case on the Pennsylvania circuit by Judge Hopkinson. He pointed out that to make a market there must be both buying and selling. Men sometimes put fantastical prices upon their property, and the asking price cannot be said to be the market value.[21] On the other hand, unaccepted offers cannot be taken as the market value. This value is "that reasonable sum which the property would bring on a fair sale by a man willing but not obliged to sell to a man willing but not obliged to buy."[22] So where a contract provided that the plaintiff might print advertising lithographs for the defendant if it met the market price, and the defendant submitted the work to a number of competitors

[21] Blydenburgh v. Welsh, 1 Baldwin, 331, 340. The court went on: "Further, the holders of an article, as flour, for instance, under a false rumor, which, if true, would augment its value, may suspend their sales, or put a price upon it, not according to its value in the actual state of the market or the actual circumstances which affect the market, but according to what, in their opinion, will be its market price or value provided the rumor shall prove to be true. In such a case it is clear that the asking price is not the worth of the thing on the given day, but what it is supposed it will be worth at a future day, if the contin-

gency shall happen which is to give it this additional value. To take such a price as a rule of damages is to make a defendant pay what never in truth was the value of the article, and to give the plaintiff a profit by a breach of the contract, which he never could have made by its performance."

[22] Allen v. Chicago & N. W. Ry. (Wis.), 129 N. W. 1094, per Winslow, C. J. "A price fixed by buyer and seller in an open market in the usual and ordinary course of lawful trade and competition." Lovejoy v. Michels, 88 Mich. 15, 23, 49 N. W. 901, 903, 13 L. R. A. 770.

for bids, it was held that the lowest *bona fide* bid represented the market price.[23]

§ 246. Value in the nearest market.

If there is no market for the article at the place where the plaintiff would be entitled to compensation, the value at the nearest market governs.[24] In addition to this, the cost of transportation of the property to the place of compensation is usually to be added,[25] and in some cases an allowance for profit.[26]

Grand Tower Co. *v.* Phillips [27] was an action for breach of contract to deliver coal at Grand Tower. The defendant company had the monopoly of the coal market at Grand Tower. It was held error to charge the jury that the measure of damages was the cash value of the kind of coal mentioned at Cairo or points below on the Mississippi River, after deducting the contract price of the coal and the cost and expenses of transporting it thither. Bradley, J., said, that although the defendant probably would have got those prices, yet the rule

[23] Cary Lithograph Co. *v.* Magazine Book Co., 127 N. Y. Supp. 300. The court said: "Where the subject of the price is an article commonly dealt in, this price will be fixed in a more or less definite sum by the consensus of all the buyers and sellers dealing in the article. The term 'market' assumes the existence of trade, and the price is fixed in trade by the highest bidder and the lowest offerer."

[24] *Illinois:* Pennsylvania R. R. *v.* John Anda Co., 131 Ill. App. 426.

Oregon: Bump *v.* Cooper, 20 Ore. 527, 26 Pac. 848.

Texas: New York & T. S. S. Co. *v.* Weiss (Tex. Civ. App.), 47 S. W. 674; Texas & P. Ry. *v.* Coggin, 99 S. W. 431, 44 Tex. Civ. App. 474; Kerr *v.* Blair, 47 Tex. Civ. App. 406, 105 S. W. 548. See, however, Missouri, K. & T. Ry. of Texas *v.* Wasson Bros., 126 S. W. 664 (Tex. Civ. App).

If there is a market value at the place, the value at another market cannot be shown. Gentry *v.* Kelley, 49 Kan. 82, 30 Pac. 186.

[25] *California:* Bullard *v.* Stone, 67 Cal. 477.

Colorado: Sellar *v.* Clelland, 2 Colo. 532.

Georgia: B. B. Ford & Co. *v.* Lawson, 133 Ga. 237, 65 S. E. 444.

Maine: Furlong *v.* Polleys, 30 Me. 491; Berry *v.* Dwinel, 44 Me. 255.

New York: Rice *v.* Manley, 66 N. Y. 82; Wemple *v.* Stewart, 22 Barb. 154. (In the latter case it appears that the value in near *and distant* markets was shown. The cost at the nearest available market, it seems, should be the only criterion.)

Virginia: Long P. L. Co. *v.* Saxon L. & L. Co., 108 Va. 497, 62 S. E. 349.

England: O'Hanlan *v.* Great W. Ry., 6 B. & S. 484, 34 L. J. (N. S.) Q. B. 154.

[26] O'Hanlan *v.* Great W. Ry., 6 B. & S. 484, 34 L. J. (N. S.) Q. B. **154.**

[27] 23 Wall. 471, 23 L. ed. 71.

was the difference between the contract price and the price at the nearest available market (to Grand Tower) where it could have been obtained, with the addition of the increased expense of transportation and hauling.

It may, however, be that the cost of transportation is to be subtracted from the value at the nearest market instead of added to it. That depends on whether the nearest market is resorted to by persons from the place where the plaintiff is entitled to the property for purchase or for sale; that is, whether the value in that market is less or greater than the value where the property should be. This is a question of fact which will never prove to be difficult of proof; the facts of the case will determine it. So where goods are purchased with a view to sending them for sale to a neighboring market, and there is no market price at the place of delivery, the market price at the place to which they were to be sent, less the cost of transportation, is the measure of their value at the place of delivery; [28] and knowledge on the part of the vendor of the destination is not necessary. [29] If, however, it is not proved that the market is in fact the *nearest*, such knowledge would seem to be necessary. [30] So in an action on the defendant's promise to pay for logs which he had converted on their way down the river to the plaintiff's mill, evidence is admissible of their market price at the mill, and of the cost of their transportation from the place of conversion thither. [31] In Harris v. Panama Railroad [32] the question was much considered. The plaintiff's race-horse was injured while being transported across the Isthmus of Panama. The evidence showed that the horse could have been sold at the isthmus for some price, but properly speaking there was no market price. The place of destination was San Francisco. Evidence of the value of the horse at San Francisco was submitted, "to enable the jury to

[28] *Alabama:* Johnson v. Allen, 78 Ala. 387.

Colorado: Union P. D. & G. Ry. v. Williams, 3 Colo. App. 526, 34 Pac. 731.

Oregon: Hodson v. Goodale, 22 Ore. 68, 29 Pac. 70.

[29] *Tennessee:* McDonald v. Unaka T. Co., 88 Tenn. 38, 12 S. W. 420.

Canada: Hendrie v. Neelon, 12 Ont. App. 41.

[30] Cockburn v. Ashland Lumber Co., 54 Wis. 619, 12 N. W. 49.

[31] Saunders v. Clark, 106 Mass. 331.

[32] 58 N. Y. 660.

estimate the value at the time and place of injury." The court said that the market value at the time and place is the proper evidence of value, but that it is reliable only where "it appears that similar articles have been bought and sold, in the way of trade, in sufficient quantity or often enough to show a market value." It was further said that in the absence of such proof, the market value in some other place is evidence, and the best evidence is the value at the place of destination, but that a great deduction should be made for the risk and expense of further transportation. It is said by the Supreme Court of Georgia to be the legal presumption, in the absence of positive evidence, that a commodity is worth as much at the place of destination as at that of shipment; and in an action against a carrier for the loss of cotton, where the plaintiff, instead of proving the former of these values, proved the latter only, it was held by that court that the defendant, not having contradicted this evidence, could not justly complain.[33]

Where the value of a stranded vessel was to be determined, the Supreme Court of Massachusetts held that her value at a neighboring port should be taken as a basis, and that reasonable allowance should be made for the probable cost of getting her off, repairing her, and getting her to market, and for the risks and chances of getting her afloat and to market; and also a reasonable allowance for her diminution in value on account of her having been ashore.[34]

§ 247. Cost of transportation—Allowance for profit.

It will be seen from the foregoing cases that there is no absolute rule fixing the value in the nearest market as the *measure of recovery* when there is no market value at the place of compensation. In some cases the cost of transportation (including, of course, all expenses such as freight and insurance) is added, while in others an allowance for a profit which it is presumed would have been made had the breach of contract or tort never occurred is given, the object of these

[33] Rome R. R. *v.* Sloan, 39 Ga. 636. *Acc., Alabama:* South & N. A. R. R. *v.* Wood, 72 Ala. 451; Echols *v.* Louisville & N. R. R., 90 Ala. 366, 7 So. 655.

New York: Richmond *v.* Bronson, 5 Denio, 55.

[34] Glaspy *v.* Cabot, 135 Mass. 435.

allowances being to reach an estimate of what the real market value at the place of compensation would have been, had there been one. In other cases again, where it appears that the nearest market value is swollen by some item of cost which could not in the nature of things enter into the market value at the place of compensation had there been one, this is subtracted. In other words, the object of the court being to get at what ought to be considered the real market value at the place of compensation, it takes in the absence of any such market the nearest market value as a part of the proof going to establish this.

When the goods are actually in transit when destroyed or injured, the value at the destination is the basis of recovery, rather than the value at the place of shipment,[35] or even at the place of injury. Thus, in an action against a carrier for injury to the goods the basis of valuation is the value at the destination, without inquiry as to the place of injury or a possible market value there;[36] and the same view has been taken where the goods were converted by a stranger while in transit.[37]

§ 248. Property in process of manufacture.

Very similar to the foregoing are a class of cases where the value of goods in process of manufacture is to be obtained; here the measure is the value of the completed goods, less the cost of completing the manufacture.[38]

§ 248a. Wholesale and retail value.

When in the ordinary case a value is to be found for a single thing, the value is what that single thing would sell for; which amounts to the retail value of it. But when a court is dealing with a stock of goods held for sale, or even with a portion of such a stock, the value to be found is its value as a stock or part of a stock of goods, that is, its wholesale value, without the profit of resale which enters into the retail value; for at the time of valuation that profit has not yet been earned,

[35] Chicago, R. I. & G. Ry. v. Rogers, 129 S. W. 1155 (Tex. Civ. App.).

[36] Post, § 844.

[37] Wallingford v. Kaiser, 84 N. E. 295, 191 N. Y. 392.

[38] Emmons v. Westfield Bank, 97 Mass. 230.

or, to put the matter in another way, the process of distribution, which brings the goods into the hands of the consumer and thus gives them their final increment of value, has not yet taken place.[39]

So where part of a stock of goods is converted, the value of goods in the retail market is not the measure of damages in an action of trover.[40] Where a stock of goods has been wrongfully sold after seizure by legal process, the retail price is not the measure of recovery; but the actual value of the stock, as a whole, in the condition in which it was, is to be recovered. As evidence of value the price brought at the sale may be shown.[41] A trustee in bankruptcy is entitled to recover the value of goods fraudulently sold by the assignee of the bankrupt under an order of the court; but the value should be fixed as of the date of the sale at what the stock and fixtures should reasonably be expected to bring at a forced sale such as ordered, and not the amount which the goods brought when sold by the purchaser at retail.[42] In an action against the mortgagee of a stock of goods for a wrongful sale, the mortgagor, recovering the value of the stock less the amount of the mortgage, is entitled only to the value of the stock in bulk, not the price at which it might be sold at retail, which would include the expense and risk of such a sale.[43] In an action for the conversion of a stock of shopworn goods which were out of date, it appeared that the goods were taken to other cities and there sold for as good a price as could be got. This was received as evidence of value.[44]

In one or two cases retail value has been allowed to be shown, not as a basis of recovery, but as evidence. Thus where a retail dealer sued for conversion he was allowed to give evidence of the retail value of the goods, but this was

[39] *Colorado:* Crymble v. Mulvaney, 21 Colo. 203, 40 Pac. 499.

Idaho: Sears v. Lydon, 5 Ida. 358, 49 Pac. 122.

Iowa: John Blaul & Sons v. Wandel, 137 Ia. 301, 114 N. W. 899.

Kansas: Bradley v. Borin, 53 Kan. 628, 36 Pac. 977.

New Mexico: Cunningham v. Sugar, 9 N. Mex. 105, 49 Pac. 910.

[40] State v. Smith, 31 Mo. 566.

[41] Perkins v. Ewan, 66 Ark. 175, 49 S. W. 569.

[42] Comingar v. Louisville Trust Co., 128 Ky. 697, 111 S. W. 681.

[43] Cerney v. Paxton & Gallagher Co., 83 Neb. 88, 119 N. W. 14.

[44] Parmenter v. Fitzpatrick, 135 N. Y. 190, 31 N. E. 1032.

to be reduced by deducting the unearned and uncertain profits.[45] Where the business carried on by the plaintiff at the time of taking was that of a retail butcher, and the stock then on hand, with the fixtures, was seized and sold by the sheriff, it was held proper to allow testimony to show the profits the plaintiff could have realized upon the sale of the stock so taken; which was much the same thing as showing the retail value. Theoretically, however, it was an allowance of the wholesale value, with a further recovery, as consequential damages, for loss of profits.[46]

§ 249. Market value artificially enhanced.

A question in regard to the "market value," not yet, so far as we are aware, directly decided, but which the operations of stock speculators are likely sooner or later to bring before the courts, is this, namely: Whether the rule which makes the "market value" the measure of damages in ordinary cases of breach of contract for the delivery of goods, is applicable to certain cases of contract for the delivery of stocks, where their value in the market is neither determined by their intrinsic value nor regulated by the natural laws of demand and supply, but is artificially inflated by the seller for the purpose of increasing his profit. It is not unfrequently the case that a number of persons combine secretly to buy up the stock of a particular railroad or other corporation, and in this way get the whole, or nearly the whole, of it into their possession or control, so that substantially it can only be purchased from them, or by their permission. Having done this, they induce other parties to agree to sell them stipulated amounts of the stock "short,"—that is, to sell them at an agreed price, deliverable on or before a certain day, stock not owned or possessed by the seller at the time of making the agreement of sale. This agreement is made by the seller in the hope or expectation of purchasing the stock before the stipulated day at a lower price than that at which he has contracted to sell. Before that day comes, however, as the stock is wholly in the buyer's control, or so far in his control that it is impossible

[45] Wehle *v.* Haviland, 69 N. Y. 448.   351, 73 N. Y. St. Rep. 448, 41 N. Y.
[46] Ebenreitter *v.* Dahlman, 18 Misc.   Supp. 559,

to procure in the general market an amount of it sufficient to satisfy the contract, the seller finds himself obliged to procure it from the buyer himself, or on the buyer's own terms, and at a price immensely beyond its intrinsic value. Perhaps the courts would be disposed to disregard, in such a case, the quotations in the market. In the cases to which we refer, the buyer cannot fairly be said to have lost anything more than the actual value of the stock by its non-delivery, and the so-called "market value," which is the result of his own secret machinations, furnishes no measure of actual damage. "A mere speculative price," observed Nelson, J., "got up through the contrivance of a few interested dealers, with a view to control the market for their own private ends, is not the true test." [47]   In Kountz v. Kirkpatrick [48] the Supreme Court of Pennsylvania said: "The market price of an article is only a means of arriving at compensation; it is not itself the value of the article, but is the evidence of value. The law adopts it as a natural inference of fact, but not as a conclusive legal presumption. It stands as a criterion of value because it is a common test of the ability to purchase the thing. . . . What is called the market price, or the quotations of the articles for a given day, is not always the only evidence of actual value, but the true value may be drawn from other sources when it is shown that the price for the particular day had been unnaturally inflated."

Where, however, the market price of property has been enhanced by such an operation it will be regarded as the value of the property, at least when the question arises between parties neither of whom has been concerned in the raising of the price. [49]   And since value is really measured by the opinion of the public, and that opinion when expressed in a free market is the market value, it would seem that if even for a short time buyers and sellers unconstrained to act are willing to pay and to receive a certain price for the com-

---

[47] Smith v. Griffith, 3 Hill, 333.
[48] 72 Pa. 376, 390, per Agnew, J.
[49] *North Dakota:* First Nat. Bank v. Red River Val. Nat. Bank, 9 N. Dak. 319, 83 N. W. 221.

Australia: Vicary v. Foley, 17 Vict. L. R. 407. In this case the court expressed its approval of the case of Kountz v. Kirkpatrick.

modity, this price is its value; but what one *constrained* to buy must pay is not necessarily the value.

§ 250. No market value.

If an article has no market value, the real value of it must be determined in some other way from such elements of value as are attainable.[50] "If at any particular time there be no market demand for an article, it is not on that account of no value. What a thing will bring in the market at a given time is perhaps the measure of its value then, but not the only one." [51] "The market price, in the ordinary sense, is generally, but not always, the test of value. For such a tort as a conversion of goods a plaintiff may be entitled to large damages, though unable to sell the goods at any price. He may be greatly injured by the loss of goods which he cannot sell, but which would be productive of great benefit, and therefore would be of great value, without a sale." [52] In Brown *v.* St. Paul, Minneapolis & Manitoba Railway,[53] it was held that the value of an annual pass over a railroad was so difficult of measurement that it could not be allowed as damages. It would seem, however, that mere difficulty in computing value should not prevent the recovery of it. In Pennsylvania the value of a pass for life over a railroad for an entire family has been allowed.[54] The court said: "It is true it is difficult to estimate its value because of two uncertainties—one the length of life and the other the number of passages he and his family would probably demand. Still this uncertainty, like many others, must be made to approximate certainty as closely as the nature of the case will admit of. The burthen of proof lay on the plaintiff, who knew the number of his family, and the customary number of trips made by himself and them." So in an action for the conversion of stereotype book plates, having little or no market value, their special value to the plaintiff, or publisher, is the measure of damages.[55] And in.

[50] Murray *v.* Stanton, 99 Mass. 345.

[51] Strong, J., in Trout *v.* Kennedy, 47 Pa. 387, 393.

[52] Doe, J., in Hovey *v.* Grant, 52 N. H. 569, 581.

[53] 36 Minn. 236.

[54] Erie & P. R. Ry. *v.* Douthet, 88 Pa. 243, 246.

[55] Lovell *v.* Shea, 18 N. Y. Supp. 193, 60 N. Y. Super. Ct. 612.

The cost of reproducing the plates would be some evidence of such value.

an action for refusal to accept school books which had no market value, the cost of production is the real value.[56] Where property not procurable in the market was bought for resale, the price realized on contracts for resale is evidence of the value;[57] and where property without market value was sent to a broker to sell with the agreement that the owner should receive a certain amount for it when sold, this amount was some evidence of its value.[58] In an action for the conversion of a box of photographic negatives having no market value, the plaintiff can show the cost of obtaining the photographs, the purpose for which they were procured and the difficulty of replacing them, and their value to the plaintiff. The fact that they were not good ones and not well taken can also be considered. On the other hand, the jury may also consider that photographs of scenery in a distant foreign country difficult to reach, or where the photograph is of some event not likely to be repeated, though poor, may have a considerable value.[59]

§ 251. Peculiar value to the owner.

Other considerations than market value may govern the measure of compensation for household goods, wearing apparel, and such things as have a peculiar value to the owner. In an action against a carrier for the loss of second-hand clothing, books, and table furniture the Supreme Court of Texas said:[60] "He could hardly have supplied himself in the market with goods in the same condition and so exactly suited to his purposes as were those of which he had been deprived. As compensation for the actual loss is the fundamental principle upon which this measure of damages rests, it would seem that the value of such goods to their owner would form the proper rule on which he should recover. Not any fanciful price that he might for special reasons place upon them, nor,

Stickney v. Allen, 10 Gray (Mass.), 352.

[56] Cody v. American Educational Co., 131 Ill. App. 240.

[57] France v. Gaudet, L. R. 6 Q. B. 199.

[58] Lehmann v. Schmidt, 87 Cal. 15, 25 Pac. 161.

[59] Wamsley v. Atlas Steamship Co., 50 App. Div. 199, 63 N. Y. Supp. 761.

[60] International & G. N. Ry. v. Nicholson, 61 Tex. 550, 553, per Willie, C. J.; acc., Dallas v. Allen (Tex. Civ. App.), 40 S. W. 324.

on the other hand, the amount for which he could sell them to others, but the actual loss in money he would sustain by being deprived of articles so specially adapted to the use of himself and his family."

In a similar case in the Supreme Court of Colorado, Stone, J., said: [61] "As to certain other goods, such as wearing apparel in use, and certain articles of household goods and furniture, kept for personal use and not for sale, while they have a real intrinsic value to the owner, they may have little or no market value whatever at the point of destination; they are not shipped as marketable goods. The market value of many such articles depends on style and fashion, irrespective of actual value for use. In some cases the owner may not be able to replace them in any market. In such cases the value is to be properly fixed by considerations of cost and of actual worth at the time of the loss, without reference to what they could be sold for in a particular market or hawked off for by a second-hand dealer where they happen to be unladed."

In the case of articles of this nature, therefore, the owner is not restricted to a recovery of the value in the second-hand market, but may recover the value for use to the owner.[62] Thus to show the value of second-hand clothing the cost, extent of use and condition, and cost of replacing may be shown.[63] The same rule has been applied to wagons and har-

---

[61] Denver, S. P. & P. R. R. v. Frame, 6 Colo. 382, 385; acc., Fairfax v. New York C. & H. R. R. R., 73 N. Y. 167.

[62] *California:* Mortimer v. Mardern, 93 Cal. 172, 28 Pac. 814.

Colorado: Colo. Midland Ry. v. Snider, 38 Colo. 351, 88 Pac. 453 (household goods).

Connecticut: Barker v. Lewis S. & T. Co., 78 Conn. 198, 61 Atl. 163, 79 Conn. 342, 65 Atl. 143 (household goods and books).

New York: Sonneberg v. Levy, 12 Misc. 154, 32 N. Y. Supp. 1130.

Oklahoma: St. Louis & S. F. R. R. v. Dickerson, 118 Pac. 140.

Texas: Lincoln v. Packard, 25 Tex. Civ. App. 22, 60 S. W. 682; St. Louis, I. M. & S. Ry. v. Green, 44 Tex. Civ.

App. 13, 97 S. W. 531 (hand-painted china); Texas & P. Ry. v. Wilson Hack Line, 46 Tex. Civ. App. 38, 101 S. W. 1042 (second-hand broughams).

Utah: Smith v. Mine & S. S. Co., 32 Utah, 21, 88 Pac. 683 (household goods); Pennington v. Redman V. & S. Co., 34 Utah, 223, 97 Pac. 115 (household goods, including heirlooms and keepsakes).

[63] *Colorado:* John Monat Lumber Co. v. Wilmore, 15 Colo. 136, 25 Pac. 556.

Illinois: Sell v. Ward, 81 Ill. App. 675; McMahon v. Dubuque, 107 Ia. 621, 77 N. W. 517.

Pennsylvania: Lloyd v. Haugh & Keenan Storage & Transfer Co., 223 Pa. 148, 72 Atl. 516.

ness which have been used.[64] So the peculiar value of pictures, manuscripts, and musical instruments may be recovered.[65] A special value may be given to paper or books by annotations or other manuscripts of the owner 'or a relative. Thus sheet music may have a special value through annotations of the owner's husband.[66]

The mere fact that the goods are second-hand goods does not bring them within this rule: the reason of it is, that the goods have a certain adaptability to the purpose for which they are used, which no other goods could have. If other goods can be bought at second-hand stores in the neighborhood which are equally suited to the purpose, the market price of such second-hand goods is the measure of compensation.[67] And if the goods in question have no such adaptability to use, no evidence of "value to the owner" or of peculiar value to the particular plaintiff can be admitted.[68]

§ 251a. Sentimental value—Pretium affectionis.

It may happen that the property is of such a nature that it cannot be replaced at all, or only with difficulty; for example, a family portrait. In that case "the just rule of damages is the actual value to him who owns it, taking into account its cost, the practicability and expense of replacing it, and such other considerations as in the particular case affect its value to the owner."[69] But this "actual value to the owner" means its value as a painting, not the satisfaction and pleasure which the possession of it gives. That feeling, like the satisfaction which comes from having a contract respected and performed,

[64] Union P. D. & G. Ry. v. Williams, 3 Colo. App. 526, 34 Pac. 731.

[65] Bateman v. Ryder, 106 Tenn. 712, 64 S. W. 48, 82 Am. St. Rep. 910.

See Southern Exp. Co. v. Owens, 146 Ala. 412, 41 So. 752, 8 L. R. A. (N. S.) 369.

[66] Leoncini v. Post, 13 N. Y. Supp. 826, 37 N. Y. St. Rep. 255. Here the cost of replacing the annotations and transcriptions may be shown.

[67] Iler v. Baker, 82 Mich. 226, 46 N. W. 377.

[68] *New York:* Eastman v. Mayor, 152 N. Y. 468, 46 N. E. 841; Prignitz v. McTiernan, 43 N. Y. Supp. 974, 18 Misc. 651.

Texas: Missouri, K. & T. Ry. v. Crews (Tex. Civ. App.), 120 S. W. 1110.

So the value of a picture to the artist as a design cannot be shown. Wade v. Herndl, 127 Wis. 544, 107 N. W. 4, 5 L. R. A. (N. S.) 855.

[69] *Massachusetts:* Green v. Boston & L. R. R., 128 Mass. 221, 226.

Texas: Houston & T. C. R. R. v. Burke, 55 Tex. 323; Ladd v. Ney, 36 Tex. Civ. App. 201, 81 S. W. 1007 (busts).

is of a nature which the law does not recognize as a subject for compensation.[70] In other words, a *pretium affectionis* can never be recovered.[71]

§ 252. Special value for a particular use.

The value of property is to be estimated with reference to the most remunerative use for which it is adapted. Thus where a building was equipped with power and fitted for a machine-shop, but was used by the defendant merely for storage, the owner, in an action for use and occupation, was allowed to recover the value of the premises as a machine-shop, not merely their value for storage.[72] So in New Jersey, where the value of a horse was in question, Whelpley, C. J., said:[73] "They were entitled to have the value of the horse as a horse to be used in their business, and fitted for that use. Perhaps he would not have been worth anything as a fast trotter or as a gentleman's carriage horse, because not adapted to the work; but that would not depreciate his value as a cart horse, for which purpose he was to be used."[74] Where liquor used for tanning was converted, it was held that it had a value equal to its value for use, though it had no salable value.[75] And where defendant's raft collided with, sank and destroyed the cargo of one of two boats of plaintiff's, packed with ice and lashed together to save expense in running, it was held that the measure of damages, that is, the difference in value before and after the injury, must be got at by taking into consideration all the circumstances upon which the value depended, *e. g.*, the fact that the expense of running the remaining boat to the point of destination would be greatly increased, and that the lost boat had no value for any other purpose than the shipment of ice.[76]

[70] Missouri, K. & T. Ry. *v.* Dement, (Tex. Civ. App.), 115 S. W. 635 (family portraits and Bible with family records).

[71] *California:* Central Pac. Ry. *v.* Feldman, 152 Cal. 303, 92 Pac. 849.

Connecticut: Barker *v.* Lewis Storage & T. Co., 78 Conn. 198, 61 Atl. 163.

Mississippi: Moseley *v.* Anderson, 40 Miss. 49.

[72] Horton *v.* Cooley, 135 Mass. 589.

[73] Farrel *v.* Colwell, 30 N. J. L. 123, 127.

[74] *Acc.*, Central B. U. P. R. R. *v.* Nichols, 24 Kan. 242; *post*, § 495.

[75] Washburn *v.* Carthage Nat. Bank, 86 Hun, 396, 33 N. Y. Supp. 505.

[76] McCabe *v.* Knapp, 23 Ia. 308.

In the case of blooded animals, which have a value as such, this is to be taken as their value.[77]   Where land has a special adaptability to a particular purpose, since the fact of such adaptability enters into its value, it may be shown to establish the value.[78]   So where land was used to dump on it refuse for a mine, its value was the value for that purpose, not its

[77] *Indiana:* Wea Twp., Tippecanoe County v. Cloyd, 91 N. E. 959 (Ind. App).

Missouri: Council v. St. Louis & S. F. R. R., 100 S. W. 57, 123 Mo. App. 432.

[78] *For farming:*
Alabama: Long Distance Tel. & Tel. Co. v. Schmidt, 157 Ala. 391, 47 So. 731.

Kansas: Kansas City, O. L. & T. Ry. v. Weidenmann, 77 Kan. 300, 94 Pac. 146.

Or *other special* cultivation:
California: Sacramento Southern R. R. v. Heilbron, 156 Cal. 408, 104 Pac. 979 (nursery).

Pennsylvania: Cox v. Philadelphia, H. & P. R. R., 215 Pa. 506, 114 Am. St. Rep. 979, 64 Atl. 729 (duck breeding).

Washington: Seattle & M. Ry. v. Murphine, 4 Wash. 448, 30 Pac. 720 (growing hops).

For bridge abutments:
Arkansas: Little R. J. Ry. v. Woodruff, 49 Ark. 381, 5 S. W. 792.

California: Arcata & Mad R. Ry. v. Murphy, 71 Cal. 122.

Illinois: East S. L., C. & W. Ry. v. Illinois S. Co., 248 Ill. 559, 94 N. E. 149.

West Virginia: Shenandoah Valley R. R. v. Shepherd, 26 W. Va. 672.

See *Mississippi:* Sullivan v. Lafayette Co., 61 Miss. 271.

For special business, as *wharf or dock:*
Illinois: Calumet R. Ry. v. Moore, 124 Ill. 329, 15 N. E. 764.

Mississippi: Louisville, N. O. & T. R. R. v. Ryan, 64 Miss. 399, 8 So. 173.

Elevator:
Russell v. St. Paul, M. & M. R. R., 33 Minn. 210, 22 N. W. 379.

Railway:
Johnson v. F & M. Ry., 111 Ill. 414.

Dye works or print mill:
Cochrane v. Com., 175 Mass. 299, 56 N. E. 610, 78 Am. St. Rep. 491.

Factory:
Illinois: Dupuis v. Chicago & N. W. Ry., 115 Ill. 97.

Minnesota: King v. Minneapolis N. Ry., 32 Minn. 224.

Rubber business:
Conness v. Com., 184 Mass. 541, 69 N. E. 341.

Building brick and stone houses:
Dickenson v. Fitchburg, 13 Gray, 546.

Restaurant:
Chicago, E. & L. S. R. R. v. Catholic Bishop, 119 Ill. 525, 10 N. E. 372 (though the owner has forbidden that use).

Other use of land:
South Dakota: Chicago, M. & St. P. Ry. v. Mason, 23 S. D. 564, 122 N. W. 601 (gravel pit).

Vermont: Hooker v. Montpelier & W. River R. R., 62 Vt. 47, 19 Atl. 775 (quarry, mine, or building lots).

West Virginia: Norfolk & W. R. R. v. Davis, 58 W. Va. 620, 52 S. E. 724 (gas wells).

In Five Tracts of Land v. United States, 101 Fed. 661, 41 C. C. A. 580, the question was as to the value of land on which part of the battle of Gettysburg was fought. It was held that the value of the land as affected by the historical associations could be recovered.

less value for agricultural purposes.[79] Where land taken for a way is specially adapted to the purpose through having been graded (as when a private way is taken for a public way) the value given to the land by the grading may be recovered. So in the case of Beale v. Boston [80] the fact that a private way which had been taken for a public highway had been graded, and that a sewer had been laid in it, was shown as bearing on the value of the land. The value of a waterworks system which is in operation is its value as a going concern.[81]

This general principle must, however, be modified where goods held for sale are rendered unsalable, though not otherwise affected in value, even though the value for sale may not be greater than the value for use. So in Collard v. Southeastern Railway,[82] some hops, consigned to a purchaser, were injured in transit by the rain. They were dried, and after this process they were as valuable for use as before the wetting, but not as valuable for sale. The consignor was allowed to recover from the carrier their depreciation in value for sale. In a case in Massachusetts, the defendant ordered goods for a certain purpose; goods were furnished which were not adapted for the purpose, and were retained by the defendant with knowledge of that fact. The plaintiff was allowed to recover the value of the goods in general (that is, for the most remunerative use for which they were clearly adapted), and not their value for the special use for which they were ordered but were not adapted.[83]

§ 253. Possible future use.

The present value of property may be enhanced by the possibility of making a more remunerative use of the property than the present use. Such possible future use is to be considered.[84] In Montana Ry. v. Warren, the Supreme Court

[79] Whiteham v. Westminster, B. C. & C. Co., [1896] 1 Ch. 894.

[80] 166 Mass. 53, 43 N. E. 1029; acc., Colusa Co. v. Hudson, 85 Cal. 633.

[81] In re Monongahela Water Co., 72 Atl. 625, 223 Pa. 323.

[82] 7 H. & N. 79.

[83] Bouton v. Reed, 13 Gray (Mass.), 530.

[84] Georgia: Ellington v. Bennett, 59 Ga. 286.

Illinois: Reed v. Ohio & M. Ry., 126 Ill. 48.

Pennsylvania: Shenango & A. R. R. v. Braham, 79 Pa. 447.

England: Moore v. Hall, 3 Q. B. D. 178; Holland v. Worley, 26 Ch. D. 578.

of Montana said [85]: "The respondent was allowed to prove the value of the land for town-lot purposes. He had the right to do so, whether he had built upon it or not. As we have seen, the question is not to what use the land had been put. The owner has a right to obtain the market value of the land, based upon its availability for the most valuable purposes for which it can be used, whether or not he so used it." [86] In Mississippi & R. R. Boom Co. v. Patterson, [87] the plaintiff in error had taken land of the defendant in error by the right of eminent domain, and compensation was sought in this action. The jury found that the land was worth but $300 for any other than boom purposes, but a very much larger sum for such purposes: and the Supreme Court of the United States held that the larger sum should be awarded. Field, J., said:

"In determining the value of land appropriated for public purposes, the same considerations are to be regarded as in a sale of property between private parties. The inquiry in such cases must be what is the property worth in the market, viewed

[85] 6 Mont. 275, 284, 12 Pac. 641, per Bach, J.; affirmed 137 U. S. 348, 34 L. ed. 681, 11 Sup. Ct. 96.

[86] *Arkansas:* St. Louis, I. M. & S. R. R. v. Theodore Maxfield Co., 94 Ark. 135, 126 S. W. 83.

Illinois: South Park Comrs. v. Dunlevy, 91 Ill. 49.

Indiana: Ohio Valley R. & T. Co. v. Kerth, 130 Ind. 314, 30 N. E. 298.

Kansas: Kansas C. & T. Ry. v. Splitlog, 45 Kan. 68, 25 Pac. 202; Chicago, K. & N. R. R. v. Davidson, 49 Kan. 589, 31 Pac. 131; Missouri, K. & T. Ry. v. Roe, 77 Kan. 224, 94 Pac. 259, 15 L. R. A. (N. S.) 679.

Kentucky: West Virginia, P. & T. R. R. v. Gibson, 94 Ky. 234, 21 S. W. 1055; Chicago, St. L. & N. O. R. R. v. Rottgering, 26 Ky. L. Rep. 1167, 83 S. W. 584.

Louisiana: Opelousas, G. & N. E. R. R. v. Bradford, 118 La. 506, 43 So. 79.

Minnesota: Blue Earth County v. St.

Paul & S. C. R. R., 28 Minn. 503, 11 N. W. 73; Sherman v. St. Paul, M. & M. R. R., 30 Minn. 227, 15 N. W. 239; Cedar Rapids, I. F. & N. W. Ry. v. Ryan, 37 Minn. 38, 33 N. W. 6.

New Jersey: Somerville & E. R. R. v. Doughty, 22 N. J. L. 495.

New York: In re Simmons, 141 App. Div. 120, 125 N. Y. Supp. 697; *In re* Simmons, 121 N. Y. Supp. 113, 66 Misc. 204.

North Dakota: Petersburg School Dist. v. Peterson, 14 N. Dak. 344, 103 N. W. 756.

Ohio: Cincinnati & S. Ry. v. Longworth, 30 Ohio St. 108.

Pennsylvania: Wilson v. Equitable Gas Co., 152 Pa. 566, 25 Atl. 635; Hamory v. Pennsylvania, M. & S. R. R., 222 Pa. 631, 72 Atl. 227.

Wisconsin: Washburn v. Milwaukee & L. W. R. R., 59 Wis. 364, 18 N. W. 328; Alexian Bros. v. Oshkosh, 95 Wis. 221, 70 N. W. 162.

[87] 98 U. S. 403, 407, 25 L. ed. 206.

not merely with reference to the uses to which it is at the time applied, but with reference to the uses to which it is plainly adapted; that is to say, what is it worth from its availability for valuable uses? Property is not to be deemed worthless because the owner allows it to go to waste, or to be regarded as valueless because he is unable to put it to any use. Others may be able to use it, and make it subserve the necessities or conveniences of life. Its capability of being made thus available gives it a market value which can be readily estimated. So many and varied are the circumstances to be taken into account in determining the value of property condemned for public purposes, that it is, perhaps, impossible to formulate a rule to govern its appraisement in all cases. Exceptional circumstances will modify the most carefully guarded rule; but as a general thing, we should say that the compensation to the owner is to be estimated by reference to the uses for which the property is suitable, having regard to the existing business or wants of the community, or such as may be reasonably expected in the immediate future."

This question usually arises in cases of condemnation of land for public purposes, under the statutes of eminent domain, and will be examined more in detail hereafter. Of course no merely speculative possibility can be considered, but only such possible future use as will be considered to enter into and affect the present market value.[88]

[88] *Illinois:* Alexander *v.* Colcord, 85 Ill. 323 (possible future use as pasture, for which it has not been fenced, cannot be considered); East S. L., C. & W. Ry. *v.* Illinois S. Co., 248 Ill. 559, 94 N. E. 149 (possible use as bridge approach: *semble*).

Iowa: Everett *v.* Union P. R. R., 59 Iowa, 243, 13 N. W. 109.

Louisiana: Louisiana Ry. & Nav. Co. *v.* Sarpy, 125 La. 388, 51 So. 433 (possible use for factory sites).

New York: In re Simmons, 114 N. Y. Supp. 575, 130 App. Div. 356 (possible use as reservoir site).

Pennsylvania: Pennsylvania Schuylkill Valley R. R. *v.* Cleary, 125 Pa. 442, 11 Am. St. Rep. 913, 17 Atl. 468;

Gorgas *v.* Phila., H. & P. R. R., 64 Atl. 680, 215 Pa. 501, 114 Am. St. Rep. 974 (possible use for house lots, according to an unrecorded plan made many years before).

Washington: Grays Harbor Boom Co. *v.* Lownsdale, 54 Wash. 83, 102 Pac. 1041 (possible use as mill site or for commercial purposes); Grays Harbor Boom Co. *v.* Lownsdale, 54 Wash. 83, 104 Pac. 267 (possible use for boom purposes, after getting permission from the public authorities).

Wyoming: Edwards *v.* Cheyenne, 114 Pac. 677 (possible use for erecting dam and storing water, or for mining).

In Richmond & P. E. Ry. *v.* Seaboard A. L. Ry., 103 Va. 399, 49 S. E.

§ 254. Value of good will.

The good will of a business has an established value, which in the proper case may be estimated by a jury.[89] A basis for such an estimate is proof of the past profits; but an amount based on such an estimate may be reduced by showing such depression in trade or other circumstances as would make the business less valuable.[90]

In Llewellyn v. Rutherford [91] the method of determining the value of the good will of premises is discussed. The plaintiff had had possession of the premises under a lease in which there was a proviso that at the expiration the defendant should pay the best he could get for the good will of the business. On regaining possession, the lessor relet the premises to a third party for the same use to which the plaintiff had put them. Coleridge, C. J., said, that as the defendant had not sold the good will, the amount of recovery should be such a sum as persons who are in the habit of estimating such things would fix as the value of the good will of the premises under ordinary circumstances. It was held that in estimating the amount, the improved value of the neighboring property could be taken into consideration as increasing the value. What is called in this case the good will of premises resembles very closely the good will of a business: indeed, it could probably be resolved into two simpler elements—the value of the lease, and the good will of the business carried on. The rule laid down by Coleridge, C. J., indicates another method of plac-

512, it was claimed that it was the purpose of promoters to develop the land in question as a public park, to be used in conjunction with an electric railway, by the expenditure of thousands of dollars in the erection of a summer hotel, casinos, pleasure buildings, ball ground, golf links, and other improvements; and that its value for such uses was practically destroyed. The court, however, held such use too conjectural for consideration, and a value for that purpose too speculative. See also Schuylkill R. R. R. v. Stocker, 128 Pa. 233, 18 Atl. 399; Rumsey v. New York & N. E. R. R., 133 N. Y. 79, 30 N. E. 654, 136 N. Y. 543, 32 N. E. 979. Where the land was valuable for saloon purposes, for which it was being used, its value for such purposes might be considered, though by a change in the entrance to a neighboring bridge, which the city might at any time make, that value might be diminished. *In re* Manhattan Terminal, 120 N. Y. Supp. 465. The fact that the land is in fact acquired to use for the purpose is immaterial. Edwards v. Cheyenne (Wyo.), 114 Pac. 677.

[89] § 182.

[90] Chapman v. Kirby, 49 Ill. 211.

[91] L. R. 10 C. P. 456.

ing before the jury a basis upon which to estimate the value of good will.

§ 254a. Fixtures.

There is generally a very great difference between the value of fixtures *in situ* and the same fixtures out of place. Where defendant converted the plaintiff's store fixtures which had remained in position after plaintiff's lease expired, the measure of damages in conversion was held to be the value of the fixtures when removed, plaintiff having no right to leave them in the store.[92] But where the fixtures might rightfully remain *in situ*, and have the additional value which fixtures have in that condition, the value of them is taken to be the value *in situ;* as where store fixtures are wrongfully seized and converted.[93] For an engine left by the owner in a building and converted by a third party, the measure of damages is the value *in situ;* the possibility that the owner of the building would take it away might, however, enter into the estimate.[94] The original cost may be shown as bearing upon the value.[95]

§ 255. Time and services.

When the value of the time of a man, or of his personal services, is to be found, the jury must determine, in the light of all the circumstances proved, what the value of such a man's labor is worth. In the case of a common laborer the matter is simple: the value of his time or services is governed by the current rate of wages. Where, however, the value of the services is enhanced by the skill or education of the man whose time is to be paid for, the case is one of more difficulty. Where compensation is sought for services, the value of the services is not governed by the benefit actually received from them; [96] nor is the value of time necessarily measured by the compensation which it was bringing in at the time of the injury.[97] The value of time and services, where there is no current rate ap-

---

[92] Johnston *v.* Albany Dry Goods Co., 12 App. Div. 608, 43 N. Y. Supp. 164.

[93] Johnston *v.* Albany Dry Goods Co., 12 App. Div. 608, 43 N. Y. Supp. 164.

[94] Fleischmann *v.* Samuel, 18 App. Div. 97, 45 N. Y. Supp. 404.

[95] Hawyer *v.* Bell, 141 N. Y. 140, 36 N. E. 6 (machinery).

[96] Stowe *v.* Buttrick, 125 Mass. 449.

[97] Fisher *v.* Jansen, 128 Ill. 549.

plicable to the case, must be fixed by the jury; and the past earnings of the party may be shown, not as fixing the value in themselves, but as evidence to assist the jury in fixing it.[98]

§ 256. Choses in action—Bills, notes, and checks.

The value of a bill, note, or check is *prima facie* the amount due on the security,[99] the defendant being at liberty to reduce that valuation by evidence showing payment, the insolvency of the maker, or any fact tending to invalidate the security.[100] But the maker himself cannot give evidence of his pecuniary circumstances to reduce the damages.[101]

[98] See cases cited, § 180.

[99] *United States:* First Nat. Bank *v.* Felker, 185 Fed. 678.

Alabama: St. John *v.* O'Connel, 7 Port. 466.

Arkansas: Ray *v.* Light, 34 Ark. 421.

Georgia: Thompson *v.* Carter, 6 Ga. App. 604, 65 S. E. 599.

Illinois: American Ex. Co. *v.* Parsons, 44 Ill. 312.

Indiana: Harlan *v.* Brown, 4 Ind. App. 319, 30 N. E. 928.

Kansas: Davies *v.* Stevenson, 59 Kan. 648, 54 Pac. 679.

Maine: Buck *v.* Leach, 69 Me. 484.

Minnesota: Hersey *v.* Walsh, 38 Minn. 521, 38 N. W. 613, 8 Am. St. Rep. 689.

Missouri: Menkens *v.* Menkens, 23 Mo. 252; Bredow *v.* Mutual S. I., 28 Mo. 181; Skeen *v.* Springfield E. & T. Co., 42 Mo. App. 158.

New York: Decker *v.* Mathews, 12 N. Y. 313; Metropolitan E. Ry. *v.* Kneeland, 120 N. Y. 134, 24 N. E. 381; Griggs *v.* Day, 136 N. Y. 152, 32 N. E. 612, 32 Am. St. Rep. 704, 18 L. R. A. 120; Panson *v.* Miller, 66 App. Div. 12, 72 N. Y. Supp. 1011; Deri *v.* Union Bank, 65 Misc. 531, 120 N. Y. Supp. 813.

South Dakota: Cosand *v.* Bunker, 2 So. Dak. 294, 50 N. W. 84.

Texas: Ramsey *v.* Hurley, 72 Tex. 194 (see Brightman *v.* Reeves, 21 Tex. 70).

Vermont: Robbins *v.* Packard, 31 Vt. 570.

England: Evans *v.* Kymer, 1 B. & A. 528.

Canada: McDonald *v.* Everitt, 3 Kerr, 569.

If the plaintiff owns only a limited interest, the proper proportion of the face value is to be recovered. So a pledgor recovers the face value less the amount of the debt for which it is pledged. Powell *v.* Ong, 92 Ill. App. 95. And a part owner recovers his share of the face value. Grigsby *v.* Day, 9 S. D. 585, 70 N. W. 881.

[100] *California:* Zeigler *v.* Wells, 23 Cal. 170.

Illinois: American Ex. Co. *v.* Parsons, 44 Ill. 312.

Iowa: Latham *v.* Brown, 16 Ia. 118.

Missouri: O'Donoghue *v.* Corby, 22 Mo. 393 (audited claim).

New York: Potter *v.* Merchants' Bank, 28 N. Y. 641; Griggs *v.* Day, 136 N. Y. 152, 32 N. E. 612, 18 L. R. A. 120, 32 Am. St. Rep. 704; Thompson *v.* Halbert, 40 Hun, 536 (right to plead statute of limitations); Cothran *v.* Hanover Nat. Bank, 40 N. Y. Super. Ct. 401.

Utah: Walley *v.* Deseret Nat. Bank, 14 Utah, 305, 47 Pac. 147.

Wisconsin: Terry *v.* Allis, 20 Wis. 32 (city order).

[101] *Maine:* Stephenson *v.* Thayer, 63 Me. 143.

Lord Ellenborough held [102] that the damages in actions for bills of exchange were to be estimated at the amount of the principal and interest due on the bills at the time of the demand and the refusal; in other words, at the time of conversion. No doubt seems to have been entertained that the face of the bills was the *prima facie* measure of damages; and the same point was ruled in New York, with no limitation, however, as to the time to which interest was to be computed.[103]

Where trover was brought to recover a bill of exchange for £1,600, which the bankrupt had deposited with the defendant, and on which, after a demand had been made for it and refused, he had raised the sum of £800, it was insisted that the damages should be only this latter sum; but it was held otherwise at the trial; and upon argument for a new trial, Lord Abinger, C. B., said: "If the defendant will bring £800 into court and deliver up the bill, the verdict may be entered for a nominal sum; but he converted the whole bill, and the plaintiffs are entitled to recover the value of the whole at the time of the conversion. The defendant cannot be less liable for having destroyed the property to the amount of one-half." [104]

In an action of trover for certain *billetes*,[105] being Peruvian paper money, it appeared that the billetes were at a great discount; but the matter being referred to the prothonotary for adjustment, the plaintiffs insisted, on affidavit, that the billetes were worth *to them* the value expressed on their face, and claimed a recovery to that amount. And the court allowed it. This, however, hardly seems in analogy to other cases; for the general rule which we have laid down is to be taken with the qualification that the note, or other chose in action, is still an available security for the amount claimed.

New York: Outhouse v. Outhouse, 13 Hun, 130.

Oklahoma: Capps v. Vasey Bros., 23 Okla. 554, 101 Pac. 1043.

Texas: Ramsey v. Hurley, 72 Tex. 194, 12 S. W. 56.

Vermont: Robbins v. Packard, 31 Vt. 570.

Wisconsin: Kalckhoff v. Zoehrlaut, 43 Wis. 373.

[102] Mercer v. Jones, 3 Camp. 477.

[103] Ingalls v. Lord, 1 Cowen, 240. It should, perhaps, be noticed, that, in this case, the defendant was a constable, who had illegally levied on the note in question; and the court said, "That it viewed with great jealousy the conduct of officers holding executions against defendants."

[104] Alsager v. Close, 10 M. & W. 576.

[105] Delegal v. Naylor, 7 Bing. 460.

Where trover was brought for a £300 check, drawn by a bankrupt on his bankers, and delivered after his bankruptcy to the defendant, a creditor, and paid by the drawees, the jury found a verdict for the face of the bill. On a motion to set aside the verdict and enter a nonsuit, Chambre, J., said: "How can you sue for a piece of paper of no value?" and Mansfield, C. J., said: "The plaintiffs proceed on the ground that the check is worth nothing, being drawn without authority; how can they recover on it the sum of three hundred pounds?" and a nonsuit was entered.[106] In Thayer v. Manley [107] the defendant had obtained from the plaintiff three promissory notes by false representations. The plaintiff, on discovering the fraud, and before the maturity, demanded their return; on refusal, brought an action for their conversion. The court held, that, as the defendant might, by transfer to a *bona fide* purchaser, render the plaintiff liable to pay the notes, the measure of damages was their face value, and this was not changed by the fact that, after the commencement of the action and before the trial, one fell due and had not been transferred. It held, however, that the defendant might have the option of satisfying the judgment by delivering up and cancelling the notes. Where the defendants converted a note, by transferring it to a *bona fide* purchaser, and a recovery was had against the plaintiff, it was held he could recover the amount paid to satisfy the judgment.[108]

As we have seen, a defendant, in trover for a note, can show the insolvency of the maker, and any evidence will be admitted which tends to show such insolvency. This, however, means insolvency at the time when the value is to be found. So in an action for the conversion of a promissory note, not due for several months, evidence of the financial condition of the maker at maturity has no tendency, it was held, to show the value of the note when converted.[109] A mere probability that a note would not have been paid, is perhaps not enough;[110] but evidence is admissible to show that the plaintiff took the

---

[106] Mathew v. Sherwell, 2 Taunt. 439.
[107] 93 N. Y. 305.
[108] Comstock v. Hier, 73 N. Y. 269.

[109] Kellogg v. Thompson, 142 Mass. 76, 6 N. E. 860.
[110] Knapp v. U. S. & C. Ex. Co., 55 N. H. 348.

necessary steps to present the note for payment, and that the makers resided at the place in which the bank was situated at which the note was payable.[111]

Since a material alteration releases the parties to a note from liability, only nominal damages can usually be recovered for the conversion of an altered note. But a qualification of this general rule was made in the case of Booth v. Powers.[112] The evidence showed that a note made payable to "A or order" had been changed so as to read to "A or bearer." It was held that that material alteration invalidated the note, and therefore reduced its value and the damages for its conversion. Folger, J., said that the alteration was one that would vitiate the instrument. He pointed out, however, that if the alteration was not fraudulent, the payee might resort to the original indebtedness, but in that case he must have the note, and the note would therefore be worth the amount of the original indebtedness. He further said, that the plaintiffs could also show a readiness by the makers to waive or ratify the alteration. So if in any case the note was available to the plaintiff to its full amount, that amount will remain the measure of damages.[113]

The measure of recovery is not affected by the fact that the note is held merely as collateral.[114]

§ 257. Bonds and shares of stock.

In an action for the conversion of a common-law bond for the payment of the amount of a judgment, the measure of damages is *prima facie* the amount of the judgment. In the case of bonds of a municipal or other corporation having a market value, such value is the measure of compensation.[115]

---

[111] Brown v. Montgomery, 20 N. Y. 287.

[112] 56 N. Y. 22.

[113] Rose v. Lewis, 10 Mich. 483.

[114] Richardson v. Ashby, 132 Mo. 238, 33 S. W. 806.

But see Fisher v. George S. Jones Co., 108 Ga. 490, 34 S. E. 172; Johnson v. Dun, 75 Minn. 533, 538, 78 N. W. 98.

[115] *Illinois:* Hayes v. Massachusetts L. I. Co., 125 Ill. 626, 18 N. E. 322, 1 L. R. A. 303 (*semble*); First National Bank v. Strang, 28 Ill. App. 325.

Iowa: Callanan v. Brown, 35 Ia. 138; Griffith v. Burden, 35 Ia. 138; Dooley v. Gladiator, C. G. M. & M. Co., 134 Ia. 468, 109 N. W. 864.

New York: Wintermute v. Cooke, 73 N. Y. 107 (*semble*); Roberts v. Berdell, 61 Barb. 37.

So in an action for the conversion of some San Francisco Waterworks Company's bonds, the plaintiff was held not to be confined in his recovery to the face value of the bonds, on the assumption that the waterworks would pay them in legal tender, as allowed by the United States statutes. The jury could, it was said, take into consideration the fact that the company received all its dues in gold, that gold was practically the currency of California, and any other facts from which the probability that they would be paid in gold could be estimated. Johnson, C., said: "These considerations go to fix the market value where there is one. In the absence of an actual market value, I know no reason why they may not be considered by any tribunal." [116] Here, as elsewhere, the market value is not an absolute standard. The market is only taken as usually the best indication of value. This it may not be at all. So where in an action for damages, by the vendee of stock purchased in consequence of the vendor's false representations as to its intrinsic value, it appears that the stock was *actually* worthless, the price at which it sold in the market is entitled to no weight on the question of value.[117] In a case of this sort in the English Court of Appeal,[118] Cotton, L. J., said: "It must not be taken that the value of the shares must be what they would have sold for in the market, because that might not show the real value at all. I do not know whether there was any market in this case, but the market might have been affected by the representations which were made by the defendants, which induced the plaintiff to act and which might have induced others to act." And Sir J. Hannen added that the value was "not what the shares might have sold for, because he was not bound to sell them, and subsequent events may show that what the shares might have sold for was not their true value, but a mistaken estimate of their value."

In Redding v. Godwin,[119] a case of the same nature, Dickinson, J., said: ·

See Henry v. North American R. C. Co., 158 Fed. 79, 85 C. C. A. 409.

[116] Simpkins v. Low, 54 N. Y. 179.

[117] Hazelton v. Carolus, 132 Ill. App. 512.

[118] *New York:* Hubbell v. Meigs, 50 N. Y. 480.

England: Peek v. Derry, 37 Ch. Div. 541, 591.

[119] 46 N. W. 563, 44 Minn. 355.

"If such property has a definite market value, for which it can be readily sold, that is to be taken as its value, as in the case of other kinds of property. The market value and the intrinsic value are not necessarily the same. It is contended that, in the absence of proof of the market value of the stock, or that it had no market value, a recovery cannot be predicated upon proof of its intrinsic value. If it were shown that the stock was of no intrinsic value, it would be inferable that it had no market value.[120] And while it may be possible that the stock of an insolvent private corporation, a corporation which is unable to discharge its liabilities in the usual course of business, may have some definite market value different from its intrinsic value, this is not to be presumed; and in such a case the intrinsic value, ascertained from the value of the corporate assets, and the amount of its liabilities, may be taken as the basis for the assessment of damages. If in fact such stock had a definite market value different from its intrinsic worth, that may be shown by the adverse party." Where there is no market value, the value of shares must be found by an examination of the affairs of the company;[121] and in the absence of any evidence the par value, it is said, will be presumed to be the value.[122] Where the defendant converted stock having no market value and all the assets of the corporation were afterwards sold out by him on foreclosure for a small sum, it was held that the price realized at this sale was not conclusive as to the actual value of the property.[123]

Where a call on the stock has been legally made before the injury, the amount of the unpaid call is to be deducted from the market value.[124]

---

[120] Miller v. Barber, 66 N. Y. 558, 568.

[121] *Arizona:* Tevis v. Ryan, 108 Pac. 461.

Michigan: Feige v. Burt, 124 Mich. 565, 83 N. W. 367.

Missouri: Deck v. Feld, 38 Mo. App. 674; acc., Huse & Loomis Ice Co. v. Heinze, 14 S. W. 756 (Mo.), where the value of stock in a *projected* corporation was to be found.

[122] *Arizona:* Tevis v. Ryan, 108 Pac. 461.

Indiana: Walker v. Bement (Ind. App.), 94 N. E. 339.

Missouri: Moffitt v. Hereford, 132 Mo. 513, 34 S. W. 252.

Pennsylvania: Harris' Appeal, 12 Atl. 743.

[123] Feige v. Burt, 124 Mich. 565, 83 N. W. 367, 74 Am. St. Rep. 390.

[124] *Oregon:* Budd v. Multnomah St.

A wrongful dealing with the certificate amounts to the same dealing with the shares themselves; and the value of a certificate of stock is the value of the shares.[125]

§ 258. Other securities for the payment of money.

So the value of a savings-bank book is *prima facie* the amount of the deposits;[126] the value of an account is *prima facie* the face value.[127] For failure to give security for a purchase, the value of the security is the measure of damages, and that is *prima facie* the amount of the sum to be secured.[128]

§ 259. Policies of insurance.

The value of a policy of insurance was involved in an action to recover damages for the fraud of an agent, who had represented to his principal that he had effected an insurance, when in fact he had not. In trover for the policy, Lord Mansfield would not permit the defendant to contradict his own representation, and laid down the rule of damages as being the same as if the policy had been actually effected. "I shall consider," he said, "the defendant as the actual insurer, and therefore the plaintiff must prove his interest and loss."[129] So, on the Pennsylvania circuit,[130] in an action of trover for a policy of insurance, by consent of parties, the rule of damages was considered the same as if the suit had been on the

Ry., 15 Ore. 413, 15 Pac. 659, 3 Am. St. Rep. 169.

England: Van Dieman's Land Co. *v.* Cockerell, 1 C. B. (N. S.) 732.

[125] *Arizona:* Salt River Canal Co. *v.* Hickey, 4 Ariz. 240, 36 Pac. 171.

Illinois: Barth *v.* Union Nat. Bank, 67 Ill. App. 131.

Michigan: Morton *v.* Preston, 18 Mich. 60.

Missouri: Deck *v.* Feld, 38 Mo. App. 674.

New York: Ormsby *v.* Vermont C. M. Co., 56 N. Y. 623 (*semble*).

Pennsylvania: Delany *v.* Hill, 1 Pittsburgh, 28.

South Carolina: Connor *v.* Hillier, 11 Rich. 193.

In Daggett *v.* Davis, 53 Mich. 35, 18 N. W. 548, 51 Am. Rep. 91, it was said that in an action for conversion of the certificate the value of the shares could not be recovered, since the title to the shares was not affected, and it would seem, therefore, that the value of the certificate should not necessarily be considered as equal to the value of the shares.

[126] Wegner *v.* Second W. S. Bank, 76 Wis. 242, 44 N. W. 1096. But see Newman *v.* Munk, 36 Misc. 639, 74 N. Y. Supp. 467.

[127] Sadler *v.* Bean, 37 Ia. 439.

[128] Barron *v.* Mullin, 21 Minn. 374.

[129] Harding *v.* Carter, Park on Insurance, 4.

[130] Kohne *v.* The Insurance Co. of North America, 1 Wash. C. C. 93.

policy.[131]   In Wheeler *v.* Pereles,[132] it was held, in an action
for the conversion of a life insurance policy by the pledgee,
that the measure of damages was the value of the policy less
the amount of the notes for which it was pledged.[133] If the
insured is still insurable the value is the difference between
the rate of premium paid for the old insurance and what another company of equal credit would charge to issue a new
policy, with the difference in the rates of premium calculated
on the expectancy of life. But if plaintiff, by reason of ill
health, has become non-insurable, this fact may be shown
and evidence of experts taken as to his expectancy of life.
Then the difference between the present value of the benefit
named in the policy and the premiums to be paid thereon
during such life will be the measure of damages.[134] Stated
in another way the value is such sum as at the reasonable
rate of compound interest would equal the face of the policy
at the end of the period of expectancy; and if not paid up,
allowance would have to be made for payment of premiums.[135]
If the insured had ceased to be an insurable risk, and subsequently died before the action was brought, the face value of
the policy, less payment of a premium which fell due before the
death of the insured occurred, would be the measure of damages.[136]

For the conversion of a matured policy the value is *prima
facie* the face of the policy;[137] and where the insured is dead
at the time of conversion, the measure of damages for conversion of the policy is *prima facie* the face value; if its col-
lectible value is less, the latter would be the true measure.[138]

[131] *Acc.*, Hayes *v.* Massachusetts L. I. Co., 125 Ill. 626, 18 N. E. 322, 1 L. R. A. 303, where for conversion of the policy after the death of the assured the face value of the policy was given.

[132] 43 Wis. 332, citing Halliday *v.* Holgate, L. R. 3 Ex. 299; Fisher *v.* Brown, 104 Mass. 259.

[133] *Acc.*, Woodworth *v.* Hascall, 59 Neb. 124, 80 N. W. 483.

[134] Barney *v.* Dudley, 42 Kan. 212, 21 Pac. 1079, 16 Am. St. Rep. 476.

[135] Supreme Lodge K. of P. *v.*

Neeley (Tex. Civ. App.), 135 S. W. 1046.

[136] Toplitz *v.* Bauer, 161 N. Y. 325, 336, 57 N. E. 1059, 34 App. Div. 526, 55 N. Y. Supp. 29.

[137] *Illinois:* Mutual Life Ins. Co. *v.* Allen, 212 Ill. 134, 72 N. E. 200.

Rhode Island: Stafford *v.* Lang, 25 R. I. 488, 59 Atl. 684.

[138] Hayes *v.* Massachusetts Mut. L. Ins. Co., 125 Ill. 626, 18 N. E. 322, 1 L. R. A. 303, *n.*

§ 260. Other sealed instruments.

The defendant agreed to purchase of the plaintiff, for £73 19s., the unexpired term of a lease of twenty years, and the plaintiff delivered to him the indenture of lease for the purpose of having an assignment made out. The defendant subsequently made an agreement with the original landlord, and broke off the bargain with the plaintiff, and declined to accept an assignment. The plaintiff demanded the lease (but not the purchase-money), which, being refused, he brought trover. The jury found a verdict for £73 19s., the price agreed on as the value of the lease, deducting the amount of some fixtures which the plaintiff's under-tenant had removed, and no question was made but the measure of damages was correct.[139] The defendant had executed a bond to one H. Clowes, which was assigned to the plaintiff, in the penalty of $1,000, conditioned to convey a lot of land. Trover was brought for this instrument, and the conversion proved. The plaintiff having been nonsuited at the trial, on the ground that none but nominal damages could be given, the court set the nonsuit aside, saying that the plaintiff, as the assignee of the obligee, having been entitled to the performance of the condition, the damages sustained would be the value of the land.[140] From this amount must be subtracted the cost of performing a condition attached to the conveyance.[141] Where a bond to secure the faithful performance of a clerk's duties was converted by the obligor tearing off the seal, the measure of damages was held to be the penalty of the bond.[142]

§ 261. Documents.

The value of a receipted account in the absence of special circumstances is nominal only.[143] The value of abstracts of title and searches is the cost of procuring other similar searches.[144] The value of a solicitor's docket and papers, containing evidences of bills of costs against certain parties, is

[139] Parry v. Frame, 2 B. & P. 451.
[140] Clowes v. Hawley, 12 Johns. 484.
[141] Rogers v. Crombie, 4 Me. 274.
[142] Bank of Upper Canada v. Widmer, 2 Up. Can. Q. B. (O. S.) 222.
[143] Moody v. Drown, 58 N. H. 45.
[144] Watson v. Cowdrey, 23 Hun (N. Y.), 169.

the value of the documents *to the owner;* [145] and the same is true of a set of vouchers, accompanied by an affidavit of their correctness,[146] and of land scrip, so called.[147]   In the case of cancelled documents the value is nominal. So where A., the maker of a promissory note in favor of F., becomes F.'s executor, and the note is thereby paid, and the defendant converts the note, and A. as executor sues in trover, it is held that he is entitled to recover nominal damages. And where an action of trover was brought [148] for a policy which it appeared was cancelled, a verdict was recovered and sustained for 2*d.*, the value of the parchment only.[149]

§ 262. Title-deeds.

The rule of damages in trover for title-deeds has not been much discussed in the reports. There can be little doubt that, in this country, the ordinary rule of damages in trover would not apply, both because the judgment would not, as in actions for the conversion of goods, effect a transfer of the title to the defendant, and because the title of the plaintiff, if recorded, as is generally the case, would be unaffected by the conversion, and if not recorded, the deed would still be unavailable to the defendant, and the plaintiff can usually have redress in equity. Dixon, C. J., in delivering the opinion of the Supreme Court of Wisconsin, said: [150]

"No case can be found, I think, where the recovery and satisfaction of a judgment, in an action for the conversion of them (title-deeds), have been adjudged to pass the legal title. I should think that in those cases where the title is unaffected, and the conduct of the defendant has not been fraudulent or oppressive, but where the deed or other written instrument was lost or destroyed through his mistake, negligence, or slight omission, the more just rule of damages would be such sum as would recompense the plaintiff for any actual

---

[145] Doyle *v.* Eccles, 17 Up. Can. C. P. 644.

[146] Drake *v.* Auerbach, 37 Minn. 505, 35 N. W. 367.

[147] Nelson *v.* King, 25 Tex. 655.

[148] Robinson *v.* Ferguson, 23 N. B. 332.

[149] Wills *v.* Wells, 8 Taunt. 264.

[150] Mowry *v.* Wood, 12 Wis. 413, 421.

In Towle *v.* Lovet, 6 Mass. 394, trover was brought for title-deeds, but the *quantum* of damages was settled by consent.

loss he may have sustained, and for his trouble and expenses in going into a court of equity, or elsewhere, to establish and perpetuate the evidence of his title, with the costs of the action." [151]

In England the case is different, since, owing to the absence of a registry system, the title-deeds are the only evidence of title. The whole value of the land is therefore allowed to be recovered, but satisfaction of the judgment is entered on the roll, on the defendant delivering up the deeds and paying costs, as between attorney and client, and otherwise placing the plaintiff in as good a situation as before the cause of action arose. [152]

§ 263. Life.

It was a rule of the common law that no action would lie for the death of a human being. But since the modern statutes giving a remedy for the wrongful taking of human life, no greater difficulty has been found in estimating the value of a life than in determining many other questions of a like nature which are constantly presented to juries. The rules for estimating the value of a life, however, concern so exclusively the actions which are brought upon the statutes just referred to that they will be discussed in connection with those actions. [153]

§ 264. Money.

The value of money, and of the use of it, come frequently before the courts for determination. The rules governing the value of money are, however, of such a peculiar nature as to require separate treatment. The subject will be discussed in the chapters immediately following.

§ 265. Illegal and noxious property.

* The character of the property may be such that the law

---

[151] *Acc.*, Edwards *v.* Dickinson, 102 N. C. 519. In an action of replevin for half-breed land scrip, the owner was allowed to recover the value of the land *to him*, though the patent could be issued only to him. Bradley *v.* Gammelle, 7 Minn. 331. This seems opposed to the cases upon title-deeds.

[152] Coombe *v.* Sansom, 1 D. & R. 201; Loosemore *v.* Radford, 9 M. & W. 657 (*semble*).

[153] Chap. xxiv.

will not give it any protection at all, or at best a partial one. In an action of trespass for cutting and destroying a picture, it appeared that it was a valuable painting, but it also appeared that it was a gross libel on the defendant's sister; and Lord Ellenborough told the jury that they must only award the value of the canvas and paint which formed its component parts.[154] ** So in an action for the conversion of irreligious and illegal pamphlets, it was held that the value *as pamphlets* could not be recovered; the plaintiff was restricted to the value of the materials.[155] So, where trespass was brought against officers of the customs for taking a portfolio and drawings, it has been held by the King's Bench, that the defendant may justify by showing that the portfolio contained drawings liable to seizure for non-payment of duty, which the plaintiff was in the act of carrying ashore out of a foreign packet. The jury found one farthing damages. On this the plaintiffs were nonsuited, and the court refused liberty to enter a verdict for the amount found.[156] So in Iowa, in an action of trespass for breaking into the plaintiff's close and taking certain liquors, which had been adjudged to be forfeited in a judicial proceeding to which the plaintiff was a party, it was held that he could not recover the value of the liquors, and, if the defendants acted in good faith, he could recover nominal damages only.[157] In Pennsylvania, in an action for pulling down a building, evidence that the building was peaceably taken down, and its materials preserved, in conformity with the directions of the commissioners of the township, during a period of great public excitement and disorder, with a view of saving the neighborhood from threatened violence, is admissible in mitigation of damages. But in such action evidence that the commissioners had by law the power to abate and remove nuisances, and that a grand jury, after instructions by a competent court, presented the building as a public

[154] Du Bost *v.* Beresford, 2 Camp. 511. See, also, Davis *v.* Nest, 6 Car. & P. 167.

[155] Boucher *v.* Shewan, 14 Up. Can. C. P. 419.

[156] De Goudouin *v.* Lewis, 10 A. & E. 117.

[157] Plummer *v.* Harbut, 5 Ia. 308; *acc.,* Jones *v.* Fletcher, 41 Me. 254; Lord *v.* Chadbourne, 42 Me. 429, 66 Am. Dec. 290.

nuisance, and recommended its abatement, is not admissible in mitigation of damages.[158]

Where the owner of the fee in a street maintained trees and shrubs thereon, liable however at any time to be removed at the will of the abuttors, this fact would be considered in determining the value of his right to the trees and shrubs.[159] And where the value of premises for a certain use is claimed, if that use is maintaining an illegal gambling house it cannot be had.[160]

In order, however, to be considered upon the question of value the illegality must be connected with the owner of the property. Ganson v. Tifft [161] was an action for breach of covenant by a lessor to rebuild. The plaintiff's testator had leased premises of the defendant, and sublet them at an increased rent. The buildings, consisting of an elevator and warehouse, were burnt down, and the sublessees terminated their lease under the statute. It was held that, in determining the amount of damages, the rent reserved in the sublease should be taken into consideration. It appeared that there was an association of elevator owners, formed mainly for the purpose of regulating prices, to which, at times, the elevators were all leased. It was held that the future profits or continued value of the lease which might arise from this cause could not be excluded from the consideration of the jury, either on the ground of remoteness or speculativeness, or because such associations are *illegal*. On the question of illegality, the court says:

"A party who has a contract for the sale of an article of property at the market value, cannot be prevented from recovering the actual value, because the price has been raised by a combination and conspiracy of strangers, to which he is not a party. He is entitled to the real value, without regard to any such consideration; and the alleged conspiracy or combination is too remote to affect such right, so long as he has no association or connection with the conspirators. It is no defence to an action brought to recover the price of property

[158] Reed v. Bias, 8 W. & S. (Pa.) 189.
[159] Pinkerton v. Randolph, 200 Mass. 24, 85 N. E. 892.
[160] McKinney v. Nashville, 102 Tenn. 131, 52 S. W. 781, 73 Am. St. Rep. 589.
[161] 71 N. Y. 48.

sold, that the vendor knew it was bought for an illegal purpose, provided that it is not made a part of the contract that it shall be used for that purpose, and that the vendor has done nothing in aid or furtherance of the unlawful design.[162] Within this rule, the plaintiff was not guilty of an act which prevented a recovery of the value of the lease; and the real question was, what was the unexpired term worth, under all the circumstances, and for what amount could the premises be sublet?"

Similarly, though the property had been used by the owner for an unlawful purpose, yet if this did not lead to the forfeiture of the property or in other ways affect its value, as if it had an equal value for other and legal uses, its value for such legal uses could be shown.[163] So where game cocks were converted, and though cock fighting was illegal the cocks themselves were a legal article of property, their value could be recovered.[164]

Where a member of a board of health wrongfully seized and destroyed furniture in a boarding-house where there had been smallpox, the measure of damages was held to be the value of the furniture as it then was, the value as affected by the exposure to the contagion.[165]

[162] Tracy v. Talmage, 14 N. Y. 162, 176.

[163] *Arkansas:* Young v. Stevenson, 73 Ark. 480, 86 S. W. 1000.

Maine: Johnson v. Farwell, 7 Me. 370, 22 Am. Dec. 203.

[164] Coolidge v. Choate, 11 Met. (Mass.) 79.

[165] Brown v. Murdock, 140 Mass. 314, 3 N. E. 208.

CHAPTER XIV

MEDIUM OF PAYMENT

§ 266. Primitive substitutes for money.

The ordinary medium of payment is, and in modern times has almost universally been, money. In primitive societies, before the introduction of money, one of the commonest measures of value appears to have been cattle. In Greece, as appears from the Homeric poems,[1] oxen were the measure of value. So in the early ages of Rome, certain fines were payable in sheep and oxen; but in the fourth century of the city money was substituted.[2] The same was true in the early Celtic and Saxon times,[3] and even as late as the seventeenth century, the colonies in this country were forced by the scarcity

---

[1] Iliad, bk. 23, vs. 1815.

[2] Aul. Gell. xi. 1; see also Cic. de Rep.

II. 36; 1 Niebuhr, Hist. of Rome, p. 223.

[3] See § 10.

of specie to adopt other standards of value. So in Massachusetts, on December 18, 1631, it was ordered "that corne shall
pass for payment of all debts at the usuall rate it is solde for except money or beaver be expressly named." [4] And on March 4,
1634, "ordered that muskett bullets of a full bore shall pass
currently for a farthing apeece provided that noe man be
compelled to take above xiid at a tyme in them." [5] In Virginia,
while a colony, tobacco was at one time a measure of value.
"Virginia was then not only throughout a slave-holding, but
a tobacco-planting Commonwealth. You can't open the
Statute Book—I mean one of the old Statute Books—not
those that have been defaced by the finger of Reform—and
not see that tobacco was in fact the currency as well as the
staple of the State. We paid our Clerks' fees in tobacco;
verdicts were given in tobacco and bonds were executed
payable in tobacco." [6]

At the present day, payment is to be made in money unless
some other medium is stipulated in the contract. That this
is still sometimes the case will be seen in this chapter. But
all verdicts must now be given in money, all damages are
pecuniary, and a study of the medium of payment becomes
practically a study of the value of money.

§ 267. Medium in which a payment may be made.

In case of a contract to pay a specified sum of money there
is usually no difficulty in estimating the amount to be paid.
The monetary system of a country may, however, between
the time of contract and the date of payment, be disturbed
and altered in one of two ways: the currency may become
depreciated, or a new standard may be adopted. In such
cases the contract will be discharged by a due payment in
any money which by law is made of equivalent value at the
time of payment.[7]

---

[4] 1 Col. Rec. 92.

[5] 1 Col. Rec. 137.

[6] Mr. Randolph in the Virginia Convention, Nov. 14, 1829. Proceedings
of the Virginia State Convention, p.
375.

    So also in *Maryland:* Crain *v.* Yates,
2 Har. & G. 332.

[7] Story on Notes, § 390, where the
opinion of the continental jurists will
be found. Case of Mixed Moneys, Sir
John Davies' Reports, 18, s. c. 2 Bligh,
98; Pilkington *v.* Commissioner for
Claims on France, 2 Knapp, 7, 18;
Cockerell *v.* Barber, 16 Ves. 461, 465;
Story on Con. of Laws, § 312; on Bills,

§ 268. Adoption of a new standard of value.

Where an entirely new standard of value is adopted by the government, the amount to be paid is found by giving such a sum in the new currency as shall be declared by law equal in value to the amount due in the old currency. A notable instance occurred in the change in this country to the decimal system of coinage, when an arbitrary ratio between the old and the new standards was adopted in each State.

A new standard may be adopted more indirectly by the issue of a paper currency, nominally but often not actually equal to the gold standard. If the government does only this, without making the new money legal tender for the payment of existing debts, it would seem that the creditor should be able to enforce payment on the earlier standard; for it is really a case of adoption of a new standard of value.

Where rent was reserved in "current money of Virginia," and the legislature of Virginia debased the currency in the way just described, it was held that the value of the rent reserved at the time of the lease should be found in gold or other stable medium, and judgment be given for that amount.[8]

§ 269. Adoption of a new legal tender—Double standard.

The most important question, however, because the case is the commonest, arises when the government not only issues a new sort of money, but makes it a legal tender for the payment of debts. This question was presented during the civil war by the passage of the Legal Tender Acts.

Congress, early in the war, passed a law declaring certain Treasury notes, to be issued by virtue of the law, a legal tender in payment of debts,[9] the principle of which was again repeatedly acted on by Congress.[10] Until this legislation, gold and silver coin had been the only legal tender known

§ 163. The American cases are to the same effect.

United States: Searight *v.* Calbraith, 4 Dall. 325; Thompson *v.* Riggs, 5 Wall. 663, 18 L. ed. 704.

Connecticut: Bartsh *v.* Atwater, 1 Conn. 409.

Virginia: Warder *v.* Arell, 2 Wash. 282; Taliaferro *v.* Minor, 1 Call, 524.

[8] Faw *v.* Marsteller, 2 Cranch, 10, 2 L. ed. 191.

[9] Act of February 25, 1862, ch. 33; 12 U. S. Stat. at Large, 345.

[10] 12 Stat. at Large, 709 (Act of March 3, 1863), 13 Stat. at Large, 218 (Act of June 30, 1864).

to the law, and had been not only understood by the profession and the public, but also assumed by high authority to be the only one sanctioned by the Constitution of the United States.[11] Indeed, subject to the constitutional restriction against impairing the obligation of contracts, the rights under them and the remedies upon them had been always regarded as matters exclusively for State regulation and control. But the exigencies of the civil war led to the expedient of giving to the notes of the government the same legal efficacy with gold and silver coin in the discharge of debts; and after a sharp and general controversy in the State courts, which, with rare exceptions, upheld the constitutionality of these laws, they were at last sustained by the highest tribunal in the land.[12] These decisions, however, so far as they applied to contracts made before the passage of the acts, overruled one made shortly before by the same court, in which, by a majority of five to three, the law had been declared unconstitutional as to such contracts.[13] They were brought about, moreover, not by an alteration in the opinions of the original majority, but by a change in the members of the court. One of the justices (Mr. Justice Grier), who had concurred with the majority, having resigned, and the number of judges in the court having, by an act of Congress, which took effect on the first Monday of December, 1869, been increased from eight to nine, the two vacancies thus created were supplied by judges who united with the previous minority of the court in overruling, by a vote of five to four, the principle of the former decision. Nevertheless, the later decision was again affirmed, and the constitutionality of the act finally settled, by the case of Juilliard v. Greenman.[14]

The result of making paper money a legal tender was to establish two standards of money. Money of either sort was held to pay a debt, and money of neither sort to overpay. In the ordinary case the debtor, being anxious to pay the debt

---

[11] See Gwin v. Breedlove, 2 How. 29, 11 L. ed. 167.

[12] Knox v. Lee, Parker v. Davis (Legal Tender Cases), 12 Wall. 457, 20 L. ed. 287; Dooley v. Smith, 13 Wall. 604, 20 L. ed. 547.

[13] Hepburn v. Griswold, 8 Wall. 603, 19 L. ed. 513.

[14] 110 U. S. 421, 28 L. ed. 204.

as cheaply as possible, tendered the less valuable sort of money. Cases arose, however, where the more valuable was tendered.

In Hancock *v.* Franklin Ins. Co.[15] a pledgee held a gold bond as security for a debt not specifically payable in gold. Having collected the bond, he applied a certain proportion to his debt, as though the debt were payable in gold (gold was at 174,—*i. e.*, 74 per cent. premium). He was required to account to the debtor, in an action for money had and received, only for the surplus after paying the debt in gold, the court saying that gold was still legal tender, and did not overpay a debt though worth more than paper currency. So where an accounting party collected debts in gold it was held that he might set it off by credits, though they were not payable in gold.[16] In the converse case, if a creditor having the right to demand payment in gold chose to demand payment out of a fund of paper money, it was held that he must take it dollar for dollar.[17]

The effect of the Legal Tender Act then was to create another legal standard of payment, and in the ordinary case the debtor had the option of paying the debt in the less valuable medium. Thus where a general deposit was made in a bank, it was held that the bank might pay it in paper, though the paper was less valuable than the medium in which the deposit was made; [18] and so, though the legal tender became more valuable in comparison with the money deposited.[19] So where gold was brought into court and was deposited by the prothonotary in a bank before the Legal Tender Act, it was held that on an order for the payment of the money to the claimant after the act when gold was at a premium payment might be made in paper.[20]

Paper was held good payment for a judgment rendered in 1858,[21] for a debt created by a loan of gold,[22] or for any other debt contracted while gold was the only standard of value.[23]

[15] 114 Mass. 155.

[16] Stanwood *v.* Flagg, 98 Mass. 124.

[17] Stark *v.* Coffin, 105 Mass. 328.

[18] Thompson *v.* Riggs, 5 Wall. 663, 18 L. ed. 704.

[19] Marine Bank *v.* Fulton Bank, 2 Wall. 252, 17 L. ed. 785.

[20] Aurentz *v.* Porter, 56 Pa. 115.

[21] Bowen *v.* Clark, 46 Ind. 405.

[22] McInhill *v.* Odell, 62 Ill. 169, overruling Morrow *v.* Rainey, 58 Ill. 357.

[23] *United States:* Legal Tender Cases, 12 Wall. 457, 20 L. ed. 287, overruling

So where a seaman had shipped at St. John, New Brunswick, on board an American ship for a voyage to London and back, he was in the lower court held entitled to recover in the United States double the stipulated wages, gold having been at a premium of one hundred per cent. But on appeal the judgment was modified by the Circuit Court of the United States for the first circuit, which held that the libellant could recover no more than the amount in dollars and cents specified in the contract.[24]

§ 270. Contract payable in gold.

There is nothing in the letter or the spirit of the Legal Tender Acts to prevent a special contract for payment of *gold* money; and a contract for the payment of coin must therefore be paid in coin. The earlier cases did not recognize this rule. They held that the spirit of the Legal Tender Act required all debts to be payable in legal tender paper, and that this could not be waived by parties to a contract; and therefore that every debt, though expressly payable in coin, could be discharged by tender of paper.[25] But these cases were overruled by the Supreme Court of the United States. By the terms of a mortgage, executed in 1851, the mortgagor agreed "to pay the sum of one thousand five hundred dollars in gold or silver coin, lawful money of the United States." The obligation had been held by the Court of Appeals of New York to be satisfied by the tender of the amount due in legal tender notes, at their nominal value; [26] but this judgment was reversed by

Hepburn *v.* Griswold, 8 Wall. 603, 19 L. ed. 513.

California: Mendocino County *v.* Morris, 32 Cal. 145; Belloc *v.* Davis, 38 Cal. 242.

Ohio: Longworth *v.* Mitchell, 26 Oh. St. 334.

[24] Trecartin *v.* The Rochambeau, 2 Cliff. 465.

[25] *Alabama:* Munter *v.* Rogers, 50 Ala. 283.

Illinois: Humphrey *v.* Clement, 44 Ill. 299.

Indiana: Brown *v.* Welch, 26 Ind. 116.

Iowa: Troutman *v.* Gowing, 16 Ia. 415.

Louisiana: Galliano *v.* Pierre, 18 La. Ann. 10, 89 Am. Dec. 643.

Massachusetts: Wood *v.* Bullens, 6 Allen, 516.

Missouri: Wright *v.* Jacobs, 61 Mo. 19.

New York: Murray *v.* Gale, 52 Barb. 427.

Pennsylvania: Shollenberger *v.* Brinton, 52 Pa. 9.

South Carolina: Gist *v.* Alexander, 15 Rich. 50.

[26] Rodes *v.* Bronson, 34 N. Y. 649.

the Supreme Court of the United States [27] in a decision based on two grounds: *first*, that by the various acts of Congress regulating the currency, a contract, payable in gold and silver coin, lawful money of the United States, was equivalent to one to deliver an equal weight of bullion of the same fineness as required by law for the coin; *second*, that as there were two kinds of money at the time the tender was made, both of which were by law a legal tender, but which were, in actual value, far from equivalent to each other, a contract stipulating for payment in the most valuable kind, namely, gold and silver, could only be satisfied by such a payment.[28] The same principle was subsequently applied by the same court to the case of a breach of covenant for the payment of rent, contained in a lease of certain premises, in the city of Baltimore. The lease was for ninety-nine years, renewable forever, upon an "annual rent of fifteen pounds current money of Maryland, payable in English golden guineas, weighing five penny-weights and six grains, at thirty-five shillings each, and other gold and silver, at their present weights and rates established by act of Assembly." [29] In the opinion of the majority of the court, delivered by Chase, C. J., in this case, the rule as to the assessment of damages for the breach of such agreements is thus declared: "When, therefore, it appears to be the clear intent of a contract that payment or satisfaction shall be made in gold and silver, damages should be assessed and judgment rendered accordingly. It follows that, in the case before us, the judgment was erroneously entered. The damages should have been assessed at the sum agreed to be due with interest, in gold and silver coin, and judgment should have been entered in coin for that amount."

Again, when a yearly rent of a specified number of ounces,

[27] Bronson *v.* Rodes, 7 Wall. 229, 19 L. ed. 141.

[28] *United States:* Trebilock *v.* Wilson, 12 Wall. 687, 20 L. ed. 460.

Illinois: McGoon *v.* Shirk, 54 Ill. 408, 5 Am. Rep. 122.

Louisiana: Poindexter *v.* King, 21 La. Ann. 697.

Missouri: Opinion of court in response to Governor, 49 Mo. 216.

New York: Cooke *v.* Davis, 53 N. Y. 318.

Ohio: Smith *v.* McKinney, 22 Oh. St. 200.

Virginia: Turpin *v.* Sledd, 23 Gratt. 238.

[29] Butler *v.* Horwitz, 7 Wall. 258, 19 L. ed. 149.

pennyweights, and grains of pure gold, in coined money, was reserved in a lease, it was held, by the same court, that judgment for the breach of the covenant should be "entered for coined dollars and parts of dollars instead of treasury notes, equivalent in market value to the value in coined money of the stipulated weight of pure gold." [30] So it was held that the Legal Tender Acts did not prevent a State from collecting its taxes in gold and silver coin.[31]

In California and Nevada, accordingly, a law, known as the Specific Money Act, requiring judgments to be paid in the coin or currency stipulated in the contract, was held to be valid, and not in conflict with the Legal Tender Acts.[32] Where, however, there was no contract to pay in coin, but the defendants had wrongfully sold to a third party, real estate which, although not held by them, as the court considered, in a fiduciary capacity, yet equitably belonged to the plaintiff, and which was valued at $5,200 gold, it was held by the Supreme Court of California that the Specific Money Act did not apply.[33]

§ 271. Form of judgment on a contract payable in gold.

A difficulty arose when the courts attempted to enforce payment in gold. A judgment for the value of the gold in currency was objectionable in two respects. In practice it did not do justice, for the value of paper fluctuated to such an extent that a judgment which represented the true value of the gold at one time would not represent it at another; in principle such a judgment would be equally objectionable, since it allowed the courts themselves to make a distinction between two sorts of currency declared to be equal by statute.[34] This difficulty was neglected in a few States; gold was treated like any merchandise, and damages assessed for failure to have it at the time appointed. The value of the gold at the time of

---

[30] Dewing v. Sears, 11 Wall. 379, 20 L. ed. 189.

[31] Lane County v. Oregon, 7 Wall. 71, 19 L. ed. 101.

[32] *California:* Carpentier v. Atherton, 25 Cal. 564; Harding v. Cowing, 28 Cal. 212; Spencer v. Prindle, 28 Cal. 276; McComb v. Reed, 28 Cal. 281, 87 Am. Dec. 115; Reese v. Stearns,

29 Cal. 273; Tarpy v. Shepherd, 30 Cal. 180; Poett v. Stearns, 31 Cal. 78.

Nevada: Linn v. Minor, 4 Nev. 462; Clark v. Nevada L. & M. Co., 6 Nev. 203, overruling Milliken v. Sloat, 1 Nev. 573.

[33] Price v. Reeves, 38 Cal. 457.

[34] Kellogg v. Sweeney, 46 N. Y. 291, 7 Am. Rep. 327.

performance of the contract was assessed in paper, and judgment was given for that amount.[35] The difficulty was met elsewhere in another way. Judgment was given for the amount due, in gold, a new writ being framed for the purpose, and this judgment could be satisfied only by payment in gold.[36]

This form of writ was used in California for the purpose of wholly frustrating the intent of the law. In that State, owing to the universal opposition of the community and its determination not to abandon a gold standard, the Legal Tender Act was never enforced; and notwithstanding its provisions, and the decisions of the courts elsewhere, the State courts allowed damages in ordinary actions to be computed in gold, and judgment to issue for gold. The Federal courts, though not upholding the practice, refused to reverse such judgments merely on that ground.[37]

§ 272. Actions of tort for the loss of gold.

Analogous to actions upon contracts payable in gold were actions of tort for the loss of gold. In an action against common carriers for the value of ninety double eagles of U. S. coinage, intrusted to them as common carriers, to carry from Acapulco to Newburyport, the measure of damages was the value in legal tender notes of the coin as a commodity, at the time when and place where it should have been delivered, with interest on the amount from the date of the demand.[38] But

[35] *North Carolina:* Dunn v. Barnes, 73 N. C. 273.

Pennsylvania: Baker's Appeal, 59 Pa. 313; Frank v. Colhoun, 59 Pa. 381.

Tennessee: Wills v. Allison, 4 Heisk. 385; Bond v. Greenwald, 4 Heisk. 453.

[36] *United States:* The Emily Souder, 17 Wall. 666, 21 L. ed. 683.

Alabama: Chisholm v. Arrington, 43 Ala. 610.

Florida: Bowen v. Darby, 14 Fla. 202.

Maine: Stringer v. Coombs, 62 Me. 160, 16 Am. Rep. 414.

Maryland: Chesapeake Bank v. Swain, 29 Md. 483.

Massachusetts: Independent Ins. Co.

v. Thomas, 104 Mass. 192; Warren v. Franklin Ins. Co., 104 Mass. 518; Stark v. Coffin, 105 Mass. 328; Currier v. Davis, 111 Mass. 480; Whitney v. Thatcher, 117 Mass. 523.

New York: Chrysler v. Renois, 43 N. Y. 209; Phillips v. Speyers, 49 N. Y. 653; Stephens v. Howe, 34 N. Y. Super. Ct. 133; Quinn v. Lloyd, 1 Sweeney, 253.

Ohio: Phillips v. Dugan, 21 Oh. St. 466, 8 Am. Rep. 66.

Texas: Bridges v. Reynolds, 40 Tex. 204; Johnson v. Stallcup, 41 Tex. 529.

[37] Edmondson v. Hyde, 2 Sawy. 205.

[38] Cushing v. Wells, 98 Mass. 550.

in an action against a hotel-keeper for the loss of a bag of gold coin, it was held by the Court of Appeals of New York, modifying the judgment below,[39] that the judgment should be entered in *coin*, and not in its equivalent in currency.[40]

§ 273. Contract payable in foreign currency.

Where a contract is expressly payable in the currency of a foreign country, since judgment must be given in the currency of the forum, the court does not estimate the damages in the foreign currency; but that currency is treated like any other commodity and judgment is given for its value at the time of performance.[41]

In one or two cases it has been said that the value of the foreign currency should be estimated at the date of trial, not at the date of performance.[42]   So in an action on a note made by the defendant in Canada, payable in Canadian currency, which at and continually subsequent to the date of the note was at a premium over the United States currency, it was held by the Supreme Court of Wisconsin that the premium might be recovered, and should be calculated at the rate current at the date of the judgment, which should be for a sum that would purchase Canadian funds to the amount found due on the note.   Any payment previously made on the note should be credited at the rate of premium current at the time of such payment.[43]   But this theory overlooks the fact that the foreign currency is only a commodity.   The contract is to deliver this commodity; if after breach the defendant had tendered the

---

[39] 1 Lans. 397.

[40] Kellogg v. Sweeney, 46 N. Y. 291, 7 Am. Rep. 327.   It may be remarked that in this case, Peckham, J., delivering the opinion of the court, observes that he sees no reason for calling the gold coin "merchandise."   It is, however, held by the Supreme Court of the United States, that gold coin, during the rebellion, was "an article of merchandise," within the meaning of the acts of July 13, 1861, and May 20, 1862 (12 Stat. at Large, 255, 404), prohibiting the taking of "goods, wares, and merchandise to an insur-

rectionary district."   Gay's Gold, 13 Wall. 358, 20 L. ed. 606.

[41] *Kentucky:* Pollock v. Colglazure, Sneed, 2.

Michigan: Sheehan v. Dalrymple, 19 Mich. 239.

New York: Fabbri v. Kalbfleisch, 52 N. Y. 28; Colton v. Dunham, 2 Paige, 267.

Pennsylvania: Mather v. Kinike, 51 Pa. 425; Christ Church Hospital v. Fuechsel, 54 Pa. 71.

[42] Robinson v. Hall, 28 How. Pr. (N. Y.) 342.

[43] Hawes v. Woolcock, 26 Wis. 629.

debt and interest in foreign currency, it would not have been a good tender. The plaintiff's claim has become one for damages for breach of contract, and the damages, of course, are estimated in the money of the forum.

That the foreign currency is only a commodity is strikingly shown by a case in Nova Scotia, where the Supreme Court of that Province held that United States treasury notes were not a legal tender for rent there payable in dollars and cents of United States currency.[44]

§ 274. Contract payable in a foreign country in currency of that country.

Where suit is brought in one country upon a contract payable in a foreign country, the plaintiff must of course recover damages in the currency of the *forum litis;* and he should recover such amount as will compensate him for his failure to get the foreign money at the time and place of payment. This, generally speaking, is the value of the foreign money in domestic money, estimated at time of payment.[45]

A difficulty arose in connection with the Legal Tender Act. It was urged on the one hand that as the legal tender currency was without intrinsic value, no equivalent in that currency to foreign coin could be furnished. The value of the foreign debt, therefore, could not be directly estimated in paper currency, but must necessarily be estimated in gold or silver dollars or units of value. After being thus ascertained in dollars, the acts of Congress which make all debts payable in certain paper currency would become applicable. And the foreign creditor having an ascertained claim of a certain number of dollars, would necessarily be compelled, like any other creditor, to accept payment of the amount in notes which are made by law a legal tender for all debts. This reasoning was adopted by the courts of Massachusetts and New York,

[44] Nova Scotia T. Co. *v.* American T. Co., 4 Am. Law Reg. (N. S.) 365.

[45] *Maryland:* Marburg *v.* Marburg, 26 Md. 8, 90 Am. Dec. 84.

Massachusetts: Burgess *v.* Alliance Ins. Co., 10 All. 221; Nickerson *v.* Soesman, 98 Mass. 364.

Michigan: Comstock *v.* Smith, 20 Mich. 338.

Pennsylvania: Benners *v.* Clemens, 58 Pa. 24.

Canada: Campbell *v.* Wilson, Berton (N. B.), 265.

which accordingly gave judgment for so many dollars as in gold would be equal to the amount of foreign money due, and refused to add the premium of gold.[46]

This view, however, does not conform to the principle of compensation. There never was a contract to pay the number of dollars allowed by the judgment. The suit is brought on a claim for damages which accrued at the breach of the contract, and which was equal to the amount which the plaintiff would have obtained at the time and place of performance. The Legal Tender Act has no application to the measure of damages. As in an action for the conversion of property, the judgment must be for the value of the property which the plaintiff should have had, measured in the common money standard. The cases first cited are therefore correct in principle, and the Massachusetts and New York decisions are erroneous.

So where suit was brought in Canada to recover a debt due in the United States before the Legal Tender Act, the plaintiff should recover such amount of Canada money as would be equivalent to the amount of the debt in gold, that is, to its amount at the time and place of payment,[47] but in a suit on such a debt payable after the Legal Tender Acts the plaintiff should recover an amount equal only to the value of the specified amount of paper money at the time of payment.[48]

It has been held that where a contract is payable in foreign gold, the judgment should be for the proper amount of gold, as in the case of a contract to pay gold in the United States; [49] but the weight of authority is the other way,[50] and it seems rightly. The common standard is paper money, and damages are estimated in that standard unless there is something to

---

[46] *Massachusetts:* Bush *v.* Baldrey, 11 All. 367; Cary *v.* Courtenay, 103 Mass. 316, 4 Am. Rep. 559.

New York: Swanson *v.* Cooke, 45 Barb. 574; Rice *v.* Ontario Steamboat Co., 56 Barb. 384.

[47] Massachusetts Hospital *v.* Prov. L. Ins. Co., 25 U. C. Q. B. 613; Judson *v.* Griffin, 13 U. C. C. P. 350; White *v.* Baker, 15 U. C. C. P. 292.

[48] Hooker *v.* Leslie, 27 U. C. Q. B.

295; Crawford *v.* Beard, 14 U. C. C. P. 87.

[49] Stringer *v.* Coombs, 62 Me. 160, 16 Am. Rep. 414.

[50] *Maryland:* Marburg *v.* Marburg, 26 Md. 8, 90 Am. Dec. 84.

New York: Ladd *v.* Arkell, 40 N. Y. Super. Ct. 150.

Pennsylvania: Benners *v.* Clemens, 58 Pa. 24.

prevent it. The express agreement of the parties must be respected, and consequently in contracts to pay gold dollars judgment is given for the gold. In the case under consideration, however, there is no contract for gold dollars, and no more reason for a judgment in gold than there would be in an action for the conversion of a gold cup.

§ 275. Exchange.

The value of foreign money is often arbitrarily regulated by statute.[51] If there is such a statute, however, it gives the value of the foreign money not in the foreign country, but in the domestic forum. And proof of the actual value of the foreign money, based on comparative weight of the standards

[51] The former rule as to damages on a bill of exchange drawn in this country and payable in England in pounds sterling, was to estimate the pound at $4.44 (which was originally the valuation for revenue purposes, Act March 2, 1799, ch. 22, § 61, 1 Stat. at Large, 673), adding what was known as the "rate of exchange" between this country and England at the time of the trial, with interest. By an act of Congress, however, passed July 14, 1832 (4 Stat. at Large, 583), the value of the pound sterling, in calculating the rates of duties, was fixed at $4.80, and subsequently, for the purpose of payments into the United States treasury, and the appraisement of imported merchandise, it was made equal to $4.84 (Act July 7, 1842, 5 Stat. at Large, 496). And by the second section of a statute, entitled "An act to establish the custom house value of the sovereign or pound sterling of Great Britain, and to fix the par of exchange," approved March 3, 1873 (17 Stat. at Large, 602), it is provided as follows: That in all payments by or to the treasury, whether made here or in foreign countries, where it becomes necessary to compute the value of the sovereign or pound sterling, it shall be deemed equal to four dollars eighty-six cents and six and one-half mills, and the same rule shall be applied in appraising merchandise imported, where the value is, by the invoice, in sovereigns or pounds sterling, and in the construction of contracts payable in sovereigns or pounds sterling; and this valuation shall be the par of exchange between Great Britain and the United States; and all contracts made after the first day of January, eighteen hundred and seventy-four, based on an assumed par of exchange with Great Britain of fifty-four pence to the dollar, or four dollars forty-four and four-ninths cents to the sovereign or pound sterling, shall be null and void. At the time of the passage of this act (which, it will be observed, is much broader in its scope than its predecessors), the English sovereign, owing to the changes in the value of the precious metals, had come to be worth a little over $4.86 in gold coin. To correct the error caused in our accounts with Great Britain, by the difference between the actual value and the legal value of $4.44, about nine and a half per cent., under the name of "exchange," was added to the legal value. By the act in question, this element of confusion is eliminated.

of value, also gives the value of the foreign currency in the domestic forum. But recovery should be had for the value of the foreign currency at the place of payment. This value is obtained by adding to or subtracting from the real or statutory value, as the case may be, the rate of exchange. On this question authorities differ. The better opinion is that the rate of exchange should be included in the recovery.[52] In New York and Massachusetts, however, it has been distinctly held that the debt is to be paid according to the par and not the rate of exchange, and that the creditor is not entitled to any allowance on account of the difference of exchange between the country where the suit is brought and the country where the debt was payable;[53] and that in an action here on a contract to pay money in another country (not a bill of exchange), no exchange can be recovered, although there were no tribunals in that country in which the plaintiff could sue.[54]

§ 276. Contract payable in bills, notes, stock, and other securities.

Where payment is to be made in notes which are not money, the notes are mere commodities; the contract becomes one for the delivery of chattels, and upon breach of it the measure of damages is the value of the notes at the time of the breach. So where a contract was payable in "solvent notes and accounts of other men," the measure of damages was not the amount to be paid, but the money value of that amount of "solvent notes of other men."[55] Where a note was payable in railroad stock, the measure of damages was the market

[52] *United States:* Lanusse v. Barker, 3 Wheat. 101, 147, 4 L. ed. 343; Woodhull v. Wagner, 1 Bald. 296, 302; Grant v. Healey, 3 Sumner, 523; Smith v. Shaw, 2 Wash. C. C. 167, 168; Cropper v. Nelson, 3 Wash. C. C. 125; Jelison v. Lee, 3 W. & M. 368; Hargrave v. Creighton, 1 Woods, 489.

Pennsylvania: Lee v. Wilcocks, 5 S. & R. 48.

England: Ekins v. East India Co., 1 P. Wms. 395; Cash v. Kennion, 11 Ves. 314; Scott v. Bevan, 2 B. & A. 78; Delegal v. Naylor, 7 Bing. 460.

Story, Confl. Laws, §§ 308, 312; Story, Notes, § 396; 3 Kent's Com. 116, n.

[53] *Massachusetts:* Adams v. Cordis, 8 Pick. 260; Cary v. Courtenay, 103 Mass. 316, 4 Am. Dec. 559.

New York: Martin v. Franklin, 4 Johns. 124; Scofield v. Day, 20 Johns. 102; Guiteman v. Davis, 45 Barb. 576, n.; Ladd v. Arkell, 40 N. Y. Super. Ct. 150.

[54] Lodge v. Spooner, 8 Gray, 166; Hussey v. Farlow, 9 All. 263.

[55] Williams v. Sims, 22 Ala. 512.

value of the stock at the time of payment.[56] Under a written contract, by which the defendant undertook to deliver the plaintiff two notes "on" certain named persons, or if he failed to do so, "to make satisfaction" within four weeks, it was held that the measure of damages was the value of the designated notes, and that the burden of proof of their value was on the plaintiff, as an essential ingredient in his case.[57] So in Kentucky, the measure of damages for breach of an obligation to pay in cash notes is the value of the notes.[58] In a suit in Indiana, for non-delivery of notes under an agreement to pay $900 in cash notes on "good solvent" men, it was held that the measure of damages was not the sum named, but the value of the notes to be found by a jury.[59] So, in the same State, in a suit on a note payable in "good judgments on good men," the value of the judgments is held the measure of damages.[60] So the measure of damages for breach of a covenant to pay a given sum in a particular species of paper, as Tennessee, Alabama, or Mississippi bank notes, is the specie value of such notes.[61] But an obligation to pay in "current bank notes" is an obligation to pay in legal tender currency,[62] current bank notes being of course the equivalent of money.

§ 277. Rule varied by principle of estoppel.

If, however, the payment stipulated for is a note or other obligation of the defendant himself, it is to be estimated at

[56] *Indiana:* Parks v. Marshall, 10 Ind. 20.

Vermont: Jones v. Chamberlain, 30 Vt. 196.

[57] Moore v. Fleming, 34 Ala. 491.

[58] Marr v. Prather, 3 Met. (Ky.) 196.

The same decision was reached in *Tennessee:* Murry v. M'Mackin, 4 Yerg. 41.

[59] Williams v. Jones, 12 Ind. 561.

[60] Pierce v. Spader, 13 Ind. 458.

[61] Hixon v. Hixon, 7 Humph. (Tenn.) 33.

So on an obligation to pay in "bankable paper" or "current bank paper:" Coldren v. Miller, 1 Blackf. (Ind.)

296; Van Vlut v. Adair, ib. 346. In "state indebtedness:" Smith v. Dunlap, 12 Ill. 184. In "militia certificates:" Clay v. Huston, 1 Bibb (Ky.), 461. In "Brandon money:" Gordon v. Parker, 2 Sm. & M. (Miss.) 485. In state securities or their equivalent in other money: Doak v. Snapp, 1 Cold. (Tenn.) 180. So on a duebill for "three hundred dollars in Watertown Railroad Stock" the measure of damages is the market value of stock of the par value of $300: Noonan v. Ilsley, 17 Wis. 314.

[62] Osgood v. McConnell, 32 Ill. 74.

par and not at its actual value.[63]   Thus in an action brought by a railroad company on a note, the defendant pleaded in set-off an obligation of the plaintiff company to deliver him a certain amount in its bonds.   It was held that the set-off should be allowed for the par value of the bonds, though at the time of payment their market value was less.[64]   This must be rested on grounds of estoppel.

§ 278. Confederate States money.

It seems that the cases involving payment of Confederate money must be rested on the same principle with those involving payment in mercantile securities.   That money consists simply of the notes of an illegal but *de facto* government; contracts to pay such currency were not invalid,[65] and payments received in such notes by an agent were good, and bound the principal.[66]   Confederate notes, then, were recognized for this purpose as the notes of a *de facto* corporation. It would therefore seem on principle that the measure of damages for a failure to pay such notes would be the value of the notes at the time of payment; to be obtained by esti-

[63] *Georgia:* Savannah & C. R. R. *v.* Callahan, 56 Ga. 331.

Illinois: Dunsworth *v.* Wood M. Co., 29 Ill. App. 23.

Massachusetts: Worthy *v.* Jones, 11 Gray, 168.

Texas: Texas W. Ry. *v.* Gentry, 69 Tex. 625.

[64] Memphis & L. R. R. R. *v.* Walker, 2 Head (Tenn.), 467.

[65] *United States:* Thorington *v.* Smith, 8 Wall. 1, 19 L. ed. 361; Confederate Note Case, 19 Wall. 548, 22 L. ed. 196.

But see Hanauer *v.* Woodruff, 15 Wall. 439, 21 L. ed. 224.

Arkansas: Leach *v.* Smith, 25 Ark. 246.

In Green *v.* Sizer, 40 Miss. 530, the doctrine is adhered to in that State, and applied to the case of a deposit with a banker during the late civil war, of Confederate treasury notes, Mississippi cotton notes, and Missis-

sippi military treasury notes; the validity of which obligations, although issued by authority of the insurgent government, is maintained on the ground that this government existed *de facto* before the notes were issued, and that at the time of the deposit they passed from hand to hand as representatives of value.

[66] *New York:* Robinson *v.* International L. I. Soc., 52 Barb. 450.

North Carolina: Baird *v.* Hall, 67 N. C. 230.

Texas: Rodgers *v.* Bass, 46 Tex. 505.

But *contra,* Mangum *v.* Ball, 43 Miss. 288.

A mere promise to pay money, if made in those States during the existence of the Confederacy, would usually be found to have been intended as a promise to pay such currency, but not always.   See Confederate Note Case, 19 Wall. 548, 22 L. ed. 196.

mating the value in gold (the common standard), and then reducing the gold to legal tender paper.[67]

There is a seeming hardship in this case, for the notes came finally to be valueless; and plaintiffs might therefore be utterly without remedy. This on reflection will appear to be a risk taken by the plaintiff, who made a contract to receive such notes in the future with full knowledge that their value depended on the success of the Confederate States. But the apparent hardship of the case has so forcibly appealed to the courts that they have modified what seems to be the true principle. Thus in some cases the value of the consideration was held to be the measure of damages.[68] The prevailing view, however, which was finally adopted by the Supreme Court of the United States, is that the measure of damages is the value of the currency at the time of entering into the contract.[69]

There was much dispute as to whether the value of the Confederate currency should be estimated by the value of the currency in United States notes, in gold or by its purchasing power. The legislatures of many of the Southern States passed scaling acts, as they are called, by which the currency received an arbitrary valuation, and those acts must be examined. There is a *quære* as to their constitutionality in The Confederate Note Case.[70] In Thorington *v.* Smith [71] the value was taken in lawful money of the United States. In Wilming-

[67] *United States:* Keppel *v.* Petersburg R. R., Chase's Dec. 167.

Alabama: Powe *v.* Powe, 42 Ala. 113.

Tennessee: Bowers *v.* Thomas, 6 Heisk. 553; Moore *v.* Gooch, 6 Heisk. 104.

[68] *Alabama:* Whitley *v.* Moseley, 46 Ala. 480; Wharton *v.* Cunningham, 46 Ala. 590.

Texas: Thompson *v.* Bohannon, 38 Tex. 241; Shearon *v.* Henderson, 38 Tex. 245.

Virginia: Moore *v.* Harnsberger, 26 Gratt. 667.

[69] *United States:* Thorington *v.* Smith, 8 Wall. 1, 19 L. ed. 361; Stewart *v.* Salamon, 94 U. S. 434, 29 L. ed. 275; Effinger *v.* Kenney, 115 U. S. 566, 29 L. ed. 495.

Alabama: Kirtland *v.* Molton, 41 Ala. 548; Toulmin *v.* Sager, 42 Ala. 127; Marshall *v.* Marshall, 42 Ala. 149; Herbert *v.* Easton, 43 Ala. 547; Whitfield *v.* Riddle, 52 Ala. 467.

Florida: Barclay *v.* Russ, 14 Fla. 372.

South Carolina: Fleming *v.* Robertson, 3 S. C. 118.

Texas: Short *v.* Abernathy, 42 Tex. 94.

Virginia: Fultz *v.* Davis, 26 Gratt. 903.

West Virginia: Brightwell *v.* Hoover, 7 W. Va. 342; Bierne *v.* Brown, 10 W. Va. 748.

[70] 19 Wall. 548, 22 L. ed. 196.

[71] 8 Wall. 1, 19 L. ed. 361.

35

ton & W. Railroad *v.* King[72] this question would appear to have been finally settled. The defendants had contracted to pay for wood at a dollar per cord, in Confederate currency. It was held that the purchasing power of specie, which that currency had, was the amount to be recovered, and that it was not proper to instruct the jury that the plaintiff could recover the value of the wood without reference to the value of the currency. It was further held that an act of North Carolina, which allowed the jury to look to the consideration of the contract in such cases, was unconstitutional. Bradley, J., dissented, on the ground that specie was not a proper standard, for there was no specie in the country; that the proper standard was the purchasing power of the currency, and that the value of the wood was good evidence of the purchasing power.

A special deposit of Confederate notes could be discharged by the same notes, though they had at the time of demand little or no value;[73] and so in case of refusal to return such a deposit the measure of damages was held to be, not the value of the notes at the time they were given, but the value at the time of the demand.[74]

§ 279. Commodities as a medium of payment.

The attempts which have been made at a complete classification of contracts payable in commodities have not been successful, partly because they have attempted to follow the superficial form of the contract; while the true classification depends sometimes upon the form of words used, sometimes upon the theory taken by the courts as to the nature and interpretation of the contract upon the whole evidence.[75]

Common-law pleading and the forms of action were long obstacles to a view of the contract in all its bearings. Now that they have been swept away or greatly modified, a clearer view of the underlying principles governing contracts payable in commodities or specific articles can be obtained.

---

[72] 91 U. S. 3, 23 L. ed. 186.

[73] *Louisiana:* Turner *v.* Beall, 22 La. Ann. 490.

Mississippi: Richardson *v.* Futrell, 42 Miss. 525.

[74] Planters' Bank *v.* Union Bank, 16 Wall. 483, 21 L. ed. 473.

[75] See Parsons on Contracts, 9th ed., 240, * 215; note on Roberts *v.* Beatty, 2 Pen. & Watts, 63, 21 Am. Dec. 410.

§ 279a. No distinction on principle between a commodity and any other medium of payment.

All the contracts which we have just been considering are discharged in law by damages representing the value of the stock, money, or security which the contract makes the medium of payment. The mere fact that the medium resorted to is not a promissory note or a stock certificate, but salt, or wheat, or lumber, or bricks, should make no difference in the rule of damages; and this is no doubt the law. The difficulties that have arisen have come from the fact that the question usually does not present itself in this simple way. There is no limit to the different sorts of contracts that may be made, and their terms produce modifications in the rule of damages, immediately applicable though they do not alter the fundamental principle.

§ 279b. Contracts regarded simply as agreements for the sale or delivery of specific articles.

Wherever the view of a contract taken by the court is that it is of this species, we think the measure of damages in commodity contracts will be found to be virtually identical with the rule just stated; that the value of the commodity fixes it.

The case which has introduced most confusion into the whole subject, for a reason that will be mentioned in the next section, is Clark v. Pinney.[76] The contract was in the form of a note promising to pay, in salt, a sum of money at a fixed rate, but it was a contract for delivery. This was held to be a case of sale, and at that time the measure of damages in cases of sale was very much in question; but the fact that it was a sale, and that the money was regarded as representing the purchase price, determined the measure of damages in accordance with the general principles applicable to sales.

In Price v. Justrobe[77] the contracts were construed to be for the delivery of rice, the money mentioned being the price, and the measure of damages being the value.

[76] 7 Cow. (N. Y.) 681.
[77] Harper (S. C.), 111; cf. Rose v. Warner, 14 Ark. 345.
Bozeman, 41 Ala. 678; Cockrell v.

In a Rhode Island case [78] the contract was one of sale and exchange. Cotton was exchanged for the note of a third person at an agreed price. The damages were held to be the value at this price of the note in money.

In an Iowa case [79] the contract was a due bill payable in flour, no rate being mentioned. This was treated as an agreement to deliver on the day fixed, and the measure of damages was held to be the market value at that time.

In Meserve v. Ammidon [80] the same view is taken of the contract, and the same conclusion is reached. The case might have been decided otherwise in other jurisdictions.

§ 279c. Option to discharge indebtedness in commodities at a rate or price fixed.

This species of contract has been at the root of the confusion which runs through the cases. It was a special form of contract which grew up in agricultural communities, where money was scarce, and payment in kind a common substitute, and was formerly quite common in this country. It took the form, usually, of a note or due bill for a certain amount of money, payable, however, in kind at a fixed rate, e. g., "I promise to pay $79.50 on the first day of January, in salt, at 14 shillings per pound." [81]

It was generally held by the judges before whom this species of contract was brought, to be the acknowledgment of a sum of money actually due from the maker; the provision for the payment in kind being intended for the benefit of the debtor only; and the understanding of the parties being that if he failed to avail himself of it, he must pay the note at its face value in money. The measure of damages therefore would not be the actual value of the salt. This interpretation is the dividing line which separates this special class of contracts from the others, considered above, when the measure of damages is the value of the security or commodity.

All cases of this sort seem to be construed as contracts in

[78] Bicknell v. Waterman, 5 R. I. 43.
[79] Davenport v. Wells, 1 Iowa, 598.
[80] 109 Mass. 415.
[81] Gleason v. Pinney, 5 Cowen 152, 5 Wend. 393. See this case fully ex-

plained in Dowdney v. McCullom, 59 N. Y. 367, 371. The contract was not the same in form with that in Clark v. Pinney, 7 Cow. 681, for it was not a contract for delivery.

which the person promises to do one of two things: if he does not do one he must do the other.

In Vermont the same view of these contracts is taken, and Poland, J., speaking of their judicial interpretation, refers to it as that "generally understood in the community," the note being commonly said to "run into money." [82]

In Pennsylvania, the same view was taken of a contract for the sale of land for $2,300, payable in axes.[83] The defendant not having paid in axes, the plaintiff was not allowed to recover the profit which he might have made on the axes, but only the balance of the purchase money and interest.[84]

The same conclusion has been reached as to this class of contracts in several other jurisdictions.[85]

§ 280. Where no rate is fixed.

When no rate or price is fixed, e. g., a note payable in wheel-wright work, the case does not belong to this class at all, and the normal rule of damages governs.[86]

§ 281. Alternative contracts—Liquidated damages—Rule of least beneficial alternative.

In this special class of cases the contract is in the alternative and suggests questions which will be more fully gone into in a subsequent chapter.[87]   As the defendant has an option

---

[82] Perry v. Smith, 22 Vt. 301.

[83] White v. Tompkins, 52 Pa. 363.

Meason v. Phillips, Add. 346, a *nisi prius* case, is opposed to the general rule.

[84] For a curious case involving the construction of a contract acknowledging an indebtedness of "two bureaus," see Roberts v. Beatty, 2 P. & W. 63; *cf.* Fleming v. Potter, 7 Watts, 380; Mattox v. Craig, 2 Bibb. 584.

[85] *Alabama:* Plowman v. McLean, 7 Ala. 775.

California: Cummings v. Dudley, 60 Cal. 383, 44 Am. Rep. 58; Delafield v. San Francisco & S. M. Ry. (Cal.), 40 Pac. 958.

Connecticut: Brooks v. Hubbard, 3 Conn. 58.

Kentucky: Cole v. Ross, 9 B. Mon. 393, 50 Am. Dec. 517, following Mattox v. Craig, 2 Bibb. 584; Mitchell v. Waring, 4 J. J. Marsh. 233.

Maine: Heywood v. Heywood, 42 Me. 229, 66 Am. Dec. 277 (rent payable in kind); Strout v. Joy, 80 Atl. 830.

Ohio: Trowbridge v. Holcomb, 4 Oh. St. 38.

Texas: Short v. Abernathy, 42 Tex. 94.

[86] *Iowa:* Davenport v. Wells, 1 Ia. 598.

Maryland: Lyles v. Lyles, 6 H. & J. 273.

New Hampshire: Wilson v. George, 10 N. H. 445.

[87] Ch. xvii.

to do a certain thing or pay a stipulated sum of money, some courts have spoken of it as a case of liquidated damages.[88] Most of the decisions proceed upon the theory that it is simply a case of a contract to do something, or failing this, to pay a sum of money, which, as we shall see, is now, if the contract is not otherwise objectionable, generally considered a liquidation of the damages by valuation and pre-ascertainment. In some of them the matter is complicated by the introduction of what is called the rule of the least beneficial alternative. Thus, in a Tennessee case, it was held that for a breach of a covenant to pay a sum of money, in Tennessee, Georgia, or Alabama bank notes, or notes of "good men," the measure of damages is the specie value of notes such as it would be most for the interest of the covenantor to pay in.[89]

Again, in a Kentucky case [90] the contract was to pay $800 in bank notes of a certain sort, and the measure of damages was held to be the market value of the cheapest notes of this sort amounting to $800.

In all cases of this kind the rule of least beneficial alternative gives the debtor not only the advantage of an option, but of a double option.

Thus in Brooks v. Hubbard [91] the court says that if it did not follow the rule requiring the money to be paid, the debtor having failed to exercise the option, the result would be to give the defendant the benefit of "the abnegated option" in another shape, i. e., he would have his option twice over.

We have collected these cases of an option to pay in commodities, or money, here, because they furnish a striking contrast to the normal rule, growing out of special circumstances; perhaps their most interesting aspect, however, is in connection with the rule of the least beneficial alternative.[92]

---

[88] Brooks v. Hubbard, 3 Conn. 58.

[89] Hixon v. Hixon, 7 Humph. (Tenn.) 33.

So far as the rule of least beneficial alternative is concerned, it makes no

difference whether the payment is to be made in commodities or securities.

[90] Anderson v. Ewing, 3 Litt. 245.

[91] 3 Conn. 58, 62.

[92] See ch. xvii.

CHAPTER XV

INTEREST

§ 282. What interest is.

§ 282. What interest is.

Interest is the value of the use of money: the amount of compensation for withholding money.[1] It bears the same relation to money that rent does to land, wages to labor, and

[1] *United States:* Loudon v. Taxing District, 104 U. S. 771, 26 L. ed. 923.

hire to a chattel. It may be secured by an agreeement, or it may be allowed as damages: in the former case the rate is usually stipulated in the agreement, in the latter it is usually fixed by legislation. It is not necessary, however, that the amount should be fixed by statute: for in the absence of a statute rate, the court will admit proof of the current rate, and will allow interest as damages at that rate.[2]

Where interest is secured by an agreement it is given by the court, not by way of damages, but as a substantive part of the debt;[3] the consideration of this branch of the subject, therefore, does not come within the scope of this treatise. But in all cases where damages are claimed for the wrongful detention of money the allowance of interest is governed by the law of compensation, and, therefore, will be treated here: for a full understanding of the rules which govern the allowance of interest as damages, however, it will be necessary also to consider some cases where interest is allowed on a contract to pay it. The English courts are less liberal in the allowance of interest than the American; and it would be confusing to consider the English and American cases together. The English law will therefore first be considered.

I.—ENGLISH LAW

§ 283. Origin of the allowance of interest.

* Interest was originally introduced into English jurisprudence by statutory provision. "Before the statute of Henry VIII.,"[4] says Lord Mansfield,[5] "all interest on money lent was prohibited by the common law, as it is now in Roman Catholic countries."[6] This statute provided that none should take for any loan or commodity above the rate of ten pounds for one hundred pounds for one whole year, which rate was

Pennsylvania: Minard *v.* Beans, 64 Pa. 411.

[2] *California:* Davis *v.* Greely, 1 Cal. 422.

Utah: Perry *v.* Taylor, 1 Utah, 63.

[3] *United States:* Jourolman *v.* Ewing, 80 Fed. 604, 47 U. S. App. 679, 26 C. C. A. 23.

Pennsylvania: Hummel *v.* Brown, 24 Pa. 310.

[4] 37 Hen. VIII., c. 9.

[5] In Lowe *v.* Waller, Douglass, 736, 740.

[6] This conclusion, notwithstanding a contrary dictum of Lord Hale (Anon., Hard. Rep. 420), is arrived at by Mr. Senator Spencer, in his very able dissenting opinion in the Rensselaer Glass Factory *v.* Reid, 5 Cowen, 587, 604, hereafter cited.

reduced to five per cent. by a subsequent act.[7] ** The general usury statute was repealed in 1854.

§ 284. English law—Rule laid down by Lord Mansfield.

* Where a principal sum is to be paid at a specific time, the English law was held by Lord Mansfield to imply an agreement to make good the loss arising from a default, by the payment of interest. Thus he expressly said,[8] in an early case:

"Where money is made payable by an agreement between parties, and a time given for the payment of it, this is a contract *to pay the money at the given time, and to pay interest for it from the given day in case of failure of payment at that day.* So that the action is, in effect, brought to obtain a specific performance of this contract. For pecuniary damages upon a contract for the payment of money, are, from the nature of the thing, a specific performance, and the relief is defective so far as all the money is not paid."

And Lord Thurlow said,[9] "All contracts to pay undoubtedly give a right to interest from the time when the principal ought to be paid." This language has been cited with approbation in this country,[10] though, as we shall see, it has not been followed in England.**

§ 285. Time of payment indefinite.

* On the other hand, where money is due, without any definite time of payment, and there is no contract, express or implied, that interest shall be paid, the English rule, independent of statute, has always been, that it cannot be claimed. In the Common Pleas,[11] it was early said, that in an action for money had and received, the plaintiff could recover nothing but the net sum without interest. In the King's Bench,[12] Lord Ellenborough said: "Lord Mansfield sat here for upwards of thirty years, Lord Kenyon for above thirteen years, and I have now sat here for more than nine years; and during this long course of time, no case has occurred, where, upon a mere

---

[7] 12 Anne, stat. 2, c. 16.

[8] Robinson *v.* Bland, 2 Burr. 1077, 1086.

[9] Boddam *v.* Riley, 2 Bro. C. C. 2.

[10] Williams *v.* Sherman, 7 Wend. 109.

[11] Walker *v.* Constable, 1 B. & P. 307; Tappenden *v.* Randall, 2 B. & P. 467.

[12] Calton *v.* Bragg, 15 East, 223.

simple contract of lending, without an agreement for payment of the principal at a certain time, or for interest to run immediately, or under special circumstances from whence a contract for interest was to be inferred, interest has ever been given." The interest here claimed was on money lent.[13] **

The same principle applies to an action for work and labor,[14] and for goods sold and delivered.[15]

§ 286. English law—Fraud.

* The rule here laid down has been, as we shall see, a good deal modified in this country; but the English courts have adhered to the doctrine with considerable rigor. Thus they have refused interest where property has been unjustly detained, or payment improperly refused, even in cases of fraud; Lord Ellenborough [16] saying, that the fraud did not take this case out of the rule which he had previously laid down,[17] that there must be an agreement, express or implied; and the same principle was afterwards adhered to.[18] **

But where the trustees of an infant holding money for him lent it on private security, they were held responsible for failure of the security, and obliged to pay interest at the current rate.[19] In another case plaintiff had been surety for a company paymaster in India. As he was about to leave India for his health, he was informed that his principal had defaulted, and that he could not leave India until he paid. Having paid, he sued to recover. The principal had not been sued, though solvent. It was held that he should be repaid with interest at the current rate, on giving surety for repayment, if found liable in a subsequent action. The court would not give interest at the rate current in India.[20]

[13] *Acc.*, Arnott *v.* Redfern, 3 Bing. 353; but *contra*, Trelawney *v.* Thomas, 1 H. Bl. 303.

[14] Milsom *v.* Hayward, 9 Price, 134. And in an action for rent of tithes it was held that as there was no agreement to pay on a particular day, but simply a general agreement for so much a year, no time for payment being specified, no interest could be recovered. Shipley *v.* Hammond, 5 Esp. 114.

[15] Chalie *v.* Duke of York, 6 Esp. 45.

[16] Crockford *v.* Winter, 1 Camp. 124, 129.

[17] De Havilland *v.* Bowerbank, 1 Camp. 50.

[18] De Bernales *v.* Fuller, 2 Camp. 426.

[19] Holmes *v.* Dring, 2 Cox Ch. 1.

[20] Law *v.* East India Co., 4 Ves. Jr. 824, 31 Eng. Reprint, 427. And see also Gowland *v.* De Farria, 17 Ves. Jr. 20, 34 Eng. Reprint, 8.

§ 287. Mercantile securities.

Where a note is not paid when due, it was said in the old cases that interest was not recoverable as matter of law, nor as part of the debt, but that the jury could give damages for the non-payment, and could give as damages interest on the amount, but that doing so was in their discretion. The law is settled that, if it is not payable by the terms of the note, it is only recoverable as damages.[21]   In Cameron v. Smith,[22] Bayley, J., said: "Although by the usage of trade, interest is allowed on a bill, yet it constitutes no part of the debt, but is in the nature of damages, which must go to the jury, in order that they may find the amount." He proceeded to say, that the jury could allow what interest they pleased, according to the damage; and that, if the non-payment was due to the default of the holder, they need not allow any.[23]   So, in Dent v. Dunn [24] it was held that interest stopped from the time an offer to pay was made, for there was no wrong after that, and therefore no damages were recoverable.   Lord Ellenborough, referring to interest on promissory notes, said: "It is more frequently recovered in the shape of damages for money improperly retained by the debtor contrary to the request of the creditor." [25]   The jury has, accordingly, been allowed to give much more than the usual rate of interest.   So in Keene v. Keene [26] the court refused to disturb an assessment of damages where the plaintiff had recovered interest at the rate of ten per cent., the rate of the note, although the usual rate was much less; Willes, J., saying: "Until the maturity of the bill, the interest is a debt; after its maturity, the interest is

[21] See, for a full discussion, the arguments in *In re* Burgess, 2 Moore, 745, 2 Parsons' Notes & Bills, ch. xi, p. 391.

[22] 2 B. & Ald. 305.

[23] So it was refused where a promissory note had been overdue thirty years; and the court on motion, would not increase the verdict by giving it. Du Belloix v. Lord Waterpark, 1 Dow. & Ry. 16.

[24] 3 Camp. 296.

[25] Chitty on Bills, 11th ed., p. 433; De Havilland v. Bowerbank, 1 Camp. 50; De Bernales v. Fuller, 2 Camp. 426;

Walker v. Constable, 1 B. & P. 306; Du Belloix v. Lord Waterpark, 1 Dow. & Ry. 16; Bann v. Dalzell, Mood & M. 228; Arnott v. Redfern, 3 Bing. 353; Calton v. Bragg, 15 East, 223; Higgins v. Sargent, 2 B. & C. 348; Page v. Newman, 9 B. & C. 378, 4 Man. & Ry. 305; Laing v. Stone, 2 M. & R. 561.   On the other hand, in Blaney v. Hendricks, 2 W. Black. 761; Lowndes v. Collins, 17 Ves. 28; Parker v. Hutchinson, 3 Ves. 134, it was said that interest should be allowed as matter of law.

[26] 3 C. B. (N. S.) 144.

given as damages, at the discretion of the jury." In *Ex parte* Charman,[27] an appeal from the Bankruptcy Court, the nature of interest on overdue paper was considered. Lord Esher, M. R., said that interest could not be claimed on a bill of exchange or a promissory note as part of the contract, unless there was an express agreement to pay interest. Interest could only be given by way of damages. In an action on the bill, the jury could give interest as damages, but they were at liberty to refuse to do so. The interest was no part of the debt. Now that actions could be tried by a judge without a jury, the judge could give or refuse to give interest. If under any circumstances a Court of Equity gave interest on a bill, it must have been given as a species of equitable damages. According to the ordinary meaning of the word "debt," interest, which could only be given by way of damages, was not a "debt."

And in an action on a demand note, in which there was no stipulation for interest, it was held that interest would run only from the day of issuing summons.[28]

§ 288. Contract, express or implied.

Even where money was payable at a definite time, it was early settled, in England, that interest, as *matter of law*, could not be given except on mercantile securities, or where there was a contract express or implied to pay it. In Higgins *v.* Sargent [29] the plaintiff brought covenant on a policy of life insurance for £4,000, payable six months after proof of death. The jury having found a general verdict for the plaintiff without any question being raised as to the allowance of interest, it was then for the first time claimed that interest should be added from the time the sum became due. But the court said that as the money was not due by mercantile instrument, and as there was no contract to pay interest, it could not be said that the jury should have been told to allow interest.

In Shaw *v.* Picton [30] the plaintiff sued for work and labor,

---

[27] W. N. (1887), 184.
[28] Pierce *v.* Fothergill, 2 Bing. N. Cas. 167, 1 Hodges, 251, 2 Scott, 334, 29 E. C. L. 485.

[29] 2 B. & C. 348.
[30] 4 B. & C. 715, 723.

and money lent, and on an account stated. Abbott, C. J., said:

"We are all of opinion that the plaintiff cannot substantiate any claim for interest. The general rule is, that interest is not due by law for money lent, unless, from the usage of trade or the dealings between the parties, a contract for interest is to be implied. Here no such contract is to be implied, for there is no usage of trade; and it does not appear by the case that any interest had ever been brought into the account on either side."

In Page v. Newman [31] the plaintiff sued on the following instrument: "Gueret, April 18th, 1814, one month after my arrival in England, I promise to pay Captain W. E. Page, or order, the sum of £135, as sterling for value received. C. Newman." Lord Tenterden, C. J., said: "It is a rule sanctioned by the practice of more than half a century, that money lent does not carry interest. . . . I think that we ought not to depart from the long-established rule, that interest is not due on money secured by a written instrument, unless it appears on the face of the instrument that interest was intended to be paid, or unless it be implied from the usage of trade. . . ."

In an action of assumpsit for money lent, and on account stated, it appeared that accounts were balanced yearly, interest then being added to the principal and interest calculated for the next year on the total amount. Held that this was evidence to show a course of dealing, and interest thus calculated would be allowed.[32]

In De Visme v. De Visme [33] land was sold and a time fixed for delivery of the abstract and payment of the purchase money, interest to run if the money was not paid at that time, from whatever cause delay might arise. The seller did not deliver the abstract at the time set, and the buyer was held not liable for interest until a good title was shown. In a sim-

[31] 9 B. & C. 378.

[32] Newell v. Jones, 4 C. & P. 124. In one case an agreement subsequent to the original transaction was held sufficient to give plaintiff a right to interest. Hicks v. Mareco, 5 C. & P. 498, 24 E. C. L. 674. And in a case for money lent plaintiffs proved their custom to charge interest on half yearly rests, but the court held that interest could not be so calculated without proof that defendant knew of the custom. Moore v. Voughton, 1 Stark. 487.

[33] 1 Macn. & G. 336.

ilar case [34] where the buyer had gone into possession before receiving conveyance, he was held liable for interest, his going into possession being held a waiver of the contract.

A mortgagor covenanted to pay on such a day with interest at 5 per cent. to that day. Neither principal nor interest was paid on the day set. After fourteen years an action for foreclosure was brought. It was held that to redeem the mortgagor must pay interest at 5 per cent. for the whole fourteen-year period. [35]

§ 289. Interest by statute—Discretionary power of jury.

In many cases the allowance of interest is governed by the statute 3 & 4 W. IV., c. 42, §§ 28, 29, which declares "that upon all debts or sums certain, payable at a certain time, or otherwise, the jury on the trial of any issue, or on any inquisition of damages, *may, if they shall think fit*, allow interest to the creditor, at a rate not exceeding the current rate of interest, from the time when said debts or sums were payable, if such debts or sums be payable by virtue of some written instrument at a certain time; or if payable otherwise, then from the time when demand of payment shall have been made in writing, so as such demand shall give notice to the debtor that interest will be claimed from the date of such demand until the time of payment, provided that interest shall be payable in all cases in which it is now payable in law." The act also allows interest, in the discretion of the jury, in actions of trover, trespass *de bonis asportatis*, and on policies of insurance, and expressly provides for the allowance of interest wherever it was previously allowed. This statutory regulation recognizes the hardship of the old rule, but leaves the matter in great uncertainty, the whole thing being given to the discretion of a jury in the particular case.

In an action of debt for goods sold and delivered, [36] it was found that the defendant had agreed, at the time of the contract, to give a bill or note for the price. The jury gave in-

---

[34] Fludyer *v.* Cocker, 12 Ves. Jr. 25.

[35] Mellersh *v.* Brown, 45 Ch. Div. 225.

See also Morgan *v.* Jones, 8 Exch.

620; Burnell *v.* Brown, 1 Jac. & W. 168, 21 Rev. Rep. 136, 37 Eng. Reprint, 916.

[36] Davis *v.* Smyth, 8 M. & W. 399.

terest, and it was held right. In a similar case it was held that as the bills would have carried interest, and performance would have entitled plaintiff to interest, he should have interest though the bills had not been given.[37]

In Hill v. South Staffordshire Ry.[38] the question of the allowance of interest, both at common law and under the statute, was considered. The plaintiff agreed to build a road for the defendant, payments to be made monthly as the work proceeded, on the engineer's certificate. There was no provision about interest. The plaintiff made a demand for a sum as the balance due him, with interest. His accounts were disputed, and, on a bill filed, he was proved to be entitled to about one-half his claim. Sir Charles Hall, V. C., in his opinion, said: "According to the contract, if it went on that, apart from the statute, there must be an express contract for the payment of interest except in the case of mercantile contracts,—bills of exchange and promissory notes, and some cases which are subject to special usage in trade. It must be in the contract itself, and no case has been made out for interest in that view." After stating that the bill must be considered as a claim for damages for not making out the certificate and for the detention of money, he referred to the case of Higgins v. Sargent, supra, as settling the liability to pay interest, irrespective of the contract and the statute, "that in the absence of any express provision in the contract to pay interest, there was no liability to do so."[39] With reference to the statute, he held that the amount could not be considered a sum certain, as it was only ascertained after examination of a long account, and therefore could not be considered within its provisions. He also said:

"Even supposing that I could treat the present as a case within the 28th section, that section is not imperative; it merely empowers a jury, if 'they shall think fit,' to allow in-

---

[37] Marshall v. Poole, 13 East, 98, 12 Rev. Rep. 310. For similar cases, see Rhoades v. Selsey, 2 Beav. 359, 17 Eng. Ch. 359, 48 Eng. Reprint, 1220; Lowndes v. Collens, 17 Ves. Jr. 27, 34 Eng. Reprint, 11; Farr v. Ward, 6 Dowl. P. C. 163, 3 M. & W. 25.

[38] L. R. 18 Eq. 154, 167, 170.

[39] The Vice-Chancellor then reviewed two cases, Mildmay v. Methuen, 3 Drew. 91, and Mackintosh v. Great W. Ry., 4 Giff. 683, which seemed to be opposed to this view, holding them to be poorly considered cases.

terest at a rate not exceeding a certain amount. These words give a discretion to the jury to say whether it be, under all the circumstances of it, a case in which interest ought to be allowed or not. A new trial would not, I think, be granted, because the jury had not allowed interest under that section in a case like the present. I do not believe that any twelve men dealing with and considering all the circumstances of this case, would say that interest ought to be allowed; and acting as a jury in this case it appears to me that I cannot allow interest."

§ 290. By way of damages for detention of money.

Interest is, however, sometimes allowed *by way of damages* for the detention of money where it is laid as special damage in the declaration. In Watkins *v.* Morgan [40] the plaintiff brought an action of debt on an indenture dated June 15, by which the defendant covenanted to pay £270, with lawful interest for the same on the 15th of December next following. The declaration alleged that there was due the plaintiff on account of the said sum and interest, the sum of £300. It concluded to the plaintiff's damage of £10. The plea was *non est factum.* Littledale, J., said he could not allow a verdict for £300, as the contract was to pay £270 with six months' interest, which would be £276 15s., and all the rest was damages for the detention; and the plaintiff having only laid these at £10, could recover no more. In Price *v.* Great W. Ry. [41] the plaintiff sued on an agreement to pay a certain sum on January 15th, 1844, and interest till that date. The principal was not paid, and a special case was made for the court on the question whether interest after January 15th, 1844, could be recovered. It was stipulated that the court should have the same powers as a jury. Parke, B., said: "This is substantially a mortgage. The constant and invariable practice is to give interest by way of damages in such cases."

In a case in the House of Lords [42] the plaintiff had received from one Bevan a warrant of attorney, dated May 2d, to secure payment of money on June 2d, with interest till that

[40] 6 C. & P. 661.
[41] 16 M. & W. 244.
[42] Cook *v.* Fowler, L. R. 7 H. L. 27, 32.

36

time at 5 per cent. per month. Bevan died before June 2d, and no payment was made, but the plaintiff did not enter judgment. Bevan's executors did not know of the warrant of attorney. By various means the plaintiff, after the executors knew he had a claim, kept the nature of it concealed for a long time. When obliged to make it known he claimed interest at 5 per cent. per month, but Vice-Chancellor Stuart allowed it at this rate for one month only, and at 4 per cent. per annum for the rest of the time. The Lord Chancellor, Lord Cairns, said that any claim for interest after the day to which interest was stipulated for, could be considered a claim for damages, it then being a question for the court, looking at all the circumstances of the case, to decide the amount of the damages. And it was his opinion that since plaintiff had kept back his security in order to be able to claim a great rate of interest for as long a time as possible, only the usual rate of interest could be given. The appeal was therefore dismissed.

§ 291. Result of the English cases.

The result to be obtained from these cases is as follows: Interest is allowed in England as a matter of law: *First*, on commercial paper; *Second*, on contracts expressly providing for it; *Third*, where an agreement to pay it is implied from usage, or the dealing of the parties. It is allowable in the discretion of the jury: *First*, in cases provided for by the statute, *supra; Second*, as special damages for the detention of money.

II.—AMERICAN LAW

§ 292. Difference between English and American law.

In the American courts interest is allowed as damages more liberally than in England. The leading difference seems to grow out of a different consideration of the nature of money. The American cases look upon the interest as the necessary incident, the natural growth of the money, and therefore incline to give it with the principal, while the English courts treat it as something distinct and independent, and only to be had by virtue of some positive agreement or statute.[43]

§ 293. Interest as damages—Frequently regulated by statute.

It is almost universally held in this country that interest is in the proper case given as damages by the common law. A large part of the subject is, however, covered by statute in every State, and the rate of interest is probably everywhere regulated by the legislature. In some States, e. g. Georgia and California, the subject is so thoroughly covered by statute that the common law is practically superseded.

In some States it has been held that interest is never allowed by the common law where there is no agreement for the payment of it; and therefore that it can be allowed in no case except on express agreement or unless it comes within the language of the statute allowing it.[44] And in other States it is held that in statutory actions no interest can be recovered unless it is allowed by statute.[45] In at least one State the time from which interest shall be allowed was by statute left for the judgment of the court.[46]

[43] For an examination of the early English and American decisions, see Wood *et al. v.* Robins, 11 Mass. 504, and Pope *v.* Barret, 1 Mason, 117, in which latter case it was held by Mr. J. Story, that interest was due when money was improperly withheld after demand. See the subject discussed, and the cases collected and cited in Alabama, in Boyd *v.* Gilchrist, 15 Ala. 849.

[44] *Colorado:* Denver, S. P. & P. R. R. *v.* Conway, 8 Colo. 1; Greeley, S. L. & P. Ry. *v.* Yount, 7 Colo. App. 189, 42 Pac. 1023; Hurlburt *v.* Dusenbury, 26 Colo. 240, 57 Pac. 860.

Illinois: Sammis *v.* Clark, 13 Ill. 544; Hitt *v.* Allen, 13 Ill. 592; Chicago *v.* Allcock, 86 Ill. 384.

Mississippi: Hamer *v.* Kirkwood, 25 Miss. 95; Warren Co. *v.* Klein, 51 Miss. 807.

Missouri: Kenney *v.* Hannibal & S.

J. Ry., 63 Mo. 99; Marshall *v.* Schricker, 63 Mo. 308; Atkinson *v.* Atlantic & P. R. R., 63 Mo. 367; De Steiger *v.* Hannibal & S. J. Ry., 73 Mo. 33; Kimes *v.* St. Louis, I. M. & S. Ry., 85 Mo. 611; State *v.* Hope, 121 Mo. 34, 25 S. W. 893; Neosho City Water Co. *v.* Neosho, 136 Mo. 498, 38 S. W. 89.

Montana: Randall *v.* Greenhood, 3 Mont. 506.

Nevada: Flannery *v.* Anderson, 4 Nev. 437.

[45] *Kansas:* Atchison, T. & S. F. R. R. *v.* Gabbert, 34 Kan. 132.

Missouri: Atkinson *v.* Atlantic & P. R. R., 63 Mo. 367.

Pennsylvania: Weir *v.* Allegheny County, 95 Pa. 413.

Contra, New York: Orr *v.* New York, 64 Barb. 106.

[46] Lewis *v.* Arnold, 13 Gratt. (Va.) 454.

§ 294. Money vexatiously withheld—Statutory rule.

Many States by statute allow interest when money is vexatiously withheld.[47] The question whether it has been so withheld is for the jury;[48] if it has, interest is then allowed, not from the time the delay became vexatious, but from the time payment was due.[49] "Wrongfully and unreasonably withheld," a phrase used in some States, seems to add nothing to the common law; it appears to mean, withheld after payment was due.[50]

§ 295. Allowance and amount of interest formerly matter for the jury.

It was formerly held in this country that when not secured by contract, that is, when claimed as damages, the allowance and amount of interest was in the discretion of the jury. This was especially urged when interest was asked upon the value of property. "There are two classes of cases," said the Supreme

[47] *Colorado:* Corson *v.* Neatheny, 9 Colo. 212, 11 Pac. 82.
Illinois: Chicago Macaroni Mfg. Co. *v.* Boggiano, 202 Ill. 312, 67 N. E. 17 (affirming 99 Ill. App. 509); Pieser *v.* Minkota Milling Co., 94 Ill. App. 595.
Montana: Ruff *v.* Rader, 2 Mont. 211.
[48] Devine *v.* Edwards, 101 Ill. 138; Levinson *v.* Sands, 74 Ill. App. 273.
Where defendant opposes a disputed claim in good faith, but does nothing to hinder or delay proceedings for collection, there is no vexatious delay.
Illinois: Imperial Hotel Co. *v.* H. B. Claflin Co., 175 Ill. 119, 51 N. E. 610; Moshier *v.* Shear, 15 Ill. App. 342.
Montana: Nixon *v.* Cutting Fruit Packing Co., 17 Mont. 90, 42 Pac. 108.
Merely appearing and defending the suit is not vexatious delay: Aldrich *v.* Dunham, 16 Ill. 403; Hatterman *v.* Thompson, 83 Ill. App. 217; neither is refusal to pay an excessive charge, Patrick *v.* Perryman, 52 Ill. App. 514; nor delay by a stakeholder to pay back

a wager on plaintiff's demand. Corson *v.* Neatheny, 9 Colo. 212, 11 Pac. 82.
In an action of contract for failure to convey land the damages were not settled and the court held that in such case there could be no unreasonable and vexatious delay of payment, and so no allowance of interest. Palmer *v.* Bennett, 96 Ill. App. 281.
The mere lapse of time does not indicate vexatious delay. Keys *v.* Morrison, 3 Colo. App. 441, 34 Pac. 259; Haitt *v.* Allen, 13 Ill. 592.
But long delay may of itself, by reason of the time elapsed, become vexatious. A delay of a month is not long enough to be vexatious from this cause. McCormick *v.* Elston, 16 Ill. 204. But longer delays have been held vexatious, where there was no dispute as to the liability. Newlan *v.* Shafer, 38 Ill. 379 (three years); Jassoy *v.* Horn, 64 Ill. 379 (ten years); Daniels *v.* Osborn, 75 Ill. 615 (three years).
[49] Chicago *v.* Tebbetts, 104 U. S. 120, 26 L. ed. 655.
[50] Killian *v.* Eigenmann, 57 Ind. 480; Hazzard *v.* Duke, 64 Ind. 220.

Court of New Hampshire, "in which interest may be recovered. The first is where it is incident to the debt, founded upon the agreement of the parties, and is a legal claim, which the court is bound to allow. The other class is where interest may be allowed by a jury in the nature of damages." [51] This was generally so in actions of *tort*, as trover or trespass for taking goods, where interest was allowed at the discretion of the jury. So, in an action of trespass, the Supreme Court of New York said: "The plaintiff ought not to be deprived of his property for years without compensation for the loss of the use of it; and the jury had a discretion to allow interest in this case as damages. It has been allowed in actions of trover, and the same rule applies in trespass when brought for the recovery of property." [52] So, in Kentucky, in case of a fraudulent refusal to convey land.[53] And so declared, also, in North Carolina, in cases of trover and trespass.[54]

The discretionary rule was applied in many cases of contract. So, in an action on an agreement to deliver wheat, the value of the wheat with interest thereon was given.[55] And the Supreme Court, on the argument of the case, said: "The judge who tried the cause did not *direct the jury* to allow the interest on the sum which they should find the wheat to be worth after the demand; but in ascertaining the plaintiff's damages, he observed they *might if they thought proper*, from the nature of the transaction, include interest as an item in making up the amount of damages. There was not in this remark any direction contrary to law." "Interest," said Washington, J., on the Pennsylvania circuit, "is a question generally in the discretion of a jury." [56]

So, in two actions against the master of a ship for the non-delivery of goods, it was held in New York that the jury might give damages if the conduct of the defendant was im-

---

[51] McIlvaine *v.* Wilkins, 12 N. H. 474.

[52] Beals *v.* Guernsey, 8 Johns. 446. So in trover, Hyde *v.* Stone, 7 Wend. 354; Bissell *v.* Hopkins, 4 Cow. 53; Kennedy *v.* Strong, 14 Johns. 128; Hallett *v.* Novion, 14 Johns. 273, and 16 Johns. 327. And in replevin, Rowley *v.* Gibbs,

14 Johns. 385. So, in case for negligence, Thomas *v.* Weed, 14 Johns. 255.

[53] Handley *v.* Chambers, 1 Littell, 358.

[54] Devereux *v.* Burgwin, 11 Iredell, 490.

[55] Dox *v.* Dey, 3 Wend. (N. Y.) 356.

[56] Gilpins *v.* Consequa, Pet. C. C. 85.

proper, *i. e.*, where fraud or gross misconduct could be imputed to him; but it appearing that such was not the fact, it was not allowed; and the court in the former case said: "Interest is not in every case and of course recoverable, because the amount of the loss is unliquidated, and sounds in damages to be assessed by the jury." [57] In a case in which a man covenanted to convey lands, and it afterward appeared that in truth he had no title to the land, but there was no fraud, it was held in Virginia, that whether the jury should allow interest on the value of the land from the date of the contract must depend on the circumstances of the case, of which they were the proper judges; and that it is competent for the defendant to give in evidence any circumstances tending to show that interest should not be allowed.[58]

In Dotterer *v.* Bennett [59] the plaintiff sued on a *quantum meruit.* The jury found a verdict for $1,756, with interest from the time the right of action accrued. This was held to be error; but the jury might, if they deemed proper, give a verdict for a sum which would include interest on the true value. So generally in the earlier and in some of the later cases the allowance of interest is said to be in the discretion of the jury.[60]

§ 296. Now usually a question of law.

Language is no doubt to be found in many cases which seems

[57] Watkinson *v.* Laughton, 8 Johns. 213; Amory *v.* McGregor, 15 Johns. 24.

[58] Letcher *v.* Woodson, 1 Brock. 212.

[59] 5 Rich. (S. C.) L. 295.

[60] *United States:* Willings *v.* Consequa, Pet. C. C. 172; Oakes *v.* Richardson, 2 Low. 173.

Arkansas: Crow *v.* State, 23 Ark. 684.

California: Brady *v.* Wilcoxsen, 44 Cal. 239.

Delaware: Black *v.* Reybold, 3 Harr. 528.

Indiana: Rogers *v.* West, 9 Ind. 400.

Kentucky: Morford *v.* Ambrose, 3 J. J. Marsh. 688; Marshall *v.* Dudley, 4 J. J. Marsh. 244; Bell *v.* Logan, 7 J. J. Marsh. 493; Stark *v.* Price, 5 Dana, 140;

Guthrie *v.* Wickliffe, 4 Bibb, 542, 7 Am. Dec. 142.

Maryland: Frank *v.* Morrison, 55 Md. 399.

Mississippi: Howcott *v.* Collins, 23 Miss. 398.

New York: Richmond *v.* Bronson, 5 Den. 55.

North Carolina: Hunt *v.* Jucks, 1 Hayw. 173.

Ohio: Hogg *v.* Zanesville Canal and Manuf. Co., 5 Oh. 410.

Pennsylvania: Obermyer *v.* Nichols, 6 Binn. 159; McCormick *v.* Crall, 6 Watts, 207; Eckert *v.* Wilson, 12 S. & R. 393.

Texas: Close *v.* Fields, 13 Tex. 623; Heidenheimer *v.* Ellis, 67 Tex. 426.

to imply that the court has the same discretion that the jury formerly had, and to place the allowance of interest on grounds of general equity. In Rensselaer Glass Factory v. Reid,[61] Colden, Senator, said: "As often as the question of interest has been before a court, the judges seem to have considered it as depending on general equitable principles; and, in most instances, to have decided each case in reference to its particular circumstances, without attempting to give any rule which might be generally applicable." But it is now perfectly well settled that in most classes of cases the allowance of interest is a question of law.[62]

In Dana v. Fiedler,[63] Johnson, J., used the following language:

"In all cases, unless this be an exception, the measure of damages in an action upon a contract relating to money or property is a question of law, and does not at all rest in the discretion of the jury. If the giving or refusing interest rests in discretion, the law, to be consistent, should furnish some legitimate means of influencing its exercise by evidence, as by showing that the party in fault has failed to perform, either wilfully or by mere accident, and without any moral misconduct. All such considerations are constantly excluded from a jury, and they are properly told that in such an action their duty is to inquire whether a breach of the contract has happened, not what motives induced the breach. . . . The right to interest, in actions upon contract, depends not upon discretion, but upon legal right."

§ 297. Gradual extension of principles allowing interest as matter of law.

The gradual extension of the principles allowing interest

---

[61] 5 Cow. (N. Y.) 587, 596; Mansfield v. New York C. & H. R. R. R., 114 N. Y. 331, 21 N. E. 735, 4 L. R. A. 566.

[62] *Alabama:* Broughton v. Mitchell, 64 Ala. 210.

California: Hamer v. Hathaway, 33 Cal. 117.

New York: Andrews v. Durant, 18 N. Y. 496; De Lavallette v. Wendt, 75 N. Y. 579; Mansfield v. New York C. & H. R. R. R., 114 N. Y. 331, 21 N. E.

735, 4 L. R. A. 566; Robinson v. Corn Exchange Insurance Co., 1 Abb. (N. S.) 186; Wehle v. Butler, 43 How. Pr. 5.

Utah: Rhemke v. Clinton, 2 Utah, 230.

In Utah the giving or withholding of interest by way of damages is said to be often in the discretion of the trial court, and this discretion will not be reviewed on appeal. Culmer v. Caine, 22 Utah, 216, 61 Pac. 1008.

[63] 12 N. Y. 40, 50.

as damages is clear. Beginning with a denial of interest in any case except where it was allowed by contract, the law first gave discretion to the jury to give interest as damages, and then allowed it as a matter of law in a constantly increasing number of cases. This has led the Supreme Court of North Carolina [64] to say:

"Although it [65] has not in cases like this yet been defined by clearly cut rules, and has therefore usually been left to the discretion of a jury, yet in the progress of the law as a science it must and will be so defined; and the question in what cases interest shall be allowed, and in what not, will be recognized as properly coming within the duty of judicial instruction, just as the question of the measure of damages now is, although until recently questions of that sort were considered too versatile and various to admit of being governed by certain principles, and were left, necessarily as was supposed, to the discretion of a jury."

§ 298. Interest by custom.

Where by custom known to the defendant interest is charged, a contract will be implied to pay the interest, and the defendant will be held to pay it. Thus, in New York,[66] interest has been allowed on the account of a forwarding merchant, on the ground of a universal custom to charge interest on such accounts, the custom being known to the defendant; and Savage, C. J., said: "Interest is always properly chargeable when there is either an express or an implied agreement to pay it." [67] A custom not proved to be known to the debtor at the time of contracting the debt will not be sufficient to charge him with

[64] Rodman, J., in Lewis v. Rountree, 79 N. C. 122, 128.

[65] That is, the allowance of interest.

[66] Meech v. Smith, 7 Wend. (N. Y.) 315.

[67] *Illinois:* Ayers v. Metcalf, 39 Ill. 307.

Iowa: Veiths v. Hagge, 8 Ia. 163.

New York: Reab v. M'Allister, 4 Wend. 483, 8 Wend. 109.

But under a statute which forbids the recovery of interest at more than a certain rate unless expressly stipulated, no more than that rate can be recovered though the custom allows a higher rate. Turner v. Dawson, 50 Ill. 85. In a case where defendant advanced for plaintiff on a bill payable in Louisiana, plaintiff was held to be entitled to interest according to the course of trade and agreement of the parties, though it exceeded the legal rate in Louisiana. Carson v. Alexander, 34 Miss. 528.

interest.[68] But a general custom is presumed to be known, and upon such a custom the debtor may be charged with interest.[69] Thus the general custom of Philadelphia merchants to charge their country customers interest on each item after six months seems to have become part of the law; no knowledge need be shown on the part of the debtor.[70] And the same is true of a custom in Vermont, to charge interest on each item of an account a year after it is entered.[71] And where it appeared that plaintiff was accustomed to charge interest after 90 days, defendant as one of plaintiff's customers, was held liable for interest after that time, on the ground that he was presumed to know of the custom.[72]

A.—LIQUIDATED DEMANDS

§ 299. Liquidated and unliquidated demands.

Having now examined the subject of interest in its historical aspect, and shown how, beginning with a general disallowance of it, the law has now come to admit principles the establishment of which render its allowance necessary in certain classes of cases, we proceed to inquire into the particular rules governing this allowance. And here we shall find that the determination of the question whether interest can or cannot be allowed, is by no means free from difficulty. The most general classification of causes of action with reference to interest is into liquidated and unliquidated demands. And it was formerly attempted to lay down the rule that interest could be recovered only on liquidated demands. But it will be perceived that not only is the distinction itself not by any means easy to keep in view, but besides this there is no reason in the nature of things why the fact of a demand being unliquidated should debar the plaintiff from receiving or exempt the defendant from paying interest. And finally, we do not

---

[68] *Illinois:* Rayburn *v.* Day, 27 Ill. 46.

South Carolina: Dickson *v.* Surginer, 3 Brev. 417.

[69] Fisher *v.* Sargent, 10 Cush. (Mass.) 250.

[70] *United States:* Bispham *v.* Pollock, 1 McLean, 417.

Pennsylvania: Knox *v.* Jones, 2 Dall. 193; Koons *v.* Miller, 3 W. & S. 271; Watt *v.* Hoch, 25 Pa. 411; Adams *v.* Palmer, 30 Pa. 346.

[71] Wood *v.* Smith, 23 Vt. 706; Davis *v.* Smith, 48 Vt. 52.

[72] M'Alister *v.* Reab, 4 Wend. (N. Y.) 483.

find as a matter of fact that the line between cases in which interest is allowed, and cases in which it is refused, corresponds with the line between liquidated and unliquidated demands. That there is a broad, general distinction between a claim sounding in damages and entirely unliquidated, and what is called a liquidated demand, is not to be denied. For an example, we may take the case of a claim for damages for personal injury arising from assault and battery, or a case of seduction, or libel. Here the elements from which to ascertain the amount of the demand are wholly at large. The defendant has no means of knowing in advance of proof what the precise pecuniary damage has been, still less what should be allowed for pain and suffering. Even the plaintiff, short of an assessment of damages by a jury, cannot give him the necessary information. Down to the time of verdict the claim is entirely unliquidated. On the other hand, the commonest example of a liquidated demand is an action of debt, where there is an express contract to pay a sum certain at a fixed time. Here all the conditions are reversed. The claim is wholly liquidated; both parties know exactly what it is and when it is to be paid. Interest in such a case represents the exact value of the use of an ascertained sum of money for a fixed period during which the plaintiff is deprived of it. Between these two extreme cases the whole body of the law lies, and it will be found that in this middle ground the demands approach or depart from the type of a liquidated demand in different degrees. Thus in the ordinary case of conversion of property, if the property be money, or mercantile securities, the case closely resembles, in its relation to interest, one of debt; if it be property of a fluctuating or peculiar value, the resemblance is not nearly so close. In the case of trespass on lands, the claim is generally of the kind which cannot be liquidated short of a verdict.

§ 300. Unsatisfactory character of the test.

But the objection to this classification lies not only in its difficulty of application, which might perhaps be surmounted; but in the fact of its unfairness. There is no reason why a person injured should have a smaller measure of recovery in one case than the other. There is no reason why the damages to be paid by the defendant should be mitigated or reduced by the circumstance that his tort or breach of contract was of such an aggravated or cunningly perfidious character as to make a liquidation of the claim against him difficult. On general principles, once admit that interest is the natural fruit of money, it would seem that wherever a verdict liquidates a claim and fixes it as of a prior date, interest should follow from that date. We shall now examine the rules laid down by the courts more in detail. As we proceed in this inquiry we shall find that there are two tests which are constantly applied by the courts, having been found by them more useful than the attempted division into liquidated and unliquidated demands. Of these the first is whether the demand is of such a nature that its exact pecuniary amount was either *ascertained,* or *ascertainable* by simple computation, or by reference to generally recognized standards such as market price; second, whether the time from which interest, if allowed, must run,—that is, a time of definite default or tort-feasance,—can be ascertained. This point of time is a fundamental part of the question in every case; and generally speaking, where interest is not allowed, as in actions of assault and battery, seduction, libel, and false imprisonment, the reason is connected with this.

§ 301. Liquidated demands—General rule.

Two rules for the allowance of interest on liquidated demands are to be deduced from the cases. 1st. Wherever there has been a contract to pay money at a given time, interest is to be allowed from the time the money should have been paid. 2d. Where money has been wrongfully acquired or detained, interest is to be computed from the time of the wrongful acquisition, or detention. Both cases depend upon the principle that the defendant has been guilty of a legal default in not paying over money to which he had no right.

When a debtor makes default in the payment of a liquidated sum of money, the creditor recovers interest by way of compensation from the time the money should have been paid.[73] "Whenever the debtor knows what he is to pay, and when he is to pay it, he shall be charged with interest if he neglects to pay." [74] "By the law as settled in this commonwealth, interest is to be allowed in all cases where, either by express contract or by implication, it is the duty of a party to pay over money due without any previous demand by the creditor. When a definite time is fixed for the payment of a sum of money, the law raises a promise to pay damages, by way of interest at the legal rate for the detention of the money after the breach of the contract for its payment." [75] "Whenever it is ascertained that at a particular time money ought

[73] *United States:* Curtis *v.* Innerarity, 6 How. 146, 12 L. ed. 146; Armstrong *v.* American Exch. Nat. Bank, 133 U. S. 433, 10 Sup. Ct. 450, 33 L. ed. 747.

Alabama: Whitworth *v.* Hart, 22 Ala. 343; Cheek *v.* Waldrum, 25 Ala. 152; Flinn *v.* Barber, 64 Ala. 193; Broughton *v.* Mitchell, 64 Ala. 210; Caldwell *v.* Dunklin, 65 Ala. 461; Talladega Ins. Co. *v.* Peacock, 67 Ala. 253; Park *v.* Wiley, 67 Ala. 310.

California: Jones *v.* Gardner, 57 Cal. 641; Pacific Mut. L. Ins. Co. *v.* Fisher, 106 Cal. 224, 39 Pac. 758.

Illinois: Peoria, M. & F. I. Co. *v.* Lewis, 18 Ill. 553; Bishop Hill Colony *v.* Edgerton, 26 Ill. 54; Clark *v.* Dutton, 69 Ill. 521; Harper *v.* Ely, 70 Ill. 581; Dobbins *v.* Higgins, 78 Ill. 440; Knickerbocker Ins. Co. *v.* Gould, 80 Ill. 388; Stern *v.* People, 102 Ill. 540; Plumb *v.* Campbell, 129 Ill. 101, 18 N. E. 790; Braun *v.* Hess, 187 Ill. 283, 58 N. E. 371, 86 Ill. App. 544.

Kentucky: Richardson *v.* Flournoy, 7 J. J. Marsh. 155; Gregory *v.* Sewing Mach. Co., 86 S. W. 529, 27 Ky. L. R. 741.

Louisiana: Duplantier *v.* Pigman, 3 Mart. 236; Daquin *v.* Coiron, 8 Mart. (N. S.) 608; Willey *v.* St. Charles Hotel Co., 52 La. Ann. 1581, 1602, 28 So. 182; Jackson, F. & M. Ins. Co. *v.* Walle, 105 La. 89, 29 So. 503.

Maine: Hall *v.* Huckins, 41 Me. 574; Maine Cent. Inst. *v.* Haskell, 73 Me. 140.

Maryland: Newson *v.* Douglass, 7 H. & J. 417.

Massachusetts: Harris *v.* Clap, 1 Mass. 308, 2 Am. Dec. 27; Bassett *v.* Sanborn, 9 Cush. 58.

Minnesota: Judd *v.* Dike, 30 Minn. 380.

New Hampshire: Buzzell *v.* Snell, 25 N. H. 474.

New York: Stuart *v.* Binsse, 10 Bosw. 436; Gutta Percha & R. M. Co. *v.* Benedict, 37 N. Y. Super. Ct. 430; Sans *v.* New York, 31 Misc. 559, 64 N. Y. Supp. 681.

Pennsylvania: West Republic Mining Co. *v.* Jones, 108 Pa. 55.

Rhode Island: Spencer *v.* Pierce, 5 R. I. 63.

Texas: Good *v.* Caldwell, 11 Tex. Civ. App. 515, 33 S. W. 243; Texarkana & F. S. Ry. *v.* Hartford Ins. Co., 17 Tex. Civ. App. 498, 44 S. W. 533.

Vermont: Hauxhurst *v.* Hovey, 26 Vt. 544; Vermont R. R. *v.* Vermont C. R. R., 34 Vt. 1; Sampson *v.* Warner, 48 Vt. 247.

Wisconsin: Butler *v.* Kirby, 53 Wis. 188.

[74] People *v.* New York, 5 Cow. (N. Y.) 331. See to the same effect McCormack *v.* Lynch, 69 Mo. App. 524.

[75] Bigelow, C. J., in Foote *v.* Blanchard, 6 All. (Mass.) 221.

to have been paid, whether in satisfaction of a debt, or as compensation for a breach of duty, or for the failure to keep a contract, interest attaches as an incident."[76] Thus in an action of debt, interest is assessed as damages for detention of the debt.[77] In an action on a promissory note interest is allowed after maturity though the note does not in terms bear interest.[78] So where the note provided for interest at an usurious rate, and by statute such interest was forfeited, interest at the legal rate was allowed after maturity.[79] Where a certain sum is due as liquidated damages on a contract, interest may be recovered upon it from the breach of the contract.[80] So interest is allowed on the amount due on an insurance policy from the time it was payable.[81]

[76] Brickell, J., in Alabama v. Lott, 69 Ala. 147, 155.

[77] *Georgia:* Robins v. Prior, 20 Ga. 561.

Illinois: Wilmans v. Bank of Illinois, 6 Ill. 667.

New Jersey: North R. M. Co. v. Christ Church, 22 N. J. L. 425; Rogers v. Colt, 21 N. J. L. 19.

New York: Sayre v. Austin, 3 Wend. 496.

Vermont: Sumner v. Beebe, 37 Vt. 562.

England: 1 Wms. Saund. 201, *n.;* Osbourne v. Hosier, 6 Mod. 167.

[78] *United States:* Loudon v. Shelby County Taxing Dist., 104 U. S. 771, 26 L. ed. 923; Crescent Min. Co. v. Wasatch Min. Co., 151 U. S. 317, 14 Sup. Ct. 348, 38 L. ed. 177; Thorndike v. United States, 2 Mas. 1.

Alabama: Murphy v. Andrews, 13 Ala. 708; Kitchen v. Branch Bank at Mobile, 14 Ala. 233.

Louisiana: Pawling v. Howren, 1 Rob. 229; Crosby v. Morton, 13 La. 357; Collins v. Sabatier, 19 La. Ann. 299; Citizens' Bank v. Baltz, 27 La. Ann. 106.

Maine: Swett v. Hooper, 62 Me. 54.

Massachusetts: Wood v. Corl, 4 Met. 203.

Missouri: Sturgess v. Crum, 29 Mo. App. 644.

New Jersey: Van Giesen v. Van Houten, 5 N. J. L. 822.

New York: Putnam v. Lewis, 8 Johns. 389.

North Carolina: McKinley v. Blackedge, 3 N. C. 28.

South Carolina: Ash v. Brewton, 1 Bay, 243.

England: Gibbs v. Fremont, 9 Ex. 25.

[79] Fisher v. Bidwell, 27 Conn. 363.

[80] *New Hampshire:* Mead v. Wheeler, 13 N. H. 351.

New Jersey: Hoagland v. Segur, 38 N. J. L. 230.

New York: Little v. Banks, 85 N. Y. 258; Winch v. Mutual B. I. Co., 86 N. Y. 618.

In *Texas,* from the filing of the suit. Yellow Pine L. Co. v. Carroll, 76 Tex. 135. In *Iowa,* interest is not allowed. Dunshee v. Standard Oil Co., 126 N. W. 342.

[81] *United States:* Field v. Insurance Co. of N. A., 6 Biss. 121; New Zealand Ins. Co. v. Earnmoor S. S. Co., 24 C. C. A. 644, 79 Fed. 368; Guarantee Co. v. Mechanics' Savings Bank & Trust Co., 80 Fed. 766.

Illinois: Home Ins., etc., Co. v. Myer, 93 Ill. 271; Catholic Knights of America v. Franke, 137 Ill. 118, 27 N. E. 86.

Interest is not allowable on the recovery of the whole amount of a premium note for the non-payment of an assessment, because it is a penalty and in no sense money due.[82]   But where the suit on the note is only for the amount of the assessments for losses actually incurred, interest is chargeable from the date when the assessments were payable.[83]

It is immaterial whether the contract broken was a parol or a written contract.[84]

§ 301a. Stockholders' liability.

A proceeding to hold a stockholder liable for the debts of the corporation may either be an action on a particular debt or a proceeding to compel the stockholder to pay to the corporation or its representative a fixed amount, assessed upon him.   In the former case if the stockholder is directly liable for the debt, and it is in itself a debt which bears interest, the stockholder is liable for interest as well as principal,[85] up to the total amount for which he is liable, at least from the beginning of action against him.[86]   Where an assessment is levied on the stockholder, interest runs upon the amount of the assessment from the time it is laid and payable.[87]

Louisiana: Gettwerth *v.* Teutonia Ins. Co., 29 La. Ann. 30; Pratt *v.* Manhattan L. Ins. Co., 47 La. Ann. 855, 17 So. 341.

Maryland: Baltimore F. Ins. Co. *v.* Loney, 20 Md. 20.

Massachusetts: Hardy *v.* Lancashire Ins. Co., 166 Mass. 210, 33 L. R. A. 241, 44 N. E. 209, 55 Am. St. Rep. 395.

New Hampshire: Swamscot M. Co. *v.* Partridge, 25 N. H. 369, 380.

Tennessee: Knights of Pythias *v.* Allen, 104 Tenn. 623, 58 S. W. 241.

Texas: Southwestern Ins. Co. *v.* Woods Nat. Bank, 107 S. W. 114 (Tex. Civ. App.).

[82] Bangs *v.* McIntosh, 23 Barb. 591; Bangs *v.* Bailey, 37 Barb. 630.

[83] Hyatt *v.* Wait, 37 Barb. 29.

[84] Cartmill *v.* Brown, 1 A. K. Marsh. 576, 10 Am. Dec. 763; Wells *v.* Hobbs, 122 S. W. 451 (Tex. Civ. App.).

[85] *California:* Knowles *v.* Sandercock, 107 Cal. 629, 40 Pac. 1047; Wells *v.* Enright, 127 Cal. 669, 60 Pac. 439.

Michigan: Grand Rapids Savings Bank *v.* Warren, 52 Mich. 557, 18 N. W. 356.

New York: Wheeler *v.* Miller, 90 N. Y. 353.

South Carolina: Sackett's Harbor Bank *v.* Blake, 3 Rich. Eq. 225.

[86] *Kansas:* Pine *v.* Western Nat. Bank, 63 Kan. 462, 65 Pac. 690.

Missouri: Millisack *v.* Moore, 76 Mo. App. 528.

New York: Burr *v.* Wilcox, 22 N. Y. 551; Handy *v.* Draper, 89 N. Y. 334.

[87] *United States:* Casey *v.* Galli, 94 U. S. 673, 24 L. ed. 168; Bowden *v.* Johnson, 107 U. S. 251, 2 Sup. Ct. 46, 27 L. ed. 386.

Nebraska: Davis *v.* Watkins, 56 Neb. 288, 76 N. W. 575.

See Berger *v.* Commercial Bank, 5

§ 301b. Contracts for the sale of land.

In actions upon contracts for the sale of land, and on claims growing out of such contracts, the possession of the land is ordinarily regarded as equivalent in value to the possession of the purchase money, and the rents of the land offset interest on the purchase-money. So where the purchaser of land took possession of it, but the time for conveyance was delayed, though without his fault, he was required to pay interest on the purchase-money; for though the delay was not his fault, and he was therefore not called upon to pay compensation on account of the delay, yet since he had taken the rents and profits (if any) he was bound to pay interest by way of compensation for the use of the land.[88] So a buyer of land who retains part of the price to secure removal of incumbrances by the seller, is chargeable with interest.[89] And interest runs on unpaid installments of the purchase-money.[90] If the pur-

Ohio S. & C. Pl. Dec. 277, 5 Ohio N. P. 176 (from time of action).

In Illinois no interest is allowed, as the statute does not provide for it. Munger v. Jacobson, 99 Ill. 349.

[88] *United States:* Sohier v. Williams, 2 Curt. C. C. 195; Jourolman v. Ewing, 80 Fed. 604, 26 C. C. A. 23.

Alabama: Broughton v. Mitchell, 64 Ala. 210.

Indiana: Conwell v. Claypool, 8 Blackf. 124.

Kentucky: Breckenridge v. Hoke, 4 Bibb, 272; Boyce v. Pritchett, 6 Dana, 231.

Louisiana: Liddell v. Rucker, 13 La. Ann. 569.

Massachusetts: Haven v. Grand J. R. R., 109 Mass. 88.

Missouri: Stephens v. Burgess, 69 Mo. 168.

New York: Stevenson v. Maxwell, 2 N. Y. 408.

North Carolina: McKay v. Melvin, 1 Ired. Eq. 73.

Oregon: Hoefler v. McGlinchy, 20 Ore. 360, 25 Pac. 1067.

Pennsylvania: Fasholt v. Reed, 16 S. & R. 266.

South Carolina: Rutledge v. Smith, 1 McCord Ch. 399 (*semble*).

Virginia: Selden v. James, 6 Rand. 665; Brockenbrough v. Blythe, 3 Leigh, 619.

West Virginia: Steenrod v. Wheeling P. & B. R. R., 27 W. Va. 1.

England: Ballard v. Shutt, 15 Ch. D. 122.

In Letcher v. Woodson, 15 Fed. Cas. No. 8,280, 1 Brock. 212, the allowance of interest was said to be within the discretion of the jury. And in Toms v. Boyes, 59 Mich. 386, 26 N. W. 646, under the special circumstances interest was not allowed, the possession being regarded as of no value.

[89] Bates v. Wynn, 7 Pa. Cas. 190, 11 Atl. 448.

[90] Lang v. Moole, 31 N. J. Eq. 413.

So if the purchaser has given a note for the purchase-money, he must pay interest on the note during the period of possession.

Alabama: Cullum v. Branch Bank, 4 Ala. 21, 37 Am. Dec. 425.

Texas: Yaws v. Jones, 19 S. W. 443.

chaser goes into possession and the contract is eventually wholly or in part rescinded or fails, either at the option of the purchaser because of fraud or breach of warranty or defect of title, or at the option of the vendor because the contract was invalid, and the purchaser recovers the purchase-money paid, he is not entitled to interest on the purchase-money during the time he had possession of the land and received the rents and profits; [91] but if he is compelled by the true owner to refund the rents and profits, he is entitled to interest.[92] So if the vendee was wrongfully kept out of possession by the vendor, in a suit for specific performance of the contract he may recover as damages the rents and profits during the time the land was withheld, but in that case the vendor would be allowed interest on the purchase-money during the same period; [93] but if the rents and profits are less than the interest, the vendee will not be called upon to pay interest, but the vendor will keep the rents and profits.[94]

Special circumstances may affect the obligation to pay interest. So a party may be barred of interest by his own

[91] *Georgia:* Whitlock *v.* Crew, 28 Ga. 289; Phillips *v.* O'Neal, 85 Ga. 142, 11 S. E. 581.

Kentucky: Talbot *v.* Sebree, 1 Dana, 56; Fox *v.* Longly, 1 A. K. Marsh. 388; Meriwether *v.* Lewis, 9 B. Mon. 163.

Oregon: Layton *v.* Hogue, 5 Ore. 93.

Contra, New York: Gillet *v.* Maynard, 5 Johns. 85, 4 Am. Dec. 329. See Warrall *v.* Munn, 38 N. Y. 151.

[92] Interest is recovered on the purchase-money of the land taken by the paramount owner for as many years back as the owner is entitled to recover the mesne profits.

Georgia: Fernander *v.* Dunn, 19 Ga. 497, 65 Am. Dec. 607.

New York: Caulkins *v.* Harris, 9 Johns. 324; Bennet *v.* Jenkins, 13 Johns. 50.

Pennsylvania: Rich *v.* Johnson, 2 Pin. 88, 52 Am. Dec. 144.

If the title to part of the land failed

and no possession was had, interest should be allowed on the part of the purchase-money recovered.

Iowa: McNear *v.* McComber, 18 Ia. 12.

Texas: McElyea *v.* Faires, 79 Tex. 243, 14 S. W. 1059.

And see Robbins *v.* Westmoreland Coal Co., 198 Pa. 301, 47 Atl. 873.

[93] *United States:* Hepburn *v.* Dunlop, 1 Wheat. 179, 4 L. ed. 65.

Minnesota: Abrahamson *v.* Lamberson, 68 Minn. 454, 71 N. W. 676.

Virginia: Huntley *v.* Lyons, 5 Munf. 342, 7 Am. Dec. 685.

[94] *Illinois:* Lombard *v.* Chicago Sinai Congregation, 64 Ill. 477.

New Jersey: King *v.* Buckman, 24 N. J. Eq. 556.

New York: Dias *v.* Glover, Hoff. Ch. 71; Selleck *v.* Tallman, 11 Daly, 141.

See Meagher *v.* Puckett, 42 S. W. 737, 44 S. W. 389, 19 Ky. L. Rep. 879.

fraud or laches or other misconduct.[95] A valid tender by the party in possession will of course put an end to his liability to interest.[96]

§ 301c. Legacies.

Interest is allowed on a pecuniary legacy from the time it should be paid over; which in most States is a year after the death of the testator.[97] This is true even though it is im-

[95] *Georgia:* Phillips v. O'Neal, 85 Ga. 142, 11 S. E. 581 (*semble*).

Kentucky: Grundy v. Grundy, 12 B. Mon. 269.

Montana: Finlen v. Heinze, 32 Mont. 354, 80 Pac. 918.

And see Faile v. Crawford, 30 App. Div. 536, 52 N. Y. Supp. 353.

[96] *United States:* Cheney v. Libby, 134 U. S. 68, 10 Sup. Ct. 498, 33 L. ed. 818 (tender at bank where note was payable).

South Carolina: Rutledge v. Smith, 1 McCord Ch. 399.

So if the money is set apart and appropriated to the use of the vendee, as by deposit in a bank; but only if due notice of that fact is given to him.

New York: Bostwick v. Beach, 103 N. Y. 414, 9 N. E. 41, 57 Am. Rep. 755.

West Virginia: Steenrod v. Wheeling, P. & B. R. R., 27 W. Va. 1.

England: Powell v. Martyr, 8 Ves. 146.

In Warren v. Banning, 140 N. Y. 227, 35 N. E. 428, an action to recover part of the purchase price of real estate, the money had been deposited with a trust company, to draw interest at 3%. Plaintiff obtained an order directing that the money remain on deposit until further order. It was held that this order was equivalent to a payment into court, and as plaintiff had restrained the defendant from using the money in any way except leaving it on deposit, he was not entitled to recover any greater rate of interest than the money earned. As

the bank paid 3% interest he could recover only at that rate.

[97] *Connecticut:* Bartlett v. Slater, 53 Conn. 102, 55 Am. Rep. 73, 22 Atl. 678.

Delaware: Custis v. Adkins, 1 Houst. 382, 68 Am. Dec. 422.

Kentucky: Chambers v. Chambers, 87 Ky. 144, 7 S. W. 620.

Massachusetts: Ogden v. Pattee, 149 Mass. 82, 14 Am. St. 401, 21 N. E. 227; Welch v. Adams, 152 Mass. 74, 25 N. E. 34, 9 L. R. A. 244; *In re* Bartlett, 163 Mass. 509, 40 N. E. 899.

Mississippi: Brownlee v. Steel, Walk. 179.

New Hampshire: Rice v. Boston, P. & S. A. Soc., 56 N. H. 191.

New Jersey: Dutch Church v. Ackerman, 1 N. J. Eq. 40; Hennion v. Jacobus, 27 N. J. Eq. 28; Welsh v. Brown, 43 N. J. L. 37.

North Carolina: Moore v. Pullen, 116 N. C. 284, 21 S. E. 195.

Ohio: Gray v. Case School of Applied Science, 62 Ohio St. 1, 56 N. E. 484.

Pennsylvania: King v. Diehl, 9 S. & R. 409.

Rhode Island: Wood v. Hammond, 16 R. I. 98, 17 Atl. 324.

South Carolina: Ingraham v. Postell, 1 McCord Ch. 94.

Tennessee: Mills v. Mills, 3 Head, 705; German v. German, 7 Cold. 180.

Vermont: Vermont S. B. C. v. Ladd, 58 Vt. 95.

In New York a legacy is payable one year from the granting of letters, not a year from the testator's death; and after some difference of opinion among

37

possible to get in the estate and pay out the legacy within the time,[98] and even if there is no one to receive the legacy at the time it is payable;[99] though any laches or unreasonable delay on the part of the legatee may bar his claim to interest.[100]

Interest on a legacy is not allowed because the executor is in default for not paying it, but merely because such is supposed to be the intention of the testator; and if by interpretation of the will a different intention appears, interest will not be allowed as in the ordinary case.[101] Thus if a time is fixed in the will for payment of the legacy later than the end of the year, interest will run from the time so fixed.[102] On the other

the courts it was finally held that interest does not run until the year from taking out administration. Matter of McGowan, 124 N. Y. 526, 26 N. E. 1089; Hiscock v. Fulton, 17 N. Y. Supp. 408; *In re* Austin's Will, 45 N. Y. Supp. 984.

The earlier cases had allowed interest from one year after death. Campbell v. Cowdery, 31 How. Pr. 172; Lawrence v. Embree, 3 Bradf. 364; Dustan v. Carter, 3 Dem. 149; Carr v. Bennett, 3 Dem. 433, 457; Devlin's Estate, Tucker, 460.

The year runs from the granting of temporary or special letters. Matter of McGowan, 124 N. Y. 526, 26 N. E. 1089.

In a few jurisdictions a distinction is made between general and specific legacies, and interest on specific legacies is allowed from the death of the testator.

Georgia: Graybill v. Warren, 4 Ga. 528.

Michigan: Wheeler v. Hatheway, 54 Mich. 550, 20 N. W. 579.

Tennessee: Darden v. Orgain, 5 Cold. 211 (*semble*).

Virginia: Quarles v. Quarles, 2 Munf. 321 (profit from use of slave).

In *Canada* no interest is allowed on arrears of an annuity. Goldsmith v. Goldsmith, 17 Grant Ch. 213; Crone v. Crone, 27 Grant Ch. 425.

[98] *New Jersey:* Hoagland v. Ex'r of

Schenck, 16 N. J. L. 370; Davis v. Rake, 44 N. J. Eq. 506, 16 Atl. 227; Warwick v. Ely, 59 N. J. Eq. 44, 44 Atl. 666.

Pennsylvania: Martin v. Martin, 6 Watts, 67.

Tennessee: Chappel v. Theus, 3 Tenn. Cas. 457.

[99] *Rhode Island:* Esmond v. Brown, 18 R. I. 48, 25 Atl. 652 (legatee had died and no administrator had been appointed).

Virginia: Lyon v. Magagno, 7 Gratt. 377.

[100] *District of Columbia:* Bohrer v. Otterback, 21 D. C. 32.

New Jersey: Adams v. Adams, 55 N. J. Eq. 42, 35 Atl. 827.

New York: Haight v. Pine, 10 App. Div. 470, 42 N. Y. Supp. 303.

[101] *In re* Vedder's Estate, 15 N. Y. Supp. 798, 17 N. Y. Supp. 93.

[102] *Connecticut:* Duffield v. Pike, 71 Conn. 521, 42 Atl. 641.

Illinois: Valentine v. Ruste, 93 Ill. 585 (on settlement of estate).

Kentucky: Trustees' Church Home v. Morris, 99 Ky. 317, 36 S. W. 2 (on condition).

Maryland: Von der Horst v. Von der Horst, 88 Md. 127, 41 Atl. 124 (on children coming of age).

Massachusetts: Kent v. Dunham, 106 Mass. 586 (three years after probate).

New Hampshire: Doten v. Doten,

hand, when the will shows an intention to have the legacy payable at once, as when it is a provision for the maintenance of the legatee, interest will be allowed from the date of the death.[103] And where the testator sets apart a particular fund to be used for paying the legacy or directs that a fund be invested for the legatee, interest will begin to run at once.[104] Since interest is not given for default of the executor, it cannot be claimed from the estate of a deceased executor.[105]

The rate of interest allowed on a legacy is the legal rate, regardless of the actual return on investments,[106] and is not compounded.[107]

66 N. H. 331, 20 Atl. 387 (on legatee reaching age of 18).

New York: Bradner v. Faulkner, 12 N. Y. 472.

Ohio: Langhorst v. Ahlers, 12 Ohio Dec. 405 (on legatee reaching age of 24).

South Carolina: Stephenson v. Axon, Bail. Eq. 274 (on legatee reaching age of 21).

Tennessee: Cannon v. Apperson, 14 Lea, 553 (on condition precedent).

But *contra, New Jersey:* Bonham v. Bonham, 38 N. J. Eq. 419 (after death of widow).

Where the estate is turned over to the residuary legatee on condition that he pay the legacies, he has been held not to be chargeable with interest on a legacy until demand. Gilbert v. Taylor, 148 N. Y. 298, 42 N. E. 713.

[103] *Annuity for maintenance:*

New York: Cooke v. Meeker, 36 N. Y. 15.

England: Newman v. Auling, 3 Atk. 579.

Provision for support of widow:

Delaware: Buson v. Elliott, 1 Del. Ch. 368.

Massachusetts: Pollard v. Pollard, 1 Allen, 490.

Provision for support of child, or one to whom the testator stood *in loco parentis:*

Delaware: Flinn v. Flinn, 4 Del. Ch. 44.

Maryland: Webb v. Webb, 92 Md. 101, 48 Atl. 95.

New Jersey: Howard v. Francis, 30 N. J. Eq. 444; Marsh v. Taylor, 43 N. J. Eq. 1, 10 Atl. 486.

New York: Brown v. Knapp, 79 N. Y. 136.

Pennsylvania: Magoffin v. Patton, 4 Rawle, 113.

This principle does not apply where the legatee has other means of support: Thorn v. Garner, 113 N. Y. 698, 21 N. E. 149; Morgan v. Valentine, 6 Dem. Surr. 18, 19 N. Y. St. 515; or where for other reasons the legacy does not appear to have been intended for support: *In re* Barnes' Estate, 7 App. Div. 13, 40 N. Y. Supp. 494.

[104] *Massachusetts:* Ayer v. Ayer, 128 Mass. 575.

Tennessee: Darden v. Orgain, 5 Cold. 211; Ensley v. Ensley, 105 Tenn. 107, 58 S. W. 288.

West Virginia: Couch v. Eastham, 29 W. Va. 784, 2 S. E. 23.

[105] *New Jersey:* Adams v. Adams, 55 N. J. Eq. 42, 35 Atl. 827.

England: Blogg v. Johnson, L. R. 2 Ch. 225.

[106] Welch v. Adams, 152 Mass. 74, 25 N. E. 34, 9 L. R. A. 244. If the estate does not earn the legal rate, it has been held within the discretion of the court to allow the rate actually received. *In re* Stanfield's Estate, 18 N. Y. Supp. 913.

[107] *Massachusetts:* Welch v. Adams,

Interest is not usually charged on advancements,[108] unless there are exceptional circumstances or special provisions in the will.

§ 302. Time from which interest runs.

In each case all the circumstances of the transaction must be considered in order to determine when the defendant was in default. Where the money is payable at a fixed time, interest is allowed from that time.[109] Where payment is postponed to some future day, or till the happening of some event, interest should be allowed from that day, or from the happening of that event. So where an insurance policy makes the loss payable sixty days after notice and proof of loss, interest is to be allowed from the expiration of the sixty days, and not from the adjustment of the loss.[110] Similarly on a contract

152 Mass. 74, 25 N. E. 34, 9 L. R. A. 244.

New York: Brown *v.* Knapp, 79 N. Y. 136.

Pennsylvania: English *v.* Harvey, 2 Rawle, 305.

[108] *Virginia:* Cabell *v.* Puryear, 27 Gratt. 902.

England: Middleton *v.* Moore, [1897] 2 Ch. 169.

So where a son had his debts paid by his father it was held that the payments by the father, being advancements to the son, would draw interest only from his death. Steele *v.* Frierson, 85 Tenn. 430, 3 S. W. 649.

[109] *United States:* Tilden *v.* Blair, 21 Wall. 241, 22 L. ed. 632; *In re* Bartenbach, 2 Fed. Cas. No. 1,068.

California: Martin *v.* Ede, 103 Cal. 157, 37 Pac. 199; Knowles *v.* Baldwin, 125 Cal. 224, 57 Pac. 988.

Florida: Hanover F. I. Co. *v.* Lewis, 28 Fla. 209, 10 So. 297.

Georgia: Ainsley *v.* Jordan, 61 Ga. 482.

Illinois: Heiman *v.* Schroeder, 74 Ill. 158.

Minnesota: Owsley *v.* Greenwood, 18 Minn. 429.

Mississippi: Wheeless v. Williams, 62 Miss. 369, 52 Am. Rep. 190.

Missouri: Ayres *v.* Hayes, 13 Mo. 252; Lancaster *v.* Elliott, 55 Mo. App. 249.

Oregon: Hawkins *v.* Citizens' Investment Co., 38 Ore. 544, 64 Pac. 320.

Wisconsin: Atkinson *v.* Richardson, 15 Wis. 594; Shipman *v.* State, 44 Wis. 458.

England: Fooks *v.* Horner, [1896] 2 Ch. 188.

In Louisiana there must be some act to put the debtor in default. Gas Bank *v.* Desha, 19 La. 459; Burton *v.* Chaney, 3 La. Ann. 338.

[110] *United States:* Unsell *v.* Hartford L. & Annuity Ins. Co., 32 Fed. 443.

Alabama: Home Ins. Co. *v.* Adler, 71 Ala. 516.

Arkansas: Southern Ins. Co. *v.* White, 58 Ark. 277, 24 S. W. 425.

New Hampshire: Nevins *v.* Rockingham M. F. I. Co., 25 N. H. 22.

New York: Hastings *v.* Westchester Fire Ins. Co., 73 N. Y. 141.

But see Knights Templars & M. L. I. Co. *v.* Crayton, 110 Ill. App. 648, affirmed 209 Ill. 550, 70 N. E. 1066, where interest was allowed from proof of loss.

for work and labor, when the balance was due under the contract act in thirty days after full completion, plaintiffs were entitled to interest by way of damages from the time when the balance should have been paid according to the contract.[111] Where plaintiff built a party wall under agreement with defendant, who then used it to support his building without paying his share, the court held that defendant was liable for interest from the time when he failed to pay the amount due under the contract.[112] Where defendant promised in writing to pay a certain sum out of the proceeds of his present crop when sold, the sum bears interest from the time of sale of the crops or a reasonable time thereafter.[113] Where labor was to be paid for in mortgages and promissory notes, it was held that interest could only be allowed from the time the notes would have fallen due.[114] Where a lunatic transferred stock, and afterward sued the corporation to recover dividends, interest was held recoverable on the dividends from the time the lunacy was judicially established, to the knowledge of the corporation.[115] And so generally, when anything is to be done or to happen before a sum of money is payable, interest runs from the event.[116] Where the original contract was barred by

On a similar policy where there was waiver of proof of loss, interest should run from the end of sixty days after the waiver. East Texas F. Ins. Co. v. Brown, 82 Tex. 631, 18 S. W. 713. For similar cases see Queen Ins. Co. v. Jefferson Ice Co., 64 Tex. 578. But in a Washington case it was held that the provision itself was waived by an agreement to arbitrate so that assured would be entitled to interest from the time when the loss occurred. Glover v. Rochester German Insurance Co., 11 Wash. 142, 39 Pac. 380.

See also: Rogers v. Manhattan Life Insurance Co., 138 Cal. 285, 71 Pac. 348. Where the insurance company denied all liability it was held that despite such a provision interest would run from the date of the loss. W. & A. Pipe Lines v. Home Insurance Co., 145 Pa. 346, 22 Atl. 665.

[111] Donahue v. Partridge, 160 Mass. 336, 35 N. E. 1071.

[112] Huston v. DeZeng, 78 Mo. App. 522.

[113] Hutchins v. Wade, 20 Tex. 7. So where money was to be paid out of the profits of a patent, interest runs only from the time the profits are received. Howard v. Johnston, 82 N. Y. 271.

[114] Tiernan v. Granger, 65 Ill. 351.

[115] Chew v. Bank of Baltimore, 14 Md. 299.

[116] *United States:* New Orleans v. Warner, 175 U. S. 120, 147, 20 Sup. Ct. 120, 44 L. ed. 96 (drainage warrants, not payable until presentation for payment, no interest until presentation); Smythe v. U. S., 188 U. S. 156, 28 Sup. Ct. 279, 47 L. ed. 425, affirming 107 Fed. 376, 46 C. C. A. 354 (bond of public officer, no in-

the statute of limitations, but the debt was acknowledged by a new promise in writing, it was held that interest could be recovered from the time when the debt was first due, since recovery was on the original debt.[117]

§ 302a. Interest on money payable on demand.

When a sum of money is payable on demand, or no time of payment is fixed, interest runs only from the time of demand.[118]

terest on balance of account till account stated).

Alabama: Folmar *v.* Carlisle, 117 Ala. 449, 23 So. 551 (purchase price of land, not payable until incumbrances removed, no interest until land freed from incumbrances).

California: Tally *v.* Ganahla, 151 Cal. 418, 90 Pac. 1049 (contract price payable on architect's certificate. Interest payable from time certificate given).

Illinois: Phillips *v.* Edsall, 127 Ill. 535, 20 N. E. 801 (attorney's fee due when amount of an award made by commissioners; interest from decree fixing the award); Hall *v.* Virginia, 91 Ill. 535 (subscription for building; no interest until building constructed); Pearson *v.* Sanderson, 128 Ill. 88, 21 N. E. 200, affirming 28 Ill. App. 571 (price of improvements, value to be fixed by appraisers according to terms of lease. Interest from date of appraisal).

Kentucky: Schmidt *v.* Louisville & N. R. R., 95 Ky. 289, 25 S. W. 494, 26 S. W. 547, 15 Ky. L. Rep. 785 (bonds payable out of net earnings of a branch road; interest from time net earnings were realized which should have been applied on the bonds).

Missouri: Risley *v.* Andrew County, 46 Mo. 382 (payment to be made as soon as bridge is finished; no interest till that time).

Nebraska: Murphy *v.* Omaha, 33 Neb. 402, 50 N. W. 265 (balance of contract price payable six months after completion of work; interest from expiration of the six months).

New York: Lawrence *v.* Church, 128 N. Y. 324, 28 N. E. 499 (payment of $3,000 in such manner as might be acceptable: no liability until demand or suit); Palmer *v.* North, 35 Barb. 282 (amount payable if plaintiff does not contest will; interest from time will is allowed); Binsse *v.* Wood, 47 Barb. 624 (time for rent to begin to be fixed by arbitration; no interest until award).

Wisconsin: Morawetz *v.* McGovern, 68 Wis. 312, 32 N. W. 290.

England: Pinhorn *v.* Tuckington, 3 Campb. 468 (award fixed amount and time of payment; interest from the time fixed).

Canada: Towsley *v.* Wythes, 16 U. C. Q. B. 139 (indebtedness fixed by award to be paid at certain time; interest from the time fixed).

[117] Suber *v.* Richards, 61 S. C. 393, 39 S. E. 540.

[118] *Arkansas:* Parker *v.* Gaines, 11 S. W. 693.

California: Buttner *v.* Smith, 36 Pac. 652.

Minnesota: Horn *v.* Hansen, 56 Minn. 43, 57 N. W. 315, 22 L. R. A. 617.

Missouri: Burgess *v.* Cave, 52 Mo. 43; York *v.* Farmers' Bank, 105 Mo. 127, 79 S. W. 968.

New York: Hanley *v.* Crowe, 3 N. Y. Supp. 154; Irlbacker *v.* Roth, 25 App. Div. 290, 49 N. Y. Supp. 538.

Canada: Jones *v.* Brown, 9 U. C. C. P. 201.

When the time of payment is to be fixed by a future event, and the debtor

So upon a demand note interest runs from time of demand only.[119] And sureties on a bond are liable for interest only from the time demand is made on them for payment.[120] And interest when recoverable on a claim against a city can be exacted only from the time of demand for payment, where such demand is necessary.[121] So on a bank check, bank note, or deposit interest is due only from the time of presentment or demand for payment;[122] and a sum of money deposited

has no means of knowing when the event happens, interest does not run until demand or notice of the event.

Kentucky: Hodges v. Holeman, 2 Dana, 396 (note payable after all incumbrances removed).

Michigan: Stevens v. Corbitt, 33 Mich. 458 (subscription payable after completion of railroad).

[119] *Kentucky:* Bartlett v. Marshall, 2 Bibb, 467 (see Francis v. Castleman, 4 Bibb, 383; Dillon v. Dudley, 1 A. K. Marsh. 65; Nelson v. Cartmel, 6 Dana, 7; Gore v. Buck, 1 T. B. Mon. 209; Cook v. Clark's Committee, 21 Ky. L. Rep. 316, 51 S. W. 316.

Massachusetts: Taft v. Stoddard, 142 Mass. 545, 8 N. E. 586.

Michigan: Nye v. Lothrop, 94 Mich. 411, 54 N. W. 178.

New York: Sanford v. Crocheron, 8 N. Y. Civ. Proc. 146.

Pennsylvania: Breyfogle v. Beckley, 16 S. & R. 264.

South Carolina: Cannon v. Beggs, 1 McCord, 370, 10 Am. Dec. 677.

Contra, Arkansas: Pullen v. Chase, 4 Ark. 210; Causin v. Taylor, 4 Ark. 408; Walker v. Wills, 5 Ark. 166.

Connecticut: Curtis v. Smith, 75 Conn. 429, 53 Atl. 902.

Texas: Henry v. Roe, 83 Tex. 446, 18 S. W. 806 (from date by statute).

In Adams v. Adams, 55 N. J. Eq. 42, 35 Atl. 827, it was held that such a note does not bear interest in any case.

A note payable on demand after a certain future day has been held to bear

interest from that day. Larrabee v. Southard, 95 Me. 385, 50 Atl. 20.

[120] *Georgia:* Frink v. Southern Exp. Co., 82 Ga. 33, 8 S. E. 862, 3 L. R. A. 482.

Massachusetts: Heath v. Gay, 10 Mass. 371.

Pennsylvania: U. S. v. Poulson, 19 W. N. C. 500.

South Carolina: Stevens v. Simmons, 1 McCord, 28.

Where, however, a bond is given, conditioned for the payment of money, and it is not made payable either upon demand or at a fixed time, it is held that interest runs from the date of the bond.

New York: Purdy v. Philips, 11 N. Y. 406.

North Carolina: Freeland v. Edwards, 3 N. C. 49, 2 Am. Dec. 620.

Tennessee: Collier v. Gray, 1 Overt. 110.

Virginia: Kent v. Kent, 28 Gratt. 840; McVeigh v. Howard, 87 Va. 599, 13 S. E. 31.

[121] *Massachusetts:* Boott Cotton Mills v. Lowell, 159 Mass. 383, 34 N. E. 367 (abatement of tax).

New York: Phillips v. Cudlipp, 50 How. Pr. 363 (award for land).

[122] *United States:* New York Nat. Bank v. Mechanics' Nat. Bank, 94 U. S. 437, 24 L. ed. 176; Andrus v. Bradley, 102 Fed. 54.

Arkansas: Ringo v. Biscoe, 13 Ark. 563.

California: Anderson v. Pacific Bank, 112 Cal. 598, 44 Pac. 1063, 53 Am. St. Rep. 228, 32 L. R. A. 479.

with the defendant as security for a debt does not bear interest.[123]

As to what will constitute a demand for the purpose of giving interest, anything which calls the attention of the debtor to the creditor's desire for payment is enough. A meeting of the parties at which a settlement is attempted will operate as a demand;[124] so will calling for and taking security.[125] A written acknowledgment by the debtor of a demand by the creditor is enough; so is a partial payment.[126] If no demand is made prior to the commencement of the action,

Colorado: Patten *v.* American Nat. Bank, 15 Colo. App. 479, 63 Pac. 424.

Illinois: Niblack *v.* Park Nat. Bank, 169 Ill. 517, 48 N. E. 438; Springfield Nat. Bank *v.* Coleman, 11 Ill. App. 508.

Iowa: Hall *v.* Farmers' Sav. Bank, 55 Ia. 612, 8 N. W. 448.

Louisiana: Faucette *v.* New Orleans, 11 La. Ann. 199; Fogle *v.* Delmas, 11 La. Ann. 200.

Michigan: Beardsley *v.* Webber, 104 Mich. 88, 62 N. W. 173.

New Hampshire: Bank of Commissioners *v.* Security Trust Co., 70 N. H. 536, 49 Atl. 113 (assignee of insolvent bank should allow interest from date of appointment).

New York: Cooper *v.* Townsend, 59 Hun, 624, 13 N. Y. Supp. 760; Bank Comrs. *v.* La Fayette Bank, 4 Edw. 287.

North Carolina: Crawford *v.* Wilmington Bank, 61 N. C. 136.

Ohio: Citizens' Nat. Bank *v.* Brown, 45 Ohio St. 39, 11 N. E. 799, 4 Am. St. Rep. 526.

Oregon: Baker *v.* Williams Banking Co., 42 Ore. 213, 70 Pac. 711.

England: In re Herefordshire Banking Co., L. R. 4 Eq. 250.

Where checks could not be paid because there was no money in bank, it was held that interest would run from the day when the checks were payable.

Culver *v.* Marks, 122 Ind. 554, 23 N. E. 1086.

And where the deposit was paid out on a forged order interest was held to run from the time of such payment. German Savings Bank *v.* Citizens' Nat. Bank, 101 Iowa, 530, 70 N. W. 769, 63 Am. St. Rep. 399.

[123] Hellman *v.* Merz, 112 Cal. 661, 44 Pac. 1079 (deposit on purchase price).

Deposit to secure a bid:

Colorado: Denver *v.* Hayes, 28 Colo. 110, 63 Pac. 311.

New York: Delafield *v.* Westfield, 169 N. Y. 582, 62 N. E. 1095 (affirming 41 App. Div. 24, 58 N. Y. Supp. 277.

Deposit in court: Oliphant *v.* Frost, 9 Pa. 308.

But where on a purchase of land earnest money was paid, to be returned if examination showed defective title it was held that plaintiff could recover interest from the time when the title was found to be defective. Fields *v.* Baum, 35 Mo. App. 511.

Interest may be recovered from demand for return:

Barrere *v.* Somps, 113 Cal. 97, 45 Pac. 177.

[124] Gleason *v.* Briggs, 28 Vt. 135.

[125] Etheridge *v.* Binney, 9 Pick. (Mass.) 272.

[126] *Louisiana:* Levistones *v.* Marigny, 13 La. Ann. 353 (demand).

Canada: Hard *v.* Palmer, 21 U. C. Q. B. 49 (payment).

interest from that time can be recovered; the commencement of the action is a demand.[127]

§ 303. Money illegally acquired or used.

Where a party knowingly keeps money which he has no right to, he is chargeable with interest from the time he should have paid it over.[128] Thus where a defendant is sued for money fraudulently obtained, he is chargeable with interest from the time of receiving the money.[129] So he is chargeable with in-

---

[127] *United States:* New Orleans *v.* Warner, 175 U. S. 120, 147, 44 L. ed. 96, 20 Sup. Ct. 44; Kaufman *v.* Tredway, 195 U. S. 271, 25 Sup. Ct. 33, 49 L. ed. 190; Gammell *v.* Skinner, 2 Gall. 45; U. S. Bank *v.* Magill, 2 Fed. Cas. No. 929, 1 Paine, 661.

Alabama: Hunter *v.* Wood, 54 Ala. 71.

Colorado: Mulligan *v.* Smith, 32 Colo. 404, 76 Pac. 1063.

Indiana: Smith *v.* Blair, 133 Ind. 367, 32 N. E. 1123; White River School Township *v.* Dorrell, 26 Ind. App. 538, 59 N. E. 867.

Iowa: Hall *v.* Farmers' & C. S. B. 55 Ia. 612; Hubenthal *v.* Kennedy, 76 Ia. 707, 39 N. W. 694.

Kentucky: Patrick *v.* Clay, 4 Bibb, 246.

Maine: House *v.* McKenney, 46 Me. 94.

Massachusetts: Hunt *v.* Nevers, 15 Pick. 500; Harrison *v.* Conlan, 10 All. 85; Thwing *v.* Great Western I. Co., 111 Mass. 93; Gay *v.* Rooke, 151 Mass. 115, 23 N. E. 835, 21 Am. St. Rep. 434, 7 L. R. A. 392.

Michigan: Brion *v.* Kennedy, 47 Mich. 499, 11 N. W. 288; Nye *v.* Lothrop, 94 Mich. 411, 54 N. W. 178; Beardsley *v.* Webber, 104 Mich. 88, 62 N. W. 173.

Missouri: Wolff *v.* Matthews, 98 Mo. 246, 11 S. W. 563; Patterson *v.* Missouri Glass Co., 72 Mo. App. 492; Shinn *v.* Wooderson, 95 Mo. App. 6, 75 S. W. 687.

New Jersey: Scudder *v.* Morris, 3 N. J. L. 318, 4 Am. Dec. 322.

New York: Rawson *v.* Grow, 4 E. D. Smith, 18.

[128] *United States:* Bischoffsheim *v.* Baltzer, 21 Fed. 531; New Orleans *v.* Fisher, 34 C. C. A. 15, 91 Fed. 574 (city kept money raised for school purposes; creditors of school board may get interest).

Alabama: Whitworth *v.* Hart, 22 Ala. 343 (widow having estate withheld it).

Colorado: Enterprise Loan Bldg. Society *v.* Balin, 12 Colo. App. 304, 55 Pac. 740 (building society refused to pay withdrawal value of stock).

Illinois: Jenkins *v.* Doolittle, 69 Ill. 415 (defendant given money to pay debts withheld portion, on claim it was compensation for services).

Iowa: Howe *v.* Jones, 71 Iowa, 92, 32 N. W. 187 (holder of disputed fund must pay interest from date of judgment settling disposition of fund).

[129] *United States:* Doggett *v.* Emerson, 7 Fed. Cas. No. 3,962, 1 Woodb. & M. 195.

Massachusetts: Wood *v.* Robbins, 11 Mass. 504, 6 Am. Dec. 182; Eaton *v.* Mellus, 7 Gray, 566; Atlantic N. B. *v.* Harris, 118 Mass. 147; Manufacturers' N. B. *v.* Perry, 144 Mass. 313, 11 N. E. 81.

Missouri: Arthur *v.* Wheeler & W. Mfg. Co., 12 Mo. App. 335.

North Carolina: Silver V. M. Co. *v.* Baltimore G. & S. M. & S. Co., 99 N. C. 445.

terest on money illegally exacted and paid under protest,[130] as for instance on taxes illegally assessed;[131] and generally on money improperly received.[132]

When money is received by a party who improperly converts it to his own use, he must pay interest from the time of such conversion.[133] So when money has been improperly withheld

But according to a South Carolina case, interest will not be due if defendant can show he did not use the money, the burden of proof being on him. Southern R. R. v. Greenville, 49 S. C. 449, 27 S. E. 652.

[130] *United States:* Stewart v. Schell, 31 Fed. 65.

South Carolina: Goddard v. Bulow, 1 Nott & McCord, 45, 9 Am. Dec. 663 (overpayments of freight).

Texas: Galveston County v. Galveston Gas Co., 72 Tex. 509, 10 S. W. 583.

Wisconsin: Graham v. Chicago, M. & S. P. Ry., 53 Wis. 473, 10 N. W. 609 (overpayment of freight).

[131] *United States:* Erskine v. Van Arsdale, 15 Wall. 75, 21 L. ed. 63; Burrough v. Abel, 105 Fed. 366 (where suit delayed for 30 years, interest only from date of writ).

Massachusetts: Boston & S. Glass Co. v. Boston, 4 Met. 181 (but if no protest at time of payment, interest from date of writ only: Boston Water Power Co. v. Boston, 9 Met. 199; Van Hise v. Board of Supervisors, 48 N. Y. Supp. 874).

New Hampshire: Boston & M. R. R. v. State, 63 N. H. 571; Amoskeag Mfg. Co. v. Manchester, 70 N. H. 336, 47 Atl. 74.

[132] *United States:* Picketson v. Wright, 3 Sum. 335 (proceeds of cargo held on debt of former owner).

Alabama: Smith v. Alexander, 87 Ala. 387, 6 So. 51 (fund paid into court on bill of interpleader, and paid out to one party, not the prevailing one, on motion pending suit).

Connecticut: Coughlin v. McElroy, 74 Conn. 397, 50 Atl. 1025 (person illegally

acting as tax collector retained commission for his services).

Massachusetts: Atlantic Bank v. Harris, 118 Mass. 147 (defendant put in bill and received money for an expenditure which he had not in fact made); otherwise when the payment was legal when made: Walker v. Bradley, 3 Pick. 261 (claim of creditor paid in full by administrator, estate proved insolvent; interest only from demand for repayment).

New York: Cowing v. Howard, 46 Barb. 579 (rents and profits received by disseisor).

Texas: Hiedenheimer v. Johnson, 76 Tex. 200, 13 S. W. 46 (funds withdrawn from court by party finally defeated); Bennett v. Latham, 18 Tex. Civ. App. 403, 45 S. W. 934 (payment for land was too much because of deficiency in amount of land; interest on overpayment).

Wisconsin: Webster v. Douglass County, 102 Wis. 181, 77 N. W. 885, 78 N. W. 451, 72 Am. St. Rep. 870 (public officer illegally withdrew money from treasury for expenditures).

[133] *United States:* Harrison v. Perea, 168 U. S. 311, 324, 42 L. ed. 478, 18 Sup. Ct. 129.

Alabama: Kirkman v. Vanlier, 7 Ala. 217; Lewis v. Bradford, 8 Ala. 632.

California: White v. Lyons, 42 Cal. 279.

Colorado: Brown v. First Nat. Bank, 113 Pac. 483.

Georgia: American Trust & Banking Co. v. Boone, 102 Ga. 202, 29 S. E. 182, 66 Am. St. Rep. 167, 40 L. R. A. 250.

Illinois: Robbins v. Laswell, 58 Ill. 203; Stern v. People, 102 Ill. 540; Cas-

by a public officer,[134] or where a sheriff retains money after the return day of the execution,[135] he is liable for interest. So, in an action on a constable's bond, for not paying over money collected by him under an execution, it was held that interest should be allowed.[136] The same principle applies to a public officer who claims and receives fees in excess of those to which he is entitled.[137] In Jefferson City Savings Association v. Morrison,[138] the plaintiff, as assignee, brought an action for money had and received. The action was based on a receipt stating that part of the money was to be placed to the account of the assignor of the chose in action on an obligation of his to a third party. The defendant having failed to place it to his account, interest on the amount was given. In delivering the decision the following language was used by the court: "Where money is received by a party who applies it to his own use, or otherwise detains it, it is but just that he should pay interest upon the money so used or detained, and the courts of this country hold him to that liability. If,

sady v. Trustees of Schools, 105 Ill. 560; Currier v. Kretzinger, 162 Ill. 511, 48 N. E. 882, 58 Ill. App. 288.

Kansas: Cummins v. Heald, 24 Kan. 600, 36 Am. Rep. 264.

Kentucky: Taylor v. Knox, 1 Dana, 391; Kenton Ins. Co. v. First Nat. Bank, 93 Ky. 129, 19 S. W. 185.

Maryland: Andrews v. Clark, 72 Md. 396, 20 Atl. 429; McShane v. Howard Bank, 73 Md. 135, 20 Atl. 776, 10 L. R. A. 552.

Massachusetts: Hubbard v. Charlestown B. R. R., 11 Met. 124; Goff v. Rehoboth, 2 Cush. 475; Hill v. Hunt, 9 Gray, 66; Dunlap v. Watson, 124 Mass. 305; Crabtree v. Randall, 133 Mass. 552; Moors v. Washburn, 159 Mass. 173, 34 N. E. 182.

Mississippi: Tarpley v. Wilson, 33 Miss. 467.

New Hampshire: Hudson v. Tenney, 6 N. H. 456.

New York: Lynch v. DeViar, 3 Johns. Cas. 303; People v. Gasherie, 9 Johns. 71; Greenly v. Hopkins, 10 Wend. 96; White v. Smith, 54 N. Y. 522; Griggs v.

Griggs, 56 N. Y. 504; Holden v. New York Central Bank, 72 N. Y. 286; New York v. Sands, 39 Hun, 519.

Pennsylvania: Com. v. Crevor, 3 Binn. 121.

Vermont: Crane v. Thayer, 18 Vt. 162; Blodgett v. Converse, 60 Vt. 410, 15 Atl. 109.

Wisconsin: School Dist. v. Dreutzer, 51 Wis. 153.

England: London Bank v. White, L. R. 4 App. Cas. 413.

[134] *Colorado:* Gartley v. People, 28 Colo. 227, 64 Pac. 208.

Louisiana: Natchitoches v. Redmond, 28 La. Ann. 274.

Maine: Brunswick v. Snow, 73 Me. 177.

[135] Slingerland v. Swart, 13 Johns. (N. Y.) 255; Crane v. Dygert, 4 Wend. (N. Y.) 675; Paige v. Willet, 38 N. Y. 28; Thompson v. Sweet, 73 N. Y. 622.

[136] Magner v. Knowles, 67 Ill. 325.

[137] Tucker v. State, 163 Ind. 403, 71 N. E. 140.

[138] 48 Mo. 273.

therefore, the defendant in this cause applied the funds intrusted to him to his own use, or otherwise improperly detained them, he should be held liable for the interest." And so generally interest is due upon money retained after it should have been paid over.[139]

§ 304. Money paid out for the defendant.

Where money is advanced to a party at his request, or by one who is entitled to make such advances (as an agent or trustee), the money advanced bears interest from the time it is paid out.[140] So where the plaintiff has been compelled to pay money for which, in equity, he must be reimbursed by the defendant (as when he was surety for the defendant), he may recover interest from the time of payment.[141] Since this

[139] Haines v. Stilwell, 40 Pac. 332 (money retained after rescission of contract).

Minnesota: Perkins v. Stewart, 75 Minn. 21, 77 N. W. 434 (surplus received by mortgagee on foreclosure sale).

Missouri: Benton v. Craig, 2 Mo. 198 (retainer paid to lawyer; interest due from time he failed to perform the services).

[140] *Georgia:* Howard v. Behn, 27 Ga. 174.

Illinois: Underhill v. Gaff, 48 Ill. 198; Cease v. Cockle, 76 Ill. 484; Perrin v. Parker, 126 Ill. 201, 9 Am. St. Rep. 571, 18 N. E. 747, 2 L. R. A. 336.

Iowa: Goodnow v. Litchfield, 63 Ia. 275, 19 N. W. 226; Goodnow v. Plumbe, 64 Ia. 672, 21 N. W. 133.

Kentucky: Taylor v. Knox, 1 Dana, 391.

Massachusetts: Winthrop v. Carleton, 12 Mass. 4; Weeks v. Hasty, 13 Mass. 218; Gibbs v. Bryant, 1 Pick. 118; Isley v. Jewett, 2 Met. 168; Haven v. Grand Junction R. R., 109 Mass. 88; French v. French, 126 Mass. 360.

Missouri: Chamberlain v. Smith, 1 Mo. 718.

New Hampshire: Ashuelot R. R. v. Elliot, 57 N. H. 397.

New York: Jackson v. Campbell, 5 Wend. 572; Gillet v. Van Rensselaer, 15 N. Y. 397; Woerz v. Schumacher, 161 N. Y. 530, 56 N. E. 72; Eldred v. Eames, 48 Hun, 253.

Pennsylvania: Milne v. Rempublicam, 3 Yeates, 102; Sims v. Willing, 8 S. & R. 103; Dilworth v. Tinderling, 1 Bin. 488, 2 Am. Dec. 469.

Rhode Island: Hodges v. Hodges, 9 R. I. 32.

South Carolina: Cheesborough v. Hunter, 1 Hill, 400; Sollee v. Meugy, 1 Bail. 620; Walters v. McGirt, 8 Rich. 287; Barr v. Haseldon, 10 Rich. Eq. 53.

Texas: Grimes v. Hagood, 19 Tex. 246.

Wisconsin: Fisk v. Brunette, 30 Wis. 102.

England: Craven v. Tickell, 1 Ves. Jr., 60.

So simple interest will run on overdraft on a bank. Dawes v. Dinger, 2 Camp. 486. And on advancements by an administrator for the estate, *post,* § 311b.

[141] *Arkansas:* Collier v. Cowger, 52 Ark. 322, 12 S. W. 702.

California: Smith v. Johnson, 23 Cal. 63.

Kentucky: Miles v. Bacon, 4 J. J. Marsh. 457.

is recovered as damages, it should be at the legal rate, no matter what was the rate due on the obligation discharged by the surety.[142]

In a suit for contribution between co-sureties, the plaintiff may recover interest;[143] so in a suit against a co-tenant for recovery of the defendant's share of the expenditure for improvements, or plaintiff's share of the profits.[144] Where two parties are to advance money equally for a common undertaking, one who advances more than his share is entitled to interest on the excess.[145] And where plaintiffs had satisfied mechanics' liens which had attached to their buildings because defendant, a contractor, had failed to pay his workmen, it was held that they were entitled to interest from the time of the

New York: Hastie v. De Peyster, 3 Cai. 190; Corn Exch. Bank v. Nassau Bank, 91 N. Y. 74, 43 Am. Rep. 655; Foley v. Foley, 15 App. Div. 276, 44 N. Y. Supp. 588; McKeon v. Wendelken, 25 Misc. 711, 55 N. Y. Supp. 626.

South Carolina: Thompson v. Stevens, 2 N. & McC. 493; Sims v. Goudelock, 7 Rich. 23.

Texas: Texarkana & F. S. Ry. v. Hartford Ins. Co., 17 Tex. Civ. App. 498, 44 S. W. 533.

Virginia: Garland v. Garland, 24 S. E. 505.

England: Petre v. Duncombe, 15 Jur. 86, 20 L. J. Q. B. 242.

Canada: Munsie v. Lindsay, 11 Ont. 520.

[142] *California:* Smith v. Johnson, 23 Cal. 63; Randall v. Duff, 107 Cal. 33, 40 Pac. 20.

Missouri: Newman v. Newman, 29 Mo. App. 649. It has been held in Georgia, however, that the surety, being substituted for the principal creditor, could recover interest only if it was due on the principal obligation, and at the rate there stipulated. Knight v. Mantz, 1 Ga. Dec. 22. And this is provided by statute in Indiana. Goodwin v. Davis, 15 Ind. App. 120, 43 N. E. 881.

[143] *United States:* Allen v. Fairbanks, 45 Fed. 445.

Kentucky: Goodloe v. Clay, 6 B. Mon. 236; Breckinridge v. Taylor, 5 Dana, 110.

South Carolina: Aikin v. Peay, 5 Strobh. 15.

So in a suit for contribution between stockholders. Allen v. Fairbanks, 45 Fed. 445.

[144] *California:* Young v. Polack, 3 Cal. 208.

New York: Myers v. Bolton, 157 N. Y. 393, 52 N. E. 114; Scott v. Guernsey, 60 Barb. 163, 180.

Pennsylvania: McGowan v. Bailey, 179 Pa. 470, 36 Atl. 325.

Virginia: Early v. Friend, 16 Gratt. 21.

West Virginia: Vance v. Evans, 11 W. Va. 342.

But where the plaintiff had acquiesced in defendant's claim of sole ownership for many years, and finally claimed co-ownership successfully it was held that he was entitled to interest on his share of the rents and profits only from the commencement of the suit. Clark v. Hershy, 52 Ark. 473, 12 S. W. 1077.

[145] *Illinois:* Buckmaster v. Grundy, 8 Ill. 626.

Pennsylvania: Harris v. Mercur, 202 Pa. 318, 51 Atl. 971.

judgment under which the liens attached.[146]　A joint debtor who has paid more than his share of the debt, can also recover interest on whatever he has paid beyond his share.[147]

It is usually held that money lent by the plaintiff to the defendant in the absence of agreement bears interest from the time of the loan.[148]　But it is different where money is advanced as a family arrangement, without the expectation of profit, as in case of advancement.[149]　So where plaintiff had supported his father, with the agreement that he should be paid out of the father's estate, it was held that he could not recover interest from the estate, after his father's death.[150]

§ 305. Money had and received by the defendant.

Where a defendant, as for instance a mere depositary or disbursing agent, rightfully held money belonging to the plaintiff, he is liable for interest only after a demand for payment.[151] So where an agent receives money for his principal and is under no obligation, by contract or otherwise, immediately to pay it over, the principal can recover interest only after demand.[152]

[146] McFall v. Dempsey, 43 Mo. App. 369. In Fawcett v. Purcell, 27 Grant Ch. (U. C.) 445, plaintiff had made improvements on property which he believed to be his wife's in fee; but in which it appeared on her death that she had only a life estate. The court held that plaintiff was entitled to interest on any amounts by which he had enhanced the value of the property from the time when he made the expenditure.

[147] Aikin v. Peay, 5 Strobh. (S. C.) 15, 53 Am. Dec. 684.

[148] *Rhode Island:* Butler v. Butler, 10 R. I. 501.

England: Trelawney v. Thomas, 1 H. Bl. 303.

Canada: Secor v. Gray, 3 Ont. L. Rep. 34.

But *contra, Massachusetts:* Hubbard v. Charlestown B. R. R., 11 Met. 124.

[149] *Ante,* § 301c.

[150] Sprague v. Sprague, 30 Vt. 483; *acc.,* Bell v. Rice, 50 Neb. 547, 70 N. W. 25.

[151] *United States:* U. S. v. Curtis, 100

U. S. 119, 25 L. ed. 571; U. S. v. Denvir, 106 U. S. 536, 27 L. ed. 264; Williams v. Baxter, 29 Fed. Cas. No. 17, 715, 3 McLean, 471; United States v. Butler, 114 Fed. 582.

Alabama: Ingersoll v. Campbell, 46 Ala. 282.

Connecticut: Jones v. Mallory, 22 Conn. 386.

Illinois: Myers v. Walker, 24 Ill. 133; Jessoy v. Horn, 64 Ill. 379.

Massachusetts: Ordway v. Colcord, 14 Allen, 59; Talbot v. Com. N. Bank, 129 Mass. 67.

Pennsylvania: Gravenstine's Estate, 18 Phila. 9.

South Carolina: Black v. Goodman, 1 Bail. 201.

Texas: Close v. Fields, 13 Tex. 623.

Vermont: Haswell v. Farmers' & M. B., 26 Vt. 100.

Wisconsin: Rice v. Ashland County, 114 Wis. 130, 137, 89 N. W. 908.

[152] *United States:* Pope v. Barret, 1 Mason, 117.

So where the defendant received payment for services rendered jointly by himself and the plaintiff, the plaintiff could not recover interest on his share without demand.[153]   But where it is the duty of the party into whose hands money of another comes to pay it over in a reasonable time, or at least to inform the owner of its receipt, interest is allowed after the lapse of a reasonable time.[154]

In Stacy v. Graham [155] the defendant was instructed by a third party to remit some money he held to one Adams. The money was for the use of the plaintiff, although this was not known to the defendant. On failing to remit it, it was held that he must be charged with interest. Ruckman v. Pitcher [156] was an action against a stakeholder who, under plaintiff's direction, had paid over the money to the winner of a wager. It was held that the plaintiff could recover interest from the time of a demand, on the ground that he had never lost his

District of Columbia: Dale v. Richards, 21 D. C. 312.

Iowa: Johnson v. Semple, 31 Iowa, 49.

Maine: Wheeler v. Haskins, 41 Me. 432.

Massachusetts: Ellery v. Cunningham, 1 Met. 112.

Michigan: Beardslee v. Horton, 3 Mich. 560.

New York: Williams v. Storrs, 6 Johns. Ch. 353.

North Carolina: Neal v. Freeman, 85 N. C. 441; Porter v. Grimsley, 98 N. C. 550.

Vermont: Hauxhurst v. Hovey, 26 Vt. 544.

If the principal makes a demand, interest runs from the time of demand.

District of Columbia: Dale v. Richards, 21 D. C. 312.

Illinois: Fish v. Seeberger, 154 Ill. 30, 39 N. E. 982, 47 Ill. App. 580.

So where a wife sent money to her husband to be accounted for when required, the amount would bear interest from demand. Witte v. Clarke, 17 S. C. 313.

When the agent renders an account

showing a balance due, interest runs from that time on the balance. Miller v. McCormick Harvesting Machine Co., 84 Ill. App. 571.

[153] *Kentucky:* Neal v. Keel, 4 T. B. Mon. 162.

Massachusetts: Hunt v. Nevers, 15 Pick. 500, 26 Am. Dec. 616.

[154] *Illinois:* Chapman v. Burt, 77 Ill. 337.

Massachusetts: Clark v. Moody, 17 Mass. 145, 149; Dodge v. Perkins, 9 Pick. 368.

Michigan: Youmans v. Heartt, 34 Mich. 397.

Missouri: Jefferson City Savings Assn. v. Morrison, 48 Mo. 273; Bates v. Hamilton, 144 Mo. 1, 45 S. W. 641.

Nebraska: Hazelet v. Holt County, 51 Neb. 716, 71 N. W. 717.

New Jersey: Board of Justices v. Fennimore, 1 N. J. L. 242; Sheridan v. Van Winkle, 43 N. J. L. 125.

Virginia: Hawkins v. Minor, 5 Call, 118.

[155] 14 N. Y. 492. See also Pasley v. Catterlin, 64 Mo. App. 629.

[156] 20 N. Y. 9.

right to the money and was entitled to its return when demanded. In Dodge v. Perkins [157] the defendant, an agent, had collected money for his principal, but had neglected to pay it over, or to notify his principal that he had received it. In an action for money had and received, it was held that the agent should have notified his principal of the receipt of the money after a reasonable time, and having failed to do so interest should be allowed. The court, after reviewing many of the cases on the subject, said: "Upon the principles of the common law we think it clear that interest is to be allowed where the law by implication makes it the duty of the party to pay over the money to the owner without any previous demand on his part. Thus, where it was obtained and held by fraud, interest should be calculated from the time when it was received. So where there has been a default of payment according to agreement, express or implied, to pay on a certain day, or after demand or after reasonable time." [158] In Thompson v. Stewart [159] the court used the following language: "Had it become the duty of the defendant to pay the money to his principal, if through *wrong* or *neglect* he had detained it, it would be reasonable that interest for the detention should be allowed."

On this basis a wife cannot recover from her husband interest on her separate estate which he has received, the presumption being that the money was spent with her consent for the support of herself and her family. [160] And where a creditor receives usurious interest, the debtor who sues to recover it cannot get interest on the amount before the time

[157] 9 Pick. 368, 388.

[158] See *acc.*, Chapman v. Burt, 77 Ill. 337; Close v. Fields, 13 Tex. 623.

[159] 3 Conn. 171.

[160] Kittel's Estate, 156 Pa. 445, 26 Atl. 1116. And so where a wife took a conveyance of land bought with her husband's money her administrator was held not to be chargeable with interest on rents collected and appropriated by her. Columbia Savings Bank v. Winn, 132 Mo. 80, 33 S. W. 451. And see Roper v. Wren, 6 Leigh

(Va.), 38. Under the Oregon statutes a wife may recover interest on money voluntarily loaned to her husband. Grubbi v. Grubbi, 26 Ore. 363, 38 Pac. 182. See Pierce v. Dustin, 24 N. H. 417.

So where a father uses his son's money, while supporting and paying the expenses of his son, interest cannot be recovered until demand. Thurber v. Sprague, 17 R. I. 634, 24 Atl. 48.

of a demand for payment.[161] So where a creditor, having in his hands property of the debtor, was allowed by the debtor to sell it and pay his claim, and another creditor appeared later who was entitled to a share of the amount, it was held that the latter was not entitled to interest on the amount due him until demand, which in the actual case was the beginning of the action.[162]

§ 306. Money received or retained by mutual mistake.

Where the defendant has received money of the plaintiff through mutual mistake, there can be no interest till demand.[163] So where an account is underpaid by mutual mistake, there can be no interest on the balance till demand.[164]

The same principle applies in cases involving the transfer of land under a mutual mistake as to title.[165]

§ 307. Rent—Distraint.

Where rent due by an agreement is not paid, interest may be recovered on the amount from the day on which it should

[161] Savings Bank v. Hodgdon, 62 N. H. 300.

[162] Kittel v. Augusta, T. & G. R. R., 84 Fed. 386, 28 C. C. A. 437.

[163] *Alabama:* Florence Cotton, etc., Co. v. Louisville Banking Co., 138 Ala. 588, 36 So. 456, 100 Am. St. Rep. 50.

Connecticut: Northrop v. Graves, 19 Conn. 548.

Georgia: Georgia R. R. & B. Co. v. Smith, 83 Ga. 626, 10 S. E. 235.

Louisiana: Smith v. Conrad, 15 La. Ann. 579.

Massachusetts: Haven v. Foster, 9 Pick. 112, 19 Am. Dec. 353.

Minnesota: Sibley v. Pine County, 31 Minn. 201, 17 N. W. 337; Corse v. Minnesota Grain Co., 94 Minn. 331, 102 N. W. 728.

New Jersey: Ashhurst v. Field, 28 N. J. Eq. 315; Ashhurst v. Potter, 29 N. J. Eq. 625.

New York: Leach v. Vining, 18 N. Y. Supp. 822.

Pennsylvania: Jacobs v. Adams, 1 Dall. 52.

South Carolina: Simons v. Walter, 1 McC. 97.

But in Illinois interest is payable (by statute) only where there is an unreasonable or vexatious delay *after* demand. Devine v. Edwards, 101 Ill. 138.

In Cummings v. Bradford, 22 S. W. 548, 15 Ky. L. Rep. 155, interest was allowed from the original payment; so in Porter v. Russek (Tex. Civ. App.), 29 S. W. 72.

[164] *Pennsylvania:* Second & T. S. P. Ry. v. Philadelphia, 51 Pa. 465.

Vermont: Brainerd v. Champlain Transp. Co., 29 Vt. 154.

Wisconsin: O'Herrin v. Milwaukee County, 67 Wis. 142, 30 N. W. 239.

And the same rule applies to overpayment on a mortgage, which the mortgagor seeks to recover back. Leach v. Vining, 18 N. Y. Supp. 822.

[165] Boykin v. Ancrum, 28 S. C. 486, 13 Am. St. Rep. 698, 6 S. E. 305.

But see: McKibbon v. Williams, 24 Ont. App. 122.

have been paid.[166] So in an action for use and occupation, or for mesne profits, where the recovery is of a sum in the nature of rent, interest is allowed on each annual sum from the end of the year; [167] or where rent was payable quarterly, from the quarter day.[168] And so on breach of a contract to hire rooms at a certain price the defendant was held to pay interest from the end of the term on the difference between the contract price and that obtained on reletting the rooms.[169] But where the landlord distrains, it must be only for the amount of the rent, without interest; that remedy is to recover the rent, not damages for delay in paying it.[170] In Skipwith v.

[166] *United States:* Houghteling v. Walker, 100 Fed. 253.

Delaware: Stockton v. Guthrie, 5 Harr. 204.

Illinois: Walker v. Hadduck, 14 Ill. 399; West Chicago Alcohol Works v. Sheer, 8 Bradw. 367.

Kentucky: Honore v. Murray, 3 Dana, 31; Elkin v. Moore, 6 B. Mon. 462; Burnham v. Best, 10 B. Mon. 227.

Maryland: Dennison v. Lee, 6 G. & J. 383.

Mississippi: Howcott v. Collins, 23 Miss. 398.

New York: Lush v. Drouse, 4 Wend. 313; Clark v. Barlow, 4 Johns. 183; Van Rensselaer v. Jones, 2 Barb. 643; Ten Eyck v. Houghtaling, 12 How. Pr. 523.

Pennsylvania: Albright v. Pickle, 4 Yeates, 264; Obermyer v. Nichols, 6 Binn. 159; Buck v. Fisher, 4 Whart. 516; Naglee v. Ingersoll, 7 Pa. 185; Newman v. Keffer, 33 Pa. 442.

Contra in Virginia: Cooke v. Wise, 3 H. & M. 463; but by a statute immediately afterwards passed interest is allowed on arrears of rent, Brooks v. Wilcox, 11 Gratt. 411, 419. See also: Kyle v. Roberts, 6 Leigh, 495.

[167] *United States:* Gaines v. New Orleans, 17 Fed. 16, 4 Woods, 581.

Alabama: Cooke v. Farinholt, 3 Ala. 384.

Michigan: Hack v. Norris, 46 Mich. 587, 10 N. W. 104.

New York: Worrall v. Munn, 38 N. Y. 137.

Virginia: Early v. Friend, 16 Gratt. 21; Bolling v. Lersner, 26 Gratt. 36.

Where the amount was unliquidated until the verdict, no interest was allowed until that time in Skirving v. Stobo, 2 Bay (S. C.), 233. But where the lease fixed rent for a certain time and provided that after that time it would be fixed by referees, and the referees could not agree, it was held that interest could be recovered at the legal rate on what was found to be a fair rent for the premises. Heissler v. Stose, 131 Ill. 393, 23 N. E. 347.

Where the defendant was kept out of the possession of premises by proceedings in appeal, and recovered compensation on the appeal bond for loss of use of the premises, interest on the amount was allowed. Turner v. Johnson, 106 Ky. 460, 50 S. W. 675.

[168] *Massachusetts:* Hodgkins v. Price, 141 Mass. 162.

New York: Jackson v. Wood, 24 Wend. 443; Vandevoort v. Gould, 36 N. Y. 639.

[169] De Lavalette v. Wendt, 75 N. Y. 579.

[170] *Illinois:* Tanton v. Boomgaarden, 89 Ill. App. 500.

New York: Lansing v. Rattoone, 6 Johns. 43.

And in a case in ejectment it was

Clinch [171] plaintiff brought a bill for payment of rent and performance of covenants in a lease. It was held that no interest could be allowed on unpaid rents, because plaintiff might have distrained and prevented accumulation of interest, and because the rent was uncertain. In a New York case [172] where rent was to be paid in wheat and services the value of neither of which was stated by the contract, interest was allowed from the day of breach, even though the damage had to be fixed by the court. But where there is no fixed rent, nor can the compensation for use and occupation be made certain by computation, interest is refused.[173]

§ 308. Sale of goods at a fixed price.

There can be no doubt (though it has not always been so held) that where goods are sold at a fixed price, the demand is a liquidated one, and interest may be recovered on the amount from the time payment is due. So where goods are sold for cash, interest may be recovered on the price from the time of sale; [174] and if no time of credit is given, it will be held a cash sale, and interest will be given from the time of the sale.[175] Where goods are sold on credit, interest may be

held not to be allowed on rent accruing from month to month. Allen v. Smith, 63 Mo. 103.

See also: Crooks v. Dickinson, 1 Can. L. J. (N. S.) 211.

[171] 2 Call (Va.), 252.

[172] Van Renssalaer v. Jewett, 2 N. Y. 135, 51 Am. Dec. 275; acc., Pujol v. McKinlay, 42 Cal. 559.

[173] Moore v. Calvert, 6 Bush (Ky.), 356. In *North Dakota* in ejectment proceedings the jury fixing the amount to be recovered for use and occupation, may add interest in their discretion. Heger v. De Groat, 3 N. D. 354, 56 N. W. 150.

[174] *United States:* Atlantic Phosphate Co. v. Grafflin, 114 U. S. 492, 5 Sup. Ct. 967, 26 L. ed. 221; Lumber Co. v. Daniel, 109 Fed. 39, 48 C. C. A. 204.

Alabama: Waring v. Henry, 30 Ala. 721.

District of Columbia: District v. Camden Iron Works, 15 D. C. App. Cas. 198, 222.

Illinois: Lurton v. Gilliam, 2 Ill. 577, 33 Am. Dec. 430; Maltman v. Williamson, 69 Ill. 423.

Kansas: Wyandotte & K. C. G. Co. v. Schliefer, 22 Kan. 468.

Kentucky: Henderson C. M. Co. v. Lowell Machine Shops, 86 Ky. 668.

Maryland: Smith v. Shaffer, 50 Md. 132.

Massachusetts: Foote v. Blanchard, 6 Allen, 221, 83 Am. Dec. 624.

New York: Pollock v. Ehle, 2 E. D. Smith, 541.

Texas: Howard v. Emerson (Tex. Civ. App.), 65 S. W. 382; Schuwirth v. Thumma (Tex. Civ. App.), 66 S. W. 691 (interest in discretion of jury).

See Heidenheimer v. Ellis, 67 Tex. 426, 3 S. W. 666.

[175] *United States:* Atlantic P. Co. v.

recovered from the expiration of the credit.[176]   If no time is
fixed for payment, interest may be recovered from the time
of demand,[177] or from the date of the writ if there has been
no demand.[178]

In accordance with these cases, where a purchaser refuses
to accept goods bought, he is held to pay interest on the difference between the price and that obtained on a resale.[179]
If the price is fixed by the contract, the fact that there is a
dispute about the quantity or quality of the goods delivered
does not relieve the defendant from the payment of interest
on the sum due.[180]

Grafflin, 114 U. S. 492, 5 Sup. Ct.
967, 26 L. ed. 221.

Alabama: Shields v. Henry, 31 Ala.
53.

Arkansas: Roberts v. Wilcoxson, 36
Ark. 355.

Kansas: Sturges v. Green, 27 Kan.
235.

New York: Pollock v. Ehle, 2 E. D.
Smith, 541.

[176] *United States:* Mine & Smelter
Supply Co. v. Parke & Lacy Co., 47
C. C. A. 34, 107 Fed. 881.

Delaware: Bate v. Burr, 4 Harr.
130.

Florida: Milton v. Blackshear, 8
Fla. 161.

Iowa: Lessenich v. Sellers, 119 Iowa,
314, 93 N. W. 348.

Massachusetts: Lambeth Rope Co.
v. Brigham, 170 Mass. 518, 49 N. E.
1022.

Mississippi: Wiltburger v. Randolph, Walker, 20.

New Hampshire: National Lancers
v. Lovering, 30 N. H. 511.

New York: Blakeley v. Jacobson, 9
Bosw. 140.

Pennsylvania: Knox v. Jones, 2 Dall.
193.

Vermont: Raymond v. Isham, 8 Vt.
258; Porter v. Munger, 22 Vt. 191.

Washington: Arnott v. Spokane, 6
Wash. 442, 33 Pac. 1063.

But *contra, Texas:* Gammage v.
Alexander, 14 Tex. 414.

[177] *United States:* Cooper v. Coates,
21 Wall. 105, 22 L. ed. 481.

California: Lane v. Turner, 114 Cal.
396, 46 Pac. 290.

Florida: Milton v. Blackshear, 8
Fla. 161.

New Hampshire: Livermore v. Rand,
26 N. H. 85.

[178] *Kentucky:* Leisman v. Otto, 1
Bush, 225.

Maine: Patten v. Hood, 40 Me. 457.

New Hampshire: McIlvaine v. Wilkins, 12 N. H. 474.

In Gammon v. Abrams, 53 Wis. 523,
10 N. W. 479, interest was allowed on
the value of a reaper from commencement of the suit to recover the price,
even though the value had to be found
by evidence.

[179] *Auction:* Blackwood v. Leman,
Harp. (S. C.) 219; Wolfe v. Sharp, 10
Rich. (S. C.) 60.

The same principle applies in any
case of failure or refusal to receive and
pay for goods bought.   McCall v. Icks,
107 Wis. 232, 83 N. W. 300.

[180] *Pennsylvania:* West Republic Mining Co. v. Jones, 108 Pa. 55.

Wisconsin: Vaughan v. Howe, 20
Wis. 497.

In an Illinois case where goods were
sold under a contract which designated
times for payments, it was held that
interest would be allowed on sums not
paid when due, as on an instrument
in writing, whether the delay was un-

It has been held in some jurisdictions that interest may be recovered after a reasonable time for payment has expired. Thus in Beers v. Reynolds [181] the plaintiff sold some goods to the defendant for a fixed price. Gardiner, J., said: "No precise time of credit was given. When, therefore, after a reasonable time had elapsed, and the account was presented, and impliedly admitted, the defendants were in default for withholding payment, and interest was properly chargeable from the time of the demand."

§ 308a. Work and labor done for a fixed price.

The same is true in actions to recover for work done at an agreed price. Where the price was to be paid on a fixed day, interest runs from that time.[182] And in action on a contract for professional services, where defendant had failed to pay

reasonable and vexatious or not. Rouse v. Western Wheel Works, 66 Ill. App. 647, 169 Ill. 536, 48 N. E. 459. See also Simms v. Hampson, 2 Ariz. 233, 12 Pac. 868, the contract being in writing.

[181] 11 N. Y. 97.

[182] *United States:* Richmond & I. Const. Co. v. Richmond, etc., R. R., 15 C. C. A. 289, 68 Fed. 105, 34 L. R. A. 625.

Alabama: Moore v. Patton, 2 Port. 451; Parker v. Parker, 33 Ala. 459.

California: Mix v. Miller, 57 Cal. 356; Mullenary v. Burton, 3 Cal. App. 263, 84 Pac. 159.

Colorado: Baldwin Coal Co. v. Davis, 15 Colo. App. 371, 62 Pac. 1041.

Connecticut: Loomis v. Gillett, 75 Conn. 298, 53 Atl. 581 (part of charge undisputed, interest may be recovered on that part).

Georgia: Robins v. Prior, 20 Ga. 561.

Iowa: Sullivan v. Nicolin, 113 Iowa, 76, 83, 84 N. W. 978.

Kentucky: Whitehead v. Brothers Lodge No. 132, I. O. O. F., 71 S. W. 933, 24 Ky. L. Rep. 1633.

Maryland: Lee v. Pindle, 12 Gill & J. 288.

Michigan: McCreery v. Green, 38 Mich. 172.

Nebraska: Mullahy v. Dingman, 62 Neb. 702, 87 N. W. 543.

New Jersey: Ruckman v. Bergholz, 37 N. J. L. 437.

New York: Martin v. Silliman, 53 N. Y. 615; Carpenter v. Brand, 40 N. Y. Super. Ct. 551.

South Carolina: Kennedy v. Barnwell, 7 Rich. 124.

Texas: Galveston, etc., R. R. v. Henry, 65 Tex. 685.

Utah: Sandeberg v. Victor Gold, etc., Mining Co., 24 Utah, 1, 66 Pac. 360.

Washington: Happy v. Prickett, 24 Wash. 290, 64 Pac. 528.

Canada: McCullough v. Newton, 27 Ont. 627.

Where work was done by a son under an agreement that he should be satisfied at his father's death, but the son was sent away before his father died, it was held that the contract was repudiated and that plaintiff should be allowed interest from the end of each year's service. Updike v. Ten Broeck, 32 N. J. L. 105.

as the contract stipulated, he was held liable for interest from the dates when payments were due.[183] Where no time is fixed for payment, interest runs from demand;[184] or if there has been no demand, not until the date of the writ.[185] And where suit was brought for work done on a building which was destroyed before completion by no fault of plaintiff, interest was allowed from commencement of the action.[186] Where a person is employed at an annual salary, and no time of payment is fixed, no interest can ordinarily be recovered until demand.[187] But where plaintiff was engaged at a fixed monthly salary, the court said there ought to be settlements at least once a year, and allowed interest on annual balances due, though no bill had been presented or demand made for payment.[188] And where payment for work has been long delayed

[183] Adams v. Ft. Plain Bank, 36 N. Y. 255; Church v. Kidd, 6 Hun, 475. In Georgia, under a statute, interest on a physician's account runs from the end of each year. Woodfield v. Colzey, 47 Ga. 121. And when the amount of attorney's fees is undisputed interest will run thereon from demand, and on disbursements from the time when they were made: Rexford v. Comstock, 3 N. Y. Supp. 876.

See, also, *Missouri:* Lanning v. Peters Shoe Co., 71 Mo. App. 646.

South Carolina: Ryan v. Baldrick, 3 McCord, 498.

In Tennessee it has been held that if the amount of the fee is not liquidated interest can only be allowed in the discretion of the court. Gribble v. Ford, 52 S. W. 1007.

[184] *United States:* Gammell v. Skinner, 2 Gall. 45.

Maine: Amee v. Wilson, 22 Me. 116.

Massachusetts: Barnard v. Bartholomew, 22 Pick. 291; Ford v. Tirrell, 9 Gray, 401, 69 Am. Dec. 297; Pierce v. Charter Oak Life Ins. Co., 138 Mass. 151.

New Jersey: Ruckman v. Bergholz, 37 N. J. L. 437.

New York: Robbins v. Carll, 93 N. Y. 656; Chase v. Union Stone Co., 11 Daly, 107; Sweeney v. New York, 173 N. Y. 414, 66 N. E. 101; Adams v. Fort Plain Bank, 36 N. Y. 255.

Wisconsin: McCall Co. v. Icks, 107 Wis. 232, 83 N. W. 300; Remington v. Eastern R. R., 109 Wis. 154, 84 N. W. 898, 85 N. W. 321.

[185] *Alabama:* Moore v. Patton, 2 Port. 451.

California: McFadden v. Crawford, 39 Cal. 662.

Massachusetts: Brewer v. Tyringham, 12 Pick. 547; Barstow v. Robinson, 2 Allen, 605.

Montana: Nixon v. Cutting F. P. Co., 17 Mont. 90, 42 Pac. 108.

New York: Feeter v. Heath, 11 Wend. 477; McCollum v. Seward, 62 N. Y. 316; Case v. Osborn, 60 How. Pr. 187.

Vermont: Newell v. Keith, 11 Vt. 214.

[186] Braas v. Springville, 100 N. Y. App. Div. 197, 91 N. Y. Supp. 599.

[187] *Kentucky:* Paducah L. C. & I. Co. v. Hayes, 15 Ky. L. Rep. 517, 24 S. W. 237.

Massachusetts: Soule v. Soule, 157 Mass. 451, 32 N. E. 663.

[188] Spencer v. Woodbridge, 38 Vt. 492; acc., Butler v. Kirby, 53 Wis. 188, 10 N. W. 373.

it has been held that the jury may give interest from the expiration of a reasonable time; the allowance of interest being said to rest in the discretion of the jury in the sense that they can fix the time for it to begin running.[189]

§ 309. Demand prevented by defendant's act.

Where the defendant, by his acts, makes a demand impossible or useless, interest may be recovered from the date of such act. In Chemical National Bank v. Bailey [190] the plaintiff had been a depositor in a bank of which the defendant was the receiver. On winding up the affairs of the bank, there proved to be sufficient assets to pay the depositors in full and leave a surplus. The question arose, whether the depositors should be allowed interest before dividing the surplus. Wallace, J., after saying that interest was allowed as a matter of right where there was a wrongful detention of a debt, said: "Ordinarily, an action cannot be maintained by a depositor against a bank, until a formal demand has been made; and, of course, no interest can be recovered except that arising after the demand. . . . But if the bank, by words or conduct, denies the depositor's right to his balance, it becomes presently liable to an action, without formal demand, and interest would be recoverable as damages." In this case it was held that putting its assets in the hands of a receiver was a wrongful act as regards the depositors, and they were, therefore, entitled to interest.[191] In a case where the defendant absented himself from the State, so that a demand could not be made upon him, it was held that interest might be recovered from the time the services were rendered.[192]

---

[189] *Delaware:* Black v. Reybold, 3 Harr. 528.
Indiana: Young v. Dickey, 63 Ind. 31; Rend v. Boord, 75 Ind. 307.
New Jersey: Wills v. Brown, 3 N. J. L. 411.
[190] 12 Blatch. 480. See also Frazer v. Bigelow Carpet Co., 141 Mass. 126, 4 N. E. 620.
[191] See also Jenkins v. Armour, 6 Biss. 312.

[192] Graham v. Chrystal, 2 Keyes, 21; s. c. 2 Abb. App. 263.
And where plaintiff was impeded in the collection of rents by defendant, he was allowed interest on the rents already due: Graham v. Woodson, 2 Call (Va.), 249. Where defendant denies liability, no demand is necessary, but interest will run from the time when defendant refuses payment: Perine v. Grand Lodge, A. O. U. W., 51 Minn. 224, 53 N. W. 367.

§ 310. Simple running account.

It has often been said that a running account does not bear interest,[193] without an agreement or custom that it shall.[194] Where there is an open running account—for example, an account for domestic supplies—it is reasonable to suppose that it was the intention to allow credit; the fact of a charge being in an account, in other words, shows that an indefinite credit was allowed. No interest should therefore be given, generally, until demand for payment,[195] or if there is no demand,

---

[193] *United States:* Davidson v. Mexican Nat. R. R., 58 Fed. 653; South Carolina v. Port Royal, etc., R. R., 89 Fed. 565.

Alabama: Tyree v. Parham, 66 Ala. 424.

California: State Bank v. Northam, 51 Cal. 387; Heald v. Hendy, 89 Cal. 632, 27 Pac. 67.

Connecticut: Phenix v. Prindee, Kirby, 207; Selleck v. French, 1 Conn. 32; Day v. Lockwood, 24 Conn. 185; Crosby v. Mason, 32 Conn. 482.

Illinois: Clement v. McConnell, 14 Ill. 154; Phillips v. Rehm, 64 Ill. App. 477.

Indiana: Shemel v. Givan, 2 Blackf. 312.

Iowa: Raymond v. Williams, 40 Iowa, 117.

Kentucky: Harrison v. Handley, 1 Bibb, 446; Tobin v. South's Adm'r, 18 Ky. L. Rep. 350, 36 S. W. 1039.

Massachusetts: Hunt v. Nevers, 15 Pick. 500; Goff v. Rehoboth, 2 Cush. 475.

Missouri: Compton v. Johnson, 19 Mo. App. 88.

Nevada: Flannery v. Anderson, 4 Nev. 437 (by statute).

New Hampshire: Morrill v. Weeks, 70 N. H. 178, 46 Atl. 32.

New York: Doyle v. St. James' Church, 7 Wend. 178; Kane v. Smith, 12 Johns. 156; Van Beuren v. Van Gaasbeck, 4 Cow. 496; Tucker v. Ives, 6 Cow. 193; Newell v. Griswold, 6 Johns. 45; Trotter v. Grant, 2 Wend.

413; Wood v. Hickok, 2 Wend. 501; Esterly v. Cole, 3 N. Y. 502; Hadley v. Ayers, 12 Abb. Pr. (N. S.) 240; Salter v. Parkhurst, 2 Daly, 240.

Pennsylvania: Henry v. Risk, 1 Dall. 265; Williams v. Craig, 1 Dall. 313; Graham v. Williams, 16 S. & R. 257.

South Carolina: Bennet v. Johnson, 1 Speers, 209; Holmes v. Misroon, 3 Brev. 209; Knight v. Mitchell, 3 Brev. 506; Goddard v. Bulow, 1 N. & McC. 45; Conyers v. Magrath, 4 McC. 392; Farrand v. Bouchell, Harp. 83.

Texas: Cloud v. Smith, 1 Tex. 102.

Wisconsin: Marsh v. Fraser, 37 Wis. 149; Shipman v. State, 44 Wis. 458; Martin v. State, 51 Wis. 407.

Canada: Bentley v. West, 4 U. C. Q. B. 98.

But *contra, Vermont:* Houghton v. Hager, Brayt. (Vt.) 133.

In an action on current account where 5% interest was contracted for, it was held that no greater rate could be allowed, since interest is not recoverable at all in the absence of contract: Baxter v. Waite, 2 Wash. Terr. 228, 6 Pac. 429.

[194] *Massachusetts:* Smith v. Butler, 176 Mass. 38, 57 N. E. 322.

England: Wilmot v. Gardner, [1901] 2 Ch. 548.

[195] *Alabama:* Tyree v. Parkham, 66 Ala. 424.

Kentucky: Henderson Cotton Mfg. Co. v. Lowell Mach. Shops, 86 Ky. 668, 7 So. 142, 9 Ky. L. Rep. 831.

Where plaintiff claimed more than

until the date of the writ; [196] but where by agreement or otherwise an item is due at a fixed time, interest accrues from that time.[197]

Interest is sometimes allowed from the time the account is closed, that is, from the date of the last item.[198] In Vermont, interest is allowed at the expiration of a year; [199] but if the defendant was ignorant of an item of charge, interest does not run till demand.[200] In Mississippi, by statute, the jury may allow interest on open accounts.[201] And interest is often allowed upon accounts by statute, from a certain date, as from the date of the last item,[202] or six months after such date.[203] But where by statute plaintiff is entitled to interest on balance of an account on demand, if he claims no interest in his petition, he can recover none.[204]

---

was actually due, no interest was allowed between the date of demand and the commencement of suit. Lusk v. Smith, 21 Wis. 27.

[196] *Louisiana:* Merieult v. Austin, 3 Mart. 318.

Massachusetts: Quin v. Bay State Distilling Co., 171 Mass. 283, 50 N. E. 637.

Missouri: Evans v. Western Brass Mfg. Co., 118 Mo. 548, 24 S. W. 175; Dempsey v. Schawacker, 140 Mo. 680, 34 S. W. 954; Henderson v. Davis, 74 Mo. App. 1.

Montana: Hefferlin v. Karlman, 29 Mont. 139, 74 Pac. 201.

[197] *Iowa:* Dubuque Lumber Co. v. Kimball, 111 Iowa, 48, 82 N. W. 458.

Louisiana: Vance v. Shreveport First Nat. Bank, 51 La. Ann. 89, 29 So. 607.

[198] *United States:* Blackfeather v. United States, 28 Ct. of Cls. 447.

Alabama: Prestridge v. Irwin, 46 Ala. 653.

Connecticut: McKeon v. Byington, 70 Conn. 429, 39 Atl. 853.

Minnesota: Leyde v. Martin, 16 Minn. 38; Bell v. Mendenhall, 78 Minn. 57, 80 N. W. 843.

Vermont: Dickenson v. Gould, 2 Tyler, 32.

[199] Bates v. Starr, 2 Vt. 536, 21 Am. Dec. 569.

[200] Wood v. Smith, 23 Vt. 706; Davis v. Smith, 48 Vt. 52; Hammond v. Hammond, 76 Vt. 437, 56 Atl. 724; Holt v. Howard, 77 Vt. 49, 58 Atl. 797; Langdon v. Castleton, 30 Vt. 285.

[201] Houston v. Crutcher, 31 Miss. 51; Thompson v. Matthews, 56 Miss. 368; McCutcheon v. Dougherty, 44 Miss. 419.

[202] Col. Gen. St., § 1707; Bergundthal v. Bailey, 15 Colo. 257, 25 Pac. 86.

[203] Neb. Comp. St., c. 44, § 4; Weston v. Brown, 30 Neb. 609, 46 N. W. 826; Lepin v. Paine, 15 Neb. 326, 18 N. W. 79; Staker v. Begole, 34 Neb. 107, 51 N. W. 468; Garneau v. Omaha Printing Co., 52 Neb. 383, 72 N. W. 360.

In Texas interest is allowed from the first of January after the account is made. Fort Worth & D. C. Ry. v. White (Tex. Civ. App.), 14 S. W. 1068; Mills v. Hass (Tex. Civ. App.), 27 S. W. 263.

[204] Van Riper v. Morton, 61 Mo. App. 440.

When an account is stated and a balance found, or a balance admitted by a party, interest on the balance runs from the time the account is adjusted.[205] While the rule stated above is generally followed, the distinction between a running account and a single transaction is often lost sight of.[206]

§ 310a. Partnership accounts.

In the case of a trading partnership it is generally held that one partner who makes advances to the firm, or puts in more than his share of capital, cannot, in absence of agreement or custom, recover interest,[207] though in some States he is allowed

[205] *United States:* Bainbridge v. Wilcocks, 2 Fed. Cas. No. 755, Baldw. 536; York v. Wistar, 30 Fed. Cas. No. 18,141; Sayward v. Dexter, 19 C. C. A. 176, 72 Fed. 758; Mine & S. S. Co. v. Parke & Lacy Co., 107 Fed. 881, 47 C. C. A. 34.

Colorado: Bergundthal v. Bailey, 15 Colo. 257, 25 Pac. 86, 453.

Illinois: Underhill v. Gaff, 48 Ill. 198.

Kentucky: Richardson v. Parrott's Heirs, 7 B. Mon. 379, 383.

Louisiana: Ledoux v. Goza, 4 La. Ann. 160; Keane v. Branden, 12 La. Ann. 20; Conrad v. Burbank, 24 La. Ann. 17; Brodnax v. Steinhardt, 48 La. Ann. 682, 19 So. 572.

New York: Case v. Hotchkiss, 3 Keyes, 334, 3 Abb. Pr. (N. S.) 381, 1 Abb. App. 324.

Pennsylvania: Crawford v. Willing, 4 Dall. 286, 1 L. ed. 836.

South Carolina: Barelli v. Brown, 1 McCord, 449, 10 Am. Dec. 683.

So interest is due on the balance of an official account after it is rendered: *United States:* United States v. Eggleston, 4 Sawyer, 199; U. S. v. Fitzsimmons, 50 Fed. 381.

Illinois: Stern v. People, 102 Ill. 540.

In the case of agreement to pay royalties on a trade-mark, quarterly statements being provided for, it was held that rests should be allowed every quarter, and interest computed on amounts then due. Miller v. Billington, 194 Pa. 452, 45 Atl. 372.

[206] Thus in cases previously cited, in which interest was allowed, the plaintiff's demand was in form an account: e. g., Moore v. Patton, 2 Port. 451; Young v. Dickey, 63 Ind. 31; Rend v. Boord, 75 Ind. 307; Barnard v. Bartholomew, 22 Pick. 291; Wiltburger v. Randolph, Walk. (Miss.) 20; Blakely v. Jacobson, 9 Bosw. 140; Chase v. Union Stone Co., 11 Daly, 107. See also Jones v. Galigher, 9 Utah, 126, 33 Pac. 417; Ryan Drug Co. v. Hoambshal, 92 Wis. 62, 65 N. W. 873.

[207] *California:* Tirrell v. Jones, 39 Cal. 655.

Georgia: Prentice v. Elliott, 72 Ga. 154.

Iowa: Smith v. Knight, 88 Iowa, 257, 55 N. W. 189.

Kentucky: Lee v. Lashbrooke, 8 Dana, 214.

Michigan: Godfrey v. White, 43 Mich. 171, 5 N. W. 243; Sweeney v. Neely, 53 Mich. 421, 19 N. W. 127.

Minnesota: St. Paul Trust Co. v. Finch, 52 Minn. 342, 54 N. W. 190.

Nebraska: Clark v. Warden, 10 Neb. 87, 4 N. W. 413; McCormick v. McCormick, 7 Neb. 440.

to do so.[208] Interest may, however, be allowed by trade usage [209] or by special agreement,[210] or in case of a loan which is not intended or received as a contribution to capital.[211]

A partnership account is of course an unsettled mutual account; and for this reason interest is generally disallowed as between partners, in accounts of the partnership.[212] But if there is anything to put an end to the currency of the account the case is different. On dissolution, either by death of a partner or otherwise, an accounting should at once be taken; and if a surviving or settling partner fails to render an account within a reasonable time, he is chargeable with interest on a

New Jersey: Morris v. Allen, 14 N. J. Eq. 44 (*semble*).

New York: Rodgers v. Clement, 162 N. Y. 422, 45 N. E. 901, 76 Am. St. Rep. 342, affirming 15 App. Div. 561, 44 N. Y. Supp. 516 (see Beach v. Colles, 85 N. Y. 511).

North Carolina: Jones v. Jones, 1 Ired. Eq. 332; Holden v. Peace, 4 Ired. Eq. 223.

Pennsylvania: Bremier v. Carter, 203 Pa. 75, 52 Atl. 178, 10 Pa. Dist. Rep. 457.

Wisconsin: Gilman v. Vaughan, 44 Wis. 646.

[208] *Alabama:* Reynolds v. Mardis, 17 Ala. 32; Desha v. Smith, 20 Ala. 747.

Illinois: Ligare v. Peacock, 109 Ill. 94.

Maryland: Matthews v. Adams, 84 Md. 143, 35 Atl. 60.

Mississippi: Berry v. Folkes, 60 Miss. 576 (partnership in managing real estate).

Vermont: Hodges v. Parker, 17 Vt. 242.

[209] Morris v. Allen, 14 N. J. Eq. 44.

[210] *Michigan:* Wells v. Babcock, 56 Mich. 276, 22 N. W. 809.

Minnesota: St. Paul Trust Co. v. Finch, 52 Minn. 342, 54 N. W. 190 (even then no interest will be allowed after dissolution).

See Tutt v. Land, 50 Ga. 339 (agreement to pay interest on increase of capital does not apply to partner's

share of annual profits not withdrawn at end of year).

[211] *Nevada:* Folsom v. Marlette, 23 Nev. 459, 49 Pac. 39 (partner just before dissolution pays creditors).

New York: Rodgers v. Clement, 162 N. Y. 422, 45 N. E. 901, 76 Am. St. Rep. 342.

[212] *United States:* Dexter v. Arnold, 3 Mas. 284.

District of Columbia: Baker v. Cummings, 8 D. C. App. Cas. 515.

Georgia: Wilson v. Wilkinson, 97 Ga. 814, 25 S. E. 908.

Illinois: Gage v. Parmelee, 87 Ill. 329; Brownell v. Steere, 128 Ill. 209, 21 N. E. 3.

Iowa: Kemmerer v. Kemmerer, 85 Iowa, 193, 52 N. W. 194; Wendling v. Jennisch, 85 Iowa, 392, 52 N. W. 341.

Maryland: Juillard v. Orem, 70 Md. 465, 17 Atl. 333.

Massachusetts: Freeman v. Freeman, 142 Mass. 98, 7 N. E. 710.

Minnesota: St. Paul Trust Co. v. Finch, 52 Minn. 342, 54 N. W. 190.

New York: Ledyard v. Bull, 19 N. Y. 62, 63 N. E. 444.

Pennsylvania: Brenner v. Carter, 203 Pa. 75, 52 Atl. 178.

Texas: McKay v. Overton, 65 Tex. 82.

Wisconsin: Gilman v. Vaughan, 44 Wis. 646; Smith v. Putnam, 107 Wis. 155, 82 N. W. 1077, 83 N. W. 288.

balance afterward found against him.[213] So interest runs after accounting on a balance found due on an accounting; [214] and when an accounting is properly demanded, interest may be had on the balance from the time of demand for settlement.[215] So interest may be allowed if it is so agreed between the partners.[216] And interest will be allowed on money misappropriated by a partner [217] or otherwise illegally withheld.[218] Where one partner fails to advance his share of capital, according to agreement, the measure of damages is interest on the amount that should have been furnished.[219]

§ 311. Balance of a mutual account.

Where there is a mutual account, a different principle governs. Until the account is gone over and balanced, there is usually no means of telling which party is the debtor and what the amount of the debt is. Consequently, as a general rule no interest can be recovered upon a mutual account until it is balanced.[220] It would seem that no interest should be re-

---

[213] *Connecticut:* Buckley v. Kelly, 70 Conn. 411, 39 Atl. 601.

Rhode Island: Allen v. Woonsocket Co., 13 R. I. 146.

Canada: McCullough v. Clemow, 26 Ont. 467.

[214] Juillard v. Orem, 70 Md. 465, 17 Atl. 333.

When after the accounts were balanced a partner received more than his proper share he was charged with interest on the excess. Atherton v. Cochran, 11 Ky. L. Rep. 185, 9 S. W. 519.

[215] *Illinois:* Derby v. Gage, 38 Ill. 27.

Pennsylvania: Magilton v. Stevenson, 173 Pa. 560, 34 Atl. 235.

From the beginning of suit:

Massachusetts: Freeman v. Freeman, 142 Mass. 98, 7 N. E. 710; Gould v. Emerson, 160 Mass. 438, 35 N. E. 1065, 39 Am. St. Rep. 501.

Wisconsin: Carroll v. Little, 73 Wis. 52, 40 N. W. 582; Green v. Stacy, 90 Wis. 46, 62 N. W. 627.

From dissolution: Wells v. Babcock, 56 Mich. 276, 22 N. W. 809.

[216] *Illinois:* Ligare v. Peacock, 109 Ill. 94.

Massachusetts: Cole v. Trull, 9 Pick. 325.

[217] *Kentucky:* Masonic Sav. Bank v. Bangs, 10 S. W. 633, 10 Ky. L. Rep. 743.

Maryland: Trump v. Baltzell, 3 Md. 295.

Missouri: Wolfort v. Reilly, 133 Mo. 463, 34 S. W. 847.

New Jersey: Coddington v. Idell, 30 N. J. Eq. 540.

[218] *California:* Falkner v. Hendy, 80 Cal. 636, 22 Pac. 401.

Missouri: Campbell v. Coquard, 93 Mo. 474, 6 S. W. 360; Powell v. Horrell, 92 Mo. App. 406.

[219] Krapp v. Aderholt, 42 Kan. 247.

[220] *Connecticut:* Clark v. Clark, 46 Conn. 586.

Florida: Pearson v. Grice, 8 Fla. 214.

Kansas: Williams v. Hersey, 17 Kan. 18.

Kentucky: Hays v. Williams, 10 Ky.

covered until the verdict, unless the defendant was in fault for not having the account sooner liquidated. It is, however, held in Massachusetts that interest may be recovered from the commencement of legal proceedings.[221] If, however, it became the defendant's duty to have the account adjusted on a certain day, and he failed to do so, interest on the balance found due will be allowed from that time. So where the defendant agreed that the account should be adjusted on a certain day; [222] and where the plaintiff, after a reasonable time made a demand for an accounting. So in Gleason v. Briggs [223] there had been mutual charges and credits. At one time the parties met to make a settlement, but none was effected. Redfield, C. J., said:

"The interest seems to have been cast upon what the auditors found to be due to the plaintiff in 1836, at the time they met and attempted to settle, and which was fairly enough, perhaps, regarded as a demand or claim of payment upon both sides for what should happen to be due. And if it had turned out that the plaintiff owed the defendant at that time a balance, it would seem just to give him interest, and that is what the auditors did for the plaintiff. The law will always imply a contract to pay interest upon a debt payable upon demand, after demand made, by way of damages for the delay. The cases upon this subject may not all be reconcilable, but this is almost the universal rule."

Where the account has been stated by the parties and a

L. Rep. 319; Bale v. Mudd, 63 S. W. 451, 23 Ky. L. Rep. 594.

Michigan: Davis v. Walker, 18 Mich. 25.

New York: Matter of Strickland, 5 N. Y. Supp. 851, 1 Conolly, Surr., 435; Button v. Kinnetz, 88 Hun, 35, 34 N. Y. Supp. 522.

Oregon: Catlin v. Knott, 2 Ore. 321; Pengra v. Wheeler, 24 Ore. 532, 34 Pac. 354.

Vermont: Raymond v. Isham, 8 Vt. 258.

Plaintiff, a tailor, rented a shop from defendant and it was agreed that the rent should be applied to defend-ant's bill with plaintiff for making his clothes. Held that the plaintiff could recover the balance due him with interest from the day that the mutual accounts closed to the date of judgment. McKeon v. Byington, 70 Conn. 429, 39 Atl. 853.

[221] Stimpson v. Greene, 13 All. 326; Freeman v. Freeman, 142 Mass. 98.

[222] Scroggs v. Cunningham, 81 Ill. 110. So where defendant's principal directed defendant to pay plaintiff the balance due, interest runs from that time. Brem v. Covington, 104 N. C. 589, 10 S. E. 706.

[223] 28 Vt. 135, 140.

balance struck, it is payable at once, and interest runs from the accounting; [224] and where an account was rendered by the plaintiff showing a balance due, and was received and kept by the defendant without objection so long that it is found to have been acquiesced in, interest runs from the time the account was rendered. [225] So where a balance is admitted by one party, interest runs on the balance from that time. [226] The cases on the subject of account seem to show that the question of whether interest is to be allowed, and the date from which it is to run, must be determined by all the circumstances of the case, including the usual course of dealing between the parties, and any custom applicable. There may be, for example, as in some stockbrokers' accounts, a custom to charge or credit each entry on both sides of the account with interest. And whenever by business custom interest is charged on the items of a mutual account it will be allowed by the court. [227]

§ 311a. Interest by a fiduciary.

Where a person holding a fiduciary relation to another retains money after being bound to pay it over, interest runs from the time when it should have been paid over. [228] Upon

[224] *United States:* Young v. Godbe, 15 Wall. 562, 21 L. ed. 250.

Illinois: Underhill v. Gaff, 48 Ill. 198; Haight v. McVeagh, 69 Ill. 624; Hartshorn v. Byrne, 147 Ill. 418, 35 N. E. 622 (affirming 45 Ill. App. 250).

Maine: Crosby v. Otis, 32 Me. 256.

Michigan: Emerson v. Atwater, 12 Mich. 314.

New York: Walden v. Sherburne, 15 Johns. 409.

England: Blaney v. Hendricks, 2 W. Bl. 761.

Contra, South Carolina: Chisolm v. Neyle, Harp. 274.

[225] *United States:* Bainbridge v. Wilcocks, Bald. 536.

Iowa: David v. Conard, 1 Greene, 336.

New York: Case v. Hotchkiss, 3 Keyes, 334.

Pennsylvania: Porter v. Patterson, 15 Pa. 229.

[226] *United States:* Vose v. Philbrook, 28 Fed. Cas. No. 17,010, 3 Story, 335.

Illinois: Luetgert v. Volker, 153 Ill. 385, 39 N. E. 113.

New York: Patterson v. Choate, 7 Wend. 441.

[227] *United States:* Barclay v. Kennedy, 2 Fed. Cas. No. 976, 3 Wash. 350.

California: Auzerais v. Naglee, 74 Cal. 60, 15 Pac. 371.

Iowa: Islett v. Oglevie, 9 Iowa, 313.

Louisiana: Thompson v. Mylne, 4 La. Ann. 206.

[228] *Connecticut:* Shipman v. Miller, 2 Root, 405.

Indiana: Sanders v. Scott, 68 Ind. 130.

Massachusetts: White v. Ditson, 140 Mass. 351, 4 N. E. 606.

New Hampshire: Pickering v. De Rochemont, 60 N. H. 179.

New York: Slingerland v. Swart, 13 Johns. 255; Lyons v. Chamberlin, 25

this principle anyone who holds money of another for which he is accountable may be charged with interest, but this is the case only if he is guilty of some wrongful act or neglect. If he has acted properly he cannot be called upon to pay interest.[229] Common instances of persons holding property in a fiduciary capacity are executors, trustees, guardians, assignees for creditors, and agents, and their position will be considered at length; but the same rules apply to all persons who hold property in a fiduciary capacity.[230] Upon this principle an executor whose duty it is to hold a fund as trustee and pay over the proceeds may be charged with interest personally though as executor he would not be liable; and his executor may be called upon to pay such interest, though he would not be liable for interest ordinarily charged on a legacy.[231] Simple interest only can be recovered ordinarily; but if the defendant's conduct was fraudulent, or if he used the property and made a profit from it, he may be charged with compound interest.[232]

§ 311b. Executor or administrator.

An executor or administrator is not usually chargeable with interest on money or on the value of other property of the estate in his hands,[233] unless he mingles the money with

Hun, 49; Monroe County v. Clarke, 25 Hun, 282.

North Carolina: Neal v. Freeman, 85 N. C. 441; McRae v. Malloy, 87 N. C. 196.

Pennsylvania: Rapelie v. Emory, 1 Dall. 349.

Rhode Island: Hazard v. Durant, 14 R. I. 25.

South Carolina: Simpson v. Feltz, 1 McC. Eq. 213.

[229] *United States:* United States v. Butler, 114 Fed. 582.

Illinois: Sampson v. Neely, 106 Ill. App. 129.

New Jersey: Johnson v. Eicke, 12 N. J. L. 316.

[230] County treasurer: Clark v. Sheldon, 134 N. Y. 333, 32 N. E. 23.

Disbursing officer: United States v. Butler, 114 Fed. 582.

Officer of a corporation: Hazard v. Durant, 14 R. I. 25.

Mortgagee in possession: Southern W. L. Co. v. Haas, 76 Ia. 432, 41 N. W. 63.

Creditor given property to sell: Cower v. Lehman, 87 Ala. 362, 6 So. 264.

Surety: Sampson v. Neely, 106 Ill. App. 129.

[231] *California:* Bemmerly v. Woodward, 124 Cal. 568, 57 Pac. 561.

England: Bloss v. Johnson, L. R. 2 Ch. 225.

[232] *Missouri:* Cruce v. Cruce, 81 Mo. 676.

Rhode Island: Hazard v. Durant, 14 R. I. 25.

[233] *United States:* Wade v. Wade's Adm'r, 1 Wash. C. C. 477.

his own,[234] uses it for his own purposes,[235] or is guilty of other misconduct in connection with the estate.[236] If, however, the nature of the administration or the provisions of the will make it necessary for the executor to invest the principal of the estate, he is chargeable with interest if he fails to invest.[237] And when a balance has been found and the executor ordered to pay it over, interest will be due on the balance from that time.[238] Interest is due the estate upon a debt owed to the

Kentucky: Adams v. Bement, 29 S. W. 22, 16 Ky. L. Rep. 676.

Massachusetts: Wyman v. Hubbard, 13 Mass. 232.

New Jersey: Lake v. Park, 19 N. J. L. 108.

Virginia: Dilliard v. Tomlinson, 1 Munf. 22.

England: Blogg v. Johnson, L. R. 2 Ch. 225.

Canada: Boys' Home v. Lewis, 3 Ont. L. Rep. 208.

In a few jurisdictions, however, an executor appears to be chargeable with interest on an annual balance.

Florida: Moore v. Felkel, 7 Fla. 44.

South Carolina: Koon v. Munro, 11 S. C. 139; Tucker v. Richards, 58 S. C. 22, 36 S. E. 3.

[234] *District of Columbia:* Mades v. Miller, 2 D. C. App. Cas. 455.

Massachusetts: Jennison v. Hapgood, 10 Pick. 77.

New York: In re Essex's Estate, 20 N. Y. Supp. 62.

[235] *Alabama:* Pearson v. Darrington, 32 Ala. 227.

California: In re Hilliard, 83 Cal. 423, 23 Pac. 393.

Massachusetts: Stearns v. Brown, 1 Pick. 530.

Missouri: Cruce v. Cruce, 81 Mo. 676.

New York: In re Myers, 131 N. Y. 409, 30 N. E. 135; Matter of Babcock, 9 N. Y. Supp. 554, 2 Connoly, Surr., 82.

Tennessee: Turney v. Williams, 7 Yerg. 172, 24 Am. Dec. 556.

Virginia: Rosser v. Depriest, 5 Gratt. 6, 50 Am. Dec. 94.

[236] *Alabama:* May v. Green, 75 Ala. 162 (delay in distribution).

Arkansas: Price v. Peterson, 38 Ark. 494 (court in discretion may compound interest).

California: Miller v. Lux, 100 Cal. 609, 35 Pac. 345, 639 (improper expenditure).

Nebraska: Bell v. Arndt, 24 Neb. 261, 38 N. W. 750 (failure to pay on order of court).

North Carolina: Jackson v. Shields, 87 N. C. 437 (failure to keep proper accounts).

Tennessee: Torbet v. McReynolds, 4 Humph. 215 (failure to get in property of estate).

[237] *Alabama:* Pearson v. Darrington, 32 Ala. 227.

Florida: Sherrell v. Shepard, 19 Fla. 300; Eppinger v. Canepa, 20 Fla. 262.

Illinois: Hough v. Harvey, 71 Ill. 72.

Missouri: Cruce v. Cruce, 81 Mo. 676.

New Jersey: Halsted v. Meeker, 18 N. J. Eq. 136.

Pennsylvania: Breneman v. Frank, 28 Pa. 475.

Rhode Island: Almy v. Probate Court, 18 R. I. 612, 30 Atl. 458.

[238] *Alabama:* Pettit v. Pettit, 32 Ala. 288.

Louisiana: Sargent v. Davis, 3 La. Ann. 353; St. Andre v. Rachal, 3 La. Ann. 574; Graves v. Barnes, 7 La. Ann. 69.

Maryland: Thomas v. School, 9 Gill & J. 115.

North Carolina: Grant v. Edwards, 93 N. C. 488.

§ 311c TRUSTEE 609

estate by an executor or administrator until it is actually paid.[239] Where one of two executors owes money or does an act which makes him responsible for interest, his fellow executor, if he was cognizant of the facts, is also chargeable.[240] Interest which would otherwise be payable may be expunged because of laches on the part of the beneficiary.[241]

An executor who makes advances to the estate is entitled to charge interest on such advances.[242]

§ 311c. Trustee.

Where a trustee mingles the trust funds with his own, he must pay interest on the amount.[243] So an investment of trust money in stock by a trustee in his own name is a breach of trust, and he may be required to pay interest on the amount invested.[244] *A fortiori* if the trustee uses the trust funds for

South Carolina: Griffin v. Bonham, 9 Rich. Eq. 71 (no interest on balance found due from deceased executor until a successor is appointed to receive it); Tompkins v. Tompkins, 18 S. C. 1.

[239] *Kentucky:* Com. v. Bracken, 17 Ky. L. Rep. 785, 32 S. W. 609.
New Jersey: Terhune v. Oldis, 44 N. J. Eq. 146, 14 Atl. 638.
New York: In re Clark, 11 N. Y. Supp. 911.
Pennsylvania: Rodenbach's Appeal, 102 Pa. 572.
South Carolina: Tompkins v. Tompkins, 18 S. C. 1.
[240] Wilmerding v. McKessom, 103 N. Y. 329, 8 N. E. 665, 28 Hun, 184; In re Clark, 11 N. Y. Supp. 911.
[241] Cook & Brinkley v. Willis, 22 Ark. 1.
[242] *New Jersey:* Liddell v. McVicker, 11 N. J. L. 44, 19 Am. Dec. 369.
New York: Mann v. Lawrence, 3 Bradf. 424.
Pennsylvania: Callaghan v. Hall, 1 S. & R. 241.
South Carolina: Teague v. Dendy, 2 McCord Eq. 207, 16 Am. Dec. 643.
Tennessee: McNairy v. McNairy, 1

Tenn. Cas. 329 (in Alvis v. Oglesby, 87 Tenn. 172, 10 S. W. 313, an administrator who was charged with interest on items against him was allowed interest on credit items).
Vermont: Rix v. Smith, 8 Vt. 365.
Contra, Massachusetts: Storer v. Storer, 9 Mass. 37.
Missouri: McPike v. McPike, 111 Mo. 216, 20 S. W. 12.
[243] *Kentucky:* Singleton v. Singleton, 5 Dana, 97.
Minnesota: St. Paul Trust Co. v. Strong, 85 Minn. 1, 88 N. W. 256.
Mississippi: Banks v. Macher, 40 Miss. 256.
New Jersey: Aldridge v. McClelland, 36 N. J. Eq. 288.
New York: Manning v. Manning, 1 Johns. Ch. 527; Duffy v. Duncan, 35 N. Y. 187.
Pennsylvania: Hess' Estate, 68 Pa. 544; Norris' Appeal, 71 Pa. 106, 123.
Vermont: Perkins v. Hollister, 59 Vt. 348.
Wisconsin: Speiser v. Bank, 110 Wis. 507, 86 N. W. 243.
[244] Morris v. Wallace, 3 Pa. 319, 45 Am. Dec. 641.

39

his own profit he may be called upon to pay interest on them,[245] or the beneficiary may at his option recover the profits of such use.[246] The trustee is chargeable with interest also for failure to invest the trust estate properly,[247] or for other breach of trust.[248] Interest is allowed ordinarily from the time the trustee becomes chargeable.[249]

Compound interest may be allowed for misconduct according to the general rule already stated.[250]

§ 311d. Guardian.

A guardian is bound to make his ward's funds productive;

[245] *Maine:* Abbott v. Stinchfield, 71 Me. 213.

Massachusetts: McKim v. Blake, 139 Mass. 593, 2 N. E. 157.

New Jersey: Voorhees v. Stoothoff, 11 N. J. L. 145.

New York: In re Myers, 131 N. Y. 409, 30 N. E. 135.

[246] *Alabama:* Kyle v. Barnett, 17 Ala. 306.

Illinois: Whitney v. Peddicord, 63 Ill. 249.

[247] *United States:* Barney v. Saunders, 16 How. 535, 14 L. ed. 1047.

Alabama: Andrews v. Huckabee, 30 Ala. 143.

Illinois: Hooper v. Winston, 24 Ill. 353.

New Jersey: Voorhees v. Stoothoff, 11 N. J. L. 145.

New York: Peyster v. Clarkson, 2 Wend. 77.

Australia: Adamson v. Reid, 6 Vict. L. R. (Eq.) 164.

[248] *Illinois:* Ogden v. Larrabee, 57 Ill. 389 (failure to account).

New York: Davidson v. Mexican Nat. R. R., 11 App. Div. 28, 42 N. Y. Supp. 1015 (delay in payment).

[249] Judden v. Dike, 30 Minn. 380, 45 N. W. 672. In Stone v. Framingham, 109 Mass. 303, a trust fund was created for the benefit of a certain academy, the capital to go to the heirs of the donor if the corporation should be dissolved. On dissolution of the corporation, the heirs filed a bill to recover the fund, and it was held that interest could be recovered only from the time when the bill was filed, if no demand or adverse claim had previously been made.

[250] *Ante,* § 311a. So for wrongful sale of the trust property. Adams v. Lambard, 80 Cal. 426, 22 Pac. 180.

But not without some particular misconduct.

United States: Barney v. Saunders, 16 How. 535, 14 L. ed. 1047.

Missouri: Ames v. Scudder, 83 Mo. 189, 11 Mo. App. 168; Gas Light Co. v. St. Louis, 84 Mo. 202.

In Barney v. Saunders, *supra,* Grier, J., said:

"On the subject of compounding interest on trustees there is not, and indeed could not well be, any uniform rule which could justly apply to all cases. When a trust to invest has been grossly and wilfully neglected; where the funds have been used by the trustees in their own business, or profits made of which they give no account, interest is compounded as a punishment, or as a measure of damage for undisclosed profits and in place of them. For mere neglect to invest, simple interest only is generally imposed. Six months' rests have been made only where the amounts received were large and such as could be easily and at all times invested."

and he is therefore chargeable with interest on such funds in his possession after a reasonable time for investment.[251] He is also chargeable with interest on money which he might have collected for his ward,[252] and on a balance which he should have paid over when the ward came of age.[253]

A guardian should at once invest any income which accrues over and above what is appropriated to the support or education of the ward. He is therefore held for interest on any such balance of income, or, as it is usually expressed, for compound interest.[254] Such compounding of interest should cease when the ward comes of age.[255]

The guardian may be charged with interest for misuse of the funds.[256] After a final accounting it is his duty to pay the balance to the ward, and he is chargeable with interest from that time.[257] He is of course not chargeable with interest on money expended for the benefit of the ward.[258] Simple interest only is allowed, unless there is gross abuse of trust.[259]

If the guardian advances money of his own for the support

---

[251] *Alabama:* Bryant *v.* Craig, 12 Ala. 354.

Kentucky: Karr *v.* Karr, 6 Dana, 5.

Minnesota: Crosby *v.* Merriam, 31 Minn. 542, 17 N. W. 950.

Missouri: Frost *v.* Winston, 32 Mo. 489.

North Carolina: Latham *v.* Wilcox, 99 N. C. 367, 8 S. E. 711; (but see *Mississippi:* Neill *v.* Neill, 31 Miss. 36; Roach *v.* Jenks, 40 Miss. 754).

[252] Latham *v.* Wilcox, 99 N. C. 367, 8 S. E. 711.

[253] *Michigan:* Moyer *v.* Fletcher, 56 Mich. 508, 23 N. W. 198.

Missouri: State *v.* Richardson, 29 Mo. App. 595.

[254] *Kentucky:* Karr *v.* Karr, 6 Dana, 5.

Missouri: Frost *v.* Winston, 32 Mo. 489; State *v.* Richardson, 29 Mo. App. 595.

North Carolina: Latham *v.* Wilcox, 99 N. C. 367, 8 S. E. 711.

[255] *Kentucky:* Tanner *v.* Skinner, 11 Bush, 120.

Missouri: State *v.* Richardson, 29 Mo. App. 595.

[256] *Alabama:* Brewer *v.* Ernest, 81 Ala. 435, 2 So. 84 (lending with insufficient security).

Illinois: Winslow *v.* People, 117 Ill. 152, 7 N. E. 135 (improper investment).

Tennessee: Sutton *v.* Cotham, 2 Tenn. Cas. 137 (use in own business).

[257] *Florida:* Fuller *v.* Fuller, 23 Fla. 236, 2 So. 426.

Illinois: Kattelman *v.* Guthrie, 142 Ill. 357, 31 N. E. 589, 43 Ill. App. 188.

Kentucky: Carter *v.* Thorn, 18 B. Mon. 613.

[258] *In re* Flynn, 20 N. Y. Supp. 919, 66 Hun, 628 (discharging mortgage on ward's land).

[259] *Alabama:* Vaughan *v.* Bibb, 46 Ala. 153.

Illinois: Kattleman *v.* Guthrie, 142 Ill. 357, 31 N. E. 589, 43 Ill. App. 188.

Tennessee: Sutton *v.* Cotham, 2 Tenn. Cas. 137.

of the ward, he has been held entitled to interest on such advances.[260]

§ 311e. Agent.

An agent entrusted with money or other property for the use of his principal is not generally chargeable with interest on it.[261] But an agent is chargeable with any income which he actually receives from the use of such money;[262] otherwise he would be making a profit at the expense of his principal;[263] and he is chargeable with interest on money he misuses.[264] An agent is entitled to interest on advances made by him in the principal's business.[265]

§ 311f. Receiver or assignee of insolvent estate.

When an insolvent estate is placed in the hands of a receiver or assignee for distribution, interest ceases upon the claims of creditors from the time the property thus passes.[266] When

[260] Hayward v. Ellis, 13 Pick. (Mass.) 272.

[261] *United States:* Sneed v. Hanly, 22 Fed. Cas. No. 13,136, Hempst. 659.

Kentucky: Riley v. Riley, 14 Ky. L. Rep. 895.

England: Harrington v. Hoggart, 1 B. & Ad. 577, 9 L. J. K. B. O. S. 14, 20 E. C. L. 606.

But in Capital National Bank v. Coldwater National Bank, 49 Neb. 786, 69 N. W. 115, 69 Am. St. Rep. 572, a bank received money in payment of a note which it had for collection, and failed without remitting the money to the party entitled. It was held that this was a trust fund on which interest could be recovered at the legal rate, even though the bank was insolvent and the interest would have to be deducted from the amount to be distributed to the general creditors.

Interest is due from the time of a demand for payment:

Shepherd v. Shepherd, 108 Mich. 82, 65 N. W. 580.

[262] *Connecticut:* Bassett v. Kinney, 24 Conn. 267.

Kentucky: Taylor v. Knox, 1 Dana, 391.

Contra, England: Harrington v. Hoggart, 1 B. & Ad. 577, 9 L. J. K. B. O. S. 14.

So where one is given an interest-bearing claim to collect, he is chargeable with interest: Horne v. Allen, 27 N. C. 36.

[263] Munson v. Plummer, 59 Iowa, 136, 438.

[264] *Georgia:* Nisbet v. Lawson, 1 Ga. 275 (attorney collects money and uses for himself).

Wisconsin: Rogers v. Priest, 74 Wis. 538, 43 N. W. 510.

England: Burdick v. Garrick, L. R. 5 Ch. 233, 39 L. J. Ch. 369, 18 W. Rep. 387 (attorneys used money of client for themselves).

[265] Taylor v. Knox, 1 Dana (Ky.), 391.

[266] *United States:* Thomas v. Western Car Co., 149 U. S. 95, 116, 13 Sup. Ct. 824, 37 L. ed. 663; Hersey v. Fosdick, 30 Fed. 44.

a debt is approved and ordered paid, interest again accrues upon the amount of the dividend until it is paid,[267] even though the payment of it is delayed by an unsuccessful appeal against the allowance;[268] and interest will also run after payment is refused on the amount of the dividend finally allowed on appeal.[269]

The receiver or assignee is personally liable for interest on the funds if he mingles them with his own [270] or uses them for his own purposes,[271] or improperly delays distribution when ordered.[272]

B.—UNLIQUIDATED DEMANDS

§ 312. Unliquidated damages in actions of contract.

The classes of cases already examined are of a simple character. We have now to examine those in which the demand, though arising from breach of contract, is unliquidated, and in which other tests have to be applied; finally ending our examination with torts, some of which, as already explained, are of such a nature that interest is, by the nature of the case, excluded.

Where no price has been agreed upon for goods or services, and the plaintiff recovers on a *quantum meruit* or *quantum*

Massachusetts: Commonwealth *v.* Massachusetts Mut. Ins. Co., 119 Mass. 45.

Montana: Guignon *v.* First Nat. Bank, 22 Mont. 140, 56 Pac. 1051, 1097.

[267] *United States:* Central Trust Co. *v.* Condon, 67 Fed. 84.

Montana: Knatz *v.* Wise, 16 Mont. 555, 41 Pac. 710.

See *Pennsylvania:* McCruden *v.* Jones, 6 Pa. Dist. 146, where on the peculiar form of the award it was held that no interest could be allowed though further proceedings delayed payment.

[268] *United States:* Armstrong *v.* Bank, 133 U. S. 433, 470, 10 Sup. Ct. 450, 33 L. ed. 747.

New York: In re Ilion Nat. Bank, 12 N. Y. Supp. 829.

Where payment was stayed by order

of court it was held that interest would not be allowed. Grand Trunk R. R. *v.* Vermont Central R. R., 91 Fed. 569.

[269] Chemical Nat. Bank *v.* Armstrong, 8 C. C. A. 155, 59 Fed. 372.

[270] *Missouri: In re* Assignment of Murdoch, 129 Mo. 488, 31 S. W. 942.

New York: Livermore *v.* Wortman, 25 Hun, 241.

[271] *Kentucky:* Hodge *v.* Quiry, 9 Ky. L. Rep. 650.

Missouri: In re Assignment of Murdoch, 129 Mo. 488, 31 S. W. 942 (compound interest).

[272] *United States:* Wilkinson *v.* Washington Trust Co., 102 Fed. 28.

Georgia: Anderson *v.* State, 2 Ga. 370.

Illinois: McCune *v.* Hartman Steel Co., 87 Ill. App. 162.

valebant, we have an unliquidated demand; yet on the principle that has been stated this fact alone does not prevent the recovery of interest. Interest is given *from the time when the defendant should have paid the amount due,* and this explains the frequent disallowance of interest in cases of this kind, for it is not generally the duty of a party to pay money until the amount to be paid is ascertained. Consequently unless the amount due is or should be ascertained, the defendant is not in default. But there must be some time within which the account ought to be liquidated; otherwise the creditor must in every case sue, a result which the courts would not look on with favor.

Generally speaking, no interest can be recovered for breach of a contract, where the damages are in their nature unliquidated,[273] until the amount is ascertained. So in an action for services, where the amount of compensation was not fixed [274]

[273] *California:* Hewes *v.* Germania Fruit Co., 106 Cal. 441, 39 Pac. 853.

Colorado: Dexter *v.* Collins, 21 Colo. 455, 42 Pac. 664.

Illinois: Flake *v.* Carson, 33 Ill. 518.

Louisiana: Foster *v.* Dupre, 5 Mart. 6, 12 Am. Dec. 466; Blymer Ice Mach. Co. *v.* McDonald, 48 La. Ann. 439, 19 So. 459.

Michigan: People *v.* Wexford, 37 Mich. 351; Coburn *v.* Muskegon Booming Co., 72 Mich. 134, 40 N. W. 198.

Missouri: Wiggins Ferry Co. *v.* Chicago & A. R. R., 128 Mo. 224, 27 S. W. 568.

Nebraska: Wittenberg *v.* Mollyneaux, 59 Neb. 203, 80 N. W. 824.

Nevada: Vietti *v.* Nesbitt, 22 Nev. 390, 41 Pac. 151.

New Jersey: Speer *v.* Vanorden, 3 N. J. L. 652.

New York: Gray *v.* Central R. R., 89 Hun, 477, 35 N. Y. Supp. 378; Bagley *v.* Stern, 92 N. Y. Supp. 244; Note Co. *v.* Hamilton B. N. E. & P. Co., 92 App. Div. 427, 87 N. Y. Supp. 200.

South Carolina: Devereux *v.* Taft, 20 S. C. 555; Sullivan *v.* Susong, 30 S. C. 305, 9 S. E. 156.

Texas: Wetmore *v.* Woodhouse, 10 Tex. 33.

Virginia: McCommico *v.* Curzen, 2 Call, 301; Waggoner *v.* Gray, 2 Hen. & M. 603; Kerr *v.* Love, 1 Wash. 172.

But see Tifton, T. & G. Ry. *v.* Butler, 60 S. E. 1087, 4 Ga. App. 191, where it is said that the jury may allow interest in such a case.

[274] *California:* Cox *v.* McLaughlin, 76 Cal. 60, 18 Pac. 100, 9 Am. St. Rep. 164; Swinnerton *v.* Argonaut Land & Development Co., 112 Cal. 375, 44 Pac. 719.

Illinois: Griggs *v.* Ganford, 50 Ill. App. 172.

New York: Reid *v.* Rensselaer Glass Factory, 3 Cow. 393; McCollum *v.* Seward, 62 N. Y. 316; Carricarti *v.* Blanco, 121 N. Y. 230, 24 N. E. 284; Godfrey *v.* Moser, 3 Hun, 218, 5 Thomps. & C. 677; Littell *v.* Ellison, 17 N. Y. Supp. 294; *In re* Hartman's Estate, 35 N. Y. Supp. 495; Chambers *v.* Boyd, 101 N. Y. Supp. 486, 116 App. Div. 208; Devine *v.* Kerwin, 102 N. Y. Supp. 841, 52 Misc. 535.

Oregon: Hawley *v.* Dawson, 16 Ore. 344, 18 Pac. 599.

or for work, labor, and materials,[275] no interest can be recovered; nor can it be recovered in an action for failure to deliver goods which have no market value,[276] or to convey land,[277] or to recover the value of goods sold; [278] or for injury to property by breach of contract; [279] or upon an unvalued policy of insurance, as a fire policy; [280] or in general, for breach of contract where by the nature of the case the damages are uncertain.[281]

South Carolina: Sullivan v. Susong, 30 S. C. 305, 9 S. E. 156.

Virginia: Shields v. Anderson, 3 Leigh, 729 (services of slave).

Wisconsin: State v. Warner, 55 Wis. 271, 9 N. W. 795, 13 Md. 255.

But see *Montana:* Leggat v. Gerrick, 35 Mont. 91, 88 Pac. 788.

[275] *California:* Macomber v. Bigelow, 123 Cal. 532, 56 Pac. 449, 126 Cal. 9, 58 Pac. 312.

New York: Anthony v. Moore & Munger Co., 120 N. Y. Supp. 402, 136 App. Div. 933; Weber v. Hearn, 49 App. Div. 213, 63 N. Y. Supp. 41.

Canada: Peters v. Quebec Harbor Com'rs, 19 Can. 685.

[276] *United States:* Barrow v. Reab, 9 How. 366, 13 L. ed. 177.

California: Hewes v. Germain Fruit Co., 106 Cal. 441, 39 Pac. 853.

Missouri: Nelson v. Iron, etc., Co., 102 Mo. App. 498, 77 S. W. 590.

New York: Sloan v. Baird, 162 N. Y. 327, 56 N. E. 752.

[277] Harvey v. Hamilton, 155 Ill. 377, 40 N. E. 592.

[278] *Kentucky:* South v. Leary, Hardin, 518; Harrodsburg Water Co. v. Harrodsburg, 28 Ky. L. Rep. 625, 89 S. W. 729.

South Carolina: Conyers v. Magrath, 4 McCord, 392; Dotterer v. Bennett, 5 Rich. 295.

[279] *Louisiana:* Morgan v. Bell, 4 Mart. 615.

New York: Bleakley v. Sheridan, 115 App. Div. 657, 100 N. Y. Supp. 1029; Shafer, F. & C. S. Co. v. E. M. Upton C. S. Co., 133 App. Div. 796, 118 N. Y. Supp. 8.

[280] *Louisiana:* Nicolet v. New Orleans Ins. Co., 3 La. 366, 23 Am. Dec. 458.

Oregon: Stemmer v. Scottish Ins. Co., 33 Ore. 65, 49 Pac. 588.

[281] *United States:* Gilpins v. Consequa, 10 Fed. Cas. No. 5,452, Pet. C. C. 85, 3 Wash. 184 (breach of warranty of quality of goods sold); Easton v. Houston, etc., R. R., 38 Fed. 784 (breach of contract to hire a car).

California: Coburn v. Goodall, 72 Cal. 498, 14 Pac. 190, 1 Am. St. Rep. 75 (breach of covenant in a lease); Ferrea v. Chabot, 121 Cal. 233, 53 Pac. 689, 1092 (failure to supply water for irrigation and other purposes).

Michigan: Coburn v. Muskegon Booming Co., 72 Mich. 134, 40 N. W. 198 (interfering with performance of contract).

Minnesota: Swanson v. Andrus, 83 Minn. 505, 86 N. W. 465 (breach of contract by plaintiff to construct building).

New York: Holliday v. Marshall, 7 Johns. 211 (agreement by defendant to take buildings at expiration of lease); Mansfield v. New York Central & H. R. R. R., 114 N. Y. 331, 21 N. E. 735, 1037, 4 L. R. A. 566 (failure to complete in time foundations of building); Gray v. New Jersey Cent. R. R., 157 N. Y. 483, 52 N. E. 555 (affirming 82 Hun, 523, 31 N. Y. Supp. 704); Docter v. Darling, 68 Hun, 70, 22 N. Y. Supp. 594 (breach of covenant against incumbrances); Crawford v. Mail, etc.,

§ 313. Damages capable of computation—New York rule.

A rule has been established by the Court of Appeals of New York in the leading case of Van Rensselaer v. Jewett,[282] which covers a large class of cases; namely, those cases where the amount can be ascertained by computation, together with a reference to well-established market values. In such cases interest will be allowed.[283] This rule was commented upon in the case of McMahon v. New York & Erie Railroad.[284] The action was for work, labor, and services under a contract for building part of the defendants' road. The contract provided for three classes of work, and at certain periods the engineer of the company was to make estimates of the amount of each class of work done, and these estimates were to form the basis of payment. The engineer did not make the estimates, and the plaintiff brought suit on the contract. The referee allowed interest on the amount found due by him, and to this an exception was taken. Selden, J., delivered the opinion of the court on this point, as follows:

"The old common-law rule which required that a demand

Pub. Co., 22 App. Div. 54, 47 N. Y. Supp. 747 (breach of contract to employ).

North Carolina: Lewis v. Rountree, 79 N. C. 122, 28 Am. Rep. 309 (breach of warranty of quality of goods sold).

Oregon: Pengra v. Wheeler, 24 Ore. 532, 24 Pac. 354, 21 L. R. A. 726 (deduction from rent for failure to furnish agreed water power); Poppleton v. Jones, 42 Ore. 24, 69 Pac. 919 (agreement to pay for property in building materials).

Virginia: Stearns v. Mason, 24 Gratt. 484 (bonds dischargeable in depreciated currency).

Canada: McCullough v. Clemow, 26 Ont. 467 (contract for division of profits of a business).

[282] 2 N. Y. 135.

[283] *California:* Ryland v. Heney, 130 Cal. 426, 62 Pac. 616.

Nebraska: Missouri, etc., R. R. v. Clark, 60 Neb. 406, 83 N. W. 202.

New York: DeLavallette v. Wendt, 75 N. Y. 579, 31 Am. Rep. 494; Clegg v. New York Newspaper Union, 73 Hun, 395, 25 N. Y. Supp. 565; Kervin v. Utter, 120 App. Div. 610, 104 N. Y. Supp. 1061.

Pennsylvania: Noblit v. Briggs, 8 Phila. 275.

Wisconsin: Paycock v. Parker, 103 Wis. 161, 186, 79 N. W. 327.

Wyoming: Kuhn v. McKay, 7 Wyo. 42, 49 Pac. 473, 51 Pac. 205.

See Kelly v. Fall Brook Coal Co., 67 Barb. (N. Y.) 183.

So where the amount of the claim is undisputed, the contest being on liability only: Locomobile Co. v. De Witt, 59 Misc. 221, 110 N. Y. Supp. 413.

[284] 20 N. Y. 463, 469. In an action by a discharged employee, the term not having expired, the damages are unliquidated, and consequently the New York courts do not allow interest. Crawford v. Mail & Express Pub. Co., 47 N. Y. Supp. 747.

should be liquidated, or its amount in some way ascertained, before interest could be allowed, has been modified by general consent, so far as to hold that if the amount is capable of being ascertained by mere computation, then it shall carry interest; and this court, in the case of Van Rensselaer *v.* Jewett, went a step further, and allowed interest upon an unliquidated demand, the amount of which could be ascertained by computation, together with a reference to well-established market values; because such values, in many cases, are so nearly certain, that it would be possible for the debtor to obtain some proximate knowledge of how much he was to pay. That case went, I think, as far as it is reasonable and proper to go in that direction. So long as the courts adhere even to the principles of that case, they are not without a rule which it is possible to apply. The rule itself is definite, and the only uncertainty which it introduces is that which necessarily attends the settling of market rates and prices. In the present case, the plaintiff's demand was neither liquidated, nor capable of being ascertained by computation merely; nor could its amount be determined by any reference to ordinary market rates, and hence interest could not be recovered here, upon the principle adopted in the case of Van Rensselaer *v.* Jewett." [285]

In Sipperly *v.* Stewart [286] the plaintiff sued to recover the value of the use of a canal-boat. Miller, J., held that, on the principle of McMahon *v.* New York & Erie Railroad, interest should be allowed, as the value of the use could be ascertained by reference to market rates. It seems, however, that the rule cannot be extended to cover cases of mutual accounts. In Smith *v.* Velie [287] the plaintiff sued for services rendered as housekeeper. There had been payments on account, and Grover, J., held that interest on the balance could not be allowed, as the case showed that the accounts were open and unliquidated. He then said that McMahon *v.* New York & Erie Railroad was a direct authority against the allowance of interest. "There was no time fixed for payment. The case shows that there was no fixed market value by which the

[285] *Acc.*, Mansfield *v.* New York C. & H. R. R. R., 114 N. Y. 331.

[286] 50 Barb. 62.

[287] 60 N. Y. 106.

rate of wages could be determined. There was no default in the intestate or appellant in determining the balance due the claimant. Under such a state, the learned judge says, in the case cited, interest cannot be allowed." These last two cases are, we think, only distinguishable by the fact that the account in the latter was mutual, and not in the former. It is true that Grover, J., says, in the latter, that there was no market value for the services, and nothing is said on that point in the former. But the decision in the latter case was based on the ground that there was an open account between the parties, and the judge cites, in support of his decision, two cases [288]—both of which were cases of mutual accounts. Interest was disallowed in them on this ground, and in one of them, at least, the articles had a market value.

On breach of a contract to buy personal property, the vendor has a choice of three remedies. He may sue for the contract price, in which case he recovers interest; he may sell the property and recover the difference between the amount realized and the contract price; or he may sue for damages, in which case he recovers the difference between the contract price and the market value. In this case, the damages are unliquidated, but on principle, under this rule mentioned above, interest would seem to be recoverable. But the New York Court of Appeals has, in the case of the sale of a ferryboat, held otherwise. [289]

This decision appears to rest on the ground that there was no clear evidence of market value, and the same conclusion was subsequently reached in the case of the breach of a contract to convey real estate. [290] The principle of these cases seems to be that whenever the defendant cannot know in advance the exact sum he should pay, as by reference to market value, he need not pay any; but in that sense every

[288] Holmes v. Rankin, 17 Barb. 454; McKnight v. Dunlop, 4 Barb. 36.

[289] Gray v. Central R. R., 157 N. Y. 483, 52 N. E. 555. See the dissenting opinion of O'Brien, J., p. 487.

In International Contracting Co. v. Nichol, 105 Fed. 553, interest was allowed.

[290] Sloan v. Baird, 162 N. Y. 327, 56 N. E. 752. O'Brien, J., again forcibly dissents, pointing out that in this case (which was against the vendor of real estate) the plaintiff had been deprived of his rents and profits.

demand for damages is unliquidated until a verdict has been rendered.   In New York a defendant may by statute, in an action of contract, defeat all claim for damages, or limit the recovery, by serving on the plaintiff an offer to liquidate the damages at a specified sum.[291]

§ 313a.   Failure to deliver goods.

Where property is paid for in advance and the seller fails to deliver it, the purchaser recovers interest on the value from the time it should have been delivered.[292]   And so in case of any failure to deliver property.   Thus in a case already cited, where the rent was payable in wheat and services, the Court of Appeals of New York held this language: [293]

"Whenever a debtor is in default for not paying money, delivering property, or rendering services, in pursuance of his contract, justice requires that he should indemnify the creditor for the wrong which has been done him; and a just indemnity, though it may sometimes be more, can never be less than the specified amount of money or the value of the property or services at the time they should have been paid or rendered, with interest from the time of the default until the obligation

[291] Code Civ. Proc., §§ 736, 737.

[292] *California:* Pujol v. McKinlay, 42 Cal. 559.

Georgia: Garrard v. Dawson, 49 Ga. 434.

Maryland: Andrews v. Clark, 72 Md. 396, 20 Atl. 429.

Mississippi: Bickell v. Colton, 41 Miss. 368.

Rhode Island: Bicknall v. Waterman, 5 R. I. 43.

Virginia: Merryman v. Criddle, 4 Munf. 542; Enders v. Board of Public Works, 1 Gratt. 364, 390.

Contra, United States: Gilpins v. Consequa, 10 Fed. Cas. No. 5,452, Pet. C. C. 85, 3 Wash. 184.

Indiana: Dobenspeck v. Armel, 11 Ind. 31.

Interest allowed from date of writ: *California:* Packing Co. v. Canty, 141 Cal. 692, 75 Pac. 564.

Wisconsin: Gallum v. Seymour, 76 Wis. 251, 45 N. W. 115.

Interest allowed in discretion of jury: *United States:* District of Columbia v. Camden Iron Works, 181 U. S. 453, 21 Sup. Ct. 680, 45 L. ed. 948.

Kentucky: Stark v. Price, 5 Dana, 140.

New York: Dox v. Dey, 3 Wend. 356. *Tennessee:* Noe v. Hodges, 5 Humph. 103.

Where the goods have no market value, no interest can be recovered, *ante*, § 312.

[293] Van Rensselaer v. Jewett, 5 Denio, 135, 2 N. Y. 135, overruling Van Rensselaer v. Platner, 1 Johns. 276. See, also, an able opinion of Willard, J., in Van Rensselaer v. Jones, 2 Barb. 643, where the whole subject is examined, and a note to Lattin v. Davis, Hill and Denio Suppl. 9.

is discharged. And if the creditor is obliged to resort to the court for redress, he ought in all such cases to recover interest, in addition to the debt, by way of damages. It is true that on an agreement like the one under consideration, the amount of the debt can only be ascertained by an inquiry concerning the value of the property and services; but the value can be ascertained, and when that has been done, the creditor, as a question of principle, is just as plainly entitled to interest after the default as he would be if the like sum had been payable in money." [294]

So in McKenney v. Haines [295] the plaintiff sued for breach of contract to return borrowed stock on demand. It was held that he could recover interest on the value at the time of demand. [296] And in Canton v. Smith, [297] where the plaintiff had given bonds to the defendant, under an agreement to complete a railroad or return the bonds, it was held "clearly correct" to charge the jury that interest should be allowed on the value of the bonds.

When property sold and not delivered has not been paid for, interest is allowed on the difference between the contract and market price. [298] In Dana v. Fiedler, [299] Johnson, J., said:

"Interest is a necessary item in the estimate of damages in this class of cases. The party is entitled, on the day of performance, to the property agreed to be delivered; if it is not delivered the law gives as the measure of compensation then due the difference between the contract and market prices. If he is not also entitled to interest from that time as matter of law, this contradictory result follows, that, while an indemnity is professedly given, the law adopts such a mode

[294] Acc., *Illinois:* Sanderson v. Read, 75 Ill. App. 190.

New York: Livingston v. Miller, 11 N. Y. 80.

[295] 63 Me. 74.

[296] See also Savannah & C. R. R. v. Callahan, 56 Ga. 331.

[297] 65 Me. 203.

[298] *United States:* Barrow v. Reab, 9 How. 366, 13 L. ed. 177.

Illinois: Cease v. Cockle, 76 Ill. 484; Driggers v. Bell, 94 Ill. 223.

Massachusetts: Thomas v. Wells, 140 Mass. 517, 5 N. E. 485.

New York: Clark v. Dales, 20 Barb. 42; Hamilton v. Ganyard, 34 Barb. 204; Fishell v. Winans, 38 Barb. 228; Currie v. White, 6 Abb. (N. S.) 352, 385.

Wisconsin: Jones v. Foster, 67 Wis. 296, 30 N. W. 697.

[299] 12 N. Y. 40.

of ascertaining its amount, that the longer a party is delayed in obtaining it, the greater shall its inadequacy become."

§ 314. Demand for settlement or payment.

In some cases it has been held that interest runs from the time the plaintiff demanded a settlement, i. e., when the demand is reasonable and puts the defendant in default. Thus in Pennsylvania, in Gray v. Van Amringe,[300] the court held a demand sufficient to entitle the plaintiff to interest. The action was for services rendered. An account had been presented, but payment had been refused, on the ground that the charges were excessive. The plaintiff recovered the full amount demanded. In delivering the opinion of the court, Kennedy, J., said: "In a case, therefore, where the plaintiff has performed work, labor, and services of any kind, no matter what, at the special instance and request of the defendant, without any express agreement between them fixing the prices or sums of money that shall be paid therefor, and after having performed the same, demands of the defendant what shall be deemed afterwards, by a court and jury, a reasonable compensation, which the latter refuses to pay, it would seem to be just that the plaintiff should recover interest on the amount so demanded, from the time of the demand."

A demand, not for an accounting and agreement on the amount due, but for a sum assumed by the plaintiff to be due, is sometimes said to be enough to put the defendant in default if the sum is a reasonable one. So where an attorney presents a bill for his services, the charges being found to have been reasonable, interest is allowed from the presentment of the bill.[301] This may be supported, upon the ground that it is really a proper demand for a settlement. A demand for the payment of an unreasonably large sum of money will cer-

[300] 2 W. & S. 128.

[301] *Illinois:* Casey v. Carver, 42 Ill. 225.

Massachusetts: Barnard v. Bartholomew, 22 Pick. 291.

New York: Adams v. Fort Plain Bank, 36 N. Y. 255; Mygatt v. Wilcox,

45 N. Y. 306; Hand v. Church, 39 Hun, 303; Richmond County Soc. v. New York, 73 App. Div. 607, 77 N. Y. Supp. 41.

But *contra*, People v. Supervisors, 9 Abb. (N. S.) 408.

tainly not put the defendant in default, so as to subject him to the payment of interest.[302]

In other cases, it has been held that interest is recoverable from the beginning of the suit;[303] while still others hold that interest can be allowed neither from demand nor from the beginning of the suit, but only from the verdict, since the defendant did not know before that how much he must pay.[304] It is well said in New York that if a demand will not set interest running, the bringing of a suit should not.[305]

If no demand is made for settlement or claim presented by the plaintiff, the defendant is not in default, and interest cannot be recovered;[306] and this is especially true where the plaintiff is himself to blame for unreasonable delay in presenting his claim.[307]

§ 314a. Duty to liquidate claim.

Where by the contract it was the defendant's duty at a certain time to liquidate the debt, and he fails to do so, interest

[302] *Massachusetts:* Goff *v.* Rehoboth, 2 Cush. 475.

Wisconsin: Shipman *v.* State, 44 Wis. 458.

[303] *United States:* Goddard *v.* Foster, 17 Wall. 123, 21 L. ed. 589; Dwyer *v.* United States, 93 Fed. 616, 35 C. C. A. 488.

Louisiana: Brownson *v.* Fenwick, 19 La. 431.

Massachusetts: Quin *v.* Bay State Distilling Co., 171 Mass. 283, 50 N. E. 637.

Missouri: Trimble *v.* Kansas City, P. & G. R. R., 180 Mo. 574, 79 S. W. 678; Berner *v.* Bagnell, 20 Mo. App. 543; Nelson *v.* Hirsch & S. I. R. R., 102 Mo. App. 498, 77 S. W. 590.

New York: Mercer *v.* Vose, 67 N. Y. 56; Hand *v.* Church, 39 Hun, 303.

Wisconsin: Gammon *v.* Abrams, 53 Wis. 323; Tucker *v.* Grover, 60 Wis. 240.

[304] *California:* Cox *v.* McLaughlin, 76 Cal. 60, 18 Pac. 100, 9 Am. St. Rep. 164.

Kentucky: Murray *v.* Ware, 1 Bibb, 325.

Massachusetts: Needham *v.* Wellesley, 139 Mass. 372, 31 N. E. 732 (under the special circumstances).

New York: McKnight *v.* Dunlop, 4 Barb. 36; Pursell *v.* Fry, 19 Hun, 595; Day *v.* N. Y. C. R. R., 22 Hun, 412.

Wisconsin: Martin *v.* State, 51 Wis. 407.

[305] White *v.* Miller, 78 N. Y. 393; McMaster *v.* State, 108 N. Y. 542.

[306] *Kentucky:* Adams Exp. Co. *v.* Milton, 11 Bush, 49.

Missouri: Southgate *v.* Atlantic & P. R. R., 61 Mo. 89.

New York: Gallup *v.* Perue, 10 Hun, 525; People *v.* Supervisors, 9 Abb. (N. S.) 408; People *v.* Clinton County, 19 N. Y. Supp. 642.

Wisconsin: Marsh *v.* Fraser, 37 Wis. 149; Lowe *v.* Ring, 123 Wis. 370, 101 N. W. 698.

[307] 11 Vt. 214.

can without doubt be recovered on the balance found due from that time.[308]   Such a consideration seems to have governed the court in Robinson *v.* Stewart.[309]   The action was to set aside certain conveyances made to the defendant by his father, in fraud of the latter's creditors.   The father had been indebted to the defendant on an account for services rendered, and conveyed the property to him nominally in payment. The property, however, greatly exceeded the services in value. The defendant claimed, as set-off, the value of his services, with interest.   Denio, J., said: "The demand being wholly unliquidated, interest should not have been allowed prior to the conveyances.   The deceased attempted to pay this debt by the conveyances, by means of the property conveyed on the 15th of January, 1842.   From that time, I think, the defendant was entitled to interest."   So where an insurance company instead of adjusting the loss, denied all liability, it was held bound to pay interest upon the amount eventually found due.[310]   This principle seems to have been overlooked in the early case of Holliday *v.* Marshall.[311]   By the terms of a lease the buildings erected on the leased premises were to be taken at the end of the lease by defendant, the landlord, at an appraised valuation.   At the expiration of the lease defendant refused to join in the appraisal; and the court refused to give interest until the amount was liquidated by verdict.   It would seem that interest should have been allowed from the time the appraisal should have been made.

§ 314b. Amount payable subject to reduction by unliquidated sum.

Where the defendant claims a reduction and succeeds in reducing the amount of damages by recoupment, or other abatement, we have a case of *quantum meruit* on both sides, analogous to a mutual account out of court.   The cases generally allow no

---

[308] *Alabama:* Moore *v.* Patton, 2 Port. 451.

New York: McMahon *v.* New York & E. R. R., 20 N. Y. 463; Davidson *v.* Mexican Nat. R. R., 11 App. Div. 28, 42 N. Y. Supp. 1015.

Canada: Ansley *v.* Peters, 1 All. (N. B.) 339.

[309] 10 N. Y. 189, 197.

[310] Bernhard *v.* Rochester G. I. Co., 79 Conn. 388, 65 Atl. 134.

[311] 7 Johns. (N. Y.) 211.

interest before verdict.[312]　It would seem, however, that it may in such cases be a question of the time when the balance is payable; and that the court should allow interest from that time.　Nor is it easy to see how it can be held that the balance is not payable at least as early as the beginning of the suit.[313] If one claim is liquidated in amount, interest will run on that claim though the counterclaim is unliquidated;[314] but in such a case interest is often allowed on the balance only, from the time the counterclaim accrued, or, what amounts to the same thing, interest is allowed on both sides of the account.[315]

§ 315. General conclusion.

The subject is without doubt a difficult one, and the decisions, as have been seen, are not harmonious.　But by keeping in mind the fundamental principle much of the difficulty may be avoided.　As soon as it is the legal duty of the defendant to pay, he is liable for interest.　As the defendant must have been in default before the action is brought, if the plaintiff

[312] *United States:* The Isaac Newton, 1 Abb. Adm. 588.
California: Brady v. Wilcoxson, 44 Cal. 239.
Illinois: McCormick v. Elston, 16 Ill. 204.
Minnesota: Bull v. Rich, 92 Minn. 481, 100 N. W. 213.
New York: Still v. Hall, 20 Wend. 51; McMaster v. State, 108 N. Y. 542; Blake v. Krom, 128 N. Y. 64, 27 N. E. 977; Excelsior Terra Cotta Co. v. Harde, 181 N. Y. 11, 73 N. E. 494, 106 Am. St. Rep. 493; H. G. Vogel Co. v. Lockport Glass Co., 118 N. Y. Supp. 351, 64 Misc. 343.
Tennessee: Stamps v. Tennessee Producers' Marble Co., 59 S. W. 769.

[313] *Massachusetts:* Palmer v. Stockwell, 9 Gray, 237 (from the date of the writ).
Nevada: Skinker v. Clute, 9 Nev. 342 (from the filing of the answer setting up the counterclaim).
New York: Sickels v. Herold, 149 N. Y. 332, 43 N. E. 852 (from the filing of the answer).

South Carolina: Greer v. Latimer, 47 S. C. 176, 25 S. E. 136 (from the time the amount was settled).
See Brown v. Brown, 124 Mo. 79, 27 S. W. 552.

[314] *Connecticut:* Healy v. Fallon, 69 Conn. 228, 37 Atl. 495 (contract price).
New York: Van Buren v. Van Gaasbeck, 4 Cow. 496 (bond).
Oregon: Smith v. Turner, 33 Ore. 379, 54 Pac. 166 (note).
South Carolina: Morse v. Ellerbe, 4 Rich. 600 (note).
Wisconsin: Thorn v. Smith, 71 Wis. 18, 36 N. W. 707 (note); Hewitt v. John Week Lumber Co., 77 Wis. 548, 46 N. W. 822 (goods sold).

[315] *Arkansas:* Rogers v. Yarrell, 51 Ark. 198, 10 S. W. 622.
Kentucky: Lee v. Reed, 4 Dana, 109.
Minnesota: Minneapolis Harvester Works v. Bonnallie, 29 Minn. 373, 13 N. W. 149; Brown v. Doyle, 69 Minn. 543, 72 N. W. 814.
Texas: Adkins v. Waite, 35 Tex. 577.

recovers, and as his default consisted in withholding money due, plaintiff should, it seems, get interest at least from the date of the writ. There seems to be good reason for going further, and holding defendant to be in default from a demand by the plaintiff for an accounting (made after a reasonable time) and a refusal to account. From that time the defendant cannot claim any right to withhold whatever balance was in fact due, and would have been found due if he had acceded to the plaintiff's demand; before that, the plaintiff cannot claim any right to payment. Where interest is refused in actions of contract on the ground that the claim is unliquidated, it is in fact usually allowed from the date of the writ;[316] and where the claim, though unliquidated in the beginning, was fixed in amount by a later event, interest runs from the time it became liquidated.[317] In all such cases, since the allowance of interest is necessary for full compensation, the inclination of the court should be to allow it.

"The purpose sought in awarding damages other than vindictive is to make a fair compensation to one who has suffered an injury.[318] Courts are more and more coming to recognize that a rule forbidding an allowance for interest upon unliquidated damages is one well calculated to defeat that purpose in many cases, and that no right reason exists for drawing an arbitrary distinction between liquidated and unliquidated damages.[319] There are actions to which the suggested rule is applicable.[320] Others, however, present conditions where without an allowance for interest, although the demand may be unliquidated, fair compensation for the injury done would not be accorded and justice thus denied. The determination of whether or no interest is to be recognized as a proper element of damage is one to be made in

[316] *New York:* McCollum v. Seward, 62 N. Y. 316; Mercer v. Vose, 67 N. Y. 56.

Wisconsin: Tucker v. Grover, 60 Wis. 240; Hewitt v. John Week Lumber Co., 77 Wis. 548, 46 N. W. 822.

[317] *Maryland:* Pearce v. Wallace, 1 Harr. & J. 48.

New York: Ryckman v. Parkins, 5 Paige, 543.

Texas: Craig v. Dumars, 7 Tex. Civ. App. 28, 26 S. W. 743.

[318] Citing Barker v. Lewis Storage & Transfer Co., 78 Conn. 198, 200, 61 Atl. 363.

[319] Citing Sedgwick on Damages (8th ed.), §§ 299, 300, 312, 315.

[320] Citing Regan v. New York & N. E. R. R., 60 Conn. 124, 142, 22 Atl. 503, 25 Am. St. Rep. 306.

40

view of the demands of justice rather than through the application of any arbitrary rule." [321]

§ 316.[a] Interest in actions of tort.

It sufficiently appears from what has been already said that there is no general principle which prevents the recovery of interest in actions of tort. The fact that the demand is unliquidated has been shown to be insufficient to exclude interest, and there is nothing in the mere form of the action which renders it unreasonable that interest should be given. Nevertheless it is in the region of tort that we find the clearest cases for the disallowance of interest.

There are many actions of tort which are not brought to recover a sum of money representing a property loss of the plaintiff, and it is frequently said broadly that interest is not allowed in such actions.[322] It is certainly not allowed in such actions as assault and battery,[323] or for personal injury by negligence,[324] libel, slander, seduction, false imprisonment. But where the tort is of a sort to deprive the plaintiff of property, though not (as in the case of conversion) taking away his title to any specific thing, interest is frequently, and perhaps generally, allowed. Thus, where the value of property

---

[a] For § 316 of the eighth edition see § 317.

[321] Prentice, J., in Bernhard v. Rochester G. I. Co., 79 Conn. 388, 65 Atl. 134; citing on the final paragraph: New York, N. H. & H. R. R. v. Ansonia L. & W. P. Co., 72 Conn. 703, 705, 46 Atl. 157.

[322] Plymouth v. Graver, 125 Pa. 24, 17 Atl. 249; Emerson v. Schoonmaker, 135 Pa. 437, 19 Atl. 1025.

[323] *Georgia:* Ratteree v. Chapman, 79 Ga. 574.

Massachusetts: Winslow v. Hathaway, 1 Pick. 211.

Pennsylvania: Pittsburgh S. Ry. v. Taylor, 104 Pa. 306.

[324] *Georgia:* Central R. R. v. Sears, 66 Ga. 499; Ratteree v. Chapman, 79 Ga. 574, 4 S. E. 684; Western & A. R.

R. v. Young, 81 Ga. 397, 7 S. E. 912, 12 Am. St. Rep. 320.

Iowa: Jacobsen v. United States Gypsum Co., 130 N. W. 122.

Kentucky: McMurtry v. Kentucky Cent. R. R., 84 Ky. 462, 1 S. W. 815, 8 Ky. L. Rep. 455.

Maine: Sargent v. Hampden, 38 Me. 581.

Tennessee: Louisville & N. R. R. v. Wallace, 91 Tenn. 35, 17 S. W. 882, 17 L. R. A. 548.

Texas: Texas & N. O. R. R. v. Carr, 91 Tex. 332, 43 S. W. 18.

Utah: Nichols v. Union Pac. Ry., 7 Utah, 510, 27 Pac. 693.

West Virginia: Fowler v. Baltimore & O. R. R., 18 W. Va. 579.

But see *Arkansas:* St. Louis, I. M. & S. Ry. v. Cleere, 77 Ark. 377, 88 S. W. 995.

is diminished by an injury wrongfully inflicted, it has been held that the jury may give interest on the amount by which the value was diminished, from the time of the injury.[325] So interest has been allowed on the money spent in repairing property injured,[326] or in repurchasing property wrongfully taken and sold by the defendant.[327] In an action against a carrier for delay in the delivery of goods, interest is allowed on the amount found due at the time they were delivered.[328] In an action for false representations, by which the

[325] *Connecticut:* New York, etc., R. R. *v.* Ansonia Land, etc., Co., 72 Conn. 703, 46 Atl. 157 (on any item which could be ascertained by computation).

Illinois: Chicago, etc., R. R. *v.* Shultz, 55 Ill. 421. (But see Chicago, etc., R. R. *v.* Davis, 54 Ill. App. 130.)

Iowa: Burdick *v.* Chicago, etc., R. R., 87 Iowa, 384, 54 N. W. 439; Black *v.* R. R., 122 Iowa, 32, 96 N. W. 984.

Massachusetts: Gillett *v.* Western R. R., 8 All. 560.

Texas: Galveston, H. & S. A. Ry. *v.* Johnston (Tex. Civ. App.), 19 S. W. 867; Gulf C. & S. F. Ry. *v.* Calhoun (Tex. Civ. App.), 24 S. W. 362; Gulf, C. & S. F. Ry. *v.* Dunlap (Tex. Civ. App.), 26 S. W. 655; Gulf, C. & S. F. Ry. *v.* Graves, 45 Tex. Civ. App. 375, 101 S. W. 488.

Contra, Kansas: Atchison, T. & S. F. R. R. *v.* Ayers, 56 Kan. 176, 42 Pac. 722.

Kentucky: Ormsby *v.* Johnson, 1 B. Mon. 80.

Missouri: Somenfield Millinery Co. *v.* People's R. R., 59 Mo. App. 668. (But see Goodman *v.* Missouri R. R., 71 Mo. App. 460, interest allowed because action sounded in contract.)

Interest was held to be in the discretion of the jury in the following cases:

Georgia: McConnell Bros. *v.* Slappey, 134 Ga. 95, 67 S. E. 440.

New York: Wilson *v.* Troy, 135 N. Y. 96, 32 N. E. 44; Black *v.* Camden & A. R. R. & Tr. Co., 45 Barb. 40; Reiss *v.* New York Steam Co., 128 N. Y. 103, 28 N. E. 24, 12 N. Y. Supp. 557. (But see Walrath *v.* Redfield, 18 N. Y. 457; Parrott *v.* Knickerbocker Ice Co., 46 N. Y. 361; Ludlow *v.* Yonkers, 43 Barb. 493; Fitch *v.* Livingston, 4 Sandf. 492.)

North Dakota: Ell *v.* Northern Pac. R. R., 1 N. D. 336, 48 N. W. 222, 26 Am. St. Rep. 621, 12 L. R. A. 97.

[326] Whitehall T. Co. *v.* New Jersey S. B. Co., 51 N. Y. 369.

[327] *Kansas:* Dodson *v.* Cooper, 37 Kan. 346.

New Hampshire: Felton *v.* Fuller, 35 N. H. 226.

Pennsylvania: McInroy *v.* Dyer, 47 Pa. 118.

[328] *Arkansas:* St. Louis, etc., R. R. *v.* Mudford, 44 Ark. 439; St. Louis, etc., R. R. *v.* Phelps, 46 Ark. 485.

Georgia: East Tennessee, V. & G. Ry. *v.* Johnson, 85 Ga. 497, 11 S. E. 809.

Mississippi: Illinois C. R. R. *v.* Haynes, 64 Miss. 604, 1 So. 765.

Texas: Houston & T. C. Ry. *v.* Jackson, 62 Tex. 209; Gulf, C. & S. F. R. R. *v.* McCart, 82 Tex. 608, 18 S. W. 716; Dorrance & Co. *v.* International & G. N. R. R. (Tex. Civ. App.), 125 S. W. 561.

Vermont: Newell *v.* Smith, 49 Vt. 255.

From beginning of action in *Louisiana:* Ryder *v.* Thayer, 3 La. Ann. 149.

defendant obtained money from the plaintiff, interest on the money is allowed,[329] and so where by false representations of the defendant the plaintiff was induced to keep his money idle; [330] and where property is fraudulently obtained from the plaintiff by the defendant, interest on the value will be allowed.[331] So where the defendant, by his refusal to perform an official duty, prevented the plaintiff from recovering money due him, the plaintiff was entitled to interest on the money from the time he should have had it.[332] So where the principal's property is, by the misconduct or negligence of the agent, disposed of for less than its value, the agent is liable for interest on the balance that he should have procured for his principal.[333] In an action for waste, it was held that interest could be recovered from the date of the writ, there having been no demand for payment.[334]

So in actions for breach of warranty of an article sold, which, though in form contract, closely resemble actions for false representations, interest is allowed upon the difference between what the article is actually worth and what it would have been worth had it been as represented.[335] Stoudenmeier

[329] *Colorado:* Mayor v. Wahlgreen, 9 Colo. App. 506, 50 Pac. 40.

Illinois: Pungs v. American Brake Beam Co., 102 Ill. App. 76, affirmed 200 Ill. 306, 65 N. E. 645.

Missouri: Arthur v. Wheeler & W. M. Co., 12 Mo. App. 335.

So where fraud was used by bankers to conceal the fact that they held on deposit money belonging to the estate of a deceased: Leake Orphan House v. Lawrence, 11 Paige (N. Y.), 80.

[330] Place v. Dodge, 54 Ill. App. 167.

[331] *Illinois:* Steere v. Hoagland, 50 Ill. 377 (taking goods in fraud of creditors); Deimel v. Brown, 136 Ill. 586, 27 N. E. 44 (taking goods in fraud of creditors).

Maryland: Andrews v. Clark, 72 Md. 396, 20 Atl. 429 (deceit).

Michigan: Cook v. Perry, 43 Mich. 623, 5 N. W. 1054 (deceit).

Missouri: McBeth v. Craddock, 28 Mo. App. 380 (deceit).

Wisconsin: Shaw v. Gilbert, 111 Wis. 165, 195, 86 N. W. 188 (deceit).

Contra, Virginia: Burgh v. Shanks, 5 Leigh, 598 (deceit).

Interest in such cases in the discretion of the jury:

United States: Lincoln v. Claflin, 7 Wall. 132, 19 L. ed. 106 (deceit).

New York: Nichols v. Coleman, 96 App. Div. 353, 89 N. Y. Supp. 234 (deceit).

[332] Clark v. Miller, 54 N. Y. 528. *Contra* in the case of a debt lost through delay of a telegraph company: Pacific P. T. Co. v. Fleischner, 66 Fed. 899, 14 C. C. A. 166; and see State v. Harrington, 44 Mo. App. 297.

[333] *Massachusetts:* Greenfield Savings Bank v. Simons, 133 Mass. 415.

New York: Milbank v. Dennistoun, 1 Bosw. 246.

[334] Dawes v. Winship, 5 Pick. 97, *n.*

[335] *Alabama:* Kornegay v. White, 10 Ala. 255; Marshall v. Wood, 16 Ala.

v. Williamson [336] was an action for breach of warranty of a slave. The court said: "We hold that, in this State, whenever one party has a legal right to recover of another a debt or damages as due at a particular time, he is also entitled to interest as an incident, from the maturity of the demand until the trial." In an action for breach of warranty of title of a slave, where the seller had a life interest only, it was held that interest on the value of the slave could be recovered from the time the use of the slave was lost; that is, from the death of the seller. [337] So, in an action for breach of warranty of title to land, the plaintiff may recover interest on the damages recovered. [338] In an action for trespass on land, interest may be recovered from the date of the trespass; [339] though in ac-

806; Rowland *v.* Shelton, 25 Ala. 217; Buford *v.* Gould, 35 Ala. 265.

Arkansas: Tatum *v.* Mohr, 21 Ark. 349.

Florida: McKay *v.* Lane, 5 Fla. 268.

Georgia: Badgett *v.* Broughton, 1 Ga. 591.

Iowa: Pitsinowsky *v.* Beardsley, 37 Ia. 9.

Michigan: Briggs *v.* Brushaber, 43 Mich. 330, 5 N. W. 383; Snow *v.* Nowlin, 43 Mich. 383, 5 N. W. 443.

South Carolina: Ancrum *v.* Slone, 2 Spear, 594.

Contra, New York: Riss *v.* Messmore, 58 N. Y. Super. Ct. 23, 9 N. Y. Supp. 1, 320.

In White *v.* Miller, 71 N. Y. 118, the decision was based on the New York rule as to unliquidated damages. The action was for breach of warranty of cabbage seed. The measure of damages was held to be the difference in value between the crop produced and that which would have been produced had the seed been of the quality represented. On this sum the court, overruling the decision of the referee, refused to allow interest, on the ground that the damages were unliquidated and could not be estimated by computation or by reference to market values.

The point was not fully considered, as there was another ground for reversing the decision; but the decision comes within the reason of the rule, as stated in McMahon *v.* N. Y. & Erie R. R. The reason there stated is, that *the debtor* can, by reference to the market values, ascertain the amount due. But in White *v.* Miller, the crop which would have been produced would first have to be ascertained, and this would depend upon conditions of soil and weather, about which the defendant could know nothing.

[336] 29 Ala. 558, 569.

[337] Crittenden *v.* Posey, 1 Head (Tenn.), 311.

[338] *Louisiana:* Bach *v.* Miller, 16 La. Ann. 44.

New York: Staats *v.* Ten Eyck, 3 Caines, 111.

Oregon: Stark *v.* Olney, 3 Ore. 88. And so for misrepresentation as to value of land: Snow *v.* Nowlin, 43 Mich. 383, 5 N. W. 443.

[339] *Connecticut:* New York, N. H. & H. R. R. *v.* Ansonia L. & W. P. Co., 72 Conn. 703, 46 Atl. 157.

Nebraska: Fremont, etc., R. R. *v.* Marley, 25 Neb. 138, 40 N. W. 948, 13 Am. St. Rep. 482.

Ohio: Longworth *v.* Cincinnati, 48 Ohio St. 637, 29 N. E. 274.

tions for flooding land [340] or for diverting water,[341] it has been held that interest cannot be allowed. And by the prevailing view interest may be allowed in all actions of tort where the loss is pecuniary.[342]

§ 317.[a] Value of property destroyed or converted.

Where property is destroyed, or is converted, so that the title either is, or is regarded as, out of the former owner, damages are the pecuniary representative of the property, and take its place. The plaintiff has lost or abandoned his claim to the *property;* his claim against the defendant is for an equivalent sum of *money.* In this point of view, a conversion very nearly resembles a sale. In this case, compensation for being

Interest in the discretion of the jury in such a case:

United States: Gulf, C. & S. F. R. R. v. Johnson, 54 Fed. 474, 4 C. C. A. 447.

District of Columbia: District v. Robinson, 14 App. D. C. 512.

Georgia: Gress Lumber Co. v. Coody, 104 Ga. 611, 30 S. E. 810.

New York: Duryee v. New York, 96 N. Y. 477.

Contra, that no interest can be allowed:

Alabama: Glidden v. Street, 68 Ala. 600.

Utah: Lester v. Min. Co., 27 Utah, 470, 76 Pac. 341, 101 Am. St. Rep. 988; Evans v. Min. Co., 27 Utah, 475, 76 Pac. 1135.

Where the tort is a statutory one, damages may be refused because of the language of the statute.

Alabama: Jean v. Sandiford, 39 Ala. 317.

Indiana: New York, C. & S. L. R. R. v. Zumbaugh, 12 Ind. App. 272, 39 N. E. 1058.

[a] For § 317 of the eighth edition, see § 318.

[340] *Missouri:* Gerst v. St. Louis, 185 Mo. 191, 84 S. W. 34, 105 Am. St. Rep. 580; Brink v. Kansas City, etc., R. R., 17 Mo. App. 177.

New York: Sayre v. State, 123 N. Y. 291, 25 N. E. 163.

But see *Ohio:* Toledo v. Grasser, 12 Ohio Cir. Ct. 520, 6 Ohio Cir. Dec. 782 (interest in discretion of jury).

[341] In the following cases interest was allowed only from the beginning of the action:

Maine: Union W. P. Co. v. Lewiston, 101 Me. 564, 65 Atl. 67 (in discretion of jury *semble,* from time of injury).

Rhode Island: Lonsdale Co. v. Woonsocket, 25 R. I. 428, 56 Atl. 448.

[342] *United States:* Crosby Lumber Co. v. Smith, 2 C. C. A. 97, 51 Fed. 63 (excluding plaintiff from a corporation).

Ohio: Hogg v. Zanesville Canal, etc., Co., 5 Ohio, 410 (obstructing river).

Wisconsin: Allen v. Murray, 87 Wis. 41, 57 N. W. 979 (prevention by third party of performance of contract).

See *Missouri:* Sparr v. Wellman, 11 Mo. 230 (loss of goods from inn: interest in discretion of jury).

Contra, United States: Pacific Postal Tel. Cable Co. v. Fleischner, 14 C. C. A. 166, 66 Fed. 899 (delay in delivering telegram: because damages unliquidated).

Wisconsin: Tyson v. Milwaukee, 50 Wis. 78, 5 N. W. 914 (damages from change in grade of street: because unliquidated).

kept from what rightfully belongs to the plaintiff is not compensation for being kept out of the use of property (the value of its use), but for being kept out of the use of money (interest). In actions of trover, therefore, the plaintiff recovers the value of the property, with interest from the time of conversion; [343] which in a case of conversion by demand and refusal

[343] *United States:* Dows v. National Exchange Bank, 91 U. S. 618, 23 L. ed. 214; New Dunderberg Mining Co. v. Old, 38 C. C. A. 89, 97 Fed. 150.

California: Hamer v. Hathaway, 33 Cal. 117.

Connecticut: Clark v. Whitaker, 19 Conn. 320.

Florida: Skinner v. Pinney, 19 Fla. 42, 45 Am. Rep. 1.

Georgia: Riley v. Martin, 35 Ga. 136; Tuller v. Carter, 59 Ga. 395. (See Macon, etc., R. R. v. Meador, 67 Ga. 672.)

Kentucky: Sanders v. Vance, 7 T. B. Mon. 209.

Louisiana: New Orleans D. Co. v. De Lizardi, 2 La. Ann. 281.

Maine: Hayden v. Bartlett, 35 Me. 203; Moody v. Whitney, 38 Me. 174; Robinson v. Barrows, 48 Me. 186.

Maryland: Hepburn v. Sewell, 5 H. & J. 211; Thomas v Sternheimer, 29 Md. 268; Maury v. Coyle, 34 Md. 235.

Massachusetts: Kennedy v. Whitwell, 4 Pick. 466; Negus v. Simpson, 99 Mass. 388.

Michigan: Winchester v. Craig, 33 Mich. 205; Johnson v. Gillen, 14 Mich. 152, 103 N. W. 547.

Missouri: Watson v. Harmon, 85 Mo. 443; Lack v. Brecht, 166 Mo. 242, 65 S. W. 976.

Montana: Montana Min. Co. v. St. Louis M. & N. Co., 183 Fed. 51 (by Montana statute).

New Hampshire: Chauncey v. Yeaton, 1 N. H. 151.

New York: Kennedy v. Strong, 14 Johns. 128; Hyde v. Stone, 7 Wend. 354, 22 Am. Dec. 582; Baker v. Wheeler, 8 Wend. 505; Stevens v. Low, 2

Hill, 132; Andrews v. Durant, 18 N. Y. 496; McCormick v. Pennsylvania Central R. R., 49 N. Y. 303; McDonald v. North, 47 Barb. 530; Pease v. Smith, 5 Lans. 519; Wehle v. Butler, 43 How. Pr. 5.

Oklahoma: Drumm-Flats Com. Co. v. Edmission, 17 Okla. 344, 87 Pac. 311.

Texas: Commercial Bank v. Jones, 18 Tex. 811; Gillies v. Wofford, 26 Tex. 76; Grimes v. Watkins, 59 Tex. 140; Hudson v. Wilkinson, 61 Tex. 610; Willis v. McNatt, 75 Tex. 69; Worsham v. Vignal, 5 Tex. Civ. App. 471, 24 S. W. 562; B. C. Evans Co. v. Reeves, 6 Tex. Civ. App. 254, 26 S. W. 219.

Utah: Rhemke v. Clinton, 2 Utah, 230.

Vermont: Grant v. King, 14 Vt. 367; Thrall v. Lathrop, 30 Vt. 307, 73 Am. Dec. 306.

Virginia: Schwerin v. McKie, 5 Rob. 404.

West Virginia: Shepherd v. McQuilkin, 2 W. Va. 90.

Wisconsin: Bigelow v. Doolittle, 36 Wis. 115; Arpin v. Burch, 68 Wis. 619, 32 N. W. 979; Ingram v. Rankin, 47 Wis. 406, 2 N. W. 755, 32 Am. Rep. 762.

England: Ekins v. East India Co., 1 P. Wms. 395.

Contra, Montana: Palmer v. Murray, 8 Mont. 312.

Interest in discretion of the jury:
Arkansas: Crow v. State, 23 Ark. 684.
Colorado: Perkins v. Marrs, 15 Colo. 262, 25 Pac. 168; Humbert v. Mason, 46 Colo. 430, 104 Pac. 1037.
Indiana: Kavanaugh v. Taylor, 2 Ind. App. 502, 28 N. E. 553,

is of course the time of demand.[344] And in any action for destroying or carrying off property, the plaintiff recovers interest from the time of the wrongful act.[345] So in an action

Kentucky: Newcomb-Buchanan Co. v. Baskett, 14 Bush, 658.

Missouri: Carson v. Smith, 133 Mo. 606, 34 S. W. 855 (but see Kamerick v. Castleman, 29 Mo. App. 658).

North Carolina: Stephens v. Koonce, 103 N. C. 266. (See Satterwhite v. Carson, 25 N. C. 549.) And see Clement v. Spear, 56 Vt. 401.

[344] *Georgia:* Garrard v. Dawson, 49 Ga. 434.

Illinois: Northern T. Co. v. Sellick, 52 Ill. 249.

Massachusetts: Johnson v. Sumner, 1 Met. 172.

New Hampshire: Clement v. Little, 42 N. H. 563.

New York: Schwerin v. McKie, 51 N. Y. 180.

[345] *United States:* New Dunderberg Min. Co. v. Old, 97 Fed. 150, 38 C. C. A. 89.

Alabama: Fail v. Presley, 50 Ala. 342; Burns v. Campbell, 71 Ala. 271.

California: Hamer v. Hathaway, 33 Cal. 117.

Connecticut: Oviatt v. Pond, 29 Conn. 479; Regan v. New York, N. H. & H. R. R., 60 Conn. 124, 22 Atl. 503, 25 Am. St. Rep. 306.

Georgia: Collier v. Lyons, 18 Ga. 648; Brown v. Southwestern R. R., 36 Ga. 377; Rutherford v. Irby, 57 S. E. 927, 1 Ga. App. 499.

Iowa: Mote v. Chicago & N. W. Ry., 27 Ia. 22, 1 Am. Rep. 212; Johnson v. Chicago & N. W. Ry., 77 Ia. 666; Burdick v. Chicago, M. & S. P. Ry., 87 Ia. 384, 54 N. W. 439.

Maine: Brannin v. Johnson, 19 Me. 361.

Maryland: Moore v. Schultz, 31 Md. 418.

Mississippi: Black v. Robinson, 61 Miss. 54.

Missouri: Walker v. Borland, 21 Mo. 289.

Nebraska: Union Pac. Ry. v. Ray, 46 Neb. 750, 65 N. W. 773.

New Jersey: Hopple v. Higbee, 23 N. J. Law, 342.

New York: Buffalo & H. T. Co. v. Buffalo, 58 N. Y. 639; Mairs v. Manhattan R. E. Assoc., 89 N. Y. 498; Campbell v. Woodworth, 26 Barb. 648.

Pennsylvania: Allegheny v. Campbell, 107 Pa. 530.

Texas: Texas & P. Ry. v. Tankersley, 63 Tex. 57; Gulf, C. & S. F. R. R. v. Dunlap (Tex. Civ. App.), 26 S. W. 655; Clarendon Land, etc., Co. v. McClelland (Tex. Civ. App.), 31 S. W. 1088; Gulf, C. & S. F. R. R. v. Jagoe (Tex. Civ. App.), 32 S. W. 717 [but see Galveston, H. & S. A. Ry. v. Dromgoole (Tex. Civ. App.), 24 S. W. 372].

Utah: Rhemke v. Clinton, 2 Utah, 230.

Vermont: Blumenthal v. Brainerd, 38 Vt. 402, 91 Am. Dec. 350.

Canada: Maxwell v. Crann, 13 U. C. Q. B. 253.

But *contra,* Green v. Garcia, 3 La. Ann. 702, on the ground that the amount is unliquidated.

The allowance of interest is in the discretion of the jury:

United States: Brent v. Thornton, 106 Fed. 35, 45 C. C. A. 214.

Alabama: Hair v. Little, 28 Ala. 236.

California: King v. Southern Pac. R. R., 109 Cal. 96, 41 Pac. 786, 29 L. R. A. 755.

Illinois: Bradley v. Geiselman, 22 Ill. 494.

Kentucky: Schulte v. Louisville & N. R. R., 128 Ky. 627, 108 S. W. 941.

New York: Beals v. Guernsey, 8 Johns. 446, 5 Am. Dec. 348; Wehle v. Haviland, 42 How. Pr. 399.

against a common carrier for the loss of goods, interest is allowed on their value; [346] and in an action of trespass for removing material from land, the owner may recover interest on the value of the material removed.[347] In Parrott v. The Knickerbocker Ice Co.[348] the plaintiff's boat had been lost by collision with the defendant's boat.

Pennsylvania: Reed v. Rodgers, 40 Pa. Super. Ct. 171.

Tennessee: Louisville & N. R. R. v. Fort, 112 Tenn. 432, 80 S. W. 429.

In case the property taken was returned and accepted by the owner, interest may be recovered on the balance: Woodham v. Gelston, 1 Johns. (N. Y.) 134.

And upon the money spent to secure the return: Fields v. Williams, 91 Ala. 502, 8 So. 808.

Where the judgment is for the value of securities, the legal rate should be allowed, although the rate earned by the securities may have been less. Govin v. de Miranda, 140 N. Y. 474, 35 N. E. 626.

[346] *United States:* Mobile & Montgomery R. R. v. Jurey, 111 U. S. 584, 4 Sup. Ct. 566, 28 L. ed. 527; King v. Shepherd, 14 Fed. Cas. No. 7,804, 3 Story, 349; Bazin v. Liverpool, etc., Steamship Co., 2 Fed. Cas. No. 1,152, 3 Wall. Jr. 229; Woodward v. Illinois C. R. R., 1 Biss. 403; Fraloff v. New York C. & H. R. R. R., 10 Blatch. 16; The Gold Hunter, 1 Blatch. & H. 300; Western Mfg. Co. v. The Guiding Star, 37 Fed. 641; Southern Pac. Co. v. Arnett, 126 Fed. 75, 61 C. C. A. 131.

Connecticut: Parrott v. Housatonic R. R., 47 Conn. 575.

Iowa: Mote v. Chicago & N. W. R. R., 27 Ia. 22; Robinson v. Merchants' D. T. Co., 45 Ia. 470.

Minnesota: Cowley v. Davidson, 13 Minn. 92.

Missouri: Gray v. Missouri River Packet Co., 64 Mo. 47 (gross negligence only).

New York: McCormick v. Pennsyl-

vania C. R. R., 49 N. Y. 303; Duryea v. Mayor, 26 Hun, 120; Sherman v. Wells, 28 Barb. 403.

Ohio: Erie Ry. v. Lockwood, 28 Oh. St. 358.

South Carolina: Walker v. Southern Ry., 76 S. C. 308, 56 S. E. 952.

Utah: Fell v. Union Pac. Ry., 32 Utah, 101, 88 Pac. 1003.

Vermont: Newell v. Smith, 49 Vt. 255.

Wisconsin: Whitney v. Chicago & N. W. Ry., 27 Wis. 327.

Contra, Illinois: Patton Paint Co. v. Erie R. R., 148 Ill. App. 410.

Missouri: De Steiger v. Hannibal & St. J. Ry., 73 Mo. 33.

New York: Richmond v. Bronson, 5 Denio, 55 (discretionary with jury); Lakeman v. Grinnell, 5 Bosw. 625.

Texas: Fowler v. Davenport, 21 Tex. 626; Wolfe v. Lacy, 30 Tex. 349.

[347] *Alabama:* Lowery v. Rowland, 104 Ala. 420, 16 So. 88 (trees).

Indiana: Pittsburgh, F. W. & C. Ry. v. Swinney, 97 Ind. 586 (gravel).

Maine: Longfellow v. Quimby, 33 Me. 457 (trees: damages equal to interest).

Michigan: Winchester v. Craig, 33 Mich. 205 (trees); Dayton v. Estate of Dakin, 103 Mich. 65, 61 N. W. 349 (crops); Gates v. Comstock, 107 Mich. 546, 71 N. W. 515.

New Hampshire: Adams v. Blodgett, 47 N. H. 219, 90 Am. Dec. 569 (trees).

Wisconsin: Ingram v. Rankin, 47 Wis. 406 (trees).

Contra, Louisiana: Robertson v. Green, 18 La. Ann. 28 (unliquidated).

[348] 46 N. Y. 361, 369.

Rapallo, J., said: "In cases of trover, replevin, and trespass, interest on the value of property unlawfully taken or converted is allowed by way of damages, for the purpose of complete indemnity of the party injured, and it is difficult to see why, on the same principle, interest on the value of property lost or destroyed by the wrongful or negligent act of another may not be included in the damages."

In an action brought against a municipality, on a statute, for destruction of the plaintiff's property by a mob, it is held in New York that interest may be recovered,[349] at least in the discretion of the jury;[350] in Pennsylvania, that interest may not be recovered.[351] In an action of replevin, where the prevailing party does not succeed in securing the property, but recovers its value, he may also recover interest from the time it was taken from him.[352] But both damages for detention and interest on the value cannot be recovered;[353] and when the action is brought to establish a right to take the goods as security for a debt, interest has been held to be in the discretion of the jury.[354]

§ 318.[a] Property destroyed by negligence.

There seems to be no reason why any difference should exist in the rules governing the allowance of interest on the value of property destroyed, whether the destruction was caused by the misfeasance or by the negligence of the defendant,[355] that is, whether the suit is such that at common law an action would have lain, on the one hand of trover, trespass,

[a] For § 318 of the eighth edition, see § 331a.

[349] Greer v. Mayor, 3 Robt. (N. Y.) 406.

[350] Orr v. Mayor, 64 Barb. 106.

[351] Weir v. Allegheny, 95 Pa. 413.

[352] *Colorado:* Hanauer v. Bartels, 2 Colo. 514.

Indiana: Yelton v. Slinkard, 85 Ind. 190.

Missouri: Woodburn v. Cogdall, 39 Mo. 222 (but see Andrews v. Costican, 30 Mo. App. 29).

Nevada: Blackie v. Cooney, 8 Nev. 41.

New York: Brizsee v. Maybee, 21 Wend. 144.

Pennsylvania: McDonald v. Scaife, 11 Pa. 381, 51 Am. Dec. 556.

Wisconsin: Bigelow v. Doolittle, 36 Wis. 115.

Interest in discretion of jury: Patapsco Guano Co. v. Magee, 86 N. C. 350.

[353] McCarty v. Quimby, 12 Kan. 494.

[354] *Missouri:* Feller v. McKillip, 109 Mo. App. 61, 81 S. W. 641.

North Carolina: Patapsco Guano Co. v. Magee, 86 N. C. 350.

[355] Parrott v. Knickerbocker Ice Co., 46 N. Y. 361, per Rapallo, J.

replevin, or detinue; on the other, of trespass on the case. In some jurisdictions interest is in fact allowed in cases of negligence;[356] but in others interest in such cases is held to be in the discretion of the jury,[357] or even refused altogether.[358]

[356] *United States:* Deems v. Albany, etc., Line, 7 Fed. Cas. No. 3,736, 14 Blatchf. 474.

Alabama: Alabama G. S. R. R. v. McAlpine, 75 Ala. 113; Georgia Pac. R. R. v. Fullerton, 79 Ala. 298.

Connecticut: Regan v. New York, N. H. & H. R. R., 60 Conn. 124, 142, 25 Am. St. Rep. 306, 22 Atl. 503.

Florida: Jacksonville, etc., R. v. Peninsular Land, etc., Co., 27 Fla. 1, 157, 9 So. 661, 17 L. R. A. 33, 65.

Indiana: Wabash R. R. v. Williamson, 3 Ind. App. 190, 29 N. E. 455.

Indian Territory: Missouri, K. & T. R. R. v. Truskett, 2 Ind. Terr. 633, 53 S. W. 444.

Iowa: Arthur v. Chicago, R. I. & P. Ry., 61 Iowa, 648, 17 N. W. 24 (as value was capable of exact computation); Johnson v. Chicago, etc., R. R., 77 Iowa, 666, 42 N. W. 512.

Michigan: Kendrick v. Towle, 60 Mich. 363, 27 N. W. 567, 1 Am. St. Rep. 526; Coan v. Brownstown, 126 Mich. 626, 86 N. W. 130.

Minnesota: Varco v. Chicago, M. & S. P. Ry., 30 Minn. 18, 13 N. W. 921.

Missouri: Fisher v. New Orleans Anchor Line, 15 Mo. App. 576.

Nebraska: Fremont, etc., R. R. v. Marley, 25 Neb. 138, 40 N. W. 948, 13 Am. St. Rep. 482; Union Pacific R. R. v. Ray, 46 Neb. 750, 65 N. W. 773.

New York: Lackin v. Delaware & H. C. Co., 22 Hun, 309.

North Carolina: Rippey v. Miller, 46 N. C. 479, 63 Am. Dec. 177.

Texas: Texas & P. R. R. v. Tankersley, 63 Tex. 57; Gulf, C. & S. F. Ry. v. Holliday, 65 Tex. 512; Galveston, etc., R. R. v. Horne, 69 Tex. 643, 9 S. W. 440; Gulf, C. & S. F. Ry. v. Jagol (Tex. Civ. App.), 32 S. W. 717; International G. N. R. R. v. Barton, 93 Tex. 63, 53 S. W. 117; Texas, etc., R. R. v. Dunman, 6 Tex. Civ. App. 101, 24 S. W. 995; Gulf, C. & S. F. Ry. v. Wedel (Tex. Civ. App.), 42 S. W. 1030; (Houston & T. C. R. R. v. Muldrow, 54 Tex. 233 and Texas & N. O. Ry. v. Cunningham, 4 Tex. Civ. App. 262, 23 S. W. 332, contra, are overruled. But see Texas & P. Ry. v. Payne, 15 Tex. Civ. App. 58, 35 S. W. 297; Galveston, H. & S. A. Ry. v. Vaughan, 54 S. W. 1055; St. Louis S. W. Ry. v. Guthrie (Tex. Civ. App.), 103 S. W. 211. In St. Louis & S. F. R. R. v. Hooser, 44 Tex. Civ. App. 229, 97 S. W. 708, interest was refused because not claimed in the pleadings).

In *Wisconsin* interest is allowed from the beginning of the action. Chapman v. Chicago & N. W. Ry., 26 Wis. 295, 7 Am. Rep. 81; Dean v. Chicago & N. W. Ry., 43 Wis. 305.

So in *Utah:* Woodland v. Union Pac. R. R., 26 Pac. 298.

[357] *California:* King v. Southern Pac. Co., 109 Cal. 96, 41 Pac. 786.

Georgia: Western & A. Ry. v. McCauley, 68 Ga. 818 (*semble*); Western, etc., R. R. v. Brown, 102 Ga. 13, 29 S. E. 130; Albany & N. Ry. v. Wheeler, 6 Ga. App. 270, 64 S. E. 1114.

[358] *Colorado:* Denver & R. G. R. R. v. Conway, 8 Colo. 1, 5 Pac. 142, 54 Am. Rep. 537; Denver & R. G. R. R. v. Moynahan, 8 Colo. 56, 5 Pac. 811 (amount being unliquidated).

Illinois: Toledo, P. & W. Ry. v. Johnston, 74 Ill. 83 (in the absence of circumstances of aggravation).

Kansas: R. R. v. Holmes, 68 Kan. 810, 74 Pac. 606.

Missouri: Damhorst v. Missouri Pac. R. R., 32 Mo. App. 350.

www.ingramcontent.com/pod-product-compliance
Lightning Source LLC
Chambersburg PA
CBHW021542210326
41599CB00010B/280